ACCOUNTING INFORMATION SYSTEMS

Accounting Information Systems

Edward Lee Summers Ph.D., CPA

Arthur Young Professor of Accounting
The University of Texas at Austin

Houghton Mifflin Company   Boston

Dallas   Geneva, Illinois
Palo Alto   Princeton, New Jersey

To Kathy

This book is written to provide accurate and authoritative information concerning the covered topics. It is not meant to take the place of professional advice.

Cover photograph by Peter Angelo Simon/Phototake—NYC.

Printed in the U.S.A.

Library of Congress Catalog Card Number: 87-80086

ISBN: 0-395-36920-7

BCDEFGHIJ-DH-9543210-89

Contents

Preface

Accounting information systems is one of the most exciting and dynamic fields in accounting today. Technological advances in hardware and commercial software are taking users of accounting information systems from a mainframe environment to one of mini- and desktop computers. This text, *Accounting Information Systems,* presents information in the context of these technologies but maintains as its foundation the traditional concepts of double-entry accounting. When students have completed a course using this text, they will be able to answer the key questions involved in understanding accounting information systems:

1. What are accounting information systems?
2. How do they work?
3. Why are they important?
4. Who uses, controls, and designs them?
5. What characteristics do they share with other systems?

Accounting Information Systems presents the up-to-date fundamentals of computer-based technology comprehensively, effectively demonstrating the relationships between today's accounting information systems and basic accounting concepts. In doing so, the text shows how accounting professionals apply management information science and data base theory to understand, design, create, and maintain accounting, reporting, and control systems. In this way, the text provides students with the skills and ways of thinking that will enable them to make informed decisions about any organization's accounting information systems needs.

Accounting Information Systems covers the traditional core topics of the accounting information systems course and the new computer environment of the accounting profession without resorting to extended flow diagrams, programming languages, mathematical proofs, or exotic technical jargon. Major topics are fully discussed in the context of their relationship to the entire accounting system. These relationships take in the principles of data base processing, internal control, and the uses of computer-generated information in management decision making. The text offers current coverage of just-in-time inventory methods, EDP auditing, local area networks, artificial intelligence, and expert systems, since a basic knowledge of these cutting-edge technologies is essential for success as an accounting professional or manager today. Techniques for protecting the accounting information system from carelessness, incompetence, and crime are also described. Coverage of mainframe systems and batch processing is minimized, as most small and medium-sized businesses no longer use them.

The text assumes that students are in a first course in accounting information systems and have taken an introductory accounting course sequence. (Background provided by an introductory survey of data processing is suggested but not essential.) The author has included more information on the relationship between basic accounting concepts and the parts of an accounting information system than one might expect in a text for this course. By linking basic accounting transactions to information about computerized systems, the text makes students continually aware that fundamental *accounting* knowledge is essential to understanding how an accounting information system works. Finally, the advent of new technologies and their inherent complexities have placed many more demands on the control elements of an accounting information system. This text includes more material on controls—including their theory, application, and analysis—than has previously been available in texts for this course.

Organization of This Text

Accounting Information Systems is organized in five parts to provide maximum flexibility for the instructor teaching the course. After covering Parts 1 and 2, instructors may assign Parts 3, 4, and 5 in any sequence they prefer.

- Part 1, Basic Accounting Systems Concepts (Chapters 1–6), lays out the essential information needed to begin a study of accounting information systems, with attention to the changing role of today's accountants. These chapters describe the system concepts, accounting processes, information requirements, computer hardware and software, and information processing concepts that are found in all accounting systems. Included in Part 1 are introductory sections on general system theory and the control elements within a system.

- Part 2, Accounting Applications (Chapters 7–10), discusses the central application areas that make up accounting information systems. Accounts receivable, accounts payable, cost accounting, and not-for-profit accounting are all covered in this section. Part 2 emphasizes selected computer concepts, equipment, operations, and software routines.

- Part 3, Controls and Accounting (Chapters 11–14), presents accounting and processing controls and discusses in detail the management of electronic data processing, computer crime, and the principles of EDP auditing. These topics comprise an essential background for designing efficient controls, anticipating the losses that may occur if controls in a system are defective or missing, and finally, testing for the presence of effective controls.

- Part 4, New Developments Affecting Accounting Information Systems (Chapters 15 and 16), assesses emerging developments in two special areas relating to system design and use: artificial intelligence and communications in local area networks. Included in these chapters are discussions of two tools that are used by accounting system designers and managers: decision support and expert systems.

- Part 5, System Design and Implementation (Chapters 17 and 18), examines the process of bringing an accounting system into existence. This section concludes with a presentation on vendor selection, detail design, and conversion.

The text concludes with a comprehensive case, Sports Products, Incorporated, which includes assignments linked to all but one of the chapters. This case is followed by an up-to-date bibliography, organized by chapter. An extensive glossary and detailed index help students use the text. The *Instructor's Resource Manual* contains suggested course syllabi, chapter outlines and lecture suggestions, solutions to all end-of-chapter materials, solutions for the comprehensive case assignments, and fifteen to twenty test items per chapter, as well as transparency masters for selected material.

Comprehensive Pedagogy

Each chapter of *Accounting Information Systems* has been carefully designed to help students understand and use the fundamental knowledge it contains. A chapter outline and list of learning objectives at the beginning of each chapter indicate what students will master by successfully completing the chapter. Key terms are listed in color and defined the first time they are mentioned in the text. More than 180 two-color drawings, figures, and charts enhance student understanding and comprehension.

At the end of each chapter a comprehensive chapter summary reviews all key concepts and is followed by a list of key terms, review questions, discussion questions, and problems. Most chapters end with a short case. The review questions focus on major concepts and terms, while the discussion questions are intended to stimulate thought and analysis. Whenever possible the problems require quantitative calculations.

The comprehensive case, Sports Products, Incorporated, provides completely independent chapter-based assignments. Because the assignments are independent of one another, instructors can select whichever assignments they choose. It is recommended that when a case assignment is used, students complete it before leaving the chapter on which it is based.

The Aurora Company Practice Set is a microcomputer-based simulation that provides the look and feel of a full-featured on-line data base accounting information system. Based on the LOTUS® Spreadsheet, this program and its accompanying workbook familiarizes students with screenforms, data structures, controls, and supports encountered in such a system. It also allows students to experience the flow and processing of data from the point of entry through the accounts to the various reports generated by the system.

Quality Control

Accounting Information Systems is a technically and conceptually accurate textbook. The author has developed and tested the manuscript and end-of-chapter materials through six semesters of classroom teaching. Throughout development, the author has made use of current professional and academic literature and discussed the topics with practitioners. Both the author and the publisher obtained independent reviews and developmental assistance. In addition, the manuscript was reviewed extensively to ensure accuracy.

Acknowledgments

A new accounting information systems textbook, summarizing the work of thousands of professionals in dozens of disciplines and describing the detailed accounting information systems used by real businesses and organizations, comes together only after years of work. I am grateful for the time my students and colleagues have taken to critique the manuscript. Their efforts have led to many significant improvements. Some of those who have been supportive and have had an impact are:

Professor Patricia Bille
Highline Community College

Dr. Owen Cherrington
Brigham Young University

Professor H. Perrin Garsombke
University of Nebraska

Ms. Jan Gillespie
Texas State Auditor's Office

Professor Roben Hatami
Pan American University

Professor Malcolm H. Lathan, Jr.
McIntire School of Commerce
University of Virginia

Mr. Joe Leung
MBA, University of Texas at Austin

Professor Richard L. Nichols
Southwest Missouri State University

Professor Dan Stone
University of Texas at Austin

Professor William O. Van Dongen
University of Wisconsin— Oshkosh

Ms. Barbara Wilson
Attorney-at-Law, Austin

I would also like to acknowledge the assistance of Daniel Jones, College of the Holy Cross, who reviewed the entire text and solutions manual to ascertain that the presentation is up to date and accurate.

Without the help of these people and others (especially all the students!) this book would not have been possible. I invite and encourage your comments on the text. Please write to me c/o Houghton Mifflin Company, College Division, One Beacon Street, Boston, MA 02108, Attention Accounting Editor.

E.L.S.

ACCOUNTING INFORMATION SYSTEMS

PART 1

Basic Accounting
Systems Concepts

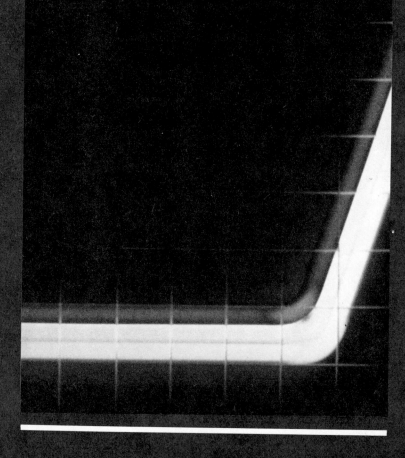

Accounting systems, which provide the information basis for financial and economic decisions, are only one kind of system. Before you can fully understand accounting systems, you must have some knowledge of general systems theory. Accounting information systems not only consist of elements of general systems, they incorporate concepts from organizational and behavioral science and mathematics and make intensive use of one of the most far-reaching developments of the twentieth century—the computer. Part 1 provides the knowledge base you need to understand accounting information systems.

The first three chapters explain how a general systems framework can be filled out to describe an accounting system and show how managers use accounting systems to secure financial and operational control over an organization. The text then explains how computers implement information processing concepts (Chapters 4 and 5). Part 1 concludes with an integrative description of the structure of an accounting system as a transaction-processing, control-enhancing, information-producing model of an organization (Chapter 6).

Part 1 contains the following chapters:

An Overview

The Changing Role of the Accountant
Technology and Controls

Accounting Information Systems
Characteristics of Systems
Information Systems
Management Information Systems

Accounting as a System
The Accounting Model
Accounting and MIS
Personnel and Equipment
Data Organization

Asking the Right Questions
Primary Users
System Objectives
System Boundaries
Information Requirements
Conflict Resolution

Summary and Overview of the Book

Learning Objectives

After studying this chapter you should be able to

- **Describe and understand the changing role of the accountant.**

- **Describe the essential components of systems in general and of information systems and accounting information systems in particular.**

- **Ask questions whose answers lead to the development of successful accounting information systems.**

- **Describe the knowledge and benefits that you should gain by studying this book.**

Chapter 1 introduces today's fast-changing, uncertain world, in which organizations depend on many kinds of information for their survival and growth. For the financial part of that information, they rely on accountants, who must be able to design and manage systems that record transactions, process data, and produce reports for internal and external users (see Figure 1.1). In order to perform in their new roles, accountants must understand the many characteristics that accounting systems share with other systems—objectives, inputs, processes, outputs, boundaries, and controls. Controls, which allow a system to be regulated, are especially important. Chapter 1 highlights the changing role of accountants as they work together with data processing and other specialists to design systems that provide just the right combination of data processing power, reporting ability, and controls—all at a reasonable cost.

Until the 1950s, accountants didn't have to concern themselves with computers—models of that day consisted of two-story monsters flashing vacuum tubes at scientists who worked inside their inventions and communicated with them in machine language understood by only a privileged few. Many of today's computers fit on a desk—or in an attaché case—and respond to commands in ordinary English. While computer experts still must learn advanced programming languages, computer users need to concentrate on accurately describing their needs and understanding how to design or select systems that can meet those needs. Contemporary software allows people with little or no programming expertise to use computer-based information systems effectively.

Figure 1.1   Accounting Activity's Relationship to Its Environment
Accounting activities take place within a larger environment of activities that fulfill an organization's needs and affect its future. Accountants specialize in providing financial information.

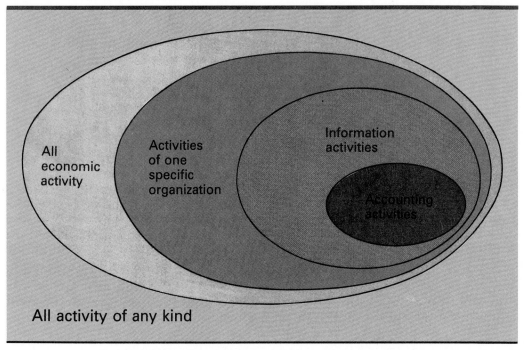

Computer technology has changed the way accountants—and students—do their work. Like students, accountants find that they are spending more time working with commercial software packages on microcomputers. Indeed, many large accounting firms, as well as industrial and service organizations, require their staff members to use microcomputers in the office and transportable computers during field audits. Price Waterhouse, a ''Big 8'' accounting firm, has had a firmwide steering committee on microcomputers since 1983. The firm now owns 3,000 micros—approximately one for every three employees nationwide—and plans to put a micro on every employee's desk by 1990.[1] Arthur Young, another large accounting firm, has made the Macintosh its standard microcomputer and anticipates that its software, when fully developed, will make possible financial audits whose working papers exist only as computer files.[2]

---

[1]*Computerworld*, February 2, 1987, p. 53.

[2]*MacWorld*, Winter 1986, p. 71.

The Changing Role of the Accountant

What does this mean for today's professional accountant? Specialized computer components have not only changed the nature of accounting; they have also made accounting a smooth, low-visibility operation. For accountants, however, the blessing has been mixed. True, they can get more detailed information, more easily and much more quickly. Expected to deliver precise information, prepared in a known way, about the economic life of their organizations, accountants are finding that the technology they use presents problems of its own: At their most detailed level of operation, most computers and software seem too complex for anyone but specialists to understand. Moreover, computer processing is impossible to observe— it takes place invisibly and silently. And computer output is not necessarily easily readable by human beings; more often, it takes the form of magnetic storage, impossible to inspect unless converted to paper or video display.

Perhaps the best way to look at the problem is to imagine that accountants have allowed a whole new generation of systems to be designed—by nonaccountants. If accountants, as financial and managerial information specialists, are to maintain control of their discipline, they will have to move beyond competence in accounting alone. They will also have to understand and apply the basic bodies of knowledge in computer science, data processing, internal and external control, and systems analysis. Only by communicating and working effectively with others in the design and installation of computer-based systems can accountants ensure that those systems meet all their needs and that they—not the systems—remain in control.

Technology and Controls

Today's accountants are called on to understand, use, evaluate, modify and/or design computer-based accounting systems. The technology and procedures used today did not even exist a few years ago; moreover, they are still changing so rapidly that improvements occur almost daily. Major changes in technology appear every three to five years. Although these products have greatly simplified some accounting tasks—people with very little skill can now process transactions and prepare accounting statements accurately—demands on professional accountants have grown enormously.

The need for effective systems—including reliable controls and competent internal administration—has never been greater. Computers are emerging not only as objects of crime but also as instruments of sophisticated white-collar crime. Organizations whose accountants do not understand how these systems can be manipulated are as defenseless as if they had no locks on their doors. And few organizations are exercising proper control over their computers. One scholar has noted that "a survey of 100 corporations by the National Association of Accountants found that only 52% of those responding said their companies had any guidelines at all dealing with the use of computers; only 22% provided their employees with any written guidelines."[3]

This book attempts to introduce the many responsibilities of contemporary accountants. It will not teach you to use particular computers or specific software packages. You can learn those skills through hands-on experience or in an introductory data processing course. Nor does it take a cookbook approach to accounting; the text assumes that you have a basic background in accounting theory and a practical understanding of accounting procedures. Throughout, the aim is to help you acquire skills and ways of thinking that will enable you to make educated judgments when you deal with accounting systems, much as an athlete learns to respond rapidly and effectively to situations normally encountered in competitive games. There is no doubt that you will need this training. Although most recent accounting graduates will take jobs in organizations whose accounting information systems are firmly in place, even the best systems undergo continuous change and have limited life spans—about six to ten years.

The reasons for this obsolescence are many. Although a system lasts well beyond the introduction of new technology, no system lasts forever. An organization will leave a system in place as long as it achieves its objectives at a reasonable cost and in a reasonable time frame, but at some point improvements in technology or changes in the environment will make a new system sufficiently cheaper, quicker, more reliable, or more sophisticated to justify replacing the old system. An organization may anticipate or experience growth through merger, acquisition, or expansion from within. It might reorganize in such a way that the new structure requires a redesigned information system. It may decentralize its operation, with a resulting need for sophisticated communications networks and security controls. More powerful and smaller computers or other devices may offer opportunities for quicker data capture. In still other cases, organizations will decide to offer more user-accessible features or to shorten the time lag between events and their appearance in accounting reports. Finally, the organization may simply want to offer new services to customers or to expand its accounting capacity because the old system has reached its limits.

In any case, if you hold any accounting job—even as an independent consultant—for more than a few years, you will probably participate in the design of a new system or the refinement of an old one. For all these reasons, the study of accounting information systems must also be considered the study of change.

---

[3]August Bequai, *Techno-Crimes*, (Lexington, Mass.: Heath/Lexington Books, 1987), as quoted in *Computerworld*, November 3, 1986, p. 88.

Accounting Information Systems

What are accounting information systems? Why are they important? Who uses, controls, and designs them? When should they be changed? What characteristics do they share with other systems? These are the questions behind the study of accounting information systems. In this chapter, we begin a discussion that will equip you to answer them by the time you finish this book.

Accounting is a collection of principles and rules that govern the transformation of data into the information used in management processes. Information is data made meaningful. The transformation is accomplished by a system consisting of people, machines, and methods. These components are organized so as to accomplish a set of specific functions.[4] Because their value lies in linking the diverse parts of an organization so it can function as a coordinated entity, accounting information systems exemplify the saying that the whole is often greater than the sum of its parts.

The study of accounting information systems is a young field. It draws from many areas of expertise—accounting, systems theory, control theory, management theory, and computer science. A book that covered every relevant aspect of each of these fields would be the length of an encyclopedia. We have set parameters by confining discussion in this text mainly to accounting systems that are modern, common, and relatively easy to understand. These systems may be found in medium-size, moderately decentralized organizations. Their operating systems allow simultaneous access by two or more users, and the accounting applications themselves are integrated and use data base principles in their design. Particular emphasis is placed on the transactions-processing aspects of computer-based accounting information systems.

We begin in this section with a brief discussion of the larger context into which accounting information systems fall—all systems, information systems, and management information systems—to lay the groundwork for understanding the way accounting information systems are organized.

Characteristics of Systems

The system concept simplifies and integrates phenomena that appear to be complex and unrelated. Systems, as noted above, combine people, machines, and methods to accomplish specific functions. Systems can also be viewed as combinations of elements that include all or some of the follow-

---

[4]American National Standards Committee, X3, Information Processing Systems, *American National Dictionary for Information Processing Systems* (Homewood, Ill.: Dow Jones-Irwin, 1984), p. 388.

ing: objectives, inputs, outputs, processes, controls and other internal relationships, and a boundary with the rest of the universe.

An **element** is the smallest part of a system that can be used in a
system description or design. An element belongs to a system if it contributes to the system's activity. For example, a spring-wound clock is a
system. Within that system, the clock's key is an element. Some elements,
like an automobile's fuel pump or a stereo's record changer, are systems
that reside within other systems. A description of a system must begin
with a description of its elements.

Objectives.   A system's **objectives** are a system's reason for being, and a
system may have one or more of them. Objectives tie each of a system's
sub-systems or elements together. Each objective consists of an effect (its
desired end result) and a time frame. For example, a clock's accuracy
objective can be viewed as having two parts: *reporting the time within plus
or minus 5 minutes* (the effect) *for a period of one year* (the time frame). A
computer's reliability objective may be *to operate without failure* (the effect)
for an average of 2,000 hours (the time frame). An organization's investment
objective may be *to earn an average annual return of 10 percent* (the effect) *for
a five-year period* (the time frame). An accounting system's objective may
be *to produce, at predictable intervals, adequate financial and managerial statements* (the effect) *for at least six years* (the time frame).

Different systems with the same objective may arrange their elements
differently. For example, systems to provide personal transportation include two-, three-, or four-wheel vehicles and even tractor-type machines;
the motive power may be electricity, steam, or internal combustion; the
engine may be in front, in the middle, or in the rear; steering might be by
means of a wheel or a stick. Although arranged differently, all these systems still meet the same objective: to provide personal transportation.

Inputs, processes, and outputs.   Not all systems contain every type of
element. Inputs or outputs, in particular, are sometimes absent. An **input**
is a phenomenon that is produced by the environment and that has a
measurable effect on the system. A **process** is a planned sequence of operations, with a beginning and an end, intended to produce certain results.
An **output** is a measurable phenomenon that is produced by the system
and that has an observable effect on the environment. For example, pressure, a hot spark, oxygen, and gasoline are inputs that cause an internal
combustion engine to operate. It then produces environment-affecting outputs of heat, work, and certain gases.

Open systems exchange inputs and outputs with their environments.
A system that does not make these exchanges is a **closed system;** it does
not interact with its environment. A locked, secure storage vault is one
example of a closed system. Even within closed systems, the internal elements do exchange inputs and outputs, although they will not be ex-

changed with the environment outside the system. The locked vault, for example, may contain a self-powered humidity control device. Closed systems do not constitute an important part of accounting information systems.

Some systems, like a "word processing" system consisting of a pencil and paper, are relatively simple. Others—such as a computerized word processing system connected through a network to a laser printer—are much more complex. A system can occupy any point on each of the continua shown in Figure 1.2.

Figure 1.2   Variable Characteristics of a System
Systems vary according to the points they occupy on many different continua. The sum of all these characteristics determines the nature of the system.

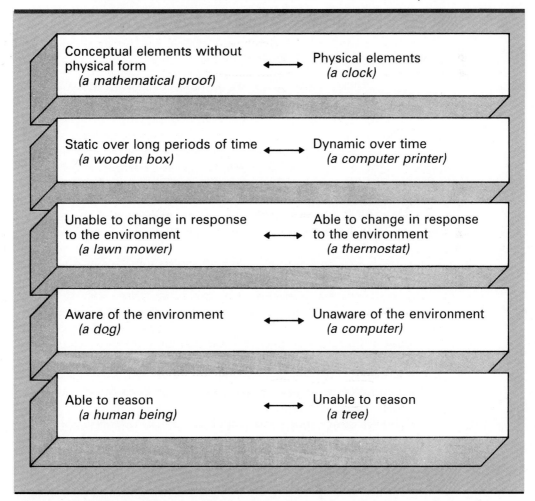

Controls. Control is the ability to regulate. The broad objective of control is to make the outcomes of routine activity more predictable. Some systems, called self-regulating, have controls so complete that they make the system entirely predictable. One example of a self-regulating system is an environmental monitoring device intended to operate unattended for long periods while recording or transmitting signals. Other systems have controls that make them only partially self-regulating; an example of such a system is an automobile with cruise control. Although the car will maintain its speed, a human driver must control its direction.

All systems change, malfunction, and break down. Houses and highways deteriorate. Production lines come to a halt. Even when changes in physical systems fall within acceptable limits, changes in the environment may make the system's inputs and outputs inappropriate. When this happens, the system fails to meet its objectives. Within a system, controls are the means to prevent or identify and correct failures to achieve system objectives.

Controls apply to all activities of a system and are always designed to include the same four control elements:

- A control objective takes the form of statements describing the desired performance of some process within the system. Control objectives differ from system objectives, which describe the system's outputs. For example, an accounting system may have the system objective of recording credit sales to customers; the corresponding control objective will be "all credit sales transactions will be recorded on a timely and accurate basis."

- The **preventive element** is determined before the process takes place. It is a value that a measurable variable in the process to be controlled will have if the control objective is achieved. Preventive controls derive their name from the earliest version of controls, which were designed to prevent an undesirable event from occurring. Other terms sometimes used in place of preventive element are *before-the-fact control element* and *ex ante control element*. For example, sequentially numbered sales invoices could be the preventive element of a control with the objective of recording all credit sales transactions. Using such invoices, one can determine at any time how many credit sales transactions occurred. This is the measurable variable's value.

- The **feedback element** (also known as the *ex post* or *after-the-fact control element*) consists of measuring the actual value of the variable chosen as the basis for the preventive element and comparing it with the expected value. The feedback element is often generated by the accounting system, for comparison with preventive elements generated by processes such as the budget. In accounting system operations, reports convey the feedback element to management, as we will see in Chapter 2 and in Chapters 7 through 11. Continuing the example of a credit sales control, the feedback element would be a count of the number of credit sales entries posted in the customer accounts.

- The **follow-up element** consists of deciding whether the control objective was achieved. This is done by comparing the values of the preventive and feedback control elements. If the objective was not achieved—that is, if there is a significant inequality between the predicted (preventive) and observed (feedback) values—controllable variables within the system should be changed to improve future performance. If the change affects the *nature* of the process, and not just the *magnitude* of the outputs, this step may be called *feedforward control*. For example, a photocopier's darkness control can be used to make copies lighter or darker (feedback control); but if the desired degree of darkness cannot be achieved, the copier may be repaired or replaced (feedforward control). In the credit sales control example, the follow-up element would compare the number of invoices used with the number of entries made. If the two numbers are the same, then the control objective was achieved.

The control objective is identified first. Then the remaining three elements are incorporated into the system design. The design must be checked and rechecked as it develops to be sure it has provided for all the elements of all the controls. Before a system is put into operation, it is tested to be sure the control elements are all present, do not conflict with each other, and achieve their control objectives.

In general, good control distributes responsibility so that different parties perform the various components of control—setting the control objective, operating the process under control, and running preventive feedback, and follow-up elements. Assigning these activities to different individuals or groups ensures that no one party can dominate the planning, conduct, and reporting of any process. Additional discussion of control appears in Chapters 12 through 14.

Boundaries. The elements in a system are separated from their environment by a **system boundary**—the "line" that an input crosses to become a system element and that an output crosses to become part of the environment. On the system side of the boundary, adding or removing elements will change the system's characteristics. Beyond the boundary, elements can be added or subtracted without necessarily affecting the system. The Earth's boundary with space is the upper limit of the atmosphere. The boundary of a phone network is the phone receiver.

Figure 1.3 shows the elements of an open system: the system's components, its inputs and outputs, its system controls, and the boundary that separates it from the external environment.

Figure 1.3   The Elements of an Open System

A system's components vary only within the ranges allowed by the system controls. The controls monitor the inputs and strive to keep outputs in ranges determined by the system's objective. Inputs must cross the system boundary to be sensed by the system components; outputs must cross the boundary to affect the environment.

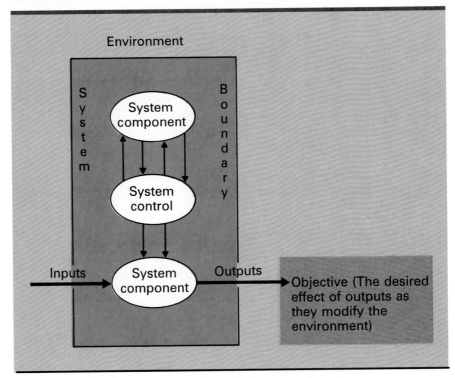

Information Systems

The topic of information systems moves the discussion of systems to a more explicit level and also adds one more concept to the definitions just given. An information system transforms data into information. Data are facts whose usefulness for designated purposes depends on further processing. A list of airline flights, including departure and arrival times, is an example of data. When the data in the list are processed to produce an itinerary for a specific journey or an organized airline guide, they have become information. Another way to view data is as system inputs that are converted, through processing, into information, the system's outputs. Often the outputs of one system become the inputs to another system. The unsorted list of airline flights—itself the output of a system that collects data on individual flights—becomes the input for an organized guide, which is in turn the input for an itinerary-planning system.

Through data collection, facts are gathered in a form that allows them to be recorded, stored, modified, deleted, and selected (processed) for specific uses. Each information system has rules that determine what data it will accept, how it will process those data to transform them into information, what information will be reported, and what form the reports will take.

Not all data can be made useful for the purposes served by a particular information system. Noise and garbage consist of useless data that result when a system design cannot reject certain inputs, much as an AM radio receiver cannot reject static during a storm, or data that the system operators have deliberately or carelessly allowed to enter the system—as when an open microphone picks up conversations and broadcasts them while music is playing. Noise and garbage are not relevant to a system objective. They can be controlled only by selecting appropriate design features and competent system operators. Spending more money on system features and operations can reduce noise and garbage, but it will not eliminate them completely. Of course, what is noise and garbage in one system may be data or information in another. Static is studied by physicists and meteorologists, and the erroneously broadcast conversation in the example above may have resolved problems that were important to the station's managers.

It is not enough, of course, merely to process some data into some information. Data processing, the series of procedures and controls that convert data to information in a specific system context, must meet the survival and profitable-growth requirements of its users while being durable, reliable, consistent, and accurate. We return to data processing operations in Chapter 5, which deals with the organization of data, and in Chapter 7, where examples of data concepts are related to accounts receivable processing.

Management Information Systems

A management information system (MIS) is a special type of information system that produces information relevant to management decision making and planning. Its objective is to help management make decisions in a knowledgeable way. Each MIS is different—defined by the activities and resources of a specific organization and tailored to the organization's needs for information. Although manual MIS do exist, our discussions are confined to computer-based information systems.

Managers use information for controlling the organization and its environment by planning, keeping records, measuring progress toward goals, controlling the environment of the organization, and analyzing problems. To serve all these purposes, most organizations operate complex information systems. In most firms, the accounting information system is one part of an overall MIS; in a very small organization, it may be the only part. In Chapters 2 and 5 we discuss some of management's needs, the ways they are implemented in accounting information systems, and how they affect report design and documentation.

Accounting as a System

Accounting systems deliver financial and managerial information, prepared in a known way, about revenues, expenses, assets, liabilities, and equity. They do so through coordinated operations, using human judgment, software instructions, and computer speed and accuracy.

The Accounting Model

Accounting systems exist wherever there is economic activity. Managers want the consistent and reliable information that an accounting system provides. Accounting information also serves as a continuous historical record, showing the results of past plans and activities so they can be evaluated and perpetuated or changed. Finally, because an organization's accounting system reflects the unique structure and needs of that particular organization, the system is sometimes said to be a **model** of that organization.

Accounting and MIS

Viewed as one part of a management information system, accounting can be seen as possessing all the elements of a system: objectives, inputs, processes, outputs, controls, and a boundary. Figure 1.4 (Part A) shows some elements of information processing systems and Figure 1.4 (Part B) shows the corresponding elements in an accounting system.

The *objective* of an accounting information system is to monitor the monetary dimension of economic activity in an organization by processing data according to known rules and delivering precise information that is useful to those who plan and manage the organization's activities as well as to interested outsiders. The information these systems supply constitutes a consistent and reliable framework for managing operations, in that it comprehensively covers revenues, expenses, assets, liabilities, and profits. By accurately keeping track of the economic life of an organization, these systems enable business activity to be undertaken and sustained.

The accounting information system accepts factual *inputs* consisting of budget and transaction data, expressed in monetary units. It produces

Figure 1.4   Information Processing Systems and Accounting Systems
Part A is a diagram of a very general system. Part B illustrates the corresponding parts of the accounting system. In some cases, the accounting system may be an organization's only management information system.

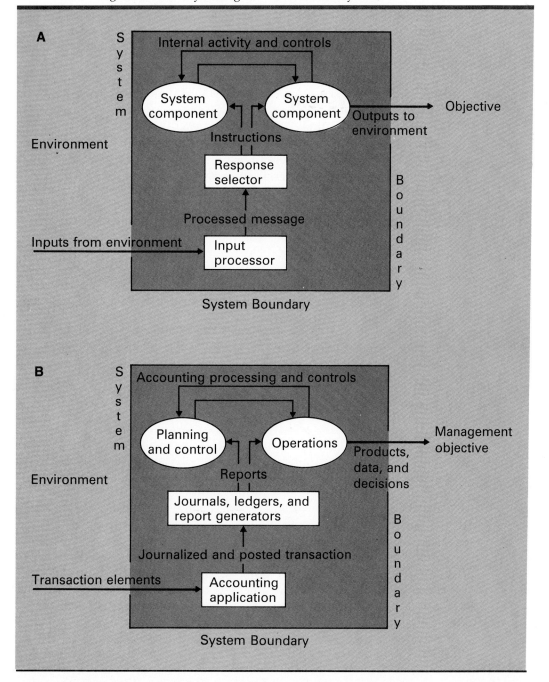

the transaction data by means of very specialized procedures—the accounting applications. These are the *processes*, typically including computer programs, that capture and control accounting data. The system's *outputs* are reports, based on the data and tailored to the needs of internal and external users. The accounting system is unique in that its output is the basis for much of the control exercised in other parts of the organization, for judgments by external parties about the organization's financial health, and for control of the accounting system's own activities.

Because its outputs are so influential, accounting is subject to an unusual degree of scrutiny, including independent audit, internal audit, and extensive controls to ensure the integrity of data and information. Like other system controls, the controls applied within an accounting information system have objective, preventive, feedback, and follow-up elements. Accounting controls can also be classified according to their pertinence to a specific application: general controls apply to the entire system, while application (or transaction) controls set standards for specific parts of the accounting system. The American Institute of Certified Public Accountants publishes an often-used (if somewhat dated) classification and description of accounting controls and of internal controls found within the accounting system.[5]

Accounting controls are just part of a hierarchy of controls that exist in the organization. Some of these controls apply to a broader spectrum of the organization and operate at a higher level of management and over a longer time span than others. **Management controls** are at the highest level. They include controls on organizational structure, long-range planning, and staffing of top-level positions. **Financial controls** have the objective of assuring that resources are available to pursue management's plans. They often include a budgeting or annual planning process, followed by performance reporting. Financial controls correspond most closely with the subject area of managerial accounting.

Internal controls, which describe the standards for day-to-day operations, are specific to particular organization segments and activities. They safeguard assets, promote operating efficiency, and encourage adherence to management's policies. They include accounting controls and data processing controls. **Accounting controls** apply to an area that corresponds most closely with financial reporting. They ensure that transaction processing occurs according to generally accepted accounting principles (GAAP) and as described by the Foreign Corrupt Practices Act and supervised by the Securities and Exchange Commission. **Data processing controls** ensure that data processing activities are adequate to support the accounting and other information systems. Internal controls also function

---

[5]American Institute of Certified Public Accountants, "Codification of Auditing Standards and Procedures," *Statement on Auditing Standards No. 1* (New York.: AICPA, 1973).

to make certain that other controls are not undermined by malfunctions in the equipment or by noise in the system. Figure 1.5 depicts the pyramidal structure of these controls, with management controls at the top of the pyramid.

When studying this hierarchy, remember that top management chooses objectives and strategies that can be achieved only if the process directed toward them can be understood and controlled at every organizational level. Financial controls, including the operating budget, define operating objectives for specific parts of the organization over short periods of time. Accounting controls ensure the kind of classifying and reporting of individual transactions that will result in GAAP-consistent reports, and other internal controls guide daily operations.

Figure 1.5   Hierarchy of Controls
The various types of controls that allow an organization to regulate its activity form a hierarchical structure in the shape of a pyramid. Accounting controls are part of the area of internal controls.

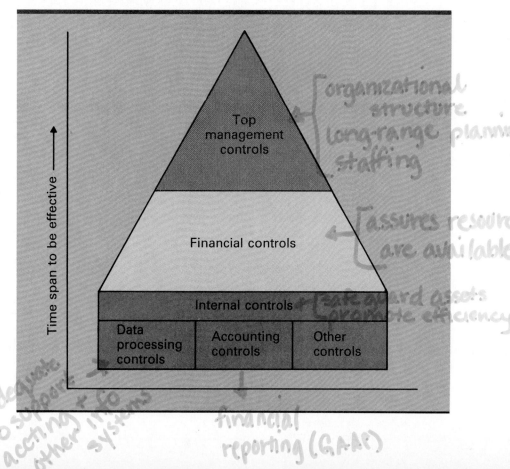

An accounting system's *boundaries* take several forms. One is the boundary crossed by inputs that describe transactions; the system boundary must consist of controls that are able to identify this type of data and reject what they cannot identify. Another boundary is crossed by output. Yet another boundary of the system permits management feedback and feedforward, which change the system's outputs and processing and even its design.

Personnel and Equipment

In addition to inputs, processes, outputs, and controls, an accounting information system has other resources: trained personnel and specialized equipment.

The *trained personnel* of the system consist of the controller and his or her staff. The controller—the chief executive of the accounting system—is responsible for its design and administration. The controller and his or her staff must have expertise in three categories: accounting, administration, and systems. Depending on the organization's size, different members of the controller's staff may specialize in one or another of those skills. The controller does not do data processing, however. That service is provided by the data processing department, which operates computers and stores programs and files for all the information systems in the organization.

The *specialized equipment* on which most accounting systems depend consists primarily of *computer systems* for data input, processing, and reporting. Computer systems include hardware, software, data files, documents, and other resources. The computer itself is an electronic device capable of rapidly carrying out a series of logical instructions. Computer systems have proved themselves cost-effective; through reduced operating costs, increased processing capacity, faster access to information, and improved reliability, they provide the means to repay the large initial investment required for equipment, planning, and software. Chapters 4 and 5 cover technology support for accounting; Chapter 11 addresses data processing management.

Data Organization

The accounting information system organizes its data by using the simple, powerful device of double entry to record the money effect of a transaction on at least two separate accounts. The number and types of accounts used must follow a few basic principles and rules if the information in accounting reports is to be relevant, complete, and timely. These attributes are achieved by recording, processing, summarizing, and reporting the monetary effect of a transaction according to generally accepted accounting principles and, in the case of internal reports, management's own rules. By means of these rules, accounts are identified and reports may be selected and related to fit a particular organization's requirements.

Asking the Right Questions

Computer systems and accounting systems that coexist happily are not the result of chance; they are carefully arranged marriages. A successful accounting system implementation requires detailed planning, based on special knowledge of the unique features of accounting systems operations. Chapters 17 and 18 explore the techniques of system design and implementation. Although it is too early in our discussion to introduce formal systems design, looking at how systems designers begin their analysis of the information needs of an organization will help clarify the various components of accounting information systems. For now, it is enough to know that systems analysts are people who work with the accountants and others in an organization to ensure that the accounting system being designed or replaced will suit the organization's needs. When systems analysts want to improve the flow of information within an organization they will try to define systems requirements by seeking answers to questions such as the following:

- Who are the primary users of the system?
- What are the system objectives?
- What are the boundaries of the system?
- What are the information requirements?
- Can conflicts between differing requirements be resolved?
- Can the information requirements be fulfilled?[6]

These questions, normally part of the planning process, can also serve as a framework for describing accounting information systems.

Primary Users

The primary users of an accounting information system are the organization's managers, who need information to identify and solve problems, as well as for profit and cost measurement. Other primary users include those with whom the organization transacts business (customers, employees, and suppliers, who receive documentary evidence of the transactions) and

---

[6]Adapted from Joan C. Nordbotten, *Analysis and Design of Computer-Based Information Systems* (Boston: Houghton Mifflin, 1985), p. 75.

the equityholders (creditors, owners, and stockholders, who must have proof of their claims on organizational assets). Each of these groups has its own information requirements, which the accounting system must meet. Information intended for primary users may find its way into the hands of secondary users, too. For example, information telling a creditor how much it owes may be used by a credit-rating agency and by other creditors. The needs of secondary users are both complex and conflicting and can rarely be satisfactorily anticipated by system designers or operators. Information for each user group is selected and reported by trained personnel under the direction of the controller. It is the controller who bears responsibility for the specialized information-producing accounting functions. The controller's staff serves as the guardians of the system, responsible for the quality of information distributed to satisfy external requirements and internal priorities.

System Objectives

Organizations expect system designers to achieve many objectives, which would be easy enough to do if unlimited resources were available to build and operate the system. With limited resources, however, the designers must often compromise. These compromises affect such important system attributes as how many details are recorded, how many reports are generated and how often they appear, how long historical data are preserved, and how quickly special information requests can be filled. The skill with which the compromises are chosen will determine how valuable the resulting system will be to management.

Broadly speaking, the system achieves its objective by the process of converting transaction data into decision and control information, while keeping noise and garbage below a disruptive level, at reasonable cost. This process requires that the system support all levels of control. The process supports top management controls by tailoring report contents and formats to the responsibilities of specific managers. It supports financial controls by including their preventive elements—such as the July sales target for the Weslaco office, the budgeted unit variable costs for the Ingram-model production run, or the planned June occupancy rate of the Fulton hotel—into reports that these operating units receive. It supports accounting controls by ensuring that accounting processing and reporting create GAAP-conforming output that satisfies the organization's external and internal needs. In turn, the accounting system relies on data processing and other internal controls to ensure that the accounting model is implemented faithfully; that all data that are processed are supposed to be processed; that no data that should be processed are overlooked; that all processing that occurs is authorized; and that other objectives relating to data integrity are supported.

System Boundaries

The boundaries of the system are not physical demarcations but sets of controls. For example, one boundary is that crossed by credit sales transactions. This boundary consists of procedures that test whether a customer has approved credit, whether the quantity and price of merchandise being sold have been identified and recorded correctly, whether delivery of the merchandise is to occur now or later, and when the customer will pay the credit balance. These procedures are designed to perform boundarylike functions by rejecting false or mishandled credit sales transactions (for example, a sale to a customer with no credit or of merchandise that is out of stock) and accounting for all credit sales that do occur (by creating complete credit sales documentation). Analogous boundaries must be designed for all inputs, outputs, and operating conditions that affect the system.

Information Requirements

Users are responsible for expressing their information requirements. Because users include people inside and outside the organization, the accounting system must meet the information requirements of both managerial and financial accounting. Those requirements are determined by the type of organization (manufacturing, retail, service, financial institution, government), its structure and legal form (centralized or decentralized, proprietorship, partnership, or corporation), and decision characteristics (degree of risk, time frame available, number of alternatives, number of people sharing decision responsibility). Whatever the requirements, the system must meet them consistently by preparing its outputs in familiar formats that correspond with the needs of the internal and external users.

Conflict Resolution

The accounting and data processing departments should share a common understanding of accounting processing requirements so that users can get information without becoming unnecessarily entangled in technological red tape. In general, technology should be used to enhance the value of information by shrinking geographical distances, reducing time delays, integrating and summarizing masses of detail, and simplifying business operations. Much conflict can be anticipated and avoided by using proven system design concepts. For example, designers typically handle the unique requirements of processing specialized types of transactions by creating up to seven commonly found accounting applications for recording transactions—sales and accounts receivable; cash receipts; purchasing and accounts payable; cash disbursements; payroll; inventory (and cost accounting); and general journal. The data organized into processed transactions by these applications can be placed in files designed to be usable in other applications and in comprehensive reports containing information from two or more applications. Data should be organized in such a way that new items can be inserted and any item in the collection can be readily located. Outputs should be accessible to users as needed. Reports should be generated in useful formats and distributed to users designated to receive them. The system should generate an **audit trail**—documentation that can be used to trace system outputs back to their supporting evidence including transaction documents—and this audit trail should be tested periodically. The process of testing, called an **audit,** acts as a feedback control element by describing how the system actually operates.

Can conflicting information requirements be resolved? For example, can data be protected from influences and people who would damage the organization's property without subjecting management to long delays in receiving information or driving up the cost of the system beyond the value of the benefits it will bring to the organization? This answer must be tailored to each system. You will have a chance to try your hand at this type of problem in a comprehensive case at the end of the book.

Summary and Overview of the Book

This book consists of eighteen chapters, organized into five parts. Part 1, Basic Accounting Systems Concepts (Chapters 1 through 6), describes the changing role of today's accountants, systems concepts, accounting processes, information requirements, computer hardware and software, and information processing concepts that are found in all accounting systems. This material provides a necessary background for understanding an accounting information system and a map of the territory covered by the modern profession of accounting. Depending on your background, Part 1 may occasionally seem overly technical or it may seem to merely review familiar concepts. Either way, bear in mind that the purpose of this book is not to teach you how to do accounting. It is to teach you how to make a very sophisticated technology perform to your specifications, so that accounting concepts and practices function as you and the management of your organization expect them to.

Part 2, Accounting Applications (Chapters 7 through 10), covers applications to handle accounts receivable (credit sales and cash receipts), accounts payable (purchasing and cash disbursements), cost accounting, and not-for-profit accounting. Though the prime focus of the book is accounting systems, not computers per se, there are very few manual accounting systems left. They are, in general, a dwindling breed, limited to small businesses and other operations with very few transaction or reporting requirements. For that reason, Part 2 emphasizes selected computer concepts, equipment, operations, and software routines.

Part 3, Controls and Accounting (Chapters 11 through 14), presents accounting and processing controls and discusses in considerable detail computer crime and the principles of auditing and electronic data processing. These topics are a necessary background for designing effective and efficient controls, anticipating the losses that may occur if controls are defective or missing, and testing for the presence of effective controls.

Part 4, New Developments Affecting Accounting Information Systems (Chapters 15 and 16), covers emerging developments in two special areas related to systems design and use: artificial intelligence and communications networks. Artificial intelligence, the field that seeks to enable machines to replicate human intellectual capabilities, has produced two tools that can be used by accounting system designers and managers—decision support systems and expert systems. Computer-based expert systems can store, as a set of rules, the kinds of logical, judgmental, inferential, and subjective knowledge that experts gain from experience. These expert systems can be used to conduct audits, analyze controls, prepare reports, and design data processing applications.

Since accounting systems of the type described in this book typically have many components and users, their effectiveness can be improved by incorporating them into linked networks, which make system services and technology available to all users within a defined office or geographical area. No system designer can afford to ignore the power available through a system implemented using a correctly designed network.

Part 5, System Design and Implementation (Chapters 17 and 18), looks at the process of bringing an accounting system into existence. The book concludes with a comprehensive case designed to test your skills before you encounter your first challenge on the job.

After you have completed this book, you should be able to

- Understand, explain, and apply the basic principles of transaction processing.
- Identify control objectives that are essential for the success of many different management processes.
- Design controls to ensure that your organization is in compliance with management intent and policy.
- Know and apply accounting concepts that make accounting information systems operate more effectively under specialized circumstances (a specific industry, size, technology, structure, or other conditions).
- Understand, explain, and apply the basic principles of creating a new accounting information system or upgrading an existing one.
- Understand the features of common accounting transaction-processing applications and how they relate to each other.

Key Terms

accounting controls
audit
audit trail
closed system
control
control element
control objective
data
data processing

data processing controls
element
feedback element
financial controls
follow-up element
garbage
input
internal controls
management controls

model
noise
objective
open system
output
preventive element
process
system boundary

Review Questions

1. Explain how the accountant's role has changed over the last four decades.

2. Name at least four ways to classify systems, based on their characteristics.

3. What is a control? What are four elements of a control?

4. How do open and closed systems differ from each other? Which category includes accounting systems?

5. Name at least four ways in which an accounting system embodies characteristics of systems in general.

6. Refer to Figure 1.3. What elements of a system does it show? What elements are not shown?

7. The same objectives can be achieved by different systems. Describe at least three different systems for getting from one's dwelling to one's place of work.

8. A boundary is one element of a system. Name four others.

9. If a system has inputs and outputs, it is a _____ system. If it is able to change, it is _____. A budget for a period not yet begun is a _____ system. If the system can drive a car to work, it is probably able to _____.

Discussion Questions

10. How is technology affecting the role of the professional accountant?

11. How does an accounting information system differ from a management information system? Can one take the place of the other?

12. In each of the following systems, identify a part of the system that would be one of its boundaries:
    (a) An automobile
    (b) A computer
    (c) An accounting system
    (d) An organization
    (e) A department in an organization

13. Can noise and garbage be eliminated from systems? If so, explain how; if not, why not?

14. Who are the accounting system's primary users? Companies try to reach people who are not primary users, such as government regulators seeking evidence of compliance with applicable rules. Can you identify some other secondary users?

15. Why does the need for conflict resolution arise in systems design and operation? How may conflicts be resolved?

16. Which of the following is information input that is used by a system to change the system outputs? Why?
    (a) An amplified noise broadcast over a public address system
    (b) Hitting the brake after a dog runs in front of the car
    (c) Authorizing overtime after reviewing the manufacturing backlog
    (d) Turning off the computer at quitting time
    (e) Watching your stock sold at a loss after placing a stop-loss sell order in a declining market
    (f) Receiving the weekly report of delinquent accounts receivable

17. Is information subject to deterioration? What is the remedy for information deterioration?

CHAPTER 2

Organizations, Decisions, and Information

Learning Objectives

After studying this chapter, you should be able to

- Define a decision and describe statistical and behavioral models of decisions.

- Describe the nature of information systems and explain why they are useful.

- Explain risk and how information is used to manage it.

- Understand how and why organization structures differ.

- Explain how management uses information produced by an accounting system.

- Describe accounting systems, using standard systems terminology and diagrams.

In his film classic "Modern Times," Charlie Chaplin satirized machines and systems that went hilariously awry. Recently IBM used a Chaplin look-alike in its ads to put a friendly face on its carefully designed and widely used computer systems. This turnabout is just one illustration of the extent to which people have become less suspicious of and more reliant on complex systems over the years. Managers are no exception to this trend.

Today's technology is such that every manager should understand how his or her organization uses information, how the organization's information systems operate, and how to use, control, and design them. Each organization's system is unique, because each system is tailored to a specific set of information needs defined by the activities and resources of a particular organization. You will recall from Chapter 1, however, that all systems share certain characteristics. Each is a set of related elements that produces information—facts, inferences, comparisons, and projections— useful to managers in making decisions. For example, each of the Fortune 500 companies is unique, yet each one has an accounting system with similar accounts, reports, transactions, processes, and controls. The accounting information system, which is part of the management information system, provides information useful for planning, keeping records, measuring progress toward goals, exercising controls, and analyzing problems. This chapter explains some of the relationships that exist among an organization, its management, and the systems that support its decision-making processes.

Management Structure

The most common user of an accounting system is an organization, which we will define here as an association of people, some of whom are managers. Organizations that engage in economic activity include profit-seeking, not-for-profit, and government entities; their activities include service, trade, selling, manufacturing, and other pursuits. Organizations take a number of forms, including corporations, partnerships, bureaus, and proprietorships. Most of the material in this book is applicable to all such organizations; Chapter 10 discusses concepts especially pertinent to not-for-profit and government organizations.

An organization is a system. It has a mission and goals, consists of elements of various types, uses scarce resources to pursue those goals, and encourages specialization of skills and responsibilities. Every organization also has a management structure—an assignment of responsibility for specific jobs, tasks, projects, and processes. These assignments are made to **responsibility centers**, or positions designating offices, departments, and divisions that can make decisions and wield other forms of authority. An organization may be centralized (most decisions are made by one person or committee) or decentralized (decision making is spread throughout the organization) or a combination of the two.

A **matrix management** structure is suited to handling multiple projects. All the projects will be managed and accounted for in the same way, enabling comparison of their revenues and costs on a two-dimensional matrix. In such a matrix, each column will represent a project, and each row will represent a responsibility center that works on the project. The intersections of rows and columns show each center's responsibility for a particular project cost.

An organization's management structure can be portrayed on an organization chart like the one shown in Figure 2.1. The boxes represent positions; the lines show which positions report to others. These lines define authority to make and review decisions, with the most authoritative positions at the top of the diagram. Management structures may also be market-oriented (see Figure 2.2, page 30), geography-oriented (see Figure 2.3, page 31), manufacturing-oriented (see Figure 2.4, page 32), or some combination of these forms. An international company may be organized geographically, but within nations or regions it may exhibit a market-

Figure 2.1 Functional Organization Structure
The functional organization structure emphasizes control over such specialized activities as sales, manufacturing, and finance. It is appropriate for simpler and smaller organizations.

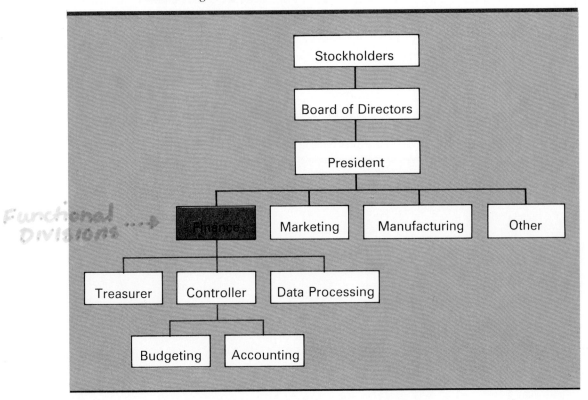

Functional DIVISIONS ···→

oriented structure. Whatever the organization's structure, its purpose is to channel management responsibilities to those best able to handle them to achieve its mission and goals.

The president or chief executive typically reports to a Board of Directors, which in some cases is elected by stockholders. The Board sets companywide objectives and reviews progress. In the organization shown in Figure 2.1, Finance, Marketing, and Manufacturing are major responsibility centers, at this level called **functional divisions** or functional specializations. In Figure 2.1 they are responsible to the president. Giving executive authority to the functional divisions is one way to organize a business; other ways are to allocate executive authority by markets, by geography, or by production activities. Note, however, that the finance function need not be distributed equally among the organization's components: it may be wholly or partially centralized or distributed, regardless of the organization's overall structure.

Organizational structures have one main purpose: to ensure that operations contribute to objectives. To achieve this goal, many organizations undergo considerable internal structural tinkering as they experiment with varying degrees of centralization that shift decision-making authority

Figure 2.2   Market-Oriented Organization Structure
This market-oriented organization structure emphasizes control over sales in differentiated markets. Each marketing unit controls its own finances and contracts for manufacturing outputs. A stronger form of this structure would place manufacturing directly under product-group control.

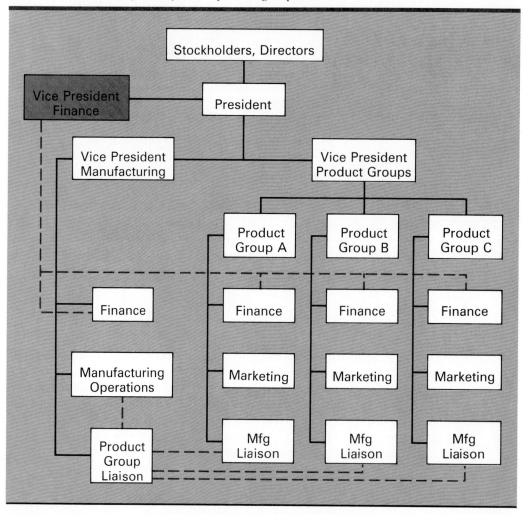

Figure 2.3   Geography-Oriented Organization Structure
A geography-oriented organization structure must be used where factors of distance, language, culture, and business objectives make it necessary to operate differently in different locations. The dotted line shows a staff relationship through which the finance function is coordinated companywide.

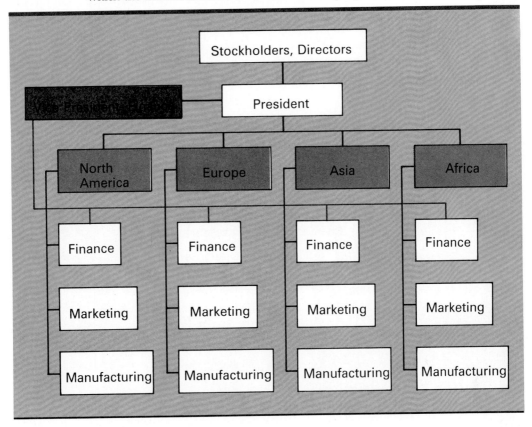

among responsibility centers. The eventual complexity of the structure will be determined not by size but by interaction between *people* and *purpose*. As the organization changes, the accounting system adapts by changing its data inputs, internal processing, and information outputs. A decentralized organization does not necessarily imply a decentralized accounting system; experience has shown that the critical factor in an accounting system's performance is not its internal structure but its ability to deliver information where and when it is needed.

Real organizations are seldom as orderly and precise as writers portray them. Organization charts don't show the overlapping or overlooked responsibilities, unreported information, absent-minded managers, personal distractions, conflicts, uncertainties, and inefficiencies. Such imperfections make an organization's survival (let alone its growth according to plan) a major achievement. An accounting system with orderly files, consistent reliability, and performance-report capability contributes to this achievement and is the essential basis for managerial success. Numerous studies and government reports show that the largest cause of business failure is the lack of an effective accounting system, the controls it includes, and the reports, documents, and resources it generates.

Accounting systems help management handle both internal problems and external uncertainties. Some uncertainties, such as the possibility of

Figure 2.4   Manufacturing-Oriented Organization Structure
Manufacturing-oriented organization structures are rarer than they used to be. In this one, the manufacturing divisions control their finances (which are coordinated by a staff relationship) and their production output is all transferred to one marketing function.

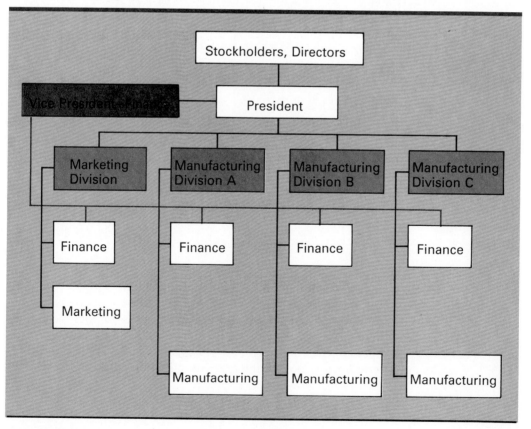

worldwide recession, will always remain uncontrollable. Others can be controlled if management uses information, including that available through its accounting system. When, for example, a business's sales of certain products rise suddenly, the managers can use accounting reports of sales and inventory levels to adjust purchases and manufacturing to appropriate levels.

Executives search for relevant information to make predictable the behavior of as many variables as possible. Often this attempt to reduce uncertainty takes the form of creating systems—such as the accounting system—to produce relevant information and use it to influence otherwise independent variables. **Risk management** is the process of using information to identify and reduce risk in decisions.

How Management Views Information

A **decision** is a choice between alternatives. In Chapter 1, we defined information as processed data, a system output. We could also define **information** as any *input* that will change management's response or output (decision) to its environment. This definition implies that managers have a choice. If one does not have or recognize a choice, there can be no decision.

In a decision, a fact qualifies as information if awareness of it could change a manager's preferences among alternatives. Information systems are designed and operated to produce messages that may prompt their recipient to make, or at least to consider, different choices. Accounting systems produce financial-information messages—records of activity, statements of expectations, and measures of performance—that encourage executive commitment to one of several alternatives.

Suppose that auditors must decide whether to accept a client's valuation of the provision for pension liabilities that is based at least in part on information generated through the accounting system. While the auditors are at work, the Securities and Exchange Commission issues a new ruling. If the ruling is about pension liabilities and covers the type of situation represented by the client, it is information the auditors must use in their decision. Otherwise, the ruling is not information so far as *this decision* is concerned. If the auditors ignore the ruling when it applies to their decision, they run the risk of accepting an incorrect client position. This type of risk occurs whenever information is omitted from a decision.

We could also say that the information was relevant. *Relevance* is information's property of being pertinent in specific circumstances. We shall examine information from two viewpoints: relevance to a particular decision and relevance to a process. In general, decision relevance applies to one-of-a-kind decisions and process relevance applies to ongoing responsibilities.

Decision relevance is the property of information that may affect a particular decision. It can best be illustrated by an example. The Winters Blanket Company must decide what materials it will use to manufacture its sleeping bags. Information relevant to this decision will include details about the properties of the materials, manufacturing operations, intended use of the product, and the risks, costs, and benefits associated with each material. The cost difference per unit of materials would be relevant information; the distribution cost of the product would probably not be relevant.

An information system should send decision-relevant information in time for those responsible for the decision to consider it fully. Facts that cannot be identified as pertinent to the risks, costs, or benefits of a decision are not relevant and should not be reported to those individuals (though they may be relevant to some other decision).

A *process*, you may recall from Chapter 1, is a planned sequence of operations intended to produce certain results. **Process relevance** characterizes information that enables a manager to administer and control a specific process or to carry out sets of related decisions. Managers with responsibilities such as those of the Chief Financial Officer or the Director of Marketing or the Day Shift Packing Supervisor are really in charge of processes—their decisions tend to run together and mingle with tasks such as preparing reports, reviewing records, sustaining morale, and acting as an advocate or critic. Accounting information may be helpful in such processes, and the manager will want to receive accounting information even when it is not relevant to a specific decision.

Managers use the accounting system to create both decision-relevant and process-relevant information. Specifically, they design the system to make its data and information searchable, so that the data and information can be examined and identified as relevant. They will also structure the system to ensure that it issues regular reports containing information relevant to the needs of those responsible for making decisions and managing processes. As part of this design process, managers strive to minimize noise, garbage, and other undesirable information system outputs. For example, the unprocessed details of a firm's sales transactions would certainly qualify as data. Processed to show sales by periods, products, districts, and customer use of credit, these details are truly information. If, however, the sales personnel were able to change the dates of certain sales to cause themselves to qualify for bonuses under a seasonal sales-incentive program, the changes would distort the seasonal picture of sales activity and would constitute noise and garbage. Such incorrect and/or irrelevant inclusions in system outputs increase the difficulty of using an information system.

Models of Decision Making

Decision making requires an adequate supply of relevant information but does not end when that information has been produced. Decisions occur only when one *chooses*. The human decision-making process is very complex, and theoretical models of it are numerous. Among the disciplines that have developed such models are psychology, political science, education, and statistics. Because the statistical and behavioral decision making models are developed most fully, we will confine our discussion to them.

As stated earlier, a decision is a choice among alternatives. The usual intent of a decision is to secure a benefit for the decision maker (manager, in our case) or for the party on whose behalf the decision maker acts (the supervisor, customer, owner, or public interest). Ordinarily, one selects an alternative without complete certainty about the exact nature of the benefit or even that the benefit will be forthcoming. The absence of complete certainty imposes risk on decision makers, who differ in their individual abilities to tolerate risk.

By offering constantly updated information, accounting systems may be able to reduce uncertainty and therefore reduce risk in decision making. In the next section, we will see how this can happen.

The Statistical Decision Model

The statistical decision model lends itself to quantitative analysis of the costs and benefits associated with available alternatives. It also offers an understanding of decision risk. According to the **statistical decision model**, five elements—a decision objective, a decision maker, a set of alternatives, one or more independent variables, and a payoff—must be present for a decision to occur.

- A **decision objective** is the goal or target the decision maker hopes to achieve and the desired end for which the decision is undertaken. If one's objective is to possess a means of personal transportation, one will undertake a decision to acquire a bicycle, motorcycle, car, boat, airplane, or some other vehicle.

- A **decision maker** chooses an alternative and is responsible for its consequences. The decision maker has the ability to act and a desire to pursue beneficial outcomes (measured as profits, assets, and so on). The decision maker—who can be one person, a group, or an entire organization—must have the means to put a choice into effect. One cannot be a decision maker seeking transportation unless one has access to and can pay for the means of transportation being considered. An eight-year-old child may want transportation but has neither access to it nor the means to move from desire to decision.

- A set of **alternatives**, among which the decision maker must choose, consists of values the decision maker assigns to controllable variables. The decision choice is the alternative the decision maker chooses. For instance, a business manager may consider different levels of investment in inventory, or a transportation seeker may select models of automobiles to consider buying or leasing.

- The values of the one or more **independent variables** are unknown until the decision maker implements the chosen alternative. Some writers, somewhat grandly, characterize each set of independent-variable values as a "state of nature." At the time of purchase, for example, the transportation seeker really does not know how a particular car will perform, in spite of estimates of its gas mileage, repair record, and braking ability. Similarly, in a business setting, a manager buying an accounting system computer does not know the organization's future transaction-processing volume. The manager must regard that future volume as an independent variable, a state of nature. If it were known, the exact value could help determine the size of the new computer; since the volume is not known, the manager must estimate it. Because the estimate may be wrong and may therefore result in a decision that does not fully achieve the decision maker's objectives, the responsibility for estimating introduces *risk*. Any improvement in the accuracy of the processing-volume estimate increases the information available, reduces uncertainty, and reduces decision-making risk.

- The **payoff** consists of a consequence to the decision maker, determined entirely by the interaction between the alternative chosen and the independent variables; it is expressed in the same units used to measure the decision maker's welfare. The payoff may not be entirely quantifiable; what formula can weigh the pleasure of owning an exotic sports car against the possibility that it may be unreliable and have high repair costs? However, when decisions are primarily economic, the payoff can be quantified in accounting terms—as though the alternative had been chosen and the independent variables had assumed their values. These values can then be used to reach a decision.

The decision maker may create one or more **decision rules** relating the independent variables to the alternatives. These decision rules indicate which alternative to select if particular values of the independent variables are expected. The decision rules are usually constructed to produce either large payoffs or small direct costs.

These rules are best understood when they are expressed as a matrix, as shown in Figure 2.5. In that figure, the independent variable combinations (the processing volume) each head a column, and the alternatives, the choices available to the decision maker (the computer models), each claim a row. The numbers inside the matrix represent the cost savings to be expected when a particular computer model (row) is chosen and must process a certain transaction volume (column). The decision rule must specify the decision alternative (the computer model) that will be chosen for each independent variable value (processing volume). It can be made up of any combination of row and column intersections that includes every

Figure 2.5   Statistical Model of the Computer-Selection Decision
This model of a computer hardware selection decision illustrates the statistical decision model. The payoffs associated with various choices are shown in the cells.

Processing volume (the independent variable) expressed as 000s of transactions/hour

Computer models	N1 200	N2 300	N3 400	N4 500	N5 600
A1	20	50	10	40	20
A2	120	40	20	0	0
A3	0	0	0	200	0
A4	30	30	30	30	30
A5	80	10	80	30	20

Computer models under consideration (decision-maker alternatives)

The payoffs (values in cells above) are the cost savings that are predicted to occur if the row-model computer is chosen and the column-processing volume occurs column and does not repeat or overlook any column. In Figure 2.5, the decision rule (N1: A2); (N1: A1); (N3: A5); (N4: A5); (N5: A4) is not acceptable because it repeats N1 (for A1 and A2) and does not show any action if N2 occurs. The decision rule that consistently selects the largest payoffs is (N1: A2); (N2: A1); (N3: A5); (N4: A3); (N5: A4). The decision maker who seeks the largest payoff rule in one or a series of decisions is said to be **optimizing**. The decision maker can achieve a satisfactory payoff only by predicting how the decision choice (which is controllable) will interact with the state of nature (which is beyond control). When such prediction is difficult or impossible, the decision is said to involve risk and decision outcomes may be unsatisfactory or harmful to the decision maker. In Figure 2.5, if the decision maker were to choose computer model A3 in anticipation of processing volume N4, but N1 occurred instead, the payoff to the decision maker would be zero.

When the decision maker can produce an information summary in the form of a model such as Figure 2.5, several strategies—none of them completely satisfactory—may be used to compensate for the presence of risk. We discuss three of these strategies below. Others are described in advanced texts listed in the bibliography at the end of the book.

Maximin Strategy.   *Maximin* is an abbreviation for *"maxi*mize the *mini*mum possible gain." **Maximin strategy** is suitable for the conservative decision maker who wants primarily to ensure some gain and avoid the worst outcomes. Loyal savings account investors follow the maximin strategy. In Figure 2.5, alternative A4, with the highest minimum outcome (30), is the appropriate choice. The maximin strategist will sacrifice the possibility of higher payoffs in the other alternatives (200, 120, 80, 50, or 40) in order to avoid the risk of an even lower payoff (20, 10, or zero).

Maximax Strategy.   *Maximax* is an abbreviation for *"maxi*mize the *maxi*mum possible gain." **Maximax strategy**—appropriate for the risk-seeking, go-for-broke decision maker—selects the alternative with the possibility, however remote, of the highest payoff and disregards the risks attached to that alternative. In Figure 2.5, A3 would be the right choice for the maximax strategy. The maximax strategist would accept as necessary the risk that the payoff could be zero in order to aim for the possible payoff of 200.

Weighted-Outcomes Strategy.   A decision maker who makes the same decision repeatedly (such as a data processing expert whose specialty is to forecast transaction-processing volume) may conclude that the five outcomes [N1...N5] are not equally likely. In fact, he or she might conclude that there is a known or estimable relative likelihood of these independent-variable values, and that using this information might result in a higher average payoff. For example, the computer buyer, concerned about the future volume of transactions, may select the five volume values from 200,000 to 600,000 transactions per hour as shown in Figure 2.5 and forecast that 400,000 transactions per hour (N3) is three times more likely than N1's 200,000. This strategy is called the **weighted-outcomes strategy**; to use it, one must assign weights to the independent-variable values, adding up to 1.0, and then calculate the expected value of each alternative as a weighted average.

Assume, for instance, that the weights are [N1: 0.1, N2: 0.2, N3: 0.3, N4: 0.3, N5: 0.1]. This situation is shown in Figure 2.6. By using these values to weigh A1's payoffs, you find that the expected value of buying computer model A1 is $E(A1) = 0.1*20 + 0.2*50 + 0.3*10 + 0.3*40 + 0.1*20 = 29.$[1] In a similar fashion, the other computer-model choices have expected values of $E(A2) = 26$; $E(A3) = 60$; $E(A4) = 30$; and $E(A5) = 45$. Because the computer model with the highest expected value is A3, a decision maker following the weighted-outcomes strategy would choose it.

Of course, since processing volume is uncertain, the decision must be made repeatedly in order for this average payoff to be achieved. Meanwhile, the decision maker must have considerable resources on reserve for those times when the high payoff is not achieved. The weighted-outcomes strategy is sometimes called Bayesian decision making.

Behavioral Decision Models

The behavioral sciences view decision making as an outcome of exchanging and processing information. A **behavioral decision model** emphasizes the relationships among variables influencing human information processing. The various models differ in how they treat individual and group responses (such as learning, thinking, problem solving, and frustration) to diverse inputs—influence (including incentives, manipulation, and authority), goal setting, risk, competition, conflict, technology, and structure. Predictions about decision outcomes may also differ, depending on the information processing model used.

The statistical model's concept of decision-making optimization gives way in behavioral decision models to **satisficing**—pursuing an acceptable rather than an optimal decision. Decision makers develop criteria for acceptability by reviewing the way past decisions were handled, what happens in other organizations, and what they believe other people will accept. Representative criteria for a decision might include maintaining a consensus and using quantitative (including financial) information.

Within an organization unit that is in the process of making decisions,

---

[1]The * represents multiplication.

Figure 2.6   The Computer-Selection Statistical Model with Weights Assigned to Independent Variables   This figure is based on Figure 2.5. It adds weights reflecting the expected relative likelihood of processing volume values and, in the free-standing right-hand column, shows the result of calculating expected values of the available choices. These expected values can be used to help make the decision.

Processing volume (the independent variable) expressed as 000s of transactions/hour

Weights showing relative likelihood of processing-volume values

		N1 200	N2 300	N3 400	N4 500	N5 600	
		0.1	0.2	0.3	0.3	0.1	Sum = 1.0
Computer models under consideration (decision-maker alternatives)	A1	20	50	10	40	20	29
	A2	120	40	20	0	0	26
	A3	0	0	0	200	0	60
	A4	30	30	30	30	30	30
	A5	80	10	80	30	20	45

The payoffs (values in cells above) are the cost savings that are predicted to occur if the row-model computer is chosen and the column-processing volume occurs

This column shows E(A), the expected values of the available choices, assuming the production-volume value relative likelihoods are represented by the weights shown.

individuals tend to band loosely together to seek new leads, exchange information, and check one another's ideas. The loose group forms a kind of network, which expands or contracts in response to the decision's urgency and resource requirements. The network also competes for the decision payoff and tries to avoid bearing its cost. For example, a network consisting of strategic planners and top executives within Childress Enterprises may decide to start a new chain of bookstores; then delegate implementation to a network of lower-level staff (say, the mid-continent retail marketing division); then, if there are profits, award bonuses and profits to an expanded network of staff and the firm's stockholders. This process could extend over twelve to twenty-four months. While it continues, the three networks exchange information. Childress Enterprises' formal organization may even change to accommodate and support the networks if the bookstore chain shows unusual promise; for example, the firm might create a separate bookstore division.

Although one person may belong to several networks, no one is likely to belong to all the networks in an organization. A network member will communicate most often with other members of the same network and will tend to give greater weight to the decision criteria of other members of the same network. This may lead to disagreements within decision-making groups whose members belong to different functional areas or have different technical backgrounds. In such cases, compromise must occur; under poor control, the decision process may be prolonged and imprecise, with the result that no one is quite sure who made the decision or when.

Higher-level managers may seek to bring the values of informal networks into conformity with those they believe serve the best interests of the organization. In selecting networks to join, managers may seek to reinforce their own values and to influence other network members to accept the same values. In making decisions, a manager may seek approval from others, including those with control over the allocation of salaries, promotions, and perquisites. When managers believe their own well-being is synonymous with the organization's welfare, the situation is said to exhibit **goal congruence**. Risk and unreasonable goals can degrade decision making because they reduce goal congruence. Under such conditions, a decision maker may respond by avoiding a decision or choosing an excessively conservative alternative.

If an organization's goals are achievable and accompanied by reasonable incentives, management and staff will nearly always try to reach them. What happens when goals are unreasonably high and incentives are held constant or reduced? Employees may then feel unable to advance their own welfare by pursuing the organization's goals, and they will tend to seek reinforcement of these attitudes from members of their networks. Goal congruence will diminish even more if network members condone or encourage disregard of the organization's interests.

Human Responses to Risk

As we have seen, risk entails the possibility of an unacceptable outcome. Not everyone tolerates risky decisions, and some decision makers feel more comfortable than others with higher levels of risk. The best decision-making performance should occur when the risk inherent in the decision matches the decision maker's level of risk tolerance. Very few investors, for example, would feel comfortable with an entire portfolio of the riskiest investments; similarly, very few would be so averse to risk as to want an entire portfolio of short-term government securities. When any risky decision must be made, the decision maker seeks ways to reduce risk and to make the outcome more predictable. In Figure 2.6, alternative A4, which promises *some* payoff no matter which state of nature occurs, is a low-risk choice.

Accounting systems are useful to decision makers because they produce information that helps identify and reduce the level of risk in decisions. Figure 2.7 charts the way executives use information to manage decision-making risk.

Figure 2.7   Risk Management in Decision Making
Decision risk is managed by either accepting it, modifying it until it is acceptable, or shifting the decision elsewhere to avoid the risk.

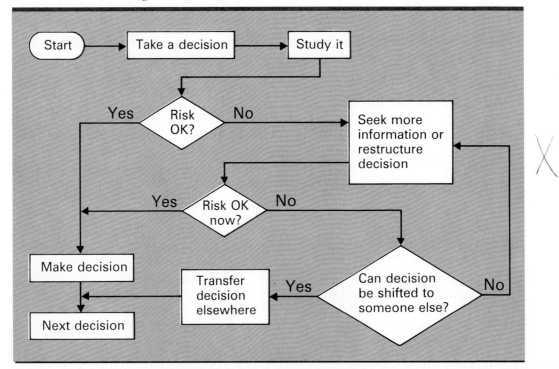

Viewed in the context of risk management, control over accounting and information processing serves to make information *predictably and routinely* reliable, objective, and consistent in its portrayal of all factors important to evaluating risks and selecting alternatives. Management and system designers expect that adequate controls can be designed to achieve these goals in most decision situations. Situations where controls fall short of these goals and prove inadequate are treated in one of two ways: the controls may be improved, with a resulting related benefit, or they may be improved but no benefit will result—in the worst case, the consequence may even be a penalty. Situations in which the controls can be improved are known as *control risks*. When strengthening the controls alone will not produce satisfactory results, the organization has a *control weakness*. You will learn more about control risks and weaknesses in Chapter 12.

Management Information and Controls

Information is plentiful. However, information certain to make the outcome of particular decisions more predictable is difficult to identify and often scarce. As we have seen, information of unknown background or source and unrelated in context to the decisions at hand typically does not improve decisions. In fact, such information can make decisions riskier by increasing the load of irrelevant data. Accounting system designers plan their systems so that the information produced will have a known background and managers can use it to make specific decision outcomes more predictable. The designers treat the information as inputs to financial, accounting, and processing controls. These controls are built into and around accounting systems, and they require specific responses from managers.

Objectives of Management Control Using Information

Information promotes management goals by pointing to areas where more effort will be needed if the goals are to be reached. This additional effort then takes the form of management intervention in the interests of conserving assets, reducing costs, stopping waste, and even improving planning. One type of information produced by accounting systems signals the possibility of significant theft, fraud, inefficiency, or carelessness. This information is a comparison of actual inventory counts with the inventory level calculated from the records. Another information output is a comparison of expected and actual utility expenses: a larger-than-expected gap could be interpreted as a sign of a problem. In either case, the usefulness of the information depends on *whether the accounting system has been operated with adequate controls to ensure its reliability.*

Control as a Part of Routine Activity.   All controls require managerial participation in order to work and have the same objective: making the outcomes of routine activity more predictable. The controls should be an integral part of routine activity; such activity must embody the controls. There should be appropriate incentives and penalties to support compliance with the controls. Support for controls also includes management and clerical analysis of the information they produce and follow-up when controls either indicate an operational failure or fail themselves. Finally, controls will not be successful unless management fully understands how they should function, what different information signals mean, and what responses are appropriate for each signal. In a retail store, for example, a managerial goal of conserving assets may entail the related control processes of mirrors installed over the shelves and merchandise tagged to set off detectors should anyone try to remove it from the store without paying for it. Unless the mirrors are watched, the checkout aisles staffed, and the detectors working and turned on, the control processes will not accomplish their goal of conserving assets. And, of course, if management fails to commit resources adequate to the tasks involved, the controls will exist in theory only.

A Hierarchy of Controls

Controls operate over different time horizons, with the long-horizon controls generally applying to higher levels of management. Thus, a five-year planning control would apply to top management and its staff. A customer-credit granting control would apply to the short-run operation of the consumer credit department. Whatever its time horizon, a control must enable management to influence and therefore predict the result of organization activities, thereby reducing the risk inherent in such activities. At the same time, the control must operate as unobtrusively and automatically as possible. Management embeds many self-controlling processes in its activities, reserving its own time for those issues of management and financial controls (often called administrative controls) that require its attention, such as setting objectives, strategies, programs and policies, and troubleshooting. Table 2.1 characterizes different types of management controls and their corresponding objectives, beginning with the long-horizon controls.

Let's examine these controls in the context of an event you may already be familiar with, the arrival of cash receipts in the mail. These receipts arrive because of objectives and activities that top management selected (top-management controls) and because of a credit policy to generate sales (financial controls). The cash receipts are handled by clerks trained to follow specific procedures (internal controls). The receipts are recorded so that accounting records reflect their amounts and origins (accounting controls). The ability of internal and accounting controls to ensure proper handling of cash receipts allows credit-extension to be an

Table 2.1   Types of Management Control and Their Objectives

Control	Objective
Top-management	Determine objectives; limit business operations to those that generate progress toward the objectives.
Financial	Establish a financial plan and compare the financial results of operations with those predicted by the plan.
Internal	Embed safeguards in everyday procedures to achieve operating goals, such as producing revenue and protecting assets.
Accounting (a class or type of internal control)	Establish and implement an accounting system that performs its processing and reporting functions in predictable and desirable ways.

acceptable way of stimulating sales; in turn, the ability of credit-extension to do this enables top management to select objectives and organization structures where credit extension is necessary.

The internal operating and accounting controls reinforce each other. By making the handling of cash receipts a controlled process, management enhances the ability of the accounting records to measure the balance of cash actually available. Management can rely on these measurements if it has installed the proper procedures for, and controls over, cash receipts handling.

Controls pay off for management by collecting process-describing information for periodic review and by saving the time and energy that would otherwise be expended on intensive, ongoing monitoring of cash receipts handling. Management can then concentrate on other matters instead.

Control over a top-management process—long-range planning, for example—differs in form *but not in effect* from control over a routine procedure like cash receipts. In each case, control seeks to make the outcome more predictable and reliable. This is a matter of specific control objectives. A long-range planning process may have as its objective reliably estimating the values of key variables (such as future market size). Suitable procedures and controls would call for using several independent estimates, projecting recent sales trends, polling customers, reviewing technology, looking for convergence of the estimates, and reviewing estimates for reasonableness.

Most variables in the business environment are not under the direct and total control of any executive or organization. Executives may spend a good deal of time trying to bring such variables under control (to turn them into alternatives, in other words) or to anticipate the behavior of uncontrollable variables.

Explaining and Describing Accounting Systems

Accounting systems and their control features can be complex. Fortunately, there are several methods to explain and describe them, the most prominent of which are narrative descriptions, entity diagrams, and data-flow diagrams.

Narrative Description.   A narrative description is a precise, sentence-by-sentence, step-by-step description of a system's components and the interaction of those components. The description can be brief (an "executive summary"), long and detailed (a user's manual), or anything in between; the form will be geared to the intended users. Examples of narrative descriptions appear in all subsequent chapters. Here is a short example of one common activity:

> The pants-retainment device is a thin, flexible piece of leather, cloth, or plastic about 35 inches long. It is inserted in cloth loops found at intervals at the top of the leg-covering device. One end of the pants-retainment device has holes in it and is tapered; to install the device, insert this end in the loop on the left nearest to the wearer's center, then in the loop left of this one, and so on until the tapered end emerges just to the right of the wearer's center. Notice that the smoothest side of the pants-retainment device should always face outward. The untapered end of this device has a fastener attached. The fastener consists of a short point and a tapered-end retainment device. After installing the pants-retainment device, pull on both ends until a pleasant tension results, then place the short point through a hole in the tapered end and let it rest against the retainment device. If pants-retainment does not occur, reinstate the short point in another tapered-end hole and check again, repeating this step as necessary.

Entity Diagram.   An entity diagram is a pictorial representation of the system. It consists of entities and relations between entities. Figure 2.1 on page 29 is an entity diagram showing the responsibility centers in an organization and the relationships among them. The entities are represented by rectangles, and the relationships by lines; a line from a higher point on the diagram to a lower point signifies a supervisory relationship. Figure 2.8 is an entity diagram of a payroll system. In this diagram, although the rectangles again are entities, the relationships are shown as diamonds. The entity diagram identifies the parties, or users, of a relationship and shows where relationships must exist. Entity diagrams can exist at several levels; the "paid by" relationship, for instance, could become the subject of its own entity diagram, and so on, until at the lowest and most detailed level, individual steps and data values are mapped.

Data-flow Diagram.   A data-flow diagram is a pictorial representation of data groupings and the processes that create, modify, and use them. Figure 2.9 shows the data flows of a simple asset information system. This diagram shows data collections as open-ended rectangles, and the

Figure 2.8　An Entity Diagram

An entity diagram is used by system designers to give a precise description of exactly how a system entity, such as *employee,* relates to other entities in the system, such as *personnel, treasurer,* and *department head.*

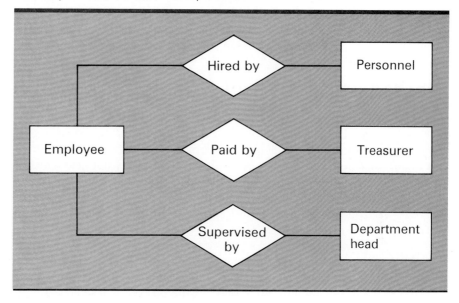

Figure 2.9　A Data-Flow Diagram

The data-flow diagram shows the data used and produced by various processes and, again, is used by system designers.

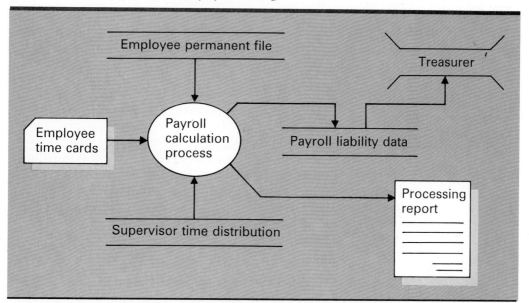

processes that modify them as ovals. Data may enter or leave through documents, reports, or interfaces with systems not shown in the data-flow diagram. Data-flow diagrams show how a system handles data.

A data-flow diagram is really another sort of entity diagram; now, however, the entities are data collections, processes, documents, reports, and interfaces. Each of these entities could be rendered in even more detailed diagrams, as we shall see in Chapters 17 and 18.

Mechanism of Control Using Information

To operate, a control mechanism needs information as an input. An organization's plan for achieving its goals is the "objective" part of many controls; it serves as an information input to the budget control mechanism. Part of this plan is the organization's budget, which is prepared in advance and expresses annual expected achievement in terms of easily measured financial variables. It specifies revenues, expenses, assets, and equities as they should appear at certain near-future dates if the plan is on schedule. By offering future values for these variables, the budget constitutes the control's "preventive" element.

The management information system, particularly the accounting system, will later produce actual figures derived from operations for the same variables that appear in the budget. These actual figures constitute the "feedback" control element. The differences between the expected budget values and the measured actual values (usually called *variances*) represent the "follow-up" control element. By analyzing these variances, a manager can determine how well a responsibility center is achieving its designated budget goals and where and how the organization or the center should concentrate effort to increase its success. Comparing actual operations with the budget and summarizing the comparison by means of variance analysis is called **performance reporting.** This topic and the related budgeting process are discussed in detail in Chapter 3.

Report Design

To select their goals and to design activities to further those goals, managers need financial information. Managers should help design the reports they will receive, specifying their content and frequency. Managerial participation of this kind integrates performance reporting with data gathering, processing, and other functions of the accounting system. Operating management and system designers must consider the following integrated functions and be sure they are designed into the system:

- The facts needed for performance evaluation should be identified and collected when transactions occur.
- Data processing capacity must be geared to the expected volume of transactions and reports.

- Data accuracy should be "locked in" by means of error checking (manual and automated) and editing at the time data are recorded.
- The variances calculated and reported must have clear relevance to the efficiency of the operations they describe.
- Administrative channels must be adequate to allow fine tuning of business operations to control the causes of large unfavorable or negative variances.

The Information-User Interface

Financial information is generated by the accounting system when it records data generated by business activities and processes them in keeping with agreed-upon accounting principles and rules. In summary form, the system then returns the processed information to managers, who exercise control by comparing their goals with these accounting descriptions of actual operations and taking action to narrow any performance shortfalls. The means of passing data into a system and getting information back from it is called the **system-user interface**. Figure 2.10 shows how

Figure 2.10   The System-User Interface
A system-user interface makes it possible for the system to be useful to nontechnical managers.

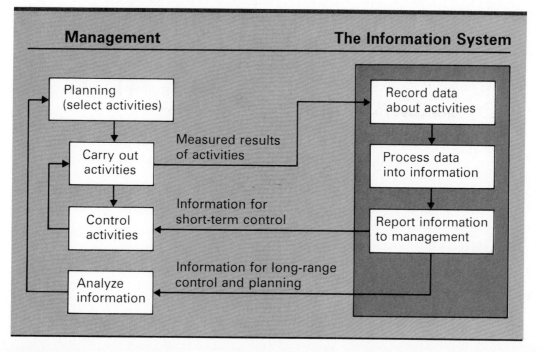

managerial processes and specific elements of the information system use this interface to give management control over operations. In brief, managers try to improve their future performance through analysis: Why weren't their goals achieved? Should the goals and activities be changed? As the figure shows, the system provides information that goal-oriented managers can use to change their responses to the environment. This feedback ability is an important capability of a good information system. It is the means by which managers develop better goal-achieving responses to their internal and competitive environments.

Responsibility for Information Systems

Management is responsible, of course, for its information systems. Every information system is structured in accordance with principles and rules that determine what data it accepts, how it processes the data, and what information it reports. The accounting system handles data according to accounting principles and rules, but a production control system handles data according to production-control principles and rules.

Different organizations handle information-system responsibility differently, but it is becoming more common for the information-system manager to be a member of top management and to be responsible for marshalling and using data processing resources to meet the organization's information needs. Besides accounting, these needs include production or service scheduling, financial scanning, product design, and more. Within this broad framework, data processing may be centralized or decentralized and can vary to suit the style and needs of the organization.

Within a system, the various functional areas are responsible for providing complete and correct data and for using the resulting information output. The data processing department is responsible for operating the system's procedures and programs. The system function is responsible for planning information systems, developing them, and keeping them up to date.

Chapter 3 describes the specific controls known as *financial controls* that are used to plan short-term activities and ensure that their outcomes are satisfactory. Financial controls are implemented by line managers in responsibility centers, who depend heavily on the data processing department, financial executives, and accounting system for support.

Summary

The desirability of predicting the behavior of as many variables as possible leads executives into a search for relevant information. Information derives from data, and the accounting system is one means of converting data into relevant information. This process explains managers' fascination with accounting systems. Indeed, some commentators now believe that information (not manufactured goods or raw materials) is the most valuable commodity of a computer-literate society.

Managers operate organizations by means of information systems. Information systems process inputs into signals that may influence managerial choices. If a system can process inputs, then modify its outputs in order to achieve a desired result, it is said to be capable of feedback. Management exercises control based on feedback to influence the outcome of specific processes, such as sales or manufacturing.

In addition to top-management control, organizations use financial, accounting, and internal controls. Organization structures deliberately foster control by distributing to different centers the responsibilities for setting objectives, conducting operations, measuring progress toward objectives, and evaluating the quality of operations.

The statistical decision model—which consists of a decision maker, a set of alternatives, independent variables, and payoffs to the decision maker—helps to explain how information affects decision-making and control activities. This model possesses other qualities, among them helping to pinpoint and visualize risk and to identify information's value in controlling risk. The behavioral decision model attempts to explain goal congruence and the extent to which managers will cooperate in an organization. Control over managerial performance relies on comparing expected operations (as described in the budget) with actual operations (as described by the accounting system) in performance reports, with special management attention to the variances discovered through the comparison.

Key Terms

alternative	independent	performance
behavioral decision	variables	reporting
model	information	process relevance
data-flow diagram	matrix management	responsibility center
decision	maximax strategy	risk management
decision maker	maximin strategy	satisficing
decision objective	narrative	statistical decision
decision relevance	description	model
decision rule	optimizing	system-user interface
entity diagram	organization	weighted-outcomes
functional divisions	payoff	strategy
goal congruence		

Review Questions

1. What is the purpose of an organization structure? What are some of the structures that have been developed to help accomplish this purpose?

2. Organization charts look very tidy. What are some of the imperfections they may not reveal? How does the accounting system help compensate for these imperfections?

3. What is the difference between decision relevance and process relevance?

4. Which decision model treats decision making as the result of exchanging and processing information? What influences on decision making does this model consider important?

5. After identifying the process to be controlled, what four steps must be taken to establish control? Are these steps performed by the same party or by different parties? Why?

6. Which decision model has five elements, including a decision maker and a payoff to the decision maker? What are the other three elements of this decision model?

7. What is an important managerial use of accounting information? How do control and scrutiny of the accounting system make its information better suited for this purpose?

8. Explain *satisficing* and give an example of it.

9. Refer to Figure 2.10 on page 49. What inputs does management receive from the information system interface?

10. What is a responsibility center? Is the accounting information system a responsibility center?

11. What four types of control characterize organizations? Name them and explain how they differ.

12. What is the difference between a decision choice and a decision rule?

Discussion Questions

13. A manager wishes to encourage goal congruence in her organization. Which of the following situations appear to promote goal congruence?
    (a) Employees submit suggestions for improving efficiency; if a suggestion is adopted, its author receives a cash award.
    (b) If a responsibility center achieves all its goals without spending its entire budget, the budget for the following year is reduced.
    (c) The Region X Division has a large computer that it does not fully use. To encourage sharing of computer facilities, the division's manager has offered to allow other divisions of the company to use the computer if they pay a fee that provides the division a modest profit. Region X Division's manager receives an end-of-year bonus based on the division's profits.
    (d) To discourage salespeople from accepting customer returns, exchanges, and requests for warranty service, their salaries are reduced by 50 percent of the amount of each such transaction.

(e) The company has set a standard purchase cost for each component. The purchasing manager receives a bonus increase when purchases occur at a lower-than-standard cost and a bonus decrease when purchases occur at a higher-than-average cost.

14. Name three methods used to describe systems. Which one describes the system components? Which one identifies information used in the system?

15. Describe the human response to risk. Name two ways that humans reduce risk in short-run decision making. Describe the intended effect of financial or administrative controls on risk.

16. Dickinson Barbecue Company is deciding how many briskets to cook for the next day's business. Each brisket weighs four pounds, costs $6.00, takes twelve hours to cook, and feeds five people. Each serving sells for $3.00. Any barbecue left over at the end of the day is donated to the county. The company has prepared the following table:

		Expected Demand (Number of Meals Sold)					
		5	10	15	20	25	30
Probability of This Demand		0.1	0.2	0.3	0.2	0.1	0.1

		Gross Profit (in Dollars)					
Number of Briskets Prepared	1	9	9	9	9	9	9
	2	3	18	18	18	18	18
	3	−3	12	27	27	27	27
	4	−9	6	21	36	36	36
	5	−15	0	15	30	45	45
	6	−21	−6	9	24	39	54

Verify that the company earns a gross profit of $36 if it prepares four briskets and sells 20 meals. Why does it also earn $36 if demand is greater for the same number of briskets?

17. If the Dickinson Barbecue Company always cooks five briskets, what will be its *average* gross profit? Use the meal-demand probabilities as weights for the profits listed in the row for five briskets, as follows: $0.1*(-15) + 0.2*0 + 0.3*15 + 0.2*30 + 0.1*45 + 0.1*45$

18. If the Dickinson Barbecue Company cannot predict demand any better than is shown in Question 17, how many briskets should it prepare each day? To find the answer, calculate the average gross profit for each row as shown for row 5 in the preceding question. The answer will be the number of briskets corresponding to the row with the highest average gross profit.

19. Consider Figures 2.1, 2.2, 2.3, and 2.4. Indicate which of the organizational forms shown in these figures would be most appropriate for each of the following businesses:
    (a) In separate plants in Wisconsin, Garfield Company manufactures office supplies, computer disk drives, and air conditioners, all of which it sells to the aircraft industry.
    (b) Sour Lake Company, a one-office political consulting firm, helps candidates for local office plan and manage their campaigns.
    (c) Mathis Service Bureau's offices all over the United States accept data processing work from small businesses, transmit it to a central location for processing, and return financial statements and other reports a few hours later.
    (d) Sarita Imports buys or produces and then markets fine furniture in seven countries; because of local regulations in these countries, it does no import or export business at all.
    (e) Edinburg Farms produces smoked meats and pickled vegetables at its 300-acre location, then markets and ships them around the world.

20. Is organization structure a control? If so, what level of control is it? Can organization structure be thought of as an element of a control? If so, and if the control objective is to provide a hierarchy of authority, what element of control does organization structure represent? Name and describe the other two elements of the control.

Problems

21. The Needville Hospital Corporation is considering expansion. It has two alternatives: to open a new facility to treat minor illnesses or to build a new wing onto its existing facility for treatment of advanced chronic diseases.

Required:

Describe the business risks of each alternative (up to six risks). Explain how the corporation could minimize these risks in making the decision.

22. Batson Electronics Corporation imports Canadian consumer electronics, such as video recorders, short-wave radios, and laser disk players. The company finds that currency fluctuations, language difficulties, low cash flow, high returns from retailers, and demand fluctuations prevent it from earning profits it hopes to attain.

Required:

(a) Which of these problems might be made more manageable by an accounting information system?
(b) How should the accounting system be used to address these problems?

23. Al Occlusion, a salesman, has a limited time to call on selected clients in September. He wants to minimize the risk of making no sales at all during these calls. His computer data base shows the following sales histories for several clients:

Client	Call and Amount of Sale
A	January–$0; March–$11,000; May–$0; July–$16,000
B	March–$18,000; April–$0; May–$0; June–$23,000; July–$0; August–$0
C	August–$0
D	January–$45,000; February through August–$0
E	New client, no history

Required:

(a) If Occlusion can make only two calls, which clients do you think he should see?

(b) Occlusion's computer is at home. He discovers that, as a prank, his children *may* have changed some of the sales data in his files. There is no way to recover the original data. How should this control failure affect his reliance on the sales data as a source of risk-reducing information?

24. Jasper Jewelry Company has developed a statistical decision model to help it decide how to market its latest shipment of gems. Its choices are to market these gems as a few large pieces or as many smaller ones. The decision depends on the type of jewelry that fashion and economic activity will favor in the coming year. Provided the company makes the right decision, it can make money either way. The model below shows the alternatives:

Jasper's Profit If It Creates	When Fashion and Economic Conditions Favor	
	Large Pieces	*Small Pieces*
Large pieces	$ 500,000	$ 200,000
Small pieces	(100,000)	600,000

Required:

(a) What arguments do you see for and against each alternative?

(b) Assume that five of the last ten years have favored large pieces and five have favored small pieces. Calculate the average annual profit if Jasper had always selected (1) large pieces and (2) small pieces. Which alternative would have produced the largest average annual profit?

(c) Now assume that, over the last ten years, Jasper had a marketing and business consultant who predicted with perfect accuracy whether the coming season would favor large or small pieces. If the company had followed the consultant's advice each time, what would its average annual profit have been?

(d) To what factor would you attribute the difference in profit between (b) and (c)? How much was the consultant's advice worth to Jasper? Judging from this problem, do you think information has value?

Case: Palacios Map Company

The Palacios Map Company was founded in 1921 by a group of surveyors to provide maps of the surrounding region to developers, roadbuilders, and real-estate agents. Today, the company has competent management and a modern facility, advertises extensively, and is in good financial condition, with an annual budgeting and performance-reporting system. It has become the leading map and engineering supply firm in its state.

About twenty years ago, however, the company's management did a self-study and realized it was in trouble. The self-study showed that sales had been level over the previous five years; management's average tenure with the company was 18 years; the average sales to the average major customer were declining; there was no planning or budgeting process; inventory was limited to local maps; the business facility was over sixty years old, in an inconvenient part of town, and too small; the firm had no advertising program; and two newly established map-service firms in the same city appeared to be growing. After the self-study, management hired a systems expert to analyze their company.

Required:

Assume that you are the systems expert. Analyze Palacios Map as it existed twenty years ago in terms of its system elements, characteristics, and resources. Then, using the same terminology, explain how the company changed in order to become the company it is today.

Case: Mineral Wells Company

The Mineral Wells Company is a chain of ten auto parts and maintenance stores, recently purchased by J.B. Jody. Not long after the change of ownership, Jody told a meeting of employees that he would establish a management structure in which "all of you feel free to come to me with your ideas to make this a better company. I want you to understand that your store manager is the boss. Nevertheless, the manager's performance depends on your support, as well as on the decisions he or she makes. I am approving an incentive plan whereby each store's employees share in bonuses amounting to 10 percent of that store's contribution to company profits."

Two days later, Jody announced certain controls as part of the new organization plan. Thenceforth, all purchasing would be done centrally, and incoming shipments of merchandise would all be delivered to a central warehouse. Each store would send a truck to pick up what it required. However, the home office would collect an "inventory charge" of 1 percent per week of the average value of a store's inventory in stock. This charge would encourage store managers to keep much less inventory on hand.

As for cash management, each store would deposit its cash daily in a central bank account. The store's petty cash funds would be reimbursed from company headquarters, not out of receipts from cash sales.

To strengthen financial controls, the position of companywide Budget Director was created. All store managers were to develop an annual budget, according to policies approved by the budget director, and to submit it to the Budget Committee for approval. The position of Company Controller was also established, and a new chart of accounts was created requiring all stores to use the same account numbers in recording sales and expenses; these account numbers corresponded to categories on the new budget forms. It was obvious that the new forms and account codes would allow actual and budgeted performance to be readily compared on a uniform basis from store to store.

Three store managers protested to Jody. "We think your new policies are very unfair," they said. "First you said we store managers would stand or fall on the decisions we made. Now you have announced a lot of rules that will tie our hands and force us to do things the way some second-level staff at headquarters want it done. We can't possibly succeed under these rules and we know we will be blamed when we fail. Furthermore, the morale of our employees will drop when they realize that they cannot win a large bonus."

Required:

(a) Comment on (1) Jody's opening statement, (2) whether the new policies are consistent with his statement, and (3) whether there is any substance to the three store managers' complaints.

(b) Write the reply you think Jody should make to the complaint, explaining the difference between controls and authority, the purposes each accomplishes, and why the new controls at Mineral Wells Company do or do not constrain the managers from running their stores.

CHAPTER 3

Financial Controls

Purpose of a Budget
Budget Process and Management Participation
    Building a Budget
    Financial Planning Models
    Budget Contents
Performance Reports
    Performance Report Structure
    Behavioral Effects of Financial Controls
    Control Time Horizon

Learning Objectives

After studying this chapter, you should be able to

■ Explain who should use performance reporting and why they would find it valuable.

■ Describe the purpose and process of budgeting as a financial control.

■ Participate in the use of budgets for planning and as an operational control.

■ Organize budget and accounting information into performance reports tailored for each manager and explain how to interpret and use the reports.

■ Relate different types of controls to differing time horizons.

As you learned in Chapter 2, organizations use controls to regulate their activities and make them more predictable. Every organization has controls of three types: top management, financial, and internal. (Accounting controls, sometimes treated as a fourth type of control, are treated here as a type of internal control.)

Top management controls include the basic distinguishing features of the enterprise: its mission, long-range goals and objectives, organizational structure, position descriptions, and staffing. Internal controls specific to each of the organization's activities—for example, quality control in manufacturing and security control in data processing—ensure that these activities are conducted properly. Accounting system controls are one kind of internal controls; they reduce garbage and noise in accounting information and make certain it will conform to the requirements set for its use in financial reporting and in operating the other control processes. In this chapter, we concentrate on financial controls, which support top-management controls and rely on accounting controls to assure accounting-information integrity.

Financial controls help ensure that financial resources will be available to carry out management's operational plans. The main instruments of financial control, budgeting and performance reporting, require management to plan and then to compare its plans with the actual results of its operations. Like other controls, financial controls are not mechanical; they succeed because of creative design and conscientious application. The success of a control procedure flows from a dynamic interaction within management and between management and its environment—its organization, technology, and cultural environment. In short, financial controls work not because they have the right structure—although that is essential—but because *people want them to succeed.*

Purpose of a Budget

The budget is the principal means by which many financial controls are implemented. The activities that produce the budget are called the **budget process**. The budget process leads to performance reports, which compare budgeted (expected) and reported (actual) performance at frequent intervals during the budget period.

Management uses the budget as a performance profile or bench mark, analogous to an airliner's flight profile prepared before each takeoff. Both the budget and the flight profile involve objective setting, planning, and control.

The aircraft crew sets an objective of traveling from, say, Pittsburgh to Chicago. They then plan their flight, setting direction of travel, speed, and en route checkpoints. The crew controls the flight by frequent comparisons of the aircraft's actual position with its expected position. If weather, airport congestion, or some other event causes the aircraft to stray from its expected position, the aircraft crew, which is responsible for the flight, restores the plane to the position called for in the flight profile.

An organization's budget operates very similarly. Management sets goals for the coming operating period, plans how to achieve the goals, and compares current performance with expected performance (the budget plan) to measure the success of operations. These activities form an ongoing process of preparing a detailed operating plan—a plan that covers a specific period of time and contains instructions and performance goals for each division or department in the organization. This plan, which typically covers one or more operating periods, is called the **budget.** The structure and contents of the budget are known as the **budget organization.** Management uses the budget as a basis for actual resource allocation and administrative decisions.

Goal Setting and Planning.   Every organization's leaders face a continuing challenge of *goal setting*—identifying goals and objectives that will sustain the organization's existence and bring it growth, profits, and resources without taking unnecessary chances. As part of the planning process, organizations should define what they want to achieve and how they want to achieve it. The budget is a plan of progress toward these goals, showing how the organization will use its financial and other resources to achieve short-term objectives in the course of its operations over a defined period, usually one year. The long-term goals and objectives set by the board of directors or the managing partners (or, in government, by the legislative or executive body) determine the scope of activities and alternatives that can be included in annual budgets.

The organization may have publicly stated goals that it expresses in qualitative terms: "We make things happen for go-getters" or "Our objective is to bring back pride in workmanship." It may also express its broad goals as a series of quantitative targets: a return on investment of at least 20 percent, a market share no less than third biggest in the industry, or total assets between $10 million and $12 million.

Long-range goals should be challenging yet consistent with the organization's character, which is determined by its top management. To ensure this consistency, top management should institute a regular, recurring formal process to review and restate its long-range goals. A financial or accounting executive should participate in the goal-setting process as a member of top management and as a provider of financial information.

The goals of the organization as a whole are the consolidated product of the goals of its various divisions, which in turn are the product of the goals of departments within the divisions, in an increasingly detailed plan down to the level of the smallest units. Management can take advantage of this structure to arrange goals according to the organizational unit to which they belong. At higher management levels, the goals are aggregated from the goals of units at lower levels.

Goal setting leads to *planning*, which is the systematic anticipation and description of the activities that will lead to goal achievement. Executives may engage experts—economists, forecasters, statisticians, consultants, and others—and set aside special time for retreats or regular meetings in order to develop acceptable plans. These plans specify the short-term objectives, or milestones, that will mark progress toward long-term goals.

One purpose of planning is to be certain that management is aware of any emerging developments that could have an impact on the achievement of its goals. Planning is a powerful risk-management tool, because it forces managers to look at the future, to anticipate all the possible environments in which they might have to perform successfully, and to devise plans suitable to any environment they will actually face. Planning helps management to avoid taking chances that might unnecessarily endanger the organization.

Planning also has a second purpose: to mold the organization's structure, resources, and activities so as to create a reasonable likelihood of achieving goals. In larger organizations, planning may become to some extent a contractual process, wherein managers propose or agree to accept obligations, with the understanding that other managers in supportive, supervisory, or cooperative roles will adhere to complementary obligations. If the overall planning process proves successful, those responsible may expect and receive rewards in the form of money, perquisites, responsibility, and status. The planning process may encourage a reward expectation through performance evaluation or incentive policies. At one large manufacturing company, for example, the salespeople could promise quick delivery because they knew the factory and distribution managers would cooperate and fill their orders on time. When occasional snafus prevented filling orders, the factory would quickly inform the sales force so unfillable orders did not stack up. Top management recognized this cooperation and rewarded it through an annual bonus program.

Controlling.   A good flight plan alone is no guarantee that an aircraft's crew will land in Chicago, and efficient objective setting and planning will not ensure an organization's future. In both cases, success will depend on controls. As a financial control, the budget serves the following functions:

- It forces management to describe for the budget period its fundamental plans and policies concerning human resources, products, capacities, cash flow, and other resources.
- It describes, in accounting-statement format, the expected results of operations. It predicts what the financial statements will show at the end of the period if operations proceed smoothly and achieve their objectives.
- It enables management to make frequent comparisons of its expectations with the results of actual operations. It compares operating *objectives* with *achievements*.

To implement the budget as a control, an organization must regard every component of the budget process as a control element and assign specific responsibility for it to some part of management. The most common distribution of these responsibilities is shown in Figure 3.1. A good budget will have desirable effects on individual managers' performance. For example, it will improve morale by describing their objectives and leaving no doubt or uncertainty about what they must achieve. It will encourage managers to participate in the planning process, giving them some influence over the description of performance expected of them.

As a control device, the budget process is the framework in which management can include the four elements of control:

- *Objective*: anticipate which operations or actions to perform.
- *Preventive*: assess whether ongoing operations are producing satisfactory performance.

Figure 3.1   Responsibility for Financial Control Elements
To be effective, controls must involve multiple managers and levels in the organization. This figure shows five types of control information (in gray) and four management centers or levels (rectangles) used to control operations processes (the oval). Arrows indicate the flow of information.

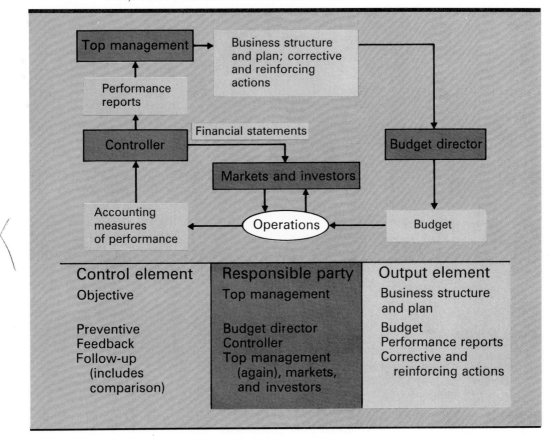

- *Feedback*: determine whether changes are necessary to restore satisfactory performance.
- *Comparison and follow-up*: determine when actual performance equals or even surpasses the performance projected in the budget.

These elements and their inclusion in the budget process are the keys to controlling the direction of the enterprise. They give management the freedom to plan and even to improvise and innovate within a clearly understood and accepted framework of goals and constraints. Goals and constraints exist in every organization. In the most centralized organizations, the goals and constraints tend to be very limiting; in decentralized organizations, they are less limiting but still present.

Budget Process and Management Participation

The **budget process** is the sequence of events that occur in the preparation of a budget. Its objective is to produce an operating plan for a complete period (usually one year), which management can compare with actual results of operations as soon as possible after they take place. The budgeting process can establish goals by either a top-down or a bottom-up process. In the top-down approach, top management articulates goals that are then progressively disaggregated into component goals for the next-lower management level. The disaggregation occurs as follows: A **budgeting unit** is a responsibility center that prepares a budget. It receives its goals from the next-higher level and determines what inputs it needs to achieve these goals. *These inputs become the goals of other budgeting units at the same and at lower levels of management.* These subsidiary goals, if they are achieved at lower levels of management, will result in successful operations by the budgeting units and achievement of top management's original goals. For example, a CPA firm's managing partners may specify revenues of $3 million as a goal for the coming year. To achieve this goal, one necessary input is hiring 35 new staff members. Hiring this many new staff people becomes the goal of the partner in charge of recuitment, who in turn determines that an input of 350 interviews of prospective staff by the audit, tax, and consulting partners will be required. These people accept the interview goals and make available time inputs of two hours per interview. If the interview time is available, if the interviews take place, and if offers are made and accepted, the original revenue goal should be that much closer to realization.

In the bottom-up approach, goal-setting begins at the lowest management levels, and the resulting goals are progressively integrated and aggregated until they can be expressed in terms of overall benefits to the entire organization. Using the bottom-up approach, the CPA firm above would ask its offices how much time each plans to spend in recruiting activities. From this and other inputs it would calculate the expected revenues for the coming year.

The bottom-up approach makes budgetary control difficult and uncertain. For this reason, the remainder of this chapter discusses top-down budgeting exclusively.

Building a Budget

At the end of each period, the goals and plans of each responsibility unit are compared with the unit's operating results, as collected and reported by the accounting system, in a *performance report*, a document that is meant for internal use. Although a performance report compares goals and results for one unit, that unit, for purposes of the report, may consist of several subsidiary units, such as a marketing region that includes a number of sales offices. Just as aggregated transactions form meaningful totals and balances, the performances of smaller entities coalesce to form the performance of the next-larger responsibility unit and the basis for performance reports. For example, the sales-performance reports of all sales departments may be aggregated to produce the sales-performance report of the entire marketing division. The controller can prepare the performance reports as often as necessary. They usually appear weekly or monthly, but some may appear daily, twice a month, or quarterly. We will look further at performance reports later in this chapter.

The lower the level of responsibility, the shorter the planning and control horizon. The organization as a whole should set goals for ten or more years; the smallest responsibility centers, depending on their function, may define goals for only two to five years.

All the budget components contain data and formats that, when included in performance reports, will allow them to be compared with the accounting system's record of operations. This means that the completed budget schedules and reports take forms similar to accounting statements. Figure 3.2 illustrates the complete process of budget preparation, showing that the process is guided at every stage by coordination and support from the controller's budget office and by uniform budget assumptions and goals created by top management. Figure 3.2 shows budget preparation beginning with expressions of long-range objectives, forecasts of business conditions, and uniform budget policies (to ensure that all parts of the budget will fit together). The budget preparation process is closely integrated with the organization's structure of divisions and departments. The division and department units may receive assistance from a "budget office," usually supervised by the controller or some other top financial executive, to help them interpret and follow uniform budget policies and finish their own detailed budget schedules. These detailed schedules reflect how each unit decides to achieve the goals assigned to it in the overall budget. The finance function may prepare cash flow, capital, and other schedules from the operating budget components. In reviewing these schedules, top management must judge whether the departmental and divisional efforts will be sufficient to support achievement of top management's original operating goals. If these efforts prove insufficient, either the goals must change or the departments and divisions must revise their budgets.

Figure 3.3 on page 67 shows, in simplified form, the order in which these components of the budget are prepared. This order is dictated by the fact that components prepared earlier contain data that are necessary in preparation of subsequent components. For example, the cash budget cannot be prepared until one knows the cash required for purchases and payroll. In practice, many budget components prepared earlier are reviewed and revised during budget preparation to support other components prepared later.

Figure 3.2   Budget Preparation Sequence and Responsibilities
The budget process sequence moves from long-range objectives through several intermediate steps to current-period operating budgets and projected financial statements. Several revisions of the latter may be necessary before final approval, which signifies management's expectation that these plans will achieve its objectives.

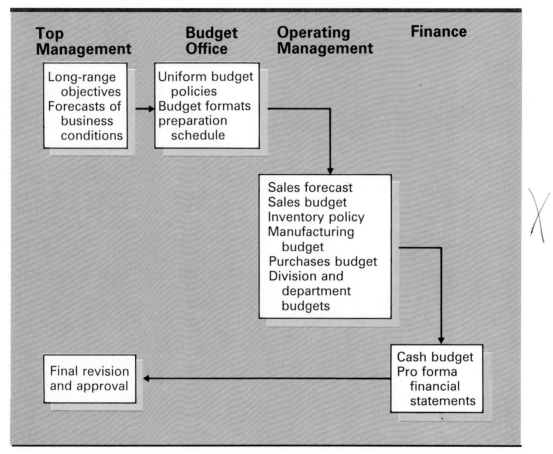

For an example of the process of building a budget, examine the figures in the Budget Contents section on page 70 in terms of Figures 3.2 and 3.3. In this section, the organization's long-term goals and strategy call for doubling the market share of the company's product within five years. This information is communicated to operating departments by the top management, accompanied by budget schedule formats and a time-table from the budget office.

Any budget built up in this way should be intensively reviewed by top management as it nears completion. The usual tests of financial performance apply to the pro forma financial statements: return on investment, cash flow, rate of sales growth, gross margin, projected market share, and the like. The key question management must ask is *if the coming year's activities produce the projected performance outputs, will the financial community, including owners of the business, accept them as satisfactory performance?* Most equityholders see a business only through the window of its published financial statements. Management must constantly keep in mind how the financial community will perceive its performance through the lens of the accounting model, with its prevailing financial reporting rules and principles.

Figure 3.3   Operating Budget Components in Order of Preparation
This figure shows that the sales forecast determines the budgeted operating levels of the marketing and manufacturing functions, which in turn determine the cash-flow requirements. Together, these allow preparation of the projected (pro forma) financial statements.

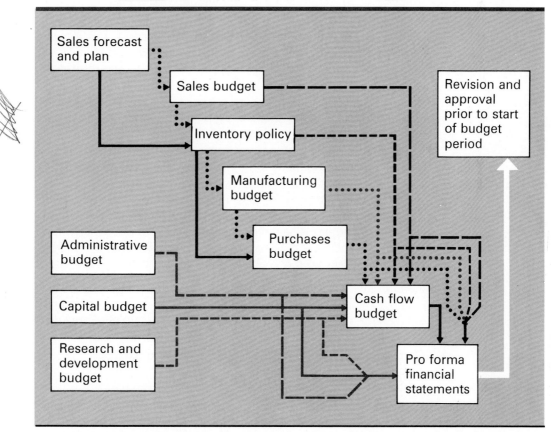

As it critically examines the budget, management reviews the quantities, forms, and timing of resource inputs and product outputs as reflected in the draft pro forma statements (prospective financial statements that project circumstances at a future date). Some or all investment and responsibility centers may be asked to revise their activities. The review and revision continue until, from the top down, management accepts the budget as a plausible plan for achieving the organization's goals during the period it covers. Among the changes that management will have weighed during the planning process that precedes budgeting are the following:

- Entry into new markets
- The balance between older cash-producing (but declining) activities and newer cash-consuming (but growing) activities
- The balance between debt and ownership financing
- The balance between long-term and short-term debt financing
- Expenditure on research and development for the future, perhaps weighed against advertising or customer service to prolong the economic life of existing technologies
- Investment in equipment, information management, office facilities, and other long-term uses of capital, weighed against lowering prices, increasing product quality, or paying higher returns to owners
- Maintaining investor and market confidence. For example, in a company that planned a major stock issue during the coming year, the plans and policies underlying the first budget led to pro forma financial statements that showed a rate of return on owners' equity several points lower than the industry average. Management realized it had to show a better performance in order to issue its stock. So, the company revised its plans to cut costs, stimulate demand, and postpone several low-priority projects; then it recalculated the budget. When even these revisions were not sufficient, a second round of revision and a third budget were undertaken; these finally produced acceptable projections.

No one model will serve to analyze such a wide variety of potential changes. However, it is fundamental to compare the financial results of status quo operations with the projected results of implementing the change:

$$\begin{matrix} \text{Difference} \\ \text{to be} \\ \text{evaluated} \end{matrix} = \begin{matrix} \text{Financial results} \\ \text{of status quo} \\ \text{operations} \end{matrix} - \begin{matrix} \text{Financial results of} \\ \text{operations implementing} \\ \text{the proposed change} \end{matrix}$$

The final budget may be the only (or the most important) means for considering the financial impact of all organization plans. This budget embodies both the planned activities and the underlying relationships between controllable variables and independent variables (such as economic conditions, inflation, and technology) that cannot be controlled. These underlying relationships are expressed via the budget assumptions. If the assumptions change or become inconsistent with reality as it emerges during the budget period, they can be restated and the budget revised to establish new operating goals as the preventive element of financial controls.

Financial Planning Models

A **financial planning model** is a set of equations that describes, in monetary terms, the relationships between an organization and its environment and the changes that occur in these relationships as time passes. A financial planning model can assist managers in their budget review by allowing them to explore the financial effects of varying sets of assumptions and strategies. Although the output of a financial planning model often appears as pro forma financial statements, the model differs from the budgeting process in two important ways. First, the model does not allow as much participation by managers as does the budget process. As a result, the model's output represents the work of a smaller group, usually staff technical experts. Second, the model cannot consider as many variables and relationships as the budget process does.

A financial planning model that is implemented on a computer does offer one advantage in the planning process. It can be operated more quickly than a new budget can be prepared, allowing management to understand the probable interactions of many different combinations of economic conditions and operating policies. In the process of such exploration, a computerized financial planning model should help management to identify a range of productive goals and policies that can serve as a starting point for the next budget preparation cycle. Computerized financial planning models apply formulas supplied by the user to calculate forecasted values of important variables such as product price, unit sales, productivity, and materials costs. These calculated values are then inserted into other formulas. A typical formula for forecasting sales might be:

> Unit sales = (110,000 * monthly index factor) + (sales growth per month * months since base period) + (price elasticity factor * base price/our forecast price) − (competition factor * average market price/our forecast price) − (market age factor * months since product was introduced)

The result of the above formula could be used as input to formulas that compute revenues and profits. Variables like the "monthly index factor" and "competition factor" may themselves have been computed using other formulas, or they may have resulted from expert guesses by the planners.

Computerized financial planning models such as IFPS (Interactive Financial Planning System, developed and marketed by Execucom Systems Corporation) translate assumptions and predictions into prospective financial statements. Managers can use these models to store the extensive data they want to use in financial planning. Such data can represent more factors than could be considered in any manual calculation done in the same amount of time. Much of this data will originate in the accounting system, having been collected during transaction recording and other activities. Decision-aid programs such as Decision Map (SoftStyle, Inc.) can help a manager decide what budget assumptions and predictions to make when using the financial planning models.

Budget Contents

A completed budget in good form will consist of the following:

1. Budget components related to company structure. (These three items, developed in a separate long-range planning process, are typically included for reference purposes in the annual budget.)

   - long-term goals
   - long-term strategy
   - organization chart

2. Budgets with different time horizons. (These two items are developed in the budget process by the budget director and top management.)

   - multiperiod (perhaps five-year) budget
   - annual budget (or annual profit plan)

3. Budgets for the responsibility centers. (The budget includes a separate statement of objectives, activities, inputs, and outputs for each responsibility center.)

   - comprehensive annual budget (for the entire organization)
   - divisional or functional budgets
   - budgets for departments, offices, and other smaller units

The comprehensive annual budget reflects the organization's structure. It includes budgets for each division or function, and, within these, for each responsibility center. Figure 3.4 shows how a comprehensive budget would be composed of divisional budgets, which in turn are composed of departmental budgets. Assuming an uncomplicated organization, the comprehensive annual budget might contain the following sections:

sales forecast and plan	sales budget
inventory policy	purchases budget
manufacturing budget	administrative budget
capital budget	research and development
cash flow budget	(or engineering) budget
pro forma financial statements	

Figure 3.4   Overall Budget and Responsibility Center Budgets
As this figure shows, each organizational responsibility center prepares its own budget, and these budgets are combined to form the budget for the entire organization.

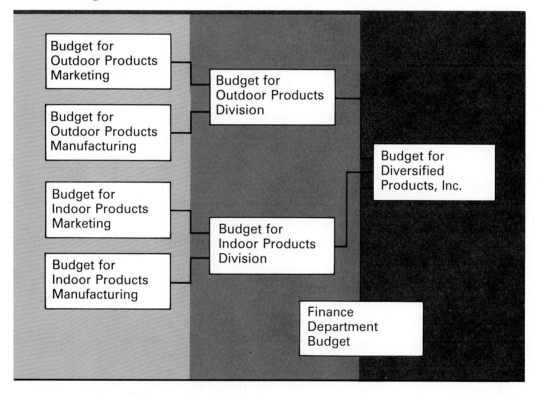

Marketing Budget.   Exhibit 3.1 is one of the first schedules prepared. Prepared by the marketing function, it shows the coming year's goal: a 10 percent increase over last year's actual unit sales of 10,000. The marketing function believes this goal is achievable provided there are a 4 percent demand-stimulating unit price reduction from last year's actual average price of $98, *and* a 25 percent increase over last year's $100,000 advertising expenditures. Last year's $50,000 actual direct marketing costs other than advertising will be increased in the budget by 10 percent, and indirect marketing costs of $100,000 will be increased by 5 percent. Thirty percent of the indirect marketing costs will be depreciation expense.

All the above assumptions are included in the marketing budget schedule, which is shown in Exhibit 3.1. Note that the lower part of the schedule contains the assumptions. The budget itself, which precedes the assumptions, includes revenue, less direct selling expenses, less indirect selling expenses. In Exhibit 3.1, the lines have numbers that correspond to the explanations below the figure.

Exhibit 3.1   Sales Forecast and Marketing Budget
This exhibit shows the calculations (top) and assumptions (bottom) necessary to
produce a marketing budget. The budget depends on the sales forecast embodied
in the assumptions and would have to be revised if these assumptions change.

		Line
Sales revenue: 11,000 units at average unit price of $94.08	$1,034,880	1
Less direct selling expenses	(55,000)	2
Budgeted revenue after direct selling expenses	$ 979,880	3
Less indirect selling expenses—cash	(73,500)	4
Less depreciation expense on equipment used in selling	(31,500)	5
Less advertising expenses	(125,000)	6
Budgeted contribution after marketing costs	$ 749,880	7

Assumptions
  1. 10 percent increase in unit sales to 11,000 units
  2. 4 percent decrease in average unit price
  3. 25 percent increase in advertising expenses (all cash)
  4. 10 percent increase in direct selling expenses (all cash)
  5. 5 percent increase in indirect selling expenses (70 percent cash)

Line 1: The result of applying assumptions 1 and 2. (Last year's unit price
    was $98; 96 percent of 98 is 94.08.) *STRATEGIC PLANNERS*
Line 2: 110 percent of last year's direct selling expenses of $50,000; see
    assumption 4.   DETERMINE THE RELIABILITY — Apply to variable costs,
    fixed costs or both
Line 3: The difference between lines 1 and 2.
Line 4: The result of applying assumption 5 to the cash portion (70 percent)
    of last year's indirect selling expenses of $100,000.
Line 5: The result of applying assumption 5 to the noncash portion (30
    percent) of last year's indirect selling expenses of $100,000.
Line 6: The result of applying assumption 3 to last year's advertising ex-
    pense of $100,000.

   This schedule, the annual budget, could be supported by more detailed schedules showing sales by month and by region or industry. A key
number that the inventory, manufacturing, and purchases budget (Exhibit
3.2 on page 74) will require from the marketing budget is the budgeted
unit sales.

Inventory, Manufacturing, and Purchases Budget.   This budget must relate budgeted unit sales to desirable inventory levels, and relate these two
in turn to the number of units to be manufactured:

$$\begin{array}{l} \text{Units to be} \\ \text{manufactured} \end{array} = \begin{array}{l} \text{Budgeted} \\ \text{unit sales} \end{array} + \begin{array}{l} \text{Units in} \\ \text{beginning} \\ \text{inventory} \end{array} - \begin{array}{l} \text{Units in} \\ \text{ending} \\ \text{inventory} \end{array}$$

Now, the manufacturing function has inventories not only of finished units but also of raw materials and of work in process. Marketing and manufacturing agree that the inventory levels of these should be the following:

Finished goods inventories:	Remain constant throughout the year at a dollar value of $70,000.
Work-in-process inventories:	Increase from 2,500 to 3,500 units. For budgeting purposes, the average cost of a unit of work in process is assumed to be $10, all in materials.
Raw materials inventories:	Increase from $20,000 to $28,000.

Before one can calculate manufacturing costs, one must establish the assumptions regarding average direct manufacturing costs per unit. The manufacturing function believes that acquisition of $80,000 worth of automated production control equipment, economies of scale, and production experience will allow budgeting of a 7 percent reduction from last year's actual $20 per unit direct manufacturing and shipping costs to $18.60 per unit. This cost, which consists of 60 percent direct materials and 40 percent direct labor, will not change during the year. Despite the savings in the direct costs, last year's $200,000 actual indirect manufacturing costs will be increased in the budget by 6 percent. Twenty percent of the indirect manufacturing budget will be depreciation expense; the remaining 80 percent will be indirect labor, materials, insurance, and taxes.

Exhibit 3.2 contains all these assumptions and the results of calculations made from them. In this figure, the lines again have numbers that correspond to the explanations below.

Line 1: The budgeted number of units to be sold comes from the marketing budget.

Line 2: Since units in finished goods inventory remains the same, no units need be produced to increase this inventory.

Line 3: Manufacturing has scheduled an increase in work-in-process inventory of 1,000 units.

Line 4: The sum of lines 1, 2, and 3. This is the total number of units that will be started by manufacturing. This line is the end of the *inventory* part of the schedule.

Line 5: This line calculates the direct materials that will be included in units started and completed by manufacturing— 11,000 units. It takes into account the scheduled cost savings of 7 percent.

Exhibit 3.2   Inventory, Manufacturing, and Purchases Budgets

This exhibit, constructed the same way as Exhibit 3.1, shows the cost and inventory assumptions (bottom) and calculations that lead to the inventory, manufacturing, and purchases budgets. Note that the sales figure on line 1 is taken from Exhibit 3.1, line 1.

		Line
Manufacturing required:		
To support sales	11,000	1
To support changes in finished goods inventory	0	2
To support change in work in process inventory	1,000	3
Total units to be started	12,000	4
Direct materials 11,000 units @ 60 percent of $18.60	$122,760	5
1,000 units @ $10.00 each (work in process)	10,000	6
Direct labor 11,000 units @ 40 percent of $18.60	81,840	7
Direct cost of goods manufactured	$214,600	8
Indirect manufacturing costs @ 80 percent of 106 percent of $200,000	169,600	9
Depreciation expense on equipment used in manufacturing	42,400	10
Total cost of goods manufactured	$426,600	11
Purchases		
To support goods manufactured for finished goods inventory	$122,760	12
To support increase in work in process 1,000 * $10	10,000	13
To support increase in raw material inventory	8,000	14
Total raw materials purchases required	$140,760	15

Direct cost assumption:
   7 percent reduction in direct cost from $20 to $18.60 per unit.
Indirect cost assumption:
   6 percent increase in indirect manufacturing costs, which are 80 percent cash
      expenditures.
Inventory assumptions:
   No change in finished goods inventory;
      1,000-unit increase in work in process inventory
         consisting of $10 per unit raw materials only.
   $8,000 increase in raw materials inventory.

Line 6: The units in process will have a scheduled increase. These partially completed units will have an assumed $10 worth of direct material in each one.

Line 7: This line calculates the direct labor that will be included in units started and completed by manufacturing— 11,000 units. It takes into account the scheduled cost savings of 7 percent.

Line 8: The sum of lines 5, 6, and 7; also the total budgeted direct costs of scheduled manufacturing.

Line 9: This line and line 10 calculate indirect costs. Last year these costs were $200,000; this year they will increase by 6 percent. Eighty percent of these costs are nondepreciation; to simplify the schedule, all of these costs are put together on this one line.

Line 10: Depreciation expense, an indirect cost, at 20 percent of 106 percent of $200,000.

Line 11: The sum of lines 8, 9, and 10. This line is the end of the *manufacturing* part of the schedule.

Line 12: The remainder of the schedule is the *purchases* budget. This line repeats line 5.

Line 13: This line repeats line 6.

Line 14: This line reflects the inventory assumption in respect to raw materials.

Line 15: The sum of lines 12, 13, and 14; and the total purchases budgeted for the year.

Cash-Flow Forecast.   The forecast of cash flow is drawn from the two previous schedules and from the information given in the explanations below. In an actual budget, much of this information would come from budget schedules, such as the administrative budget, not shown here. Exhibit 3.3 shows the cash-flow forecast and its typical format. The *sources* of cash appear first, followed by operating and then by other *uses* of cash. Depending on the organization, this schedule could be prepared by the treasurer or the budget office. The explanations below correspond to line numbers in Exhibit 3.3.

Line 1: This estimated cash balance was provided by the treasurer.

Line 2: Budgeted sales from the marketing budget were $1,034,880. From these, the treasurer has subtracted $12,000 that, as a result of an expected increase in Accounts Receivable from $120,000 to $132,000, will not be collected during the year.

Line 3: Remember that the manufacturing function will receive new equipment costing $80,000. The treasurer expects to borrow 90 percent of this amount, as shown.

Line 4: The total of lines 1, 2, and 3.

Line 5: The sum of lines 2 and 4 in Exhibit 3.1, the marketing budget.

Line 6: Line 6 from the marketing budget.

Line 7: Line 7 from Exhibit 3.2.

Line 8: Line 9 from Exhibit 3.2. Note that this is the nondepreciation, or out-of-pocket, portion of indirect manufacturing expense.

Line 9: Line 15 from Exhibit 3.2.

Line 10: The administrative budget will remain unchanged at $250,000, of which all but $30,000 of depreciation expense is expected to be cash expenditures.

Exhibit 3.3   Cash-Flow Forecast

This exhibit shows how information in budgets previously prepared can be converted into a cash-flow forecast, showing sources and uses of cash. The assumptions underlying this exhibit are explained in the text.

			Line
Sources of Cash:			
Estimated Cash Balance at Beginning of Year		$ 70,000	1
Sales (Net of $12,000 Increase in Accounts Receivable)		1,022,880	2
Borrowing 90 percent of $80,000 to Acquire Equipment		72,000	3
Total Cash Available		$1,164,880	4
Operating Uses of Cash:			
Direct and Indirect Selling Expense	128,500		5
Advertising	125,000		6
Direct Manufacturing Labor	81,840		7
Indirect Manufacturing Expense	169,600		8
Purchases of Raw Materials	140,760		9
Administrative Expense	220,000		10
Interest Expense	25,000	890,700	11
Cash Available from Operations		274,180	12
Other Uses of Cash:			
Payment for Equipment Acquired	$ 80,000		13
Reduction of Debt	82,026		14
Payment of Dividends	35,154	197,180	15
Estimated End-of-Year Cash Balance		$ 77,000	16

Line 11: The first figure is an estimate of interest expense provided by the treasurer; the second figure is the sum of lines 5 through 11 and represents the total operating uses of cash.

Line 12: Line 4 minus the total on line 11. This cash is available for paying debts and dividends.

Line 13: Payment for equipment the manufacturing function will receive.

Line 14: This line and line 15 will be determined by the company policy of using 70 percent of excess cash to reduce long-term debt and 30 percent to pay dividends. The total to be divided this way is line 12 ($274,180) minus the sum of line 13 ($80,000) and the budgeted end-of-year cash balance, which will be $77,000; or $117,180. Seventy percent of $117,180 is $82,026.

Line 15: See the explanation for line 14. Then, 30 percent of $117,180 is $35,154.

Line 16: The difference between line 12 and line 15. In this illustration, this amount was actually determined by the treasurer before preparing the cash flow schedule.

Pro Forma Income and Retained-Earnings Statements. A pro forma statement is one whose data are forecasts of what the actual statement will be when it can be prepared. Thus, pro forma financial statements are forecasts of results the financial statements will contain. The pro forma income and retained earnings statement can be assembled by the budget office entirely from the preceding three schedules, with one exception— estimated owners' equity at the beginning of the budget period, which the treasurer estimates as $315,000. No new calculations, other than calculating budgeted profit and owner's equity, need be made. Exhibit 3.4 contains the pro forma income and retained earnings statements, which reflect how management believes the actual income and retained earnings statements

Exhibit 3.4 Pro Forma Income and Retained Earnings Statements
This is one of the final budget schedules and shows how the period income statements will appear if all the budget assumptions and planned activities occur exactly as described. Note the careful linking of all figures to previous exhibits or authority.

			Schedule
Revenue from Operations		$1,034,880	*Exhibit 3.1*
Less Direct Expenses:			
Direct Sales Expenses	$ 55,000		*Exhibit 3.1*
Direct Cost of Goods Sold	204,600	259,600	*Exhibit 3.2*
Contribution		$ 775,280	
Less Indirect Expenses:			
Indirect Sales Expenses—Cash (Including Advertising Expenses)	$198,500		*Exhibit 3.1*
—Depreciation	31,500		*Exhibit 3.1*
Indirect Manufacturing Expenses—Cash	169,600		*Exhibit 3.2*
—Depreciation	42,400		*Exhibit 3.2*
Administrative Expenses—Cash	220,000		*Exhibit 3.3*
—Depreciation	30,000		[1]
Interest Expense	25,000	717,000	*Exhibit 3.3*
Profit		$ 58,280	
Reconciliation to Owners' Equity:			
Estimated Owners Equity at Start of Year		$315,000	[2]
Add Budgeted Profit	58,280		[3]
Subtract Cash Budgeted to Be Paid to Owners	(35,154)	23,126	*Exhibit 3.3*
Estimated Owners' Equity at End of Year		$338,126	

[1] Explained in text as the depreciation portion of administrative expense
[2] Estimated by treasurer
[3] Calculated in this exhi¹ t

will appear at the end of the budget period. Instead of following a line-by-line explanation, you are encouraged to trace each line back to the figure whose number appears to its right.

Pro Forma Balance Sheet.   After the treasurer has estimated the balance sheet amounts at the beginning of the budget period, these amounts can be combined with the changes budgeted to occur from operations to produce a budgeted balance sheet as it will appear at the end of the budget period. This has been done in Exhibit 3.5. In this figure, columns 1 and 2 contain the beginning balance sheet, columns 3 and 4 contain the budgeted changes, and columns 5 and 6 contain the ending balance sheet. The origin of each change is shown in parentheses.

In practice, this budget would have all the supporting schedules listed in Figure 3.3. The only difference between the examples shown and those one might encounter in an actual organization is the degree of detail; a real budget can be dozens or even hundreds of pages long.

Figures 3.2 through 3.4 and Exhibits 3.1 through 3.5 illustrate in a simplified fashion how a budget can be built up from past experience, predictions, and modeling all the way to pro forma financial statements.

Performance Reports

Performance reports are statements for internal use within a business; they compare expected and actual results of operations (outputs and resources used) for all or part of an organization. Because performance reports incorporate the budget as the source of expected results, they are effective only to the extent that the budget is based on realistic plans and policies and contains achievable goals. When the expected results in such a budget are combined with the actual results reported by the accounting system and included in performance reports, they give managers information that they can use to appraise and modify their own performance independent of formal review by top management.

Performance Control Essentials.   Five essential elements for performance control must exist if performance reports are to be useful:

1. A responsibility center (company, division, or department) where the controls will apply
2. The responsibility center's goals and objectives
3. The manager's authority to operate in order to create output
4. The responsibility center budget relating resources available for operations to the goals and objectives of the next operating period
5. The manager's expectation that performance will be controlled by comparing actual outputs and resources used with the budget

Exhibit 3.5   Balance Sheet

This is the other final budget schedule and shows how the end-of-period balance sheet will appear if all the budget assumptions and planned activities occur exactly as described. As in Exhibit 3.4, all amounts are linked to previous exhibits or authority.

	1	2	3	4	5	6
	Beginning of Year		Changes		End of Year	
	Assets	*Equities*	*Debits*	*Credits*	*Assets*	*Equities*
Cash	$ 70,000		$ 7,000 (Exhibit 3.3)		$ 77,000 (Treasurer)	
Accounts Receivable	120,000		12,000 (Exhibit 3.3)		132,000 (Treasurer)	
Inventories						
Raw Materials	20,000		8,000 (Exhibit 3.2)		28,000 (Manufacturing)	
Work in Process	25,000		10,000 (Exhibit 3.2)		35,000 (Manufacturing)	
Finished Product	70,000				70,000 (Manufacturing)	
Equipment and Property	500,000		80,000 (Exhibit 3.3)		580,000	
Provision for Depreciation		$200,000		$103,900 (Exhibits 3.1, 3.2)		$303,900
Accounts Payable		90,000				90,000
Debt Payable at Start of Year		200,000				
Budgeted Debt Service			82,026 (Exhibit 3.3)			
Budgeted Financing				72,000 (Exhibit 3.3)		
Debt Payable at End of Year						189,974
Estimated Equity at Start of Year		315,000 (Treasurer)				
Profit from Operations				58,280 (Exhibit 3.4)		
Dividends Paid			35,154 (Exhibit 3.3)			
Budgeted Equity at End of Year						338,126 (Exhibit 3.4)
Totals	$805,000	$805,000	$234,180	$234,180	$922,000	$922,000

Let's illustrate these five essential performance control elements in terms of a familiar college-campus situation—a cooperative living arrangement. In such arrangements, each member contributes cash to pay the co-op's expenses. If an arrangement of this type is to be successful, the members must budget and monitor performance just as a business organization should. The applicable performance control elements are indicated by the numbers in parentheses. The co-op is the responsibility center (1). Its objective is to provide low-cost room and board for 25 people who will tolerate and respect each other's life styles and privacy (2). The manager's authority arises from the co-op members and includes having access to cash and other resources to attract members, maintain living quarters, and prepare food (3). Each semester the co-op members prepare a budget projecting costs and allocating a share of those costs to each member (4). At the end of each semester, or more often, the members compare actual income and expenditures with those budgeted and draw appropriate conclusions about future income and expenses, services, need for additional members, and the manager's compensation or even retention (5). The co-op members can select a budget committee to oversee the co-op's activities. Such a committee would do well to make certain the performance control elements are present. Especially, the co-op's comparisons will be useful performance reports.

A performance report describes a part of the organization which, in terms of the inputs and outputs analyzed in the report, operated as a coordinated unit during the period of the report. That unit may be one center, such as a quality-control laboratory or station; several centers, such as all centers in the manufacturing division; or even several functions, such as the western products division (actually, a subsidiary).

Flexible Budget. The flexible budget's unique feature is that the budgeted dollar amounts of revenues and expenses are dependent on the actual level of activity. As the basic building block of performance reports, the *flexible budget* allows you to calculate the magnitude of resources (the inputs) that should have been used to create the actual performance outputs. A flexible budget is frequently expressed, at least in part, as formulas, illustrated here for an item we will call *direct input type 1*:

$$\begin{array}{c} \text{Allowed} \\ \text{total cost of} \\ \text{input type 1} \end{array} = \begin{array}{c} \text{Number of} \\ \text{units of type 1} \\ \text{input per unit} \\ \text{of output} \end{array} \times \begin{array}{c} \text{Cost per unit} \\ \text{of type 1} \\ \text{input} \end{array} \times \begin{array}{c} \text{Actual} \\ \text{units of} \\ \text{output} \end{array}$$

Each type of input will have its own formula. The formula would be known to the manager, but only its calculation result would appear in a performance report. For example, if the responsibility center assembles bicycles, if "input type 1" is a bicycle wheel costing $10, and if 55 bicycles were assembled, the allowed total cost for bicycle wheels would be:

$1,100 = 2 wheels per bicycle x $10 per wheel x 55 bicycles produced

The total flexible budget formula should also include such indirect costs as depreciation and fixed salaries:

$$
\begin{matrix}
\text{Total responsibility} \\
\text{center budgeted} \\
\text{costs}
\end{matrix}
\quad = \quad
\begin{matrix}
\text{Budgeted} \\
\text{indirect} \\
\text{costs}
\end{matrix}
\quad + \quad
\begin{bmatrix}
\text{Total budgeted} & \text{Actual} \\
\text{direct input} & * \ \text{units of} \\
\text{cost per unit} & \text{output}
\end{bmatrix}
$$

Follow-up. There are three kinds of follow-up to performance reports: routine, analytic, and remedial.

Routine follow-up is typically associated with review of routine periodic performance reports by the manager and his or her immediate supervisor. Let's imagine that a company, Sundata Electronic Systems, manufactures a series of electronic bird whistles, which it markets nationally. (See Exhibit 3.6 on the following page.) Every western division sales performance report should be examined and discussed by the western division sales manager and by Sundata's marketing vice president. As a result of this discussion, both executives should have the same understanding of what occurred in the western sales division during the period covered by the performance report and why it occurred. The discussion should cover any follow-up actions that are indicated, such as whether an incentive program is necessary to increase sales of PN7045 in California. If sales performance is a factor in the formula that determines the western division manager's bonus or incentive compensation, the sales manager should explicitly understand the effect of this quarter's sales performance on compensation. Such a discussion fulfills the control requirement that expected and actual performance should be compared and understood, and that any necessary responses be selected and implemented.

Analytic follow-up is also done on a regular basis, but it differs from routine follow up in that it usually takes a longer time perspective. An example would be a study by Sundata's western division manager of second-quarter sales compared with budget over the last five years. Such a study would provide a historical perspective on second-quarter sales variances and could lead to changes in the budgeting process or in second-quarter sales strategies. Analytic follow-up, then, seeks to identify opportunities for improving performance before failure to do so results in acute short-run performance problems.

Remedial follow-up occurs when a routine or an analytic follow-up has identified faults to correct or problems to solve. An organization may need to make major unexpected changes in the way it responds to its business environment. Both environment and responses must be studied quickly with a view to changing the organization's policies, procedures, structure, budgets, or other major variables. Most remedial follow-up will involve requests for more information, usually originating with the manager or immediate superior. The result of remedial follow-up should be a concise description of the situation, a list of available alternatives, criteria for decision making, and projected consequences of each alternative.

The ongoing need for performance reporting and follow-up underlines the importance of the accounting system's ability to provide information on demand, outside the regular reporting structure. The following example is based on the performance report in Exhibit 3.6.

Exhibit 3.6   Partial Performance Report
This performance report was prepared to allow many different types of analyses, such as comparing dollar and unit sales to budgeted sales by products, periods, and regions. For an example of a specific application, see the text. The format and content of this exhibit illustrate many of the suggestions made in the text.

Prepared by Controller 7-3-XX

Sundata Electronic Systems
Western Marketing Division
Period April 1, 19X1 to June 30, 19X1

Sales District and Product	Second Quarter 19XX			Year 19XX to date		
	Budget	Actual	Variance	Budget	Actual	Variance
California (Detail on page 3)						
PN6866	$ 60,000	$ 66,000	$ 6,000	$130,000	$125,000	($ 5,000)
units	600	660	60	1,300	1,250	(50)
PN7045	70,000	68,000	(2,000)	178,000	174,400	(3,600)
units	350	340	(10)	950	900	(50)
PN9099	35,000	44,000	9,000	55,000	68,000	13,000
units	7,000	8,800	1,800	12,000	14,800	2,800
$ Subtotals	$165,000	$178,000	$13,000	$363,000	$367,400	$ 4,400
Oregon (detail on page 4)						
	–	–	–	–	–	–
	–	–	–	–	–	–
Washington (detail on page 4)						
	–	–	–	–	–	–
	–	–	–	–	–	–

At the Sundata company, the western marketing division manager wonders if other divisions have surplus inventories of PN9099, which is in short supply and has been selling strongly in this region. The manager contacts the controller to request a summary of PN9099 inventories in the past three months and notices that the eastern division has a large inventory. The western division works out a partial transfer of this inventory and, in August, registers higher sales as a result of the transfer. The western division manager is better off because of the increased sales; the eastern division manager is better off due to the reduced inventory. The manufacturing plant is also better off because it could devote scarce production capacity to PN6866, which is also a good seller.

Performance Report Structure

A performance report describes and analyzes two basic aspects of performance: the extent to which the unit achieved the outputs set for it, and the efficiency of resources used to achieve the actual level of output. The **report period** is any interval covered in the performance report— a day, a week, a month, a quarter, or an even longer period. The interval chosen will depend on the time horizon required to influence the magnitude of reported items. For example, daily reports are appropriate for manufacturing defects because the frequency of such defects, if unacceptable, can and should be reduced quickly. Depreciation expense, on the other hand, could be reported quarterly without loss of relevance. An organization that experiences regular seasonal changes might vary its reporting intervals with the season.

A performance report usually looks something like Exhibit 3.6, which shows a partial second-quarter sales-performance report for Sundata's western marketing division. Sales are shown by state and, within states, by product. Product sales are shown in dollar amounts and in units. The report compares budgeted and actual sales for the second quarter and for the year to date and calculates the variance for each comparison. The unfavorable variances appear in color. If the report were complete, the western marketing division manager could easily pick out the high and low performers in that division.

Two of the three products Sundata sold in its western region during the quarter did better than expected, and one did worse. Although this report compares the second quarter with the year to date, other options would be to compare the most recent quarter with the preceding four quarters or to show the variances as percentages of the budget. The $5,000 variance on the top line could, for example, be shown as 3.84 percent (of the total $130,000).

Other regularly issued performance reports for Sundata's marketing effort include eastern region sales, in dollars and units, by states and products, this quarter and year to date; international sales excluding the United States, in dollars and units, by nations and products, this quarter and year to date; combined world sales including the United States, in dollars and units, by nations and products, this quarter and year to date; marketing expenses, in dollars, by nations (regions shown in the United States), this quarter and year to date; inventories, in units and in dollars at projected sales prices, by storage locations, end of this quarter and end of last three quarters.

Performance reports have considerable value in cost accounting, operational auditing, management, and marketing. These reports can be prepared if the accounts classification plan has provided ways to distinguish budget and real balances, the date of the balance, the nation and region in which a sale occurred, and the type of revenue or expense. An account number format which includes these classifications is A-BB-CC-D-EEEE, in which

A   = one digit, whose value shows whether the balance is budgeted or actual
BB   = two digits, which shows the last month included in the balance
CC   = two digits, which show the nation
D   = one digit, which shows the district
EEEE = four digits, which show the type of revenue or expense

We will show in Chapters 7 and 8, among others, how such reports can be prepared and to whom each would be of interest. Chapter 6 discusses the process of constructing a code of accounts.

Formatting.   The format of a performance report has a significant impact on its usefulness. The following guidelines should meet most organizations' needs.

- Prominently label the unit described in the report.
- Designate the period covered by the report.
- On the first page, show the origin of the report.
- Label each column.
- Label each row in the left-hand column.
- Indent any row-descriptive labels that represent a breakdown of detail (for instance, in Exhibit 3.6, the product numbers are breakdowns of California sales).
- Make liberal use of row and column totals to summarize information, building toward an overall row-column total in the lower right-hand corner of the page.

■ If possible, confine each performance report to one side of one page. If necessary, show only summary categories on the first page. Back up the summary categories with additional detail on subsequent pages, allowing one page for each summary category.

Content. The content of a performance report should support as many analyses as its recipient is likely to make and should be limited to only the information needed. These general rules apply:

1. Show direct revenues and expenses first. Show indirect or allocated revenue or expense later, as near the end of the report as possible, after a subtotal line that summarizes the direct revenues and expenses.
2. Show all information of the type the report conveys for the unit in question.
3. Omit any information irrelevant to the purpose of the report (such as, in Exhibit 3.6, manufacturing costs).

Behavioral Effects of Financial Controls

TEST

At the beginning of this chapter, we pointed out that successful control procedure flows from dynamic interaction within management, and between management and its market, organization, technology, and cultural environment. Joseph A. Maciariello outlined six dynamic organization behaviors that interact through successful controls and performance reporting follow-up. These six interacting factors consist of the following:

■ Actively *exploring* the environment (as contrasted with passively reacting to it)
■ Defining problems so that *decisions flow* from the problem structures
■ *Avoiding uncertainty,* which no expertise exists to manage
■ Processing information to *identify key success factors* likely to apply in decisions
■ Building the organization's strength through *conflict resolution* incentives that tie individual welfare to organization success
■ Obtaining managers' *commitment* to goals and processes they perceive as valuable, difficult to reverse, and publicly accepted[1]

These points were illustrated in the Sundata example above. The western division manager did explore the environment, looking for additional inventory to sell. The manager defined the problem as finding more PN9099,

---

[1]Joseph A. Maciariello, *Management Control Systems* (Englewood Cliffs, N.J., Prentice Hall, 1984), 590 pp. 464-470.

rather than as restricting or rationing sales of this popular product. The uncertainty the manager avoided was the question of what would happen if customers could not buy their PN9099 from Sundata; the manager substituted for this uncertainty the manageable task of pulling in additional product from other regions. The western division manager identified and built on key success factors in the form of the profit and good will that come from additional sales and the other managers' incentives to cooperate. The organization certainly was stronger after the successful cooperation between the controller and the western and eastern division managers. This cooperation was possible because all three people were committed to Sundata's operations, budget, and reporting.

Information should foster managerial planning such that, if managers carry out their plans under expected environmental conditions, the managers, and therefore the organization, will achieve their respective goals. At all levels within the organization, budgets and performance reports, because they contain much of the information that influences managerial behavior, will be a motivating factor that affects the efficiency, spirit, and profitability of the organization. Managers often revise their personal expectations for their own achievement to bring them into line with what is or might appear in performance reports. Those responsible for budget and performance reporting should remember that the information they communicate has a great potential to motivate themselves and others. This information may encourage positive or negative behavior, depending on whether managers perceive it to be useful. The budget process and related performance reports can influence managers to behave in positive ways, such as finding that their individual interests coincide with those of the organization (goal congruence), pursuing performance goals contained in the budget, cooperating with other managers, and supporting the budget process. Or, these reports can produce negative results if managers decide that their individual interests conflict with and supersede those of the organization, reject the performance goals in the budget, undercut other managers, or participate indifferently in the budget process.

Clearly, the organization will benefit if managers have positive reactions. Some proven rules of thumb for encouraging the positive effects of performance reporting follow:

- Encourage broad participation in the budgeting process. Every level of management, every manager, should have some part in preparing the budget. Any manager who participates in preparing the budget will feel committed to helping achieve its goals.
- Set achievable but challenging goals for managers. These goals should be set with concurrence of the managers. In one such case, for example, a data entry department set an error goal of no more than 3 errors per 1,000 keystrokes. The operators complained be-

cause their most recently measured average was 5.2 errors, and it appeared that management expected too much improvement. The goal remained at 3, but only after data entry management promised the operators both an ongoing training program and a modest incentive program to provide flexible hours if the goal was achieved. At the same time, the computer operations department adopted a budget goal of cutting computer downtime to half its previous level. Each department's goal-setting process was reinforced by the knowledge that the other was also adopting challenging goals.

- Follow up on all performance reporting. If management checks to see what is being done about variances between expected and actual performance, everyone will know the performance reports are significant. In the data entry department, the average declined to 3.2 by the second quarter, then actually rose to 5.3 in the third quarter. When a follow-up study was made, it revealed that the temporaries hired to replace vacationing operators had made many errors. The permanent operators appreciated the adjustment that was made to compensate for this influence.

- Select managers who have a demonstrated ability to fit their responsibilities. The person who can manage data entry operations might not be able to manage treasurer operations. Managers whose abilities fit their responsibilities work more effectively and inspire better morale and commitment in their departments.

- Base rewards on the progress shown in the performance reports. In one firm, the sales bonus plan depended on salespeoples' sales as reported on a special form. In the past, no one had reconciled these forms with the sales performance reports, which were based on total sales credits. When the two were compared, it turned out that, to qualify for larger bonuses, many on the sales force were optimistically reporting sales that occurred well in the future or not at all.

- Periodically review all controls to make certain they are still applicable, effective, and necessary. If management enforces controls that do not possess these attributes, departments may lose respect for all controls, including performance reports. Employees at one company were required to prepare lengthy annual activity reports that were never read. The quarterly and monthly reports soon began to come in late, and, in a short time, the data base for activity analysis was severely deficient.

Ultimately, as we stated in the introduction to this chapter, controls succeed because people want them to. Much depends on management's desire for the controls to succeed. To have a system of controls that can work, an organization needs managers who can and will make them work.

Control Time Horizon

A **control time horizon** is the time span for future planning that attaches to a given level of control. The different types of control—management, financial, internal and accounting—have different time horizons, orientations, and objectives. Table 3.1 lists the four types of control in descending order of time span and degree of detail. Though each control is separate,

Table 3.1   Control Perspectives
The four types of controls, first introduced in Chapter 2, have complementary time horizons, orientation, and control objectives. In day-to-day operations, all these controls interact to determine activities, to report them to management, and to analyze them.

Type of Control	Time Horizon	Orientation	Control Objective
Top management	Long range	Planning	Achievable objectives Programs to achieve objectives
	Medium and short range	Operations	Analytic and remedial as indicated by performance report follow-up
Financial	Medium range	Financial management	Operating budget to implement programs Performance reporting comparing expected with actual results
Internal	Varies with the control	Functional divisions and departmental operations	Adherence to management policies
Accounting (an example of internal control)	Short range	Accounting model; processing of data	Description of current activities & available resources Recorded & actual assets are the same Recorded and actual transactions are the same

they operate together to provide all four of the necessary control elements: objective, preventive, feedback, and follow-up.

TEST Top management sets objectives and strategies—and only the passage of time will reveal whether they are successful. Financial controls, including the operating budget, define expectations for individual responsibility centers over much shorter periods, roughly a month to a year. Accounting controls ensure complete and correct recording, processing, and reporting of individual transactions, giving minute-by-minute assurance that transaction data are correctly handled. Internal controls safeguard assets, promote operating efficiency, and encourage adherence to management's policies.

Summary

Control is the ability to regulate or to make more predictable. In any organization, management wants to control business operations. It does so by supplying controls that have objective, preventive, feedback, and follow-up elements. Information is important in control because it increases the predictability of routine processes and decision making. Financial controls covered in this chapter include planning and budgeting. Planning expresses objectives, which are the first element of controls. Budgets are preventive in the sense that they are intended to prevent haphazard activities and failure: they describe in detail the organization's goals and operations to achieve these objectives during a specific period such as a year, arranged according to the unit responsible for achieving the goals by carrying out the operations, and within subintervals such as the weeks or months that comprise the main budget period.

Performance reports are part of the feedback element of control. They compare expected results with actual results as collected and described by the accounting system. Management must be the follow-up element of control by investigating and taking steps to correct processes that generate unacceptable differences between expected and actual results.

Good planning, accounting, and follow-up systems make possible a great variety of reports based on the contents of the budget and the accounting system. These systems all contribute to the quality of control.

The budget process begins with a review of long-range objectives and the plans and programs of major functions and divisions. Then follows a review of expected environmental conditions and a forecast of sales (or other output). Eventually the budgeting process, which draws on all levels of managerial authority, produces pro forma financial statements showing the projected financial position of the organization if the budget can be successfully implemented.

Key Terms

budget

budget organization

budget process

budgeting unit

control time horizon

financial controls

financial planning
   model

internal controls

pro forma statement

report period

top management
   controls

Review Questions

1. What is a budget? How does management use the budget?

2. Explain in your own words what a financial control is and how financial controls differ from accounting, management, and internal controls.

3. What is goal setting and planning? How does it differ from controlling?

4. Why should management articulate a purpose and set goals? What is the benefit to the organization owners or operators?

5. What output corresponds to the four elements of financial controls: objective, preventive, feedback, and comparison and follow-up?

6. Name three types of information that should be included in a budget and give at least two examples of each type of information. Which management document compares the results of actual operations with expectations as described in management's plans? What other two functions does this document serve?

7. What is a performance report? Where does management obtain the information about actual activities that it includes in the performance report?

8. What is a financial planning model? Can such a model replace the budget? Why or why not?

9. What ten sections comprise the annual budget? List these in the order in which they must be prepared.

10. Why must the cash flow forecast be among the last segments of the budget to be prepared? If the forecast is unsatisfactory, what options does management have?

11. What critical question must management ask itself about its developing budget? Why is this question so critical?

12. What is a flexible budget? What is its importance in performance reporting?

13. What are the three kinds of performance report follow-up? Give an example of each one.

14. Which types of control operate over the short range? What are the objectives of these controls?

Discussion Questions

15. During budget preparation, why doesn't management start with a goal oriented toward production quantity, or persons to be employed, or average salary? Why start with return-on-investment or profit?

16. Imagine that you are a new department manager in a commercial product-design consulting firm. You are responsible for encouraging existing clients to do more business with your department, seeking out suitable new clients, and supervising ongoing design work. You have been told your department's goals and objectives, authority in operations, the budget for the coming period, and how budgeted and actual performance will be compared and evaluated. You want to be an innovative and creative manager. Do the givens of your job limit your pursuit of innovation and creativity? How can you display these characteristics? How do the budget and the accounting system help you? Do they limit you in any way?

17. Each of the following statements describes a situation at the Raymondville Company. In each case, indicate whether it would best be handled by a management, financial, internal or accounting control:
    (a) The organization plan shows a division that was actually closed out two years ago.
    (b) The company's first ten-year plan has been drafted but not yet shown to the Board of Directors.
    (c) Any order for microprocessors should be shipped with 2 percent extra units to allow for defective units.
    (d) All journals must be posted weekly.
    (e) Special forms have been designed for use in recording transactions.
    (f) Special forms have been designed for use in the budgeting process.
    (g) Special forms have been designed for customer complaints.

18. The Salt Lake Grocery distributes fresh vegetables. Name at least three routine activities, and, for each one, the financial-control objective that such a business might have.

19. Drivers for City-Wide Cleaners receive some cash payments for deliveries. What three control objectives should the company have with respect to cash receipts?

20. Angleton Produce Distributors has a long-range plan, which includes the items listed on the next page. Supply a suitable managerial or financial control objective for each item.

Item covered in plan	*Control objective*
(a) Number of delivery trucks	_____
(b) Share of the fresh vegetable market	_____
(c) Ratio of debt to equity	_____
(d) Ratio of operating costs to gross revenue	_____
(e) Ratio of sales in Massachusetts to total sales	_____

21. Refer to the rules for performance report formatting and complete the following table:

Rule	*Probable benefit if rule is followed*
Prominently label the unit described in the report.	_____
Designate the period covered by the report.	_____
On the first page, show the origin of the report.	_____
Label each column.	_____
Label each row in the left-hand column.	_____
Indent any row labels that represent a breakdown of detail.	_____
Make liberal use of row and column totals to summarize information.	_____
Confine each report to one side of a page.	_____
Show direct revenues and expenses first.	_____
Show all information of the type the report conveys for the unit in question.	_____
Omit any information that is irrelevant to the purpose of the report.	_____

22. Interstate Express, a courier service, hired a major consulting firm to help set up completely new management and financial controls. Because the consultants had no expertise in accounting and internal controls, they did not change them. In your opinion, what risks is Interstate Express taking by neglecting to review its accounting and internal controls?

Problems

23. Addicks Construction Company's current year has produced the following operating results: residential development, $2,100,000; commercial development, $1,800,000; government contracts, $2,300,000; and remodeling, $500,000. In the coming year, Addicks expects residential sales to decrease 5 percent; commercial sales to decrease 8 percent; government contracts to increase 10 percent; and remodeling

to increase 15 percent. Although the company has never advertised before, it will place institutional ads for $25,000 next year. Its direct selling expenses will change, as follows: residential, from 5 percent of sales to 6 percent; commercial, from 8 percent to 6 percent; government, unchanged at 7 percent; remodeling, from 8 percent to 12 percent. Indirect selling expenses, which were $300,000 this year, are expected to drop by 20 percent.

Required:

From these figures, prepare next year's sales forecast and marketing budget. Use a format similar to that used in Exhibit 3.1.

24. Belton Imports Company is trying to forecast cash flow for the coming year. The company expects to have $250,000 in the bank on January 1, the start of the fiscal year. During the year, the company's capital budget called for purchasing equipment worth $300,000. Belton will trade in old equipment worth $70,000, pay $25,000 cash, and finance the remainder over a five-year period starting after next year. Belton has always paid a dividend; the dividend this year will be $1 per share, paid $0.25 at the end of each quarter. There are currently 300,000 shares outstanding, and the company plans a new stock issue in July of 100,000 more shares, which it hopes to sell for $20 per share (the brokers handling the sale will charge 10 percent of the proceeds for their services). Belton estimates sales next year will be 15 percent higher than this year's sales of $8,100,000. Belton's committed (fixed) out-of-pocket selling and administrative costs will be about $2,000,000 next year, as they were this year. Direct costs are 40 percent of sales and all cash. Finally, Belton's importing operations will result in currency fluctuation losses of $200,000 due to the changing value of the dollar.

Required:

Prepare next year's cash flow statement for Belton, using the format in Exhibit 3.3. Is anything missing that will prevent you from calculating the estimated end-of-year cash balance? If so, tell what the missing item is.

25. Home Insect Control Company, established in 1980, has grown rapidly. It has offices in seven cities; operates eleven trucks; mixes, uses, and sells its own insecticides; and is about to acquire two competing businesses. Management is considering the need for a budgeting process and performance reporting.

Required:

(a) Write a short paragraph describing the benefits a budget might bring to this particular company.
(b) Draw simple organization charts for this company showing two different ways it could be organized. Which do you prefer? Why?

26. Home Insect's acquisitions, described in Problem 25, did take place, and a budget process was approved. As a beginning step, the seven city office managers have been asked to develop annual budgets for their operations. Angela Diaz, manager of the Tulsa office, is trying to develop her budget. Actual results of last year's operations are shown below, along with the percentage change expected for this year:

Sales	
Home exterminations	$ 30,000 (+10%)
(Single visits to individual	
homes to apply pesticides)	
Contract exterminations	115,000 (+ 5%)
(Insect-control contracts	
whereby the company agrees	
to make monthly visits to	
apply pesticides)	
Insecticide sales	24,000 (+30%)
(Sales of pesticides to do-it-	
yourself exterminators)	
Direct Expenses	
Truck operating costs	$ 16,000 (+ 7%)
Salaries and wages	66,000 (+20%)
Insecticide costs	4,500 (+35%)
Office rent, supplies, and	10,000 (+ 6%)
expenses	

Required:

(a) Develop a budget for next year based on the information above.

(b) Design a performance report format that will show exterminations and insecticide sales as separate activities. Suggest how the office rent and other such items should be shown in the performance report.

27. Caper Instrument Company sells and services high-quality electronic instruments that use a magnetic principle to examine the interiors of solid structures, such as concrete beams. The company markets three different models— M-100, M-200, and M-300. It also services these instruments for customers who buy a maintenance contract. Four sales representatives (one for each product line and one for maintenance contracts) call on customers. All service is done at a facility in Bayonne, New Jersey.

Required:

Design formats for performance reports that will answer the following questions (use as many formats as you think necessary):

(a) What are sales in any quarter?

(b) What are sales of each product line and of maintenance contracts?

(c) Which sales representative is responsible for each product line and for maintenance contracts?

(d) To which industries were sales made?

Case: Belton Parasol

The Belton Parasol Manufacturing Company implemented a budgeting process that seemed to work extremely well in 1985, the year after it was set up. All managers participated and took pride in their performance. Many received performance-based bonuses. The company's actual and expected performance in 1985 follow:

	Revenues	Expenses	Profits
Budget	$1,300,000	$1,150,000	$150,000
Actual	1,400,000	1,050,000	350,000
Variance	100,000	100,000	200,000

For 1986, central management decided to raise the goals and levels of performance in the budget. Budget and performance figures for 1986 follow:

	Revenues	Expenses	Profits
Budget	$1,700,000	$1,150,000	$550,000
Actual	1,600,000	1,200,000	400,000
Variance	100,000	50,000	150,000

Management morale plummeted during 1986 as the negative variances kept rolling in. In the first half of the year, everyone worked very hard. By December, however, no one seemed to care anymore; budget reports were not even being picked up. No one got bonuses.

Required:

(a) Was 1986 a bad year?

(b) What mistake(s) did management make in budgeting for 1986?

(c) Was low morale predictable? Why or why not?

Case: Redoubt Company

Redoubt Company is using accounting information to try to analyze the impact of its advertising campaign. It has tracked sales in two regions, only one of which it advertised in. The advertising campaign began on March 15 and lasted five days; only two of Redoubt's four product lines were advertised. Sales were tracked from March 8 until March 27. The sales journal appears below:

Transaction number	Date of sale	Sales region	Product line	Amount of sale
3453	3-8	A	1	$2,500
3454	3-10	B	1	1,000
3455	3-10	A	4	1,500
3456	3-11	A	3	2,000
3457	3-12	B	2	500
3458	3-12	A	4	800
3459	3-15	B	4	1,200
3460	3-16	B	2	1,500
3461	3-16	B	3	2,000
3462	3-17	A	2	700
3463	3-18	B	2	1,800
3464	3-18	B	3	2,100
3465	3-19	B	2	3,000
3466	3-19	A	3	600
3467	3-19	B	3	1,500
3468	3-22	A	4	900
3469	3-24	B	2	1,100
3470	3-25	A	1	1,400
3471	3-26	B	1	1,400

Required:

(a) Design a suitable performance-report format and fill in the information from the preceding sales journal. Divide the performance report into three periods: weeks before, during, and after the experiment.

(b) Compare sales by product lines, periods, and regions. Which product lines were advertised? In which region were they advertised?

(c) How would a properly designed accounting system assist this analytical process?

Computer Hardware and Software

Learning Objectives

After studying this chapter, you should be able to

- Explain fundamental computer operations: input, processing, storage, and output.

- Describe the historical development of computer technology.

- Explain the data representation hierarchy: bit, byte, field, record, file.

- Compare and contrast the various data storage media, such as RAM, ROM, tape, and disk.

- Identify the major hardware and software components of a computer-based system, such as the CPU, the operating system, applications programs, files, and input and output devices.

No matter how carefully planned, controls will not be effective unless those responsible for the accounting system's design understand the functions, capabilities, strengths, and weaknesses of the components that comprise its mechanical and logical building blocks. Ideally, data processing technology would offer to accounting and other users a neat standardized list of options—we could choose one from column A, two from column B, specify the color and size appropriate for our environment, and then sit back and wait for delivery. Unfortunately, the field of computers has been plagued by problems of incompatibility across product lines, both in hardware and in software.

Strangely, accountants are particularly at risk in such a promising situation. Used properly, computer technology offers capabilities that would be far beyond the reach of many accounting departments that rely on manual methods and manpower. Used improperly, the technology could damage the organization's records and even open its most private files to those who would perform acts of mischief or fraud. The best protection seems to be educating ourselves so that we know what to expect from the hardware and software that make up these systems. This chapter describes the computer system components normally found in an accounting information system. Although it will not substitute for a degree program in computer science, it will briefly introduce you to the field.

A typical computer-based accounting system consists of hardware such as one or more central processing units (CPUs), external memory or data storage, input devices (keyboards, optical and magnetic character readers, and others), output devices (terminals and printers), and communications equipment that transfers data among various parts of the accounting system. The system also includes software—an operating system to organize and control all the activities that go on inside a working computer and applications programs to process accounting data and find and report accounting information. A **program** is a sequence of interrelated instructions to a computer, which have the objective of producing specific outputs, such as reports. Controls in the operating system and applications form an accounting system's boundary with its environment. The operating system and applications programs determine how the CPU will act on data that pass through the control boundary to produce the outputs reported to users.

Past and Future

The milestones of computer history have been the nineteenth-century mechanical linkages of gears and wheels (Charles Babbage's "analytical engine"), the 1940s and 1950s vacuum tube computers, often referred to as first-generation computers; the second-generation solid-state transistorized computers in the 1960s (IBM 7090); the first integrated circuit computers that marked the third generation in the 1970s (IBM 360 and VAX-11); and the fourth generation, which brought the very large-scale integrated (VLSI) circuitry of today (the Apple Macintosh Plus and Compaq PC, among many other examples). A fifth generation of computers is under development in Japan and Europe and by the MCC consortium in the United States. The goal of fifth-generation computers is to incorporate artificial intelligence so that computers can modify their own programs in response to "learning" that occurs during their use.

In the early nineteenth century, punched cards were used to control textile looms. In the 1880s, a U.S. Census Bureau employee named Herman Hollerith developed a way of using punched cards in data processing. IBM, the largest computer manufacturer in the market today, evolved in part from the company Hollerith founded to produce and sell his invention. The nineteenth-century English mathematician Charles Babbage, however, was probably the first person to conceive of a computer as a programmable machine capable of both performing calculations and following a sequence of logical instructions. Babbage's machine was never built; it was probably too complex to build in the nineteenth century. His colleague Ada Augusta, the Countess of Lovelace and the daughter of the poet Lord Byron, was a mathematician who developed programming concepts for the Babbage machine; she is recognized as the first programmer.

The first computer to be built and used was the MARK I, developed at Harvard University around 1942. ENIAC, constructed at the University of Pennsylvania in 1946, was the first all-electronic computer. In 1950 the Census Bureau used the UNIVAC I, the first commercial electronic computer, to process census results. Although remarkable for its time, UNIVAC's reliance on vacuum tubes made it a power hog, bulky, unreliable, and slow. Any modern computer easily surpasses the UNIVAC I. The first computer companies—IBM and Sperry-Rand—were joined by established manufacturers like Burroughs, NCR, RCA, and General Electric. Soon, other companies like Control Data, Data General, Datapoint, and Digital Equipment Corporation began to form and compete with each other and with IBM.

Two legal decisions in the 1960s had a profound impact on the marketing and, therefore, on the development of computers. When the courts decided that manufacturers must offer computer equipment for sale as well as for lease, IBM had to end its practice of only leasing its equipment. The courts also ruled that a computer company could no longer force a buyer to acquire both hardware and software from the same source—which meant that IBM could no longer refuse to sell hardware and software separately. These decisions opened the computer market to more producers and intensified competition. Some firms, including General Electric and RCA, eventually withdrew from the market.

In the late 1970s, development of microprocessors led to the introduction of microcomputers—small, inexpensive machines that qualified as products with mass appeal. New companies such as Apple, Heath (later acquired by Zenith), Commodore, Compaq (founded in 1982 and a Fortune 500 company in 1985), and Northstar pioneered the microcomputer market. The structure of the computer industry has now mushroomed to an extent that defies complete description. The general picture, however, includes moderate-size specialized firms, many with a short life expectancy. Some firms make chips, others assemble disk drives, others make only the keyboards, and so on. The court-ordered breakup of the Bell System in the 1980s allowed the giant communications firm AT&T to sell computers, and it began to market the equipment originally developed only for its own use.

Computer systems available to end users have changed radically over the past four decades, and they will continue to change. Although costs will continue to decline in terms of price paid per unit of memory, storage, or calculating power, new products will certainly contain progressively larger amounts of these crude measures of value. In 1982, for example, a standard "Winchester" hard-disk drive (an external storage device) cost $2,000, or $200 per million characters of external storage. In 1987 a drive of similar design and twice the capacity cost $600, a six-fold reduction in cost per unit of storage. This trend will continue until external storage costs drop to only a few dollars per million characters. The cost per unit of storage is also plummeting for other computer components such as internal memory. New high-capacity memory chips offer the prospect of a cost-per-million-characters of memory of $50 or less in the near future. Processor chips costing only a few dollars or cents promise very inexpensive and powerful computers.

One hotly competitive area is the market for "IBM compatibles"— small computers able to run the same software as the IBM PC family. IBM did not introduce a microcomputer until 1981, but its PC, PC-XT, and PC-AT have been extremely popular. IBM's PS/2 product line, introduced in 1987, runs many of the same programs as the PC family while introducing new features demanded by users. AT&T, Compaq, Columbia, Epson, ITT, Leading Edge, Panasonic, PC's Limited, Radio Shack, Wang, Zenith, and a number of other manufacturers have produced computers that nearly duplicate the basic input-output systems (BIOS) that determine the original IBM PC family's operating characteristics. Components and software for these machines are made, assembled, and marketed worldwide, making PC compatibles truly an international industry.

As computers have become less costly, they have also become physically smaller. Compactness means higher speed, since the electrical impulses have a shorter distance to travel. The small-scale components draw very little current and generate little heat, eliminating the need for the massive cooling apparatus of first- and second-generation computers. Nearly flat liquid-crystal or electroluminescent display screens could eliminate the bulky CRT (televisionlike) monitor. More components may be placed in one cabinet—many small computers now include a hard-disk drive, one or more floppy disk drives, one-half million or more characters of internal memory, a built-in operating system and other software, a thermal printer, and a modem, all in one transportable unit.

One trend that may accelerate in the future is computer specialization. Smaller and less expensive computers mean that several computers, each performing a specialized function, can be used in the same system. A modern automobile, for example, may contain one microprocessor (actually a small computer) to control engine functions and others to level the suspension, operate the brakes, control temperature and humidity, and tune the stereo. Similarly, a business may have a large computer to process inputs, several smaller computers to record inputs, and still others for economic forecasting, financial planning, product design, decision analysis, and production control. Linking such computers in a network, as we will see in Chapter 16, allows the data on one computer to be shared with authorized users on other computers. For example, an organization's financial planners could use current sales data and product manufacturing cost data to prepare a forecast. Organizations that used to plan in terms of buying "a computer" now think of multiple computers, each suited to different specific requirements.

Computer Hardware

Computers operate by accepting inputs and altering, preserving, and using them as electronically stored information. When the current is on, the computer can "read" the data stored in its internal circuits in the form of electrical charges or magnetic fields present or absent at specific locations. When the current is off, tiny magnetized locations on a disk or tape store a pattern that later serves as the starting-point to restore its electrical equivalent in the computer.

Chips, Bits, and Bytes

The building-blocks of computers are the integrated circuits familiarly known as chips. Especially designed to handle the electronic representations of data at high speed with total accuracy, chips are actually complex miniaturized integrated circuits containing thousands of diodes, transistors, capacitors, resistors, connectors, and other components. A closely controlled process similar to etching duplicates one of these circuits over and over on a silicon wafer about the size of a small saucer. A delicate cutting operation separates the wafer into fingernail-size individual chips, each of which is soldered to a base an inch or so square, large enough to allow the necessary connections to other components. Although designing a new chip is time consuming and expensive, the direct cost of making one chip becomes very low in volume production—in some cases less than a dollar. Since each chip is an integrated circuit with many components, relatively few are required for a complete computer.

A **processor chip** consists of logic circuits. A computer must contain one processor chip and may contain several. A **memory chip** stores data. The computer must possess enough memory chips to retain programmed instructions and data.

Computers process and store numbers and letters by means of electronic "switches," which can be off or on. The data amount that any one such switch contains is called a **bit**, which is a contraction for "*bi*nary dig*it*." The switch state of being on or off can be represented numerically as the value 1 or 0; the value of a bit can therefore be only 0 or 1. Accordingly, the binary number system, which employs only the two digits 0 and 1, lends itself well to the nature of computers. One bit can represent two (2^1) alternative values; two bits can represent four (2^2) alternative values, or unique combinations of 0s and 1s. Eight bits can represent 256 (2^8)

unique combinations. For example, here are some binary numbers and their decimal number equivalents:

Binary number	Decimal number
00000000	0
00000001	1
00000010	2
00000100	4
00001000	8
00001010	10 (= binary 00001000 + 00000010 or decimal 8 + 2)

Three features of bits are particularly important. First, they can be used as **flags**, a type of variable whose value corresponds to the outcome of an operation. For example, a bit set to 1 might indicate successful completion of a data processing operation; if the same bit is set to 0, then the operation was not completed successfully. Bits are used as flags at the computer system or software execution level and the user typically has no control over them.

Second, the computer design will determine how many bits the computer will read or process in one operating cycle. This number of bits, which may be called the *bus size* or *data path width* or *word size*, plays a role in determining the rate at which a computer will process data.

Third, computer data are stored in combinations of **bytes**, eight bits each in most computer systems. As one example, you may want to assign a number to each of 256 items—the upper- and lower-case alphabet, the numbers 0-9, and dozens of other symbols. Each item might correspond to a different numerical value of one byte. In the computer memory, eight switches, one byte of storage space, would hold whatever number corresponded to the symbol then in use. If your list requires the computer to uniquely identify 257 symbols, then two 8-bit bytes in computer memory would be required and in fact would suffice to represent up to 65,536 symbols.

The American Standard Code for Information Interchange (ASCII) is the agreed-upon code for assigning one-byte values to letters, numbers, symbols, and input-output operations. For example, the ASCII codes for three of these items follow:

Letter/Number	ASCII Decimal Code	ASCII Binary Code (used by computer)
3	51	00110011
A	65	01000001
a	97	01100001

Computer hardware consists of the central processing unit (CPU), external storage, input-output devices, and the connections among them. Figure 4.9 on page 122 shows these components arranged as a simple system. The CPU controls and exchanges data with all the other devices, collectively called **peripherals**. The peripherals in Figure 4.9 include a printer, two terminals, a graphics display device, an optical read-only memory, and a multiplexer to allow additional connections. Let us look at the basic components of a computer system in more detail.

The Central Processing Unit

The **CPU**, the brain of the computer, consists of a unit to execute arithmetic and logic instructions; various **buffers**, which provide temporary storage for data, input, or output, to hold the results of intermediate calculations; internal storage to hold programs and data (explained in the next section); a control unit; and input and output links to the rest of the computer system. These units are all mounted on one or more pieces of resin-impregnated cloth called a motherboard, which enables the units to be connected to each other. Figure 4.1 shows a simple CPU.

The Arithmetic-Logic Unit. The **arithmetic-logic unit (ALU)** is the part of the CPU that can carry out arithmetic calculations and make logical comparisons. Suppose, for example, that there are three buffers—*A*, *B*, and *C*. The ALU can perform operations like the following:

Take the value in *A*.
Multiply it times the value in *B*.
Place the product in *B*.
Compare the value in *B* with the value in *C*.
If the value in *B* is larger, subtract the value in *C* from the value in *B* and place the result in *A*.
If the value in *B* is smaller, subtract the value in *B* from the value in *C* and place the result in *A*.
If the value in *B* equals the value in *C*, place a zero in *A*.

Arithmetic operations make heavy demands on an ALU's resources. The ALU must convert decimal numbers to their binary equivalents, carry out the arithmetic using binary numbers, then convert the binary result back to a decimal value. Many computers achieve greater speed by including one or more processors especially designed to handle arithmetic only.

The Control Unit. The CPU **control unit** controls timing and sequencing by repeating a simple cycle over and over; during each cycle, it synchronizes to the computer clock and translates computer program instructions into signals to the ALU and other parts of the computer system. The control unit may, for example, require one cycle or more for each of the following operations:

Signal the disk drive to get ready for an instruction.

Send the disk drive the first byte of the instruction.

Receive a confirming signal from the disk drive.

Send the remainder of the instruction to the disk drive and receive from the disk drive confirming signals (several cycles).

Locate the portion of memory in which the next program instruction is stored.

Read the instruction (several cycles).

Receive from the disk drive a signal that it has completed the instruction, and so on.

The Clock.   The **clock** is a timing device, often a quartz crystal vibrating at a certain frequency as a weak electrical current passes through it. Electronic circuitry converts these vibrations into regular pulses that, when sent to the control unit, trigger its actions.

Figure 4.1   Simple CPU

All the components of a simple CPU may be placed on a single motherboard, making it easier to connect them. On an actual motherboard, RAM and ROM take up more space than other CPU components. CPUs of all types have decreased in size as computer scientists have found new ways to miniaturize their components.

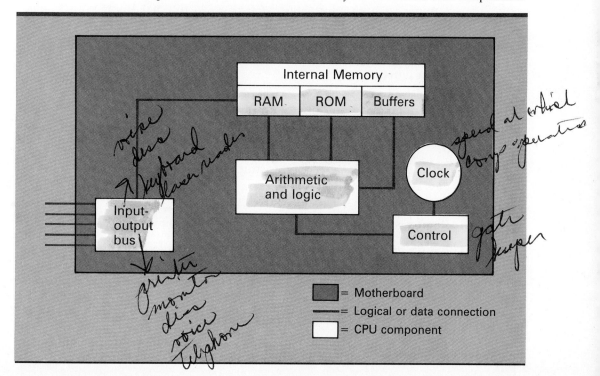

Interfaces. The computer components communicate with each other through interfaces, sometimes called *buses*. The interfaces are of two major types: serial and parallel. A serial bus sends the signal through a single wire one bit at a time. (RS-232 and RS-422 are examples of standard serial connections.) A parallel bus sends signals one byte at a time down at least eight wires, a different wire for each bit and possibly more wires for check bits and other controlling signals. You can recognize a parallel bus by its distinctive flat multistrand wire. (S-100 or "Centronics" is the best example of a standard parallel interface.) In smaller computers the printer connection usually is parallel. Although they may be either serial or parallel, the connections intended for disk drives, modem, monitor, and many printers are usually serial. The Small Computer Serial Interface (SCSI), a standard bus used by many small computers, allows connection with SCSI-standard computer accessories.

At one time, parallel connections, which are extensively used within the CPU, were thought to be capable of higher transmission rates than were serial connections. Today, however, modern high-speed serial connections will satisfy most high-volume data-handling requirements between the CPU and other system components.

Data Storage

Computers store information in two ways. **Internal storage**, also called memory, is built into the CPU. Internal storage is used extensively during processing. **External storage** resides outside the main computer unit on magnetic media. The information in external storage remains intact even when power is off.

Internal Storage in RAM, ROM, and Buffers. Random-access memory **(RAM)** is the part of the CPU that stores programs and data that are currently in use. RAM is temporary storage; its contents disappear when the electrical current goes off. The computer can change the contents of RAM according to its stored instructions: it can replace them with other data or print or display them.

RAM storage locations are identified (or addressed) by numbers that range from zero on up. Some parts of RAM may be reserved for the operating system and other special purposes such as storing the contents of the screen display, the disk cache, or the printer buffer. (The last two are specialized types of temporary storage explained later in the chapter.) Other parts may be reserved for software applications, data, and program segments.

Read-only memory **(ROM)** is also a part of the CPU. Unlike RAM, ROM's contents are inserted by the manufacturer and cannot be changed by computer operations. Its contents also remain permanently in the CPU even when the current is shut off. The three usual applications of ROM are to store the instructions the computer must follow to become usable when it is turned on; to hold very frequently used programs such as the basic input-output system (BIOS) and perhaps the operating system; and to hold applications or data that limit access to the computer, such as a program available only to users who know a password.

In modern computers, both RAM and ROM consist of very large-scale integrated (VLSI) chips. These chips each contain from 4K to 1,024K bits. Eight chips of the same size comprise a bank (or unit) of memory. Each chip will hold one bit of each byte stored in this bank of memory. Although fastest access dictates that the memory chips should be mounted on the motherboard, as close as possible to the processor itself, this sometimes proves impractical. Very large memories may require at least part of the memory to be located off the motherboard. In such cases, the CPU will be designed to make the least frequent use of the slower memory located off the motherboard.

The third type of internal memory, buffers, are temporary storage places for information that is on its way somewhere else. For example, after a multiplication operation, the product may be placed in a buffer before being sent to its memory address. Another use of buffers is to store data read from an external storage device, entered by a human through the terminal keyboard, or about to be sent to a printer. These buffers are sometimes reserved parts of RAM; at other times they actually exist in a peripheral device, such as a printer. Print buffers can store from a few kilobytes in a computer intended for producing short printed documents to many megabytes when the computer produces detailed color graphics. A print buffer enables the CPU to transmit all the data for printing quickly, then resume executing other instructions in its program. The section on peripherals later in this chapter discusses printer buffers in more detail.

External Storage on Disks and Tapes.   Disk drives represent one major storage family. Tape drives (which differ only in speed, reliability, and precision from a home tape deck) are the other. (A third type of external storage, read-only optical disks, offers an inexpensive way to access large quantities of unchangeable data; see page 123.) In effect, there are no upper limits on the size of external storage for large computers.

A **disk drive** is a mechanical device that holds and spins a disk, which has been coated with an iron-oxide compound that retains patterns of magnetized and unmagnetized areas. The disk drive incorporates one or more sensing devices called read-write heads to detect, erase, and create these magnetic patterns. The disk drive also contains electronic circuits designed to accept and execute signals from the CPU that control the disk drive. Figure 4.2 depicts these operations. The read-write head can find any location on the disk surface within hundredths of a second, allowing random access to any data stored on a disk surface. This characteristic has

Figure 4.2   Disk Drive Components
The disk rotates at about 300 r.p.m., bringing its surface at a given radius under the read-write head five times per second. By quickly moving in and out in response to the head motor, the read-write head has quick access to the whole surface of the disk, and thus to all the storage contained on the disk's surface. Despite their complexity, disk drives are very reliable.

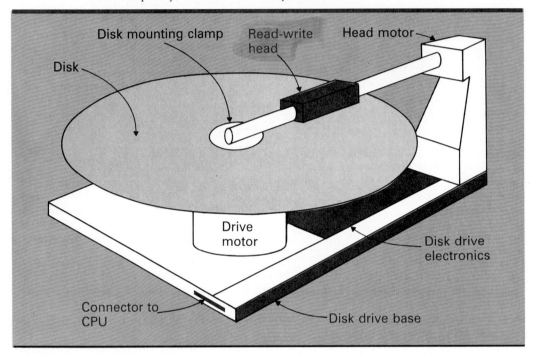

important implications for software designed for a disk-based computer system. Such software can store and find data in any order and so can operate more quickly than software designed for a tape-based system, which requires sequential access to data. The read-write head of the disk drive is driven by a tiny precision electric motor and assumes a position at a specific radius from the center to the edge of the disk's rotating surface. There it waits until the desired part of the disk circumference passes beneath it. The part of the disk scanned by the read-write head at a specific radius forms a circle called a track. The disk surface's magnetic patterns are organized into concentric tracks, each of which in turn is divided into sectors, the smallest parts of the circumference the read-write head can recognize. The read-write head senses the magnetic patterns passing beneath it and converts them into electrical pulses that the computer interprets as bits and bytes. Most disk drives can use both sides of the disk to store data. Double-sided storage is faster since the drive can write two tracks (one on each side) without moving or repositioning itself.

A magnetic **tape drive** unit is based on the same principles as a cassette-tape player. The tape drive passes a long, thin plastic tape past a read-write head at a constant speed. The tape is wide enough to accommodate several tracks and is divided lengthwise into sectors. In one track on the tape, a special sector mark identifies where one sector ends and the next begins. The tape drive may keep track of its location by counting the number of sector marks that pass beneath its read-write head. To find a particular tape sector, the tape drive computes the number of sectors it must move the tape, and in which direction, to place the start of the desired sector at the edge of the read-write head.

Tape drives excel at sequential access to data—reading or writing sectors in the order they appear on the tape. Many accounting applications work best with sequential data access. For example, when a transaction file is posted, reading the sectors sequentially ensures that none will accidentally be overlooked. And when paychecks are written, if the employee master file is read sequentially, a check will be printed for every employee. Chapter 5 discusses some of the advantages and disadvantages of data access systems.

Both tape and disk drives interface with the rest of the computer system through controllers. The controller is a circuit or module that contains a power supply, connections, and ROM and can link one or more tape or disk drives with the CPU.

Input-Output Devices

The market offers a wide variety of input and output devices, some of them targeted at very specialized audiences. A mouse, a keyboard, and an optical reader are examples of input devices; each can enter data or commands into the system. A terminal display screen, a plotter, and a printer are examples of output devices; they make the results of the computer operations available to the user. Terminal display screens often resemble television screens and, like those screens, are available in color or monochrome models.

Small printers that can produce a draft-quality page in a minute or so cost from $300 to $600; very high-quality printers often cost $1,000 and up. Printers differ in their individual features almost as much as computers do. With almost any computer, one has a wide choice of printer costs, sizes, quality, and speed of print.

Software for Data Management

The programs and instructions that guide the hardware's data operations fall into three categories—the operating system, computer languages, and the applications programs. These three software layers nest around each other, as shown in Figure 4.3. The CPU receives its instructions from the

Figure 4.3   Relationships Among Data, Software, and the CPU
The CPU (in the center of the bull's eye) operates only in response to the BIOS, which in turn responds to the operating system. This operating system responds in turn to the programs that are being run. (These programs are often written in a language or program environment that helps humans express the program logic in a computer-translatable form). The program's logic responds to data that reflect day-to-day processing and reporting requirements.

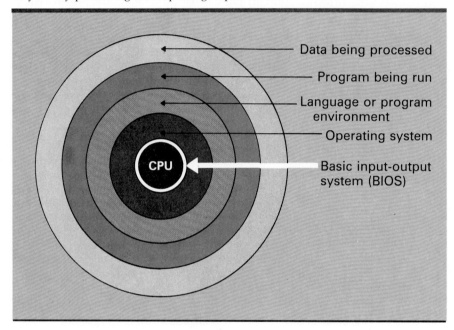

operating system. The operating system also supervises the running of applications programs that perform tasks, such as word processing or filing, for the user. These programs, which were created by programmers in terms users could understand, are sets of instructions to the CPU. The instructions are transformed by a computer language into a form the operating system and CPU can accept and carry out. Finally, the data, which form another layer surrounding the software, are processed in accordance with these instructions.

The Operating System

The **operating system**—sometimes called the disk operating system (DOS) or supervisory program—is a mediator that interacts with the CPU, the peripherals, and the computer program. It issues signals that cause the CPU to run programs, open and close files, read and save data, turn disk drives on and off, alter the screen display, protect files from deletion or change, group files in directories, and perform other tricks in its repertory. Some operating system commands may be issued by the computer user; others are issued by programs as they are run.

The operating system may reside internally in ROM, or it may be read in from a disk or tape when the computer is started and remain in RAM until the computer is turned off. Storing the operating system in ROM usually allows a much quicker computer startup. Reading in the operating system from an external memory source allows the user to change and improve the operating system more easily.

Often a computer has its own proprietary operating system and cannot be used without that system. However, the trend seems to be toward fewer operating systems, which will be compatible with more than one computer. Small computers made by IBM, Texas Instruments, Compaq, Leading Edge, and other companies use the MS-DOS operating system developed by Microsoft. Many computers of various sizes use the UNIX operating system developed by AT&T. Operating systems that will run on many computer models offer a wider range of compatible software than most proprietary systems offer and let users replace computer equipment with different models (and even different brands) with little or no modification of software.

Computer Languages

As we noted earlier, the CPU processor understands only the binary numbers of data and machine language. However, almost all processors have a built-in set of symbols, called **assembly language,** that people can understand and memorize and that the processor can translate into the appropriate binary commands. Thus *A* in an assembler program might be the symbol for the binary command-code number (01101001) that initiates the add operation. Programmers may be trained to use assembly codes.

However, assembly language symbols have a one-to-one correspondence with machine language instructions. Because a typical computer program contains thousands of such instructions, the effort of writing it in assembly language would be stupendous. To avoid this huge task, computer scientists have developed **programming languages** that create simple statements, each corresponding to many—even hundreds—of assembly language commands. These languages also allow statements to be linked together to form more complex statements and permit control of the program to be transferred temporarily to subroutines, then returned to the main program. A complete language will give full access to all of the assembly language commands in the processor. Most languages are intended for use with many different computers, and programs written in a particular language are thus "portable" from one computer to another without heavy rewriting. Each computer model has its own special compiler or interpreter program to convert language statements into the assembly commands of that particular computer. Figure 4.4 shows how languages are used to program computers.

The first computer language most users learn is BASIC, developed in the 1960s as a language for teaching programming. BASIC was conceived as a simpler version of FORTRAN, which was developed earlier for scientific programming. BASIC is a "string processor," a type of language in which the computer translates each statement into assembly or machine language and executes it before moving to the next statement. Although BASIC's authors did not expect those who learned it to write long programs, the language remains popular today and is in fact used to write many long programs. The most popular language for accounting applications is probably COBOL, which was designed especially for data processing (as compared to scientific programming).

Figure 4.4   Role of Languages in Programming Computers
Computer languages are a bridge from programmer to CPU. They also fit into the much broader scope from human data-generation to human information-use.

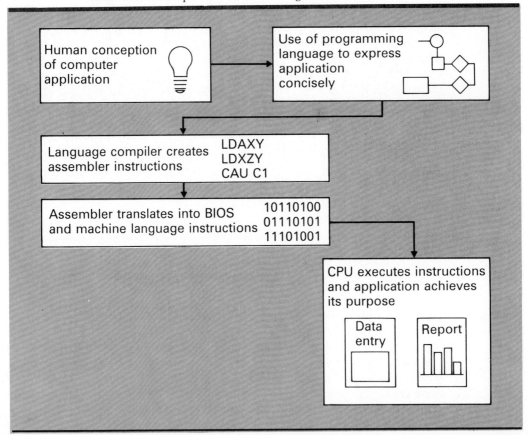

BASIC presents an example of the way a vendor can use hardware to limit the use of software. The IBM PC family uses a version of the BASIC language known as BASICA ("BASIC- advanced"). IBM designed its PCs so that, although part of this language is on a floppy disk, another essential part is contained on a proprietary ROM chip, which is legally protected against duplication and can be found only in IBM PCs. An IBM PC-compatible, therefore, cannot run programs that were written for BASICA and, for that reason, some people would not buy a PC-compatible. Users who want to run such programs on PC-compatible computers must buy a version of BASIC known as GW-BASIC, which is contained entirely on a floppy disk.

PASCAL is another language written to teach programming concepts. PASCAL is a "structured" language, harder to learn than BASIC but much more powerful and suited for large programs. Since the relative advantages of different languages are best understood after you have become familiar with the applications for which they must be used, we will delay further discussion until Chapters 17 and 18, which describe system development.

Applications Program Concepts

An application program is one written or purchased to perform tasks set by a user (such as an accounting or engineering-design program). It requires both data structure and logical structure. The data structure consists of fields, records, and files. These data structure elements must correspond to data handled by an accounting system. Accounting data are appropriately stored in this structure. Data bases, the most highly organized data structures, adapt well to accounting applications, and this section lays a foundation for their further discussion in Chapter 5.

The logical structure of a program is contained in the instructions to the operating system. The operating system passes the instructions on to the CPU. A computer program consists of commands, logical statements, constants, variables, and user interfaces. A typical logical structure organizes the program into a main segment and subroutines. The main segment contains a **user interface** describing the program and giving the user a choice of program options, usually in a form called a **menu**. The subroutines carry out the options. Figure 4.5 illustrates this logical structure and shows how the user interface presents that structure as a series of nested menus. The first menu explains the main program options. When a user selects an option on the main menu, such as "Cash receipts," the program displays another menu for the cash receipts application, showing the options available there. If the user had selected "Prepare reports," another menu would have listed the reports that could be prepared. Nested menus make it unnecessary for the program user to remember all the options and commands the program makes available. After the user has selected a specific option, such as "Print cash receipts report for

August," the report-printing routine combines information from the cash receipts journal and creates the report. When the report is complete, the program offers the options of printing the report now or saving it as a file to be printed later.

The menus also offer a "way out." After the cash receipts report generator completes the cash receipts report, it again displays the "Prepare

Figure 4.5   Menu-Based Program Structure
Menus can simplify an otherwise complex program. Here, the menu sequence takes a user from the main program interface to the general ledger menu, to the cash receipts menu, to the cash receipts application user interface, to the cash receipts report-generator menu. The user need not memorize any of the commands, only select the correct options.

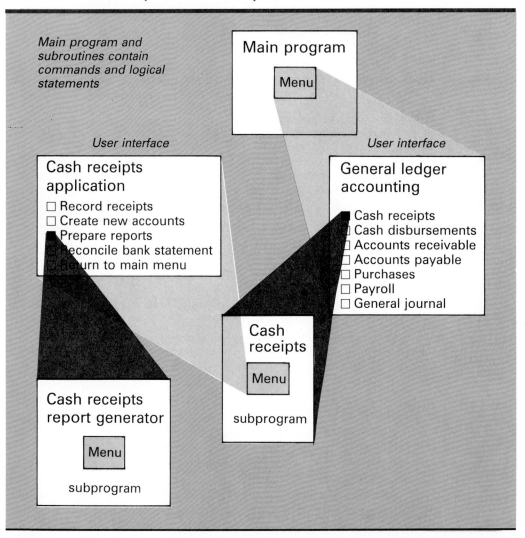

reports" menu, which contains the option "Return to cash receipts." If selected, this action will display the cash receipts menu. It, in turn, allows the user to select "Return to main menu," from which the user can select "Quit." Programs are complex, and require good design to function efficiently. If a program is well designed, it should be easy to see what the program is supposed to do.

Computer hardware is only as powerful as the software that provides its instructions. Some excellent software has been written for very small and specialized markets. However, the general-use buyer is likely to receive greater value from software written—and priced—for a large market. This rule partially explains the popularity of computers that can run software written for the IBM PC family.

Fields. The smallest meaningful unit of data that a human being would recognize is a **field**, which consists of one or more bytes representing a word, a number, or some other entity. You might use a field to represent an account number, a dollar amount, an account name, a date, an address, or any of many other possibilities. You may want to define several types of fields—large numbers, small numbers, mixed numbers and characters, dates, or logical (yes/no or equal/not equal) fields.

A field's length is specified in bytes, one byte for each character, digit, space, or symbol the field will contain. Thus, a field to store a date might contain 6 bytes—2 each for the month, day of the month, and year. A field to store an 8-character account number would have to contain 8 bytes, one for each digit. A field to store a street address might be allocated 25 or 35 bytes. A numeric field to store numbers up to $9999.99 would require 7 bytes. Bytes are so small (one character each) that most storage applications require a great many of them.

When defining the capacity of internal memory in a CPU, bytes are conventionally counted in units of "K." One K is a **kilobyte**, 2^{10} or 1,024 bytes. External storage is measured in megabytes. A **megabyte** is 1,024 kilobytes, or about one million bytes. One expresses small computer storage capacities in kilobytes, those of other computers in megabytes. A megabyte is a large but not awesome storage capability. A double-spaced typewritten page corresponds to almost 2,000 bytes, so a 512-page manuscript would occupy about one megabyte of storage.

Records. In a computerized system, a **record** consists of several related fields and corresponds closely to other records you might think of, such as the information associated together in a credit application, employment history, accounting entry, or an account. A record is a close equivalent to the information generated by a simple accounting transaction like a receipt of cash. Figure 4.6 depicts such a record. Note that the record has a beginning and an end, and that within the record, the fields are separated from each other and occur in a defined sequence. It is often convenient if the accounting system can vary the number of fields in a record to meet changing requirements. For example, a complete credit or loan history record might require added fields to cover a progressively longer time span.

Files. A **file** is a collection of related records. If all the records in the file contain the same fields in the same format, the result is called a flat file. A flat file can be represented as a matrix, as Figure 4.7 shows. All of an organization's accounting journal entries (records) constitute a file, and all

Figure 4.6   Example of a Single Record
All records have a beginning and an end. The fields within a record are separated from each other and occur in an expected sequence.

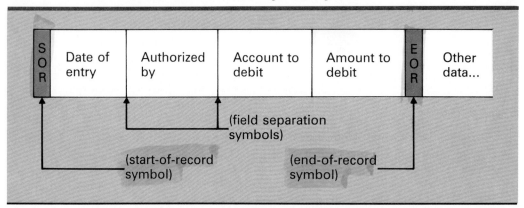

| S O R | Date of entry | Authorized by | Account to debit | Amount to debit | E O R | Other data... |

(field separation symbols)

(start-of-record symbol)

(end-of-record symbol)

Figure 4.7   Example of a Flat File
This flat file consists of three rows, each corresponding to a unique record. Each record has six columns, or fields. In each column, the same type of information is presented. A flat file can also be called a *table* or a *matrix*.

Attributes or fields

Last name	First name	Street address	City	State	ZIP
Arnold	Robert	344 West Academy	Houston	TX	77001
Barton	Charles	215 Plumb	Weslaco	OK	65432
Greenspan	Arthur	105 Tower	Beaumont	LA	11104

Records (also referred to as rows or tuples)

Figure 4.8 Bit, Byte, Field, Record, File
Here, we pluck several records from a tape and expand them into their fields. In the top record, you see the field with the value "Abilene" analyzed further; the *A* in Abilene is represented by a byte with the value 65. In this byte two bits (the solid black dots) are "1" and the others are "0."

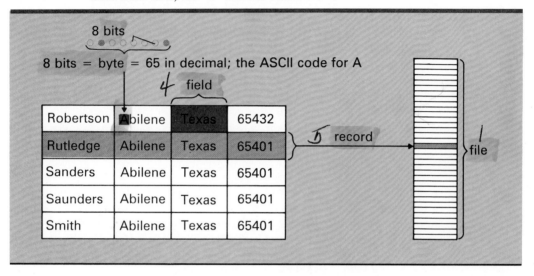

its general ledger accounts (records) constitute a file. Ordinarily, the records in a given file all have fields of the same type, although their values will differ. Usually (but not always) the records in a computerized file are the same length. The record length, number of fields, field types and lengths, and certain other parameters constitute the design of the file. Unless the file is somehow restricted, you can remove records or insert them if their designs are compatible. You can also move records from one file to another. Figure 4.8 shows the relationships among bit, byte, field, record, and file. The organization and processing of records and files is the topic of Chapter 5.

Choosing and Designing Computer Systems

Someone who expects to choose or design a computer system certainly has a broad array of features from which to choose. Still, the smallest computers have most of the features discussed above—although on a smaller scale—offered on the larger and more powerful computers. To select any system's size and power, the designer has to consider the requirements for applications software, which in turn depend on the needs for calculation speed, memory capacity, number of active users, and response to connected devices.

Computer Size and Power

Based on increasing cost and size, the four broad classes of computers are microcomputers (for instance, the IBM PS/2 and Apple Macintosh Plus, costing $3,000 to $10,000 for a complete system); minicomputers (Wang VS100 and DEC VAX 11/780, costing up to $1 million); mainframe computers (IBM 360 and 4031, costing $1 million to $5 million); and supercomputers (CDC CYBER-70 and IBM Sierra, costing $6 million and up). These classes overlap, and the distinctions have become quite blurred. At least two manufacturers, IBM and Digital Equipment Corporation, offer computers in all four broad classes. Even within a class, computer capabilities vary; IBM's new Personal System/2 microcomputers offer the computer equivalent of a range of cars in a dealer showroom. And a new class, the "workstation," a minicomputer intended for use by only one person, seems to be emerging.

Calculation Speed.   Calculation speed depends largely on the frequency at which the processor chip operates, the width of the data path through the processor, the efficiency of its command set, and the number of processors in the CPU. The processor-chip's operating frequency is usually selected at the time the computer is designed, although some microcomputers allow the user to select the processor frequency. Lower frequencies are slower but impose less stress on the computer design. Processor frequencies of 4 to 10 megahertz are common today. The width of the data path determines the number of bits that are processed during each cycle—the more bits, the faster. Popular advertising refers to data path width as the number of bits, as in "This computer has a 32-bit processor." High-speed modern processors have data path widths of 8, 16, or 32 bits.

A processor's command set, built in at the time of its design, contains a relatively small number of commands—fewer than a thousand in most cases. Each command performs a logical operation or a data movement; as a set, the commands determine the processor's capabilities. A large command set usually means that the processor contains circuits that can accomplish complex operations in response to one command, which is the equivalent of several simpler commands. Since each cycle executes one command, a larger command set implies that the same number of cycles will accomplish more data processing than the same number of cycles in a processor with fewer commands. Processing will be slower if one CPU must carry out all computer activities and faster if separate processors control input and output, create the monitor display, perform arithmetic calculations, and manage other specific tasks.

Memory Size.   A large internal storage increases computer power by allowing larger programs and more data to be stored where the processor can access them quickly. When an entire file of several megabytes can be held in RAM, its records can be accessed much more rapidly than when the records must be read individually from tape or disk. A computer without a large memory has to rely on "overlays," holding in internal storage only part of the program and data and repeatedly replacing or overlaying them with other parts. Although the overlay process seems very quick relative to human speed, it is very time-consuming in terms of computer speed. Fortunately, memory is becoming less expensive and designers are building more of it into new computers. Internal storage size in a new design is limited to the number of bytes the processor is able to address directly. Typical maximum internal storage sizes are 64K bytes for the old Z80 and 6502 processors and 16M bytes for the newer 68000 processor. However, designers can get around these limits by creating banks of internal storage and enabling the processor to switch from one bank to another. For example, a 64K-byte processor could be made to use a 256K-byte RAM by placing four 64K-byte banks in the CPU design and including instruction sets that cause the processor to address the correct bank for whatever operation is under way. Even though it is all RAM, however, bank storage is not all directly addressable at one time and, therefore, is slower than traditional internal storage.

Number of Active Users.   One measure of a computer system's power is the number of active users it can accommodate without slowing down to a pace that is unacceptable for any one user. Very large computer systems, designed for multiuser environments, and incorporating multiple disk drives, tape drives, printers, and other components, can accept hundreds of users. The ability of a computer to respond sequentially to different users while retaining the appearance that each user has exclusive control of the computer is called **multiprogramming**. One way to achieve multiprogramming is to install several processors in the CPU for program execution; another way is to link several CPUs under common control to execute programs simultaneously as they arrive from users. The latter approach is called **multiprocessing**. In general, computers are designed to give the best power-to-value ratio when the number of users falls within certain set limits; prospective computer buyers can learn these limits from manufacturers.

The number of users served need not reflect the size of the computer. Some very large computers, such as those that analyze a nation's air defenses, are intended for only one user—the authority who must activate defense or attack systems. Some small systems can serve hundreds of users comfortably (although not all at once). A system designed for multiple users will have a large memory and should have more than one processor in the CPU. One processor will do arithmetic and logic calculations: other processors will handle input and output, printers, graphics, and monitor displays. A large memory may be partitioned among various users so that each one has exclusive use of part of it. Large external storage capacity will enable each user to store programs and files not actually in use. Many serial connections will link user terminals directly to the CPU.

All of these features add complexity and cost to a computer system and so are not suitable for the lowest-cost small computers. Above that level, the majority of large and small computers have the capability for multiperson use. Chapter 16 describes various designs and features of computer-based communications systems intended to link people and computers in a data and information network.

Response to Peripherals. The efficient use of peripherals is another measure of a computer's power. Three design features that increase this efficiency are the disk cache, printer buffer, and job-queue manager. The disk cache can be either a part of RAM or a separate small memory; the CPU, as it proceeds with processing, can use the disk cache to hold programs or data normally kept in external storage but likely to be required *next* by the operations under way. By "guessing" what programs or data will be needed and placing them in the cache, the CPU will have them available and can avoid stopping its calculations to wait for the relatively slow disk access and read operations. For example, if the CPU is reading records sequentially from a file and performing calculations on them, the disk cache will detect the pattern of disk access and hold the next record. A disk cache, which may be 32K bytes or more in size, can affect processing speed dramatically.

A printer buffer, also a part of RAM or a separate memory, is sometimes located in the printer itself and stores documents to be printed. Without the buffer, the CPU would have to send each document to the printer one line at a time; the CPU would thus be tied up in slow output operations, preventing it from doing other tasks. Suppose, for example, that a computer is calculating payroll and printing paychecks. After calculating each check, the CPU inserts that check's information in the printer buffer and proceeds to the next calculation. The CPU is much faster than the printer, and it may finish payroll long before the printer finishes. Because of the printer buffer, the CPU can move on to other operations not requiring the printer.

A job-queue manager is valuable when several jobs, or user programs, must be executed on a multiuser computer. The job-queue manager analyzes the jobs and arranges them according to rules designed into it. It may hold back jobs that will take a long time or that use large files. The job-queue manager's objective is to allow most users to perform most of their jobs, holding back or executing in parts the longer jobs that would reduce the computer's service to the majority of users.

Open or Closed Architecture

Architecture refers to the way the various components, especially those of the CPU, are connected. Open architecture means the end user of the computer system may connect additional components to the CPU. Closed architecture means that the designers do not intend any additional system components to be connected. For example, early computers from IBM, UNIVAC, and other manufacturers had closed architecture: the manufacturer provided the CPU, all the peripherals, the software, and even the training and documentation. Today, nearly all small computers and many large ones are sold with the specific intention that the end user will select other components to meet specific requirements.

With closed architecture, a responsible manufacturer can harmonize all the system components to work well with each other, and the user has the comfort of knowing that one manufacturer will handle all hardware problems that arise. Closed architecture's disadvantages are that only one manufacturer's innovation and creativity can be tapped to help meet a user's needs, and that the user cannot benefit from marketplace competition in purchasing peripherals and other components.

Open architecture allows the user to choose among competing products and to improve the system and extend its life without replacing all components at once. The main disadvantage of open architecture is that the user will have difficulty establishing what product is responsible if a modified system fails to function satisfactorily.

For example, suppose that the Sealy Company acquires an open-architecture computer with one megabyte of internal storage, expandable to 6M bytes. Sealy first expands this memory to 2M bytes using Pecos Company memory chips; then Sealy expands again, to 3M bytes, using Borger Company memory chips. Random memory errors begin to appear. After Sealy expands memory a third time, to 4M bytes, using Cedar Park Company memory chips, the errors become so frequent as to degrade operations and make it difficult to operate the computer. The various chip manufacturers stand behind their individual chips (which all operate satisfactorily when tested alone) and claim the cause of the memory failure must lie with other vendors' components. Sealy probably cannot hold anyone responsible. Such situations often lead to the "Christmas-tree light solution": Sealy acquires a one-megabyte set of memory chips from the original computer manufacturer and systematically replaces each of the other sets with it until the faulty chips are found.

End users, including anyone responsible for operating an accounting system, should understand how hardware has been designed and whether the data processing department endorses open or closed architecture. The end user should also be able to exchange information with the data processing department about hardware performance problems that may be traceable to the hardware architecture.

Hardware Options

Hardware options include external storage, graphics devices, optical ROM storage, printers, terminals, and mutliplexers for connection to other systems and users. Figure 4.9 shows these options grouped in a simple computer system configuration.

Figure 4.9   Simple Computer System
Compare this with Figure 4.1. The CPU sits at the center of connections to input-output devices and other CPUs. Without these connections, all its speed and logical versatility would be inaccessible.

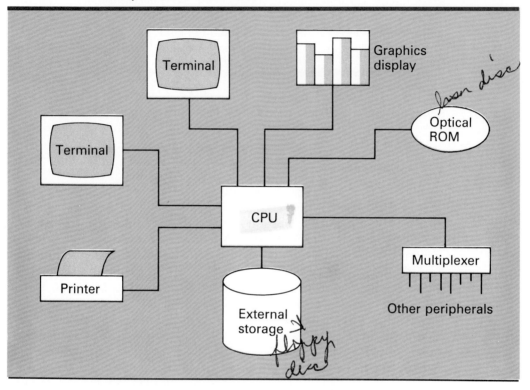

Disk Drive Options.   Designers of accounting systems face a wealth of options in choosing the appropriate external storage. Some sort of disk drive is indispensable in modern computer systems, and many computer systems have two, three, or more. Over a million disk drives were sold in a recent year.

The features that describe a disk drive are (1) whether it is a floppy or hard disk drive, and, if it is a hard disk drive, whether it is a fixed or cartridge design, (2) whether it is internal (mounted inside the computer cabinet) or external, and (3) how much data the disk will hold.

Although floppy disks and their drives were developed as a means of storing occasionally used copies of programs, they have become popular primary external storage devices. The original floppy disk drives, designed for very flexible 8-inch Mylar disks encased in a flexible rectangular case, were quickly joined by 5.25-inch disk drives of similar design. A 3.5-inch disk drive, designed to accept a flexible disk protected by a rigid plastic cover, was introduced in 1983.

A 5.25-inch floppy disk may have forty single-density or eighty double-density tracks on one side (single sided) or both sides (double sided). Applied to this size of disk, the letters *DSDD,* meaning "double sided, double density," denote the highest available capacity in wide use—about 720K bytes. A so-called high-capacity 5.25-inch floppy disk drive writes a track only half as wide as a conventional drive this size and, using special, more expensive disks, can write 1.2M bytes on one disk. High-capacity drives can read conventional 5.25-inch floppy disks but cannot write data on them in a form legible to a conventional drive.

The hard disk drive was originally introduced as a heavy, washing-machine-size cabinet containing a "disk pack" that consisted of one or more rigid disks about 12 inches in diameter. Such a disk pack could store 20M to 60M bytes. The most recent hard disk drives are lightweight, about 8 inches square, and 3 inches thick. They contain one or more rigid disks, either 3 or 5 inches in diameter, that can store 10M to 80M bytes. If they contain multiple disks (called "platters"), the multiple surfaces greatly reduce the number of moves the read-write head must make in order to record or read data. The set of tracks in the same relative position on each surface form a "cylinder" within which data operations occur very quickly. Table 4.1 compares floppy-disk and hard-disk drives. All types of disk drives can find specified data very quickly.

An **optical disk** is similar to a magnetic disk, but it transfers information to the CPU via light reflecting from a metal surface, rather than through detection of magnetic fields. At its present stage of development, the optical disk is primarily a read-only device; the user cannot record, delete, or alter data on it. Optical storage depends on laser technology. A laser is used to melt tiny pits, corresponding to data bits, into circular tracks on a thin, round disk of flat metal. This disk is the master from which others (production disks) are duplicated. The production disk drive rotates the disk and aims a tiny light beam at the desired track. The track

Table 4.1   Characteristics of Hard Disks and Floppy Disks

Floppy Disks	Hard Disks
Flexible plastic	Metal alloy disk
Encased in paper or plastic	Encased in metal, surrounded by inert gas
Stores 100K–1.2M bytes	Stores 5–80M bytes *120M Now*
Rotates at 300 r.p.m.	Rotates at 3,000 r.p.m.
Removable disks cost $1–$6 each	Some disks are removable; Winchester disks are not
Drives Cost $200–$400 each	Drives cost $600–$25,000 each, including disks; price is declining

reflects the light beam to a photosensitive detector with an intensity determined by the pattern of pits. As with the magnetic read-write head, the laser light reflector and detector move from one track to another according to signals from the computer operating system. The advantages of optical ROM, as it is sometimes called, are very high speed; huge data-storage capacity; and resistance to dirt, scratches, dust, static electricity, and other environmental hazards that can disable magnetic storage.

Tape Options. Tape drives are usually omitted from the smallest computer systems. In larger systems, they are included for backup, sequential-access processing, and off-line (archival) storage. A full-size tape drive uses a 2,400-foot tape that costs about $30 and stores 45M bytes of data, which the drive can read at 100,000 bytes a second. These full-size drives are available new and used from various manufacturers at prices from $1,000 up.

For backup purposes in smaller systems, several manufacturers offer a combined disk-drive tape-drive unit in which the tape periodically recopies the disk-drive contents. The least expensive of these units sells for about $1,800, and the tape drive accounts for about a third of this price. For backup purposes, the tape unit operates at a slower speed; backing up a 20M-byte disk takes about 15 minutes.

Input-Output Options. The two most common input and output media are paper and the display screen. In either medium, information can be displayed as text and numbers or as graphics.

Two technologies exist for screen display. The simpler technology displays only characters. It converts the character signals from the CPU into display patterns on the screen; if the CPU cannot send the signal (for example, if a character is not in the ASCII table), the screen cannot display it.

The other technology, bit-mapping, accepts a more complex signal from the CPU. This signal consists of two parts: the address of a particular location on the screen, and the code indicating the type of display to be placed there. Monitors that can accept this signal are sometimes said to be graphics capable. On a monochrome screen, a given location may only be "on" or "off," but on a color screen it may be given one of several colors. The highest resolution occurs when the location contains only one pixel, the smallest addressable point on the monitor screen. A bit-mapped monitor displays any character or shape formed by the stream of signals it receives from the CPU. Thus, a bit-mapped monitor allows much more clarity and sharpness than character displays. And because the display can be changed quickly, the bit-mapped monitor excels at showing dynamic graphic displays such as the movement of stock prices. Figure 4.10 compares character and bit-mapped displays.

For display screen and paper output, the quality of graphics depends on both hardware and software. High resolution, creating the greatest

Figure 4.10 Bit-Mapped and Character Displays

To transmit a character to a bit-mapped screen, the CPU sends the *on* or *off* status of each bit and its location on the screen. For example the coordinates (9,9) refer to one "on" bit. Thus, the display is not limited to characters already stored in the monitor's screen interface. To transmit a character to a character-display screen, the CPU sends its ASCII code. The screen interface converts this code into a representation of the complete character, which the monitor converts to a displayable signal.

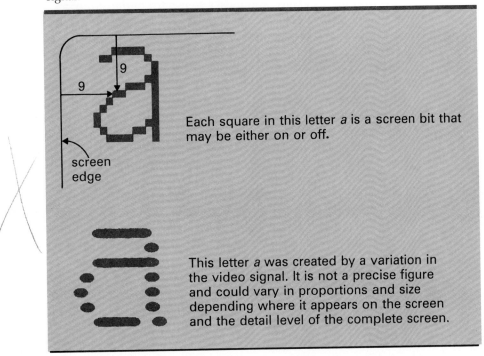

Each square in this letter *a* is a screen bit that may be either on or off.

screen edge

This letter *a* was created by a variation in the video signal. It is not a precise figure and could vary in proportions and size depending where it appears on the screen and the detail level of the complete screen.

detail and the sharpest image, is important for publishing, mapping, and computer-aided design and manufacturing applications. On a screen, the speed with which graphics may be changed (dynamics) is important in simulations and games. Graphic dynamics are affected by both processor clock speed and the presence of a dedicated graphics processor. They are also a function of programmer skill in designing efficient graphics code and in preparing software that uses this code efficiently.

When one requires printed output, there are three types of printers from which to choose: dot matrix (the cheapest), letter quality (an inexpensive printer that produces neatly typed text), and laser (the most expensive, quickest, and most flexible). A dot-matrix printer has a small "head" that contains tiny pins arranged in vertical columns. An electric current triggers a magnetic field that "fires" the pins against a ribbon as the print head moves across the page, forming characters and even graphic figures. The letter-quality printer looks like an office typewriter. It contains a wheel with characters on it; the wheel rotates and presses the proper character onto a ribbon as its carrier moves across the page. The laser printer controls a laser that activates static-electricity charges on a specially prepared drum, which uses xerographic copying technology to create an entire page of output at one time.

Although inexpensive dot-matrix printers can create excellent graphics, they are awkward and messy to use for multicolor work. Color graphics, such as bar and pie charts, may call for a plotter, which consists of one or more pens that move on controlled arms across the paper. The pens can create lettering, shaded areas, and precise shapes. If the CPU is programmed to generate the appropriate signals, a plotter can draw perspectives of a building for an architect, draft the floor plans, and print the instructions to the contractor. Programs with graphics also produce useful tabular information; the software the architect uses to design and sketch a building can also print a bill of materials, estimate the building cost, and compare actual and budgeted costs as construction progresses.

Often organizations need computer input or output that both humans and computers can read. In such cases, optical character recognition (OCR) and magnetic ink character recognition (MICR) are often employed. Optical and magnetic characters resemble their conventional equivalents closely enough for humans to recognize them. They are also recognizable by computer-controlled sensors that convert them into the appropriate ASCII signals for computer processing.

Optical bar codes—the codes on packaged food products, for instance—cannot be read by an untrained human eye, but they can be read very quickly by a computer-controlled sensor. The bar code does not actually contain the price; it merely identifies the product. When the computer receives the value of the bar code, it refers to its memory for the corresponding price. To change prices, the store need not re-mark all its products; it need only change the prices in computer memory.

Perhaps because keyboards date back to mechanical typewriter days, computer users tend to take them for granted. There are good and bad keyboard designs, however, and one should actually use several keyboards long enough to get the "feel" of each one and to develop a preference for one. Keyboards can be custom designed with special keys for common operations. For example, airline check-in computers have special keys for recalling, storing, editing, and deleting reservation data.

Summary

Computers and computer software allow accounting systems to carry out transaction recording, data processing, and reporting smoothly and efficiently. Computer hardware consists of the CPU and peripherals such as disk drives, printers, terminals, and specialized data sensing devices.

Computer operations require power-dependent internal storage within the computer. Large volumes of data are preserved in external storage, generally on magnetic tape and disk. Tape supports sequential files and data back-up, whereas disks lend themselves to rapid direct access of files. The CPU and other computer components employ VLSI microcircuits for high speed and reliability. Computer software consists of the operating system and programs to provide a logical structure for data processing. The programs that handle processing like that in accounting systems are called applications programs. Users exchange data and information with the computer through terminals, printers, and plotters.

The computer system designer has many options, including four classes of computer size and power. Within any class, there are choices of calculation speed, memory size, number of users to be served efficiently, features that affect the system's ability to respond to its peripherals, and the type of architecture (open or closed).

Key Terms

arithmetic-logic unit (ALU)	field	operating system
assembly language	file	optical disk
bit	flags	peripherals
buffer	internal storage	pixel
byte	job-queue manager	printer buffer
clock	kilobyte	processor chip
closed architecture	megabyte	program
control unit	memory chip	programming languages
CPU	menu	RAM
disk cache	multiprocessing	record
disk drive	multiprogramming	ROM
external storage	open architecture	tape drive
		user interface

Review Questions

1. What is the significance of each of the following: Babbage, ENIAC, and UNIVAC I?

2. Calculate the binary equivalents of 3, 5, 6, and 7.

3. To what quantities do *K* bytes and *M* bytes refer?

4. What is the difference between a bit and a byte? What is the largest possible decimal value of a byte containing only four bits?

5. What is the difference between a field and a record? a file and a record?

6. How can a field of two bytes represent up to 65,535 characters?

7. What is a flat file?

Discussion Questions

8. If a computer system has a closed architecture, what does it mean in practical terms? What are an advantage and a disadvantage of closed architecture? With closed architecture, would you expect locating competing suppliers of compatible additional RAM to be easier or more difficult than with open architecture?

9. Would there be any advantage to a disk drive designed to use a disk with one continuous track, like a phonograph record? any disadvantages?

10. Why have any ROM in a computer? If ROM were very inexpensive, can you think of additional uses for it that are presently served by disk and tape storage?

11. What features are sometimes used to measure a computer's power? How does a large internal memory enhance the power of a computer? Does external storage increase power in the same way as internal memory?

12. Disk drives continue to decline in price. Go to a computer store and find out which brand of disk drive offers the lowest cost per kilobyte of available storage. Is it the least expensive drive?

13. Name at least three computer components that are not part of the CPU. In your opinion, why are they designed to be physically separate from the CPU?

14. What is the advantage of a floppy disk over a hard disk as a means of external storage? When would you prefer a floppy disk drive in a computer system?

15. The Yegua Company is developing an information system. Its uses will include computer-assisted circuit design, production scheduling, and graphics-oriented performance reports. Would you recommend bit-mapped or character-display monitors for this system? Why?

Problems

16. Second Coast Computers is considering three different ways of acquiring 10M bytes of on-line magnetic storage. They will choose the one that offers the lowest purchase price per kilobyte.

   - They can buy one 10M-byte drive for $2,000.

   - They can buy as many 800K-byte floppy disk drives as they need at $400 each. Assume only four controllers at $500 each are needed and that floppy disks for this drive are $5 each.

   - They can buy as many 360K-byte floppy disk drives as they need at $180 each. Assume ten controllers at $150 each are needed and that floppy disks for this drive are $4 each.

Required:

(a) What is the purchase price per kilobyte for each type of storage?

(b) Which alternative should the company choose?

17. The Pott Hauling Company's Banana PC computer has 640K bytes of RAM, expandable to 896K bytes, and 128K bytes of ROM. Its operating system is entirely in ROM. The company's accounting applications require 500K bytes of memory. How large a file can the computer, in its current configuration, hold entirely in RAM?

18. Kellogg Company has a new double-sided double-density disk drive. This drive uses disks with 80 tracks on a side. Each track is divided into 16 sectors, and each sector will hold 256 bytes.

Required:

(a) How many bytes will this disk hold?

(b) What is the disk's capacity in kilobytes (be careful!)?

19. The disk drive in the preceding problem spins at 300 r.p.m. The read-write head can read or write on only one side of the disk at a time. The head takes 0.2 second to jump from one track to another, which it must do whenever it finishes a track.

Required:

(a) How many tracks will be required to hold a 81,920-byte file?

(b) How many seconds will it take to write this file on one side of a completely empty disk (given that the head does not have to move before or after the writing operation)?

(c) What percentage of this time will be spent moving from one track to another?

(d) How many seconds will it take to write this file half on one side of the disk and half on the other? How much time would this save compared to writing the whole file on one side only?

20. The "Winchester" disk, legend says, got its name from the design team's objective of placing 30M bytes of information on 30 tracks (recalling the Winchester 30-30 rifle) on one disk. Winchester disk drives have disks permanently mounted inside that spin at 3,000 r.p.m. or more. The great precision of these drives allows for tracks to be much closer together than usual and for much greater data density within a track. If each of the 160 tracks on a certain Winchester drive has 256 sectors, each of which contains 256 bytes, how many megabytes of capacity does the drive have?

21. A certain file contains 11,450 records. Each record consists of exactly 1,024 bytes.

Required:

(a) How many 360K-byte floppy disks will be required to hold this entire file?

(b) How much space will be left over on the last disk?

(c) Would this entire file fit on a 10M-byte hard disk? Would it fit on a 20M-byte hard disk with a 6M-byte file already stored on it?

Case: The Denison Company

The Denison Company sells, leases, rents, and services equipment for oil exploration and drilling. The firm was founded in 1948 and now has offices in five cities. The founder, Alex Denison, was a dynamic manager who pursued an aggressive, centralized management style until his death in 1980. At that time the firm was selling drilling, well-fractionating and survey services, drill bits, and pipe; and it owned one deep rig. All inventory was kept at the Midland office, but could be moved to any other office on 12 hours' notice. The services unit was located in Houston and could fly a team to any location in 4 hours.

Prior to Denison's death and for several years afterward, the company was declining along with the rest of the oil industry. During this entire period, the company relied on manual accounting and control systems. The controller, at the home office in Tulsa, was a young CPA with a staff of three; in each of the other four cities, one person trained by the controller handled all transactions and forwarded them to the home office in Tulsa, which was separate from the operations office in the same city. The major sales, rental, services, and lease transactions of Denison Company were recorded on simple triplicate forms. The salesperson, local office manager, and local accounting manager signed each form. The local office kept one copy; two were forwarded to the controller. The local offices enjoyed a good deal of autonomy, although they could call as needed on the services and inventory functions and on the marketing function's advice and expertise. Each office prepared its own budget, which was reviewed and approved by the president. The local offices also prepared their own performance reports, analyses, forecasts, and other schedules. Once a month, they sent their estimates of inventory and rental requirements to Midland and their estimates of service requirements to Houston. Any use of the drilling rig was handled through marketing. The company was audited by a major CPA firm, which commented regularly and extensively on financial and accounting controls; management always took this advice seriously and followed it completely.

In 1983, Denison's three daughters, who had inherited principal ownership, took the company public with an offering of 66 million shares; the daughters retained 34 million shares. The investment banking syndicate that managed the stock issue required a change in CPA auditors to another firm and also advised the daughters in their choice of managers to lead the Denison Company. In 1984, after some reorganization, the company's organization chart looked like the figure on the following page.

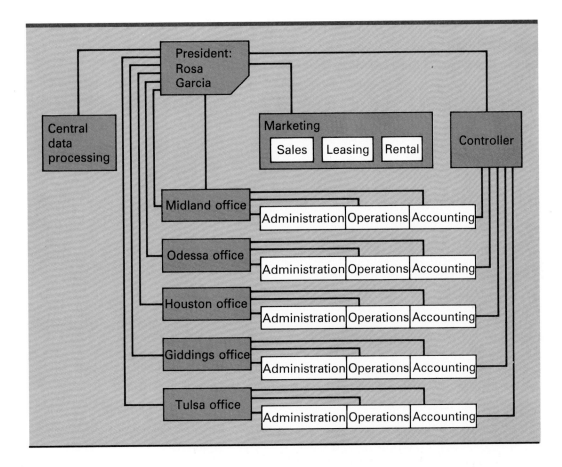

The position of data processing reflected the lack of computers in the company; data processing was only a planning and development operation. The new president, Rosa Garcia, indicated that data processing should continue to report to her while developing liaisons with the other offices and, especially, with the controller. Marketing would report directly to Garcia, who would communicate its plans and policies to the local offices. These offices had no marketing managers; the office supervisor was in effect the marketing manager.

Required:

The controller decided that the firm should acquire the newest computers. What types of computers, computer peripherals, and programs do you think this firm should have considered?

CHAPTER 5

File and Data Base Processing

Learning Objectives

After studying this chapter, you should be able to

- Compare sequential-access files, direct-access files, relational data bases, and hierarchical data bases.

- Understand and explain such data organization concepts as file index, hierarchical indexes, primary and secondary record keys, and pointers.

- Explain the difference between file processing and data base processing, and relate each to the structure of an accounting system.

- Explain how relational and hierarchical data bases manage data, and identify the parts of the accounting process to which each is best suited.

- Classify commercial data management software in terms of its concepts and features.

Data require order, and order can be imposed on them through data management. As an organization's size increases, data management becomes a progressively higher priority. When data are gathered together and organized, and arranged so new items can be added and any item in the collection can be readily located, the collection is called a **data base**. In this broad sense, any directory, file cabinet, tape or book library, or similar collection is a data base. Computerized data bases provide flexible access to data to respond to changing input, processing, and output needs.

In this chapter we will look at four data organization concepts widely used in computerized accounting systems: sequential-access file processing, direct-access file processing, relational data base processing, and hierarchical data base processing. These approaches, whether used alone or combined, offer a broad range of options for accounting processing, which is handled by programs called accounting applications. File processing is application oriented; that is, it structures the data to fit particular applications. The alternative, data base processing, is data oriented; in other words, it creates a pool of data to which applications may be tailored.

File Management

The simplest types of processing rely on files. As you learned in Chapter 4, a file is a set of records. The two types of file processing are **sequential access** and **direct access**. In sequential access, the computer processes the records in the sequence they occur, in much the same way a cassette player produces music from a tape. In direct access, the computer may process records in any order defined by the program and the data structure. As you will see, direct access allows users more flexibility in data processing at the cost of increasing processing complexity and expense. A good direct-access system allows a user to find any record quickly.

Master File

Some information is used repeatedly and kept for a relatively long time. Other information is used only once or twice and need not be kept available after that. A **master file** contains the former type of information. Each record in a master file contains relatively permanent information about one entity. For example, a customer master-file record contains a record for each customer. Each record contains the customer's name, address, and credit limit. In the employee master file, records contain fields for name, number of dependents, and salary. Less permanent information can be kept in an **update file**. Each record in an update file contains current information that relates to at least one master-file record. For example, an update file may contain records of sales transactions, and each such record would be related to a master record in the customer master file. When several update records relate to the same master-file record, the master-file record is called a **header record**. A header record typically contains information that is common to or relied upon by its related update records, and it may also summarize information contained in them.

The Record Key

The **record key** is the field or fields whose values uniquely identify a particular record. Your driver's license number is shared with no other license in your state. That number is the record key in the Registry of Motor Vehicles' driver master file. Your social security card, passport, and credit cards all have their own numbers. The IRS may use your social security number to identify you as a taxpayer. Each check in your checkbook has a unique number, thus your account number plus the check number becomes the record key for the bank.

Record keys need not be numbers, but they must be unique. Your name alone, for instance, may not uniquely identify you. Telephone books are full of people with the same name; that is why phone companies provide name plus address to uniquely identify each phone number.

A record key may consist of a single field or several fields. In the latter case, the fields are treated as a single variable for purposes of identifying the record. For example, the numbers on your checks identify

your bank (first field)
you (second field)
the particular check (third field)

These three fields constitute the complete record key of the check in the bank clearinghouse's file.

The File Index.   Ensuring that each record has a unique key guarantees only that records can be distinguished from each other. Knowing a record's key doesn't mean that the record can be found directly (without looking first at other records) or quickly. To make quick searches and direct access possible requires a separate, smaller **file index** comparable to the card catalog in a library.

In the simplest file index, each record has as few as two fields: the record key of the complete record in the larger file, and that record's physical location in the larger file. In a manual system, the physical location of record 34567 might be "second file cabinet, third drawer down, fifth folder from the front." A computer system expresses the location of the record as an "address" in terms of the disk drive, track, and sector. The computer's operating system uses the file indices as guides to the larger files and maintains a file index for each direct-access file. Table 5.1 is an example of a file index showing the locations of six records. Such an index would be read into the CPU's memory at the beginning of any processing that required the use of that file. To locate a record, the computer searches the index sequentially until it finds the record-key value matching that of the desired record; then it goes to the location shown on the disk and reads the record. An entire file index, because it consists of

Table 5.1   Example of a File Index

Record Key	Location on Disk
Start of File	
45	Disk 1, Track 7
52	Disk 1, Track 30
35	Disk 1, Track 19
72	Disk 1, Track 6
15	Disk 1, Track 9
56	Disk 1, Track 16
End of file	

very short records, can usually be stored in internal memory, where the computer can search it very quickly to locate the disk address of the main-file record. Even though the computer searches the file index sequentially, the speed of access to internal memory makes the search rapid. The desired record in the index can be located *much* faster than the corresponding record in the main file.

To conduct a search of an indexed file, one defines a **search criterion**—the value of the record key in the record that is to be located. When the record in the index file is found, the disk address of the corresponding main-file record is delivered to the computer's operating system, which causes the read-write head to move directly to the location specified by that address. The read-write head reads the record and transmits it to the CPU, which can display or process it.

Index-Sequential File Management.   A file index, although smaller and easier to search than a complete file, nevertheless needs an organizing principle to make the search process even simpler. When the records in a file can be accessed in ascending order of the value of the record key, the file is said to be arranged according to the **index-sequential-access method** (abbreviated ISAM). Don't let this fancy name obscure a very simple concept. The telephone directory, where names are arranged in alphabetical order, has sequential access but also allows you to start your search fairly close to the name you want. Similarly, the index of a book allows you to access its contents in alphabetical order by subject. Index-sequential access is a system that arranges a file to combine the simplicity of sequential access with the convenience of direct access.

Assume you start with a set of records physically arranged in alphabetical order by last name, which is the primary key. The index-sequential data-management system creates an index in which the operating system can find the external storage address by looking up the last name. For example, in Figure 5.1 the record with record-key value "Summers" has the address Drive B, Track 34, Sector 14. There are two records in each sector; the number of records per sector is called the **blocking factor**. When searching for a record, the system reads the entire sector into its memory and selects between the two (in this case) on the basis of the record key value that is the search criterion.

We stated in the introduction that one criterion of computerized data organization systems is that new items should be easily added. How do you add a record to an index-sequential data structure? The ISAM method employs pointers liberally. A **pointer** is a field in a record that indicates a related record. Suppose that the Summers record above is in an alphabetical sequence whose record-key values and disk addresses are respectively Richards (B, 34, 14), Summers (B, 34, 14), and Taylor (B, 34, 15). Assume we want to add a record with the key value Skinner between Richards and Summers. The blocking factor is 2. (You should refer to Figure 5.1 and

Figure 5.1 Adding a Record Using Index-Sequential Access
The index-sequential access method is illustrated here, inserting the record "Skinner" logically between the records "Richards" and "Summers" by means of pointers. A pointer after Richards directs us to the two-record block at the end of the file containing the new record; a second pointer then directs us to the Summers block, and a third pointer helps us resume the file sequence.

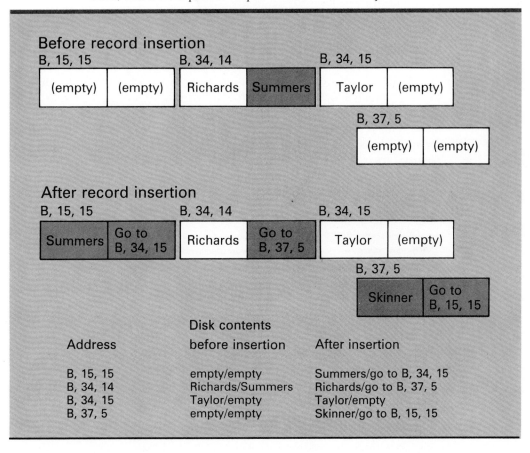

Before record insertion

Address	Disk contents before insertion	After insertion
B, 15, 15	empty/empty	Summers/go to B, 34, 15
B, 34, 14	Richards/Summers	Richards/go to B, 37, 5
B, 34, 15	Taylor/empty	Taylor/empty
B, 37, 5	empty/empty	Skinner/go to B, 15, 15

follow the path of the pointers.) The software removes the Summers record and places it in a sector saved for displaced records, say (B, 15, 15). In place of the Summers record in sector (B, 34, 14), it places the new disk address of the Skinner record, sector (B, 37, 5). In the remainder of sector (B, 37, 5), it places the disk address of the Summers record (B, 15, 15). At sector (B, 15, 15), next to the Summers record it also places the disk address of the Taylor record (B, 34, 15). These record addresses serve as pointers. To display the four records in alphabetic sequence, the system would have to use the pointers in sectors (B, 37, 5), (B, 15, 15), and (B, 34, 15). The file index is updated to show the disk address of each record so individual records can be found directly; but in accessing records sequentially, the system follows the trail of addresses. Figure 5.1 shows these moves, which would allow the index-sequential system to find all the records in record-key order. The data processing procedure of sending the search to a location where the record's disk address is stored, instead of straight to the record itself, is called **indirect addressing**

The advantages of index-sequential access are that it is simple and reliable and also faster than a simple indexed file in any application where the records should be processed in record-key sequential order (since most records are already in proper order and the index need not be used). ISAM's disadvantages are that as more records are added to a file, the file becomes much longer, and the disk operating system must move from one location to another to follow the trail of records. Also, any access in other than record-key order must search the file as if it were in random order. To overcome this disadvantage, the system must reblock the records—that is, rearrange them physically in the sequential order. This process can be time consuming for a long file in which there have been many additions or deletions.

Direct Access to Records.   Direct access to records can be achieved in many ways. We will describe three methods here. The first and simplest, **equal-length records**, requires all the records to be the same length, and then records them sequentially on a disk or tape. Given the sequence number of the record, the operating system can calculate how many bytes forward from the beginning of the file the record will start, and where, in terms of track and sector, this position is. The equal-length records method has the advantage of simplicity; the disadvantage is that it wastes external storage space if all the records are not filled completely.

The second method, **hashing**, assigns to each record an address that is calculated from the value of its record key. Thus, this method requires a hashing formula that will calculate a unique disk address for each possible value of the record key. When a record is created, this formula is used to calculate the address at which it will be stored. When a record must be found, the system calculates its disk address using the same formula and gives it to the operating system to use in locating the record. Hashing has two disadvantages: the available hashing formulas occasionally assign the same address to two or more records, requiring an overflow area or other means of locating addressable storage for the record; and the time required to locate records rises and the system slows down when a disk becomes about 80 percent or more filled with data.

The third direct-access method, **indexed files**, is actually a form of sequential access "speeded up" to give the appearance of direct access. The program searches the short file index sequentially until it locates the record-key value matching the one it seeks. Then it passes the disk address of that record to the operating system. The sequential search of the file index, which should be held in RAM, proceeds very rapidly. However, a large file will have a long file index, and the "direct" access can seem very slow; on the average, half of the index records will be searched before a given record's disk address is found.

Programmers have developed ways of organizing a file index so that fewer index records are examined before the desired disk address is found. One method that has been worked out imposes a hierarchical structure on the file index. Suppose, for example, a file contains 1,000 records, and the record key values are distributed evenly from 0 to 9,999. If all the records were in one file, an average of 500 index records would have to be read to find the disk address. But the application could be designed to create ten files, each with 1,000 possible values of the record key and containing, on the average, only 100 records. Each file would have its own index. When such an application searches for a record using the record key, it determines the first digit, then searches a short ten-record index to determine the record's file, then searches that file's index to determine the disk address. This process is shown in Figure 5.2. It would result, on the average, in only 55 index records being read; 5 in the first index, then 50 in

Figure 5.2   Hierarchical File Index
From a particular track and sector on the disk emerges a single record whose location is in the file 5 index. The operating system goes to file 5 because a short file index indicates that file 5 contains record 5072's disk location. This search of two short files takes less time than a search of one much longer file.

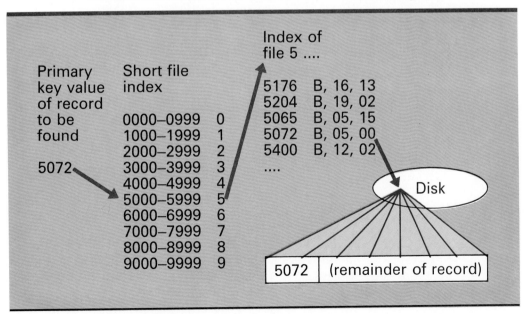

the correct file index. Varying the number of levels in the hierarchy and the number of divisions in each level allows a programmer to create a data management system to match the requirements of a specific application.

Linking Records.   Since businesses create and modify records in an order dictated by business activity and not in an order logical for processing efficiency, those who design the systems must often impose logical order by employing linking techniques. A link is any means of connecting one record with another. One type of link already mentioned is a pointer, a field in one record that contains the key of another record in the same or a different file. Pointers do not take the place of the basic file index, but they do expand and supplement it. One type of pointer appears as additional fields in each record in the file index.

In addition to their use in indirect addressing, pointers can indicate another record related by a processing application to the pointer's record, or they can point to the next record in a logical grouping. An example of the former is a field in a credit sales transaction record that points to the record in another file containing complete information about the customer, as Figure 5.3 illustrates. The specific purpose of these pointers is to allow the customer record to be easily located for each transaction record.

Figure 5.3   Pointers Linking Records in Different Files
Records in the file of credit sales are linked to the record of customers responsible for each transaction. These customer records have a different design and are in a separate file.

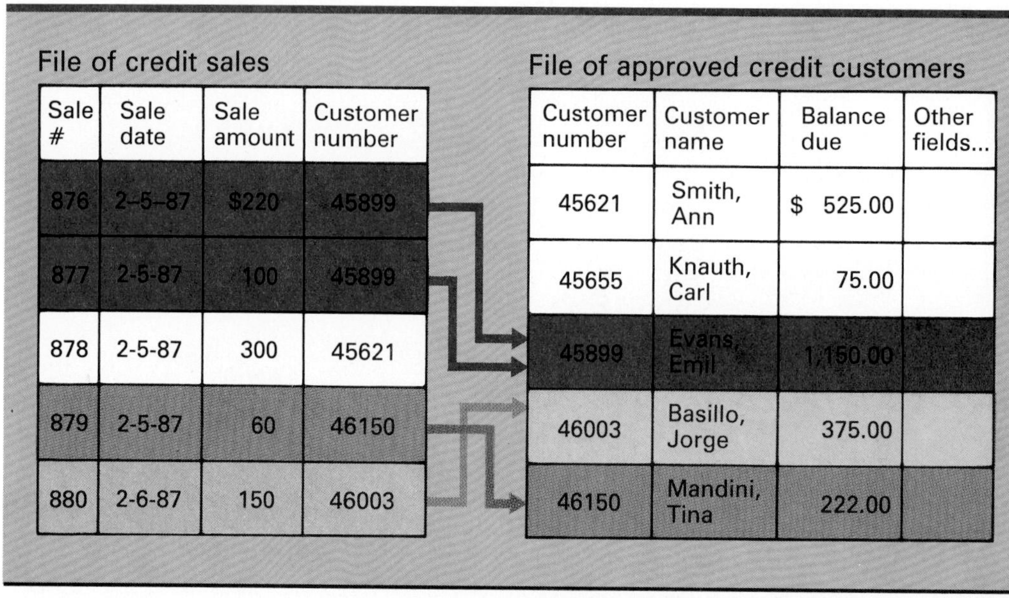

File of credit sales

Sale #	Sale date	Sale amount	Customer number
876	2-5-87	$220	45899
877	2-5-87	100	45899
878	2-5-87	300	45621
879	2-5-87	60	46150
880	2-6-87	150	46003

File of approved credit customers

Customer number	Customer name	Balance due	Other fields...
45621	Smith, Ann	$ 525.00	
45655	Knauth, Carl	75.00	
45899	Evans, Emil	1,150.00	
46003	Basillo, Jorge	375.00	
46150	Mandini, Tina	222.00	

Table 5.2   Illustration of File Index for Records Logically Sequenced via Pointers

Record Key	Location on Disk	Key of Next Record (Pointer)
Start of file		15 (start of sequence)
45	Disk 1, Track 7	46
52	Disk 1, Track 30	72
35	Disk 1, Track 19	45
72	Disk 1, Track 6	(end of sequence)
15	Disk 1, Track 9	35
46	Disk 1, Track 16	52
End of file		

An example of the second use is a file in which pointers indicate the record order. Table 5.2 shows the same six-record file as Table 5.1, still physically arranged in random sequence, but set up to be read in logical sequence according to the pointers in the last field on each line. As long as the data-management system continually revises the index in Table 5.2 to reflect the current state of its file, it can access the file records in record-key order (that is, 15-35-45-46-52-72) by following the pointers. The data-management system, if asked to supply the record that follows the one with key value 15 (that is, 35), would do so as follows: (1) search the index sequentially to find the index record with key value 15; (2) in that index record, note the value of the key of the next record, 35; (3) search the index sequentially to find the index record with key value 35; (4) in that index record, note the disk location (Disk 1, Track 19) of the corresponding main-file record, and (5) use the operating system to find it and bring its contents into the CPU.

Another example of using pointers to indicate the next logical record is linking individual credit sales transactions to the same customer. To calculate the current balance due and send a statement that shows transaction details, the accounting system must compute the total credit sales to, and cash receipts from, the customer. Since the credit-sales transaction file is not arranged in order by customer, pointers would have to link together each customer's records. Figure 5.4 shows an example of the resulting linkages.

In Figure 5.4, when the computer calculates the statement balance for Emil Evans, it first locates Evans's record in the file of approved credit customers. It reads the first sales record's key value of 876, opens the sales transaction file, and (using that file's index) locates this record. Then it reads the record-key value of the next credit-sale record for the same customer, 877; it finds this record, and then finds record 881. The "EOC" value in the last record's pointer means "end of chain" and indicates that this is the last linked record. Cash receipts transactions must also be con-

Figure 5.4   Pointers Linking Customer Records
The record of Customer 45899 in the file of approved credit customers is linked to the initial record of a three-record chain in the file of credit sales, containing current-transaction data about Customer 45899. These data can be used to calculate the customer's statement balance.

File of credit sales

Sale #	Customer number	Next sale # same customer
876	45899	877
877	45899	881
878	45621	882
879	46150	890
880	46003	950
881	45899	EOC
882	45621	EOC

File of approved credit customers

Customer number	Customer name	Balance due	First sale #
45621	Smith, Ann	$525.00	878
45655	Knauth, Carl	$ 75.00	
45899	Evans, Emil	$1,150.00	876
46003	Basillo, Jorge	$375.00	880
46150	Mandini, Tina	$222.00	879

(arrows show sequence of access to records for customer Emil Evans)

sidered. If Evans's master-file record includes a field that shows the balance due, the process just described serves to verify or update it.

Secondary Keys

Throughout this chapter we have referred to *the* record key, but in practice, one record key probably cannot serve all the needs of an accounting system that requires varying criteria to locate records. In such cases, a secondary key or keys may be used; a **secondary key** is a field whose value serves as a means for finding a record when the primary key isn't known. When there is a secondary key, the unique identifying record key we have been referring to is usually called the **primary key.** Suppose, for example, that the customer account number is the primary key in the accounts receivable file. If a customer wishes to check the account balance but doesn't know the account number, it should be possible to find the account by means of the customer's name alone. In such a circumstance, the customer's name would be a secondary key. There can be any number of secondary keys.

They work the same way as the primary key, and each one has its own file index. Unlike primary keys, however, secondary keys need not be unique. In fact, it's not unusual for several records to have the same secondary key. In the secondary-key file indexes, each short record has the following organization:

> First field: secondary key of record in main file
> Second field: primary key of record in main file
> Third field: secondary key of next complete record in main file, in secondary-key sequence

When using a secondary-key index, the file-management system must use both the primary- and secondary-key indexes. The system first finds the secondary key value (the first field) in the secondary-key file index and notes the value of the primary key (the second field). The system then looks up the disk location of the main-file record in the primary-key file index. The use of two indexes may appreciably slow down the file-management system, but this disadvantage is more than offset by the ability to find records using values not in the primary-key index.

When records are added to or taken from the main file, each file index must be revised. The additional steps required to revise the several indexes for a file with multiple keys make these operations slower than for an equivalent file with only one index.

Sorted Files

Being able to review all or part of a file in an unusual sequence is often valuable. Sorted files allow such review. A **sorted file** (or **inverted file**) has a file index arranged in some desired secondary-key sequence. The file index may be based on one field or on the chained-together values of several fields (such as last name-first name) per record. The data-management system can build as many custom indexes as the data user requires, and the inverted files can be ready for use in a relatively short time.

Here is an example. In a purchasing application, each purchase order becomes a record in the purchase order file. The unique document number of each purchase order is the primary key of the corresponding record. Suppose that you wish to review the purchase orders not in the order of their creation, but classified by vendor. Given the proper instructions, the data-management system will create an index that allows the operating system to display the records classified this way. To review the purchase orders according to the office that placed the order, the system could create an additional index making the file appear as if it has been sorted according to office.

Consider the file in Table 5.3, which shows selected fields from certain purchase order file records. If you sort the file in Table 5.3 so it can be accessed in vendor sequence, it will look like the list below the table.

Table 5.3   Secondary Keys in a Purchase Order File

Purchase Order Number (primary key)	Date of Order	Office (secondary key)	Vendor ID (secondary key)
115	3-8-86	Chicago	22
116	3-20-86	Chicago	23
117	3-31-86	Chicago	23
118	3-31-86	Boston	22
119	4-1-86	Chicago	24
120	4-4-86	Boston	22
121	4-10-86	Boston	22
122	4-15-86	Boston	23

Vendor 22
```
115   3-8-86    Chicago   22
118   3-31-86   Boston    22
120   4-4-86    Boston    22
121   4-10-86   Boston    22
```

Vendor 23
```
116   3-20-86   Chicago   23
117   3-31-86   Chicago   23
122   4-15-86   Boston    23
```

Vendor 24
```
119   4-1-86    Chicago   24
```

Sorted according to office, the file would appear as follows:

Boston
```
118   3-31-86   Boston    22
120   4-4-86    Boston    22
121   4-10-86   Boston    22
122   4-15-86   Boston    23
```

Chicago
```
115   3-8-86    Chicago   22
116   3-20-86   Chicago   23
117   3-31-86   Chicago   23
119   4-1-86    Chicago   24
```

A simple data-management system can sort a table such as the file in this example whenever you need it to be in a different order. The file will not need an index as long as you require the data-management system to access the records only sequentially. If the file in Table 5.3 were printed out in either sequence shown above, with appropriate column headings, it would be a report to management showing how vendor activity varies by vendor (the first sequence) or location (the second sequence). As the file becomes larger, though, sorting it will take more time and become less convenient. Therefore, larger files should not be physically sorted. Instead, they should be given an additional index that allows the records to be directly accessed in the same order as if they *were* sorted.

The major advantage of file inversion is probably the additional speed of access it provides. Using the appropriate index to search an inverted file in the sequence of the selected key saves the time of actually sorting it. The disadvantage of this method is that keeping many indexes current for a large file will noticeably slow down processing. To maintain acceptable processing speed without sacrificing data accessibility, data managers can use more powerful CPUs.

Inserting New Records Using a File Index

File indexes may be easily changed to add or remove records from a file without actually rearranging the records (as was necessary using ISAM). Suppose, for example, that a CPA society keeps a record of the management-training programs its members attend. Each member and each course has a unique identifying number. Since registrations arrive in random order, indexing must be used to allow arrangement of the registration records according to member. The primary key is (member number)-(course number). The records are assigned creation-sequence numbers, shown in the left-hand column. In the right-hand column, the creation-sequence numbers are shown in primary-key sequence. These columns are part of the index. Assume that the following four records are already in the file:

Creation-Sequence Number	Primary Key	Next Primary Key
	Start of sequence	2
1	567-23	4
2	324-27	1
3	702-23	End of sequence
4	567-30	3

To insert a new registration from member 640 for course 28, the registration program will add it at the end of the file and the file index:

Creation-Sequence Number	Primary Key	Next Primary Key
	Start of sequence	2
1	567-23	4
2	324-27	1
3	702-23	End of sequence
4	567-30	3
5	640-28	

Next, the program moves through the index, following the existing pointers, until it encounters the pair of records whose primary-key values bracket that of the new record; these are records 4 and 3. The program changes the pointers to appear as they do below:

Sequence	Primary Key	Next Primary Key
	Start of sequence	2
1	567-23	4
2	324-27	1
3	702-23	End of sequence
4	567-30	5
5	640-28	3

Changes of this kind can be made as often as necessary; they allow records to be added to the file sequentially but accessed in order of the values in any field the system user desires.

Sequential File Processing

The oldest and most widely used data organization concept is sequential file processing. Applications based on sequential file processing require master files that are closely integrated with the application design. The files do not have indexes. The records in each file must be physically arranged in the order in which they are to be processed. Most of the steps in processing operate on an entire file.

For example, consider the accounts receivable application. Credit sales activity produces a file of transactions (the journal). Each record in this file corresponds to a credit sale transaction. Credit sales are recorded in the order in which they occur. A credit sale transaction produces a new charge to the customer's account receivable, and this charge must be reflected in, or linked to, the file of customer accounts receivable (the subsidiary ledger, also called the accounts receivable master file). This process, called **updating**, requires the records in both files to be sorted into the same sequence, usually in an ascending order of customer identifying numbers. Since neither file has an index, the records in each file are physically sorted before processing. Sorting is a routine process, but it requires the files to be "out of service" and unavailable for any other processing. Most sequential file processing systems therefore update files when a "batch" of credit sales transactions has accumulated (rather than each time a transaction occurs) and are called *batch-update systems.*

Updating the master file of customer accounts receivable begins by taking the customer identifying number from the first record in the transaction file. The accounts receivable system examines the master file, one record after another, until it matches the batch record with the customer's master record (remember that not every credit customer will have a credit sale in any one batch). The transaction is posted; that is, the customer record is modified to include the information about the credit sale and

Figure 5.5   Sequential File Processing
In sequential file processing, all the transaction data must be saved and sorted into the same order as the accounts receivable master file, then used to perform all the updates to that file at one time in a single batch.

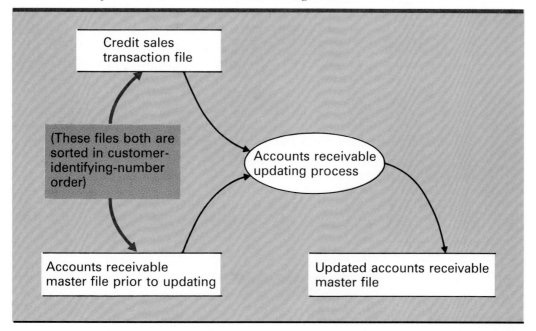

placed in a new, updated accounts receivable master file. The system then reads the next record in the transaction file and, if it is for the same customer, posts it also. If the batch update record is for another customer, the next accounts receivable master file records are read until that customer's record is found. This procedure continues until all records in both files have been processed. Figure 5.5 shows sequential file processing applied to processing credit sales.

Direct-Access File Processing

In most applications, the convenience of direct-access processing more than compensates for its additional complexity. Because records can be found quickly through their primary and secondary keys, most processing and updating can be accomplished without sorting files. Sorting becomes necessary when the master file is on tape, or when data access must be carried out in a way that was not anticipated when the primary and secondary keys and their respective indexes were created. Freedom from sorting means users can update files as the need arises, rather than in batches. Immediate updating is a feature of "on-line" systems; that is, systems in which files and records may be accessed as they are needed.

Each credit sales transaction, for example, would be used immediately to update a record in the accounts receivable master file. Then the sale transaction would be saved as a record in a credit sales transaction file. Figure 5.6 shows how a direct-access accounts receivable application would operate.

The accounts receivable file indexes and the main file itself may need reblocking, sorting, and other maintenance that requires the file to be taken off-line. However, this off-line time will be much briefer than for a sequential-access system.

Both direct-access and sequential access file processing have the advantage of lower initial cost than the data base processing we will discuss next. However, they both also have serious disadvantages. To collect new data items about a credit customer, all application software that uses the accounts receivable and credit sales transaction files has to be rewritten and the files run through a program that creates extra space for the new items. Because these procedures require systems experts and programmers, an organization may put them off until they are desperately needed. Also, file processing may limit the variety of reports the system can pro-

Figure 5.6   Direct-Access Processing
In direct-access file processing, the accounts receivable process uses transaction data immediately to update records in an accounts receivable master file. No other data or processes are involved.

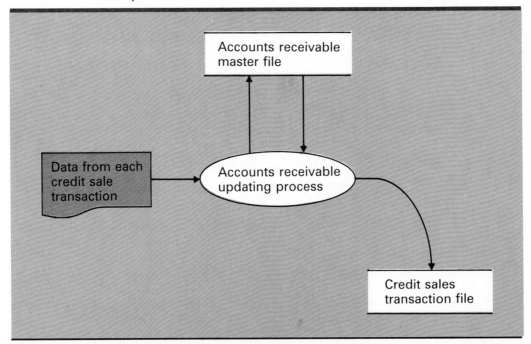

duce and its ability to add new reports. This lack of flexibility in file processing (even after much refinement) led to the development of data base management.

Data Base Management

Data base processing organizes data in such a way that it can be used by many different processes. These processes all work with the data by means of a program called a **data base manager**. The data are stored in a data pool in internal and external memory; the data base manager translates data from this structure into logical structures required by the various processes that use the data. By creating these logical "views" of the data when responding to a process's requirements, the data base manager can

- Locate information quickly, regardless of its relation to other data.
- Create and delete connections between data.
- Split a file into two or more new files.
- Create a new file from selected records of an existing file.
- Create a new file whose records consist of selected fields from one or more existing files.
- Update a given field in all files in which it occurs.
- Create reports drawn from selected records.
- Conduct sequences of operations, sometimes called *command macros*, defined by programmers or managers.

The data base manager makes all these capabilities available to the applications that form the accounting system. Figure 5.7 illustrates the role of the data base manager, which easily incorporates changes, integrating new data with old data in such a way that existing processes are affected by the new data's presence only when they must be modified to use the new data. For example, suppose the Zip Code field must be lengthened from five digits to nine. The data base manager can do so in such a way that all data groupings, processes, and reports that use the Zip Code will be compatible with its expanded length.

A data base does not use traditional files and records; instead, the data items are defined separately and independently from their uses. Pointers link data into the sets required for any processing that is occurring. As we shall see shortly, these sets take two forms, resulting in two types of data bases: relational and hierarchical. In a relational data base, the data sets are called **relations**, meaning that they are based on some property—such as their connection to the same transaction or to the same customer—that links the data items. In a hierarchical data base, the data sets called **trees**, because they show control or ownership properties in a branchlike hierarchy. (In practice, many data bases combine relational

Figure 5.7   Data Base Processing
In data base processing, any number of processes have immediate access—through the data base manager—to the same organized collection of data.

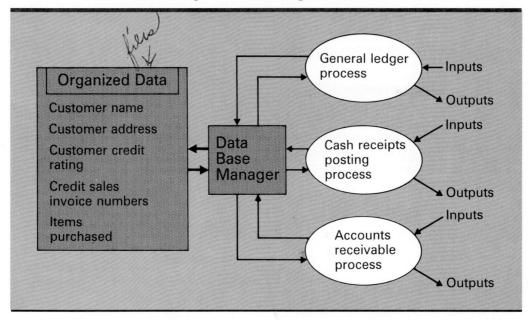

and hierarchical features so that relations and trees are both used to organize data into very powerful structures.) The logical separation between data items and their uses improves data reliability. Assume, for example, that in a credit sales and accounts receivable system a clerk recorded some credit sales incorrectly. When a user discovers the errors, it will be necessary to correct them—but should it be necessary to also reenter the customer name and account number if they were recorded correctly the first time? In many file-processing systems the answer is yes, and the records thus created are used to update the accounts receivable master file on a batch basis. In a data base system, however, one need enter only the corrections.

Relational Data Base Processing

A **relational data base** is a collection of data items organized into relations that correspond closely in the user's perception to the more traditional word file. The relational data base concept was first proposed by E. F. Codd in 1970.[1]

---

[1]E. F. Codd, "A Relational Model of Data for Large Shared Data Banks," *Transactions on Database Systems* 13 (June 1970).

Like a file, a relation can be perceived as data organized into rows and columns. No two rows should be alike, each column should contain all the same sort of data, and no two columns should contain the same sort of data. In the accounts receivable relation, each row is one customer and no customer has more than one row. Only one column contains the type of data designated as the customer account number, and that column contains only account numbers and includes no sales amounts or transaction numbers. The account number column is an example of an **attribute,** a term that is applied to a column of similar data items in a relation.

The rows and columns in any relation may be moved, distributed among several other relations, or combined with rows and columns from other relations. Thus, a need for an additional data item in one application requires only (1) that the item (and its values) be placed in the data pool and related to the items it will be associated with in applications, and (2) that use of the item be incorporated into the application that requires it. It is not necessary to modify all the other applications that use the same data base but will not use the new item.

An accounting system organized as a relational data base consists of data attributes. Each attribute may belong to many rows, and each row may have a different value of the attribute. The attributes are associated with other attributes through relations. Each relation is a defined data structure. Some of the relations in an accounting system correspond to the accounting subledgers, journals, and general ledger, but others may merely contain reference information that helps the accounting system to function, such as lists of authorized vendors, customers with approved credit, and current employees.

Relations: An Example.   Figure 5.8 is an example of relations in an accounts receivable application. The attributes are listed at the top. The three relations shown are formed by associating pointers with individual data items. Thus, an individual data item has associated with it a pointer indicating each relation to which the item belongs, and to which record in that relation it belongs. Because these pointers consume storage space and processing time, data bases require relatively more computer power than file-processing data structures that handle the same number of records. However, data bases create a much more flexible, more useful, and longer-lived system. In Figure 5.8, the arrows that connect the relations show that one customer's master relation record (or row) may have a relationship to many invoice header relation records (one for each credit sale), and each invoice header may have a relationship to many items sold relation records (one for each type of item sold in the same sale).

Many accountants and data-processing managers view relational processing as data oriented rather than application oriented. Certainly relational processing allows data to be altered with minimum disruption of applications.

Figure 5.8   Attributes Formed into Relations

Here, eleven attributes used in relational accounts receivable processing have been formed into three relations. The item sold relation has one row for each item sold; all the rows for the same credit sale have the same invoice-number attribute value as the credit sale row in the invoice header relation. In turn, all the rows for the same customer have the same customer number attribute value as the customer number row in the customer master relations.

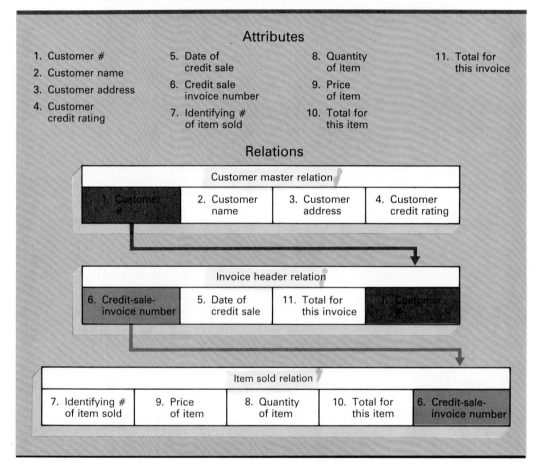

Attributes

1. Customer #
2. Customer name
3. Customer address
4. Customer credit rating
5. Date of credit sale
6. Credit sale invoice number
7. Identifying # of item sold
8. Quantity of item
9. Price of item
10. Total for this item
11. Total for this invoice

Relations

Customer master relation

| 1. Customer # | 2. Customer name | 3. Customer address | 4. Customer credit rating |

Invoice header relation

| 6. Credit-sale-invoice number | 5. Date of credit sale | 11. Total for this invoice | 1. Customer # |

Item sold relation

| 7. Identifying # of item sold | 9. Price of item | 8. Quantity of item | 10. Total for this item | 6. Credit-sale-invoice number |

Number of Files or Relations.   In theory, the entire accounting system could be encompassed in one very large relation. However, such a relation would require a very complex record key and would probably slow down data processing operations. Only a few of the relation's many fields would be used in any one transaction or process. At the other extreme, a data base could consist entirely of relations containing only one attribute. The large number of relations that would result would be difficult to remember and use. Accounting processing would require the data base system to combine relations temporarily and then to separate them, activities that require time-consuming extra steps.

The typical accounting data base processing system compromises by creating a limited number of relations that combine data items commonly used together. Creating several relations means that each relation can be shorter, with fewer records and fewer fields in each record, which makes for faster processing. Limiting the number of relations may necessitate some duplication of information among them. Although theoretically undesirable, well-thought-out duplication does not cause any difficulty in practice and seems a reasonable price to pay for data processing efficiency. For example, in Figure 5.8, the items sold relation includes the credit-sale-invoice number, even though the data base manager provides a link between each invoice header and the corresponding items-sold records.

If a newly created set of relations for data turns out to be unsatisfactory, the data items can be regrouped into new relations, and relations can be appended to or combined with one another.

Hierarchical Data Base Processing

A **hierarchical data base** differs from a relational database in how it expresses certain relationships. For example, a relational data base records the customer in a credit sale transaction by making the customer account number an attribute in the relation that contains credit sales transactions. The hierarchical data base would express the customer-transaction relationship by including a pointer from each row in the transaction relation to the appropriate credit customer row in the accounts receivable relation. In effect, each customer row *owns* certain rows in the credit sales transaction relation. Figure 5.9 illustrates this arrangement; notice that it does not include data links as in Figure 5.8; these are provided by the data base manager. The customer master relation is connected to the invoice header relation, which in turn is connected to the items sold relation. The owner record identifies and provides access to the owned records and creates control benefits because only connected relations are used in one process. Records are connected via pointers in the owner record *to* the owned records, and by pointers *from* the owned records to their owner record. Figure 5.10 (page 155) shows that multiple levels of ownership can exist in a hierarchical data base. Figure 5.11 (page 156) shows the connections that might exist among the accounts receivable, cash receipts, and general ledger applications. These connections make it possible to record a credit sale, verify the customer's credit worthiness, record a charge to the customer's account in the accounts receivable subsidiary ledger, record the customer's payment when it is remitted, and complete other processes for purchasing and payment of vendors' invoices. Hierarchical data base design clearly supports the data summarization that is the principal purpose of transaction processing.

Figure 5.9   Hierarchical Data Base Links
Compare this with Figure 5.8. Here, the rows in different relations are linked hierarchically, through indices or pointers, and not through common attributes. The end result is the same in terms of the information groupings formed during accounts receivable processing.

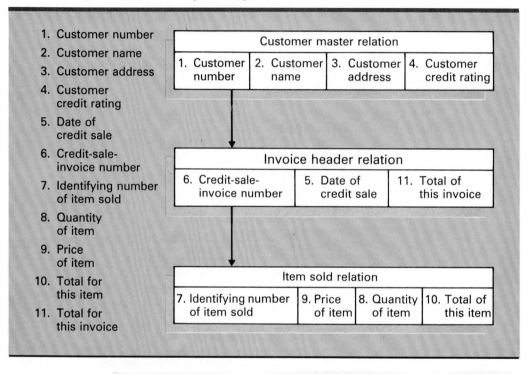

However, as we pointed out in Chapter 2, management's use of information is dominated by the search for meaningful relationships among data from different sources. Relational data base managers best promote this use because they can combine items from various relations regardless of the origins of the data. Much of an accounting system's usefulness arises from its ability to make its information available in a variety of formats on short notice. It simply is not possible to anticipate all possible useful formats. This is why so much emphasis falls on the abilities of a system to produce any format that management may want. Thus, planning and decision making are best supported when the processing of data is done hierarchically and data analysis and reporting to management are done relationally.

Network Data Bases

Network data bases allow the system user to specify many links or relationships among records. For example, product-specification records could be linked to customer sales patterns, new technology trends, and equipment-purchase requisitions. This design would make for an extremely useful accounting system, but it really transcends the boundaries of accounting; in fact, it has several disadvantages when applied to accounting:

- Designers cannot anticipate the multiple relations management might want. Nevertheless, the programmer must provide for multiple relations by reserving space for a large number of pointer fields, most of which will not be used. Thus, for a given application, network design requires more hardware and software capacity (and a greater outlay of money).

- The unused potential of a network design leaves many openings for fraud or mischief. The organization must choose either to monitor the network closely (at an ongoing cost) or to accept the risk that a conniving person will use the openings for criminal or self-serving purposes, inflicting a large one-time loss.

- The large number of possible relationships strains users' ability to recall and use them, often to the point of impairing user friendliness and possibly undermining acceptance of the system.

- Relational data base design offers, at lower cost, many of the inherent advantages of the network design.

Figure 5.10 Hierarchical Data Base Support for Transaction Processing
Compare this with Figure 5.9. The hierarchical data base structure readily accommodates the aggregation and summarization of data that characterize accounting processing.

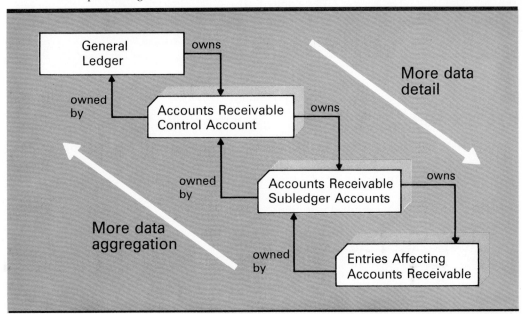

Figure 5.11 Relations in an Accounting System That Support Generation of Managerial Reports
Compare this with Figure 5.10. A complete set of accounting system relations would require many levels and file connections. For example, the link between cash disbursements and sellers' invoices would be used by a process that calculates amounts payable to vendors from whom purchases have been made and links these amounts to the checks used to effect payment.

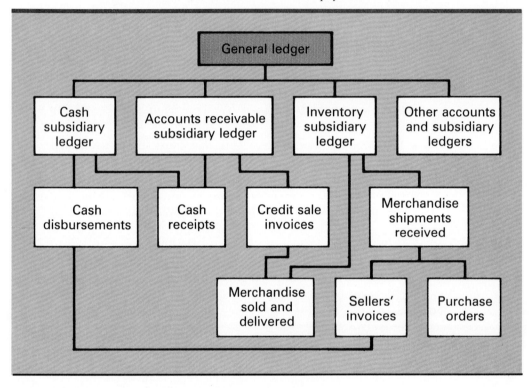

Processing Operations

Five basic processing operations—capturing, processing, storing, updating, and deleting—create a data base. This section will describe the objectives of these five operations in accounting data processing. Two additional operations discussed here, report generation and search, do not change the data base but do use its contents.

Capturing. The purpose of capturing (also called recording) is to collect all the transaction information that is required for a complete accounting entry. This is done by putting the data that support the transaction into computer-readable format and, where required, creating and filing source documents.

Processing.   Once the appropriate data have been captured, they are re-organized by placing each element of an entry in the proper subsidiary ledger. For example, the amount of a credit sale will be placed in the customer's account in the accounts receivable subsidiary ledger and also in the product category in the sales subsidiary ledger. Processing also transfers information supporting the entries—document numbers, dates, and authorizations—to the subsidiary ledgers. During processing, there are checks for errors, which are corrected if found. Processing also summarizes information, leaving the detail in the journals. Finally, processing copies records for purposes of data security.

Storing.   Processed data must be stored for ready retrieval when they are needed. Storage routines organize entries, accounts, and related information so they are properly situated relative to the other elements of the collection. They also protect the stored items from deterioration or arbitrary change.

Updating.   Updating is a form of processing that involves limited changes in previously processed data to maintain their timeliness and accuracy and hence their relevance for decision making or routine processing. An example of updating to maintain decision-making relevance is increasing a customer's credit limit; you replace the old credit limit with the new one and use the new limit to decide whether to allow the customer to make additional purchases on credit. An example of processing relevance is correcting an erroneously processed credit sale so a customer's current balance will appear on the next routine statement sent to the customer. Update operations comply with data processing controls by including routines to ensure that all specified data, and only specified data, are altered during updating.

Deleting.   Deletion removes fields, records, and relations from the data base because they are erroneous, out-of-date, or no longer needed. System procedures should detect and call to the system operator's attention items that should be considered for removal from the accounting data base. It is customary to retain a record of deleted items for a time, so that deletion can be reversed if necessary.

Report Generation.   Reports contain the distilled essence of the accounting system's stored information. Reports come in two types: *routine reports*, which are regularly produced, and *unique reports*, which are one-of-a-kind and produced on request. Creating either kind of report is called **report generation**. Both types of reports are necessary to management. Only reports that are necessary should be generated, and only those who use reports should receive them.

Search.   A search is an organized effort to locate an item in a collection of information. Some of the value of information resides in its availability when someone wants it. Almost by definition, unique reports will not exist if no means exists to create them quickly. Managers expect to find the data they want (assuming those data are in the accounting system) with only a short search.

Accountants and systems operators want these seven activities to be routine, controlled by policies and procedures. The activities, policies, procedures, and all the equipment and resources used for the activities comprise the accounting system.

Accounting System Examples of Data Base Processing

Representative examples of data base processing in accounting systems include the integrated or general ledger system, verifying customer credit, budgeting, and networking. In each of these examples, the criterion for good data organization is the ability to record, process, store, and retrieve data and report reliable information. The data organization must follow the accounting rules that govern the order of accounts: application of generally accepted accounting principles; use of journals, subledgers, and control accounts; and use of account classification numbers. Data control, security, access, and reporting requirements help keep the contents of the accounting system accessible and up-to-date.

Integration with General Ledger Systems

An *integrated* accounting system includes within a single framework all functions from transaction recording to financial statement preparation. These functions can exchange data with each other and can produce summary output to the general ledger (and thus to financial statements). A general ledger system may use the data base approach to ensure, from the user's viewpoint, the simplicity and flexibility of its functions. Table 5.4 lists some general ledger functions made simpler and more flexible by the data base approach.

Verifying Customer Credit

You have already seen that accounting systems contain much information that supports their operation but is not actually part of any transaction entry. Suppose you have many credit customers. In the process of deciding whether to accept someone as a credit customer, you acquire confidential and personal information. You must keep this information secure. Yet you must check every time the customer wants to use credit, to make certain that the customer's credit is still good and that the new purchase will not raise the total balance owed above the customer's credit limit. The best place for the confidential information is a special file, not the credit customer's subsidiary ledger account. A data base system allows you to keep a separate file of confidential customer data records, separate from the subsidiary ledger, yet available for use as needed for credit-evaluation decisions, *without* interrupting data entry or transaction processing.

Budgeting

In Chapter 3, we discussed budgets, which allow organizations to compare actual financial statements with those predicted. In data processing terms, the budget consists of the field values (projected account balances) that management would like to see appear in revenue and expense fields for the budgeted period. These projected balances cannot be intermingled with actual account balances; however, performance reports are prepared from selected actual and projected account balances, and explanations of the differences between them, as shown in Table 5.5.

A data base system can maintain separate budget and general ledger files, prepare reports drawn from selected parts of the two files, and change both the general ledger and the budget with only one alteration to the chart of accounts. Prior to data base processing, such reports had to be prepared from files that commingled actual and projected data.

Table 5.4   Integrated General Ledger System Functions

- Expand the accounting system as the organization grows.
- Create a set of accounts for a subsidiary or new office.
- Close the books.
- Post transactions whose entries affect more than one kind of account.
- Maintain connections among accounts and the multiple transactions affecting them.
- Create a new report based on information in more than one location or file.

Table 5.5   Simple Budget-Based Performance Report

Marketing Department	March 19xx
Expected sales (from the budget)	$10,000
Actual sales (from the sales subsidiary ledger)	9,000
Variance (unfavorable, due to rainy weather)	(1,000)

Networking

Networking is a natural application of data base systems, with their multiple files and flexible input and output. Networking combines one or more computers with stations for input and output, perhaps along with extra memory and extra printers, display terminals, and other peripherals. The computer and input-output stations need not be close to one another; if they are, they are called a **local-area network (LAN)** and the telephone company need not be involved. Because networking allows broader participation in data entry and information analysis, decision makers need not wait for a central data processing center's schedule or report formats; they process their own accounting data. For example, the controller's staff may use one computer to prepare and place in disk storage a file of general journal entries; meanwhile another computer, using this file as part of its input, posts the entries into subledger and general ledger accounts. In another location, a third computer prepares sales transactions for processing. A fourth computer tracks purchases and payroll. All the computers have access to the common disk storage. Other services, such as word processing and electronic mail, may also arrive through the network.

Summary

To carry out transaction recording, data processing, and reporting, accounting systems employ data organizing and access tools such as primary and secondary keys, file indexes, sorting, and file inversion. The programs that handle accounting processing are called accounting applications. They employ three basic principles, alone or in combination, to handle data: sequential file processing, direct-access file processing, and data base processing. Sequential file processing is simplest and least expensive and requires the least computer power; it is also the least flexible and most time-consuming method. Direct-access file processing is more complex, more expensive, more flexible, and in many cases consumes the least amount of time. Data base processing is about as complex and time consuming as direct-access file processing; it is also more expensive and requires the most computer capacity of the three methods. The uses of accounting for management planning and control depend on easily generated, adaptable routine and unique reports.

Relational data base processing is a data-oriented set of processes that allows data to be altered with minimal disruption to applications. Data items may be grouped or regrouped into relations, and relations may be appended or joined to one another. Relational data bases may include features drawn from hierarchical and network data bases. In general, hierarchical data base management supports transaction processing, while relational and network data base management support decision making, planning, and analysis. Thus it is increasingly common to combine different approaches.

Key Terms

attribute

blocking factor

data base

data base manager

direct access

equal-length records

file index

hashing

header record

hierarchical data base

index-sequential- access
   method (ISAM)

indexed files

indirect addressing

inverted file

local-area network
   (LAN)

master file

networking

pointer

primary key

record key

relational data base

relations

report generation

search criterion

secondary key

sequential access

sorted file

trees

update file

updating

Review Questions

1. What is a record key? What is its relation to a file index?

2. What is a search criterion? How is it used with a file index to locate a record?

3. Explain how pointers and the blocking factor function in index-sequential file management.

4. What can a direct-access file management system do that a sequential-access system cannot?

5. Two types of direct-access file systems allow the operating system to go directly to a record on disk without first searching an index. One is called hashing. Name the other method and explain how it works. Then explain how hashing works.

6. If you have two files and wish to go from a record in one file to a related record in another file, what is the name of the device or variable that you would use? What are the three types of records this device can indicate?

7. What is a primary key? Give two synonyms for a primary key. What short file associated with the main file also shares the primary key?

8. What is a secondary key? Does a secondary key require a separate file index?

9. What is a data base manager? What is its function? Why doesn't a file-processing system have a data base manager?

10. Which of the following two data base concepts is hierarchical? Which is relational? Give the reasons for your answers.
    a. Many instances of the same data attribute are linked together. Attributes may be combined, broken up, and recombined as the data base manager requires.
    b. Several records must be linked to another record in a different file.
11. Name and give examples of five basic accounting processing operations.
12. Name two types of reports that an accounting system should be able to produce.
13. Name three examples of data base processing in an accounting system.

Discussion Questions

14. Compare direct-access file processing and data base processing, naming at least one advantage and one disadvantage of each.
15. Can relational and hierarchical data base concepts be combined in one data base manager? Give an example of such a combination.
16. If the processing of accounting data is hierarchical, what data base concept best describes the *use* of accounting information? For example, to produce a list of products that have increased in price by 3 percent or more and whose sales increased 2 percent or more in the past year, one must use two files: one containing product identification number and beginning-of-year and end-of-year prices, the other containing product identification number and sales quantity.
17. A certain minicomputer with a 2M-byte internal memory is used to maintain several files, each with multiple keys, totaling 350,000 records and 18M bytes. This computer required extensive maintenance one year, so the business rented a replacement minicomputer, identical in every respect except that it had only one megabyte of memory. The data processing director noticed that the replacement computer operated much more slowly. What is the probable explanation?
18. Do you see any problems in keeping multiple copies of the same file, each copy sorted according to a different key? Answer this question for the specific case of a police department that keeps copies of its traffic-tickets-issued file sorted according to date of issue, officer who issued the ticket, date set for court hearing, and type of offense.

Problems

19. An accounting system consists of files (F1, F2, . . .), each of which contains records composed of fields (D1, D2, . . .) as follows:
    F1: (D1,D3,D4,D6,D8,D15); total of 1,000 records
    F2: (D2,D3,D6,D7,D8,D10,D11); total of 1,000 records

F3: (D1,D4,D5,D6,D7,D9,D12); total of 1,000 records
F4: (D4,D9,D12,D13,D14); total of 1,000 records
Each field has a length of 20 bytes.

Required:

    (a) How many bytes are required for these files plus a file-manager program requiring 500,000 bytes?

    (b) If all the unique data items above could be consolidated (without duplication) into one file, how many fields would each record in this file contain?

    (c) What would be the maximum and minimum total number of bytes required for this superefficient file *plus* a data base manager program requiring 540,000 bytes?

    (d) How do the space needs of *a* compare to the minimum in *c*? If each file held 15,000 records, how many bytes could be saved?

20. San Andreas No-Fault Company sells computer software. It keeps a record of every customer and the customer's purchases, payments, returns, service needs, and referrals. For each customer, the following data items are recorded: (1) customer name, (2) customer address, (3) item sold to customer, (4) date of sale, (5) amount of sale, (6) date of payment, (7) amount of payment, (8) item returned, (9) date of return, (10) amount of return, (11) name of referral (potential customer), (12) address of referral, (13) subject of comment, and (14) summary of comments. Some of these data items occur more than once.

Required:

    (a) Which items are likely to occur more than once?

    (b) Which of the items in *a* seem related to each other (such as *item sold* and *date of sale*)? Give a name to each relation you identify.

    (c) Draw a diagram showing the links between relations. Represent each relation as a labeled box and each link or pointer as a line or arrow.

    (d) Describe three reports that could be prepared from this information (for example, a report showing total current accounts receivable). For each report, indicate the relations that contain the information required to prepare it.

21. Sunshine Realty has several pieces of data that need to be processed; the list follows.

    (a) A house sale has just occurred, but no information about it has yet been entered into the accounting system.

    (b) The standard salary rates for three staff members have been increased by 5 percent.

    (c) Agent Bart Robinson has resigned, effective immediately.

    (d) Information describing the housing needs of ten potential buyers has been captured.

    (e) Payment is due on the office lease.

(f) A commission recorded as $60,000 must be corrected to $6,000.

(g) Financial statements for last month must be prepared.

Required:

For each item, indicate which of the five basic data processing operations discussed in the chapter will be used.

22. Bright and Early, CPAs, are trying to design a record key for their service and billing system. The record key should include the following:

   ■ The office where the work was done (there are six offices)

   ■ The CPA who did the work

   ■ The type of work (audit, tax, system design, compilation, review)

   ■ Unique client identifier

   ■ Client industry

   ■ Month the service was completed

Required:

   (a) Design a record key that will reflect all this information and facilitate preparation of detailed monthly reports of services billed

   (b) Suppose that several jobs of a similar nature are performed for the same client. What would you add to the record key in *a* to create a unique primary key for each job?

23. A certain direct-access disk file has a file index listing the following records:

Record Position	Record Key	Position of Next Record
Start		
1	320	
2	250	
3	500	
4	620	
5	300	
6	545	
7	805	
8	450	
End		

Required:

   (a) You want to list the file in order of ascending record key. Fill in the numbers in the "Position of Next Record" column.

   (b) Two records are added to the file (and to the file index). These records occupy positions 9 and 10 and have record-key values of 520 and 350, respectively. Make a new table showing the order of the "Position of Next Record" column.

(c) Describe the procedure for adding a record to an indexed file (the process you just performed in *b*).

Case: **The Doctor's Data Base**

Many commercial data base management systems are becoming available for computer users. These products make data base design available to those who have computers and understand their accounting system needs but lack the means to write computer programs. Commercial data base products vary greatly in features and ease of use. To give you some idea of their differences, the table below compares two hypothetical data base products intended for small computers, X Filer (a file manager) and X Manager (a relational data base).

Characteristic	X Filer	X Manager
1. Design context	File manager	Relational database
2. Typical computer used	Apple II family	IBM PC family
3. RAM required	48K bytes	128K bytes
4. Maximum number of records stored in one file	about 387,000	65,535
5. Maximum fields per record	99	32
6. Maximum characters per field	30	254
7. Maximum characters per record	990	8,128
8. Maximum number of files open at same time	one	two
9. Can carry out commands in prearranged sequence?	no	yes
10. Application design and setup	less difficult	more difficult
11. Application use	more difficult	less difficult
12. Application "power" potential	medium	high
10. Software cost	$195	$495

X Filer's limited scope makes it easy to learn and set up; it would be your preference for a simple stand-alone accounts receivable or purchases application. For a small integrated accounting system, X Manager would be your choice because of its superior ability to store and carry out commands in prearranged sequence. Of course, for any but the smallest accounting systems, you'd want more computing power than either of these two programs offer. Such power takes the form of

- More options to choose among in setting up a system.
- Faster processing, based on the greater speed of a larger computer.

- More files open at once and larger files, based on the larger internal memory and greater storage capability of a larger computer.
- The ability to store procedures or command files for later execution in processing data.

Required:

(a) Which of the two products would be best suited to a system for a doctor's office in which the information about patients, appointments, patient billing, and patient medication will be kept in separate records in different files? Learn as much as you can about how a doctor works with patients, and justify your selection.

(b) New products are coming on the market every day. Visit a computer store and choose a file manager and a data base manager. Collect for them the same information that is provided here for X Filer and X Manager. Decide which of the two products you research you would recommend for the doctor's office.

CHAPTER **6**

Accounting Systems

Generally Accepted Accounting Principles
Objectives of GAAP
Operations in an Accounting System
- Data Collection
- Entry of Transactions
- Analysis of Transactions
- Journalizing
- Posting to Ledgers
- Balancing Control Accounts with Subsidiary
  Ledgers
- Summarizing Posted Accounting Data
- Adjustments
- Creation of Statements

Tools to Implement Accounting Systems
- Chart of Accounts
- Account Coding
- Account Coding for Complex Organizations

Learning Objectives

After studying this chapter, you should be able to

- Identify the major factors that shape the accounting model.
- Identify and explain the operations of an accounting system.
- Prepare accounting statements from a general ledger trial balance.
- Design an account classification system to meet the needs of a simple organization.

No real record exists of accounting's history prior to the publication of Friar Luca Paciolo's *Summa de Arithmetica* in Venice in 1494, but accounting probably evolved as a way for management to describe a commercial venture to others, including the venture's owners. Much has changed since the fifteenth century, but accounting remains a kind of specialized language for reporting certain financial information about organizations.

In Chapter 1 we defined **accounting** as a collection of principles and rules that govern the development of information used in management processes. The result is a standardized process for recording, classifying, summarizing, and reporting financial data. As part of an information system for management and others with an interest in management's performance (shareholders, creditors, regulators, and the like), accounting principles and rules derive value from the fact that virtually all organizations adhere to the same rules to record transactions, describe assets and liabilities, prepare financial statements, ensure internal consistency of outputs, and measure management performance. A person familiar with accounting principles and rules can gain an understanding of an organization's financial position very quickly by applying these principles and rules to the organization's accounting statements. As organizations have grown more complex, the *managerial* uses of accounting have expanded greatly. Reports to owners appear annually or quarterly and include an income statement, showing how operations produced a profit or loss, and a balance sheet, showing the assets and equities. Reports to management appear much more frequently (weekly or even daily) than do reports to outsiders and consist of descriptions of specific activities, such as manufacturing or selling, and comparisons of actual results with those that management expected to occur, as described in Chapter 3.

Generally Accepted Accounting Principles

An **accounting system** is a set of elements—goals, policies, accounting principles, equipment, personnel, inputs and outputs, and controls—that can jointly perform accounting functions. We stated in Chapter 1 that accounting systems deliver precise information, prepared in a known way, about revenues, expenses, assets, liabilities, and profits. As a result, they are often viewed as a model of their organization (see Figure 6.1).

For an accounting system to fulfill its purpose, the information in accounting reports must be relevant, complete, and timely. These attributes are achieved by recording, processing, summarizing, and reporting the monetary and other measures of a transaction according to **generally accepted accounting principles (GAAP)**. As we will see shortly, accounting uses the simple, powerful device of double entry to record the money measures of a transaction in at least two accounts, the set of classifications in which these records are maintained. The number and types of accounts used must follow a few basic rules that are spelled out in GAAP.

Within the rules of GAAP, accounts and reports may be selected and related to fit a particular organization's requirements. GAAP are determined by a process for which the Securities and Exchange Commission (SEC), a federal agency, is responsible. Of the many elements that contribute to general acceptance of an accounting principle, the most important are its widespread use and approval, empirical evidence that users of accounting reports understand it, endorsement by the Financial Accounting Standards Board, and approval by other government agencies, including the Internal Revenue Service and the court system, for use in accounting reports supplied to them.

Firms whose stocks are publicly traded must adhere very strictly to accounting principles. An independent outside specialist called a *certified public accountant (CPA)* must attest that their annual financial statements were prepared according to generally accepted accounting principles. The CPA provides this opinion only after conducting an **audit**, an intensive investigation of the accounting records. As we discussed in Chapter 1, an audit traces system outputs back to their component transactions. Even businesses that are not required to submit to an independent audit should prepare financial statements that adhere to GAAP.[1] Government and not-for-profit organizations, however, may sometimes deviate from GAAP, and accounting principles for these organizations are less well defined and enforced, as we will see in Chapter 10.

---

[1] Most CPAs subscribe to a code of ethics and accept some liability for adverse consequences if they perform their work poorly. Most also belong to professional associations such as their state's CPA Society and the American Institute of CPAs. Professional accountants who are not CPAs may belong to one or more of the other associations of accountants, such as the National Association of Accountants (NAA) for managerial accountants, Financial Executives Institute (FEI) for financial executives, and American Accounting Association (AAA) for accounting academics.

Figure 6.1 Factors That Shape Accounting Systems
Components of the accounting model are directed at specific features of a single organization. The model for one organization probably will not be suitable for any other organization.

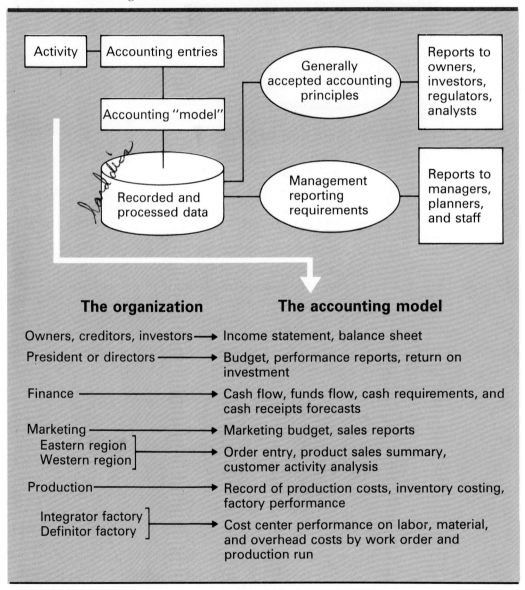

Objectives of GAAP

The objectives of GAAP are to make sure that accounting statements represent fairly the financial condition of the reporting organization and are sufficiently complete that users can rely on them to make meaningful comparisons between the financial statements of different businesses. To achieve these objectives, GAAP relies on broad implementation principles that are based on certain assumptions. The assumptions include the following: that the accounting reports apply to a definable entity such as a business, a business segment, or a group of businesses; that the entity issuing the reports will continue to exist indefinitely; and that the objectives of accounting include providing information that is useful. The implementation principles based on these assumptions provide guidelines for building accounting statements for individual businesses. For example, the materiality principle holds that other principles need apply only to the material aspects of the accounting statements; the matching principle holds that when costs are incurred to earn revenue, they are expenses and should be recognized in the same accounting period as the revenue. From these and other principles flow the rules, treatments, and procedures that determine the content of any set of accounting statements. For example, GAAP requires a distinction between assets held for use in the production of goods for sale (fixed assets) and the goods themselves (finished goods inventory). The accounting system must be able to collect and process all its inputs in such a way that this distinction can be made reliably, completely, and quickly. Minor exceptions (such as a wooden brace normally regarded as inventory but used in one instance to help support a machine) are not significant—this is the meaning of the materiality principle. As for the matching principle, the costs associated with all the braces manufactured will remain in the finished goods inventory until the braces are sold. Then the costs will be matched with the sales revenue on the income statement for that period.

Generally accepted accounting principles are only useful when applied to transaction data that have been recorded accurately, completely, and in a timely fashion. Ensuring that transaction data have these attributes is a major mission of accounting systems. It is crucial to this purpose that the accounting model be used consistently. For this reason, management imposes strict procedures and tests to be used in accounting systems, including constant monitoring of accounting processing and reporting. These procedures and tests follow the control structure described in Chapters 1–3 and are called **accounting controls**. As we noted in Chapter 1, they belong to the broad category, internal controls. An example of an accounting control objective is to ensure that the organization's depreciation rules, which are consistent with GAAP, are being correctly applied to record the periodic depreciation expense.

Operations in an Accounting System

Accounting systems rely on operations that include data collection, entry of transactions, transaction analysis and authorization, preparing journals, posting to ledgers and balancing control accounts, summarizing accounting data, making adjustments to the summarized data, and preparing accounting statements. This section discusses each of these operations.

Data Collection

Chapter 1 explained that the word *data* is used to describe unprocessed facts whose usefulness depends on further processing. *Data collection* is the process of gathering and retaining data in a processable and durable form. You will recall that we used an unorganized list of airline flights as an example of data for planning a trip. When the data in the list of flights are *processed* to produce a guide or an itinerary for a specific journey, the guide or itinerary represents *information.* Organizations require many kinds of information, and accounting is only one means of collecting it. The organization will also collect raw economic data; monitor the performance of its competitors, suppliers, and customers; and keep abreast of new techniques pertinent to the design and manufacture of its products or services. Ultimately, in the course of decision making and other administrative processes, it will evaluate and judge information by relying on the knowledge of its managers and knowledge gleaned from experience.

Any data collection process should be tailored to a particular type of data. Those who operate the collection process should specify the items of data to be collected, how precise the data should be, their form and level of aggregation, how often to collect them, and from what sources they may be collected and over what time horizon. A payroll data collection process, for example, would require the employee name, the hours worked, and the pay rate. The name and pay rate must be completely accurate; company rules may allow the hours worked to be precise only to the nearest quarter-hour. All data will be quantitative and unaggregated; that is, work hours must be measured for each employee individually, not for the work force as a whole. Hours-worked data may be collected every week. The hours worked will be collected from the employee (a primary source); the names and pay rates from the personnel office (a primary source for the employee pay rate and a secondary source for the name, since personnel got the name from the employee). This collection process will continue as long as there are active employees.

Entry of Transactions

The accounting system deals only with business activities that can be treated as transactions. We have used the term *transaction* in earlier chapters, and you probably have a good idea of its basic meaning. You should remember, though, that in an accounting system a transaction must have certain very specific attributes. A **transaction** is an event involving a change in resources, usually an exchange or transfer of an asset or a claim on an asset, with offsetting changes in the status of assets or claims on assets. The transaction must take place or be recognized as complete at one instant in time, and must involve an increase or decrease in at least one type of asset or claim on assets and a related offsetting equal increase or decrease in at least one other type of asset or claim on assets. These offsetting changes are incorporated into an **accounting entry**. The concept that the changes must offset each other within an entry is called the debits-equal-credits or **double-entry rule**. An example of a transaction is a purchase of materials. Completed when the seller delivers the materials the buyer has agreed to purchase, this transaction results (for the purchaser) in an increase in materials inventory offset by the seller's claim on sufficient cash to cover the agreed purchase price. An accounting entry expresses these changes in units of currency, such as dollars. So if the agreed transaction was that the seller would transfer materials to the buyer and the buyer would later pay $500 to the seller, the buyer's accounting entry would show the following:

Purchases	$500	
Accounts Payable		$500

Thus, **transaction processing** consists of recording the details of transactions (data input), then restating them as accounting entries (data input) and classifying and summarizing these details (data processing) to become part of an accounting system's data and information content.

The accounting entries record only those business activities that can be treated as transactions according to generally accepted accounting principles. Since most business activities do not fit the model of a single transaction, much of what a business does cannot be learned by looking only at its accounting entries, or at least not in the form and order in which they were originally recorded. For example, a business may be developing a new product, an ongoing endeavor resulting in a number of apparently unconnected events that can be recorded as accounting entries: salaries paid to engineers, travel costs, purchases of supplies and equipment, payment of taxes, maintenance and utilities for the product-development facility, and payments to consultants for product advice. While the business is interested in each of these individual transactions, it primarily wants the product development effort to be successful and complete. The product development, in turn, will become part of a larger activity, perhaps an investment center or business division, and over a period of years the business will try to determine the profitability of the product it developed. To get the information it needs to measure the cost of the product development and the product's subsequent profitability, the business must identify the accounting entry elements related to the product's development and link them to the elements related to production and marketing. As this example illustrates, recording transactions as accounting entries, while critical, is by no means the major part of an accounting system. Nevertheless, most other accounting system operations depend on complete, correct transaction recording, either in the form of entries or in a form from which accounting entries can be written.

Analysis of Transactions

Every organization tends to specialize in a certain mix of transactions and designs procedures to handle them with a minimum of inconvenience. For most transactions, recording and documentation are simple and routine. Transaction analysis is a very important process—if done incorrectly, the subsequent accounting outputs will have no meaning or will be misleading. Whatever the type of accounting entry, the accountant analyzes it for processing by asking five important questions:

1. What type of entry is this?
2. What accounts will be affected, and by what amounts?
3. What information in addition to accounts and amounts (such as names and addresses) is needed, and is it present?
4. Is this entry authorized?
5. Is the transaction complete and are all its accounting details known?

Since the answers to these questions determine what kind of processing the entry receives, the types of answers possible receive close attention here.

Types of Entries. Accounting data processing uses three types of entries: (1) *exchange entries*, arising from exchanges with independent outside parties, such as sales, purchases, receipts, and payments; (2) *internal entries*, resulting from purely internal activities, such as manufacturing, and (3) *time interval entries*, arising from the passage of time, such as depreciation. Each type of entry will be processed differently.

Exchange entries, describing transactions with outside parties, are recorded from source documents provided by both parties and acknowledging that an exchange took place. For example, Alan Hurst sells 40 acres of his property to Marjorie Tow, who pays him $30,000 in cash and gives a two-year note for the balance of $40,000. Hurst's assets increase by $30,000 cash and the right to receive an additional $40,000. His assets decrease by 40 acres of property. Hurst records this transaction as follows:

Cash	$30,000	
Note Receivable from Tow	40,000	
Land (here would appear a legal description)		$70,000

In the land sale, both parties will have a sales contract. The buyer will have the property deed; the seller will have the buyer's note and cash.

An internal transaction should be supported by written authorization for the transfer. For example, in the manufacturing process, a transfer of lumber from the wood yard to the carpenter shop is supported by an internal materials requisition form that has been signed by the carpenter using the wood.

A time interval entry is made at regular intervals, as though a transaction had occurred, to record the result of a process that takes place continuously. An accounting entry that reduces the net carrying value of equipment and increases the depreciation expense is a time interval entry. These entries require no outside documentation or authority, and the accounting department processes them automatically.

For ease of handling, each type of entry can be subdivided into the most frequently encountered kinds of transactions. As a result, several major classes of transaction handling exist and, in accounting data processing, are called **applications**. (You will recall from Chapter 4 that the term *application* also refers to computer programs that do specialized processing.) The following list describes the major classes of applications in transaction processing:

Type 1: Exchange Entries

1. Credit sales (and accounts receivable)
   Normal activity: sales to customers with approved credit
   Normal entry: debit to a customer account receivable, credits to one or more sales accounts

2. Credit purchases (and accounts payable)
   Normal activity: purchase of assets, materials, and supplies from vendors on credit
   Normal entry: debits to purchases or asset or expense accounts credits to a vendor account payable

3. Cash receipts
   Normal activity: receipt of payment from credit customers or a sale for cash
   Normal entry: debit to a cash account
   credit to a customer account receivable **or** credit to a cash sale account

4. Cash disbursements
   Normal activity: payment of debts or acquisition of goods and services for cash
   Normal entry: debit to a seller account payable **or** debit to Wages Payable **or** debit to some other current liability account
   credit to a cash account

5.   Payroll
     Normal activity: payment to employees for services performed
     Normal entry: debit to Payroll Expense
                          credit to Wages Payable

Type 2: Internal Entries

6.   Inventory (and cost accounting)
     Normal activity: management of inventory
     Normal entries: debits to various purchase or inventory accounts;
                          credits to others; transfers of work in process among
                          work centers in manufacturing

Type 3: Time Interval Entries

7.   General journal
     Normal transactions: those involving the passage of time, such as
                          depreciation, amortization, and accrued in-
                          come; those involving preparation of state-
                          ments, such as adjusting and closing entries;
                          error corrections and all other unusual trans-
                          actions, such as issuing new stock or acquiring
                          another company

Each of these categories of activity involves specialized procedures. The circumstances under which the activity occurs usually determine the transaction type and related procedures. For example, retail sales usually originate at a cash register. Thus, the sales procedures are typically performed there and not in the payroll department or on the factory floor.

Affected Accounts and Amounts.   Transaction analysis identifies the accounts affected and the amounts recorded for each account. A straightforward and established procedure nearly always exists for doing this. Each of the seven accounting applications affects only certain accounts. Credit sales, for instance, affects only the sale and accounts receivable accounts; payroll affects only wages and withholdings payable and wages, taxes, and benefits expense accounts. Rules for each case determine exactly what the amounts recorded should be. For example, in payroll,

Jones's hourly wage rate ($11.00) $\times$ total hours worked by Jones
   (37 hours) = $407.00
Total wages payable to Jones: $407.00 credit to Wages Payable
Offsetting debit: $407.00 to Wages Expense

In each transaction, the sum of all debits must equal the sum of all credits. If any account has been omitted, or the amount calculated incorrectly, the entry's debits and credits may not balance. *However, equality of debits and credits is not sufficient to ensure that the entry is correct.* The application must correctly select the accounts to receive the debits and credits. For example, debits would equal credits if the wages payable to Jones were credited incorrectly to Smith's account. Accounting systems use other controls to make this kind of error unlikely. For example, see Chapter 12 for an extended discussion of accounting and processing controls.

Necessary Additional Information. In the payroll example above, the accounting system requires more information about Jones and the nature of Jones's work. For example,

> Is Jones really an employee?
> What type of work did Jones do during those hours?
> What deductions from his gross pay has Jones authorized?
> Where does Jones want his paycheck sent?

The payroll procedure can be designed to answer these questions in the course of normal processing. Jones's name and employee number should be on a master employee list maintained in the personnel office. Every employee time card should be compared with this master list. Jones's supervisor can describe what Jones did during the hours worked and will submit a time distribution sheet for every employee. This record can be checked against the hours shown on the employee time cards. Authorizations for payroll deductions, dated and signed by Jones, should be on file in the personnel office. The treasurer's office, which prints the paychecks, should have a signed authorization from Jones and every other employee designating where to send each check; these authorizations are used to address the envelopes for the checks.

Authorization. If you were asked to issue cash to someone claiming payment for goods or services, you would ask for some evidence (documentation) in support of this claim. If the evidence satisfied you, you would pay—otherwise you would not pay. This rule applies to all accounting transactions and is stated as an explicit control objective: "There must be satisfactory evidence to support a cash disbursement." Before the accounting system accepts any transaction and its corresponding entry for processing, it must be established first of all that the transaction was authorized, and second that it is consistent with applicable company policies and procedures. The people responsible for the transaction are supposed to collect and present this evidence.

Most organizations have policies for each type of transaction, specifying the facts and procedures required to record a transaction. Specialized preprinted forms can help in recording these facts. Collectively, the forms, reports, approvals, and papers that support a transaction and its processing are called **source documents**. Table 6.1 lists the source documents associated with each transaction processing application.

Organizations usually preserve source documents for at least a year after their transaction. Doing so makes it possible to recover data if the accounting system is lost or damaged and to trace any questionable matter back to its origins.

Journalizing

A **journal** is a collection of accounting entries for similar transactions. Its purpose is to make it easier to record and post similar transactions. The process of placing an accounting entry into a journal is called **journalizing**. There are two types of journals: transaction journals and the general journal. Transaction journals record exchanges and some internal entries; the general journal records all other entries. The seven most common journals correspond to the seven applications listed in Table 6.1.

Transaction Journals.   Any accounting entry must affect two or more accounts, each of which contains its portion of the transaction. Rather than making it necessary to look up the appropriate accounts for each transaction, the accounting system simply records each entry completely in a journal designed for that type of entry. Each journal allows access only to the accounts its type of transaction could affect. The accounting entries are recorded in the sequence in which they occurred. As a result, routine transactions are recorded smoothly and efficiently, without complications that could hamper accuracy.

Other accounting courses may have introduced you to journals as manually compiled notebooks. No doubt some notebooklike journals exist. In practice, however, a journal may consist of either the source documents themselves or a computer-generated summary of information from the source documents. The credit sales journal, for example, may consist of copies of all credit sales receipts or a summary of all credit sales transactions. Only in a small system would the credit sales journal, or any other transaction journal, be a manually kept notebook. Table 6.2 depicts part of a computer-generated credit sales journal.

In the first entry of Table 6.2, the date indicates when the transaction was recorded (it should be a matter of policy to record a transaction as soon as it occurs). The receipt number refers to the credit sales receipt that is the primary source document. Arrow Manufacturing Co. is the party to whom merchandise was sold. The addresses for shipping and billing are recorded elsewhere. The customer account number identifies the specific account receivable assigned to that customer by the organization. Total sale is the total amount (including tax and shipping) that the customer will owe; this amount, then, is the debit to Accounts Receivable. (As we will see, another operation is necessary to actually *make* the debit.) Item ID is the number uniquely identifying each item purchased by the Arrow Man-

Table 6.1   Common Source Documents

These source documents are created as a transaction occurs; without them, a transaction should not be recorded as an accounting entry.

Application	Typical Source Documents
Credit sales	Credit sales receipt—2 or more copies Credit authorization—on file, verified prior to sale
Credit purchases	Purchase order—3 or more copies Vendor authorization—on file, verified prior to purchase Vendor invoice—2 copies Receiving report
Cash receipts	Remittance advice—accompanies payment Deposit slip—2 or more copies
Cash disbursements	Vendor invoice—received from creditor entitled to payment Purchase order copy—showing that goods or services were ordered Receiving report copy—showing that goods ordered were received Employees time distribution sheet and/or supervisor's affirmation of time worked Voucher—to organize data to support cash disbursement
Payroll	Employee time cards—prepared by employees, approved by supervisors Authorized employee roster Schedule of wage rates and authorized deductions Payroll voucher—to organize data supporting payroll payment
Inventory	Standard cost schedule Bills of materials for products Overhead allocation plan Material requisition—2 or more copies Labor distribution (of time to specific jobs, tasks, or activities)
General journal	General journal voucher Supporting documentation (varies due to wide variety of transactions handled through general journal)

ufacturing Co. in this transaction. These numbers correspond to accounts for recording sales. The Qty (quantity) and Item Unit Price columns specify that 4 units of item A100 were sold at $990.12 each, and 2 units of item A205 were sold at $300 each. Note that tax and shipping charges are also recorded in the Amount column, and that the total of all merchandise,

Table 6.2   Computer-Generated Credit Sales Journal

Date	Receipt Number	Sold to	Customer Account	Total Sale	Item ID	Item Unit Price	Qty	Amount
2/3	02265	Arrow Mfg. Co.	5678	$ 5129.36	A100	$990.12	4	$3960.48
					A205	$300.00	2	$ 600.00
					Tax		6%	$ 273.63
					Shipping			$ 295.25
2/3	02266	Bright Instr. Co.	4325	$ 3910.05	A100	$990.12	2	$1980.24
					A450	$500.00	3	$1500.00
					Tax		6%	$ 208.81
					Shipping			$ 221.00
2/3	02267	Morris Distr.	1178	$20622.07	A205	$990.12	10	$9901.20
					T006	$ 75.00	20	$1500.00
					W015	$205.00	36	$7380.00
					Tax		6%	$1126.87
					Shipping			$ 714.00
2/4	02268	Ball Bros.	5401	$ 3239.58	A100	$990.12	3	$2970.36
					Tax		6%	$ 178.22
					Shipping			$ 91.00
2/4	02269	Acme Foods	5617	$ 6842.20	A205	$300.00	4	$1200.00
					W015	$205.00	24	$4920.00
					Tax		6%	$ 367.20
					Shipping			$ 355.00

Table 6.3   Textbook Form of an Entry

Accounts Receivable—Arrow Mfg. Co.	$5,129.36	
Sales—A100		$3,960.48
Sales—A205		600.00
Tax @ 6% collected		273.63
Shipping charges collected		295.25
To record credit sale to Arrow Mfg. Co. 2/3/XX		

tax, and shipping adds up to the total sale, which will be the debit to Account Receivable number 5678. To offset this single debit, there will be four credits: two to sales accounts, the third to a sales tax collected account, and the fourth to an account for shipping. In textbook form, this first entry would look like Table 6.3.

General Journal.   The purpose of the general journal is to record entries that do not fit into any other journal, like time interval and some internal transactions. If new common stock is issued, the general journal will be used to place the new shares into the general ledger. The general journal will also record the accounting entries required at the end of the period to prepare financial statements. (See page 188 for a description of the process of preparing financial statements.)

Posting to Ledgers

A sales, purchase, or payroll journal may accumulate many entries in a short time. The accumulated entries in each journal are copied, or *posted*, to the accounts at regular intervals varying from a few seconds to a few days. Since accounting statements are prepared not from the journals but from the accounts, an accounting system's ability to deliver timely information to management may depend on the efficiency of journal posting to accounts.

Most organizations, even small ones, have so many accounts that the accountant must impose some order and organization on them. Accountants do this by grouping similar accounts together in ledgers. There are two types of ledgers: the subsidiary ledgers and the general ledger.

Subsidiary Ledgers.   A group of similar accounts, such as all the accounts receivable, is called a **subsidiary ledger** or **subledger**. Each subsidiary ledger consists of accounts posted from one or more principal journals. The subsidiary ledgers are named for the accounting application to which they belong, for example,

Accounts receivable subledger
Accounts payable subledger
Cash subledger
Inventory subledger
Fixed assets (property, plant, and equipment) subledger

The basic purpose of the subsidiary ledgers is to accept data from the journals and aggregate it in orderly fashion with similar data already in the accounting system. The ultimate result is that individual debits and credits are posted to the accounts designated for them. After posting, the accounts have new balances. In this way, the effects of economic events, interpreted as transactions and translated into accounting entries, find their way to the proper accounts.

For example, consider the plant, property, and equipment subledger. Its purpose is to provide an individual record for each tangible asset controlled by the organization. This record will include, as a minimum, the asset's unique name or description, date acquired, location, original cost, life expectancy, depreciation method, accumulated depreciation to date, salvage value, and information about maintenance, renovation, rebuilding, or other kinds of enhancement.

If the organization controls 100 assets, each will have an account in this subsidiary ledger. At least three general ledger accounts will reflect

Figure 6.2   General and Subsidiary Ledgers and Journals (facing page)
Here, the large rectangle represents the general ledger and each row in it represents
a control account. The balances shown are for October 31 unless otherwise noted.
Carl's accounts receivable balance was zero at September 30. In (Part b) some of
these control accounts are shown connecting to their subsidiary ledgers. In (Part
c), two credit sales to Carl have increased Carl's debit balance in the accounts-
receivable subsidiary ledger and a payment by Carl has reduced this balance. These
transactions have affected the accounts-receivable control account balance.

---

the contents of this subsidiary ledger: (1) Property, Plant, and Equipment,
(2) Provision for Accumulated Depreciation, and (3) Depreciation Expense.
Entries affecting these accounts, such as the one that follows reflecting
acquisition of a new asset financed by a note payable, will be made in the
general journal.

Property, Plant, and Equipment	$29,950	
Note Payable		$ 29,950

General Ledger.   The **general ledger**, which is the set of accounts from
which the trial balance and the financial statements emerge, summarizes
the subsidiary ledgers. Figure 6.2 illustrates this relationship. Note that
each subsidiary ledger shown corresponds to one account in the general
ledger. These general ledger accounts are called **control accounts**. The
balance of a control account must equal the sum of all the account balances
recorded in the corresponding subsidiary ledger. For example, if the accounts receivable subsidiary ledger contains accounts with debit balances
of $40, $50, $100, and $75, as in Figure 6.2b, the control account balance
will be $265. The accounts receivable subledger may contain hundreds or
even millions of accounts—one for each credit customer. That many accounts in the general ledger would make working with it difficult, and
make financial statements too detailed to be meaningful. Summing the
balances of all the accounts in the accounts receivable subledger produces
a single control account balance for all accounts receivable. Linking the
general and subsidiary ledgers in this way allows relatively few accounts
to summarize information from many current and past transactions and
from other accounts. One can verify the control account balances by reviewing the original detailed transaction data and how it was processed
into the summarized accounts.

Balancing Control Accounts
with Subsidiary Ledgers

When the sum of all the account balances in a subledger equals the balance
of the control account, the subledger is *in balance* with its control account.
This is a happy state of affairs compared with the out-of-balance condition

A. General ledger alone

Debit	General Ledger	Credit
$ 300	Cash	
$ 265	Accounts Receivable	
$ 500	Inventory	
$1,100	Fixed Assets	
$ 200	Other Assets	
	Accounts Payable	$ 600
	Wages Payable	$ 350
	Owners' Equity	$1,200
	Revenue	$5,000
$3,000	Purchases	
$1,285	Labor Expense	
$ 500	Depreciation Expense	
$7,150	Balance	$7,150

B. General ledger summarizing supporting subsidiary ledgers

Cash Receipts Subsidiary Ledger

Fixed Assets Subsidiary Ledger

Purchases Subsidiary Ledger

Debit	General Ledger	Credit
$ 300	Cash	
$ 265	Accounts Receivable	
$ 500	Inventory	
$1,100	Fixed Assets	
$ 200	Other Assets	
	Accounts Payable	$ 600
	Wages Payable	$ 350
	Owners' Equity	$1,200
	Revenue	$5,000
$3,000	Purchases	
$1,285	Labor Expense	
$ 500	Depreciation Expense	
$7,150	Balance	$7,150

Accounts Receivable Subsidiary Ledger

Debit	
$ 40	Amos
$ 50	Carl
$100	Della
$ 75	Fran
$265	Balance

Accounts Payable Subsidiary Ledger

Payroll Subsidiary Ledger

C. General ledger, subsidiary ledger, and journals

Debit	General Ledger	Credit
$ 300	Cash	
$ 265	Accounts Receivable	
$ 500	Inventory	
$1,100	Fixed Assets	
$ 200	Other Assets	
	Accounts Payable	$ 600
	Wages Payable	$ 350
	Owners' Equity	$1,200
	Revenue	$5,000
$3,000	Purchases	
$1,285	Labor Expense	
$ 500	Depreciation Expense	
$7,150	Balance	$7,150

Accounts Receivable Subsidiary Ledger

Debit	
$ 40	Amos
$ 50	Carl
$100	Della
$ 75	Fran
$265	Balance

$80 total credit sales to Carl
− $30 cash paid on account
$50 balance

Credit Sales Journal

Name	Date	Account
Amos	10-6	$ 10
Fran	10-6	$ 30
Carl	10-7	$ 20
Amos	10-10	$ 30
Della	10-12	$ 50
Della	10-15	$ 30
Fran	10-20	$ 40
Della	10-22	$ 20
Fran	10-25	$ 5
Carl	10-30	$ 60
October total		$295

add Sept 30 balance $4,705
$5,000

Figure 6.3   Testing Whether the Control Account and Subsidiary Ledger Are in Balance   A control account balance should equal the previous balance plus total postings from journals, and as a check, should also equal the sum of account balances in the subsidiary ledger.

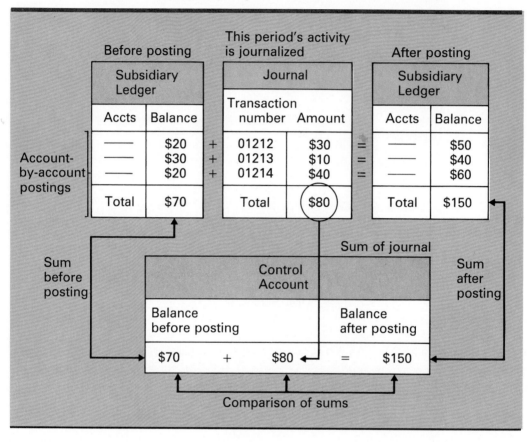

that will exist if posting errors occur. Figure 6.3 diagrams the procedure set out in the following steps for preventing an out-of-balance situation from occurring during processing, assuming that prior to processing the control account and subledger were in balance.

1. Post each journalized entry to the proper accounts in the subledger.

2. Add up all the account balances in the posted subledger to obtain the updated sum of the subledger account balances.

3. For each class of account (for example, all cash receipts or all accounts receivable), add up all the amounts posted from the journal to obtain the cumulative sum.

4. Post the cumulative sum of each type of posting to the corresponding control account (cash receipts control account, accounts receivable control account) to obtain the new control account balance.

5. The new control account balance (4) and the updated sum of the subledger account balances (2) should agree. If they do, the state of balance still exists.

Summarizing Posted Accounting Data

The first performance requirement of accounting systems is to organize and summarize data. The listing of all the general ledger account names and their balances, from which accounting statements are prepared, is called the **trial balance**. Because in each accounting entry the debits equaled the credits, each journal's debits and credits should be equal. Therefore, in the trial balance, the total of debit account balances should equal the total of credit account balances; if these totals are equal, the entries have probably been made correctly. Figure 6.4 illustrates the process of data summarization. Data that have been organized and sum-

Figure 6.4 Accounting Data Summarization
Accounting transaction processing organizes and summarizes data so they can be found and incorporated into reports to management (including the accounting statements).

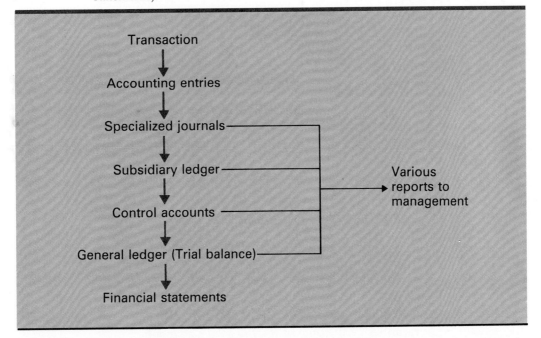

marized can be used to prepare internal management reports and external financial statements; the same body of summarized transaction data supports both functions. The trial balance summarizes all the information produced by the accounting system. An exact and simple two-part process converts the trial balance to financial statements. The first part brings the trial balance completely up-to-date, to reflect the company's position on the date of the financial statements. The second part calculates the financial statements.

Inevitably, summarization excludes detail. To compensate, the accounting system retains the ability to access higher or lower levels of summarization, so that detail is actually recoverable at a lower level and excludable by moving to a higher level. The journals reveal transaction detail, subledgers contain account detail, control accounts summarize subledgers, and the general ledger presents a summarized accounting perspective on the whole organization. The trial balance—the basis for preparing financial statements—comes from the general ledger and includes the control accounts, but not the accounts in subledgers. Financial statements are based on the information summary in the general ledger; management reports include much of the detail in the journals and subledgers.

Adjustments

Adjusting entries record transactions that occur at the end of the accounting period and that are necessary to include the effect of as yet unrecorded revenues and expenses. Adjusting entries appear first in the general journal. These entries can be classified into three major groups: accrual and deferral, valuation, and error correction.

Accruals and Deferrals.   An *accrual* recognizes all at once revenue or expense that has accumulated gradually over the reporting period or is practically certain to occur, such as depreciation expense or the conversion of prepaid insurance from an asset to an expense. A *deferral* delays recognition of revenue or expense to another period. The *accrual basis* of accounting requires accruals and deferrals to enter revenue in the period when it is earned, not necessarily the period in which cash is received, and to enter expense in the same period as the revenue to which it is most closely associated. Here are some examples:

1. *Purchase of maintenance service on credit*

> Maintenance Expense
> Accounts Payable

> This entry is made when the seller's invoice is received or if maintenance service was received but the liability has not been recorded by the date of the financial statements.

2. *Purchase on credit of labor for production*

> Work in Process (asset)
>> Wages Payable

This entry is made if the date when financial statements are issued differs from the date when payroll is normally recorded and paid.

3. *Use of an automobile during the year*

> Depreciation Expense—Automobile
>> Accumulated Depreciation—Automobile

This entry is made at the end of each accounting period.

4. *Hold certificate of deposit on which interest is declared and paid annually*

> Interest Receivable
>> Interest Income Earned

This entry is made if the date when financial statements are issued differs from the date when interest is paid.

Valuation.   Inevitably, a few good-faith transactions are not completed as an organization expects. Although a bank, for example, makes loans only to entities its loan officers believe will repay the debt, imperfect judgment renders a few loans uncollectible. In its financial statements, the bank reports total loans outstanding as an asset, and it also estimates the amount that will prove uncollectible. A business may allow customers to buy on credit, and a few of the accounts receivable thus created may prove to be uncollectible. When the business reports total accounts receivable, it will estimate the amount it expects it will be unable to collect. Such deductions from assets appear in a **valuation account**. The words *provision for* or *allowance for* usually appear in the titles of valuation accounts. Each time the bank issues a financial statement, it reviews and recalculates the balance of the valuation accounts and, if necessary, makes entries that change the balances. If the bank has decided that the provision for uncollectible loans should increase from $42,000 to $47,000, the entry would look like this:

Expense of Uncollectible Loans	$5,000	
Provision for Uncollectible Loans		$5,000

On the balance sheet, the loans amount and its valuation account would appear something like this:

Loans Outstanding	$1,200,000	
Less: Provision for Uncollectible Loans	(47,000)	$1,153,000

A similar case is the valuation account for Accounts Receivable. The same pattern occurs, with different account titles. Assume that the provision for uncollectible accounts should rise from $15,000 to $20,000:

Bad-Debt Expense	$5,000	
Provision for Uncollectible Accounts		$5,000

And of course, in the balance sheet:

Accounts Receivable	$245,000	
Less: Provision for Uncollectible Accounts	(20,000)	$225,000

Error Correction. In preparing to issue financial statements, errors may be discovered. Errors should be corrected immediately. To correct an error, identify the accounting entry that contains the error, cancel the entry's effect by recording and posting an opposite entry (called a **reversing entry**), and record and post the correct entry.

Creation of Statements

Financial statements convey important information about an organization's assets, equities, revenues, expenses, profits, and cash and funds flows. The **balance sheet** shows the assets and the equities (claims of creditors and owners) on a specific date. The **income statement** shows changes in assets and equities (in the form of revenues, expenses, and profit) since the date of a previous balance sheet (that is, during a period bracketed by two balance sheets). A **statement of retained earnings** explains changes in that category of owners' equity. The **statement of cash flows** shows how operating, investing, and financing activities during a period have affected cash. Other specialized statements may be produced if managers, creditors, or other parties request them. Starting with a complete trial balance, you can produce the balance sheet, income statement, and statement of retained earnings.

Division of the Trial Balance and Closing Entries. Financial statements result from dividing the trial balance into two or more categories. The simplified trial balance in Exhibit 6.1 can be divided into two groups of accounts, as shown in Exhibit 6.2, where you will note that in the balance sheet (top) group, debits exceed credits by $3,000; in the income statement (bottom) group, credits exceed debits by exactly the same amount. As you may have guessed, this is the amount by which retained earnings have increased since December 31, 19X5. You can recognize this change with a closing entry that removes the old retained earnings (Dec. 31, 19X5) and replaces it with the new retained earnings figure:

Retained Earnings	$6,800	
Net Addition to Retained Earnings, 19X6	3,000	
Retained Earnings		$9,800

Exhibit 6.1   Simplified Trial Balance
The trial balance, a listing of control-account balances, is the starting-point for preparation of accounting statements. The sum of debits should equal the sum of credits.

Trial Balance
As of December 31, 19X6

Account	Debit	Credit
Cash	1,000	
Accounts Receivable	3,000	
Provision for Uncollectible Accounts		200
Inventory	5,000	
Property, Plant, Equipment	12,000	
Provision for Depreciation		4,500
Accounts Payable		4,000
Loans and Other Long-Term Debt		500
Common Stock		2,000
Retained Earnings as of 12-31-X5		6,800
Dividend Declared	1,000	
Revenue		15,000
Cost of Sales	7,000	
Selling & Administrative Expense	4,000	
Totals	$33,000	$33,000

When this entry is incorporated into the partitioned trial balance, debits equal credits for both the balance sheet and the income statement portions, as shown in Exhibit 6.3. The changed lines are shown in italics. Net income is the net addition to retained earnings plus dividends, or $4,000.

Detailed descriptions of how to prepare accounting statements can be found in most principles of accounting textbooks.

Closing Entries.   Closing entries such as the one above do not record transactions; made after financial statements have been prepared, they "reset" the revenue and expense accounts to zero at the beginning of the next accounting period. For the trial balance illustrated in Exhibits 6.1, 6.2, and 6.3, another closing entry would be

Revenue	$15,000	
Cost of Sales		$7,000
Selling and Administrative Expenses		4,000
Dividends Declared		1,000
Net Addition to Retained Earnings, 19X6		3,000

Exhibit 6.2 Trial Balance Partitioned into Balance Sheet and Income Statement Accounts

The first step in accounting-statement preparation is partitioning the trial balance. Note that the difference between debits and credits is the same in both balance-sheet and income-statement account groups, but offset each other.

Trial Balance
As of December 31, 19X6

Account	Debit	Credit
Balance sheet accounts		
Cash	1,000	
Accounts Receivable	3,000	
Provision for Uncollectible Accounts		200
Inventory	5,000	
Property, Plant, Equipment	12,000	
Provision for Depreciation		4,500
Accounts Payable		4,000
Loans and Other Long-Term Debt		500
Common Stock		2,000
Retained Earnings as of 12-31-X5		6,800
Subtotals	$21,000	$18,000
Income statement accounts		
Revenue		15,000
Cost of Sales	7,000	
Selling & Administrative Expense	4,000	
Dividend Declared	1,000	
Subtotals	$12,000	$15,000
Totals	$33,000	$33,000

Tools to Implement Accounting Systems

As far as an accounting system is concerned, business activity consists of individual transactions. The attributes of these transactions need to be properly recorded, processed, and reported, as we have seen, to be meaningful and useful. In terms of accounting systems, then, the *data* (the input to the accounting system) consist of the unprocessed details of transactions; and the *information* is the output reports and summaries relevant to specific purposes.

An accounting system's most important feature is the classifications, or accounts, it contains. Reports consist of the titles of certain accounts

Exhibit 6.3   Trial Balance Partitioned and Modified to Prepare Balance Sheet and Income Statement
The italicized accounts have been adjusted (by $3,000 each) to equalize debits and credits in each group of accounts. This $3,000 is the income earned through operations.

	Modified Trial Balance	
	December 31, 19X6	
Account	**Debit**	**Credit**
Balance sheet		
Cash	1,000	
Accounts Receivable	3,000	
Provision for Uncollectible Accounts		200
Inventory	5,000	
Property, Plant, Equipment	12,000	
Provision for Depreciation		4,500
Accounts Payable		4,000
Loans and Other Long-Term Debt		500
Common Stock		2,000
Retained Earnings as of 12-31-X6		9,800
Subtotals	$21,000	$21,000
Income statement		
Revenue		15,000
Cost of Sales	7,000	
Selling & Administrative Expense	4,000	
Dividend Declared	1,000	
Net Addition to Retained Earnings, 19X6	3,000	
Subtotals	$15,000	$15,000
Totals	$33,000	$33,000

and their balances. The more accounts there are, the more detailed the reports can be. But since excessive detail can be as harmful to decision making and control as too little detail, the accounts in the system must be no more numerous than necessary to provide enough detail for operational control and reporting.

Chart of Accounts

To implement accounting procedures and maintain an accounting system, organizations adopt a **chart of accounts,** a diagram or list showing the relationships of all the accounts in the accounting system and usually indicating the structure by which detailed accounts are summarized in the general ledger or trial balance by control accounts. Most organizations require hundreds of detailed accounts, some of which undergo many postings, or changes in their balances, each period. Moreover, accounts are created and canceled throughout the year. And accounts may be divided. If the organization collects cash in more than one location, it will partition the cash receipts application among those locations and find a way to combine the parts to produce one trial balance for the entire organization (even if the locations are countries apart and require currency translations prior to consolidation). Other applications may also have multiple parts to handle decentralized, multiple-location purchasing, credit sales, cash disbursements, manufacturing, shipping, and so on. Clearly, there is a crucial need for a systematic means of identifying and keeping track of accounts and of summarizing them so as to end up with a trial balance of reasonable size. The remainder of this section discusses such a means.

The organization should prepare the chart of accounts before the accounting system begins operations. A typical small chart of accounts (with the most common control accounts noted) might begin as follows:

Cash	(control account)
Accounts Receivable	(control account)
Inventory	(control account)
Property, Plant, & Equipment	(control account)
Accounts Payable	(control account)
Bank Loans	
Shareholders' Equity	(control account)
Retained Earnings	
Revenue	
Purchases	(control account)
Selling and Administrative Expense	
Taxes Expense	
Interest Expense	
Other Expense	

This chart of accounts is too imprecise to be of practical value after a business develops a history and has attained a level of vigorous activity. Note that every general ledger account could be used to summarize a subsidiary ledger, in which accounts may be entered or deleted *without affecting the overall chart-of-accounts structure.* This gives the chart of accounts the necessary flexibility to change with an organization's operational and planning requirements.

Now imagine that it becomes necessary to provide for recording transactions and formulating accounting entries at multiple sites. The revised chart of accounts in Table 6.4 shows how to do so. The indented accounts, which belong to the preceding control account, are used to record elements of transactions that occur at the location in question. For

Table 6.4   Multisite Chart of Accounts
The accounts necessary for branches in Baltimore, Philadelphia, Chicago, Minneapolis, and St. Louis are included in this chart of accounts.

Cash (master control account)
  Baltimore (control account)
    Operating account
    Money Market Investment
    Payroll A (hourly employees)
    Payroll B (salaried employees)
  Philadelphia First National Bank (control account)
    Operating account
    Payroll B (salaried employees)
  Philadelphia Franklin Savings (control account)
    Certificate of Deposit 5678 Investment
    Certificate of Deposit 5679 Investment
    Money Market Investment
Accounts Receivable (master control account)
  Baltimore (control account)
  Chicago (control account)
Inventory (master control account)
  Baltimore Production Plant (control account)
  Minneapolis Production Plant (control account)
  St. Louis Warehouse (control account)
Property, Plant, & Equipment (master control account)
  Baltimore (control account)
  Philadelphia (control account)
  Chicago (control account)
  Minneapolis (control account)
  St. Louis (control account)
Accounts Payable (master control account)
  Philadelphia (the only location from which cash disbursement may be authorized)
Bank Loans
Shareholders' Equity (control account)
Retained Earnings (beginning of period)
Revenue
  Baltimore Philadelphia Chicago Minneapolis St. Louis
Purchases (master control account)
  Baltimore (control account)
  Philadelphia (control account)
  Chicago (control account)
  Minneapolis (control account)
  St. Louis (control account)
Selling & Administrative Expense
Taxes Expense
Interest Expense
Other Expense

example, in Table 6.4 Baltimore has the following accounts for its exclusive use:

>Cash—Baltimore (control account)
>   Operating account
>   Money Market Investment
>   Payroll A (hourly employees)
>   Payroll B (salaried employees)
>Accounts Receivable—Baltimore
>Inventory—Baltimore Production Plant
>Property, Plant, & Equipment—Baltimore
>Purchases—Baltimore
>Revenue—Baltimore

The chart of accounts in Table 6.4 shows a *hierarchical relationship* between master and subsidiary control accounts. The same relationship exists between each subsidiary control account and the accounts in the corresponding subledger.

Account Coding

A code is an identifying number or designation for an account. An account's properties and type determine the fashion in which codes are assigned. The accounts in Table 6.4 have names that are satisfactory for use in conversation. In any automated accounting system, though, the account names should be supplemented by a classification code based on numbers or letters. *The classification and code should be such that when the accounts are arranged in numerical or alphabetical order, they are in the sequence found in a trial balance,* as are the accounts in Table 6.4. The code should indicate whether its account belongs to a control account or an account in a subledger. If the account belongs to a subledger, the code should indicate the subledger containing the account. The code should also identify the account as a revenue, expense, asset, liability, or equity account. Finally, the classification code should allow new accounts to be created, with codes that are consistent with existing accounts. For the chart of accounts in Table 6.4, the classification might be a simple matter of numbers, as shown in Table 6.5.

Block Codes.   The intervals in Table 6.5 are sometimes called **block codes** to signify that they are blocks or intervals of numbers set aside for identifying similar accounts. The control accounts could be those ending in one or two zeros. This plan will succeed as long as there are no more than 100 cash accounts, 100 receivables accounts, and so on. If there are three accounts receivable control accounts (one master plus one each in Baltimore and Chicago) this particular classification will allow up to 97 credit-customer accounts. When the 98th account must be created, however, a

Table 6.5 Block Coding of a Chart of Accounts
An account coding system that sets aside a block or range of numbers for similar accounts is called block coding; it is easy to set up but has limited flexibility.

0–99	Cash
100–199	Accounts Receivable
200–299	Inventory
300–399	Property, Plant, & Equipment
500–599	Accounts Payable
600–649	Other Liabilities
650–699	Shareholders' Equity
700–799	Revenue
800–999	Expenses (900–999 reserved for purchases)

problem arises! This problem could be solved by employing a four-digit code, which would allow for 10,000 possible accounts. But another problem would remain. Suppose that one assigns the four-digit accounts receivable codes as follows:

1000	Master control account
1001	Baltimore control account
1002-1499	Baltimore accounts receivable subledger
1500	Chicago control account
1501-1998	Chicago accounts receivable subledger
1999	Allowance for uncollectible accounts

Now the Baltimore accounts receivable subsidiary ledger has a capacity of 497 accounts (1002–1499). Assume that 200 of these accounts already exist. You could arrange them in any order you wish (alphabetic, by industry, by region, or whatever) and assign the account numbers. However, this order will last only until a new account needs to be created that forces changes in the codes of already existing accounts. In other words, this simple numerical classification will not allow for the creation of new accounts whose codes are consistent with those of existing accounts.

Also, if your firm experiences more credit customer growth in Chicago than in Baltimore, you would run out of numbers in one subsidiary ledger while open numbers still exist in the other subsidiary ledger. Perhaps you could change the dividing point by changing the number of the Chicago control account to, say, 1250, making more accounts available for Chicago. However, this would involve changing computer programs and revising files—a lot of work. The same problem could arise in any of the subledgers, or all of them, quickly eroding the advantages of numbering the accounts.

Despite the weaknesses of simple three- and four-digit account numbering with arbitrary partitions between account types, this approach is popular with small organizations. It lends itself to implementation on inexpensive microcomputer accounting software. As long as there is only one location and very few accounts, the accounting system investment can remain modest. However, as such a business grows, it will eventually need a more flexible account numbering plan.

Flexible Numbering Systems.   Flexible account numbering systems usually partition the account number, assigning a meaning to each part. The additional partitions are sometimes called **group codes**, since groups of similar accounts are controlled by a single block of numbers within the account code. Flexible systems require more digits than simple ones; it is the additional digits that give them their flexibility. Some flexible systems produce account numbers with sixteen, thirty-two, or more digits.

Suppose the account number has eight digits. These digits might be partitioned to produce an account number such as 12-3-4-5678, which is commonly deciphered as follows:

12 (100 numbers)	*Major account or master control account:* Each of these is a block-number code for up to 10 values of the location identifier that follows it.
3 (10 numbers)	*Location identifier:* Each of these is a block-number code for up to 10 values of the subledger identifier that follows it.
4 (10 numbers)	*Subledger identifier:* Each of these is a block-number code for up to 9,999 values of the individual account identifier that follows it.
5678	*Identifier of individual accounts in subledger.* Each set of 9,999 of these is controlled by the subledger identifier that precedes it.

This system is more flexible than a simple three- or four-digit one because it allows for the creation of many more accounts, while still tying into the small number of accounts in the trial balance. Further, the accountants can change the number of digits in any group code to meet a need (for example, add a third digit to the major or master control account block to allow for more accounts in the trial balance). Table 6.6 shows the accounts listed in Table 6.4 coded according to this eight-digit system.

Modest though it is, the flexible account coding system has many advantages. It permits a very large number of control accounts, locations, and subledger accounts. If a subledger becomes full, the controller may establish second, third, and subsequent subledgers reporting to the same

Table 6.6 Numerical Account Codes

01-0-0-0000	Cash (master control account)
01-1-1-0000	Baltimore (control account)
01-1-1-0001	Operating account
01-1-1-0002	Money Market Investment
01-1-1-0003	Payroll A (hourly employees)
01-1-1-0004	Payroll B (salaried employees)
01-2-1-0000	Philadelphia First National Bank (control account)
01-2-1-0001	Operating account
01-2-1-0002	Payroll B (salaried employees)
01-2-2-0000	Philadelphia Franklin Savings (control account)
01-2-2-0001	Certificate of Deposit 5678 Investment
01-2-2-0002	Certificate of Deposit 5679 Investment
01-2-2-0003	Money Market Investment
02-0-0-0000	Accounts Receivable (master control account)
02-1-1-0000	Baltimore (control account)
02-3-1-0000	Chicago (control account)
03-0-0-0000	Inventory (master control account)
03-1-1-0000	Baltimore Production Plant (control account)
03-4-1-0000	Minneapolis Production Plant (control account)
03-5-1-0000	St. Louis Warehouse (control account)
04-0-0-0000	Property, Plant, & Equipment (master control account)
04-1-1-0000	Baltimore (control account)
04-2-1-0000	Philadelphia (control account)
04-3-1-0000	Chicago (control account)
04-4-1-0000	Minneapolis (control account)
04-5-1-0000	St. Louis (control account)
50-0-0-0000	Accounts Payable (master control account)
50-2-1-0000	Philadelphia (the location for all cash disbursements)
60-2-0-0000	Bank Loans
70-2-0-0000	Shareholders' Equity (control account)
75-2-0-0000	Retained Earnings (beginning of period)
80-2-0-0000	Revenue
80-1-1-0000	Baltimore (control account)
80-2-1-0000	Philadelphia (control account)
80-3-1-0000	Chicago (control account)
80-4-1-0000	Minneapolis (control account)
80-5-1-0000	St. Louis (control account)
90-0-0-0000	Purchases (master control account)
90-1-1-0000	Baltimore (control account)
90-2-1-0000	Philadelphia (control account)
90-3-1-0000	Chicago (control account)
90-4-1-0000	Minneapolis (control account)
90-5-1-0000	St. Louis (control account)
91-0-0-0000	Selling & Administrative Expense
92-2-0-0000	Taxes Expense
93-2-0-0000	Interest Expense
94-2-0-0000	Other Expense

master control account, even in the same location. For example, if Accounts Receivable in Chicago exceeds 9,999, by simply starting a new control account with the number 02-3-2-0000, and starting a new subledger with numbers 02-3-2-0001 through 02-3-2-9999, the problem disappears, temporarily at least. Should a new location be required for Accounts Receivable, there are five more location codes available for assignment to it and its successors.

Account Coding for Complex Organizations

Complex organizations can make good use of flexibility in an account numbering system. For example, the geographically organized firm whose organization chart is shown in Figure 2.3 in Chapter 2 may wish to use the chart of accounts demonstrated in the preceding section to show the revenues produced and the costs incurred by specific responsibility centers and the assets they control. To see how the firm can use the account classification numbers to handle this situation, assume that it establishes a wholly owned subsidiary in Kansas City to manufacture and sell wind turbines to wheat farmers. The code for this location (third digit) is 6; the chart of accounts for this subsidiary will contain a 6 as the third digit of every account number. For all practical purposes, this chart of accounts is that of an independent company: the Kansas City enterprise has its own accounts receivable, inventory, cash, revenue, and other accounts. Yet its accounts easily consolidate with those of the parent company whenever necessary. Local management will process its own transactions yet be subject to overview by the parent firm.

Incidentally, it's not necessary for the facility responsible for transactions actually to process them. That is, the data processing itself could all be done elsewhere (centrally) or it, too, could be decentralized. The degree of decentralization in accounting operations does not depend on the degree of decentralization of the business organization.

The remainder of this section briefly explains manufacturing and project management, two other common applications for account coding systems.

Manufacturing.   The company using the chart of accounts we have been examining has two production plants and a separate warehouse. We will cover accounting for manufacturing costs, a very extensive subject, in Chapter 9. In brief, however, manufacturing involves the transfer of materials from one work station to another. Each work station adds more materials, labor, mechanical operations, and quality-control checks until a completed product emerges into Finished Goods Inventory. The process proceeds more or less as shown in Figure 6.5.

Figure 6.5   Simplified Manufacturing Diagram
Most manufacturing processes resemble this diagram. Manufacturing responsibility centers work together to combine materials, labor, and indirect inputs to produce finished outputs.

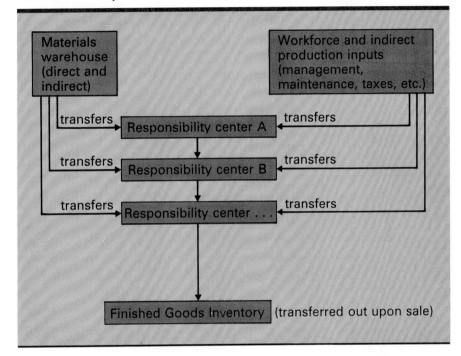

Specific entries exist to record each type of transfer, such as materials to each work station, labor and indirect inputs to each location, work in process from one location to another, and completed work to Finished Goods Inventory. Each transfer is from one account to another account. For the system to be effective in describing and recording manufacturing activity, the balance in each account must be identified with one location and one or more production activities or inputs. The Baltimore inventory control account code is 03-1-1-0000. This code allows for 9,999 manufacturing account numbers in subledger 1, and eight more subledgers may be created if required. Table 6.7 shows a design for these numbers. According to Table 6.7, the code 03-1-1-2456 refers to direct labor performed at site B in Baltimore. This system makes it possible to infer from the account code what type of production-cost information the account contains and to assign codes for new inputs or transfers logically.

Project Management Structure.   A project-management structure, sometimes called a matrix-management structure, is one in which the respon-

Table 6.7   Manufacturing Account Numbers Showing Work Site and Expense Classification   The inputs, work in process, and outputs of a manufacturing activity can all be assigned account identification numbers in a systematic way.

Site	First Digit	Work in Process or Raw Materials	Labor	Indirect Inputs	Other
Materials Warehouse	0	0001–0299	0300–0599	0600–0899	0900–0999
Site A	1	1001–1299	1300–1599	1600–1899	1900–1999
Site B	2	2001–2299	2300–2599	2600–2899	2900–2999
Sites	4–8	*001–*299	*300–*599	*600–*899	*900–*999
Finished Goods	9	9001–9299	9300–9599	9600–9899	9900–9999

* = 4, 5, 6, 7, 8 for the entire row, corresponding to the site

sibility centers work on several different projects at the same time. You can use account numbers to reflect the multiple activities of a firm with a project-management structure. Imagine that your construction firm has a number of construction projects going on simultaneously for different clients. The firm's framers, plumbers, electricians, and other specialists all work on the various projects. Management must keep track of each project and its specialized framing, plumbing, electrical, and other costs.

Table 6.8   Block Organization of Project-Management Group in Account Number   This block code structure allows any type of cost to be further classified into four broad categories, and then into from 100 to 300 subsidiary categories. Another group of numbers (not shown) could identify a project on which the costs were incurred.

Type of Service	First Digit	Direct Materials	Direct Labor	Indirect Costs	Other
Foundation	1	1000–1299	1300–1599	1600–1899	1900–1999
Framing	2	2000–2299	2300–2599	2600–2899	2900–2999
Electrical	3	3000–3299	3300–3599	3600–3899	3900–3999
Plumbing	4	4000–4299	4300–4599	4600–4899	4900–4999
Roofing	5	5000–5299	5300–5599	5600–5899	5900–5999
Heating/cooling	6	6000–6299	6300–6599	6600–6899	6900–6999
Interior	7	7000–7299	7300–7599	7600–7899	7900–7999
Finishing	8	8000–8299	8300–8599	8600–8899	8900–8999
Architectural	9	9000–9299	9300–9599	9600–9899	9900–9999
Special	0	0000–0299	0300–0599	0600–0899	0900–0999

To serve this purpose, you create separate accounts receivable and cost control accounts and related subledgers for each project. Focusing only on costs, suppose the first two digits for Construction Work in Process are 33. The third and fourth digits identify the specific job, and the last four digits identify expenses, as shown in Table 6.8.

The number 33-43-5750 would refer to Construction Work in Process indirect costs incurred during the roofing of job 43. This table looks a lot like the one for manufacturing, because the principle of design remains the same, using the first group of digits to denote the account's position in the general ledger or trial balance, the middle group of digits to denote the major project involved, and the third group of digits to denote specific types of costs.

Summary

Computer-based accounting systems record, process, and report the information managers use to make decisions, control the risk inherent in their pursuits, and plan for the future. Accounting systems function in agreed-upon ways so that the financial information they provide to external users meets standards known as generally accepted accounting principles, and so that financial information used by internal managers is relevant, complete, and timely.

An organization's accounting system consists of goals, policies, accounting principles, equipment, personnel, inputs and outputs, procedures, and controls. Every organization has a unique system, often viewed as a model of the organization. The factual inputs to accounting systems consist of transaction data. These data, expressed in monetary units, are classified and compiled during processing into performance reports, which describe specific processes or organizational units. A double-entry journalizing system of placing each transaction's monetary amount into at least two accounts helps assure the accuracy of accounting reports. Other requirements found in all accounting systems include collecting data, keeping ledgers, recording supplementary nonfinancial information to describe transactions completely, and preparing financial statements. To speed up accounting processing, an accounting system often groups similar accounts into subsidiary ledgers and represents their cumulative total as the balance of a control account in the general ledger. From the general ledger's summary of assets, equities, revenues, and expenses come the accounting balance sheet and income statement; management performance reports draw on ledgers, subsidiary ledgers, and journals.

Processed accounting information consists of balances classified according to their attributes. These classifications are called accounts and are chosen to preserve and make available information needed for decision making and control. Account numbers help to organize and identify large numbers of accounts. They should follow a consistent hierarchical structure and should identify the general ledger account (block code), location, local control account, and individual account (group codes). Account numbers help to summarize information and link portions of the summarized information to create accounting reports. If the account numbering system is flexible, the chart of accounts can accurately reflect the organization's structure and the decision-making and control responsibilities within it.

Key Terms

accounting controls
accounting entry
accounting system
adjusting entries
applications
audit
balance sheet
block codes
chart of accounts
closing entries
control accounts
double-entry rule
general ledger
generally accepted accounting principles
 (GAAP)

group codes
income statement
journal
journalizing
reversing entry
source documents
statement of cash flows
statement of retained
 earnings
subledger
subsidiary ledger
transaction
transaction processing
trial balance
valuation account

Review Questions

1. Why do virtually all organizations adhere to the same rules to record transactions, describe assets, and prepare financial statements?

2. Why do managers and investors consider it essential to receive information, such as financial statements and performance reports, from an accounting system?

3. Name some elements of the accounting model and the parts of the organization to which they correspond.

4. What are generally accepted accounting principles, and how do they influence accounting systems? Name some of the objectives, and assumptions that lead to accounting principles.

5. What is data collection? What six decisions must be made about data that are to be collected?

6. What is the difference between a transaction and an accounting entry? Name three types of accounting entries that accounting systems

record. Name seven classes of transaction-processing systems, or applications.

7. Identify two purposes of a source document. Name at least one source document for each class of transaction processing system.

8. Describe a journal entry. If source documents exist, what is the point of having journal entries?

9. Name two types of ledgers and explain the difference between them.

10. What are the two major types of data collecting and summarizing accounting books in each transaction processing application?

11. Give an example of an accounting entry for each transaction processing application.

12. Which transaction processing applications handle most internal transactions?

13. Which transaction processing application records unusual or unique accounting entries?

14. Why do organizations need a systematic means of identifying accounts? Why should it be possible to add and delete accounts without affecting the overall structure of the account identifying system?

15. What are the characteristics of a good account classification code?

16. Explain the difference between block and group codes, and identify the uses for which each type is best suited.

Discussion Questions

17. In any accounting entry, the total debits must equal the total credits. Although this requirement promotes the accuracy of accounting, it does not guarantee accuracy. Discuss why not and what additional measures the accounting system should include to improve the accuracy of recording transactions.

18. Why not record all accounting entries in one journal, or at least in journals with the same format?

19. Consider the computer-generated sales journal in Table 6.2. Why are the sales transaction numbers in sequential order, while the customer account numbers are not? Why do you suppose the items sold are listed individually? To what account will the total amount of the sale be posted? Will it be posted as a debit or a credit?

20. The Austin Company purchases manufacturing materials. List at least ten details (such as the type of material) that the Austin Company will want to record about each such purchase. For each detail, state whether it can be part of the accounting entry for that purchase or whether it must be included in the explanation of the accounting entry.

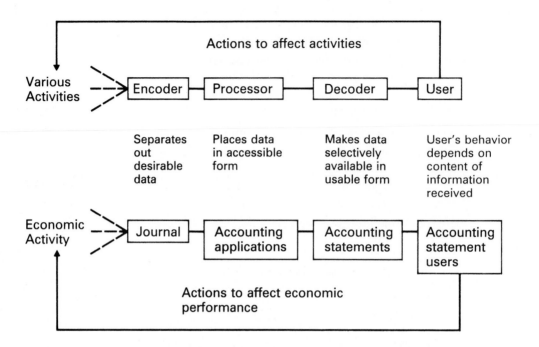

21. Look at the figure at the top of the page, which diagrams a generalized information system and an accounting system, and discuss the analogies between them.

22. What is the relationship between a control account and a subsidiary ledger? How does the control account serve as an interface between the information in the subsidiary ledger and that in the general ledger?

23. Explain how information from two or more transaction processing applications comes together in the general ledger.

24. When financial statements are prepared, the trial balance is divided into two groups of accounts. What is the basis for the division? What is the importance of the imbalance between debits and credits in each of the groups thus created?

25. What do we mean by a "flexible" account coding system? Are account codes in a flexible system hierarchical? What implication does this have for data processing?

26. If an account code contains an identifier for the location to which an account refers, do transactions affecting this account have to be processed there? Why or why not?

27. Refer to Problem 27 in Chapter 3. Here is a sales-account code intended to classify data so that it can be used to answer the questions in that problem.

Digit Significance
  1,2 General-ledger control account identification (one control account for sales)
    3 Product identification (3 products plus maintenance agreements)
    4 Quarter of the year (4 quarters)
    5 Salesperson (four salespeople)
  6,7 Industry (allows up to 99 industries)

Evaluate whether this code actually does enable data to be classified so as to answer the four questions in Problem 27 in Chapter 3.

Problems

28. The following accounting and budget data apply to the Austin Company's semiconductor division for March 1987. Using the performance-report format discussed in Chapter 3, arrange these data into a performance report showing March, year-to-date, and variance totals. Show profit also. Indicate whether variances are favorable or unfavorable.

    Budgeted sales for March were $54,000. The actual cost of sales for the same month was $32,000. Budgeted administrative costs were $20,000; actual administrative costs were $25,000. Budgeted cost of sales were $30,000. Actual March sales were 110% of the amount budgeted. All year-to-date budgeted amounts are 280% of the budgeted March amounts. Year-to-date actual sales were $150,000; cost of sales, $90,000; administrative costs, $75,000.

29. Which transaction processing application would handle each of the following transactions by the Alabama Company?
    (a) Purchase of office supplies from Acme Company for $1,100.
    (b) Payment of $12,300 in taxes to the city of Mobile.
    (c) Mr. Smith remits $3,200 owed on account.
    (d) Employees' wages for the week of January 23, in the amount of $19,500, set up as Wages Payable.
    (e) Premium of $14,000 on three-year property-damage insurance policy paid to Harper Insurance Agency.
    (f) One thirty-sixth of the $14,000 insurance premium, amortized and charged to January expense.

30. Which transaction processing application would handle each of the following transactions for the Alabama Company?
    (a) Eastern Division of Alabama Company sells one of its tractors to Fred Farmer on credit for $13,000.
    (b) Alabama Company refinances $350,000 of its accounts receivable in exchange for $300,000 in immediate cash.

(c) Alabama Company's Menard tractor plant transfers $250,000 from various work-in-process accounts to several finished goods inventory accounts.

(d) The company is successful in winning a tax refund of $346.28 from the local school board, in the form of a check for deposit.

(e) Checks are processed for $15,200 total wages for the week of January 23. (Why would the total of these checks be less than the total payroll for the same week, $19,500?)

(f) Three checks for a total of $4,300 are sent to the U.S. Treasury, the Medical Insurance Company, and the Pension Assurance Corporation, representing partial fringe-benefit remittances for the January 23 payroll.

31. For each of the Alabama Company's following activities, name the appropriate transaction processing application and show the journalized transaction.

(a) The company remits the interest for one month at 9.1 percent on a $1.2 million debt to Superbank, Inc.

(b) A new frame bender is acquired from Clark Machinery, Inc., in exchange for a four-year note at 13 percent annually in the amount of $400,000.

(c) The company sells 350 box blades to dealers for $500 each in exchange for promises to pay in full in thirty days.

(d) Last year Alabama Company bought a $1.5-million corporate jet. The pilot's annual salary is $48,000, paid monthly. His paycheck is written along with the executive payroll. (Two applications and accounting entries)

(e) Full remittance is received on Root and Hogg's purchase of two F-41 earth movers, sold three month ago for $110,000 each. The remittance includes interest at 1.5 percent per month compounded monthly, for two full months.

(f) A certificate of deposit of $500,000, which bore interest for three months at 12-percent annual simple interest, comes due and is cashed.

32. The table on the next page shows a complete journal of credit sales transactions for Mesquite Company, a retailer of auto supplies, for June 24, 19X6.

Required:

(a) Why are the receipt numbers in sequential order?

(b) What were the total sales of Item A100?

(c) What were the total postings to the credit sales subledger?

(d) Assume that the accounts receivable control account is $315,000 before these entries are posted. How much will it be after they are posted?

Date	Receipt Number	Sold to	Customer Account	Total Sale	Item ID	Unit Price	Qty	Item Amount
6/24	02265	Arrow Mfg.	5678	$ 5129.36	A100	$ 990.12	4	$3,960.48
					A205	$ 300.00	2	$ 600.00
					Tax	6%		$ 273.63
					Shipping			$ 295.25
6/24	02266	Marx Bros.	1268	$ 1112.80	A350	$ 98.00	10	$ 980.00
					Tax	6%		$ 58.80
					Shipping			$ 74.00
6/24	02267	Alabama Co.	3258	$ 966.00	B005	$ 34.95	24	$ 838.80
					Tax	6%		$ 50.28
					Shipping			$ 76.92
6/24	02268	Elk Co.	5578	$20,917.87	A100	$ 990.12	10	$9,901.20
					B006	$8,200.00	1	$8,200.00
					C003	$ 9.50	80	$ 760.00
					Tax	6%		$1,131.67
					Shipping			$ 925.00

(e) Assume that the shipping payable control account is $13,215 before the merchandise in the above entries is shipped. How much will it be after they are shipped?

(f) Who would be responsible for journalizing these transactions? For posting them?

Case: Kathy's Art Productions

Kathy Ndebe needs a system to keep track of her business expenses. She does painting, matting, and framing in her studio and sells paintings and prints at art shows, through galleries, and by mail order in response to ads placed in various art publications. She buys paper, brushes, and paints from local suppliers and travels to galleries, painting sites, and supply stores.

Required:

(a) Make a short list of the financial information Kathy should have about her art business.

(b) List the subledgers and general ledger accounts Kathy should have.

(c) List the source documents and journals she should have.

(d) Describe an account coding plan that would meet her requirements.

PART 2

Accounting Applications

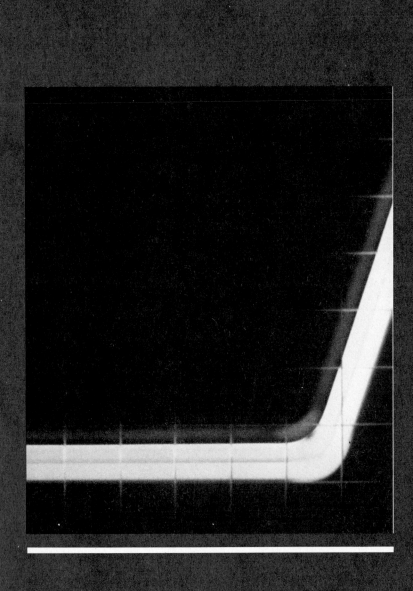

If management is to benefit from the ideas presented in Part 1, it cannot be content with a general ledger system alone. The accounting system must group similar transactions into specific processing activities, called "applications." Each application is created to handle one class of transactions very efficiently. Thus, Chapter 7 describes systems that focus on transactions arising from credit sales; Chapter 8, transactions arising from purchasing; Chapter 9, transactions arising from manufacturing and maintaining inventories; and Chapter 10, fund-accounting systems used by certain not-for-profit and government entities.

Each chapter in Part 2 starts by describing the underlying business function that its application serves and then presents the data elements and structure required by the application, the application processes that use the data, and the application reports used by management. In addition, each chapter emphasizes a particular type of detail as it describes its application. For example, Chapter 7 emphasizes data base structure; Chapter 8 emphasizes computer-implemented data links; Chapter 9 emphasizes account codes as record keys; and Chapter 10 emphasizes reporting from the processed data.

Part 2 contains the following chapters:

7 Credit Sales, Accounts Receivable, and Billing
8 Purchasing and Accounts Payable
9 Manufacturing, Cost Accounting, and Inventory
10 Fund Accounting Systems for Not-for-Profit (NFP) Organizations

Credit Sales, Accounts Receivable, and Billing

Learning Objectives

After studying this chapter, you should be able to

- Define and explain examples of linked records, a data flow diagram, process descriptions, and report formats.

- Describe the files, processes, and reports in an on-line credit sales, accounts receivable, and billing application.

- Explain the advantages and disadvantages, in a given situation, of using centralized or decentralized data processing, batch or on-line processing, cycle billing, and lockboxes.

- Describe and explain the use of various management reports, including the processing report and reports of unprocessed transactions, aging of accounts receivable, cash collections, and sales performance.

- Construct an account code number that captures much of the information required for sales performance reports.

- Make and justify the major accounting entries, including correction of data entry errors.

The credit sales, accounts receivable, and billing application (often abbreviated to credit sales application or accounting receivable application) supports specialized organizational functions, in this case the marketing and cash flow activities. The data and information processing any application provides is called *support*. The credit sales, accounts receivable, and billing provides support by recording credit sales transactions, calculating total sales of various product types, and tracking the credit status and balances due from credit customers. This support is important because most sales take place on a credit basis—that is, cash changes hands *after* delivery of goods or services.

This application creates reports that provide valuable control feedback to management planning, financial planning and control, production or purchasing, customer service, credit approval, and in some cases, product design (about features and services customers prefer). The reports support marketing, in particular, by locating buyers, encouraging sales, authorizing shipment of goods or services, and preparing invoices and statements for credit customers.

The accounts receivable application includes the following processes:

- Credit approval (deciding to whom to allow credit privileges, and in what amount)
- Order entry (accepting sales transactions on a credit basis)
- Billing (informing credit customers that it is time to pay, and how much to pay)
- Crediting accounts (posting cash remittances)
- Reporting to management (summarizing to management the credit sales and accounts receivable activity)

This chapter describes these processes in detail. It also shows how they help fulfill management's financial control, reporting, and informa-

Figure 7.1   Four Ways to Represent the Same Credit Sales Data for One Customer   All four of these representations show how to represent accounts-

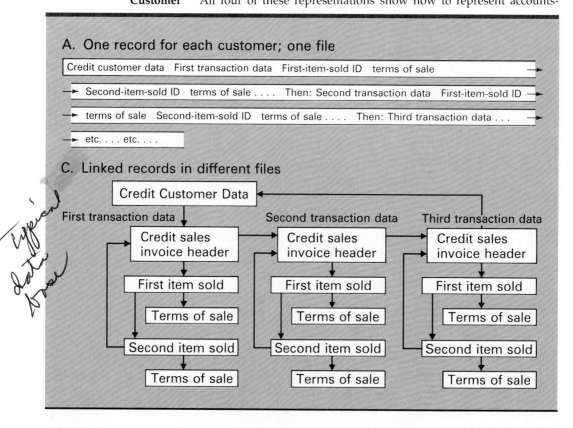

tion needs, and it demonstrates how to prepare reports, explains the use of account codes, and discusses how credit sales records can help in analyzing an organization's sales activities. Specific accounting entries are also described.

The Data Base Approach

There are numerous ways to organize, process, and store accounts receivable data in a computer. Three of these are shown in Figure 7.1. The first way would be to store all data in one file, with one record per customer. Each customer record would be very long. In practice this way is not used because of the difficulty of anticipating how many transactions will occur. The second way would be to use multiple records per customer in a single file without record links. If you could not use record links and were limited

receivable transaction data. Parts A, B, and C are logically different; part D is logically equivalent to C, which is the most flexible and modern.

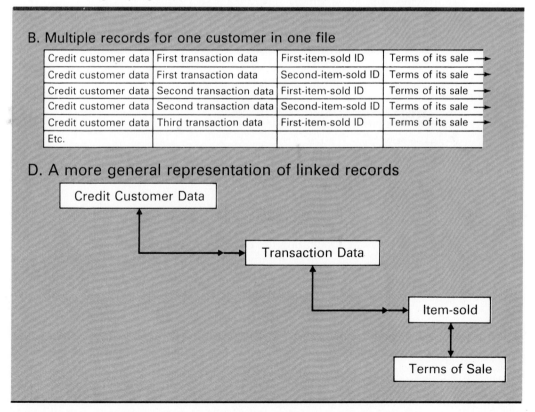

B. Multiple records for one customer in one file

Credit customer data	First transaction data	First-item-sold ID	Terms of its sale →
Credit customer data	First transaction data	Second-item-sold ID	Terms of its sale →
Credit customer data	Second transaction data	First-item-sold ID	Terms of its sale →
Credit customer data	Second transaction data	Second-item-sold ID	Terms of its sale →
Credit customer data	Third transaction data	First-item-sold ID	Terms of its sale →
Etc.			

D. A more general representation of linked records

Credit Customer Data

Transaction Data

Item-sold

Terms of Sale

to one file to hold records both on accounts receivable customers and on credit sales transactions, you would have to establish a separate record for each item sold in each distinctive transaction. The complete credit customer information that would appear once in a master file record (as described in Chapter 5) would be repeated in each of these records. If the organization made fifty credit sales to the customer, each credit sale would create a record, and each record would contain all the customer's master file information plus the data unique to this credit sale. Clearly, such a file would contain mostly repetitive information.

The third way utilizes the data base approach to avoid this excessive repetition. Similar data are placed in separate records and then linked to other data as required by the specific transactions. In Figure 7.1, part C, the credit-sale process uses four files to store data from transactions it processes. To make the information stored in these files usable, the data base approach uses links to connect records in the same and different files. Chapter 5 introduced you to techniques used in linking records and files. This section discusses how these techniques can be applied in an accounts receivable application to establish appropriate connections between files. In general, a design incorporating links is desirable when a large and growing number of similar records is associated with a single record of a different type. This kind of one-to-many relationship exists, for instance, between the credit-customer data record and the transaction-data records of transactions with that customer.

Linking Records in Different Files

If separate linked records were used for each accounts receivable transaction, they would contain four kinds of data:

1. Credit customer data such as name, address, and credit limit. These data will appear in the approved-credit-customer record.
2. Transaction data such as invoice number, date of sale, location of sale, salesperson, and shipping instructions. These data will appear in the credit-sales-invoice-header record.
3. Item-sold data, including the item identifying number and description. These data will appear in the items-sold record.
4. Terms-of-sale data, such as the quantity, price, and payment terms of each item sold. These data will appear in the terms-of-sale record.

In Figure 7.1, part C, the credit-customer-data record is a master record and contains permanent information such as customer name, address, and credit limit. It contains a link, shown as an arrow, to the first transaction record, shown on the left. This transaction record contains information about the transaction as a whole—such as its date, its location, and the person making the sale. It in turn is linked to the second transaction record, which is linked to the third transaction record. In the illustration, the third transaction record is also the last one, so it is linked back to the credit-customer-data record.

Each transaction record is linked to the items that were sold in that transaction. In the illustration, each transaction involved the sale of two items. These are identified as first item sold and second item sold. The item-sold records contain the identity of the item. To reflect unit price, discount, quantity sold in that transaction, shipping terms, and other details, a terms-of-sale record is linked to each item-sold record. Examine Figure 7.1, part C carefully to find all these records and links.

How are links established? The general principle of linking relies on each record, in each file, including a unique identifying key field. The link between the credit-customer-data record and the first transaction record then consists of a field in the credit-customer-data record that contains the value of the key field of the first transaction record. The first transaction record contains a field reserved for the key-field value of the second transaction record for this same customer. The number of the credit-sale invoice can serve as the unique transaction key field, since no two transactions have the same invoice number. The last transaction—the third one in Figure 7.1, part C—contains only the customer identifying number to signify that it is the final transaction for this customer. The links from transaction record to item-sold records are formed in the same manner; the linking field could contain the unique inventory numbers assigned to products offered for sale. The terms-of-sale records are linked by unique numbers based on the inventory number of the product to which they apply. For example, if an item's inventory number is 8808, the corresponding terms-of-sale record could be identified by the value 8808-TOS.

There are many ways to represent record links; Figure 7.1, part D shows the same situation as part C in a more general way. In this representation, the number of arrowheads and the directions in which they point convey important information about the links. The double arrowhead means that multiple records of that type can link to the type of record at the other end of the arrow. One arrowhead means that only one record of that type can link. Since a customer can have multiple credit sale transactions, two arrowheads point from the credit-customer-data record to the transaction data record. Since only one customer can be involved in a transaction, only one arrowhead points back from the transaction data record to the credit-customer-data record.

Links also connect all records required to describe a *single* transaction. The credit-sale invoice record for a given credit sale does not contain a list of the items sold; instead, it contains a *link* to a record in the items-sold file. This record contains a description of the first item sold and a link to the record of the next item sold, and so on, for all the items in the trans-

Figure 7.2   Chains of Data
In this figure you can find the following chains: customers, invoices for a single customer, items sold and listed on one invoice, and items paid for by a single remittance. Although not shown, there would also be a chain of remittances for a single customer.

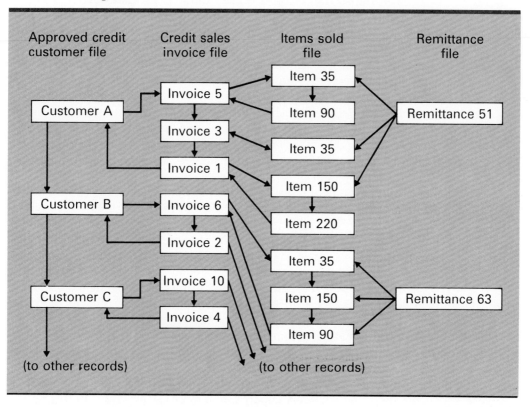

action. Each item-sold record contains a link to a record in the terms-of-sale file that shows the quantity of each item sold and general information such as a price change or a discount for quantity purchases. Other relevant records, such as remittances or late charges, are similarly linked. This sequence of links combines all the records describing each transaction into a chain. All transactions are linked together to create a single chain of data, as shown in Figure 7.2.

Links in Processing and Reporting

To prepare a customer statement, the billing process reads the chain of data generated by the customer's activity. The process moves through each customer's chain, accumulating the individual pieces of data from numerous records and files—the sale amounts, payments recorded, returns, allowances, interest, late charges—and transferring these data to a customer statement form.

Chaining keeps large quantities of data from numerous files readily available for computer use. It also has another advantage. System designers can easily insert special pointers to link invoice records in new combinations. Thus the computer can be directed to produce special reports listing, for example, all sales over a specified dollar amount (for purposes of thanking those customers), or all sales in a certain geographic area or industry (so that the organization's sales can be compared with those of competitors), or sales made by specific salespeople (for comparison of performance and computation of competitive bonuses).

The same report output could be generated from direct-access files in two other ways. First, the system could undertake special sorts or searches of entire files to locate, separate out, and summarize the desired items. The second method is to use temporary pointer and index files called *report generators*, which instruct the system to review each file and find all data that meet the search criteria, compile a list of pointers to those data, copy these links into a report format, and use them to prepare the report.

Table 7.1 compares three commonly used structures for linking information: the data base method, the files-only method, and the file-of-report links method. In the data base method, which requires more mem-

Table 7.1   Comparison of Three Information Linking Structures

Structure	Advantages	Disadvantages
Data base method of embedded pointers	Fast and convenient Adapts easily to changing requirements	Requires a lot of internal and external memory Requires more computer power
Files only—sorts and searches	Simple file structure Efficient use of storage Lower startup cost	Complex instructions to system Repetitive effort each time a report is needed; higher operating cost Time consuming to use Least flexible
File of report links	Simple file structure Inexpensive setup	Report formats valid for current data structure only

ory and computer power than the other two methods, pointers are embedded in the file design. In the files-only method, selective sorts or searches substitute for pointers. In the file-of-report-links method, pointers reside only in an external report-related file, not in the data file.

The remainder of the chapter illustrates the use of pointers embedded in a data base. However, you will benefit from keeping the other two methods in mind and envisioning how they would handle the same requirements. In general, the data base approach is preferable as a general-purpose way to provide frequently issued, frequently changing reports. The other two approaches may serve system developers who prefer not to use the data base approach, perhaps in an application that has a narrow scope and less need for flexibility.

Data Flow Diagram

As we indicated in Chapter 2, a data flow diagram shows the relationships between files, processes, reports, and interfaces with other applications. These relationships involve additional files beyond the four already described. For purposes of simplicity, the data flow diagram in Figure 7.3 shows only the major files: stock items, approved credit customers, credit-sales-invoice headers, items sold, terms of sale, shipping advice, and customer payments on account. As you will see shortly, other files, not shown, may include unprocessed transactions (one or more for each process), back-up copies of all files, and paper documents from which information may have been transcribed. To facilitate your understanding of the relationships between the various files and processes, please study the following short explanation of Figure 7.3, then refer to the figure to locate each application component as it is described in detail in the remainder of the chapter.

Start by looking in the upper left-hand corner of Figure 7.3, at the oval shape labeled order entry. The oval shape denotes a process within an application. The order entry process may capture sales transaction data as—or even before—the sale occurs. This process uses information from a file describing the current approved credit customers and places data describing the sale into other files. The approved-credit-customers file is maintained by a process labeled credit approval.

You can recognize the files in this diagram by the horizontal parallel bars enclosing their names. Horizontal bars with "horns" denote an interface with another application; in this diagram, interfaces provide connections to the shipping application and the cash receipts application. The interface connection is actually one or more files that both applications use. The shipping application, for example, uses data from three credit sales application files and places data in a fourth file. A report generator process produces various reports, including the customer statements.

Figure 7.3 Credit Sales, Accounts Receivable, and Billing
This data flow diagram shows the relationships of files, processes, interfaces, and certain reports in this application.

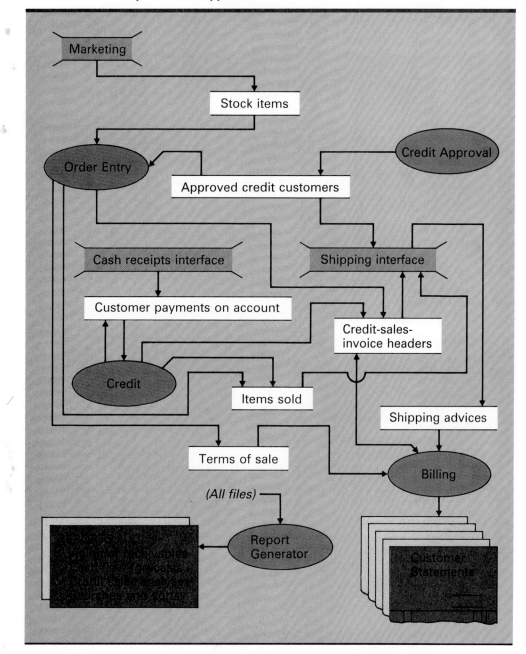

TEST

Files Used in This Application   *7 files*

1. Approved Credit Customers

The approved-credit-customers file (often called the *customer file* for short) contains one record for each customer account that has been approved for credit. Each customer record includes the information necessary to identify, ship to, bill, and correspond with that customer. The account balances of credit customers in this file are summarized in the accounts receivable subsidiary ledger's control account in the general ledger. Thus the customer file is part of the accounts receivable subsidiary ledger. The customer record should include at least the following fields:

> Unique credit account number (record key)
> Name
> Address for statements
> Date credit established
> Credit limit
> Date credit last reviewed
> Previous credit limit
> Credit-history fields: slow payment, returned checks, notes payable,
>   and other information bearing on the credit rating
> Special-needs fields that describe business customers: industry, key
>   executives, shipping address, and other data for understanding the
>   customer's needs and for sales and marketing analysis
> Current account balance
> Links to credit-sales-invoice headers (in a separate file)

2. Credit-Sales-Invoice Headers

The credit-sales-invoice header file contains one record for each credit sales invoice, which in turn represents one transaction with an approved credit customer. These records are called **headers** because each one contains information common to other records (in the items-sold file) that are linked to it. Each invoice record is related by a pointer, which can be the customer credit-account number, to a customer record in the approved-credit-customers file. A special form—either on the computer screen or paper— is the source document for each transaction. In older systems, the salesperson records a sale manually on a sales invoice form, and a data entry person transcribes the data into a computer file. In newer systems, the salesperson enters the sales data directly to a computer program, which edits the data for accuracy, creates a record in the sales journal file, and prints a paper sales invoice, a report of the sale, or both. A record in this file should include the following fields:

Unique sales invoice number (the record key)

Date of sale

Customer's account number (the record key in the approved-credit-customer file)

Location of sale

Salesperson

Total invoice amount

Pointer to customer-payment-on-account record in cash receipts file, where payment on this invoice will be shown

Pointer to first item sold

3. Items Sold

Records in the items-sold file describe all specific items sold. Items recorded on a credit sale invoice are identified in the credit-sales-invoice header by links to the appropriate items-sold record. We will review two different designs for the items-sold file.

Design 1. Since the organization knows the identity of each item it sells, the items-sold file could consist of one record for each unique product (in this case, we would more properly call it the stock-items file). Each credit-sales-invoice header record contains a separate pointer to each stock item sold in the transaction. This file structure satisfies the minimum accounting requirement of locating items sold on credit so as to bill or make adjustments on account balances. A one-to-many relationship would exist between the invoice record and the several stock-item records for items sold in that particular transaction. A given record in the stock-items file would be "pointed to" by every sales invoice header corresponding to a sale of the item in question. In other words, the sales invoice header would contain one pointer for each type of item sold. The stock-items record, however, would not point back to the large number of transactions in which that item was sold; to do so would make too large a demand on computer memory.

This data structure is efficient in its requirements for on-line storage. However, it *does not support analysis of sales of particular products*. In other words, you could not begin with product A in the stock-items file and access any of the data about transactions involving that product.

Design 2. Since many companies need exactly the kind of information design 1 does *not* provide, system designers have corrected the weakness. Producing this information requires some data duplication, namely two files that list the items sold. The first file, as in design 1, would be a complete file describing every item stocked for sale. (This file is not shown in the data flow diagram in Figure 7.3. The second file called the "items-sold" file, would be created as transactions occur. When recording a transaction, the order entry process would first generate a credit-sales-invoice header and then a separate record in the items-sold file for each item sold. This items-sold record would be short, containing fields for the following attributes:

> Unique item identifier (record key)
> Abbreviated description of item (may be omitted)
> Pointer to credit-sales-invoice header
> Pointer to record in the terms-of-sale file (see below)
> Pointer to next item sold in this transaction (or end-of-chain symbol)
> Pointer to corresponding record in the shipping-advice file (supplied after shipping occurs; see Figure 7.3)

The first two fields could be copied from the stock-items file (maintained by the marketing function, which decides which products can be sold). The links back to other files would allow this transaction-generated items-sold file to be sorted by invoice number and to be combined with data from the credit-sales-invoice header and the approved-credit-customer record to produce useful sales analyses for management. This design is preferable for its utility in the management information system, as well as for its service to the accounting function. These short items-sold records could also point to the stock-items records for quick access to a complete description of products sold to specific customers.

Figure 7.4 compares these two alternatives. In both cases, each record in the stock-items file may be referenced by many other records. In Design 1, the credit-sales-invoice header refers to the stock-items records, which do not point back to specific invoices. In Design 2, the short items-sold records are able to relate a stock item to a specific invoice and also to a record in the terms-of-sale file.

Terms of Sale

You may have noticed that the invoice and items-sold records contained no fields for quantity sold, price, or special discounts or terms. These data are recorded in a separate terms-of-sale file, which contains one or more records corresponding to each record in the stock-items file. Each items-sold record will be linked to a stock-item record, which in turn is linked to that item's terms-of-sale record. The fields in each terms-of-sale record should include the following:

> Unique item identifier
> Terms-of-sale identifier
> (these first two fields jointly constitute the record key)
> Unit price
> Quantity discount or other variables affecting price
> Quantity sold to customer in this transaction

Figure 7.4 Alternative Invoice-to-Items-Sold Relationships
In Design 1, all information about items sold is contained in the stock-items records. In Design 2, this information is partially copied into unique records linked to invoices. Design 2 allows more processing and reporting flexibility.

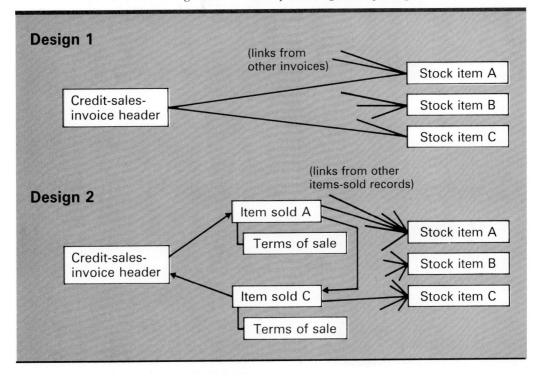

The first three or four fields might be copied from a sales contract with the customer or from records in a file of sales terms and conditions (not shown on the data flow diagram in Figure 7.3). The quantity sold would be supplied by the salesperson during order entry, and the process software would supply the pointer. By placing terms-of-sale information in special records, the organization can target specific items for temporary sales, discounts, and price changes, yet maintain control over them all.

Shipping Advice

A shipping advice file records the delivery of items to the customer. Delivery may occur in one of two ways: the customer may accept the items at the time of purchase, or a shipper may transport the items to the customer. If the customer takes the items, the shipping-advice record is created in the order entry process and may be known as a delivery receipt;

if the items are to be delivered, the record is created during the shipping process. Fields in a shipping-advice record should include the following:

Unique shipping-advice-record identifier
Credit-sales-invoice-header identifier
   (combined, these first two fields serve as the record key)
Taken by customer (yes/no)
Date of shipment
Pointer to items-sold record for each item shipped

Since some orders may be shipped in more than one batch, there may be more than one shipping advice for each invoice (and occasionally even for each item). Once the shipping-advice record exists, showing shipment or receipt by the customer, the customer receives a statement requesting payment.

Customer Payments on Account

The customer-payments-on-account file, prepared by the cash receipts application, functions as an interface between credit sales and cash receipts. The file's format can be read and used by both applications. Because customers usually pay on invoices rather than statements, records in the payments file must be related to records in the credit-sales-invoice headers file. Fields of a record in this file should include the following:

Unique payment identifier (record key)
Date received
Amount received
Pointer to corresponding credit-sales-invoice header

If customers often don't pay the full amount of an invoice, a process and the files used and maintained by it should explain the difference between invoice and payment amounts. An example would be an agreement that a buyer would remit a fixed amount monthly to the seller in exchange for prompt delivery of merchandise, with the exact sales amount to be determined later. This technique is used in long-term construction, research, and development contracts and in certain time-sensitive manufacturing situations described in Chapter 9.

Unprocessed Transactions

Occasionally, because of error, omission, or some other deficiency, input data are not processed completely. The records containing these unprocessed transactions are not posted; instead, such records enter a special file containing only transactions that could not be processed. Records sent to this file retain all the information they contained when they were created; in addition, the process adds fields that describe why the records couldn't be posted, to the extent that the computer can determine why. Later, records in this file will be examined and, if possible, made error free and processable.

Back-up Copies

Every application has the need to make back-up copies—duplicates of existing files—for data-security control and to protect against data loss. Back-up files duplicate the operating files containing processed transactions as well as other files. Because accounts receivable are a major asset of most organizations, it is especially important to protect the files that document this asset. These files should be protected by means of special back-up and security measures such as the following:

1. A duplicate copy of the current version should be stored in a secure off-site location.
2. The two previous versions and intervening update files should also be stored in secure off-site locations, but not where the duplicate of the current version is kept.
3. The supporting audit trail should be duplicated and/or stored securely off-site, so that the company can recreate the master file by processing intervening transactions against a previous copy of the accounts receivable customer file.

Back-up need not be limited to computer readable files. Many accounts receivable applications generate paper documents that describe credit sales transactions, customer account status, cash remittances, and debits and credits to customer accounts. These documents are called source documents, a term that applies to any form, approval, or other paper that supports transaction processing. As back-up material, source documents are cumbersome, yet provide the ultimate security against a catastrophic loss of all magnetic media.

Computerized Accounts Receivable Processes

As mentioned earlier, five major *processes* jointly create and maintain the records in the files described. These processes depend on computers for timely and accurate recording, posting, classification, storage, and retrieval. They are credit approval, which should precede any credit sale to a particular customer; order entry and edit, to ensure correctness of the entry; billing (sending statements to customers); credit (posting customer payments); and generating reports. Two other, less frequently used processes are revising the control account balance in the general ledger to agree with the accounts receivable subsidiary ledger and posting miscellaneous adjustments that result from shortages, lost shipments or payments, returns, or other causes. This section discusses each of these processes.

1. Credit Approval

This process adds records for new credit customers to the approved-credit-customers file, modifies existing records there to reflect changed credit terms, and deletes records of customers whose credit has been withdrawn or has not been used for a set period.

Credit approval should be the responsibility of the finance function; it should not be the responsibility of sales personnel. Therefore, this process operates independently of marketing. One benefit of this separation is that credit-granting standards cannot be relaxed or compromised to increase sales volume at the expense of account collectability.

The records in the approved-credit-customers file are an important resource for the entire organization, and management ought to emphasize keeping this file current. In most organizations, credit approvals or changes are authorized by the treasurer or someone within the marketing function who is not directly involved in sales. After a credit application has been approved, the credit manager converts the information on the credit application form into a computer record in the approved-credit-customers file. Changes in credit status—credit limit increases or decreases, or reversal of credit approval—are processed the same way. Some computer programs periodically review records of credit customer purchases and payment and automatically change credit limits. To verify that a customer has credit approval, the salesperson can refer to the approved-credit-customers file prior to every credit sale.

2. Order Entry and Edit

The order entry process adds records to the credit-sales-invoice header, items-sold, terms-of-sale, and shipping-advice files for each credit sales transaction. This process is the set of procedures and controls that governs how salespeople must record the essential attributes of each sale. It relies on the marketing function to assign identifying numbers and prices to items available for sale, which are listed in the stock-items file. Order entry reads this file but does not change it. To simplify the order entry process, the computer accepts entry of data in their natural order, then opens each file and modifies existing records or creates new ones.

To the greatest extent possible, only records that contain no common errors detectable by routine editing should enter files. The edits examine data entries to ensure that all fields have entries, that numeric fields have the proper number of digits, and that dollar values or physical quantities are reasonable.

For example, the data entered for a credit-sales-invoice header record should not be accepted until editing has made certain that

- A credit sale transaction took place.
- The customer had valid approved credit.
- All information required by the transaction was available.

If the entry does not meet all three conditions, the system should place the incomplete record in the unprocessed-transactions file. When editing and record creation are complete, this process has posted the credit sale.

Billing

The billing process produces the invoices and statements that are sent to the customer for payment. To prepare these documents, the computer scans the shipping-advices file. For each new advice that has not been previously processed, the billing process seeks the credit-sales-invoice header. The process also seeks—through pointers contained in the header—the corresponding items-sold, terms-of-sale, and customer payment records relating to that shipping advice. Then, from these records, the billing process composes the statement to the customer.

Credit (Posting Customer Payments)

The credit process updates records in the credit-sales-invoice header file. The objective of this process is to ensure that customers' remittances are deducted from their account balances. The credit process uses the records in the customer payments file prepared by the cash receipts application. Each record in this file describes a cash payment, recorded as soon as possible after receipt. The credit process selects a cash payment record, then looks in the credit-sales-invoice file for invoices of the credit customer in question. When the invoice corresponding to the remittance has been located, the process adjusts the records accordingly and selects another cash payment for processing. The process continues until it has handled all cash remittances. There are two alternative designs for adjustment of the records: balance forward and open invoice (often called "open item").

In a **balance-forward design**, the credit process reduces the customer's outstanding balance to reflect the amount in the cash remittance record. The customer's new balance will appear in the approved-credit-customers master record. Simplicity, economy, and processing speed are the strengths of the balance-forward design. Its weakness is that the supporting details for each customer balance are not in computer-accessible records. Should anyone question the accuracy of the outstanding customer balance, the supporting details would have to be found manually. In actual practice, most balance-forward applications provide open-item detail for the current period's transactions, with a beginning balance as the balance forward.

In an **open-invoice design**, the credit process recomputes the customer's outstanding balance. The customer payment is compared to the corresponding sales invoice, which is marked paid by linking it to a cash-receipts record in another file. The computer then examines all of the customer's invoices and accumulates the amount now outstanding on all unpaid invoices. Because the covered invoices have been marked paid, the customer's balance is reduced by the amount of the most recent remittance. Pointers in the sales-invoice records identify customer-payments-on-account. The open-invoice design gives the organization complete computer access to information about customer remittances. The strength of the open-invoice design is its computer-accessible record of the details of each customer's account; its weaknesses are its higher cost, relative complexity, and greater on-line data storage requirements.

Reports Generated for Management

The report-generation processes assemble information from the files for broad managerial scrutiny as well as for specific marketing, accounting, and credit-management purposes. There are three broad types of reports: periodic preformatted reports, on-request preformatted reports, and on-request custom reports. A *periodic report* is prepared automatically at regular intervals: daily, weekly, or monthly, for example. Data processing prepares an *on-request report* only when someone asks for it. *Preformatted reports* have a standard format that can be used whenever the report is prepared; *custom reports* are prepared in a form that is not used often enough to warrant advance preparation and storage of a format.

Periodic preformatted reports include regularly issued performance reports and interim financial statements. Product and regional sales analyses and capital investment analyses are examples of on-request preformatted reports. A report showing the additional capital required to finance higher product inventories is an example of an on-request custom report.

The report-generation processes can be grouped together according to report frequency and run on a regular schedule. This chapter's final section looks at examples of each type of report.

Control-Account Revision

The preceding chapter explained the role and purpose of control accounts. The **accounts receivable control account** record in the general ledger holds the sum of the cash balances customers owe as a result of credit sales. The control-account balance is the sum of all current account balances in the approved-credit-customers file; that is, it represents the amounts owed the organization for all items invoiced and shipped but not yet paid for. Obviously, after any process that involves the approved-credit-customers file, the system should adjust the control-account balance in the general ledger to agree with the total of all accounts in the subsidiary ledger (the approved-credit-customers file and open invoices linked to it). Each time the subledger is posted, the summary of postings is used to adjust the control-account balance. The following relationship should hold:

Old accounts receivable control-account balance	+	Sum of all debits (credit sales this period)	–	Sums of all credits (customer payments this period)	=	Sum of all invoices corresponding to shipping advices for which reimbursement not yet received	=	New accounts receivable control-account balance

Miscellaneous Adjustments

Miscellaneous adjustments record events such as lost shipments and the return of items sold. There is a separate process for each adjustment, but all of them should operate in a manner that fulfills these following four requirements:

- The process accepts and edits the necessary data.
- It places the data in the appropriate files and records.
- It creates and preserves an audit trail by means of a dated log showing the entries and who authorized them.
- It generates any reports that are required.

Application Design Features

The information system's ability to generate reports depends to a large extent on its design features. A few design features can potentially influence all processes and reporting capabilities. Two such features are account number encoding and the structure of an application and its segments.

Account Number Encoding

In Chapter 6, you learned how an account coding system is used to classify and find accounts in a trial balance. Account coding is also extremely valuable in a transaction journal, where it allows transactions to be classified and reclassified into sets which, on analysis, yield important information to management. For example, most organizations would like to learn as much as possible about factors that lead to or predict sales. You can manually tally much of this information by sifting through sales invoices and/or the accounts receivable master file, but it is faster, easier, and more accurate to extract summary information from data base processing of the application's files. The simplest way to do so is to use a group code account-number structure and design part of the credit sale identifying number to encode the most routine data you'll require in preparing reports. In addition to the subsidiary ledger and sales invoice groups, the transaction code could include groups to describe the region, sale date, customer, salesperson, and product information, all encoded at the time of sale by assembling the sale identification number for various attributes of the sale.

For example, look at the nine-digit number shown in Table 7.2, which, without loss of relevance, omits the subsidiary ledger and sales invoice number groups, which are not used in any of the analyses that this section describes. To unlock the power of this sale-identifying-number design, note that each of the seven elements in Table 7.2 presents a different attribute of the sale. The first element (top line) specifies whether the item is an actual sale or a sales prediction that has become part of the budget. The second element indicates when the sale was made. The remaining elements allow identification of the sales region, intra-region district, salesperson, customer industry, and the product itself.

When these elements have been assigned values and every credit sale invoice includes such an account number, they can be used to separate the records into whatever classifications management wants.

The credit-sales-invoice records, listed in record-key order, will provide budgeted and actual sales by period, region, district, salesperson, customer code, and product code. Many firms predict sales by major

Table 7.2   Design of a Nine-Digit, Seven-Element Sale Identifying Number, Omitting Subsidiary Ledger and Sales Invoice Groups
A sales number such as this one can be customized in length, elements included, and element sequence to fit the needs of individual organizations.

Element	Digit	Values	Classification
1	1	0 or 1	Budget or actual
2	2,3	1–52	Week of the year
3	4	0–9	Sales region
4	5	0–9	District within region
5	6	0–9	Salesperson within district
6	7	0–9	Customer industry classification
7	8,9	00–99	Product identification

clients, by industries, by geographical regions, and by time periods. This type of code helps sales management compare actual performance with predicted sales by comparing the actual totals of invoices representing sales with the totals predicted for the classifications corresponding to these totals. Such comparisons take the form of answers to questions like the three that follow:

- How did our sales staff in regions 4, 5, and 6 perform during weeks 6 through 10 in selling product 43 to industries 8 and 9?

  The answer to this question is calculated by summing the amounts on invoices with the numbers as shown below, where "n" means "all values in this element":

Region 4	Region 5	Region 6
1-06-4-n-n-8-43	1-06-5-n-n-8-43	1-06-6-n-n-8-43
1-07-4-n-n-8-43	1-07-5-n-n-8-43	1-07-6-n-n-8-43
1-08-4-n-n-8-43	1-08-5-n-n-8-43	1-08-6-n-n-8-43
1-09-4-n-n-8-43	1-09-5-n-n-8-43	1-09-6-n-n-8-43
1-10-4-n-n-8-43	1-10-5-n-n-8-43	1-10-6-n-n-8-43
1-06-4-n-n-9-43	1-06-5-n-n-9-43	1-06-6-n-n-9-43
1-07-4-n-n-9-43	1-07-5-n-n-9-43	1-07-6-n-n-9-43
1-08-4-n-n-9-43	1-08-5-n-n-9-43	1-08-6-n-n-9-43
1-09-4-n-n-9-43	1-09-5-n-n-9-43	1-09-6-n-n-9-43
1-10-4-n-n-9-43	1-10-5-n-n-9-43	1-10-6-n-n-9-43

- How did actual sales compare to budgeted sales during week 19?

  The answer to this question is the difference between the sum of the amounts of invoices in accounts 1-19-*nnnnnn* and the sum of the amounts of invoices in accounts 0-19-*nnnnnn*.

- In weeks 6 through 12, did salespersons with two or more years of experience sell a greater average volume than salespersons with less than two years of experience?

  To answer this question, sum sales in weeks 6 through 12 for each salesperson in each district and region. (This code structure allows up to 1,000 salespersons: 10 in each district, 10 districts to a region, and 10 regions). Then divide the salespersons into two groups according to years of experience. (This will require access to the sales personnel file.) Finally, sum the sales within each group, and divide the result by the number of salespersons in the group, to obtain the average sales for each group. To answer the question, you'd compare these average sales figures.

This coding design facilitates the generation of routine reports. In addition, managers need a powerful, easily used information search and report generator to find and compile nonroutine information.

Structure of the Application

Structure of the application includes the principles, conditions, concepts, and variables embodied in how the application is organized. These variables determine who is responsible for a particular process or activity within the application, and how and where it is performed. This section describes four structural variables: degree of centralization, use of batch or real-time processing, cycle billing, and lockboxes.

Degree of Centralization.   **Centralized data processing** locates all the processes in an application at one site, and branch or subsidiary departments have little role other than data capture and report review. In **distributed data processing**, the processes comprising an application are carried out in several locations, at branches or subsidiary departments. An application's processes can also exhibit various degrees of centralization; i.e., credit approval may be centralized while billing and report generation may be distributed.

For an illustration of how the degree of centralization affects organization of the accounts receivable application, consider the processes that use the approved-credit-customers file. This file may be centralized in one location, but it need not be. Suppose that a firm is divided into six sales regions, each of which has four districts. All twenty-four district offices are connected to the large main computer for centralized processing of credit approval, order entry, billing, credit, and reporting. District sales personnel maintain direct contacts with customers and transmit orders to the centralized credit sales application operating out of the home office. Information flows back and forth between the sales offices and the large files and rapid processing of the central facility.

Alternatively, each district could have its own approved-credit-customers master file. All procedures involving credit approval, order entry, billing, collection, and maintenance of this file would occur in the district offices using identical software on identical small computers. Each file would have its own control account. The home office's general ledger would have a master control account and an accounts receivable subsidiary ledger for each of these four district's control-account balances.

Centralized and decentralized data processing both work well, and both are compatible with centralized or decentralized organizational structures. The advantages and weaknesses of each are listed in Table 7.3.

Batch or Real-Time Processing.   The degree of centralization adopted may affect the choice of batch or real-time processing. In turn, a need for one or the other technique may influence the degree of centralization chosen. Batch processing is the technique of saving similar transactions to process them all at once. In real-time processing, each transaction is processed as it occurs, and all records affected by it are updated at that time as well.

Table 7.3 Comparison of Centralized and Distributed Processing
Neither centralized nor distributed processing is preferable in all situations. Careful analysis will show which is the best match to specific organization needs and resources.

	Centralized Processing	Distributed Processing
Financial investment in system	Higher	Lower
System controllability by management	Greater from organization headquarters	Greater from local offices
Ability to provide timely information	Higher for top management	Higher for local management
Time to develop system	Longer	Shorter
System response time	Best for top management	Best for local management
User-friendliness to management	Achieved best with skilled operators	Readily achievable without skilled operators

The shorter the wait between batches, the more closely batch processing resembles real-time processing. In batch processing, unprocessed data records for order entry, shipping, or credit accumulate in an unposted transactions file for a day, week, or other time period. Then the entire file is posted all at once, in a batch. The batch technique works best for small organizations with relatively few credit accounts, a low level of use, and a low level of inquiry. Batch processing also offers more control over data, since the master file is only in use by the computer while a batch update is taking place, and not continuously.

Real-time processing occurs when files are continuously available and current. A real-time file must be of direct-access design, since repeatedly accessing specific records in a sequential file would take too much time. An authorized person may view or change the status of any account record in an on-line direct-access file with a short access time. The real-time approach works best for organizations with many credit accounts and frequent use and inquiry.

As a compromise between pure batch and real-time processing, files may be on-line—that is, continuously available for inquiry through the computer—but updated only once or twice daily. Such a modified real-time system accommodates a high level of accesses per record while using limited computing resources.

Cycle Billing.   Batch processing can overload an organization's computer resources. One method of distributing the workload is cycle processing. An example would be the "cyclical" preparation of customer statements, called **cycle billing**. In cycle billing, statements are prepared and mailed to a few customers each day, rather than to all customers on the same day. Cycle billing allows uniformly allocated use of limited computer resources and helps avoid conflicts among competing applications; it also encourages more uniform distribution of receipts of customer cash payments throughout the month. Cycle billing is most useful for leveling the processing load of a business whose customers pay from a monthly statement rather than from invoices.

Using cycle billing in a data base system, each customer credit account is assigned a field whose value indicates the billing cycle to which it belongs. Each day, the processing program selects and processes those accounts belonging to that day's cycle. These amounts may be identified by a field that is part of the customer account number. In a file-processing system, the approved-credit-customers master file is accessed in record-key sequence to process a new batch of accounts daily (and to ensure that all accounts are actually processed).

An example will show how cycle billing works in one company and why it was the method chosen. A certain company has 30,000 credit accounts. Preparing and sending customer statements requires 2 seconds of computer time for each account, and the processing program itself requires 5 minutes to load and perform diagnostics, print reports, and maintain files, regardless of the number of records processed. To process all accounts and send out statements requires more than 16 hours of computer time. If nearly all accounts are usually active and statements are all prepared at once on the first of each month, and there is only one shift, the computer and data processing staff will do nothing but process customer statements for two full days. Nothing else will get done: *no* cash receipts, *no* purchases, *no* trade accounts payable, and *no* payroll.

The company could use any of several strategies to ease this pressure on data processing. It could acquire a new, higher quality system to process customer statements. Alternatively, occasional extra shifts could condense the processing into less calendar time. The usual solution to this problem, however, is cycle billing. Processing statements every working day allows other applications to be run on the same days. Since the average month has 21 or more working days, the firm can process 5 percent or 1,500 of its customer statements on each of the first 20 working days of each month. Processing 1,500 statements takes 55 minutes, leaving the remainder of the workday for other data processing activities.

Lockboxes. Sometimes, certain processing needs are best served by employing the resources of another firm. A company may contract out the entire data processing function or parts of an application to a processing service. Lockboxes are such a service and are used by many companies to enhance controls, reduce costs, and simplify processing of cash customer

Table 7.4   Lockbox Mailing Label
Although simple in form, this label is the key to directing remittances to the correct lockbox.

The Friendswood Company, Inc.
P.O. Box 34267
Central City, Missouri 01234
Special Code 47

payments. A **lockbox** is an address at a financial institution to which a company's customers send cash remittances. For example, Table 7.4 shows a mailing label that directs customer remittances to a lockbox.

Friendswood Company provides its customers with forms that serve as remittance advices and with envelopes addressed to the lockbox, which the customers use to send their cash remittances. A bank employee collects and sorts lockbox envelopes by the special codes; that is, envelopes with code 47 (Friendswood Company's code) are grouped together. The enclosed checks and accompanying remittance advices are copied and the copies are sent to the Friendswood Company controller for processing. The bank immediately deposits the checks to the account of Friendswood Company. The company pays a small fee to the bank, usually 1 to 2 percent of gross remittances. The Friendswood Company benefits from the savings in salaries since there is no need to hire or assign staff to handle receiving the cash. It also enjoys a higher level of security since its own employees do not handle cash. Finally, it has faster access to cash remittances. Lockboxes can be established in multiple locations, if necessary, to reduce the time customers' checks are in the mail.

To determine whether lockboxes are cost effective for a particular company, their cost should be compared with the sum of the interest income resulting from faster deposit of funds plus the internal savings from reduced processing.

Accounting Entries for This Application

Making the Entries

1. Credit Sale.   In the third week of January, C. Customer, whose accounts receivable subsidiary ledger account code is 567123789, buys 40 gonzo painters (product no. 33) at $30 each in region 3, district 8, from salesperson 5. C. Customer is in the service industry, coded 2. The sales invoice code is constructed as described in the preceding section. The first

Figure 7.5   Recording a Credit Sale
Even though a credit sale is recorded through only one set of documents, dual processing of these documents, as shown here, is consistent with debit and credit concepts.

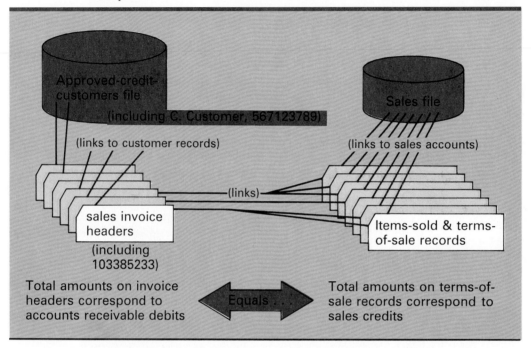

part of the customer account number is a random sequence permanently assigned to C. Customer. The second part identifies the invoice, as is required in this open-invoice system. The entry follows:

> Receivable from C. Customer,
>   Acct. 567123789-(invoice #) $1,200.00
>   Sales—Acct. (subledger)-(invoice #)-
>   103385233 $1,200.00

The debit amount in this entry would be included in the sum of additions to the open credit sales invoices (the accounts receivable subsidiary ledger) during the sales period. The credit amount would be included in the distribution of credit sales to the various sales accounts. This is shown in Figure 7.5.

2. Prompt Payment. C. Customer pays part of the invoice generated by the credit purchases of gonzo painters in time for the prompt-payment discount. This payment results in a debit to Cash and a debit to an account used to record the prompt-payment discounts. These account numbers are omitted below, but could be determined in the manner explained in Chapter 6. The credit, of course, relieves C. Customer's account.

Cash	$980.00	
Prompt-Payment Discount	20.00	
Receivable from C. Customer,		
Acct. 567123789-(invoice #)		$1,000.00

The debit to Cash is part of the debit made to record a total bank deposit. The debit to Prompt-Payment Discount and the credit to Customer's account are part of the total of remittances linked to customer accounts, as shown in Figure 7.6.

Figure 7.6   Recording Customer Payment
Dual processing of the records resulting from a customer remittance enables analysis of the transaction in terms of debits and credits. Note the absence of T accounts in this representation.

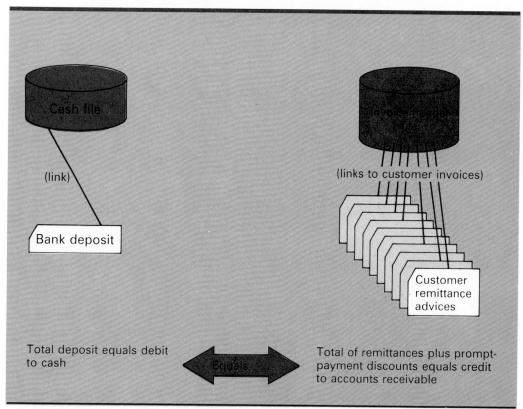

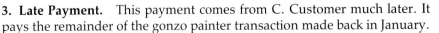

3. Late Payment.   This payment comes from C. Customer much later. It pays the remainder of the gonzo painter transaction made back in January.

Cash	$200.00
Receivable from C. Customer	$200.00
567123789-(invoice #)	

The entry is the same as the preceding one except that there is no discount for prompt payment.

4. Write-off of a Doubtful Account.   A **write-off** means that the balance is no longer shown as part of accounts receivable. Because a write-off is a voluntary reduction of the assets shown in financial statements, write-off authorization and implementation are controlled very closely. A write-off does not eliminate the right to receive payment, it simply indicates that the organization has little hope of receiving it. The organization might specify that any balance written off as uncollectible should meet all the following conditions:

- The amount has been owed for a year or more.
- No payment has been received for at least nine months.
- The debtor is adamantly uncooperative (or in bankruptcy, unlocatable, or the like).

Chapter 6 explained the use of valuation accounts to record estimates of assets that will be uncollectible. In the general ledger, credit-granting businesses maintain an account with a credit balance called **Allowance for Doubtful Accounts**. This account contains the controller's estimate of the amount of *current* accounts receivable that will prove uncollectible in the future. When the controller decides that a receivable amount finally has proved to be uncollectible, it should be removed from both the accounts receivable and the allowance for doubtful accounts. The following entry accomplishes this removal:

Allowance for Doubtful Accounts	$1,572
Accounts Receivable (specific account number)	$1,572

The accounting system handles this function by requiring a periodic review of all accounts for collectibility.

If it becomes necessary to partially reduce a customer's unpaid balance for nonpayment, the open invoice system provides a more complete documentation and audit trail than the balance-forward system. The open-invoice system, which links a customer's credit sales transactions and cash remittances to the same customer's outstanding balance, allows the removal of specific invoices (or items on invoices) from the outstanding balance. This capability is especially useful when a customer will not or cannot pay for part of a shipment.

Delinquent account collection can be pursued more aggressively. Rather than wait to analyze accounts for possible collection problems, the billing process (which operates each time a new shipment is billed, or a statement sent) could calculate the age of each component item in the total amount due. For each item aged over, for example, 60 days, the billing process could generate a letter to be sent to the customer requesting payment, a report to the credit manager, and a note to the legal department to consider legal action.

5. Response to an NSF Check.   **Not sufficient funds (NSF)** is a message from the customer's bank that the customer's account balance is too low for the bank to honor a check the customer sent. The company assumes that the checks it receives from approved credit customers will be honored, thus it treats the checks as cash and marks the accounts paid. When a check is returned NSF, the original entry crediting the customer's account receivable balance must be reversed.

Suppose C. Customer's check for $200 was deposited and processed as a debit to Cash and a credit to Customer's account. A few days later, the bank returns Customer's check NSF. You, as controller, proceed as follows:

1. Reverse the payment entry (whether discounted, as in entry 2, or not, as in entry 3) to adjust the accounting records.
2. Note the NSF check in the customer's record in the approved-credit-customers file for purposes of reviewing the customer's credit rating.
3. Request the collections department contact C. Customer and urgently request prompt payment.

Many NSF checks represent haphazard cash planning by an otherwise sound customer. Some are early indications of credit deterioration, and a few represent unethical decisions by credit customers to delay payment of current obligations. Frequent review of the approved-credit-customers file will reveal candidates for credit revocation due to slow payment, dishonored checks, and evidence of deliberate delay.

6. Return of Merchandise.   It often happens that a customer orders merchandise and then returns it. Naturally, credit sales processing should handle returns of merchandise, discounts and rebates, and the corresponding reductions in the customer's accounts receivable balance—called **sales returns and allowances**—smoothly. Customarily, the seller requires the customer to obtain approval prior to returning merchandise and to accept limits on merchandise returnability. These limits usually specify both a time interval after the sale and the condition of the merchandise. (With consumer goods, such approval and conditions may be very liberal and are often waived altogether.)

Suppose that on June 1, Customer *A* purchases from you the following items:

20 gasoline-driven spades @ $300 each
30 retrograde condensers @ $80 each
14 expansion controllers @ $50 each

You ship the order. Customer *A* accepts it. You send the invoice; *A* pays it, less a 1-percent discount for prompt payment. (The total amount of the order is $9,100, and the 1-percent discount is $91, yielding net cash receipts of $9,009.) On July 15, Customer *A* requests permission to return 10 of the condensers, which are not needed, and one of the spades, which never worked properly.

Your policy is that a customer who requests authorization to return merchandise within 60 days of the date of sale may do so. You do not charge a restocking fee, but you do require the customer to obtain a **return authorization**, which is simply a record of the seller's permission to return merchandise. The return authorization is a preventive element of control. You maintain a list of authorized returns; when a returned shipment arrives, you check it off the list. A report of authorized return shipments received is the feedback element of control.

The sales department authorizes return of the merchandise and assigns the return a number. Customer *A* places this number prominently on its return shipment. Your receiving department, instructed not to accept unauthorized deliveries, looks for this number on Customer *A*'s shipment when it is delivered. The number is the receiving department's authorization to accept the return. The receiving department completes the report of authorized returns received and a report on the condition and disposition of the returns. (The malfunctioning spade will go to your production engineers to determine why it was manufactured incorrectly. The 10 unused condensers will be inspected and, if they are in good order, returned to stock.)

The return authorization plus the receiving department's report that the returns have arrived provide the evidence for recording the return. The accounting entry will be

Credit Sale to *A*—1 spade (defective)	$300.00	
Credit Sale to *A*—10 condensers	800.00	
Account Receivable—*A*		$1,089.00
Prompt-payment Discount taken		11.00

The accounts receivable application prepares a numbered returns and allowances transaction record summarizing this information and places it in the transaction file for processing.

Data Capture Error Correction

An error made during order entry or other data capture is corrected by returning the unprocessable transaction to its point of origin for correction and resubmission. If the error is not detectable by the usual edit and logic checks (a wrong quantity or wrong but valid account number, for example, would not be detected by these checks), then the accounting system records the transaction and an additional procedure will be necessary to correct the mistake. Since errors cannot be predicted, no single procedure will cover all of them. However, all such procedures *reverse* the original erroneous postings in the records and then enter the transaction information *correctly*. Consider, for example, the following sequence of events:

1. *Transaction:* Customer A buys $100 worth of merchandise on credit.
2. *Error:* During processing, Customer B's valid credit number is accidentally substituted for that of Customer A.
3. *Error detected:* This error is detected by Customer B on the monthly statement.
4. *Error reported:* Customer B reports the error to your customer credit department by telephone.
5. *Error corrected with two records:* A data processing clerk records B's account number, the date and amount of the erroneous charge, and the location at which it occurred. Following this audit trail of the transaction's posting reveals that it originated as a transaction with A that was never posted to A's account. The data processing clerk's supervisor authorizes two new records, one canceling the erroneous charge to B's account and a second posting the correct charge to A's account.

Both of these records, and the original erroneous one, will appear in the year-to-date transactions file and will become part of the audit trail of both individuals' accounts.

Reports

Assuming that this application incorporates a useful account coding structure and appropriate design features; and that it has recorded credit sales, payments on accounts, and other types of entries correctly, it will produce a well-organized data base that will meet many reporting needs. We have already reviewed some of the potential performance reporting opportunities in an earlier section. Processing associated with credit sales, accounts receivable, and billing can also produce information that is useful to management, if assembled in a form that highlights the enlightening points. Report generation is actually a collection of processes that result in a variety of reports. The report generators should allow users the discretion to specify the content of reports and the frequency with which they are produced. The six major reports described in this section are periodic statements to customers of their account status, unprocessed transactions, changes in customer credit status, aging of accounts receivable, collections, and processing reports.

Management's ability to specify report content to fit its current needs will depend on the design of this application. The design concepts described in this chapter eliminate much of the sequential searching required in file-processing systems and thus provide for flexibility in reporting.

Apart from the application's routine processing, the credit-sales-invoice, accounts receivable, and customer payments files themselves are a valuable source of information if the transaction data are recorded in a conveniently retrievable fashion. Account codes and prenumbered documents promote the goal of retrievability. They make possible computerized sales analysis, budgeting, advance indication of purchasing or production requirements, and performance analysis of sales districts, product lines, and personnel.

Periodic Statements of Account Status

Statements notify customers of the amount they owe and result in their sending cash remittances. In addition to their cash-raising function, statements are effective preventive controls. The customers provide the feedback control element by making payments or disputing the amount owed and the activity since the last statement. Credit management completes the control cycle by providing the comparison and follow-up element.

If the posting processes are performed regularly, the generation of customer statements is a straightforward process of reading each customer's records in the six major files. The information extracted and printed on a customer statement form usually includes the following:

- Customer name and billing address
- Account number
- Balance due as of the previous statement
- Payments, purchases, and adjustments (and date of each) since previous statement
- Interest, penalty, or credit charge, if any (usually calculated immediately prior to printing statement)
- New balance due

Unprocessed Transactions

Management should receive reports of transactions which occurred but for some reason could not be processed, so that it can identify why they were not processed. If a credit sale can't be posted, for example, it may indicate

Table 7.5   Causes and Remedies for Unprocessed Transactions

Computer Message Identifying Problem	S___n
1. Two identical master file records exist	Re___ ___ both records. Change record key of one. ___ ___ess transaction.
2. Transaction number obliterated or lost	Refe___ ___ritten source documents and reenter tra___ ___on number; reprocess transaction.
3. Credit for merchandise return lacks authorization by proper code.	This ___ ___ have been caught by the editing program whe___ ___ update file was being prepared. It sugg___ ___ither a flaw in this program or a delibe___ ___ttempt to circumvent it. Refer to intern___ ___iting, which will work with technical suppo___ ___nd the explanation. Secure authori___ ___ code and reprocess transaction.

a failure of controls, or it might re___ ___ unique set of circumstances that existing procedures could not hand___ ___ either case, management should know about it.

Numerous other scenarios resul___ ___nprocessed transactions. A common problem in batch-processing sy___ ___s is that a customer's credit is canceled after a transaction is approve___ ___before merchandise is shipped. When the transaction is processed, th___ ___k of an approved-credit-customers-file record stops the process—u___ ___ an unprocessed-transactions file exists. In the latter case, the transa___ ___ goes into an unprocessed-transactions file with an indication of why ___ ___essing could not continue—"no master file record found," for exampl___ ___e report summarizing these stoppages will go to a managerial investi___ ___ for analysis and remedial action. Table 7.5 shows some other examp___

Very few credit sale transactions shou___ ___d up in the unprocessed-transactions file. A sales executive should ___ ___nine the report of these transactions for the underlying cause of error___ ___ach case, be it a careless salesperson, a defective software program, or ___ ___cenous customer. There are many ways to search for these causes. T___ ___xecutive might request that the unprocessed transactions be sorted b___ ___es point, salesperson, processing point, customer, date, or any other promising category. When the causes and impact of the errors are determined, management can take appropriate corrective action.

Changes in Customer Credit Status

Changes in customer credit status include approval for credit, increases or decreases in credit limits, and withdrawal of credit approval. As a preventive element of the controls on customer credit, any change in the status of a credit account should receive advance approval from the credit manager, who reports to the treasurer or other official in the finance function. The credit manager should receive regular reports of all changes in credit status, including new credit customers, and should verify that all such changes were properly approved. This procedure will discourage unauthorized changes and potential fraud.

4. Aging of Accounts Receivable

The **aging of accounts receivable** is the process that determines and reports how long ago each outstanding credit purchase was made. The "age" of each outstanding balance is valuable information for cash planning and credit management because the collectibility of accounts tends to deteriorate sharply as they age. An account twenty-five days old might be presumed to have a 99-percent probability of collection, whereas one more than six months old may have less than a 20-percent probability of collection. Financial management uses the aging information in three ways: *first*, to identify slow-paying customers so they can be urged or legally compelled to pay; *second*, to help forecast cash flow; and *third*, to help value the total of accounts receivable.

The amount of detail required and the accessibility of data determine the method of processing used. If you are using the balance-forward method, you may have to show the entire balance of a customer account as having a single age—usually the age of the earliest invoice. The open-invoice method allows you to age different unpaid invoices for the same customer according to their actual dates. This method may be adapted to categorize accounts by the month or week the invoices were created or by the number of days since the invoice was created. Each approach is particularly useful for a specific purpose and may give some incidental information relevant for other purposes.

Classification by Time of Creation.   You can prepare an aging report by classifying outstanding invoice amounts according to the week or month in which the sale occurred. Prior to classification, a report based on the March, April, and May invoice data would resemble the one illustrated in Table 7.6. Additional information can be shown by also classifying the invoices by sales region. The classifying program will examine every credit-sales-invoice header to extract the report information. The aging report may appear like the one illustrated in Table 7.7. You can verify that Table 7.7 reflects the data from Table 7.6.

Examining the underlying records of accounts summarized under "May" and "> 3 months" in Table 7.7 should identify the customers responsible for slow payments and nonpayments. (The invoice numbers can be found in Table 7.6.) You can then determine whether an explanation exists for each one. Possible explanations include disputes over returns or

Table 7.6 Richards Company Preaging Invoice File as of July 31
This long excerpt from the credit sales invoice file will be used to illustrate aging analysis by time period and sales region.

Invoice Number	Date of Sale	Net Balance Still Due (in millions)	Region
1043	3-15	0.3	Western
1109	4-17	0.2	Central
1113	4-17	0.5	Eastern
1118	4-29	0.2	Central
1132	5-03	0.4	Eastern
1140	5-10	0.3	Western
1150	5-14	0.2	Eastern
1160	5-20	0.5	Central
1173	5-28	0.2	Eastern
1180	5-28	0.2	Central
1181	5-28	0.3	Central
1195	6-2	0.5	Western
1199	6-4	0.5	Western
1215	6-10	0.6	Central
1225	6-12	1.1	Eastern
1226	6-12	0.2	Western
1231	6-13	0.8	Central
1235	6-15	0.2	Eastern
1237	6-16	0.4	Central
1238	6-17	0.1	Central
1239	6-17	1.1	Central
1240	6-18	0.6	Eastern
1245	6-20	0.2	Eastern
1301	7-1	0.6	Western
1310	7-5	1.0	Western
1311	7-5	5.4	Eastern
1312	7-6	2.5	Eastern
1316	7-9	2.6	Central
1317	7-10	1.5	Western
1320	7-12	2.0	Central
1322	7-14	0.5	Eastern
1325	7-15	0.3	Eastern
1330	7-15	0.2	Eastern
1335	7-18	0.4	Western
1336	7-19	1.3	Western
1340	7-20	1.8	Central
1341	7-22	2.9	Central
1350	7-25	10.0	Eastern
1352	7-26	0.8	Western
1353	7-27	2.5	Central
1354	7-27	0.4	Central

Table 7.7   The Richards Company Aging of Accounts Receivable as of July 31 (in millions)
This aging is based on the data in Table 7.6. Among other things, it shows management whether collections differ by regions. To improve it further, the report could include either year-ago or predicted collectibility data.

	Outstanding Balances				
	July	*June*	*May*	*> 3 months (all March and April)*	*Total*
Western region	$ 5.6	$1.2	$0.3	$0.3	$ 7.4
Central region	12.2	3.0	1.0	0.4	16.7
Eastern region	18.9	2.1	0.8	0.5	22.3
Total	$36.7	$6.3	$2.1	$1.2	$46.4

allowances, improper billing, and inability to pay. In the first two instances, you can take action to resolve the dispute and secure payment. In the latter case, you may want to reduce the customer's credit rating and take action to secure payment, such as use of a collection agency or legal proceedings.

Classification by Number of Days Since Creation.   Table 7.8 illustrates another technique for classifying accounts receivable, using arbitrary age brackets and collection probabilities. The estimated collectible accounts receivable will be compared with the existing accounts receivable control account balances less the balance in the provision for doubtful accounts. This kind of aging helps an organization value the balances on the year-end financial statements for three related accounts: accounts receivable, provision for doubtful accounts, and bad-debt expense, and may be a part of the independently conducted year-end audit procedure. It is not uncommon for some older account balances to be presumed uncollectible, a supposition that may require increases in the balances of the latter two accounts.

Table 7.5 shows that you expect to recover only $43,559,000 from your current accounts receivable with the face amount of $46,400,000. The allowance for doubtful accounts should therefore have a credit balance of $2,741,000, which is $46,300,000 minus $43,559,000. The current amount of the allowance balance usually does not equal the calculated amount, owing to previous write-offs. An adjustment is required, increasing the allowance and also increasing bad-debt expenses for the current period.

The information on the collectibility of accounts in reports classified by time of creation and ones classified by days since creation is similar,

Table 7.8 Valuation of Richards Company Accounts Receivable Using Aging
This valuation estimates how much cash will be collected from the current accounts receivable balances. It reflects the rule that the older a debt is, the less likely it is to be paid.

Age (days)	# of Invoices	$ Amount of Invoices	Probability of Collection	Valuation (in millions)
0–30	350	$36.7	0.99	$36.333
31–60	91	6.3	0.92	5.796
61–90	22	2.1	0.60	1.260
91–180	8	1.0	0.16	0.160
> 180	2	0.2	0.05	0.010
	473	$46.3		$43.559

Desired valuation provision: $46.300 − $43.559 = **$2,741,000**

yet the format of each report facilitates the purpose for which it is generated. A third purpose is to determine whether the company's collection of accounts is slowing down generally. A comparison of the number of invoices outstanding each month over a three-month period helps answer this question. Table 7.9 illustrates such a report.

The table shows a pattern of growing numbers of outstanding invoices in the older categories, a clear indication that customers are taking longer to pay their bills. This pattern has serious but usually controllable consequences for a business's cash flow. The decreasing number of in-

Table 7.9 Richards Company Number of Aged Invoices Compared by Months as of July 31
The number of invoices in each age group can help management judge whether the quality of credit sales is stable, trending up, or trending down.

Age (days)	# of Invoices		
	May	June	July
0–30	350	340	330
31–60	91	97	100
61–90	22	60	70
91–180	8	22	55
> 180	2	4	9
	473	523	564

voices in the 0–30 day category is a potential warning of declining sales, requiring further investigation. It may signal a downturn in the economy or difficulties in the marketing department, or even in production. If the first appears to be the cause, management must recognize that inventories tend to rise as business activity slows, requiring alertness and quick revision of production plans to keep them at target levels. If internal problems are to blame, corrective measures will depend on their exact nature. For example, if the problem is lack of salesperson enthusiasm, the solution may be to increase incentives for salespeople. If the problem is poor quality of merchandise, management may strengthen production controls.

5. Collections

A **collections report** shows the schedule of expected cash flow from accounts receivable during a particular period; it is prepared prior to that period. In real life, cash-collection estimates may prove inaccurate owing to unforeseen business growth, a change in customer profile or business conditions, or special credit terms such as prompt-payment discounts and interest calculated on overdue accounts. Because of these complications we omit the calculations and show only a typical collections-report format. Table 7.10 lists monthly sales and collections for three consecutive months, which are used to estimate collections for May. The May sales and sales discount are estimated and shown in italics.

Table 7.10 Cash Flow Forecast for May (prepared April 30)
This is one of the most important reports management can receive. Its usefulness depends on the quality of the underlying data, especially that collected and processed by the application described in this chapter.

Month	Credit Sales	Collections in February	March	April	Est. May Collections
Feb.	$110,000	$25,000	$75,000	$ 6,000	$ 2,000
discount	(250)				
interest & penalty			750	120	60
March	$112,000	—	30,000	72,000	9,000
discount		(300)			
interest & penalty				720	180
April	$ 90,000	—	—	23,000	64,000
discount			(230)		
interest & penalty					640
May (est.)	$ 97,000				$22,000
discount (est.)					(220)
Total estimated collections for May					$97,660

A well-designed, well-run information system can create many re-ports similar to Table 7.7, but with different purposes, such as identifying quick-paying customers, regions or industries with unique payment pat-terns, or the effect of quick-payment incentives on test groups. Such re-ports differ in format, as in the examples of aging reports.

The Processing Report

The **processing report** describes activity in the data processing department. Its purpose is to inform management of the data processing that has been completed and, if possible, to allow comparison of actual activity with that scheduled for the period.

As a preventive element of controls on accounts receivable, data processing operates on a predetermined schedule. As a feedback element of these controls, each time processing occurs, the processing program prepares a report showing the following:

The program that was run
The date, time, and duration of the run
The authorization to run the program (the system operator follows a
    schedule of activity prepared by the controller)
The files used and created during the run
The number of records changed, accessed, added, and deleted in a
    file, and their identifications
The number of unprocessable transactions, and their identifications
Other useful processing information

A copy of the processing report goes to the data processing supervisor, and an abridged version goes to the controller. The data processing su-pervisor, who is not directly involved in day-to-day data processing op-erations, uses the report to evaluate performance. The controller uses the report to ensure that accounting processes are being carried out appro-priately, and thus that accounting information remains reliable.

Summary

The credit sales, accounts receivable, and billing application is one of the most important for management, since it identifies and calculates cash inflows. Its processes include credit approval, order entry, billing, posting cash remittances, and reporting to management. These processes use data from credit sales transactions, customer payments, and other sources to maintain an up-to-date record of customer account balances and other information executives find useful for cash management, credit manage-ment, and asset valuation. The use of a well-designed account code and pointers to link related records in the different files eliminates or reduces the need for sorts and searches.

The organization's file of approved credit customers may be centralized or distributed. Each customer's record in this file should include a credit limit and an outstanding balance. Whenever a credit sale is made, this record is checked to make certain that credit is still approved, to verify that the balance including the sale does not exceed the credit limit, and to update the balance. An invoice is sent when the shipping-advice file shows that the customer has received the merchandise. A regular statement of each customer's account, summarizing activity since the previous statement, is generally sent monthly.

To assure consistency of the amounts recorded with the double entry principle, debits to customer accounts are based on the credit-sales invoice headers and credits to the sales file on the amounts calculated from items-sold and terms-of-sale records. Other control procedures apply to cash debits and offsetting accounts receivable credits. Important entries that can be constructed from data in this application also include recording late payments, writing off doubtful accounts, and correcting entries previously recorded with errors.

Customer cash payments may be received by the organization itself or by a bank operating a lockbox. In either case, the organization updates the approved-credit-customers-file record to show the payment. These operations provide data for sales analyses, salesperson performance reports, and accounts receivable aging.

Because of their importance to the organization, files used in this application should be carefully backed up. Duplicate copies should be made frequently and stored in an off-site location.

Key Terms

accounts receivable control account	headers
aging of accounts receivable	lockbox
allowance for doubtful accounts	not sufficient funds (NSF)
balance-forward design	open-invoice design
centralized data processing	processing report
collections report	return authorization
cycle billing	sales returns and allowances
distributed data processing	write-off

Review Questions

1. What are the five major component processes in the credit sales, accounts receivable, and billing application?

2. What particular needs of the marketing department does the credit sales, accounts receivable, and billing application satisfy? What capabilities must this application have to serve these needs?

3. What is a linked chain of records? What does a pointer do in a linked chain? Can a record contain more than one pointer?

4. Why is it preferable to use several records to contain the details of a transaction rather than one large record?

5. What is a data flow diagram?

6. What is a header record? What is the purpose of the credit-sales-invoice-headers record?

7. What is a shipping advice? What purpose does it serve if the customer immediately carries off the items purchased?

8. Distinguish between the objectives of the credit approval process and those of the credit posting process.

9. Explain why the sum of all invoices related to shipping advices for which reimbursement has not yet been received should be equal to the balance of the accounts receivable control account.

10. Why should there be a report of changes in customer credit status? Who should receive this report?

11. What financial reporting purpose does accounts receivable aging serve?

12. Explain the difference between centralized and distributed processing and between batch and real-time processing.

13. Name at least two advantages of cycle billing. What types of firms should consider cycle billing?

14. What is a lockbox? List three advantages of using a lockbox. How can a company determine whether a lockbox will be cost effective?

15. List and give examples of six types of entries in the credit sales, accounts receivable, and billing application.

16. Refer to Figure 7.3 and the related discussion to answer the following questions:
    (a) What is the purpose of the stock-items file?
    (b) What is the purpose of the items-sold file?
    (c) Is there any limit to the number of invoices that can point to a record in the items-sold file?
    (d) Is there any limit to the number of items-sold records that can point to a given record in the stock-items file?
    (e) How does the items-sold file support use of sales transaction data to prepare management information reports?

17. For at least three types of reports to marketing or credit management, describe the report contents and the uses to which the report could be put. Also, explain the relationship between marketing management and credit management, and why they must be independent of each other.

Discussion Questions

18. In your opinion, would an open-invoice system be more compatible with a very large master file record designed to hold the information of all of a customer's invoices or with a chain of invoice records linked to a relatively small master file record?

19. Early last year, Sam Spencer and Martha Bower started very similar small businesses. Each acquired a computer-based accounts receivable application similar to the one described in this chapter. Sam kept a copy of his period-to-date posted transactions file in a safe-deposit box. Every day he processed new transactions and made a new copy of the posted transactions file. Martha also updated every day. However, she copied her subsidiary ledger (account balances) file only once a month; at the same time she started a new posted transactions file containing only the transactions since the first of the month. In her safe-deposit box, she kept copies of all these monthly transactions files, including the daily updated current month's file.

    In November, freak accidents destroyed the on-site files of both companies. The only remaining records are those in the safe-deposit boxes.

    (a) Which business do you think suffered the most disruption from its disaster? Why?

    (b) Discuss the issues and variables at stake in deciding how often to copy files and where to store the copies.

20. Ruth Desk is assistant marketing manager at Planview Systems Company, a retailer of home and office furniture and electronics. For the last three weeks she has devoted her lunch hour to answering incoming phone calls while catching up on credit applications data entry at the company's computer. Yesterday, she had the following phone conversation:

    Ruth: Hello, Planview Systems.

    Customer: Yes, my name is Ms. Spender. I need some help from the credit manager.

    R: That person's not in now, but I'm in that department. May I help?

    C: There's a credit charge I don't understand on my last statement.

    R: Please tell me about it.

    C: Well, I've never had one before, it's a code 1 or something like that, and it's 32 dollars. And the only thing that might account for it is, I bought Uncle Herman a stereo last month, and we had to refurnish our den around the new wide screen TV the month before that. And I didn't answer that red card you sent me. So now there's this *charge*, and with all the things I've bought from you . . .

R: I'm looking at your account now. You have really been an active customer lately! Not many of our customers buy $4,000 worth of merchandise on credit in just two months.

C: Well, thank you, and I'm going to buy a lot more stuff too, as soon as I get another job. And what I need to know is, how can I get these *charges* off?

R: Oh, I see they've made a mistake with your credit rating. Your purchases are not on the installment plan . . .

C: I know, they discouraged me . . .

R: Well, for such a good customer . . . there's this little letter I can change here on the screen . . . there! Now, that gives you 90 more days!

C: Oh, wow, what can I say!

R: Just ask for *me* when you come in to buy again!

(a) Explain what happened here and how to prevent it in the future.
(b) If this did happen in an organization with controls, what report or control would eventually bring it to light?

21. Brief descriptions follow of the marketing functions of five companies. For each company's accounts receivable application, indicate whether (1) centralized or decentralized processing and (2) batch or real-time processing would be preferable (or are already in place). Explain the factors supporting your recommendations.

(a) Wiggins Company is an architectural design firm. It has one main office. The firm markets its four basic designs at builders' conferences and to individual contractors. Its annual net sales are about $1 million, and its three owners try to keep office expenses at a minimum.

(b) Global Wire & Cable Company serves the oil and gas industry. It has seventeen field warehouses in nine countries. The warehouses deliver on 12 hours' notice. Four purchasing offices keep the warehouses supplied; they also analyze customer order patterns to identify sales trends. Company management is convinced that its extensive range of products and rapid response to orders are what keep the company profitable.

(c) Potts Grocery uses electric cash registers at its check-out counter. Each register creates a punched paper tape of transaction data. After closing, these tapes are fed into a computer, one by one, for processing.

(d) Mr. Strength Fitness Centers has seven locations. Each location's manager sells memberships and checks the validity of customers' membership cards. Cash remittances go to a main office. Members may use any locations, not just the one at which they joined.

(e) Direct Mail Associates maintains a list of 200,000 names and addresses along with demographic attributes such as income, age, family size, and profession. Smaller lists can be generated to fit the profiles customers desire. About 8 profiles per week are run for customers. Each week, to keep the mailing list up-to-date, about 8,000 names are added, deleted, or changed by reading tapes purchased from other companies and by five data entry operators working from printed materials such as phone books and tax rolls.

22. Firm *A* uses a written, four-copy sales invoice document to record credit sales. The customer and the sales department each keep a copy, and one copy is sent to the shipping department and one to billing. Firm *B*'s sales department fills out a form on a computer terminal screen with the same sales information recorded by Firm *A*. From the screen form, the order entry application creates appropriate records. What need, if any, would Firm *B* have for hard (paper) copies of the information recorded on the screen form? How would shipping and billing learn of the sale?

Problems

23. Consider the following situation:
    Arthur and Babcock both have accounts at the Northrup Warehouse. Arthur's number is 45456 and Babcock's number is 54546. On May 1, Arthur recovered merchandise stored in the warehouse, and the clerk entered the following transaction:

Account 54546 Receivable	$105.00	
Warehouse Rental Sales		$105.00
(May 1, 19XX—to record sales invoice #11066)		

    Babcock received a May statement from Northrup Warehouse that included the following item:

      5-1-XX   #11066 $105.00

    Babcock called the customer credit phone number on the statement to report that he had no record of their invoice #11066.

    Required:
    (a) Describe the process for correcting the error.
    (b) List the accounting entries that will be necessary to correct the error.
    (c) Explain why Northrup Warehouse's check-digit control did not operate in this case.

24. Define the account called Allowance for Doubtful Accounts. Then, calculate the bad-debt expense for each of the following situations:

	Accounts Receivable Balance	Estimated Accounts Receivable Collectible	Allowance for Doubtful Accounts—Balance
(a)	$109,407	$ 99,865	$ 5,000
(b)	256,800	234,900	19,656
(c)	82,500	79,000	5,200

25. In an open-invoice system, the Driftwood Company's auditors are reviewing the software that prepares the aging of accounts receivable, which the company uses in calculating its Allowance for Doubtful Accounts and Bad-Debt Expense. As part of their review, the auditors are examining the account of Ivan Preston. Preston's invoice and payment record as of the year just ended is shown in the following table.

Invoice Number	Date of Sale	Amount Due	Amount Remitted	Date Received	Adjustments	Balance Due
0525	4-30	$456.00	$420.00	5-16		$ 36.00
0547	5-26	350.00	280.00	6-16	$ 70.00	
0604	6-22	904.00	904.00	7-16		
0725	7-10	82.00	80.00	8-17	2.00	
0800	7-30	195.00	195.00	8-17		
0873	8-18	419.00	220.00	9-15	120.00	79.00
0950	9-10	733.00	783.00	10-16		(50.00)
					(50.00)	
1005	10-21	610.00	200.00	11-15	10.00	400.00
			200.00	12-15		200.00
1108	11-03	95.00	95.00	12-15		
1191	12-15	550.00			25.00	525.00

The software program produced the following result for this account as of 12-31:

0–30 days	525.00
31–60 days	0.
61–90 days	400.00
91–180 days	79.00
181 or more days	36.00

Required:

(a) Calculate your own aging of this account. Do you think the software program does an accurate job of aging?

(b) If you discovered any disagreement between your aging and that of the software program, identify the cause of the disagreement.

26. The treasurer of Stonewall Company receives a check made out by Martin Polk in payment of his current account. The treasurer endorses

the check, deposits it, and notifies the controller, who reduces the outstanding balance in Polk's account accordingly. The check is returned marked NSF.

Required:

What actions must the treasurer take when a customer's check is returned marked NSF? Give as much detail as you can, naming files and describing entries and procedures.

27. To what accounting system component does the approved-credit-customers file correspond? What information should be in each of its records?

28. Thorndale Company is an artists' supply retailer. It has granted credit purchase privileges to about 1,200 artists. The average credit customer makes a purchase every 45 days; the average purchase amount is $300. The company processes and sends statements on the last day of each month. It offers its customers the option of paying 10 percent of the outstanding balance or paying the entire balance due. If the customer pays only 10 percent, a credit cost fee of 1.5 percent of the unpaid balance is calculated and added to the next statement. If the customer pays the entire balance, there is no credit fee. For each artist, the approved-credit-customers-file record contains five balances:

   (1) Credit sales to the artist since the date of the last statement
   (2) Balance due (total amount due at date of last statement *plus* credit cost incurred this month, *plus* credit purchases this month, *minus* cash payments since date of last statement, *minus* returns and adjustments this month)
   (3) Credit costs this fiscal year (the sum of credit costs for all months in which the total amount due wasn't paid)
   (4) Returns and adjustments this month (since the date of the last statement)
   (5) Returns and adjustments this fiscal year (this month's returns and adjustments *plus* those calculated at the date of the last statement)

Required:

   (a) Robert Monet's account on March 31, after processing, showed a total due of $1,000. Thorndale Co. received a payment from Monet of $115 on April 20. The balances shown in his approved-credit-customers record at the date of the April 30 statement were (1) $300, (2) _____, (3) $85, (4) $40, (5) $120. What will be the amount due on Monet's statement dated April 30? If he again makes a minimum partial payment, what will be the amount of the credit charge shown on the May 31 statement?
   (b) With the information given, do you think this is a balance-forward or an open-invoice system?
   (c) Propose a management use for the fifth balance—the sum of all returns and allowances.

29. Smaith Company has five files in its data base–oriented batch-processing credit sales, accounts receivable, and billing application:
    (1) Approved-credit-customers file
    (2) Credit sales invoices
    (3) Adjustments to credit sales invoices
    (4) Backorders
    (5) Cash remittances

    Smaith's controller is developing links between records in these files for purposes of preparing marketing reports. For example, each record in file 3 might be linked to the proper credit sales record in file 2. File 2 records in turn link to the customer records in file 1.

Required:

   For each report below, indicate which files' records should be linked via pointers. Also indicate to which record fields the pointers should point. Assume the availability of information you require that could be recorded when a transaction takes place. (Remember, pointers link records but do not do the calculations or prepare the report!)
   (a) East district customers who have ordered over $5,000 on credit since January 1
   (b) Customers who have ordered product 024 and 013 within the same 30-day period
   (c) Sales offices that have had a 20-percent increase in sales revenue from product 024 in any 3-month period compared with the preceding 3-month period (assume figures are available)
   (d) Any product with more than 5-percent returns, based on dollar sales, since July 1
   (e) Any product with more than 3-percent backorders, based on dollar value of sales, in any calendar month this year

30. Warda Company, which imports scientific instruments, will grant and maintain credit to any U.S. customer who (a) has a positive rating with a commercial company such as Dun & Bradstreet or TRW Credit, (b) will promise to order $10,000 worth of merchandise in any 12-month period, and (c) does not fall more than 60 days behind in paying any of its accounts.

Required:

   List the fields needed in an approved-credit-customers-file record to hold the information described, as well as other information you think should be present. For each field, state whether it is purely numerical or mixed characters and numbers. Also, estimate its length. Include fields for any pointers necessary to link a record in this file to appropriate records in other files.

31. AMFM Company has a new employee who is trying to determine on April 30 whether the accounts receivable control account is in balance with its subsidiary ledger. The following information is available:

(1) March 31 control account balance: $567,000
(2) April 30 control account balance: $1,211,000
(3) Total April Credit Sales Postings to subsidiary ledger:

4/1	$30,000
4/5	$35,000
4/10	$32,000
4/15	$40,000
4/20	$28,000
4/25	$33,000

(4) Total April Cash Receipts Postings to subsidiary ledger:

4/2	$100,000
4/8	$ 50,000
4/13	$ 75,000
4/18	$ 90,000
4/23	$ 25,000
4/28	$110,000

(5) Total April adjustments: $4,000 (net credit)
(6) Sum of invoices related to shipping advices for which reimbursement was not received by March 31: $567,000
(7) Sum of invoices related to shipping advices for which reimbursement was not received by April 30: $1,211,000

Required:
   (a) Determine whether the April 30 control account and subsidiary ledger are really in balance; if not, suggest reconciling items.
   (b) If you were the credit manager, would anything about the information shown concern you? How would you collect additional information to follow up on your concern?
   (c) If you were the sales manager, would anything about the information concern you? How would you express your concern?

32. Ringo Oil Company, with annual gasoline sales of $100 million, has 1.5 million credit card customers all over North America. To speed collections, it is considering using a lockbox operation. The delay before Ringo receives and deposits a mailed customer remittance is now 12 days. A proposed system of 6 lockboxes would reduce this delay to 3 days. A bank would typically charge an annual fee of $1,000 plus 1 percent of gross remittances to operate a lockbox. The interest rate on short-term funds is stable at 9 percent annually (0.025 percent per day). Ringo currently employs 9 cash receipts clerks at an average salary of $12,000 each and incurs direct costs of $150,000 to process remittances. Ringo's internal auditors have estimated the cash losses due to control risk in the existing cash remittance operation at $90,000 annually.

Required:

Assuming all the costs of internal handling of cash remittances could be avoided by the use of lockboxes, compare the costs of the proposed system of lockboxes with the costs (and lost interest) of the present system. Would you recommend the lockbox proposal on economic grounds?

Case: Pine Tree Furniture Company

Pine Tree Furniture Company sells its products on credit through an extensive network. The company presently has a manual accounting system. Each office keeps its own accounts receivable. The company is considering developing a nine-digit account code like the one illustrated in Table 7.2. A computer system would be acquired to implement the code. The following is part of Pine Tree's sales journal with the proposed account numbering codes assigned:

Account Number	Sale Amount
101111167	$ 980
101218166	1,100
101112167	650
001111167	1,500

Required:

(a) How many regions are identified in this segment of the sales journal?

(b) Did salesperson 1 in region 1 meet his quota of sales of product 67 to industry 1?

(c) Would the last entry really be part of the sales journal? If not, of what control is it most likely to be a part?

(d) What benefits will Pine Tree get if it adopts an account code like the one in Table 7.2? Can you think of any negative consequences of adopting such a code?

CHAPTER **8**

Purchasing and Accounts Payable

Learning Objectives

After studying this chapter, you should be able to

- Describe the roles of the purchasing function within an organization and explain how centralized purchasing may save money.

- Recognize and evaluate major purchasing documents such as the material requisition, purchase order, receiving report, and debit memorandum.

- Recognize and evaluate major purchasing files, such as approved sellers, items approved for purchase, and items requisitioned.

- Identify and describe the major purchasing application processes such as identifying purchase requirements, seller selection, purchase order preparation, and purchase order update.

- Describe the relationship between purchasing and accounts payable credits and debits.

- Explain the proper use of pointers and relations in organizing data flows within the purchasing application.

- Describe purchasing's major reports to management, their contents, and how they should be used.

Purchasing and accounts payable will be your second look at processing of a computerized accounting application. This chapter is more detailed than Chapter 7, particularly in its stress on the uses of pointers and relations. The purpose of the **purchasing function** is to identify and acquire specific materials, supplies, and services that the organization needs if it is to function; acquisition must take place in sufficient quantities, when needed, and economically. The corresponding accounting application, **purchasing and accounts payable,** seeks to achieve three objectives: make certain that no unauthorized financial obligations are recorded or paid, record accurately and pay promptly all authorized financial obligations arising from purchasing activities, and report to management as required for cash flow management, seller performance evaluation, inventory management, and payment of obligations. Although manual accounting and record-keeping procedures have enabled organizations to keep track of their obligations and purchases, manual procedures are expensive and cannot always meet the three objectives just listed. Accordingly, this accounting application was one of the first to be converted to computers on a widespread basis. Purchasing and accounts payable benefits particularly from application of data base principles to classify the transaction data and the control data as linked relations.

Overview of Purchasing

We have seen that most sales are on credit; most purchases are also made on credit. Credit purchases are used to acquire office supplies, utilities, and manufacturing materials and supplies. In addition, services such as maintenance, data processing, and consulting are typically obtained on credit rather than by immediately transferring cash to the sellers. Furthermore, most purchases are routine. Since only a few purchases require nonroutine attention, this chapter will focus on purchasing, receiving, and accounting system support for the bulk of transactions that are handled routinely. A simplified diagram of this process appears in Figure 8.1.

This figure shows that responsibility centers requisition, or request, materials through the purchasing function, which determines whether the materials should be provided; locates sellers (also called vendors; we use these terms interchangeably); and makes the purchases. The intent to purchase is signified by a purchase order that is sent to the seller. The seller ships the materials and sends an invoice, a request for payment. The shipment arrives at the buyer's receiving center, a separate responsibility that verifies that the shipment matches what was ordered. The receiving center passes these items on to the center that requested them (which could be a stockroom if the buyer stockpiles this item). The separation of using, ordering, and receiving materials is an important control over consumption of material resources by an organization. The paying function relies on evidence that items were ordered, received, and properly invoiced to support paying the seller for them. An **account payable** is a payment due a seller for goods or services received by the purchaser.

Within the accounts payable function, sellers' invoices are tested to verify that they represent actual liabilities; this process questions whether each item listed as ordered and delivered actually *was* ordered and delivered, according to the organization's own records. Amounts owed for all items that pass this test are paid; the remainder are held back until evidence of receipt appears or clearly will not appear. The management of accounts payable requires that all verified liabilities be paid, that no unverified liabilities be paid, and that no liabilities be overlooked or misclassified. Since sellers often assess penalties for delaying payment of real liabilities, accounts payable operates under time pressure.

All routine purchases, and their corresponding accounts payable operations, are documented and processed in the same way, regardless of

Figure 8.1   The Purchasing and Accounts Payable Process
Note the separation between ordering, receiving, and paying. Except for requesting
what it expects to need, an operating center has no responsibility for purchasing.

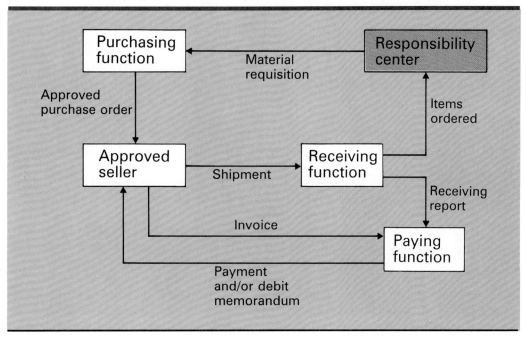

what is being acquired. Chapter 12 describes controls over the cash disbursement process. Here in this chapter we discuss the controls on purchasing and on measurement of accounts payable. Purchasing controls resemble controls on other processes and conform to the same rules: major functions like receiving, accepting, and paying are separated; major decisions like selection of the seller, approval of purchase, and acceptance of delivered goods and services are made by different individuals; and prenumbered forms are used for ordering, receiving, and paying.

The organization's style and needs determine how it organizes, positions, and supervises the purchasing function. Purchasing is a staff function and should serve the entire organization. In a small organization, one purchasing agent may suffice. In larger firms, a purchasing director may coordinate purchasing specialists who are supervised by major departments or functional directors. The purpose of such an arrangement is to make purchasing expertise and service available within the departments that generate the most purchasing activity. The immediate superior of the purchasing director might be the chief executive officer or the director of finance, marketing, or production. Whichever executive receives the purchasing director's reports, purchasing should take pains to serve the best interests of the entire organization at all times. The assembly of documents to support payment of cash to a seller is the controller's responsibility; verification of this evidence and preparation of checks is the responsibility of the treasurer.

Centralized Versus Departmental Purchasing

In a large organization, economies of scale dictate that the purchasing function be relatively specialized and centrally coordinated. Purchasing the right quantities from dependable sellers, at the right prices, and at the right times can be complex. Purchasing requires expertise that most individual departments lack the incentive or resources to obtain.

Consider this example: National Woodstove, Inc., is a manufacturing and distributing company with two manufacturing departments and eight distributing departments. It makes total annual purchases of $2 million. National Woodstove may realize significant savings by purchasing pencils, paper, typewriters, furniture, and even paper cups in bulk for the entire company from a limited number of sellers, rather than allowing all ten departments to purchase supplies individually in small lots from different sellers. Also, a staff that specializes in purchasing is more efficient than scattered individuals who attend to purchasing part-time. There are discounts for ordering larger quantities at one time; most wholesale and many retail suppliers offer discounts that increase with order size, so that a gross of pencils may generate only a 5 percent discount, whereas a case of pencils produces a 27 percent discount. Since purchasing is evaluated partly on whether it obtains the best deals, a purchasing department has reason to seek out the lowest prices. In addition, a central place for storing supplies encourages better control over waste and loss. Table 8.1 presents a comparative economic analysis of departmental and centralized purchasing.

The Responsibilities of Purchasing

The responsibilities of the purchasing function are fourfold: internal operations, purchasing policies, seller relations, and transportation and receiving (a separate activity not related to ordering). Throughout all its operations, purchasing must generate the documentation to support either acceptance or rejection of the seller's delivered merchandise and payment or nonpayment of the seller's invoices. Some representative tasks that a purchasing function would be expected to perform in each category of responsibility follow:

Internal operations: Establish policies and procedures for purchasing based on the type of goods, the urgency of the requirements, and the cost of the goods. Train regular staff to be aware of and follow the policies and procedures. Use printed forms and other documentation to encourage proper handling of transactions.

Table 8.1 Cost Comparison of Centralized Versus Departmental Purchasing

Annual Cost Using	Wages and Salary Expense	Discounts for Quantity Orders	Inventory Shrinkage and Waste from Inadequate Purchasing Controls	Total
Departmental purchasing	20 people, 25% time, salary $17,000 each = $85,000	0.5% × $2 million = ($10,000)	$150,000 average inventory × 10% = $15,000	$90,000
Centralized purchasing	3 people, 100% time, salary $20,000 each = $60,000	2% × $2 million = ($40,000)	$100,000 average inventory × 5% = $5,000	$25,000

Purchasing policies: Identify items purchased frequently or in significant quantities, and negotiate contracts with sellers for these items to be acquired on favorable terms. Consolidate many small purchase requests into larger purchase orders. When complex requirements are involved, work with managers and engineers to develop appropriate performance or design specifications.

Seller relations: Become familiar with different sellers' products and performance, and select as regular suppliers those sellers that are superior. Whenever possible, negotiate appropriate agreements with sellers specifying item description, quality, and performance; price; maximum and minimum quantities; means of shipment; seller services expected; and conditions for returns or allowances.

Transportation and receiving: Designate a centralized point at which the organization will receive shipments and verify that shipments meet the terms of the purchase agreement and are acceptable before turning them over to users. If the volume of deliveries justifies doing so, negotiate agreements with carriers about freight and service on incoming shipments. Match shipments received with purchase orders. Make certain that insurance coverage for the shipment is adequate to assure recovery for losses that exceed the carrier's liability limits.[1]

---

[1]Many carriers limit their liability per shipment. If the shipment terms are FOB shipping point (FOB stands for "free on board"), the buyer is assuming the risks of any loss or damage during transportation, above the carrier's liability limits, and should be insured appropriately. If the shipment terms are FOB destination, the seller is assuming these risks.

Key Documents and Forms

The documentary support required by the purchasing function depends on its underlying philosophy. Generally speaking, there are two distinct approaches to purchasing. First, purchases can be made often enough and in sufficient quantities to keep on hand a constant inventory that fluctuates between selected upper and lower limits. An example of this approach is a warehouse that keeps inventory on hand and fills orders quickly from it. The inventory on hand serves a relatively constant demand for small orders that must be quickly filled, buffering demand against the large incoming shipments that arrive infrequently.

The alternative is to purchase only in response to requests, maintaining almost no inventory on hand. An example of this approach is the mail-order office that keeps no inventory but accepts and forwards customer orders. There is less need for the buffer of an on-hand inventory when demand can be deferred somewhat and resupply through purchase can occur relatively quickly and frequently.

This chapter illustrates the second approach because it shows how purchases can occur in direct response to organizational needs as expressed by requisitions.

The principal documents in the purchasing function are the material requisition, the purchase order, the receiving report, and the debit memorandum. These forms enhance control by separating needs identification (the material requisition) from the act of purchasing (the purchase order), and they allow the staff to improve effectiveness by consolidating several requests into one order.

The Material Requisition

Operations, production, marketing, and administrative centers use a **material requisition** document to describe the materials, supplies, or services they need. They send the requisitions to the purchasing department, where they are either implemented or returned for additional information or appropriate approval.

A sample material requisition is shown in Figure 8.2. The request form should include enough copies so that the originator, the manager who approves the request, and the purchasing department may keep one each. Because it is an internal document, a material requisition can be very simple. The one shown in Figure 8.2 can easily be adapted for display on a computer monitor, which prompts the user to enter specific computer-usable data to prepare a request. This type of data entry mechanism is an example of a **screen form**. The originator does not need to fill in the purchase order number, and unless he or she specifies a particular seller, the purchasing application selects one from its usual approved suppliers.

Figure 8.2   A Material Requisition
This document initiates the process of acquiring materials or supplies. On this particular form, one person must prepare the requisition and one person must authorize it. The last three columns are for use by the purchasing function.

Material Requisition						066875
form revised 11-30-87						

Department _____   Date _____

Requested by _____   Authorized by _____

Item I.D.	Description	Seller	Quantity	Priority	Charge Account	Purchase Order I.D.
———	———	———	———	———	———	———
———	———	———	———	———	———	———
———	———	———	———	———	———	———
———	———	———	———	———	———	———
———	———	———	———	———	———	———
———	———	———	———	———	———	———

COPY A

If the originator wants to request more than six items using a form like the one in Figure 8.2, the computer can scroll the first part of the form up the screen and out of sight. When completed, the material requisition becomes one or more records in the pending material requisitions file.

The Purchase Order

The **purchase order** is an external document used by the purchasing department to provide a single seller with a written description of specific needed materials, supplies, or services that the buyer is offering to purchase. It often contains items from more than one material requisition but never includes items to be obtained from more than one seller. To this seller, the purchase order represents either an offer or a contract; therefore, it should include the information necessary to indicate what the terms of the agreement are. This information includes the quantity and quality of

Figure 8.3 A Purchase Order
The purchase order is actually a request to a vendor that the vendor sell the specified items on the terms described. The purchaser sends one or two copies to the vendor and keeps two to four copies for its own use. If a screen form is used, access authorization may substitute for the internal copies of the form.

Purchase Order	Date prepared __/__/__ By _____	NO.067890
Summers Distributing Company 1000 Avenue Z Austin, Texas 78700 (512) 000–0000	Date approved __/__/__ By _____ Date requested __/__/__ By _____ Capital item?☐ If yes, category no.____	This number must appear on all invoices and related documents

TO

(Name and address of vendor)

Special Instructions:
Please acknowledge ☐
Partial shipments acceptable ☐
Insure for $500 or less only ☐
Do not make substitutions
without prior notice ☐
TOP PRIORITY RUSH ☐

☐ Refer to purchase
agreement no._____
☐ OTHER: _____
_____
_____
_____

Item no.	DESCRIPTION	Units and quantity	Unit price (*)	Delivery required	Enter below quantities actually received	
					1	2
					Date	Date
					1	2
					Date	Date
					1	2
					Date	Date
					1	2
					Date	Date
					1	2
					Date	Date

Ship to:

Address of receiving dept.

* = Do not charge sales tax on this item

Send invoice to:
Invoicing address not same as purchasing or receiving, if possible

each item, the price, the date required, shipping information, and special provisions. For as long as the seller is responding to it—that is, as long as its shipments are still incomplete—the purchase order is called an **open purchase order**.

Figure 8.3 shows a typical purchase order. The purchase order, too, may be a screen form that a purchasing agent completes. If purchasing typically processes many requisitions listing numerous items from multiple vendors, the process of creating purchase orders from requisitions can and should be computerized. A computerized purchase order preparation process determines whether a requisition has been approved and, if so, searches other requisitions for similar items, items to be purchased from the same seller, and items allowing discretion on choice of seller. Then it creates the appropriate purchase orders.

The Receiving Report

The receiving report originates in the receiving area, a place set aside for deliveries. An employee in the receiving area completes the receiving report on each incoming shipment. This document itemizes what is in an incoming shipment and indicates whether the goods are damaged. It serves as evidence that a shipment with specific contents, from a specific seller, related to one or more specific purchase orders, arrived in a particular condition. The simplest receiving report is a copy of the purchase order designed so that it does not show the quantities ordered and items can be marked off as they are received in incoming shipments. (Withholding access to the quantities ordered is a control to ensure that the receiving area counts the items and that the quantities received match the quantities ordered.) In such a system, the purchasing department must provide the receiving area with copies of every open purchase order. If a computer is used to produce the purchase order, the receiving report screen form can easily display each purchase order without listing quantities.

Using the purchase order as the receiving report is complicated when not all items on an order are shipped or received at the same time. A computer can help keep track of items not yet received by sorting and reporting on backorder items by date and purchase order. To aid in computer data entry and to organize documents, the packing list that came with the shipment can be attached to the receiving report.

We show no illustration of a receiving report because even if the actual purchase order isn't used, the receiving report is based very closely on a purchase order. In Figure 8.3, the spaces for date and quantity received will make one copy of the purchase order suitable for use as a receiving report.

The Debit Memorandum

The purchaser prepares a **debit memorandum** when adjusting terms of a purchase or rejecting a shipment in whole or in part. The memorandum is sent to the seller to indicate that the buyer is decreasing all or part of the amount shown on the seller's invoice. In a typical scenario, the purchaser phones the seller for authorization to return the rejected items. By granting this authorization, the seller agrees to two conditions. First, the seller agrees to accept the return shipment of rejected items. Second, the seller agrees to a reduction in the buyer's account payable to the seller. At the same time that the shipment of rejected items begins its trip back to the seller, the buyer sends a debit memorandum to the seller, which says in effect, "We have reduced our liability to you by $xxx; please adjust your books accordingly." Copies of the debit memorandum and shipping papers also serve as the buyer's internal record to support the seller's reduced account payable. Figure 8.4 illustrates a typical debit memorandum form. In a manual accounting system, copies of the debit memorandum go to the seller, the purchasing function, the accounts payable function, and perhaps to the inventory and receiving functions. In a computerized system, the debit memorandum screen form is the basis for one or more computer records that can be displayed in the same departments and also for a printed version of the screen form that is sent to the seller.

Complexity and Files

Purchasing systems are relatively complex. To see why, consider the simplest possible purchasing system, which would limit each material requisition to one item. Each purchase order, too, would buy only the one item requisitioned. The seller would ship and deliver exactly what was ordered. When the seller's monthly statement arrived, it would agree exactly with what was ordered, shipped, and received, and would match the purchase orders and receiving reports precisely. No returns or allowances would ever be necessary. There would be no headaches over goods lost or damaged in shipping, substitutions, or long delays. Describing such an unrealistically simple system points out the numerous ways in which purchasing can become complicated in the course of ordinary business, even for a small business. As the number of items purchased and the frequency of purchases increase, so do the complexity of the purchasing process and the likelihood that the adverse circumstances mentioned will overwhelm a simple and inflexible system. Designing in enough flexibility to deal successfully with each potential pitfall contributes to the complexity of the purchasing process.

Since real purchasing systems must deal with all of the routine complications that occur, the computer program design we describe here uses

Figure 8.4   A Debit Memorandum Form
The purchaser uses this form, with the vendor's authorization, to return or exchange merchandise, claim discounts, or adjust the price of merchandise for which an invoice has already been issued.

Debit Memo   **No. 023221**

revised 12-3-85

Summers Distributing Company
1000 Avenue Z
Austin, Texas 78700
(512) 000-0000

Date: Mo. ____   Day ____   Yr. ____

- -

TO: _____   Seller No. _____
             (name of seller)

We today debit your account for the following items:

Our ID Item #	PO#	Quantity	Unit Price	Debit Amount	Your Invoice ID	Explanation Code
_____	_____	_____	_____	_____	_____	_____
_____	_____	_____	_____	_____	_____	_____
_____	_____	_____	_____	_____	_____	_____
_____	_____	_____	_____	_____	_____	_____
_____	_____	_____	_____	_____	_____	_____
_____	_____	_____	_____	_____	_____	_____

data base principles to create a system that can manage these complications. In tailoring this system to a particular business, you could omit portions of the program to accommodate a less demanding purchasing environment. The program uses hierarchically connected files (or relations) that liberally incorporate pointers. Here, the record-design function of each file is discussed so that you can compare these functions with those of the credit sales, accounts receivable, and billing application treated in Chapter 7. You will see again in this chapter and the next one that data base concepts can increase the power of any accounting application.

Figure 8.5 **Pointer Relationships (facing page)**
This diagram depicts the access from one document to others in the purchasing-function data base.

Files

The purchasing and accounts payable application uses the same item-description details for several different activities. To avoid duplicating these details each time they are used, the computer program employs pointers to create hierarchical relationships among records in different files and to link related records in the same file. Table 8.2 shows seven pairs of files. The seven files with suffix "A" are header files. A header file record contains information common to other records that are linked to it. Each linked **record** contains process-unique information about items affected by that process, such as preparing a purchase order. The set of items affected by the process, such as the ones included in a given purchase order, are linked to the header. All the items linked to a particular type of header, such as purchase order headers, constitute a set of item records, which is identified in Table 8.2 by the suffix "B."

The "B" item sets (2-B, 3-B, 4-B, 5-B, 6-B, and 7-B) consist of overlapping subsets of file 1-B. Each record in file 2-B represents one instance of one item requisitioned. The first subset, items requisitioned, includes all items in the file. Therefore, each item in this file is linked to one material-requisition-header record; that is, every record in item set (2-B) corresponds to an item that was requisitioned. Each item in set (3-B) is linked to one purchase order header; in turn, a purchase order header is linked to as many items as were ordered in the purchase order. Until an item in 2-B and 3-B is invoiced (6-B), received (4-B), and paid for (7-B), it will not appear in these sets, even though it is in the file of items. These sets do not exist independently of the file of items, even though to the user they appear to be separate files. The records in each of the item sets are distinguished and linked by appropriate pointers. Figure 8.5 graphically illus-

Table 8.2 **Structure of Relations in Purchasing and Accounts Payable**

Group	Header File	Related Item Set
1	1-A Approved-seller header	1-B Items approved for purchase (purchasable items)
2	2-A Material requisition header	2-B Items requisitioned
3	3-A Open purchase order header	3-B Items on open purchase order
4	4-A Receiving report header	4-B Items on receiving report
5	5-A Debit memorandum header	5-B Items on debit memorandum
6	6-A Seller-invoice header	6-B Items invoiced
7	7-A Authorized-payments header	7-B Items paid for

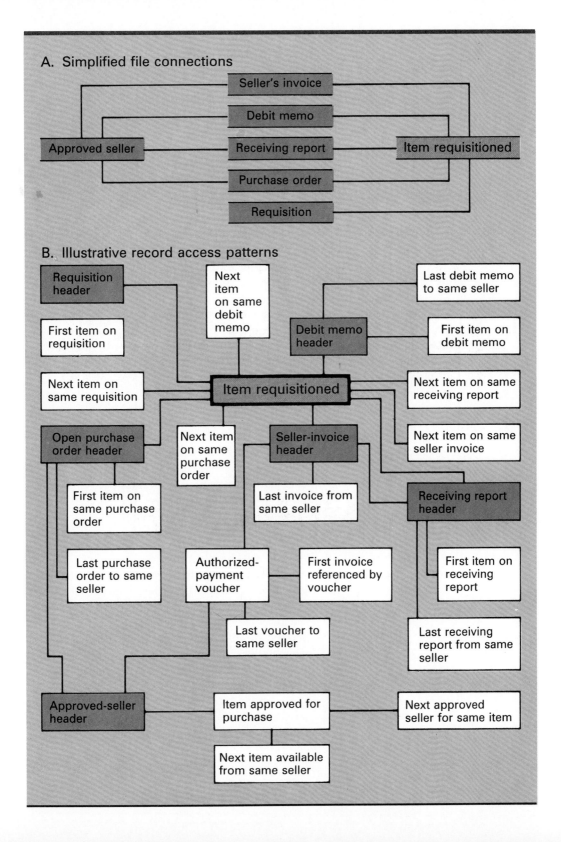

A. Simplified file connections

B. Illustrative record access patterns

trates all the pointer relationships among records in these files. It will serve as a helpful adjunct to the following verbal descriptions of individual files and the fields contained in their records.

Approved Sellers and Items Approved for Purchase. The purchasing director must identify approved sellers. An **approved seller** is one which meets the buyer's standards as one from whom purchases of specific approved items may be made. Each approved seller has a record in this file. Each seller record is linked to the items that have been approved for purchase from that seller. A record in the approved-sellers file is prepared in advance of any purchasing activity involving that seller. Preparing approved-seller records involves technical and purchasing expertise, so the authority for creating and maintaining these records generally must reside in the purchasing function.

Through an approval process, items are proposed and selected to be on a list of items approved for purchase. Because this process must occur before the item can even appear on an approved purchase order, it serves as the preventive element of controls over purchasing. Every such item will appear as a record in file 1-B, the items approved for purchase. The organization units that use these items should work with the purchasing director in deciding whether to include these items on the list.

File	*Fields*
1-A Approved sellers	Seller identification number (primary key and also the accounts payable number)
	Seller name, address, phone number
	Pointer to first item approved for purchase from this seller

File	*Fields*
1-B Items approved for purchase	Item identification number (primary key)
	Item description (code or words)
	Item order quantity (if ordered in preset quantities)
	Item price per unit
	Covered by Purchase Agreement No. _____
	Date this item last reviewed
	Pointer to first seller from whom this item may be purchased
	Pointer to next item that may be purchased from first seller
	Pointer to second seller from whom this item may be purchased
	Pointer to next item that may be purchased from second seller

[and so on]

2. **Material Requisition Header and Items Requisitioned.** The material-requisition-header record contains a field for each data value from the material requisition, plus a pointer to the first item requisitioned. There is a separate record in the file for each material requisition that is submitted.

File	*Fields*
2-A Material requisition header	Requisition number (primary key)
	Identification code of requesting department
	Date prepared
	Authorization/approval code
	Date approved
	Pointer to first item on this requisition

The items-requisitioned file contains many records, each describing a single item whose purchase has been requested, plus pointers linking the record to various header records and to subsequent requisitioned items. Several items-requisitioned records are typically linked to a single material-requisition-header record. This file is extremely important, since it enables an item to be entered only once, then connected to every significant event in the sequence of requisition, purchase, receipt, invoicing, authorizing payment, and payment or return. Thus the smooth functioning of the entire application depends on the items-requisitioned file's being properly designed. The computer software can be designed and programmed to check for all of the appropriate links to various header records as processing continues through the sequence.

File	*Fields*
2-B Items requisitioned	Item identification number (primary key)
	Description of item (words or code)
	Seller identifying code (if seller is known)
	Quantity of item requested
	Total cost of item
	Account number to be charged
	Delivery priority
	Quantity delivered
	Condition upon delivery
	Pointer to requisition header
	Pointer to next item on same requisition
	Pointer to items-approved-for-purchase-file record
	Pointer to purchase order
	Pointer to next item on same purchase order
	Pointer to receiving report
	Pointer to next item on same report
	Pointer to seller invoice
	Pointer to next item on same seller invoice
	Pointer to debit memorandum
	Pointer to next item on same memorandum

Each item requisitioned should include a purchase order number, which is the pointer to the purchase order header.

Purchase Order Header and Items on an Open Purchase Order. The purchase order header is the file that contains the categories of information on the purchase order form, plus pointers to the seller, items purchased, and purchase orders to the same seller. To prepare the purchase order, the items to be requisitioned must be located in the items-approved-for-purchase file and must be available from an approved seller; the information in these records is retrieved to prepare a purchase order. A separate purchase-order header record will exist for each purchase order prepared. As a group, these records help the accounts payable process to verify invoices from sellers.

The fields listed here correspond to headings on the purchase order in Figure 8.3, but some fields are omitted for brevity. Fields 2, 3, and 4 may be copied from the approved-sellers file.

File	*Fields*
3-A Open purchase order header	Purchase order number (serial and primary key)
	Purchasing manager name, address, phone number
	Buyer delivery address
	Buyer invoicing address
	Special instructions (may be several fields)
	Pointer to authorized seller
	Pointer to first item on this order
	Pointer to last purchase order to this seller

The data set of items included on open purchase orders is, as already explained, not a distinct group of records that stay together like a file. Here, the multiple-table data base design begins to show its efficiency. The pointer in the purchase order header to the first item on this order is the item identifier code of an item in the items-requisitioned file. That item links to the next item requisitioned on the same purchase order, which also links to the next item on the same purchase order, and so on. These pointers move the computer along the information path. The last item on a purchase order links back to the purchase-order header file, which contains the standard terms and conditions to be printed on the purchase order (or applied under a contract with the seller). The items on one purchase order may originate from several requisitions.

In other words, the records created to record items requisitioned, which were linked to material requisitions, are also linked to purchase orders. Thus, this information need not be reentered or duplicated; it is merely referenced through pointers.

File	*Fields*
3-B Items on open purchase order	Selected records from 2-B, linked to 3-A by pointer

Receiving Report Header and Items on a Receiving Report. The receiving-report header record contains fields that pertain to all goods received. It may contain links to a purchase order (if sellers have been instructed not to combine items from multiple purchase orders in a single shipment), to a seller's invoice (if the invoices do not combine two or more shipments), to the first item received in a shipment, and to the last receiving report header for a shipment from this seller. If the conditions just noted in parentheses are not met, then pointers on records in file 4-B, to be described next, may identify the purchase order and seller's invoice.

File	*Fields*
4-A Receiving report header	Receiving report identifying number (serial and primary key) Purchase order number Shipment identifying number (supplied by shipper or seller) Date shipment received Pointer to our record of seller's invoice corresponding to this shipment Pointer to first item received Pointer to last receiving report header for a shipment from this seller

The data sets for the files of items on receiving report and items on debit memorandum will work the same way as the items-on-purchase-order data set. In reviewing or printing a receiving report, the pointers in the header record start the computer along the information path, and pointers in this file link all the items connected to that report.

File	*Fields*
4-B Items on receiving report	Selected records from 2-B, linked to 4-A, representing items requisitioned, ordered, and received

Using records originally created during material requisition, it becomes possible to indicate whether an item was received simply by linking the original record to a receiving report.

Debit Memorandum Header and Items on a Debit Memorandum. The debit-memorandum header file contains one record for each group of returns to the seller from a given shipment. This record is linked to records created in the items-on-debit-memorandum file when the items are found to be unacceptable and their return has been authorized.

File	*Fields*
5-A Debit memo- randum header	Debit memorandum number (serial and primary key) Seller identification number Date prepared Authorized by Debit memorandum total dollar amount Pointer to first item Pointer to last debit memorandum to same seller

File	*Fields*

5-B Items on
    debit memoran-
    dum
	Selected records from 2-B, linked to 5-A, repre-
	    senting items requisitioned, ordered, received,
	    then returned to the seller

Seller-invoice Header and Items Invoiced by Seller. The seller-invoice header contains the fields on the seller's invoice, the document sent by the seller to the buyer to indicate the seller believes payment is due for specific goods or services, plus the seller's accounts payable identifying number and links to the receiving report header and the authorized-payment, or voucher, header. A **voucher** is a document used to bring together evidence indicating a seller's invoice should be paid. These links allow the controller to verify that items invoiced by the seller were ordered and have been received.

Normally, shipments and invoices have a one-to-one correspondence. However, a seller's invoice may reference complete or partial shipment of several purchase orders, and the file structure described here allows the application to examine the receiving report(s) and individual items. The items-invoiced file is accessed and organized only through the receiving report file. Like the files for items purchased, items received, and items on debit memos, this file is an information path rather than a separate collection of records.

File	*Fields*

6-A Seller-
    invoice
    header
	Unique invoice-identification number (primary key)
	Seller identification number
	Date received
	Gross amount billed
	Tax due
	Shipping charges due
	Debit memoranda amount
	Discount available for prompt payment
	Date prompt-payment discount expires
	Indicated net amount due
	Pointer to first receiving report invoiced
	Pointer to last invoice from same seller
	Pointer to authorized-payment record

File	*Fields*
6-B Items invoiced	Selected records from 2-B, linked to 6-A, representing items requisitioned, ordered, received, not returned to the seller, and finally invoiced by the seller

7. **Authorized-payments Header and Items Paid For.** The authorized-payments header contains the fields that appear on each payment voucher. It is the file that acts as an interface with the cash disbursements process, providing that function with the information required to create a check for the seller. The information is organized as a voucher, which organizes it as support for paying cash to the seller (or other creditor). To support the production of approved-payment vouchers, this file must rely on and access *every* file in this application. Such access comes through only three links within this header: to the approved seller, to the first invoice referenced, and to the last authorized payment to the same seller (so that only one check need be prepared for each period, or invoice, as the organization's policy dictates). The link to the seller's invoice starts the path back to the receiving report headers and the items requisitioned, from which the connected records in the purchase order and debit memo files are accessed. These links demonstrate, once again, the power of data base design and the scope of a computer's capacity to organize data.

File	*Fields*
7-A Authorized- payments header	Payment-voucher number Date voucher prepared Person approving voucher Amount of payment Number of check used to pay seller Date check prepared Pointer to approved seller Pointer to first invoice referenced Pointer to last payment for same seller

File	*Fields*
7-B Items paid for	Selected records from 2-B, linked to 7-A, representing items requisitioned, ordered, received, not returned to the seller, invoiced by the seller, and paid for

In this on-line system design, proper data entry and editing procedures (to be discussed in Chapter 12) can virtually eliminate unprocessable transactions. Nevertheless, some processes may temporarily defer acting on a record. For example, a material requisition may have to be held because no seller for it has been approved.

The flexibility of this design for purchasing and accounts payable makes it possible to deal with most complications as they arise. For example, the system is able to handle partial deliveries of items on a purchase order, which can create difficulties in matching invoices with orders and deliveries. Some purchase orders lead to substitutions, backorders, returns, allowances, and cancellations, which may extend over weeks or months before the original purchase order is fully satisfied. During this period, the seller will usually post and invoice the partial deliveries. The buyer will often pay these invoices. These complications can be recorded and processed by the system just described. Its complexity actually helps management retain control of information. On orders involving large quantities of many items, a complex computerized system may reduce but not entirely eliminate the occasional need for substantial human intervention. Sometimes the best way to control a tangled situation is to start over by making a supplementary purchase order incorporating the newest availability, pricing, and delivery information for the items still outstanding on the original order.

Inventory Maintenance System of Purchasing

As noted early in this chapter, there are two distinct purchasing philosophies. We have described in detail the requisition approach to purchasing. If an organization prefers to maintain a constant inventory within specified limits, the file organization just described can be used with only minor changes.

An items-to-be-acquired file takes the place of the items-requisitioned file (2-B). The record content remains about the same, except there is no reference to any requisitioning department. For each item, management establishes an **order point**—the inventory level at which the item should be ordered. Each time a quantity on hand drops below its order point, a record for that item will be added automatically to the items-to-be-acquired file. That record then behaves like a record in the items-requisitioned file, in the sense that pointers connect it to various header records as the item is ordered, delivered, invoiced, and paid. All references to material requisitioning are disregarded. The order point may be implemented by accumulating approved material requisitions until their combined total equals the predetermined order quantity, or by ordering a predetermined quantity when the number of items on hand reaches the "order-trigger" level. To manage inventory-requirements identification, management should formulate an inventory-control policy, which should identify the order point for each item and the order quantity approved for purchase when the inventory on hand falls below the order point.

Economic Order Quantity.   Purchasing may be responsible for determining order quantities, especially for high-volume items. Determining the correct order quantity usually requires consideration of many different factors—the seller, shipping costs, rate at which the item is used, cost of placing an order, cost of being unable to fill orders for the item, and cost of keeping the item on hand.

A common starting point for determining the correct order quantity is the formula for finding the **economic order quantity (EOQ)**—the order size that under certain conditions will yield the lowest combined cost of ordering and carrying inventory in stock. This formula assumes that demand for the item is known and constant over time; that the cost to carry one unit in stock for one period is known; that the cost to place an order is known; that purchasing wishes to minimize the sum of combined ordering and carrying costs; and that delivery of stock occurs as soon as an order is placed. The formula for calculating the optimum economic order quantity Q^* is as follows:

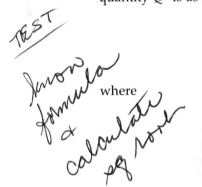

$$Q^* = \sqrt{\frac{2DC_O}{C_S}}$$

where

D = units demanded in one period

C_O = cost of placing one order

C_S = cost to carry one unit one period

For example, if D = 1,000, C_O = \$100, and C_S = \$10, the economic order quantity Q^* would equal the square root of (2 × 1,000 × 100/10) = 141.4 units.

To compute the average cost of ordering exactly 141 units each time inventory is depleted, calculate and then combine the total ordering costs and total inventory-carrying costs. Dividing annual demand by the EOQ (1,000/141.4) reveals that 7.07 (in practical terms, either 7 or 8) orders will be placed each year. At \$100 per order, average total ordering costs per year would be \$707. If reordering takes place at an inventory level of zero and delivery of the new order occurs immediately, average inventory will be 141.4/2 = 70.7 units. The average cost of carrying inventory at \$10 per unit per year also would be \$707. The average annual inventory cost would then be \$707 + \$707 = \$1,414. The EOQ might have to be modified based on quantity discounts, standard shipment size, or other factors not included in the model here. Nevertheless, the EOQ formula is widely used in inventory management.

Figure 8.6 Purchasing and Accounts Payable Data-flow Diagram (facing page)
This diagram shows the major file and process interrelationships in the purchasing and accounts payable application. Note the interfaces with inventory and cash disbursements applications.

Computerized Processes in Purchasing and Accounts Payable

The data flow diagram in Figure 8.6 shows the major processes (ovals), files (parallel lines), and data flow paths (arrows) in the purchasing and accounts payable application. The eight major processes in the illustration use the files just described to accomplish specific data entry, processing, and reporting objectives. The processes are (1) identifying requirements and approval and edit; (2) selecting approved sellers; (3) preparing purchase orders; (4) receiving incoming shipments; (5) updating purchase order data; (6) identifying accounts payable liabilities; (7) updating purchase order debits; and (8) updating general ledger/accounts payable (not shown in Figure 8.6). The following discussion of these processes shows how they work to serve the organization and also describes their major controls.

Identifying Requirements and Approval and Edit

Each operating department identifies its own needs for materials, supplies, and services. For control purposes, departments state these needs in the form of a material requisition. This requisition may be the normal way to acquire all inventory, or it may be used only for items not normally kept in inventory. In either case, the material requisition sets in motion the process of replenishing needed supplies.

An authorized individual, other than the person who prepared the requisition, should review and approve the request. This person should have organizationwide purchasing knowledge and expertise. When the system converts the approved request into computer-processable form, it should do so through an editing process that determines whether the requisitioner should actually need the requested items. For example, a quality-control department might have little need for a stereo and should not be able to purchase one routinely. The editing process should verify the item identification numbers and other purchase information. Finally, the computer should create the requisition-header record for this request and items-requisitioned records for each item in the request and add them to the appropriate files.

Selection of Approved Sellers

The purchasing function is responsible for selecting and approving sellers who can supply required items and services. Purchasing experience

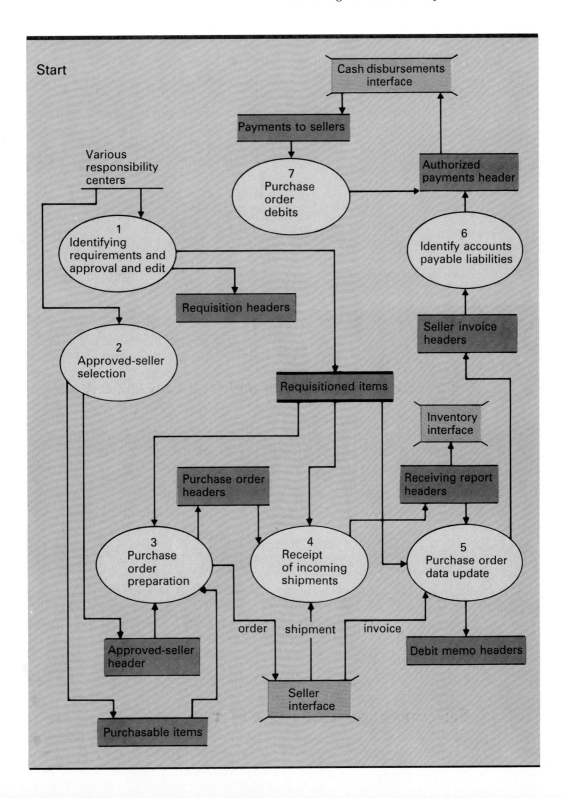

stresses the importance of following three major rules to obtain the best results:

> *First*, have two or more sources for as many items as possible. The record format described on page 272 accommodates this practice and allows pointers for two sellers for each item. Using more than two or three sellers for an item, however, may tend to generate order splitting into small quantities that do not qualify for discounts.
> *Second*, if possible, negotiate agreements with sellers that include purchase and delivery terms.
> *Third*, regular review of the sellers' performance is essential.

This process maintains two files: the approved-seller header file, which describes approved sellers, and the items-approved-for-purchase file, which describes items approved for routine purchase.

Preparation of Purchase Orders

This process uses information from the material-requisitions, items-purchased, and approved-sellers files. It consolidates separate material requisitions for the same item. A computer program might use a four-step process to create an open purchase order from various approved material requisitions. First, it would look up the approved seller for each item and fill in the item pointer to the approved seller. Second, it would create an open-purchase-order-header record. Third, via pointers, it would link this header to all requisitioned items to be acquired from the same seller. Fourth, it would consolidate items to be ordered from the same seller and print a purchase order for those items in the consolidated quantities.

To purchase an unusual item that is not in the file of items approved for purchase, and for which there is no number or approved seller, special authorization is required. Such purchases follow the same route as others, except that the seller may be selected through a bidding process or negotiations.

Receiving Incoming Shipments

The existence of a purchase order that has not been completely filled authorizes the receiving department to accept an incoming shipment citing that purchase order number. The receiving department should not have access to the quantities ordered and expected and must examine the shipment to complete the receiving report. The shipment arrives with two types of documentation: a **packing slip** describing its contents and identifying the purchase orders that serve as the seller's authority to ship the items, and a **bill of lading** instructing the shipper where and how to deliver it. The bill of lading for the shipment functions as a plane or bus ticket does for a passenger and may later become a source document to support payment of freight and insurance charges billed by the shipper.

In a computerized system, the computer terminal in the receiving department displays as a receiving report screen form the purchase order referenced on the packing slip. The quantities are blanked out. By filling in the quantities received, the receiving department documents the shipment and adds pointers connecting the corresponding records in the items-requisitioned file to the receiving report header.

The receiving report file can also be linked with the inventory application, which uses this information to maintain a record of inventory quantities, deliveries, and amounts of items still on order.

Updating Purchase Order Data

Updating the purchase order data consists of matching seller-invoice-header records with items linked to both receiving reports and purchase orders. The various pointers facilitate this process and make it possible to identify discrepancies between records.

Consider this example. You order 100 model B62 condensation units from Romney Company. Romney pays for shipping. Shortly, an invoice for 50 model B62s arrives. Correspondence reveals that 50 more should be received in three weeks. The quantity-received field in this B62 items-requisitioned record indicates that only 48 B62s arrived. The shipper apparently lost two of them, and Romney will file a claim with the shipper. Meanwhile, you create a debit memo header and link it to the B62 items-requisitioned record. The accounts payable process will interpret this header to mean that the seller's invoice referencing the original purchase order should be reduced by two model B62s.[2]

Identifying Accounts Payable Liabilities

Upon shipping, the seller sends a shipping advice to the buyer's receiving department. The **shipping advice** tells the buyer that the shipment has been sent, what it consists of, and what amount due will appear on the invoice for this shipment. The buyer keeps a file of shipping advices and compares them regularly with receiving reports. With some sellers, the shipping advice *is* the invoice, and no monthly statement is sent; in this case, the shipping advice/invoice enters the seller-invoices file and does not go to the receiving department. When a shipping advice or invoice record enters the seller-invoice header file, the computer creates pointers in it and in the appropriate records in the items-requisitioned file.

---

[2]In a system without provision for a debit-memo file, this adjustment could take the form of placing the unique identifying numbers of the transaction's receiving report and seller invoice in the appropriate items-requisitioned record (the one that shows an order for 100 B62 units). Then any search for the details will reveal a trail to these two additional records, allowing comparison of the number of items ordered with the quantity that arrived; the payment to the seller can be adjusted accordingly.

To identify accounts payable liabilities, the computer examines the file of seller-invoice headers. For each header, it finds the corresponding receiving report records and examines the item records linked to each. An accounts payable liability is defined as any amount supported by a requisitioned item with (a) a pointer to a purchase order header, (b) a pointer to a seller-invoice header, and (c) a pointer to a receiving report header. If the item records have these three pointers, the computer takes into account any debit memos linked to the items, then calculates the amount payable for this invoice.

Next, the computer creates an authorized-payment record for each seller and links to it all the invoices that it references. The process then calculates the amount due that seller, which becomes the balance of the seller's account payable. This marks the point at which the organization recognizes the liability associated with a purchase or purchases.

The authorized-payment records proceed selectively through the cash disbursements interface, and the liabilities are paid. The basis of selection may be whether a prompt-payment discount will be lost or interest will accrue on the liability if it is not processed and paid. Treasurers typically delay payment of liabilities on which discounts are not yet "ripe" as an inexpensive means of temporarily increasing working capital without borrowing money. The treasurer sorts out and prioritizes the authorized payments as part of the cash disbursements application.

Updating Purchase Order Debits

When the cash disbursements application has made a payment to a seller, the corresponding authorized-payment record will reflect the payment. The records of items, invoices, and receiving reports covered by the payment are linked with the authorized-payment record. In the case of general journal adjustments, such as an allowance for repairs or defective items, the general journal entry record will also link with the authorized-payment record. Thus, the authorized-payment record ties together all the information necessary to compute the individual account payable liabilities and to explain any cash payment in terms of its supporting order, shipments, and invoices, just as the voucher document does in a manual system. The sum of invoices paid, less debit memorandum and general journal adjustments, forms the debit to Purchases associated with the authorized-payment record and/or the voucher.

When all items listed on any purchase order have been received, adjusted, substituted, or canceled, and then paid for as appropriate, that purchase order's header is no longer needed for current operations (although it may continue to have some value in purchasing and inventory analyses). Similarly, when all items on a seller's invoice have been received or otherwise accounted for, the invoice header has no more current utility.

The file-maintenance program may remove these records and all their linked items to off-line storage on diskette or tape. If they cannot be removed, each record may contain a field indicating its open or closed status.

Reconciling the General Ledger with Accounts Payable

Periodically, the system verifies that the subsidiary accounts payable ledger is in balance with its control account in the general ledger. The open purchase order headers, receiving report headers, debit memo headers, invoice headers, and linked item records contain information about what was ordered, when it arrived, and how much the company owes for it. The processes that identify accounts payable and update purchase order debits determine the balances for individual sellers. Four steps are necessary to calculate the balance in the subsidiary ledger and the control account after a complete processing cycle.

First, the computer opens the file of authorized-payment vouchers to obtain the sum of all net amounts due on invoices linked to unpaid authorized-payment vouchers. This is the new balance of the subsidiary accounts payable ledger. Second, the computer opens the file of paid vouchers to obtain the sum of checks and adjustments issued to sellers since the last reconciliation. This is the total debit to accounts payable this period. Third, the computer opens the file of authorized-payment vouchers to obtain the sum of all net amounts due on invoices linked to paid or unpaid vouchers approved since the last reconciliation, which is the total credits to accounts payable this period. Fourth, the computer calculates the new balance for the control account. The formula is as follows:

$$
\begin{pmatrix} \text{New} \\ \text{control} \\ \text{account} \\ \text{balance} \end{pmatrix} = \begin{pmatrix} \text{Old} \\ \text{balance} \end{pmatrix} + \begin{pmatrix} \text{Total credits} \\ \text{to accounts} \\ \text{payable} \\ \text{this period} \end{pmatrix} - \begin{pmatrix} \text{Total debits} \\ \text{to accounts} \\ \text{payable} \\ \text{this period} \end{pmatrix}
$$

The new control account balance should equal the new subsidiary ledger balance. The following example shows the application of these four steps to data from the Wichita Falls Company.

Subsidiary ledger balance at last reconciliation (old balance)	$ 3,900
Sum of unpaid authorized payment vouchers (new subsidiary ledger balance)	
3454 Crocker Co.	$ 3,412
3455 Diamond Services	2,289
Total	$ 5,701

Sum of checks and adjustments issued since last
reconciliation (debits to accounts payable)

3450	Wise Co.	$ 1,100
3451	Bright Co.	2,500
3452	Henderson Co.	3,000
3453	Marathon Co.	4,000
	Subtotal	$10,600
Debit memorandum 0045 Sweeney Co.		300
	Total	$10,900

Sum of vouchers approved since last reconciliation
(credits to accounts payable)

3452	Henderson Co.	$ 3,000
3453	Marathon Co.	4,000
3454	Crocker Co.	3,412
3455	Diamond Services	2,289
	Total	$12,701

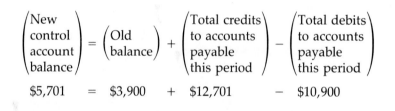

$$\begin{pmatrix} \text{New} \\ \text{control} \\ \text{account} \\ \text{balance} \end{pmatrix} = \begin{pmatrix} \text{Old} \\ \text{balance} \end{pmatrix} + \begin{pmatrix} \text{Total credits} \\ \text{to accounts} \\ \text{payable} \\ \text{this period} \end{pmatrix} - \begin{pmatrix} \text{Total debits} \\ \text{to accounts} \\ \text{payable} \\ \text{this period} \end{pmatrix}$$

$$\$5,701 \quad = \quad \$3,900 \quad + \quad \$12,701 \quad - \quad \$10,900$$

Accounting Entries for This Application

Purchasing and accounts payable generate four major accounting entries. Note that no entry is necessary to record the creation of an open purchase order. Sending a purchase order to a seller normally does not, in itself, create a liability. The liability comes into existence when the seller delivers the order; it is typically recognized in the accounts when the seller's invoice is approved for payment. The system then makes the first entry.

1. Recording an Accounts Payable Credit Owing to a Purchase

Purchases, Acct. 84-225-5678	$2,500	
Accounts Payable, Good Co.,		$2,500
Acct. 40-222-0075		

This entry is made by the process that identifies accounts payable liabilities after receipt of the shipment and verification that a corresponding purchase order and seller's invoice exist.

In the purchases account number, 84 denotes a purchase, 225 identifies the department placing the order, and 5678 identifies the merchandise. In the customer account number, 40 denotes accounts payable, 222 identifies the seller, and 0075 identifies the particular account with this seller. Additional digits representing a purchase order, invoice, or voucher number are not shown here. In an actual computer accounting entry, account numbers usually take the place of the account titles.

2. Recording an Accounts Payable Debit Owing to a Payment

Accounts Payable Smith Co., Acct. 40-232-0111	$2,500	
Cash, Voucher 02178, Acct. 41-535-0001		$2,450
Prompt-Payment Discount, Acct. 41-222-0075		50

This entry would be made in the course of updating purchase order debits on the basis of the payments-to-vendors file from the cash disbursements interface. Information for the entry comes from the authorized-payment voucher, which is the document used to collect and organize the evidence to support a cash disbursement. Vouchers are serially numbered and are used only once.

3. Correcting an Error in a Recorded Entry.   As with other applications, an incorrect or unprocessable transaction returns to its point of origin. There, the person who originated it corrects and resubmits it. Even though thorough on-line data entry edit routines exist, circumstances may occur that require correcting transaction data previously recorded in the files. To discourage unauthorized tampering with correct entries, the system should require special approval before a recorded entry may be altered. Given such approval, it should be possible to reprocess entries that contain errors. Such reprocessing is done by reversing (removing) the erroneous entry and re-entering the correct data.

4. Return of Items Ordered for Credit.   This entry is made in the course of updating purchase order data. On pages 239–240, we discussed the treatment of merchandise sold on credit, then returned by customers. Purchasing handles the inverse of this common occurrence. Using the same example as in Chapter 7, Customer *A*'s Division 231 purchased and accepted certain items from the Stock Company, whose identification number in *A*'s accounts is 224. When *A* received the invoice and prepared the payment voucher, it recorded the original purchase as:

Purchases—Spades, Acct. 84-231-7763	$6,000	
Purchases—Retrograde condensers, Acct. 84-231-5325	2,400	
Purchases—Expansion coolers, Acct. 84-231-5337	700	
Accounts Payable—Stock Co., Acct. 40-224-0082		$9,100

A asked for and received authorization to return condensers and coolers invoiced at $1,100. After turning the merchandise over to the shipper, *A* recorded the return with the entry at the top of page 290.

X

Accounts Payable—Stock Co.,	$1,100	
Acct. 40-224-0082		
Purchases Return—Retrograde condensers,		
Acct. 85-224-5325		$800
Purchases Return—Expansion coolers,		
Acct. 85-224-5337		300

This entry removes the returned merchandise from Purchases and debits Stock Company's payable account. The documentary support for this entry is the debit memorandum, which authorizes an accounts-payable-liability reduction not connected with a remittance to the seller.

Reports

The relative complexity of this application—with at least ten files, seven processes, and three interfaces with other applications shown in Figure 8.6—provides considerable scope for management to improve the conduct of purchasing and accounts payable. Because almost all reporting involves more than one file, reporting in this application is also complex. Many reports can be generated by relying on the pointer connections, but only a few of these reports are generated regularly.

The regularly produced purchasing and accounts payable reports to management serve two major purposes: they provide information needed to estimate and control cash requirements, and they assist in managing and controlling inventories. This section discusses some of the regularly generated reports.

Report of Changes in Approved Sellers

The purpose of the report of changes in approved sellers is to catch unauthorized changes, especially additions, to the approved-sellers file. This report should go to the person who approves such changes, and someone should reconcile it regularly with the authorized additions and deletions since the last report was prepared. There is a parallel control in the accounts receivable application for changes in customers with approved credit. Exhibit 8.1 shows a report of changes in the approved-sellers file.

Schedule of Accounts Payable Balances and Open Purchase Orders

A schedule of accounts payable and open purchase orders is useful in forecasting short-term cash requirements. This report describes payments currently due sellers and payments likely to become due in the near future. Exhibit 8.2 shows an abbreviated version of this report.

The report of accounts payable balances is created by taking the net amounts due but not yet paid, which are linked through receiving reports to individual items. This sum is the current accounts payable balances due.

Just as important for cash planning are the amounts likely to become due when sellers make deliveries in response to open purchase orders. This estimate of future liabilities is the sum of all items on open purchase orders not yet delivered or invoiced (the total of all items in the items-requisitioned file, less the items connected to both receiving report and invoice headers).

Exhibit 8.1 Report Showing Changes in Approved Sellers
This report goes to the person responsible for approving such changes. Actual changes should be compared with the authorized changes, and any discrepancies—especially unauthorized additions—should be investigated.

Businesses Approved as Suppliers and Sellers
Changes for March, 19XX

Seller Number	Seller Name	Date of Change	Numbers of Items Approved for Purchase	Purchase Contract	Approved By
Additions					
7823	Hereford Co.	3/12/XX	A759 A316 A969	CO-79.4	ELS
7824	Jarrell Co.	3/18/XX	L501 S100	CO-82.8	ELS
Deletions					
6215	Sugarland Co.	3/03/XX	A316 S100 S255	CO-86.3	ELS

Exhibit 8.2 Accounts Payable Balances Due and Open Purchase Orders Report
This report shows the amount now due on each invoice and relates it back to a purchase order and a receiving report. The last column shows the date by which the net amount must be paid to avoid penalty.

Vendor Number	Vendor Invoice	Our Purchase Order	Ref. Receiving Report	Gross Amount	Net Amount	Last Date for Net
Balances Due:						
7098	03672	15284	32323	$1,565.19	$1,519.00	4/10/XX
	03814	15284	32365	$ 375.00	$ 350.00	4/15/XX
7150	415	15006	32299	$2,150.00	$2,107.00	4/03/XX
7175	AAB032	15170	32325	$ 200.00	$ 200.00	4/12/XX
Total				$4,290.19	$4,176.00	
Open Purchase Orders:						
7150		15006		$ 450.00		
7180		15169		$3,000.00		
7205		15172		$2,500.00		
7212		15173	32366	$1,700.00		
Total				$7,650.00		

3. Seller Performance Report

The seller performance report summarizes seller activity over an arbitrary period, such as a quarter or a year. The report should show the number of orders, items ordered and amounts of each, time required to ship orders, returns and allowances, and other information from purchase orders open for any part of the period. Supplementary records may compare two or more sellers who supply the same item. The report may include several items as a broader basis for a seller performance comparison. Table 8.3 shows a partial seller performance report comparing the performance of three sellers for one frequently ordered item. A complete report covering all items and sellers would be in the same format but much longer.

4. Prompt-Payment Discounts Lost

Many sellers offer a discount for prompt payment or charge interest or penalties for payment after a specified date. A **prompt-payment discount**, which may be offered by the seller, is the reduction of an invoice amount if payment occurs before a certain date. The report of prompt-payment discounts lost shows how effectively the organization takes advantage of such discounts. Including the prompt-payment deadline in the item record helps the treasurer select and write vouchers for invoices that are ripe for payment. Even partial payments help reduce the cost of short-term credit. The cash disbursements application prepares and uses this report, which is illustrated in Exhibit 8.3.

5. Purchase-Activity Analysis

The purchase-activity analysis shows quantities of various items ordered, taken from approved material requisitions. This analysis is useful in evaluating both the purchasing policies for quantities, prices, and sellers and the effectiveness of purchase agreements. Part A of Figure 8.7 shows an

Table 8.3   Item S100 Vendor Performance

	Edna Corp.	Wharton Corp.	Victoria Corp.
Number of orders	3	6	4
Average order quantity	500	500	500
Average unit price including shipping and tax			
Gross	$21.00	$21.50	$21.25
Net	$21.00	$21.07	$20.83
Average days between purchase order date and receiving report date:			
	10	8	6
Units returned	0	24	0
Debit memos total		$516.00	

Exhibit 8.3 Report Showing Lost Discounts

This report helps the controller and the treasurer to evaluate the effectiveness of the accounts payable function in preparing vouchers and of the treasurer in issuing checks. The objective is to lose as few discounts as possible without making material errors.

Prompt-Payment Discounts Lost, Month Ended March 31, 19XX

Vendor Number	Vendor Invoice	Last Date for Net	Date Paid	Gross Amount	Net Amount	Amount Paid	Discount Lost
7305	841	3/15/XX	3/18/XX	$ 400.00	$ 390.00	$ 400.00	$10.00
7400	11245	3/21/XX	3/26/XX	$3,650.00	$3,577.00	$3,650.00	$73.00
	Total						$83.00

Figure 8.7 Purchase-Activity Analysis

The information in this report may help purchasing management to renegotiate purchasing contracts or to drop items that are no longer being ordered.

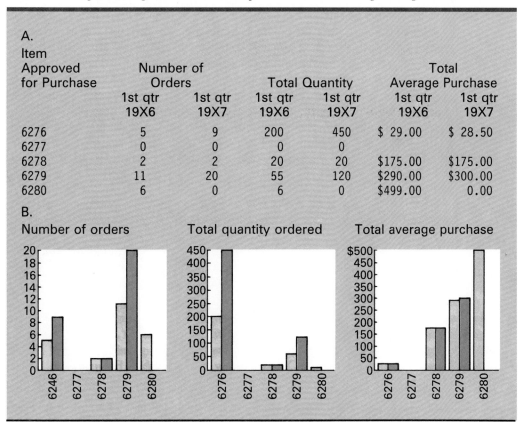

excerpt from a purchase-activity analysis comparing the purchases in the first quarter of 19X7 with those in the same quarter of 19X6. This same information could be presented graphically, as shown in Part B, which compares number of orders, quantity purchased, and average purchase size for the same five items in the first quarter of 19X6 with the first quarter of 19X7. The decision whether a report's data format should be tabular or graphic or both depends on the preferences of the managers who receive it and the ability of the system to produce graphics.

Summary

Purchasing and accounts payable is responsible for identifying the need for acquiring materials, supplies, and services; for acquiring them in an orderly fashion; and for calculating the liabilities that arise from acquiring them. Although manual procedures work adequately, computerized systems based on data base principles are superior in terms of control, speed, management of complexity, and utility of information reported to executives. The system described in this chapter uses the individual item requisitioned as the basic unit of information. It links an item with a seller, requisition, purchase order, debit adjustments, receiving report, invoice, and payment. It records for each item purchased the account number that will allow cost or administrative accounting systems to record that item's use by the organization. (These systems will be the subject of Chapter 9). The reports drawn from purchasing and accounts payable files help management control cash requirements and manage inventories. The complexity of this application depends on the demands of the organization and its operating environment.

Key Terms

account payable
approved seller
bill of lading
debit memorandum
economic order
   quantity (EOQ)

material requisition
open purchase order
order point
packing slip
prompt-payment
   discount
purchase order

purchasing and
   accounts payable
purchasing function
record
screen form
shipping advice
voucher

Review Questions

1. What is the purpose of the purchasing function? What objective does the purchasing and accounts payable application seek to achieve?

2. Which offers greater cost savings—a centralized or a decentralized organization design? Why?

3. Name at least three specific duties involving outside parties that the purchasing function would be expected to perform. Name three that involve parties within an organization.

4. In which accounting entry does a voucher play an important part? What is the function of the voucher? What is the name of the document that accompanies a return of merchandise to the vendor?

5. Look at the purchase order illustrated in Figure 8.3, and answer the following questions about it:
    (a) How many dates must be recorded on it?
    (b) How many addresses must it contain?
    (c) Can the purchase order reference a purchase agreement?
    (d) Which squares should probably be blanked out on the receiving report version of this form?

6. What is a receiving report? Can a copy of another document be used as a receiving report? If so, which document?

7. How many files pertinent to this application are named in this chapter? Identify and describe them.

8. How many distinct processes are described in this chapter? Identify and describe them.

9. What are the two purposes of the reports to management arising from this application? Name the five reports described in the chapter.

Discussion Questions

10. Name two approvals that should be performed by different persons and three functions that should be separated. In each case, describe why the separation is important.

11. Study the cost savings example in Table 8.1. Then answer these two questions:
    (a) Where do the cost savings of centralized purchasing occur?
    (b) Can you think of any types of purchasing that should *not* be centralized?

12. Explain why no accounting entry is made when a purchase order is sent to a seller. Why do you make an entry when you send a check to a creditor? Why are these situations different?

13. On page 272, the text makes the statement, "All the 'B' item sets (that is, 2-B, 3-B, 4-B, 5-B, 6-B, and 7-B) consist of overlapping subsets of one file." Explain the sense in which this is a true statement. In answering this question consider the following: If you were to print out each "B" item set, would every record be on each printout? Why or why not? What will records in any two item sets have in common? What will be different about them?

14. Refer to Figure 8.5, showing data links for this application. Then, answer the questions on the next page.

(a) If you have a seller's invoice, you create a header record for it. How do you determine which of the involved items was ordered? delivered? included on a previous invoice from the same seller? returned to the seller?

(b) In evaluating a seller invoice, you discover a debit memo for one item on the order. How do you determine whether any other items on this invoice also have debit memos?

(c) You have a requisition for a particular item. How do you find out if this is a purchasable item? How would you find out from which sellers it may be purchased?

(d) In the same situation as *c,* you want to know when this item was last ordered, from whom, and in what quantity. Describe how to find this information.

15. The description of the seller-invoice header indicates that it includes no pointer to records in file 6-B. Yet the file 6-B includes a pointer to the appropriate invoice header.

    (a) What pointers does the computer program use to verify items on an invoice? Why do you think the application works this way? Is there a control advantage? If so, what is it?

    (b) When an ordered item arrives, how might the department that requisitioned it learn of its arrival?

16. The Lampasas Company handles purchasing differently from the system described in this chapter. Department managers send their requisitions to the inventory manager. The inventory manager fills the requisitions from open stock if possible. If not, the inventory manager checks to see if any open orders for the requisitioned items large enough to cover the requisitions are expected to be delivered within five days. If so, the inventory manager does not send a new order. Otherwise, the inventory manager sends a purchase order, which usually takes the seller five days to fill and deliver. The quantity ordered is 10 percent of total demand for the item over the last six months.

    The Pipe Division of Lampasas Company has requisitioned 300 knuckle fittings. Only 100 are in stock. The inventory manager has already received requisitions for 1,000 of the same fittings. A shipment is on order, to be delivered in ten days, for 2,000 fittings. Total usage over the past six months has been 20,000 fittings.

Required:

(a) Should more knuckle fittings be ordered?

(b) Criticize this purchasing system. Comment on the advisability of keeping inventory on hand to fill requisitions quickly and of sending in a new order when an open order has not yet been delivered.

(c) Suggest ways to improve this system.

17. Bob McAllen has decided to simplify the purchasing system of his company by putting the entire purchase requisition in one record. He

is including fields for the purchasing function to specify the approved seller and purchasing approval and for the receiving department to record receipt of the items ordered. McAllen believes that the only restriction this approach will put on the operating departments is that they will have to limit each requisition to items that can be acquired from one seller. He believes the purchasing function will not have to prepare a separate purchase-order-header record and will not need an items-ordered file or a receiving-report-headers file.

Required:

Explain any difficulties McAllen's plan may pose that he has not anticipated.

18. What recorded data items, assembled in a report, would enable you to compare the quality and service between sellers for the same type of item? Suppose you are comparing a high-cost, high-quality supplier and a low-cost, low-quality supplier. What data items would you expect to be useful in this comparison? Which of these might arise from outside this application?

19. In a manual accounting system, the accounts payable subsidiary ledger consists of account balances owed to various sellers. In a data base system, the subsidiary ledger exists only as the sum of costs for requisitioned items included on vouchers prepared but not yet paid. Explain how, at the balance sheet closing date, you would determine the *total* balance due to each authorized seller, using the data base system.

Problems

20. The Presidio Luggage Company purchased briefcases at $36.25 each from Leatherworks, Inc., that proved, upon inspection, to include 24 items with torn covers. The covers were torn when a Nueces Transport Company handler dropped the shipping carton on a hook inside the delivery truck. The Presidio Luggage receiving department, which inspected the shipment upon its arrival, accepted these briefcases but got the Nueces Transport driver to sign a form acknowledging responsibility for the damage. Nueces Transport will reimburse Presidio Luggage. Presidio Luggage may order replacement briefcases from Leatherworks if it wishes. Presidio paid for the shipping and has had title to the damaged briefcases since they left Leatherworks' shipping area.

Required:

(a) What accounting entry (if any) is required by these events? The general ledger account number for adjustment credits to Purchases is 41.

(b) List the documents required to record these events and the information each should contain.

(c) Identify the links in the items-requisitioned data set (2-B) that will be affected by these events.

(d) Should the seller's invoice be held up or paid promptly, assuming that neither Nueces Transport's reimbursement to Presidio nor the replacement units ordered from Leatherworks on a separate purchase order have yet arrived?

21. Review the data in the table below and answer the following questions:
    (a) How many different items appear on purchase orders and/or have been delivered?
    (b) How many different vendors received purchase orders?
    (c) In all, how many purchase orders were there?
    (d) How many deliveries were made?
    (e) Do you see any evidence of control weakness? If so, what is it?

22. Review the data in the table below and answer the following questions:
    (a) Have any requisitions not yet been placed on purchase orders?
    (b) Purchase order 67890 has two debit memos associated with it. What is the explanation for this?
    (c) Which purchase order was sent in at least three shipments?
    (d) Which items were ordered from more than one supplier?
    (e) Which purchase order consolidates items from the largest number of requisitions?

23. In the table below, the first group in the nine-digit account numbers is the major asset group; 20 is factory–direct materials inventory, 21 is

Green River Company, Excerpt from Items-Requisitioned File

Item ID code	Quantity Required	Acct. # to Charge	Seller ID Code	Requisition Pointer	Purchase Order Pointer	Receiving Report	Seller Invoice Pointer	Debit Memo Pointer
21	100	20-225-1010	330	1225	67890	11251	45045	1205
21	200	20-129-1010	425	1230	67897		45130	
14	10	20-231-1020	213	1215	67915	11340		1208
16	48	20-225-2030	330	1225	67890		45045	
15	900	21-231-1000	250	1215	67940			
15	300	21-225-1000	250	1225	67940			
19	400	20-129-2030	425	1245		11400	45228	
21	200	20-225-1010	425	1250	67950	11405		
21	10	20-231-1010	425	1215	67950	11405		
20	100	20-231-1030	330	1225	67890	11255	45045	1209
14	30	20-129-2030		1255				
16	48	20-225-2030	250	1250	67940	11270	45040	1210

factory–indirect materials and supplies. The next group of digits signifies the department that requisitioned the item. The third group of digits is the item classification (expense account code) to which the item belongs.

(a) How many different item classifications could potentially be represented by an account number in this account numbering system?

(b) How many different departments submitted requisitions?

(c) Why, if each item has a unique identifying number, isn't this identifier included in the expense account code?

(d) If the same item is ordered for use in the factory *and* by an administrative department, should the first-group value be 20 in both cases? If you think not, recommend a way of distinguishing the two uses of the item in the item file.

(e) Which invoices, if any, appear to include items that should be placed on a payment voucher? What are these items?

24. This chapter does not discuss the contents of files that go through interfaces with other applications. Consider the file used by the inventory function, which comes through the purchasing interface. What information generated by purchasing and accounts payable is necessary in the inventory application? Remember that the purposes of the inventory function are to record all inventory additions and withdrawals, to see that these transactions are authorized, and to make certain that the actual physical inventories correspond to the amounts in the accounting records. Review the contents of the files in the purchasing and accounts payable application, and then list the records and fields that will be passed to the inventory-maintenance application.

25. Marble Falls Stone Company's purchasing manager recently established files of approved sellers and purchasable items. The purchasing manager just approved two new sellers. The first seller, Industry Blades, will supply stonecutter blades, sharpeners, abrasive powder, water cutting nozzles, and high pressure hose. The second seller, Lexington Supplies, will supply sharpeners, abrasive powder, and a flexible drive shaft. Industry Blades has been assigned the seller number 23 and Lexington Supplies, number 24.

Required:

Prepare a record format showing each record that is created or modified as a result of the facts described above. You may omit fields for which no values are given, except for pointers between records.

26. At Kingsland Lumber Company, the accountant is trying to balance the accounts payable and purchases control accounts as of April 30. The following information is available:

	March 31 Balance	April 30 Balance
Accounts payable control	$16,500	$ 17,600
Purchases control (year-to-date)	95,500	120,500
Sum of accounts payable subsidiary ledger	16,500	17,200

	Totals for the month
Total due or paid on April authorized-payment vouchers	$22,700
Total April payments and seller adjustments	22,000
Sum of net April purchase orders	22,400
Total of April debit memorandums	400

Obviously, the accounting manager has made an error or has forgotten to do something. Can you find the error?

27. Wrench Company's sales department requisitions 400 drafting kits for a promotion campaign. These kits are approved purchasable item No. 2345. The purchasing manager approved the purchase and sent purchase order No. 9805 to seller No. 23. There is only one account with this seller, and its number is 0001. This seller allows customers to deduct 1 percent of the invoice amount if payment occurs within 30 days. Wrench Company records the discount at the time it pays the invoice. Wrench Company believes that drafting kit 2345 has a standard price of $35. No tax is due, and the price includes shipping. The shipment arrives ten days after the order. The invoice, which arrives one day later, shows that the standard price has risen to $36.25. Assume that there were no other problems with the shipment and that Wrench Company pays the invoice 12 days later.

Required:

Construct the accounting entries for this order. Refer to any documents that support these entries. Use the account number coding system described on pages 288–289. Use 40 as the general ledger accounts payable code, 84 as the general ledger purchases code, 41 as the general ledger discounts-taken code, and 01-001-0001 as the cash account code.

28. Bay City Company maintains an inventory of oil-rig drilling pipe in diameters of 4 inches, 6 inches, 8 inches, and 12 inches in lengths of 50 and 75 feet. The major buyers of this pipe are oil drillers and producers. Their demand is not seasonal, but may vary with cycles in the energy business. Bay City orders the pipe from a pipe mill nearby. The cost to Bay City of each size of pipe, and the demand for it, are as follows.

Pipe	Cost per Unit	Demand per Year
4",50'	$ 100	600
4",75'	140	400
6",50'	220	800
6",75'	300	500
8",50'	400	1,000
8",75'	600	200
12",50'	1,200	400
12",75'	1,900	300

Annual variable costs of carrying an inventory of pipe are about 20 percent of the cost of pipe in stock, regardless of the size of pipe. Bay City estimates that its cost for processing an order and incoming shipment are $1,000.

Required:

Calculate Bay City's economic order quantity (EOQ) for each pipe size.

Case: Regional Chime

You are the chief accounting executive of Regional Chime, a company that provides telephone service for residents of a certain area. Regional Chime maintains a record of all long-distance calls by any of its customers. It also maintains a customer file, sorted by phone number, with mailing addresses. Every month, your accounts payable application receives a file on computer-readable, magnetic tape, of invoices from each of twelve long-distance service companies. Together, these tapes contain over 300 million invoice records! The long-distance companies itemize invoices by call: the phone number to be billed, date, time of day, originating phone number, phone number called, and applicable rate. Regional Chime must remit payment by check to each long-distance company within 60 days. The long-distance companies will be responsible for any amount that proves to be uncollectible. Meanwhile, Regional Chime verifies the records on the tape, links them to the appropriate phone-customer headers, sends monthly statements, and collects from its customers.

Required:

(a) Create a data flow diagram showing the processes and files described or implied in the description above.

(b) Find and describe as many parallels as possible to the purchasing and accounts payable application described in the chapter.

Case: Manor Builders Supply Company

Manor Builders Supply Company is a new company whose business is very seasonal. Most of its sales take place in spring and early summer, and most of its inventory build-up takes place in late fall and early winter.

Many sellers "help out" with this seasonality by allowing Manor Company to pay nothing, not even interest, for 90 days, and then pay the amount due in six payments. If Manor adopts this plan, the sellers will charge a rate of interest ranging from 0 to 2 percent monthly after delivery. Manor's accountant has hired you as a consultant to develop a data flow diagram, file descriptions, and a process description showing how it can control and account for its liabilities to these vendors.

Required:

The accountant would like to see how the calculations for Manor's account with New Sweden Company would be determined. The facts are as follows: On November 25, Manor received a shipment of window frames and an invoice for $60,000 from New Sweden. New Sweden charges 1 percent interest per month or fraction of a month after delivery on the remaining balance. Each month after the 90-day period, Manor pays ⅙ of the invoice amount plus all interest accrued and unpaid to that date.

Manufacturing, Cost Accounting, and Inventory

Learning Objectives

After studying this chapter, you should be able to

- Diagram a simple-to-intermediate manufacturing process, identifying work centers and processes and describing the related cost accounting processes.

- Identify various types of costs that are included in inventory such as direct materials and labor, overhead, work in process, and finished goods—and explain the role of each in manufacturing.

- Describe batch and continuous production.

- Explain cost suspense and cost allocation and identify cost types and assign them properly to cost pools.

- Explain the purposes of cost accounting and the procedures used to authorize production and track the progress of work orders.

- Perform cost allocation and use standard and actual costs to calculate manufacturing performance variances.

- Name the accounting entries used in cost accounting.

- Identify the relations or files used in cost accounting and the attributes or fields one should expect to find in each.

- Construct account codes that facilitate the process of keeping track of manufacturing costs and use them in cost accounting entries.

Manufacturing can be described as the organized process of assembling identical or nearly identical units, usually as a means of producing salable inventory from material, labor, and indirect inputs. There may be many units—as for automobiles—or only a few—as for the space shuttle. Most manufacturing processes require dozens—or hundreds or even thousands—of different materials, skills, facilities, and supplies. The acquisition of these inputs is supported by purchasing and by the corresponding purchasing and accounts payable application. Their transformation into finished goods must take place according to detailed plans and a timely schedule and within many strict cost limits. Manufacturing's basic techniques—precision measurement, skill specialization, and use of machines to substitute for human strength—were pioneered two centuries ago. The resulting Industrial Revolution gave rise to an abundance of low-cost manufactured products and to the development of cost accounting.

Cost accounting includes in its objectives planning and control of manufacturing, valuation of inventory, and income determination. It consists of techniques used to estimate, record, and control manufacturing costs. It involves recording and classifying manufacturing costs and allocating them among the goods produced. Cost accounting also helps to control the resources used in manufacturing processes. Although we can control the use of cash to purchase resources, it is usually not feasible to keep track of the flow of each resource as it moves through a manufacturing process and is transformed into products. Despite this difficulty, a manufacturer must know the cost of its manufactured products so that it can value inventory and find out whether its products can be sold profitably. Cost accounting techniques make this knowledge available to those who manage manufacturing. This chapter describes systems to implement cost accounting for manufactured inventory, but it is noteworthy that cost accounting has also found many applications outside manufacturing—in finance, marketing, research and development, services, and project control.

A Brief Description of Manufacturing

The purpose of manufacturing is the controlled transformation of specific inputs of material, labor, machinery, and management into designed outputs with predetermined characteristics. Manufacturing processing can typically be subdivided into separate, identifiable operations. Processing operations include chemical reactions, cooling, heating, cutting, bending, welding, assembly, quality control, testing, painting, and packing. For example, through heating, grinding, rotating, stirring, and holding operations and intensive monitoring and quality control, a chemical facility transforms native calcium phosphate, ammonia, sulfuric acid, and potash into various grades of commercial chemical fertilizer. Other firms produce computer software and financial audits by diverse processes that are structurally quite similar to those in manufacturing. Manufacturing operations usually must take place in a particular sequence. Any materials on which processing has begun but is incomplete are called **work in process**.

Manufacturing processes can be "continuous" or "batch" or some combination of the two. **Batch processing** carries one set (or batch) of units to completion, then starts another. Products like paint and pharmaceuticals are generally made in batches. **Continuous processing**, as the name implies, turns out a steady stream of output in which one unit of product is indistinguishable from another; an oil refinery is a common example of a continuous process. Manufacturing processes that combine attributes of both approaches include aircraft production, home construction, and limited production runs. Aircraft are produced through a continuous assembly process, yet each is built as carefully as if it were a single unit. A developer may construct a batch of 10, 20, or 100 homes as if they were going through a continuous assembly process, with crews moving from one site to the next to do the concrete pouring, framing, plumbing, or wiring. A manufacturer who sells 20 products may batch-produce each product in one or two production runs per year, yet may operate each production run like a continuous process while it is going on. These types of processing can apply to both high-volume and low-volume production.

Some manufacturing processes use a **production line**, whereby a product being assembled passes from one work center to another until it is completed. Partially assembled units move past work centers that perform the same brief assembly or testing operation on each unit as it passes by. The sequence of operations is determined by the configuration of work centers along the production line. Automobiles are assembled by this type of process, which is suited to producing a large number of relatively simple units each period. In manufacturing highly complex units like aircraft or ships, each work center may devote several hours or days of attention to completing the operations for which it is responsible.

Whatever the type of production, all manufacturers must control the work that is done. To define the purpose of a production activity, they use a **work order**, which is the authorization to produce a certain quantity of a specific product. This key document specifies what to produce (product identification), which responsibility centers will be involved, the production quantity, and the date when production should begin. Production should occur only if proper work orders authorize it. The work order serves as a preventive control; reports of subsequent production activity, which are the corresponding feedback control, may be compared with it. A work order may also be called a *job order*.

Because manufacturing tends to be capital-intensive in terms of land, buildings, machinery, engineering design, and training, most manufacturing processes require extensive planning and preparation before they can operate profitably. A properly controlled manufacturing operation becomes increasingly efficient once it is up and running. The greatest profitability occurs under two conditions: the manufacturing process has operated long enough to become more efficient than those of rival firms just beginning to make the same product; and the product is so unusual that it is not subject to severe competition and the manufacturer can thus exercise some control over its price. In the early and middle 1980s, the personal computer market was particularly vulnerable just because it was subject to runaway competition.

Cost Accounting Concepts

Cost accounting collects, processes, and reports the information necessary to control the costs of manufacturing. Briefly, it assigns costs to account classifications that correspond to the nature of the resource they represent and the type of process and product that generated them. These costs are transferred from one classification to another as the corresponding resources move through the manufacturing process toward completion and the status of finished goods. Reports often compare the actual costs incurred by operations to the costs management expected. This comparison, which is another application of the control model, serves to inform management whether manufacturing costs are within the expected range. Such reports usually focus on the activities of a single process, work center, or project over a short interval such as a week or a month and on the activities performed on a specific job or process.

A **responsibility center** is a work center with specific decision-making responsibility. The decisions it makes determine what type of responsibility center it is. In manufacturing, those decisions concern how to use designated inputs in specific production tasks to create designated outputs. Manufacturing responsibility centers do not sell their output, nor do they decide on the capital investment required to create it. Their decision making is limited to how to use materials and labor to produce the product. Therefore, manufacturing responsibility centers are not profit or investment centers, but work centers. A work center usually is also a **cost center**—an organizational unit responsible for control over certain costs. These are called controllable costs for that work center. As far as that cost center is concerned, all other costs are noncontrollable costs, even though they are controllable costs to *some other* work centers. Thus manufacturing responsibility centers, as work centers and cost centers, are held responsible for the costs they incur while producing their designated outputs. Their managers participate in manufacturing planning and should have significant influence over their own budgets. In effect, work-center managers "contract for" resources. For control to occur, they must account for their use of these resources as compared with the budgets they developed.

Many tasks affect the objectives of cost accounting. The company must keep accurate records of all resources used in the activity being reported on. Management must report on how resources were used; they might be used, for example, as inputs to different responsibility centers or to produce different outputs. Using these records and reports, the accountants tabulate results that provide measures of efficiency and productivity for each manufacturing responsibility center and also provide cost valuation figures for each product kept in inventories. The cost valuation allows gross profit measurement when finished goods that are sold are matched with the sales revenues of the same period.

Direct and Indirect Cost Classification

Cost accounting recognizes a distinction between direct and indirect costs. **Direct costs** are proportional to the rate or level of output and are clearly identifiable in each unit of output. Examples of direct costs are the tires purchased and installed on an automobile (and the labor to install them), keys purchased and assembled into a calculator, and the paper sack in which fertilizer is packaged. In contrast, **indirect costs** are not directly associated with the rate of output or with individual product units; they tend to be primarily a function of the passage of time. One example of an indirect cost is the maintenance cost for machinery used to make a product. Others are salaries of production managers, depreciation on the factory building and machinery, and taxes levied on work in process. None of these costs can be specifically associated with the finished product.

An objective basis can be established for assigning direct costs to output. For example, someone with a watch may determine that it takes 15 minutes to install tires during the manufacture of an automobile. If the wage rate is $28 per hour, the direct cost of tire installation is $(^{15}/_{60}) \times \$28$, or $7 per automobile.

The indirect costs of tire installation, however, cannot be calculated so objectively, so direct costs can serve as the basis for an arbitrary assignment of indirect costs to output. Typically, management will decide to establish an indirect-cost allocation rate by dividing the total of all indirect costs (supervision, insurance, taxes, depreciation, and maintenance) by a factor like the total number of direct labor hours or even the number of tires installed. Using direct labor hours of 3,000 and indirect costs of $75,000 incurred in the same month, the indirect-cost allocation rate is $25 per direct labor hour for that month. The indirect costs allocated to tire installation for each car would be $(^{15}/_{60}) \times \$25$, or $6.25.

Cost Attributes, Decision Making, and Control

Many cost attributes have specific uses in managerial decision making and control. The most common such attributes are how the cost responds to a change in the production level, the controllability of costs by a specific responsibility center, the controllability of costs within a given time period, and the relevance of a cost to a specific decision. Costs controllable by a particular responsibility center are usually easy to distinguish.

Suppose your manufacturing facility has two work centers: one assembles the product, and the other packs it for shipping. The costs of assembly are controllable by the assembly center; the costs of packing are controllable by the packing center. But from the viewpoint of each center, the costs of the other are noncontrollable.

For certain costs, a cost center must act now in order to control them in the future. **Committed costs**, such as depreciation and insurance, once committed, cannot be changed within the time period specified by the commitment. In any given month, it is unlikely a cost center could affect costs related to product design, factory layout, or the cost accounting system itself, since so much time is required to decide upon and implement such changes. Thus, changing committed costs requires a long lead time. Management could, however, increase, decrease, or cancel **discretionary costs** during a given time period. For example, over the next month a work center's managers could make and implement a decision about hiring additional employees, training them, and assigning them to manufacturing duties.

This distinction is important in deciding what information to include in cost reports and to consider in decision making. If the report appears daily or weekly, most if not all of its emphasis should be on costs that can be controlled by managerial decision making or control activities before the next reporting date. Including information on committed costs could distract the user from the important discretionary costs in the same report, resulting in errors and bad judgment. If these costs must be included, they should appear near the bottom of the report.

In most management decisions, including those in manufacturing, some costs are affected and others are not. Costs that change as the result of a particular decision are **relevant costs** for that decision. Costs that are not affected by a management or manufacturing decision are **nonrelevant costs**. Clearly, whether a cost is relevant or nonrelevant depends on the specific decision under consideration. In the manufacture of pleasure boats, a decision on changing the hull dimensions will cause costs for materials, labor, setup, interior finishing, and shipping to be relevant. A decision on modifying the sail plan will probably make only the rigging costs relevant. This distinction is important in assembling information for decision making and analysis. The accounting system design should support many different cost distinctions to allow relevant costs to be assembled for many different (and usually unanticipated) decisions.

Cost Pools

A key simplifying concept for cost processing is the consolidation into a **cost pool** of the costs of similar resources that are treated alike by the cost accounting process. Another name for the same thing is a **suspense account**. The purpose of cost pools is to make it easier to assign costs to finished goods. For example, if the various machinery-maintenance costs were consolidated into one pool, the combined maintenance costs could then be allocated among the outputs produced during that period. In this way, finished-goods inventory and, in turn, cost of goods sold would reflect the maintenance costs incurred during the period when the products or goods were manufactured. Assigning costs to a cost pool is often somewhat arbitrary. One objective of cost accounting, in fact, is to find the right compromise between simplification and arbitrariness in developing cost pools.

Several simple rules can greatly reduce the arbitrariness of assigning costs to pools. To the greatest extent possible, costs in a cost pool should have similar attributes, such as time spans of controllability, type of material or labor, and reason for incurrence. Direct and indirect costs should be kept separate because of their fundamentally different behavior. Knowing which work center *actually* controls costs is important when you assign costs to a cost pool; make certain the pool includes only costs representing services or inputs actually used by all the work centers slated to receive the costs. In sum, each cost pool should include costs controllable by work centers to which the costs will be allocated, discretionary over the same time horizon, and relevant to the same types of decisions.

For example, maintenance, safety, utility, tax, and grounds costs are common to both assembly and packing centers and are not really controllable by either center. You might combine these costs in a single pool for allocation purposes. Costs that are clearly specific to either assembly or packing should be placed in separate pools.

Flow of Costs

The hypothetically simplest manufacturing process buys one resource and requires one labor skill. All activity occurs in one facility, and one product is produced. When the product is ready for sale, the cost accounting system records the manufacturing process by adjusting the amounts in three cost pools: one each for material, labor, and facility costs. When the manufacturer acquires resources, it debits (increases) the appropriate cost pool and credits (decreases) cash or accounts payable. When the manufacturer uses up the resources to produce the product, it credits the cost pools and debits work in process (an inventory account). When the product is complete, the manufacturer credits work in process and debits finished-goods inventory. The work in process account balance should at all times agree with the total material, labor, and indirect costs of resources active in the manufacturing process at that time. This simple recording process is summarized in Figure 9.1.

Real-life manufacturing invariably entails more complexities, like multiple materials and multiple products. One important further complication is that a manufacturing operation usually involves more than one responsibility center or work center. Each responsibility center has separate costs, and the cost system should account for them to exercise control over each. Goods that flow through the manufacturing process create a corresponding flow of costs. The costs at each responsibility center are debited when it receives resources and credited when it completes its work

Figure 9.1 **The Flow of Costs in Manufacturing**
The T accounts show the liabilities and related cost classifications. Arrows trace how costs move through these classifications to reflect manufacturing activity. As finished goods emerge from production, the costs of resources included in them will also be debited to finished goods.

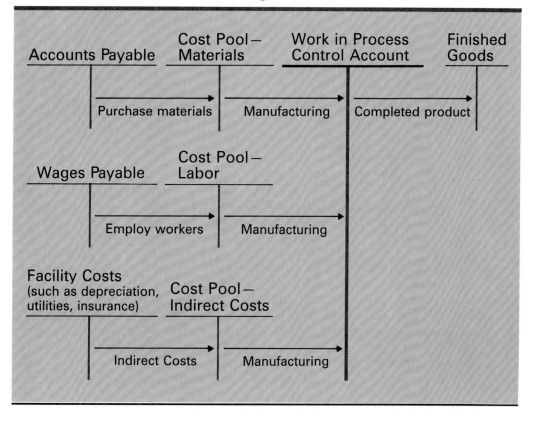

and the production activity shifts elsewhere. The equations relating inventory balances, purchases, and withdrawals apply to the flow of manufacturing costs. In other words, the beginning-of-period work in process account balance *plus* the period's cost-pool credits *minus* the period's transfers to finished goods equal the total of all open work orders still incomplete and in process. If the beginning work in process account balance was $55,000, transfers to finished goods were $78,000, credits to the material cost pool were $23,000, credits to the labor cost pool were $29,000, and credits to the indirect-costs cost pool were $30,000, the end-of-period control account balance should be $59,000 ($55,000 + $23,000 + $29,000 + $30,000 − $78,000).

Standard Costs

Actual costs are often used as the basis for inventory and cost-of-goods-sold valuation in the published financial statements. Actual costs alone, without any kind of bench mark or comparison standard, give very limited information to management. Advanced cost accounting systems incorporate a set of **standard costs**, which represent the cost of inputs per unit of output if manufacturing proceeds as efficiently and competently as management expects. Standard costs are the planned or expected bench-mark costs to which actual costs are compared. They constitute the preventive element in manufacturing cost controls; actual costs are the feedback elements, and performance reports are the comparison and follow-up element.

Allocated Costs

All indirect and many direct manufacturing costs are allocated by means of cost pools. **Allocated costs** are costs classified together and assigned to work centers on a meaningful but somewhat arbitrary basis. Their main uses are in evaluation, control, and managerial incentives. The remainder of this section illustrates cost allocation at Mid-State Company, which produces video digitizers. Its factory includes three work centers.

When all indirect manufacturing costs are placed in an indirect-cost pool, the costs in the pool are often called **overhead**. These costs are subsequently allocated to production as if they were direct costs. The cost accounting system assigns the overhead accumulated in a cost pool to the various work centers on a cost allocation basis. The **cost allocation basis** is, or should be, an objective and reasonable measure of the extent to which work centers are individually responsible for incurring these indirect costs. Two popular bases for overhead allocation are *direct labor hours* and *direct labor dollars*. When a basis has been selected, costs are allocated to the centers in proportion to the part of the basis that each center incurred. For instance, using direct labor hours as an allocation basis, a work center working twice as many direct labor hours as another work center would receive an allocation of twice as many indirect-cost dollars. This allocation represents the work center's *consumption* of indirect resources in the production of its actual outputs. The **cost allocation rate** is the number of cost dollars credited (taken) from the cost pool and debited (distributed) to the work center for every unit of the cost allocation basis.

Consider, for example, the month of July at Mid-State. Mid-State scheduled its three work centers to produce 3,000 video digitizers, and during operations the indirect-cost pool accumulated $30,000. The standard direct labor hours required to produce 3,000 video digitizers are split among the three work centers as shown in Table 9.1.

Table 9.1   Example of Cost-Allocation-Rate Calculation, Mid-State Company, Month of July

The cost pool (account 21) accumulated $30,000 in July. The actual output of 3,000 digitizers requires 600 *standard* hours to produce; thus the calculated allocation rate would exactly allocate the actual cost pool balance if no more or less than the standard number of hours was incurred.

Work Center	Standard Direct Labor Hours Required to Produce 3,000 Video Digitizers
A	300
B	100
C	200
	600 total standard direct labor hours

Indirect-cost allocation rate is

$30,000/600 hours = $50/direct labor hour

Cost Allocation Reporting

To use the data collected in the cost accounting system, the centers need reports that set out the information meaningfully. To illustrate a report, we will continue to use the Mid-State video digitizer example. The work centers met the schedule, producing 3,000 video digitizers. However, they varied in their success at doing so within the allowed standard hours; Table 9.2 shows the actual hours and the costs associated with them. A **cost variance** is a variance between actual cost and standard cost. In Table 9.2, the cost variances are the difference between the cost of actual hours incurred and the cost of standard hours. All three centers in Table 9.2 produced the required output, but Centers A and B were less efficient than

Table 9.2   Indirect-Cost Allocation Basis, Mid-State Company, for the Period Ended July 31, 19XX

Using the rate calculated in Table 9.1, the cost pool is allocated to production centers. The result shows that the cost centers were not equally efficient.

Work Center	Standard Hours	Actual Hours	Allocation Rate $50/hour	
			Actual Allocated Costs	*Cost Variance*
Center A	300	310	$15,500	$ 500 over
Center B	100	120	$ 6,000	$1,000 over
Center C	200	190	$ 9,500	$ 500 under
Totals	600	620	$31,000	$1,000 over

Figure 9.2   Data Flow Diagram for Manufacturing, Cost Accounting, and Inventory (facing page)
Here you see the major relationship between processes, interfaces, and data files. The text explains the purpose and function of each process and the contents of each file. The purchasing application, which interfaces with this application through receiving and accounts payable, was covered in Chapter 8.

---

expected, and Center C was more efficient. Each center includes the standard costs—$15,000, $5,000, and $10,000—in the cost of output, by crediting work in process for these amounts. The cost variances, the differences referred to above, remain until the accounts are closed. How cost variances are treated during financial statement preparation is beyond the scope of this text.

The Cost Accounting Application

This section discusses the entries, files, processes, and reports that make up the cost accounting application. The data flow diagram in Figure 9.2, showing eight files and six processes (excluding report generation), graphically represents the files and processes described here. Product specifications taken from engineering form the basis for creating an authorized work order (create a work order). When the work order has been placed in an active file, its work is scheduled (work scheduling) and arrangements are made for the work centers to requisition necessary inputs. Every transfer or addition of resources to the work order creates a record in one of the distribution files by the create-materials-distribution, create-labor-distribution, or create-overhead-distribution processes. These records are linked to the active-work-order header record by the link-input-distributions-to-active-work-order-headers process. Together, a header record and its linked input records in the three distribution files describe a work order's completion and cost status. General journal and payroll interfaces provide cost pool suspense accounts for overhead and labor.

Although cost accounting is basically a simple application, several of its features—especially cost pools and the use of account numbers to record the details of production—require close attention for full understanding.

Cost Accounting Entries

In cost accounting, just as in financial accounting, entries record the major events as the rules require. Cost accounting is ordinarily a very active application with many accounting entries. In cost accounting, the recorded events occur entirely within the organization, rather than between the

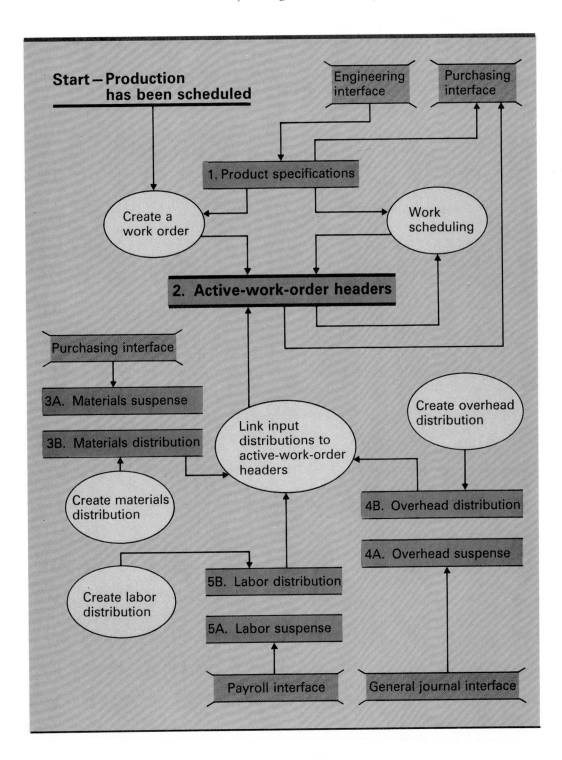

organization and external entities. Keep in mind that since performance-control information can be obtained at any time, as needed, from the files to be described in the next section, the accounting entries shown might be made only at the end of the period as part of the closing process prior to preparing financial statements.

The most frequently posted accounts in cost accounting entries are the cost pools. The cost pools receive debits from the purchasing application for direct and indirect materials and supplies, from the payroll application for direct and indirect labor, and from the general journal application for indirect costs. They receive credits when resources are used by work centers and subsequently transferred to other work centers or inventory. When you credit a cost pool, the offsetting debits are made to work in process accounts. If work centers transfer work in process to other centers, the work in process accounts keep track of where the work is. Finally, completed output results in a credit to Work in Process and a debit to Finished Goods.

Distribution is the allocation of costs to specific work centers or work orders. In Figure 9.3, notice that cost pool debits are made to a suspense account, while cost pool credits are made to a separate distribution account. Keeping the cost pool debits and credits separate in this way serves

Figure 9.3 Suspense and Distribution
The accounts on the left are the ones in which costs are first recorded. The suspense accounts (cost pool debits) reclassify the costs to reflect how the resources they represent will be used during manufacturing. The distribution accounts (cost pool credits) reflect the using-up of the resources from these classifications; the work in process accounts show how the resources have been incorporated into production output.

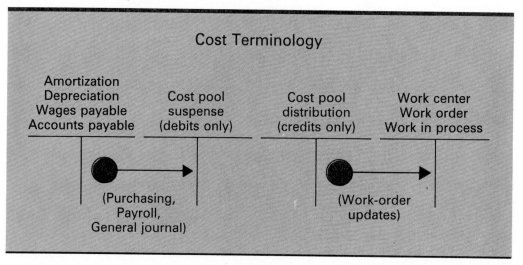

Cost Terminology

Amortization
Depreciation
Wages payable
Accounts payable

Cost pool
suspense
(debits only)

Cost pool
distribution
(credits only)

Work center
Work order
Work in process

(Purchasing,
Payroll,
General journal)

(Work-order
updates)

two important functions. First, it allows you to know at any time the total debits, or costs incurred to support manufacturing, and the total credits, or costs applied to manufacturing outputs. Second, it allows you to separate the functions that *acquire* inputs (purchasing, payroll, and asset management), on the one hand, and the functions that *assemble* these resources into salable inventory (manufacturing and cost accounting), on the other. This separation increases the reliability of the information produced by each application and enables each to perform its specialized functional responsibilities more effectively.

The sample entries and account titles that follow are for Mid-State.

1. Purchasing Direct and Indirect Materials.   This entry links the cost accounting and purchasing and accounts payable applications. The entry shown places debits in the cost pools, or suspense accounts, and records delivery of eight varieties of circuit board and seven different sizes of high-porosity electronic filters. This entry would be made after shipments are received and accepted. It acknowledges both the obligation to pay for them and their availability for manufacturing purposes.

Direct Material Suspense	$1,600	
(purchases of etched circuit boards)		
Overhead Cost Suspense	400	
(purchase of electronic filters)		
Accounts Payable—Diode Supply Co.		$2,000
To record assorted purchases from		
Diode Supply Co. as indicated on		
voucher number 750.		

2. Incurring Labor Services and Paying for Them.   This entry links the cost accounting and payroll applications. It places debits in the labor cost pools immediately after each payroll period. It also records other payroll liabilities, including fringe benefits and overtime, which most organizations treat as indirect costs.

Direct Labor Cost Suspense	$3,450	
Overhead Cost Suspense	2,500	
Factory Payroll Payable		$4,200
Other payroll liabilities		1,750
To record payroll expense for		
April 1–7, 19XX, as indicated		
on payroll voucher 223 and		
general journal entry 175.		

Note that all the "other payroll liabilities" are included in Overhead Suspense.

3. Transfer Indirect Expenses to Cost Pools.   This entry shows how the general journal can be used to create the suspense (debit) balance in a cost pool. Notice that the single debit may consolidate similar costs from many different vouchers and other accounts—an example of how cost pools summarize information.

Overhead Cost Suspense	$3,900	
Factory Building Provision for Depreciation		$600
Factory Machinery and Equipment Provision for Depreciation		700
Prepaid Insurance Premium		100
Data Processing System Service Charges		500
Engineering Group Service Charges		900
Property Tax Liability		300
Factory Utilities Payable		800

      To record expenses and charges for
overhead for week of April 1–7, 19XX,
as described in general journal voucher 176.

4. Transfers from Cost Pools to Work Centers.   Additional entries distribute to cost centers the amounts in the suspense accounts, or cost pools, based on the inputs used by the centers. The following three entries involve two work centers, both working on the same work order. The first two show direct-cost distributions; the third one shows indirect or **overhead cost distribution**:

Assembly Department Work in Process (work order 345)	$1,800	
Finishing Department Work in Process (work order 345)	1,650	
Direct Labor Cost Distribution		$3,450

      To reflect use of direct labor
according to labor hour
distribution report for April 1–7,
19XX.

Assembly Department Work in Process (work order 345, requisition 811)	$900	
Finishing Department Work in Process (work order 345, requisition 901)	700	
Direct Material Cost Distribution		$1,600

      To reflect use of direct materials
according to material
requisitions report for April 1–7,
19XX.

Assembly Department Work in Process	$1,980	
Finishing Department Work in Process	1,815	
Overhead Cost Distribution		$3,795

        To distribute overhead expense
        based on labor hour distribution
        report for April 1–7, 19XX.
        Allocation rate: $1.10 per standard
        direct labor dollar. Factory voucher
        No. 9996.

5. Transfer from One Work Center to Another.   When the assembly department completes its part of work order 345, it transfers the work order to the finishing department, where it becomes part of the work in process of that department. The following entry reflects this transfer from one work center to another:

Finishing Department Work in Process	$4,165	
(work order 345)		
Assembly Department Work in		$4,165
Process		

        (work order 345)
        To transfer costs associated with
        work order 345 from assembly to
        finishing department. Factory
        voucher No. 9998.

If the debits to cost pools do not exactly equal the credits in the entries transferring costs to work centers, the differences may be accounted for by variances. These inequalities are the source of information for work-center and work-order cost variances.

Cost Accounting Files

A typical cost accounting application includes eight files like the ones shown in Figure 9.2: (1) product specifications, including operations descriptions and input descriptions; (2) active-work-order headers; (3-A) material suspense; (3-B) material distribution; (4-A) overhead suspense; (4-B) overhead distribution; (5-A) labor suspense; and (5-B) labor distribution. We examine these first.

Product Specifications.   The product specifications file (1) contains a separate record for each product the organization regularly manufactures. These records are prepared and maintained by the engineering function. Each record lists as **product specifications** every direct input required to make its product, the product-performance specifications, a complete description of the product, how it should be manufactured, and what it takes to manufacture it. Records in this file may be pointed to by records in the file of active-work-order headers, listed next. Each product specifications record includes the following fields:

> Product identification number
> Date of last revision of this record
> Physical description of product
> Performance expected of product
> Normal size of production run
> Direct material product inputs—identity and quantity per production run
> Operations required to manufacture product—identity of each operation, its standard duration per unit, and its standard duration per production run of this product [these fields may be in another file's records, linked to the appropriate record(s) in the product specifications file]
> Other necessary information

Active-Work-Order Header.   This header file (2) contains a record for each batch, production run, project, or other unit of activity to which cost accounting can be applied. This record forms the basis for controlling the work it describes and for accumulating the corresponding costs. The record contains fields that distinguish the work order and also describe its history (both as planned and actual) and its specifications or link this record to records in other files that contain this information. These fields include the following:

> Work-order number
> Work-order date
> Work-center identification
> Scheduled start date for each work center involved
> Actual start date for each work center involved
> Scheduled completion date for each work center involved
> Actual completion date for each work center involved
> Identity of unit or product (pointer to product-specification record)
> Quantity to be produced
> Standard bill of materials for each work center
> Actual materials used by each work center on this work order
> Standard labor inputs for each work center
> Actual labor required by each work center on this work order
> Other instructions and information, or pointers to records containing them

Material Suspense.   The inventory function—which is often called "materials" or "stores" in manufacturing—maintains physical custody over materials and supplies after they have been received. These materials and supplies will be classified according to cost pool, and they will be available for requisition by work centers. The materials suspense file (3A) contains records detailing all materials and supplies acquired and available for manufacturing. The information in it is based on receiving reports prepared by the purchasing application. This account always contains a debit balance, unless it has been closed at the end of a reporting period. It contains the following fields:

> Identification number for material cost pool suspense account
> Receiving report identification number (same record as in the purchasing application)
> Material identification number (same record as in the purchasing application)
> Quantity of material
> Dollar amount of material

Material Distribution.   The material distribution file (3B) contains a record for each actual application of materials to an active work order. Such records are created when a work center knows the actual quantity of material used, usually at the completion of its part of a job. The quantities are drawn from material requisitions used to obtain specific materials for specific jobs. The requisition document could be based closely on the material distribution record. This account always contains a credit balance, unless it has been closed at the end of a reporting period. Its fields include the following:

> Identification number for material distribution record
> Active-work-order number (same as in header file)
> Identification number for material cost pool
> Work-center identification number
> Date of distribution
> Quantity of material requisitioned and distributed
> Dollar amount

Overhead Suspense.   The overhead suspense file (4A) is created by the cost accounting application, the interfaces with payroll and the purchasing/ accounts payable application, and the general journal application. It contains one record for each overhead suspense account, or cost pool, and is updated periodically, perhaps weekly or monthly. Its account codes include a description of the type of overhead expense contained in each record. It always contains a debit balance, unless it has been closed at the end of a reporting period. It includes the following fields:

> Account number for overhead cost pool suspense
> Identifying number for general journal voucher (same record as in general journal)
> Date of entry
> Cost amount transferred

Overhead Distribution.   The cost accounting application allocates overhead with the same regularity that it distributes the direct input component used as an overhead allocation basis. The most common overhead allocation bases are direct labor hours and direct labor dollars. Whenever the system distributes direct labor cost (or direct labor dollars), it also allocates overhead costs. The overhead distribution file (4B) always has a credit balance, unless it has been closed at the end of a reporting period. It contains the following fields:

> Identification number for overhead distribution record
> Active-work-order identification number (same as in the header file)
> Identification number for overhead cost pool
> Work-center identification number
> Date of distribution
> Dollar amount of overhead distributed

Labor Suspense.   The interface with the payroll application creates the labor suspense file (5A), which contains one record for each labor suspense account and is updated each payroll period. This file's account codes identify the type of labor expenses contained in the records. The file always contains a debit balance, unless it has been closed at the end of a reporting period. Its fields are as follows:

> Identification number for labor cost pool suspense account
> Number of payroll voucher
> Date of payroll voucher
> Cost amount transferred in

Labor Distribution.   The labor distribution records are created by one process. At its simplest, this process may be a work-center clerk's hand-prepared distribution sheet; at the other extreme, computer terminals in work stations may be programmed to respond to employees' individually coded identification cards. The labor distribution file (5B) contains one record for each labor cost pool and is updated as manufacturing proceeds. It always contains a credit balance, unless it has been closed at the end of a reporting period. In the following list of this file's fields, the values marked with an asterisk describe how the labor was used in manufacturing, and they may be combined to form a useful account code.

> Identification number for labor distribution record, which may be based on
>> Active-work-order number (same as in header file)
>> Account identification number for labor cost pool distribution
>> Work-center identification number
> Date of labor distribution
> Hour amount of labor distribution
> Dollar amount of labor distribution

Cost Accounting Processes

This application consists of six major processes; creating a work order, scheduling work, creating the material distribution, creating the labor distribution, creating the overhead distribution, and linking input distributions to active work orders.

Creating a Work Order. It is management's responsibility to decide when to create a work order and what its contents will be. Management bases this decision on demand and inventory factors. Once it makes the decision, the process of creating a work order sets up an appropriate record in the work-order file. This record need not be highly detailed—the product specifications can always be found in their own file. However, the application should be able to calculate and store the bill of materials and other input quantities based on the size of the order.

Work Scheduling. Using information in the work-order file about active in-process work orders, the work-scheduling process schedules and prioritizes new work orders, setting start and completion dates at each of the work centers involved in the production of the product. Of course, these schedules will be reviewed and perhaps changed by management. This work-scheduling process may also recalculate the schedules for remaining work orders if they will be affected. In smaller, simpler businesses, management may schedule work manually.

Creating Material Distribution. The process of creating material distribution accumulates requisitions for materials and supplies needed to complete open work orders, calculating and consolidating the cost of the materials used. This process should prepare the material requisitions with sufficient **lead time**—the interval between placing an order and receiving the shipment. The materials distributed to jobs during any period should equal the sum of beginning material inventories plus material purchases, less ending material inventories.

Creating Labor Distribution. The process of creating labor distribution records the various types of labor cost incurred to produce work-order outputs. The total hours and dollars distributed to work orders during any period should equal the hours and dollars incurred and shown on the payroll for that period.

Creating Overhead Distribution. The process of creating overhead distribution associates overhead costs with the allocation basis, usually direct labor hours or dollars, and distributes overhead to work orders. The total overhead distributed should equal the overhead incurred for the period, adjusted by the amounts of any variances recorded.

Linking Input Distributions to Active-Work-Order Headers.   Linking input distributions to active-work-order headers is a busy process and is the key to the cost accounting application. This process performs several important functions, including all the "accounting" in cost accounting. Its primary function is to make available at any time a classification of work in process costs by work centers and by work orders. To do so, it relies on the account coding system.

The Distribution Process: An Example

The distribution processes prepare records of inputs used by the work centers. This example will illustrate the linkage of actual distributions to active-work-order header file records for actual labor, materials, and overhead entries. It will also show transfer of a job from one work center to another at the Mid-State Company.

For work order 325, work center 34 produces 40 electronic assemblies. To do so, it requisitions and uses 240 circuit boards (from cost pool 04) costing $3 per board. Workers actually spend 80 direct labor hours (from cost pool 01) completing these assemblies. The actual hourly wage rate per direct labor hour is $8. Overhead, from cost pool 07, is applied at the predetermined rate of $6 per direct labor hour. When work center 34 completes work on this job, the job will move to work center 39.

Any information just given but not shown in the records that follow is contained in either the active-work-order header record or the product specifications file. The direct-material-cost-distribution record, the direct-labor-cost-distribution record, and the overhead-cost-distribution record are explained in Exhibits 9.1, 9.2, and 9.3, respectively. Each of these exhibits includes the groups in the account number that are used in cost accounting. These groups are explained in the next section. They can be used to classify distributions and prepare reports. The direct-material-cost-

Exhibit 9.1   Direct-Material-Distribution Record
This seven-field record starts with a unique identifying field; the remaining fields describe the distribution of certain direct materials.

Value of Field	Title of Field
8402602	Identification number for material-cost-distribution
325	Active-work-order number
04	Distribution account identification number for material cost pool
34	Work-center identification number
041488	Date of material distribution (April 14, 19XX)
240	Quantity of material distribution
720	Dollar amount of material distribution

Exhibit 9.2   Direct-Labor-Cost-Distribution Record
Similar in construction to the record in Exhibit 9.1, this record describes a distribution of direct labor, capturing the work-order number, cost pool, cost center, and other information.

Value of Field	Title of Field
6543875	Identification number for labor-cost-distribution record
325	Active-work-order number
01	Distribution account identification number for labor cost pool
34	Work-center identification number
041488	Date of labor distribution (April 14, 19XX)
80	Hour amount of labor cost distribution
640	Dollar amount of labor cost distribution (calculated from actual hours, using actual labor rate)

Exhibit 9.3   Overhead-Cost-Distribution Record
Using the same format as Exhibits 9.1 and 9.2, this record describes a distribution of overhead.

Value of Field	Title of Field
6543876	Identification number for overhead-cost-distribution record
325	Active-work-order identification number
07	Distribution account identification number for overhead cost pool
34	Work-center identification number
041488	Date of overhead cost distribution (April 14, 19XX)
480	Dollar amount of overhead cost distribution (calculated from actual hours and predetermined overhead allocation rate)

distribution record shown in Exhibit 9.1, linked with the active-work-order record, shows material costs incurred at this center on this work order. This record can be combined with other records to produce useful cost totals. Combining it with other records in the material-cost-distribution file containing the same work-order number shows the total material costs incurred to date on this work order. Combining it with other records in that file with the same cost pool number shows the total distributions to this direct material cost pool. Records can be similarly combined within a file for labor and overhead costs. According to the facts given on work order 325, there would be no other records to combine with the ones shown.

Thus, the actual costs of work order 325 are $720 for materials, $640 for labor, and $480 for overhead, for total work-order costs of $1,840.

When a work center has completed its activities on a work order, other work centers may continue working on the order. But the cost accounting records should show that the job is no longer in process for the first work center. There are many ways to accomplish this. One simple and reliable way is to link the cost distribution records to the work-order header, which contains a completion date for each center that has completed its part of the job. To transfer costs to the work center receiving the job, use a material-cost-distribution record showing the number of the work center that will receive the costs. Exhibit 9.4 illustrates a transfer from one work center to another.

For purposes of transfer, all labor, overhead, and material costs become transferred-in material costs at the work center receiving the job. All previous work-order updates remain in the distribution files, linked to their work-order headers, for use as an audit trail and to reconstruct work-order costs.

Standard Costs and Variances.   Consider some additional information. The standard cost for an electronic assembly is $50, which consists of the following:

Materials: 6 circuit boards per assembly $\times$ $3
            standard cost per board   = $18 materials content

Labor: 2 standard direct labor hours $\times$ $10
            standard wage per hour   = $20 labor content

Overhead: 2 standard direct labor hours $\times$ $6
            standard overhead allocation rate   = $12 overhead content
      Total unit standard cost $50

The only variation between the actual costs given earlier and these standard costs is that the standard wage rate is higher than the actual wage rate.

As explained earlier on page 319, the transfer of costs between work centers moves only the *standard cost* of the work done. Exhibit 9.4 uses this approach to transfer the costs at work center 34 to work center 39. Various records for center 34 show the actual inputs consumed by that center on work order 325. However, when activity on the work order transfers to center 39, only the standard costs transfer with it. These standard costs are in the last field of Exhibit 9.4, and are also shown later in Figure 9.5 (on page 330). The cost accounting application recognizes this record as a transfer when it encounters a work-center number instead of a cost pool number in the third field. The application obtains work-order quantity and standard cost in work center 34 from the product-specifications and active-work-order-header files; it then calculates the standard cost.

Exhibit 9.4 Transfer of Costs Between Work Centers
The cost-distribution format used in the three preceding exhibits can also show a transfer of work in process from one cost center to another.

Value of Field	Title of Field
6543950	Identification number for material-cost-distribution record
325	Active-work-order identification number
34	Identification of work center transferring the job out
39	Identification of work center receiving the job and its costs
041588	Date of material cost distribution (April 15, 19XX)
40	Quantity of material cost distribution
2,000	Dollar amount of material cost distribution

To see how efficiently, overall, center 34 performed, compare the $2,000 costs transferred-out balance from Figure 9.5 with the sum ($1,840) of labor ($640), material ($720), and overhead ($480) transferred in for this work order at center 34. Specifically, center 34 had a favorable balance of $2,000 − $1,840 = $160 on work order 325, achieved by using direct labor costing that was less than the standard wage rate established for it.

If a work center finds it has materials or supplies left over, it should return them to the material storage area. An appropriate material-cost-distribution record to reflect such a return shows the returning work center's number in the field normally used for the cost pool. The number of the cost pool appears in the field normally used for the work center, and the remaining fields, including the quantity and dollar amount of the return, are completed as shown in the direct-material-distribution record in Exhibit 9.1.

Report Preparation

Reports organize the information collected in the cost accounting system and present it to management. The way the data are distributed among scattered files makes efficient retrieval procedures essential. The primary mechanisms built into the application to assist in information retrieval are the account codes and identification numbers. Proper account code design greatly simplifies cost accounting, and an inadequate account code design will lead to enormous difficulties. We discussed basic coding-system considerations in Chapter 6. In this section, we build on that discussion to show how account numbers enhance control and simplify processing in cost accounting. Real account numbers can be 30 characters or more in length, but, for simplicity, we will use an 8-character code.

The purpose of an account code is to identify and describe the account. An account's identification should indicate whether it is an actual or a budget account, whether it normally has a debit or credit balance, and the characteristics of the cost it contains. The part of the account number structure used in Exhibits 9.1–9.4 and in the related discussion is the part used in cost accounting. This part is explained below:

Character Position	*Significance*
1	Actual or budget account (this character is optional)
	1 = actual account
	2 = budget account
	No other values defined
2,3,4	000 = a cost pool
	any other number = a work order
5,6	Identification number of cost pool or center transferring costs out (crediting)
7,8	Identification number of the work center receiving costs (debiting)
	00 = not identified with a work center
	99 = identified with Finished Goods Inventory
	Any other number = identification number of a cost pool or work center transferring costs in (debiting)

As an example, consider the account number segment *325-01-34*, constructed from Exhibit 9.2. The *325* is the number of the work order that gave rise to the need for the transfer. The *01* shows that the labor cost pool was credited; *34* means that work center 34 received the labor and was debited. Thus, Figure 9.4 shows this entry as a transfer from the cost pool to the work center.

This simple account structure has two weaknesses. First, it can accommodate only 999 work orders, and a combined total of 98 work centers and cost pools. Under some circumstances these low limits would be a handicap. The second weakness is that the account number contains no means to separate costs by time period and, in practice, an application should be able to separate costs at least monthly or weekly. Two additional digits, in positions 9 and 10, would permit monthly or weekly accounts. Additional character positions could denote other details important to a particular organization. For example, if an organization has scattered manufacturing plants, the additional characters could indicate the nation, region, specific plant, and product; and if all locations use the same account code system, the organization could make interplant comparisons of costs to identify plants most efficient at producing certain products.

In general, the account code is a powerful tool for making an accounting system appear simple to the user. It appears simple because there

Figure 9.4   Illustration of Sum of Credits

The numbers on the arrows are the account-code designations for the cost distributions we have been discussing. Each number can be constructed from the work-order number, the cost-pool number, and the cost-center number.

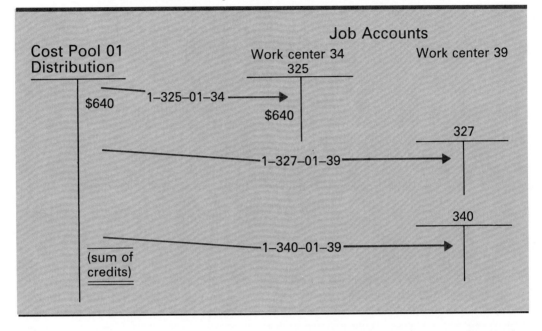

is a logical procedure for assigning account code numbers and because it handles many different reports and inquiries easily. Extra time and care spent developing a coding system for cost accounting will amply repay the user. Other parts of the account number, not shown here, identify the control account that consolidates work in process, the organizational entity to which this inventory belongs, and perhaps other information.

Logical Search

Many computer applications that store data in files are able to search all the available files and records for a logically specified sequence. They can search for sequences that include certain characters in designated positions, without regard to the content of the remaining positions. In other words, it is possible to look for an 8-character sequence with *1* as the first character and *01* as the fifth and sixth characters (the dashes do not affect the 8-character sequence).

1-(any work order)-01-(any work center)

A search often uses an asterisk to signify that any digit or character in that position will satisfy the search. Used this way, the asterisk is sometimes called the *wild-card symbol*. The number just shown, expressed with asterisks, would appear as 1-***-01-**.

As the numbers that satisfy this search criterion are found, they are listed and totaled to build a report. To determine the magnitude of all credits to cost pool 01, for instance, you would find and sum the amounts in all the accounts with numbers 1-***-01-**. Figure 9.4 illustrates the results of a search for all the credits to cost pool 01.

To determine the total of all debits to work center 39, you would find and sum the amounts in all the accounts with the numbers 1-***-**-39. Figure 9.5 shows the results of this process, with the amount shown for the entry from Exhibit 9.4.

In addition to wild cards, it is often possible to specify a range or to exclude certain values. The symbols =, ≠, >, <, ≥, and ≤ may be used to describe the conditions sought. Several of these conditions may be linked together using *and* or *&* to mean "both," and *or* to mean "either

Figure 9.5   Illustration of Sum of Debits
As work center 39 accumulates costs for the work orders in process there, each new debit is assigned the number shown on its arrow. These numbers are constructed as were the ones in Figure 9.4.

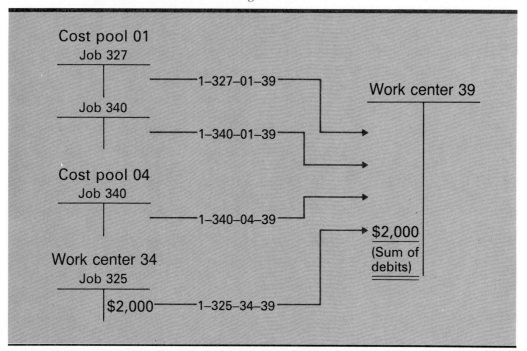

or." For example, the range "one to ninety-nine" would be specified as $0 < ** < 100$ or as $1 \leq ** \leq 99$.

Among the many other lists you can prepare using an account number of this design and the logical search are the following:

> The work in process subsidiary ledger (all accounts starting with 1)
>
> All costs of any work order in process (includes all accounts with numbers 1-(work order)-** $\neq$ 0-0 $< ** < 99$)
>
> All costs placed in any cost pool (includes all accounts with numbers 1-000-**-00)
>
> All costs at work center 22 that were transferred from cost pool 35 (includes all accounts with numbers 1-***-35-22)

Comparisons

After items have been listed and totaled, further operations can be performed on them. Some reports require data accumulation based on two or more sets of criteria. Two examples are the cost efficiency of all work on a simple work order and that of all work done by a single work center. In preparing these two reports, the lists and totals previously gathered are compared by taking the difference between the budget total and the actual total. To further illustrate how the computer assists in report preparation, we will review the operations necessary to produce these two reports.

To determine the cost efficiency of all work centers on completed work order 325, the computer performs three operations. First, it obtains the actual input quantities at standard costs by totaling in accounts all balances relating to work order 325 in any cost pool or work center. The debit balances in accounts numbered 1-325-**-0 $< ** < 99$ allocate costs to work centers from cost pools, and the total of these balances provides the required total. Second, the computer obtains the standard costs on each work by finding the sum of balances in all accounts with numbers 1-325-**-99. This provides the total of the work order's account numbers in account 99, Finished Goods. Third, the computer subtracts the total of actual input quantities at standard costs from the total of standard inputs at standard costs. If the difference is positive, actual costs were less than standard costs and overall efficiency appears good. If the difference is negative, actual costs exceeded standard costs and overall efficiency does not appear good, even though some work centers might have performed efficiently.

The next report we will consider is the cost efficiency of a specific work center on certain work orders it has completed and transferred out. To find this information for work center 24 and work orders 317, 327, 328, and 340, the computer must perform three operations. First, it obtains the total standard costs of actual inputs for each work order by computing the combined balances of all accounts numbered 1-(*** = 317 or = 327 or = 328 or = 340)-**-24. The second step is to obtain the total standard costs of standard inputs transferred out on the same work orders. This will be the combined balance of all accounts with numbers 1-(∗∗∗ = 317 or = 327 or = 328 or = 340)-24-∗∗. In the third step, the computer subtracts the sum of actual inputs at standard costs from the sum of standard inputs at standard costs. A positive balance indicates favorable performance; a negative balance indicates unfavorable performance.

Just-in-Time Manufacturing

Factories have traditionally kept substantial quantities of materials and supplies on hand, on the theory that ample inventories will buffer work centers against temporary shortages and resulting work delays and will eliminate the need for expensive rush orders for out-of-stock items.

Several criticisms can be made of the traditional approach. Large inventory levels may represent an invitation to wasteful and sloppy production techniques and may tie up valuable working capital, without totally eliminating work slowdowns. Recently, a new strategy has become prominent in Japan, where transportation services are highly developed and manufacturing activities are physically close to each other and may be closely concentrated and coordinated. This strategy of purchasing, productions, and inventory management, called *kan-ban* or **just-in-time**, attempts to reduce in-process inventories. Factories hold inventories to a minimum at all stages of production and rely on deliveries from suppliers and other parts of the factory literally *at the moment they are required* to support production. Production is planned to proceed at a volume rate tailored to maintain finished-goods inventories that exactly match sales demand. For just-in-time to work, management must plan and coordinate production very carefully. It must eliminate the problems of delivery delay, poor quality control, and unscheduled production interruption that cause cost increases in manufacturing and that large inventories tend to disguise. This planning usually produces other efficiencies. The intense attention necessary to execute the plan requires trained managers, appropriate computers, and constant communication among all areas of production and inventory. High-quality materials and components are also necessary, as are excellent working conditions.

Manufacturers that use the just-in-time approach order and arrange for delivery of materials in very small quantities. The manufacturer evaluates its suppliers regularly by inspecting their facilities and helps them to improve efficiency and quality. In keeping with this attentiveness to suppliers, the manufacturer usually selects only one supplier for each item. The manufacturer-supplier relationship tends to be long-term, to involve cooperative design of products and components, and to require the supplier to take full responsibility for the quality of the materials and components it supplies. Just-in-time promotes a different approach not only to manufacturing and scheduling but also to purchasing, accounting for purchasing and manufacturing, and doing business generally.

The accounting records that support just-in-time inventory and production methods are very similar to those we have outlined in this chapter. In addition, just-in-time requires close integration of the financial and cost accounting applications. Among the points of integration are inventory levels, bills of materials, product specifications, and order entry. These points tend to be covered by long-term agreements between manufacturer and supplier to collaborate on product design, access certain records in each other's accounting and production control systems, and devote more management attention to production efficiency and quality improvement.

Summary

Cost accounting provides management with knowledge about the cost of its manufactured products and about how resources and costs flow through production. Logical accounting codes and computer operations are the backbone of a simple system for keeping track of specific work orders and the costs incurred to complete them. Computer processing allows basic controls, such as the requirement that work be undertaken only in response to an authorized work order, to be implemented automatically.

In manufacturing, costs may be too numerous to track individually. For this reason and others, this application creates a limited number of cost pools. Similar costs are assigned to the same pool, typically on the basis of common characteristics such as being a function of production rate or time or being common to the same work center.

Through account codes, a cost accounting system can keep close tabs on processing costs. The codes also facilitate report preparation. Common cost accounting reports are those showing the status of a work order, the summations of certain costs, and the efficiency of work centers.

Key Terms

allocated costs	direct costs	product specifications
batch processing	discretionary costs	production line
committed costs	distribution	relevant costs
continuous processing	indirect costs	responsibility center
cost accounting	just-in-time	standard costs
cost allocation basis	lead time	suspense account
cost allocation rate	nonrelevant costs	work in process
cost center	overhead	work order
cost pool	overhead cost	
cost variance	distribution	

Review Questions

1. What is a production line? Name two types of production processes.

2. What do you call production costs that are a function of production volume? costs for which a cost center is responsible? costs that depend on which decision alternative is chosen? costs expected to be incurred if an operation is carried out? costs that can be affected or changed during a certain time period?

3. Why are cost pools necessary in cost accounting? What exactly *is* a cost pool? What is the nature of the arbitrariness involved in cost pool definition? Define suspense accounts and labor, overhead, and material distributions, and explain how they are related to cost pools.

4. Describe the flow of costs. (With what does it start? With what does it end? What is in the middle? How does a cost "flow"?) What "real-world" process is represented by the accounting flow of costs?

5. What are the purposes of cost accounting?

6. What is a work order? What purposes does it serve? What information must it contain?

7. What is a work center? Is it also a cost center? Is it also a profit or investment center? What factors would you use to evaluate the performance of a work center? How might budgets, actual costs, and standard costs be used?

8. What is overhead? How does the cost accounting system treat overhead? What is the difference between suspense and distribution? Is overhead part of the cost of manufactured goods and services provided?

9. How many processes and how many files that are part of this application does the chapter describe?

10. What is just-in-time inventory control? List its major features. Is it really a system limited just to inventory? If not, what other operations does it affect?

Discussion Questions

11. Are the concepts and techniques of cost accounting limited to manufacturing situations? Give at least five examples of nonmanufacturing activities in which cost accounting techniques are used or could be used.

12. What two conditions tend to produce profitable manufacturing operations? Do you think management has any control over whether its organization enjoys these conditions? Why or why not?

13. Costs can be classified in many ways. This chapter discusses direct,

controllable, discretionary, relevant, standard, and allocated costs. Classify each cost described below:

(a) Air freight on fresh fish flown to a Kansas City restaurant, from the restaurant's standpoint.

(b) Depreciation on the computer used in the data-processing cost center.

(c) Depreciation on the *same* computer considered from the standpoint of any other cost center.

(d) Compensation paid to the office-managing partner of an accounting professional corporation.

(e) The budgeted cost of labor to complete one tank in the Fabricating Department of Giddings Tank Company.

(f) Amortization of the software required for automated timekeeping and billing at an architectural firm.

14. At the Henly Company, a producer of subassemblies for aircraft avionics, the marketing director and engineering department have completed specifications for a new product. The product consists of existing subassemblies already defined and produced as products. Discuss how the product specifications file could be modified to include this product without duplicating all the existing information about its component subassemblies.

15. Many experienced production managers say they do not rely on information system reports to identify problem work centers or work orders. Such managers claim that, by keeping in close personal contact with work under way they are able to spot such problems more quickly. Assume they are correct and explain why cost accounting systems continue to exist—and expand.

16. The products of the Alto Company are made from materials that frequently fluctuate in price. The company therefore does not include material prices in its product specifications file but in a separate materials-price-list file. Explain how a standard-cost-computation process could calculate the current standard costs of the materials included in one particular product type.

17. In the Beaumont Company's factory, each work-center supervisor uses a computer screen form to enter the records of each day's labor distribution for work orders in process at that center. Each work order, each work center, and each type of labor has its own identifying number. The supervisor enters only the labor hours and not the dollar amount, which the create-labor-distribution process calculates. Design a simple screen form to accept the necessary information.

18. When Beaumont's factory completes a work order, the product becomes part of finished goods and is available for sale or delivery. Describe a process that would place the work order's costs in a finished-goods inventory account.

Problems

19. Giddings Tank Company makes various sizes of tanks. Its manufacturing process has two cost centers, fabrication and finishing. To produce 24 tanks of the standard design XAS, Giddings Company prepares work order 432. This order, prepared on May 1, specifies that production should begin in the fabrication department on May 12 and be completed in finishing by June 30. Prepare a clear, simple work order of your own design containing this information.

20. At Mid-State Company (Table 9.2) all indirect overhead occurs as a result of the activities of work center D. Work center D uses a flexible budget formula for its budget: $50 per *actual* direct labor hour worked by centers A, B, and C, which receive and use its indirect overhead outputs.

Required:

(a) What is the July budget formula for center D?

(b) Suppose that actual expenditures by work center D in July were $32,000. Relative to its budget, should work center D be evaluated as efficient?

(c) Suggest a general way of evaluating the effectiveness of departments, such as work center D, that provide services to other departments.

21. Examine Figure 9.2.

Required:

(a) Redraw this diagram, splitting the process link input distributions to active-work-order headers into two processes. The first process, update file preparation, will prepare a work-order update file. The second, work order update, will find the appropriate work-order-file record for each update file record and change it to reflect the new information.

(b) Consider two data processing strategies for accomplishing the work-order update process: (1) linking short records, each of which describes a single update operation or milestone, to the work-order record via pointers, and (2) including all the update information directly in the work-order record, which would increase in size. Present at least one advantage and one disadvantage for each strategy.

22. Andice Company has a cost accounting system similar to the one described in this chapter. However, related records in the system files are not linked via pointers. The firm wishes to gain the operational ease and convenience of software that employs such links. Programmers and systems analysts are preparing the software to make this possible. They need a list of the necessary links.

Required:

Review the cost accounting process descriptions carefully. Then

(a) Identify the links that should be inserted to allow creation of appropriate record chains.

(b) Draw a diagram for cost accounting similar to Figure 8.5, on page 273, which illustrates pointer relationships in purchasing and accounts payable. Be sure to show the relationships established by your pointers. (Your diagram will be simpler than Figure 8.5.)

23. At El Paso Air Conditioning, the following is a summary of work order 907:

Work center 68	Direct labor (14)	$4,000
	Direct materials (16)	1,200
	Overhead (18)	3,000
Work center 33	Direct labor (14)	$6,000
	Direct materials (16)	1,000
	Overhead (18)	8,000

Account numbers follow the structure described on page 328. The following excerpts from the work order update file reflect progress to date on work order 907:

Transaction Identification Number	*Account Number*	*Dollar Amount*
1231	1-907-14-68	$ 850
1234	1-907-16-68	1,200
1236	1-907-16-68	300
1239	1-907-68-16	150
1240	1-907-16-33	1,000
1241	1-907-14-68	3,050
1242	1-907-18-68	2,925
1245	1-907-68-33	8,200

Required:

(a) Calculate the variances at work center 68 on work order 907.

(b) What evidence is there that extra direct materials were first issued, then returned?

(c) The records above each have only one account number. Explain how the double-entry accounting system would produce a conventional accounting entry to describe record 1239.

(d) Update record 1245 transferred many of the costs of work order 907 to center 33. Will the costs remaining at center 68 remain there indefinitely? If not, where will they go?

(e) What event do you think caused update record 1245 to be prepared? If you are right, and that event is consistent with good manufacturing practice, how do you explain update record 1240, which precedes it in sequence and in time?

24. San Angelo Boot Company produces fine footwear. Each employee has an identifying number, which is printed on a magnetic-stripe plastic card the employee must carry. Upon arriving at work and at quitting time, the employee inserts the card into a terminal that reads it, records the time, and calculates the total hours for which pay is due. Each week, the software transfers the records of the weekly total hours plus employee number to the payroll application, which prepares pay checks. In addition to this hours-worked file, the payroll application uses an employee master file that gives information about pay rate, deductions, and deposit procedure.

The boot foreperson receives a daily report of hours worked by each employee the previous day. The foreperson states the number of hours each employee spent unassigned (64), cutting (65), sewing (66), finishing (67), or packing (68), and gives a work-order number on which each activity, except for unassigned time, was performed. The software uses this information, plus wage rates and total payroll liability, to prepare a labor distribution.

Required:
   (a) Draw a data-flow diagram depicting this process.
   (b) Which step(s) described above help assure that hours paid equal hours assigned in the labor distribution?
   (c) Most payroll and cost accounting systems include overtime in overhead for allocation to all work orders, rather than assigning it to the specific work orders on which it occurs. Suggest how this could be accomplished, using concepts discussed in this chapter.

25. At the Swiftex Company, the following account and file totals appeared on July 31:

Material inventory control account (as of 7-31)	$ 42,000
Work in process control account balance (unadjusted since 6-30)	68,000
Total of costs linked to open work orders (7-31)	73,000
Transfers to finished-goods accounts in July (at actual cost)	105,000
Total of credits to cost distributions in July	110,000
Variances	4,000

Required:

Use the information given to determine whether the work in process control account is in balance with its subsidiary ledger.

26. Dime Box Bank's management presently uses two suspense accounts for accumulating costs. The costs included in each one are as follows:

Suspense Account A	*Suspense Account B*
Teller wages	Clerical wages
Depreciation on equipment	Property taxes
Clearinghouse fees	Stationery
(on cleared checks)	Bank officer salaries
Electricity, water, and gas	Cost to print personalized checks
Investment management costs	Advertising & promotion
All data processing costs	
Interest expense (on savings)	

Required:

(a) What is wrong with these suspense accounts?

(b) Reclassify these costs into three suspense accounts that collectively exhibit less of the problem you identified in *a*.

27. During the week ended November 11, Matrix Paper Company's two work centers (02 and 04) concentrated their efforts on work orders 310, 311, and 312. At the start of the week, both centers were working on all three orders. The company has cost pool accounts numbered 50, 60, 70, and 80. The centers' efforts have resulted in the following work-order-header updates:

Transaction ID	Cost transferred: Acct.	Cost Amount
901	1-310-50-02	$ 453
902	1-310-60-02	250
903	1-312-70-02	200
904	1-311-60-02	1,100
905	1-311-04-02	3,760
906	1-312-04-80	52
907	1-311-80-04	52
908	1-312-70-04	800
909	1-310-02-04	4,700
910	1-312-80-02	600
911	1-311-04-02	52
912	1-311-02-99	4,800
913	1-000-02-50	3

Required:

(a) Explain the probable cause for entries 906 and 907, and how they are related to entry 911 (other than the same dollar amount).

(b) Assume that center 02 was the last one to work on order 311 and that it had not done any work on this order before the current week. Was this order completed in center 02 with favorable overall efficiency variances? How do you know?

(c) What happened to cause entry 913? Discuss the desirability of this entry from the control and cost-effectiveness standpoints if the direct cost of creating the record and running the update is $1.50 and the allocated overhead to these operations is $2.50.

28. Pages 317–319 illustrate a number of accounting entries without account numbers. After reading pages 327–331 on account numbers, you should be able to assign account numbers to these entries using the conventions for number structure in the chapter. If a work order is not involved, place zeroes in the appropriate spaces. Use these classification numbers where appropriate:

Accounts payable	40	Assembly department work	
Data processing service		in process	25
charges	51	Diode Supply Company	750
Direct labor suspense	12	Direct materials suspense	10
Engineering service charges	52	Factory utilities payable	44
Factory depreciation	74	Factory payroll payable	43
Finishing department work		Prepaid insurance premium	76
in process	29	Overhead suspense	11
Machinery and equipment		Purchases	84
depreciation	75		
Payroll-related liabilities	42		
Property tax liability	77		

For example, the number of the account Prepaid Insurance Premium, supported by general journal entry 555, would be 1-555-76-11.

Required:

Using the account numbers you construct, rewrite the accounting entries on pages 317–319.

Case: Selma Seat Company

Selma Seat Company has agreed to provide seats for garden tractors made by Adams Motor Company. The seats will be supplied on a just-in-time basis. The two plants are a 2-minute drive apart. Selma has a terminal linked to Adams's factory computer. This terminal allows Selma's computer to extract data from Adams's open-work-order and product-specifications files. The former file contains product identification, quantity, time, and date for each run. The latter file specifies the seat model for each tractor model.

Adams sets up production runs 48 hours in advance. A run lasts 2 or 3 days and results in production of 200–300 tractors. Selma can produce 100 tractor seats per hour. Once Selma knows Adams's production plans, it arranges its own schedule to produce the seats, load them onto a van, truck them to Adams's plant, and unload them in the assembly area only 10 to 20 minutes before they are needed. To let Adams know that it is responding, Selma's computer maintains files, which the Adams computer can access, of open work orders and work orders shipped. These files identify the components supplied by Selma and needed by Adams for its product currently in production. Selma has arrangements with its own suppliers for quick delivery of seat materials and supplies.

Required:

(a) Draw a data-flow diagram for the two companies, showing how their information systems cooperate to make just-in-time succeed.

(b) Can accounts receivable (for Selma) and accounts payable (for Adams) be integrated into this system? Write a paragraph explaining your ideas on how to do so.

(c) Do you think that Selma and Adams can make this plan work? Why or why not?

Case: Calvert Family Restaurants

Calvert Family Restaurants is a well-managed firm that operates large cafeterias in several cities. Its management theme is careful cost control as the key to profitability while charging the lowest prices in its market. Management has noticed that one restaurant has a particularly effective cost accounting system and wishes to extend its account coding system to all the other restaurants so that their costs can be compared directly for similar meals and time periods. The chain envisions that it might eventually have as many as 99 restaurants. Each restaurant has four work centers—meal preparation, cleanup, serving, and publicity. Calvert does not use work orders but would like to keep track of dates and meals in the first three areas and of publicity media in the fourth.

Required:

Suggest an account coding plan appropriate for Calvert, showing the total number of digits and the information each digit position will represent. (You need not assign actual numbers.)

CHAPTER 10

Fund Accounting Systems for Not-for-Profit (NFP) Organizations

Learning Objectives

After studying this chapter, you should be able to

- Describe the differences between profit-seeking and not-for-profit organizations and their accounting systems.

- Define the Standard Industrial Classification.

- Describe the desirable features of the accounting function, the accounting system, and the broad management structure of a not-for-profit organization.

- Explain the control concepts of fund accounting and their objectives, and illustrate the major types of entries used in fund accounting.

- Apply the concepts of account code design to not-for-profit accounting systems.

- Apply concepts of financial control to the budgeting and operating functions in a not-for-profit organization, including zero-based budgeting and sunset review.

- Show how to define programs and account for their costs, using cost pools and account codes as appropriate.

- Describe performance reports for not-for-profit managers, and show how to extract them from a properly designed accounting system.

Government and other organizations that do not seek profits (also called *nonbusiness organizations*) conduct about half the economic activity in the United States. Besides the various levels and branches of government, the not-for-profit sector includes transportation authorities, flood control districts, utility districts, trust and foundations, churches, schools, social and fraternal groups, and short-lived entities like election campaign funds. About half the U.S. work force is employed by such organizations. Many of these organizations perform the same services as certain profit-seeking entities, such as power generation and health care. Government and other not-for-profit organizations all employ the fund-accounting concepts described in this chapter in their accounting systems, because fund-accounting concepts allow for very detailed control over integrated resource planning and utilization. Profit-seeking organizations may also use fund-accounting systems, but rarely do they require such high levels of control; their control needs are met by the simpler alternative of conventional non-fund-accounting systems.

A not-for-profit nature doesn't reduce the amount of accounting detail generated by an organization's activities, nor does it relieve an organization of the need to record, process, and report accounting information in ways that are similar to those used in for-profit business organizations. Fund accounting systems for not-for-profit organizations do have certain unique characteristics with which managers and accountants in the systems area should be familiar. This chapter describes the unique characteristics of not-for-profit organizations, the performance required of their accounting systems, and the design and operation of accounting systems to deliver that performance.

Overview and Description of Not-for-Profit Organizations

Managers of not-for-profit (NFP) organizations have the same responsibilities as management in profit-seeking entities—to plan, direct, and control the activities of the organization. Yet the differences between the two types of organizations make for different processes and styles.

Unique Characteristics of Not-for-Profits

From management's point of view, the major differences that distinguish NFP organizations from profit-seeking entities are matters of economic environment; range of activities; sources of revenue; planning, budgeting, and control; criteria of organizational effectiveness; and functional differentiation within the organization.

Economic Environment.   Most profit-seeking entities experience market competition. Although many NFP organizations (such as churches and charitable organizations) also experience this competition, it is generally less intense and less likely to result in ongoing short-run adjustments of products, services, and pricing. Governments, of course, do not compete in any conventional sense. For not-for-profit managements, therefore, competitive market survival is rarely an important objective of planning or control. Instead, they plan for stability, efficiency, and maintenance of quality.

Range of Activities.   The NFP sector displays diversity of entities and of their sizes and activities. If a set of entities has characteristics in common, such as sources of revenue, markets, products, planning and control processes, technologies, criteria of success, and functional structure, it may be called an "industry." How organizations are classified into industries becomes important when one studies all the firms in a classification to identify common features, such as accounting rules or systems. The **Standard Industrial Classification**, which categorizes the different types of economic activity in the United States, has over 400 classes, each represented by a unique code. The SIC is maintained by the U.S. Department of Commerce and takes the form of a set of numerical codes, each of which identifies a unique group of products or services. The 1972 SIC contained 99 major groupings. The NFP sector is represented in many of these classes, especially ones like health, educational, and social services.

Americans tend to speak of government as if it were a single entity, but as many as six government bodies influence the life of a typical citizen. These bodies exist at the federal, state, county, city, school district, and special-purpose district levels. The same American may also deal with numerous nongovernment NFP organizations—church, professional association or union, service club, political action, recreational, cultural, and other special-interest groups. Each type of entity has a unique character and requires different accounting system capabilities.

Sources of Revenue.   Most private-sector organizations derive revenue directly from the purchasers of their products or services. Some NFP groups, such as cooperatives and credit unions, also fit this description, but most don't derive funds directly from those who benefit from their activities. Instead, they rely for support on voluntary gifts or a very few outside sources. Government agencies and departments derive their resources from a funding authority. The **funding authority** is usually a governmental (or private nonprofit) entity that collects or earns revenues and designates how those revenues may be spent.

Many communities have a single charitable fund drive administered by a board of local citizens. This board accepts contributions from businesses and individuals; then, acting as a funding authority, it authorizes local agencies to spend designated amounts. Each local agency accepts its designated amount as its budget. These allocations are called **appropriations** and are the funding authority's legal authorization to draw upon the fund for money to carry out specific activities that the funding authority has approved. The agencies themselves actually deliver services to groups or individuals with special needs. The individuals who benefit from services supported by the charitable fund drive are not likely to have been contributors to it.

Governments operate similarly, except that they rely on their legal power to assess taxes, not on volunteer contributions. A government's funding authority (usually composed of elected officials and called a council or legislature) authorizes government departments to use these funds for purposes it believes promote the general welfare. These purposes include street maintenance, police and fire protection, public health, and others. Any specific government department, such as a parks authority, may seek its sustaining appropriation from the government's funding authority, be it a city council or state legislature, or Congress. Those who benefit directly from any given department's activities have not necessarily paid taxes to support those activities.

Although NFP organizations experience little market competition, they may compete vigorously with each other for support from the relatively few available, or interested, funding authorities. For example, a parks authority may receive 85 percent of its funding from the local government, 10 percent from federal funds, and the remaining 5 percent from private contributions or miscellaneous income (such as park concession fees). These latter two sources typically have little potential for expansion. The local government confronts a long list of other agencies and departments seeking funds, each of which makes an impressive case for its objectives and enjoys the support of some segment of the public. The parks authority and the other agencies and departments compete by tailoring their proposed budgeted programs to the perceived interests and values of the funding authority (whose members are in turn supposed to represent the public). Another form of government authority operates facilities such as harbors, toll roads, or bridges and collects fees from users to finance and operate the facilities. The board of directors may be appointed by a legislature or council, to which it is accountable. This type of authority operates much like a business.

Planning, Budgeting, and Control Processes. Processes for planning, budgeting, and control differ considerably between profit-seeking and NFP organizations. The former require flexibility to earn a reasonable profit; the latter require a means to assure funding authorities that their instructions have been followed.

Profit-seeking organizations set objectives, establish programs, forecast sales, adopt budgets, produce outputs, compare operating and budgeted activities, and constantly adjust their activities to achieve objectives with available resources. The budget supports a flexible process of creating goods and services and promoting their purchase by others to produce revenue.

An NFP organization secures input commitments from its funding authority. For operational control, it compares its actual inputs with those budgeted. The budget is intended to define and support a process of using the funds solely for their intended purposes and is therefore expenditure oriented, which means that money must be spent to acquire specific inputs such as labor, office space, equipment, and services. Often, these expenditures occur in pursuit of output goals for which no objective measurements exist (such as "maintain a system of parks" or "protect public health"). Thus it is difficult or impossible to establish an economic connection between the expenditures for inputs and the quality or benefit from the outputs.

Criteria of Organizational Success. All organizations seek meaningful criteria of success. Private-sector businesses rely on profit as an indicator of their overall success, because it measures competitive strength, ability to expand operations, and stability. In contrast, NFP or government organizations cannot use profit as a measure of effectiveness or success. Nor do large surpluses in their treasuries necessarily indicate success, any more than higher than expected expenditures necessarily indicate failure.

To the extent that governments have a measure of success, it is how closely they comply with applicable laws, fulfill their charters, or fully use funds provided for intended purposes. Yet success in the sense of compliance with rules or following a rigorous discipline may not be the same as success in a broader sense. For example, community-development funds may be spent exactly as the funding authority intended, but knowledgeable critics may doubt whether they have benefited the community.

A government agency's budget is usually contained in measures passed by a legislature, city council, or other elected funding authority. The agency must comply with the budget, as with any other law, by spending the budgeted amounts as the budget directs. Unlike a profit-seeking organization, whose managers may alter their budget as circumstances indicate, a government agency may risk legal action if it fails to spend all of its budget exactly as written. Whereas a profit-seeking organization's management seeks favorable budget variances, government managers often face a presumption that money not spent means *failure* to achieve objectives.

Functional Differentiation Within the Organization. In private-sector organizations, marketing, production, and finance are typically distinct, well-differentiated functions. This strong but flexible functional structure creates favorable environment for initiative and for responsible application of the work force's technical expertise. It helps give the organization direction and leadership.

Not-for-profit organizations rarely include strong finance or marketing functions; their major organizational functions are set up to address the organization's operating objectives. The NFP organization's top leadership combines ability to work with the funding authority with experience and technical knowledge of the organization's activities and objectives. The top leadership uses this structure to control and supervise the activities of the other employees (many of whom may be part-time or volunteer workers) who carry out the organization's programs. No exact equivalent

Figure 10.1   Functional Differentiation—Private Sector and Not-for-Profit Sector
Color indicates the equivalent entity in each sector. In the NFP sector, the funding authority and treasurer functions are often further separated from the rest of the entity than the equivalent functions would be in a private-sector entity.

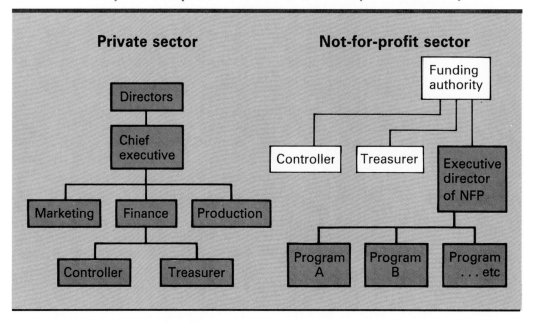

to marketing exists, and much of the finance function may be outside the organization. Figure 10.1 compares private-sector and NFP functional differentiation.

Management Responsibilities

Not-for-profit management's responsibilities differ fundamentally from those of a profit-seeking company's management. Since an NFP organization does not earn a profit, its management does not have responsibility for providing a return on investment. *Instead, it is responsible for achieving the organization's guiding purpose or* **mission** *set by those who provide its funds,* without exceeding its budget.

This mission, as we have said, may not be objectively expressed or subject to measurement. It is this nonmeasurability that leads to much of the confusion surrounding NFP activities. Consider a state agency responsible for treatment of the mentally ill. No precise statement of this responsibility establishes accountability for the resources the agency uses in the same sense that a profit or return-on-investment requirement establishes accountability in a construction company. There is no "standard cost" of caring for one patient for one day, nor is there an objective measure of "care." "Cure rate" means very little without an accepted definition of "cure" or of how a "cured" person should be able to function.

If the funding authority sets some objectives for this agency's management, they may be expressed as nutritional standards, square feet per patient of floor space, hours per day of recreation, documentation of treatments, entrance and discharge conditions, and other variables that are measurable but do not really shed much light on the success of the agency in caring for the mentally ill.

Not-for-profit management must be prepared to demonstrate that funds received have been spent to achieve the approved objectives, and no others, and that the funds were spent reasonably and competently. NFP management therefore has a strong incentive to establish and maintain a good accounting system.

The Finance and Accounting Function

As Figure 10.1 shows, NFPs may rely on the funding authority's finance function. The discussion in this section applies both to that function and to an NFP having its own finance function.

The accounting executive (or controller) in an NFP organization should report to the chief financial officer. The chief financial officer (CFO) should, if the NFP is large enough, assign authority to specialized functions within finance. If the NFP's size permits, it should separate cash and record-keeping responsibilities just as in a profit-seeking organization. The CFO typically supervises the five specialized functions of the treasurer, the controller, the internal auditor, budgeting and planning, and often (in many government entities) the tax assessor-collector.

Many internal and external variables interact to determine the exact accounting system requirements of an NFP organization. The following five groups of variables determine these requirements:

1. The major function, service, or process the organization provides
2. The relationships among the organization, its service consumers, and its funding authority
3. The major uncontrollable external variables that have an impact on the organization
4. The processes by which the organization converts resources into products and services and delivers them to its consumers
5. The management structure and practices of similar organizations in the public or private sector (For example, both electric co-ops and private utilities should have comparable services and efficiency.)

Broadly speaking, the NFP accounting system helps management do everything an accounting system in a profit-seeking organization would do, except measure profit. As a minimum, an NFP accounting system should meet these four broad control objectives:

- *Authorization:* Enable management to establish that the organization's activities are in keeping with its general or specific authorization
- *Recording:* Record and classify transactions promptly, accurately, and in sufficient detail to allow preparation of accounting statements
- *Access:* Provide access to assets in accordance with management's express or implied intentions
- *Accountability:* Allow records of accountability for organizational assets (such as cash, receivables, and equipment) to be reconciled to those assets

These capabilities and the related control requirements that support them are presented in detail in Chapter 11.

Fund-Accounting Systems

This section discusses the fund-based accounting system used by most NFP organizations. It does not cover the unique financial reporting principles applicable to entities using fund accounting.

A **fund**—the basic unit of fund accounting—is a set of resources committed to specific purposes. For accounting purposes, a fund is an entity much like a business, and it can have accounts recording cash and other financial resources as well as related liabilities and equities. **Fund accounting** is simply a system of accounting in which each fund's receipts, expenditures, assets, and liabilities are kept separately. Fund accounting can be used in the public or private sector in any application that requires this system's ability to integrate control, planning, and transactions. For example, bank trust departments may establish separate investment funds to pursue different income and growth objectives; in these funds they invest capital from individually established trust funds to fit the needs of the trusts' beneficiaries.

Fund accounting works in much the same way as private-sector entity accounting. Other than a strong integration of budgeting and operations, it presents no new twists. Typically, an organization manages several funds and is obliged to produce both individual statements for each fund and consolidated statements showing the financial condition of all the funds together. Such statements show the **fund balances** as the net amount in each fund. Specialized account coding/classification plans facilitate keeping funds separate and preparing individual and collective statements in various combinations. A church, for example, may have a building fund, an organ fund, an operating fund, and a benevolence fund. You

Table 10.1 Consolidated Funds Statement

	Dept A Fund	Dept B Fund	Consolidated
Beginning balance	$ 50,000	$30,000	$ 80,000
Appropriations	110,000	70,000	180,000
Expenditures	(120,000)	(50,000)	(170,000)
Transfer from B fund to A fund	15,000	(15,000)	0
Ending balance	$ 55,000	$35,000	$ 90,000

may have (now or later) a retirement fund. A bank's trust department may have separate growth funds for debt, equity, income, and assets in which to invest the resources of the trust it manages. An organization may have more than one fund, each serving a separate purpose.

Despite its additional features, fund accounting does not compensate entirely for the unique control problems inherent in the outputs of NFP enterprises. It does offer increased accountability over inputs and a much stronger audit trail that enables management to discover how the inputs were used to produce the resulting outputs.

Each fund should have its own accounts, be in balance with itself, and have its own financial statements. A consolidation of these individual statements describes the organization's activities. Table 10.1 shows a consolidated statement for two simple funds.

If management considers it important to distinguish between fund assets and fund income, it can create *two* funds, one for principal and one for income. All income that the assets produce goes into the income account. Often, only the income may be used to pay expenses or taxes or to make required outlays. Sometimes unexpended income can be carried over to the next period or transferred to the asset account.

Very small NFP organizations should make use of reasonably priced fund-accounting software that runs on small computers. Such systems have all the features discussed in this chapter. They differ from larger systems only in speed, number of funds, number of accounts, and price.

Government Accounting Systems

There is no single system of government accounting. The federal government operates over 300 separate accounting systems, all different. Nevertheless, all government systems are based on three types of accounts—appropriation, encumbrance, and expenditure. Using such accounts offers management a uniquely high degree of control over **compliance**—the conformance of organizational activities to budget or plans. In other words, these accounts enable management to monitor closely, through account balances, how well the organization fulfils its designated objectives and to intervene (by withholding approvals) should organizational activities appear ineffective.

The relationships among appropriation, encumbrance, and expenditure accounts and government financial processes are shown in Figure 10.2. Continue to refer to this figure as you read the rest of this section. In Figure 10.2, the funding authority and organizational management establish objectives. The appropriation and encumbrance accounts define these objectives financially, in terms of programs, budgets, spending levels, and expenses. These categories form part of the set of preventive controls. When operations occur, the accounting system records expenditures. These expenditures are incorporated, along with preventive-control information, into performance reports that act as feedback controls. In response to these reports, operating management and the funding authority may take follow-up action as appropriate.

Figure 10.2 Data Flow Diagram Showing Appropriation, Encumbrance, and Expenditure Accounts

Appropriations, encumbrances, and expenditure accounts tie together all the operations of a not-for-profit entity.

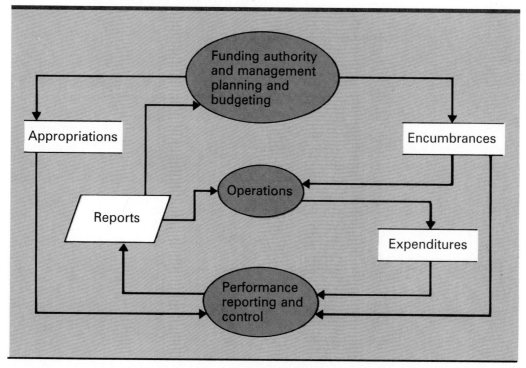

The more detailed diagram in Figure 10.3 (page 355) shows figures from the example that follows. Please refer to the figure as you go through the example.

Appropriations

Appropriation accounts are used in the budgeting process to allocate available funds to operating units. This is often called the appropriations process. Appropriations should total no more than the estimated tax revenues available during the period covered. The amount of such revenues is estimated just as carefully as sales revenue in a profit-seeking firm. For example, information about the value of property could be used to estimate property taxes, sales activity to calculate sales tax, and personal income estimates to figure income taxes.

A revenue estimate is formalized by means of an accounting entry. For example, your county tax assessor-collector would include the estimate of taxes receivable in an accounting entry as follows:

Tax Revenues Receivable	$600,000	
Revenues Available for Appropriation		$590,000
Provision for Uncollectible Taxes		10,000

You can locate this entry near the top of Figure 10.3. The balance of Revenues Available for Appropriation is $590,000. The funding authority appropriates these available funds to all the programs or units it supports. Note that the encumbrance of appropriated funds involves a different account (discussed below) from the credit-balance account Revenues Available for Appropriation. This procedure parallels the use of suspense and distribution accounts as described in Chapter 9. The use of two accounts in such situations enhances control, preserves totals, and separates responsibilities for appropriations, encumbrances, and expenditures. The resulting appropriation entry, which is not shown in Figure 10.3, may look like this:

Encumbrance of Revenues Available for Appropriation	$220,000	
Appropriation for Street Construction & Maintenance		$ 50,000
Appropriation for Sheriff's Office & Law Enforcement		100,000
Appropriation for Tax Assessor-Collector's Office		70,000

The Sheriff's Office part of this entry may be found in Figure 10.3. Note that these appropriations leave $370,000 available for later appropriation. The appropriation process may not commit all the expected revenues,

Figure 10.3 Fund-Accounting Entry and Control Relationships (on facing page)
The $400 expenditure can be traced all the way back to appropriations by the funding authority, using the audit and accounting entry trail shown at right.

leaving a planned surplus; or it may deliberately appropriate more than the expected revenues and cover the excess by issuing bonds or borrowing from a financial institution. The tax assessor-collector maintains a collection system to record tax remittances received and track down taxes-receivable outstanding. This collection system is broadly comparable to the accounts receivable and cash receipts functions in a profit-seeking organization.

Encumbrances

In the government budgeting process an **encumbrance** commits appropriated funds to use for specific programs and activities. The first example is the Encumbrance of Revenues Available for Appropriation account discussed in the previous section. Each encumbrance places a certain portion of appropriated funds into an encumbrance account—that is, it *encumbers* the funds so that they may not be used for any other purpose.

The same funds may be encumbered at several levels. Once the funding authority has encumbered expected revenues by appropriating funds for a program budget, the program manager may encumber (commit) parts of the appropriation for wages, rent, equipment, supplies, and so on, by placing the desired amounts into encumbrance accounts for these specific purposes. The following entry sets up encumbrances within the sheriff's office:

Encumbrance—Sheriff's Office and Law Enforcement	$100,000	
Appropriation—Sheriff and Deputy's Salaries		$40,000
Appropriation—Office and Jail Operations		45,000
Appropriation—Automobile Allowance		15,000

The office and jail part of this entry appears in Figure 10.3 near the bottom. The salary encumbrance could be further encumbered for the salaries of specific individuals. Each encumbrance establishes a control account for the appropriations at the next lower level. A control account (encumbrance) for Program A summarizes a subledger that includes a control account (encumbrance) for wages, which in turn summarizes the subledger of encumbrances for individual salaries.

Expenditures

An **expenditure** is the use of funds as designated by an encumbrance. Expenditures consist of transactions exchanging resources for labor, materials, space, services, utilities, and other inputs that allow the organi-

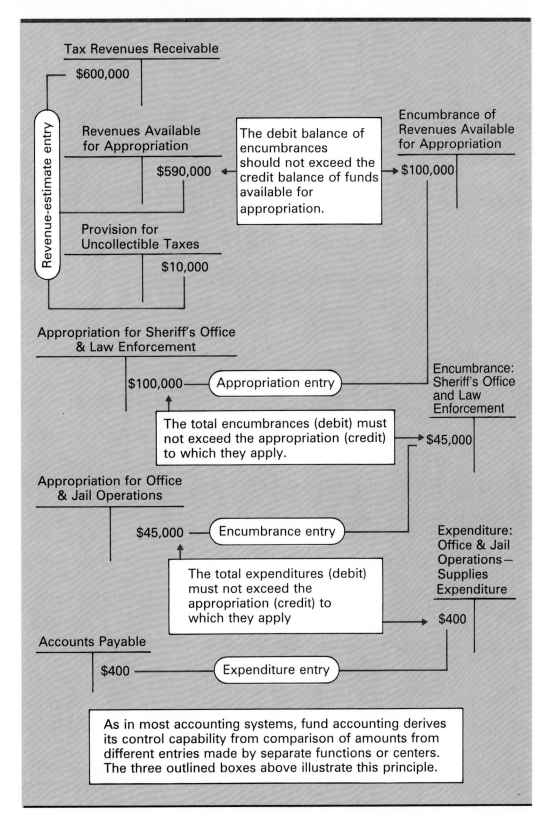

Tax Revenues Receivable

$600,000

Revenue-estimate entry

Revenues Available for Appropriation

$590,000

The debit balance of encumbrances should not exceed the credit balance of funds available for appropriation.

Encumbrance of Revenues Available for Appropriation

$100,000

Provision for Uncollectible Taxes

$10,000

Appropriation for Sheriff's Office & Law Enforcement

$100,000 — Appropriation entry

The total encumbrances (debit) must not exceed the appropriation (credit) to which they apply.

Encumbrance: Sheriff's Office and Law Enforcement

$45,000

Appropriation for Office & Jail Operations

$45,000 — Encumbrance entry

The total expenditures (debit) must not exceed the appropriation (credit) to which they apply

Expenditure: Office & Jail Operations — Supplies Expenditure

$400

Accounts Payable

$400 — Expenditure entry

As in most accounting systems, fund accounting derives its control capability from comparison of amounts from different entries made by separate functions or centers. The three outlined boxes above illustrate this principle.

zation to pursue its objectives. The parts of the accounting system that record and classify expenditures correspond very closely to the payroll, cash disbursements, purchasing, inventory, and general journal applications in a profit-seeking organization. The entries also have a similar appearance. Using the office and jail example, assume that various expenses are paid monthly. Representative expenditure entries might look like this:

Office and Jail Operations—Rental Expenditures	$500	
Accounts Payable—Commercial Properties, Inc.		$500
Office and Jail Operations—Electricity Expenditures	$200	
Accounts Payable—Smallville Electric Co.		$200
Office and Jail Operations—Supplies Expenditures	$400	
Accounts Payable—Ace Business Supply Co.		$400

The Ace Business Supply purchase appears at the bottom of Figure 10.3.

Budgeting and Control

The major elements of NFP budgeting are aimed at establishing the NFP's objectives and related budget as precisely as possible. Outside the budget process itself, the funding authority may employ both short-run and long-run spending controls. The zero-based budget is a typical short-run control on budgeting and spending; the sunset review is a widespread long-run control. This section discusses these techniques, after introducing government budgeting in general.

Budgeting Revenues and Expenses.   Government units usually receive their appropriations from a legislative body. The complete appropriation process, from the point of view of such a unit, works like this: The unit prepares a statement of goals, objectives, programs, and what it believes to be the required funding inputs. This statement is often a modification of that of the previous operating period. The estimate of required funds may be based on the resources required during the previous period, adjusted for inflation, and on changes in objectives and other factors. The unit presents this plan to the legislative body.

In large governments, a professional staff (typically called a **legislative budget board**) studies and coordinates all the budget requests of individual units before they are presented to the funding authority. This budget board is often independent of the government finance function, although it may use that function's estimates of the availability of appropriated funds. If total budget requests exceed estimated available revenues, the budget board asks certain units to revise their requests or imposes its own revisions before presenting an integrated budget, in the form of a proposed law, to the funding authority. The funding authority typically relies heavily on the recommendation of its budget board, although it may also consider pleas from government units whose requests were revised by the budget board. Those who use the services of particular units may attempt to influence the funding authority. To varying degrees, a legislative body may revise its budget board's proposals before finally approving and enacting the budget.[1]

Zero-Based Budgeting. For decades, government funding authorities have sought methods of constructing budgets closely aligned to the funding authority's objectives. **Zero-based budgeting**—the process of building up a budget based on each unit's objectives, rather than on the last period's budget—is one such method. Its name signifies that every unit begins with *no* assured appropriation. The unit reviews each of its objectives, discarding those no longer in effect and adopting new ones consistent with its designated responsibilities. It develops programs and a corresponding budget *from the ground up, every period*, to achieve its objectives. By adhering to this process, each unit should be able to identify and discontinue unnecessary programs, thus saving their costs.

In practice, zero-based budgeting has been disappointing. The expected savings have not materialized, probably because the effort of truly reviewing and justifying all operations each budget period exceeds the capabilities of the typical NFP organization. Also, some managers may resist a process *intended* to result in a lower level of funding. Zero-based budgeting pays off best when applied in a government unit with truly inefficient operations or superfluous objectives or programs. It might be preferable for a unit to review only part of its operations each budget period. Such a limited review would be more manageable and less likely to result in a major resource reduction for the entire unit. Alternatively, the unit could be reviewed in whole but less frequently.

Sunset Review. The concept of reviewing an entire unit's purposes and operations only once every several years is called **sunset review**—a control process that specifies a finite life span for a government agency, after which the agency is allowed to expire or is re-established. The term comes from the political saying, "Let the sun set on any unit for which there is no longer a need." To implement sunset review, the legislature includes in the law that creates the unit a provision giving it a limited-term existence—typically a five-to-ten-year term. At the end of the term, the unit simply ceases to exist unless the legislature enacts a new law. Of course,

---

[1]In nongovernmental NFP organizations, these same elements exist but may be named differently and handled less formally. In other such organizations, revenues may derive from dues, sale of services or products, contributions, or fees. The organization's board of directors or executive committee approves the treasurer's revenue estimates and the budget.

the legislature that reviews the unit is likely to extend its term, possibly with changes in its responsibilities that affect the services it may provide and the resources it needs.

Identifying Programs and Funding Sources

In a private-sector profit-seeking organization, control of cash is often centralized to the point that only one cash "fund" exists; all revenues flow into this fund and all activities are financed from it. In an NFP organization, legal, service, and traditional needs often require keeping several funds and separating the accounting for the cash inflows and outflows of each. In this way, any program expenditure can be traced to the fund that provided it and the outflows of any fund can be traced to the programs they supported.

Account Classification Codes

The simple eight-digit account coding system described in Chapter 6 can be adapted to distinguish among different programs and sources of funds by adding a two-digit program-identifying code and a two-digit fund-identifying code. These changes will create a twelve-digit number that can account for up to 100 funds, each with 100 million accounts. Table 10.2 illustrates the complete account classification code design.

Maintaining accountability relies heavily on the account classification structure. The classification structure is described by account codes. These account codes or numbers include a portion whose value is unique for

Table 10.2   NFP Account Classification Code Design (Code Format: AB-CD-EF-G-H-IJKL)

The characters EFGHIJKL are the original account number; combined with characters ABCD they form the full account identifying code.

Position	Purpose
AB	Program identifier
CD	Fund identifier
EF	Major class of appropriation
G	Subclass of appropriation
H	Identifies account as appropriation, encumbrance, or expenditure
IJKL	Account or voucher number of expense charged to encumbrance

each fund and which serves as a **fund identifier**. Two examples of this structure and its accompanying codes follow:

Example A

Number: 10-20-21-3-2-0050
Account Title: Salary Expenditure, Willard Aseki, Supervisor, Smallville office of state employment agency

10	Program identifier (state employment agency)
20	Fund identifier (general revenues appropriated by the legislative body)
21	Major class (supervisory salaries)
3	Subclass (Smallville office)
2	Code 2 signifies an expenditure
0050	Employee number (Willard Aseki, a specific employee)

Example B

Number: 10-10-35-1-1-0000
Account title: Encumbrance of Wages and Salaries, state employment agency, for temporary help

10	Program identifier (the state employment agency)
10	Fund identifier 10 identifies cash flow from the state's investments—income available for hiring temporary help to handle peak loads
35	Major class 35 is wages and salaries category
1	Subclass is temporary help
1	Code 1 signifies an encumbrance
0000	Signifies that this encumbrance is against the amount originally appropriated to the state employment agency for wages and salaries

Using these account numbers, the computer can be programmed to produce various accounting statements showing appropriations, encumbrances, and expenditures by funding source (such as dues, contributions, investment income), program (such as annual meeting, training program, publications), and expense classification (such as travel, printing, wages).

An Illustration of Account Codes

This section illustrates the use of fund-accounting account codes to appropriate, encumber, and record some administrative expenses. The setting is a state service agency; it could be almost any administrative unit. The agency, the State Agricultural Service (SAS), operates three programs: Crops, Herds, and Trees. The SAS has a director—Jones—and three employees—Wang, Vitorio, and Young. The legislature, relying for advice on its budget board, appropriates funds from a single source to the SAS and specifies how much the agency may spend for salaries and how much for operating expenses. It is up to the SAS director to set salaries for Wang, Vitorio, and Young, to allocate their time among the three programs, and to allocate the operating expenses appropriation to specific travel and supplies categories.

Table 10.3 shows the SAS account structure and numerical codes. The salary account codes and amounts are shown in Table 10.4, and the operating expenses codes and amounts in Table 10.5 (page 363). Only the accounts to which the legislative body has made appropriations show amounts in Tables 10.4 and 10.5. The salary of Jones, the SAS director, is set by the legislature. The other accounts are either allocated by the administrator or used to record expenses.

The appropriation accounts of this agency normally have credit balances; the balances indicated in Tables 10.4 and 10.5 are set by the legislature. The variations between programs are decided by fund allocation decisions within the SAS. The SAS makes these decisions in light of the needs of individual programs, such as how much time SAS employees will have to spend in each, how much travel they will have to do for each, and what other support the programs need. Thus, the SAS administrator budgets SAS programs using resources designated by the legislative body. The account number for the SAS total appropriation is 55-20-00-0-0-0000, and the amount is $1,200,000. This amount is the sum of the two appro-

Table 10.3   Account Code Structure for the State Agricultural Service (Format: AB-CD-EF-G-H-IJKL)
Here the characters in the general account code are given specific meaning and the classifications they represent are described.

Positions	Meaning
AB	55 = The agricultural service (These digits appear in all of the agency's accounts.)
CD	20 = Appropriations from general tax revenues, the source of the agency's funding
EF	40 = Salaries appropriation or 50 = Operating expenses appropriation
G	1 = Crops, 2 = Herds, 3 = Trees
H	0 = Appropriation, 1 = Encumbrance, 2 = Expenditure
IJKL	2000 = Salary—Jones 2100 = Salary—Wang 2200 = Salary—Vitorio 2300 = Salary—Young 8100 = Operating expenses—supplies 8200 = Operating expenses—travel

Table 10.4   SAS Salary Accounts

55-20-40-0-0-0000	$400,000
	The appropriation for salaries.
	This is the sum of the four accounts with numbers
	    55-20-40-0-0-2000, 55-20-40-0-0-2100,
	    55-20-40-0-0-2200, and 55-20-40-0-0-2300

55-20-40-0-0-2000	$100,000 Salary Appropriation—Jones (SAS director), set by legislature
55-20-40-0-0-2100	Salary Appropriation—Wang to be set by SAS director Wang's salary expense will be allocated (according to hours worked) to the following three accounts:
55-20-40-1-0-2100	Salary Allocable to the Crops Program—Wang
55-20-40-2-0-2100	Salary Allocable to the Herds Program—Wang
55-20-40-3-0-2100	Salary Allocable to the Trees Program—Wang
55-20-40-0-0-2200	Salary Appropriation—Vitorio to be set by SAS director Vitorio's salary expense will be allocated (according to hours worked) to the following three accounts:
55-20-40-1-0-2200	Salary Allocable to the Crops Program—Vitorio
55-20-40-2-0-2200	Salary Allocable to the Herds Program—Vitorio
55-20-40-3-0-2200	Salary Allocable to the Trees Program—Vitorio
55-20-40-0-0-2300	Salary Appropriation—Young to be set by SAS director Young's salary expense will be allocated (according to hours worked) to the following three accounts:
55-20-40-1-0-2300	Salary Allocable to the Crops Program—Young
55-20-40-2-0-2300	Salary Allocable to the Herds Program—Young
55-20-40-3-0-2300	Salary Allocable to the Trees Program—Young

priation accounts shown in color in Tables 10.4 and 10.5. The January 1 account balances are $400,000 and $800,000. The details of these accounts are shown in Tables 10.4 and 10.5, respectively.

The legislature's appropriation is encumbered to fund the appropriations at the next lower level. In other words, the director encumbers the legislative appropriation for the service's own internal allocations. Yet another way to put it is that the legislative appropriation is encumbered to fund the appropriations at the administrative level. This appropriation/ encumbrance relationship is replicated from one level to the next all the way down to the smallest operating units. For comparison with these appropriations, the SAS must record the expenses it incurs in the proper accounts. Examples follow of setting and paying salaries and of budgeting and paying for supplies and travel.

Set Appropriated Salaries.   The director's salary, set by the legislature, is $100,000. The director encumbers the remaining $300,000 salary appropriation to establish salaries for Wang, Vitorio, and Young. In doing so,

Jones creates three new accounts. The following accounting entry would be used to encumber salaries:

55-20-40-0-1-0000 Salary Encumbrance	$300,000	
55-20-40-0-0-2100 Salary Appropriation—Wang		$120,000
55-20-40-0-0-2200 Salary Appropriation—Vitorio		100,000
55-20-40-0-0-2300 Salary Appropriation—Young		80,000

In Table 10.6 Link 1 shows the salary appropriations made by this entry.

January Salary Expenses Recorded and Allocated to Departments.   Wang earns $10,000 per month; Vitorio, $8,333; Young, $6,667. In the lengthy entry below, the service's director allocates these monthly salaries to the various programs in which the persons participated. This allocation could be based on the amount of time spent in each program, but need not be. Notice how the account number indicates the kind of expense, the department, and the accounts normally used to record an expenditure.

55-20-40-1-2-2100 Salary Expenditure—Wang	$5,000	
55-20-40-2-2-2100 Salary Expenditure—Wang	3,000	
55-20-40-3-2-2100 Salary Expenditure—Wang	2,000	
55-20-40-1-2-2200 Salary Expenditure—Vitorio	2,000	
55-20-40-2-2-2200 Salary Expenditure—Vitorio	5,333	
55-20-40-3-2-2200 Salary Expenditure—Vitorio	1,000	
55-20-40-1-2-2300 Salary Expenditure—Young	1,333	
55-20-40-2-2-2300 Salary Expenditure—Young	2,000	
55-20-40-3-2-2300 Salary Expenditure—Young	3,334	
(Wages payable account number) Wages Payable, January		$25,000

In Table 10.6 Link 2 shows the January salary expenditure for Wang.

Set Appropriations for Operating Expenses: Supplies and Travel.   Just as salaries are allocated to specific individuals, the SAS director encumbers the operating expenses appropriation by establishing specific appropriations for its component classifications of supplies and travel. (Like salaries, these expenses are not allocated to programs until they are incurred.) The director need not choose to encumber the entire $800,000 at the beginning of the year, as the following entry illustrates:

55-20-50-0-1-0000 Operating Expenses Encumbrance	$500,000	
55-20-50-0-0-8100 Appropriation—Supplies		$300,000
55-20-50-0-0-8200 Appropriation—Travel		200,000

Link 3 in Table 10.6 shows the supply and travel appropriations made by this entry.

Table 10.5   SAS Operating Expenses Accounts

55-20-50-0-0-0000	$800,000 The appropriation for operating expenses. This is the sum of the two appropriation accounts with numbers 55-20-50-0-0-8100 and 55-20-50-0-0-8200.
55-20-50-0-0-8100	Operating Expenses Appropriation—Supplies Supplies will be allocated to the three programs according to the SAS's judgment.
55-20-50-1-0-8100	Supplies Allocated to the Crops Program
55-20-50-2-0-8100	Supplies Allocated to the Herds Program
55-20-50-3-0-8100	Supplies Allocated to the Trees Program
55-20-50-0-0-8200	Operating Expenses Appropriation—Travel Travel will be allocated to the three programs according to the SAS's judgment.
55-20-50-1-0-8200	Travel Allocated to the Crops Program
55-20-50-2-0-8200	Travel Allocated to the Herds Program
55-20-50-3-0-8200	Travel Allocated to the Trees Program

Recognize January Operating Expenses.   In practice, over the weeks and months, supplies and travel involve a series of payments to suppliers, airlines, rental-car agencies, hotels, restaurants, and the like, here summarized as Accounts Payable. The specific expenditures incurred were $30,000 for supplies and $10,000 for travel. The entry follows the format you have seen above:

55-20-50-1-2-8100 Supplies Expenditure—Crops	$12,000	
55-20-50-2-2-8100 Supplies Expenditure—Herds	14,000	
55-20-50-3-2-8100 Supplies Expenditure—Trees	4,000	
55-20-50-1-2-8200 Travel Expenditure—Crops	2,000	
55-20-50-2-2-8200 Travel Expenditure—Herds	5,000	
55-20-50-3-2-8200 Travel Expenditure—Trees	3,000	
(Various account numbers) Accounts Payable		$40,000

In Table 10.6, Link 4 shows the January supplies expenditure for the crops, herds, and trees programs.

Table 10.6 (page 364) shows the relationships among these accounts throughout the four appropriation, encumbrance, and expenditure entries just described. The entries have produced the accounts and their balances as shown in the table. Table 10.7 (page 365) is not suitable for use as a report; the next section explains how to use these account numbers to group account balances into useful reports.

Table 10.6 Legislative and Administrative Annual Appropriations for State Agricultural Service, and January Expenditures
Here you can see links that tie accounts together, utilizing the account codes.

Legislative Appropriations

Salaries—Jones and others	55-20-40-0-0-0000	$ 400,000
Other expenses	55-20-50-0-0-0000	800,000
Total appropriation	55-20-00-0-0-0000	$1,200,000

L L
I I
N N
K K
3 1

*Encumbrances and Appropriations
by the Director of the State Agricultural Service*

Supplies	55-20-50-0-0-8100	$ 300,000
Travel	55-20-50-0-0-8200	200,000
Total encumbrance	55-20-50-0-1-0000	$ 500,000
Salary—Wang	55-20-40-0-0-2100	$ 120,000
Salary—Vitorio	55-20-40-0-0-2200	100,000
Salary—Young	55-20-40-0-0-2300	80,000
Total encumbrance	55-20-40-0-1-0000	$ 300,000

L L
I I
N N
K K
2 4

*January Expenditures (Partial)
State Agricultural Service*

Salary Expenditure—Wang	55-20-40-1-2-2100	$ 5,000
(Salary expenditure for Vitorio and	55-20-40-2-2-2100	3,000
Young not shown)	55-20-40-3-2-2100	2,000
Wages Payable	(account number not given)	$ 10,000
Supplies Expenditure	55-20-50-1-2-8100	$ 12,000
(Travel expenditures not shown)	55-20-50-2-2-8100	14,000
	55-20-50-3-2-8100	4,000
Various credits	(account numbers not given)	$ 30,000

Performance Reporting

The accounts in Table 10.7 can be used to produce a variety of reports, many of which contribute to performance evaluation. This section reviews management objectives in NFP organizations and describes reports that management can use to measure progress toward those objectives.

Management Objectives and Controls

Managers of not-for-profit organizations cannot target profit or return on investment as objectives. Instead, they focus on objectives like the following:

Quantified objective Achieving a target value of some measure of activity output (for example, number of cattle vaccinated, acres of

Table 10.7   SAS Account Titles, Numbers, and Balances at 1-31-19XX
This partial listing of account codes and balances is typical of an NFP entity's trial balance as operations continue. (Note that this is not a complete trial balance.)

Account Number	Account Title	Balance @ 1-31-XX
55-20-00-0-0-0000	Appropriation—Agricultural Service	$1,200,000
55-20-40-0-0-0000	Appropriation—Agricultural Service Salaries	400,000
55-20-40-0-1-0000	Encumbrance—Agricultural Service Salaries	400,000
55-30-40-0-0-2000	Appropriation—Jones Salary	100,000
55-20-40-0-0-2100	Appropriation—Wang Salary	120,000
55-20-40-0-0-2200	Appropriation—Vitorio Salary	100,000
55-20-40-0-0-2300	Appropriation—Young Salary	80,000
55-20-40-1-2-2100	Expenditure—Salary—Wang—Crops—January	5,000
55-20-40-1-2-2200	Expenditure—Salary—Vitorio—Crops—January	2,000
55-20-40-1-2-2300	Expenditure—Salary—Young—Crops—January	1,333
55-20-40-2-2-2100	Expenditure—Salary—Wang—Herds—January	3,000
55-20-40-2-2-2200	Expenditure—Salary—Vitorio—Herds—January	5,333
55-20-40-2-2-2300	Expenditure—Salary—Young—Herds—January	2,000
55-20-40-3-2-2100	Expenditure—Salary—Wang—Trees—January	2,000
55-20-40-3-2-2200	Expenditure—Salary—Vitorio—Trees—January	1,000
55-20-40-3-2-2300	Expenditure—Salary—Young—Trees—January	3,334
55-20-50-0-0-0000	Appropriation—Agricultural Service Operating Expenses	800,000
55-20-50-0-1-0000	Encumbrance—Operating Expenses	500,000
55-20-50-0-0-8100	Appropriation—Supplies	300,000
55-20-50-1-2-8100	Expenditure—Supplies—Crops—January	12,000
55-20-50-2-2-8100	Expenditure—Supplies—Herds—January	14,000
55-20-50-3-2-8100	Expenditure—Supplies—Trees—January	4,000
55-20-50-0-0-8200	Appropriation—Travel	200,000
55-20-50-1-2-8200	Expenditure—Travel—Crops—January	2,000
55-20-50-2-2-8200	Expenditure—Travel—Herds—January	5,000
55-20-50-3-2-8200	Expenditure—Travel—Trees—January	3,000

crops inspected, number of seedlings planted, or number of information queries answered)

Legal compliance   Using the appropriated funds for the exact purposes specified in the appropriation (to pay salaries, purchase supplies, and pay for travel)

Efficiency   Protecting against waste by hiring qualified staff, writing job descriptions, and making comparisons with similar organizations (such as comparing salary cost per animal vaccinated with that in another state's agricultural service)

Legal compliance is especially amenable to monitoring using the accounting system. Nonmonetary detail captured in the course of transaction recording can be used to monitor progress toward achieving quantified objectives and efficiency. Here, for each of the three objectives, are examples of the use of accounts to help management measure and control progress toward its objectives.

Quantified Objective. As part of the Crops program, the SAS has developed a fire-ant control project. The objective of the project is to deliver 10,000 pounds of fire-ant poison to farmers. The director establishes an account with the number 55-20-50-1-1-8101 and budgets $25,000, which will buy 10,000 pounds of fire-ant poison. The SAS asks its agents to report on a monthly basis as to pounds distributed. When the 10,000-pound figure is reached, the director intends to stop buying the poison and announce that the program is complete.

Legal Compliance. The accounts can be compiled into stewardship reports to the legislature's budget board. Suppose the state experiences a funds shortage elsewhere and seeks to know the amount of appropriated but unencumbered funds in the agricultural service. This amount, called the **appropriation free balance**, is found as shown in Table 10.8.

The $300,000 free balance shown in Table 10.8, or some part of it, may be recovered by the budget board—if state law permits—by reversing the entry that created the operating expenses appropriation and replacing it with an entry for a lesser amount.

Table 10.8 Calculation of Appropriation Free Balance
This table illustrates calculation of the appropriation free balance. This balance changes, usually declining, as operations continue. Asterisks represent "wild card" values.

(1) Sum of all SAS appropriations from general tax revenues		
(sum of accounts 55-20-**-0-0-0000)		
55-20-40-0-0-0000	$400,000	
55-20-50-0-0-0000	800,000	
Total appropriations		$1,200,000
(2) Sum of all encumbrances on the appropriations		
(sum of balances of all accounts 55-20-**-0-1-0000)		
55-20-40-0-1-0000	$400,000	
55-20-50-0-1-0000	500,000	
Total encumbrances		$900,000
(3) Subtract (2) from (1), giving		
The appropriation free balance:		$300,000

Other account number combinations will reveal expenditures for any particular program, expenditures compared to appropriations, various free balances, and other potentially useful information.

Efficiency.   The number of animals vaccinated in January as part of the Herds program, recorded by Young and Vitorio on a day-by-day basis, is 14,666. The salary cost per animal vaccinated can be calculated as $7,333/ 14,666 = $0.50. The $7,333 is Young's and Vitorio's salaries for the Herds program in January. Wang did not participate in the Herds program that month. If the same statistic is collected by other state agricultural services, comparison might generate conclusions about the efficiency of the SAS vaccination program. Numerous comparisons for all of the programs may allow conclusions about the efficiency of the SAS as an agency.

External Performance Bench Marks

Because NFP organizations have difficulty developing measures that relate outputs to funds appropriated, they rely heavily on comparisons with similar operations in other organizations. The averages of such measures become performance bench marks.

For example, credit unions are NFP organizations that provide financial services to their members. Although similar in many ways to banks and other for-profit financial institutions, credit unions are member owned and rarely regard their level of earnings as the most important statistic describing their operations. *Credit Union Magazine* collects and publishes monthly updated performance bench marks, including loan delinquency rate; average loan yield; ratios of interest expense to interest income, operating expenses to income, total capital to total assets, loans to savings, notes payable to total assets; liquidity ratio; and more. Approaching or exceeding these bench marks does not guarantee a high level of performance, but it does provide some assurance to management that the organization is performing as well as or better than comparable organizations.

Performance-Report Follow-up

The performance-report follow-up portion of the budgeting process in an NFP organization proceeds much as it might in a division of a business. The appropriation and budgeting processes both allocate resources to achieve goals. Encumbrances and expenditures correspond closely to the recording and reporting of operating results. In both an NFP and a business, reports compare budgeted and actual expenditures. The main difference, other than format, is the greater reliance by NFP on controlling expenditures to correspond to predetermined appropriation (budget) levels. Clear-cut performance measures of NFP output are often lacking. Performance-report follow-up also emphasizes overruns and underruns because they represent deviations from the funding authority's instructions, which have the force of law—even to the point of subjecting an administrator to a lawsuit for not complying with them. In a business, in contrast, overruns and underruns are scrutinized for the information they provide about efficiency in producing outputs and responding to environmental changes, but they are not, by themselves, judged to be favorable or unfavorable.

Computer-Based Systems to Implement Fund Accounting

The operating procedures and data structures of fund-accounting systems resemble those of the ordinary accounting applications, such as cost accounting, with which you are now familiar. That is, they are based on files containing records that can be linked to other records. They have data entry processes to capture budget and transaction data. Transaction recording and classifying proceed along the lines of the data base formats illustrated in Chapters 7, 8, and 9. A design, such as Figure 10.3, that uses three files—one each for appropriation, encumbrance, and expenditure records—could be expanded to fit many NFP systems. Fund-accounting systems also use the same types of computer equipment and controls as other accounting systems.

Consolidation of account balances to form a set of financial statements for an NFP proceeds much more easily if the account structure is designed to combine balances from multiple accounts in the same classification. For example, to consolidate the State Agricultural Service with other state agencies, the state controller would instruct the software to sum the balances of each specific type of account—such as Salaries, Travel, and Supplies—across all fund numbers.

Summary

Not-for-profit (NFP) organizations typically employ fund accounting, a set of techniques for accounting control over funding, administering programs, and expenditures. Although in many ways similar to for-profit accounting, fund accounting has its own jargon and account structure. A unit of government, having received funds through an appropriation process, encumbers the appropriated funds for specific purposes, makes expenditures in pursuit of those purposes, and prepares reports for the funding authority and its managers comparing its appropriation, encumbrance, and expenditure account balances at the same date. Transaction journals provide supportive detail.

A well-designed account coding structure makes routine processing more manageable. By designing the data entry portion of the system with managerial reports in mind, it is possible to generate reports automatically by specifying classes of account numbers whose balances should be selected, summed, or compared.

Because NFP organizations aren't subject to pressures of market competition and profit measures, they must use some other means to measure their success. Zero-based budgeting and sunset review, two such means used by government, are only partly successful.

Fund accounting cannot compensate for the innate control difficulties of NFP organizations. It can, however, assure reasonable controls over acquisition and use of resources.

Key Terms

appropriation free balance
appropriations
compliance
encumbrance
expenditure
fund
fund accounting
fund balances

fund identifier
funding authority
legislative budget board
mission
Standard Industrial Classification
sunset review
zero-based budgeting

Review Questions

1. What six major differences distinguish not-for-profit from profit-seeking organizations? Which of these seems most important to you? Why? Which seems least important? Why?

2. What is a funding authority? How would you expect a local service agency's dealings with its funding authority to differ from a profit-seeking organization's dealings with its customers?

3. What specialized activities characterize the finance function of an NFP organization?

4. Why do public-sector managers have a strong incentive to maintain accounting controls? How does this motivation differ from that of managers in a business?

5. What accounting control objectives do NFP organizations share with profit-seeking groups?

6. Define: *appropriation, encumbrance,* and *expenditure,* and specify who is responsible for each. How do these three activities contribute to control in an NFP organization?

7. In the State Agricultural Service, who established the balance in each of the following accounts: 55-20-40-0-0-2100, 55-20-40-0-0-0000, 55-20-50-2-2-8200?

8. Name three types of performance objective that an NFP organization's accounts can be used to describe and control.

Discussion Questions

9. What is the Standard Industrial Classification? Through your library, try to obtain a copy of it. If you are successful, spend a few minutes looking it over. Can you think of a practical use for it?

10. Select any two of the six major differences between NFP and profit-seeking organizations, and explain how they influence the accounting system of an NFP.

11. What is a fund? Why might an organization require several funds? Why must such an organization consolidate its individual fund statements to produce operating reports? Are consolidated statements more desirable, in general, than individual fund statements?

12. Take stock of your own relationships to profit and not-for-profit organizations. Label the left side of a sheet of paper "profit-seeking" and the right side, "not-for-profit." On the left side, list the profit-seeking organizations you have worked for, bought major merchandise from, borrowed money from, and so on. On the right side, list the not-for-profit organizations you have joined, donated to, taken classes from, and so on. Focus only on the last five years.

13. Draw an organization chart for the finance function of a government organization. Why do you suppose tax collection is not one of the functions of the treasurer?

14. Classify each of the following not-for-profit missions as measurable or not measurable. For those you classify as measurable, give an example of a suitable measurement. For example, a mission to collect all taxes due the school district is measurable; it could be considered achieved if 98 percent of taxes due were actually collected within 90 days of the due date.
    (a) Educate the public on the dangers of drug abuse (public health department)
    (b) Protect endangered species (parks and wildlife department)
    (c) Promote fellowship among the fraternity's members (college fraternity)
    (d) Promote professionalism among CPAs (AICPA)
    (e) Offer members sizable savings on purchases (co-op store)
    (f) Improve members' working conditions and pay (labor union)

15. In small not-for-profit organizations, the fund-accounting system may be simplified to record only receipts and expenditures, not appropriations or encumbrances. What control weaknesses might result from this simplification? In your answer, keep in mind that the appropriation and encumbrance processes can play a role similar to that of the budget in for-profit organizations.

16. The town of Crockett has two hospitals, one owned by the city and the other by a profit-seeking company. What differences might you

expect between the purposes and managements of these two hospitals? Would you expect comparable differences to exist between two electric utilities, one government owned and the other investor owned? Why or why not?

17. An organization's funding authority may appropriate more funds than the revenue estimate. May the organization management encumber more funds than the funding authority appropriated? Why or why not?

18. Suppose a state wishes to improve the efficiency of its public housing agency. Discuss how each of the following might affect its (a) efficiency and (b) mission of providing affordable housing to low-income families: zero-based budgeting, sunset review, improved accounting system, sale to investors who would operate it as a privately owned company.

19. Discuss the merits of the *sequence* of information in the account code described in Table 10.2. For example, suppose the order were completely reversed: IJKL-H-G-EF-CD-AB. If the account number is the primary key of the transaction record, what difficulties, if any, would this order create in a search for specific records?

Problems

20. Table 10.1 on page 351 is a simple illustration of a consolidated funds statement. There were no transfers to a fund not shown and no liabilities. Nor are debit and credit balances identified. Assume that the revenue earned by these funds is passed into a separate fund called the revenue fund. The Department A fund earned $9,000 and the Department B fund earned $6,000. These amounts are included in Appropriations and Expenditures and should be shown separately. The revenue fund's initial balance was $12,000. Distributions to various parties from the revenue fund totaled $10,000, including $3,000 transferred to the Department B fund and currently included in Appropriations.

Required:

Revise Table 10.1 (page 351) to reflect all these changes, including the revenue fund.

21. The Smithville Charitable Association is a small organization that uses fund accounting. It has three funds: operating, capital, and income. Each fund has the following nine accounts:

Appropriation	Funds Receivable
Cash on Hand	Wages and Accounts Payable
Short-Term Investments	Other Assets
Contributions	Fund Balance
Distributions	

Required:

Use these accounts (and any others you think are needed) to journalize the following events:

(a) The budget committee estimates contributions for the coming year at $18,000, of which $5,000 will be for the capital fund.

(b) The capital fund earns $1,000, which is paid to the income fund.

(c) The association borrows $7,000 for the operating fund from Smithville Bank.

(d) The budget committee recommends that $10,000 from the operating fund and $1,500 from the income fund be appropriated for charitable projects.

(e) The projects committee approves appropriations of $900 for the Boy Scouts, $1,200 for the Salvation Army, $2,000 to the United Fund, $500 to the public school scholarship fund, and $1,000 to Smithville College. All of these are also encumbrances on the operating fund.

(f) The health care committee approves an encumbrance of $1,500 on the income fund as a contribution toward the new outpatient clinic.

(g) The capital fund receives a $3,000 cash donation.

(h) The operating fund receives a donation of $1,000.

(i) The treasurer sends checks for $900 to the Boy Scouts and $600 to the Salvation Army and pays the bookkeeping service's monthly $100 retainer.

22. The Bastrop County tax assessor-collector has a file containing a record for every known piece of taxable real and personal property in the county. This record is a header for records in other files that are linked to it and give information about (1) the owner and the address to which to send tax notices, (2) tax payments, (3) value appraisals, (4) penalties or adjustments, and (5) delinquent taxes.

Once a year the tax assessor-collector goes sequentially through the property file and sends tax notices to all owners.

When payments arrive, the treasurer processes them and creates a record in the tax payments file linked to the property record.

Once a month after tax notices are mailed, the assessor-collector goes sequentially through the property file and mails follow-up notices to owners of property for which there is no appropriately dated tax payment record. In the fourth month, the assessor-collector adds a 5-percent penalty to the amount due the previous month and creates a corresponding record in the penalty/adjustment file. Starting in the seventh month, the assessor-collector creates a record in the delinquent file if the taxes have not been paid. These records are linked to the property records. The county attorney uses the delinquent file to initiate legal action aimed at collecting the taxes.

Required:

(a) Draw a data flow diagram of your own design, showing the processes, files, and relationships described.

(b) Why do you think the assessor-collector goes *sequentially* through the property file in the tax-notice process?

(c) When the time arrives to take legal action, how does the delinquent file enhance processing efficiency?

23. Brownwood County has decided to employ zero-based budgeting in its emergency-medical-vehicle system. The eight vehicles are based at fire stations; each vehicle has three 3-person crews working 8-hour shifts. Crew members earn $25,000 annually. Each vehicle costs $55,000 and could be sold for $40,000. Annual call-response costs (vehicle and medical equipment, supplies, and operating costs other than salaries) totaled $210,000. The county levies a service charge of $50 per call and collects it 90 percent of the time. Last year the emergency service responded to 1,500 calls.

    Studies have suggested that a helicopter based at the county hospital might replace some or all of the emergency vehicles. The helicopter would cost $500,000. It would require 4 pilots (working in shifts) each earning $30,000 annually, plus four 2-person medical crews at annual salaries of $25,000. Call-response costs for the helicopter would be $250,000 annually. The $50 service charge would remain unchanged.

    A major concern is that the helicopter could not fly in fog or very bad weather. Such conditions prevail about 5 percent of the year. A study suggests that two of the existing vehicles, plus full crews, should be kept for use at these times. Another view is that very bad weather usually only lasts an hour or so, after which the helicopter could fly again.

    Required:

    (a) Prepare zero-based budgets for five different approaches: (1) no emergency service; (2) two vehicles only, responding to only 500 calls; (3) helicopter only; (4) helicopter plus two back-up vehicles; and (5) the eight existing vehicles. For each alternative, calculate the net cost for next year and prepare the required appropriation entry, using three categories: (a) salaries, (b) call-response costs, and (c) equipment cost (or sale proceeds).

    (b) Is the $50 service charge relevant to this zero-based budgeting exercise?

    (c) What criteria other than cost should be considered when budgeting this operation? How can you integrate such criteria with cost considerations?

24. The State Agricultural Service uses the account coding structure discussed in the chapter. Prepare all the accounting entries and account numbers necessary to describe the following events:

    (a) Voucher 4005, for supplies for the Crops program, is approved for payment and credited to Accounts Payable. Its amount is $7,000. The Accounts Payable code is 70-20-01-0-2-4005.

    (b) To match an offer to Vitorio of a higher salary elsewhere, the director transfers $10,000 from the travel appropriation, which was earmarked for the Herds program, to Vitorio's salary appropriation.

(c) An emergency session of the legislature reduces the other expenses appropriation by $100,000 and orders that travel and supplies be reduced by identical amounts.

25. Examine Table 10.6 on page 364.

Required:

(a) Designate each number as a debit or a credit.

(b) Supply the missing expenditures for January.

(c) Draw a diagram similar to Figure 10.3 (page 355), starting with the legislative appropriation for salaries and tracing Wang's salary completely through the accounts until it becomes an expenditure in the Trees program in January. Place correct account numbers at the top of the T accounts.

(d) In your diagram, identify the comparisons between entries for control purposes.

26. Refer to the list of accounts and balances for the State Agricultural Service in Table 10.7 (page 365).

Required:

(a) What is the appropriation free balance for Operating Expenses?

(b) How do you distinguish between a legislative appropriation account and an appropriation made by the SAS director?

(c) What was the total expenditure on Herds in January?

(d) Suppose the SAS director's budget for the Trees program in January was: Wang, 20 percent time; Vitorio, 10 percent time; Young, 60 percent time; supplies, $11,000; and travel, $4,000. Prepare a comparison of this budget with actual expenditures.

(e) Suggest a way to use the existing account numbers to set up a budget within the fund-accounting system so that preparation of performance reports could be automated.

27. After the legislature passes an appropriations bill, each account in it corresponds to a record in a computer file called the legislative appropriations (LA) file. Agency administrators' appropriations become records in the agency accounts (AA) file. Vouchers for expenditures are prepared within the agency and sent to the state treasurer, where they are examined, paid, and entered as records in the expenditures accounting (EA) file. Pointers link appropriate records in each file.

Required:

(a) Create a data flow diagram showing the three files mentioned above plus the appropriation, encumbrance, expenditure, and cash payment processes.

(b) Refer to Table 10.6 on page 364, which shows linkages among data elements. Create a similar diagram for the SAS. You will have to decide what links should be established between records. For example, there should be a link between debits and credits in the same transaction, and between a legislative appropriation and all the encumbrances against it.

28. To encourage industry to locate within its borders, a certain state operates an agency that undertakes research and development projects for its businesses. This agency is in the process of designing a new computerized fund-accounting system.

    The agency may undertake as many as 80 projects at once and wishes to store records of up to 800 current and completed projects online. Each project may have up to 90 steps or phases. Within each step, the agency wants to keep track of as many as 5 types of salary or wage expense, 15 types of direct material or service input, and 15 types of indirect input. The agency also wants to prepare accounting reports weekly.

    When the agency accepts a project, it sets up an internal appropriation, with a debit to Project Billings Receivable. The managerial staff will specify the encumbrances against this appropriation, one encumbrance for each step. Finally, the project manager will authorize expenditures.

Required:

   (a) Design an account code that will provide for all the procedures described. Specify its length and the placement of digits corresponding to various items. Describe your code thoroughly.
   (b) Assume that the agency has five work centers, which do all the actual work on projects. Each work center has a special code. Modify your account code to incorporate this information.
   (c) Which values of your code would have to be specified to prepare a cost report on one project for the past three most recent weeks?

Case: **Fort Stockton College**

You and several other students decide to organize a housing and food coop. You write a constitution and bylaws, stating that the purpose of the coop is to provide good-quality room and board to members. Several weeks later, the coop has enrolled its quota of 100 members, each of whom has agreed to pay dues of $176 per month during the 9-month school year. These members elect a 5-person board of directors, who in turn appoint a member to serve as coop manager. The manager will receive a salary of $300 per month. The manager finds a suitable apartment building, which the board agrees to lease for $5,600 per month, utilities included.

The board asks you to serve as coop treasurer (without compensation). You prepare the following budget for the coop.

Membership dues $176 × 100 × 9		$158,400
Apartment building rent $5,600 × 9	$ 50,400	
Food $3 per member per day for 250 days	75,000	
Housekeeping supplies $0.50 per member per day	12,500	
Improvements and repairs on building	6,000	
Used car for utility transportation	3,600	
Small computer and accounting software	2,500	
Manager	3,600	
Miscellaneous and contingencies	4,800	
		$158,400

The board of directors, upon seeing the budget, realizes how much money the coop will have to handle. The board asks you to describe some reasonable controls for handling and accounting for coop resources, including the type and frequency of reports the coop board and members should receive.

Required:

Prepare the information the board has requested. Draw an organization chart for the coop. Describe at least ten controls (including all four elements of each control) and design formats for at least two reports of your choice that the manager should find useful (for example, you might suggest review of the budget to be sure it is consistent with the charter and bylaws and takes into account such things as member resignations and failure to pay dues, since about 5 percent of dues can be expected to become uncollectible). Describe how each piece of information on a report will be produced.

Case: The State Society of Lawyers and Doctors

The State Society of Lawyers and Doctors has 34,000 members. It receives income from dues, from training programs sponsored by its Educational Foundation, and from interest earned on cash placed in short-term investment accounts.

    The society consists of three councils: the Educational Council, the Council of Doctors, and the Council of Lawyers. Every society member is a member of the Educational Council and of one of the two other councils. Each of these entities sponsors a set of programs, supported by an appropriation from the State Society Coordinating Board, which sets the dues rate and acts as a funding authority. Each council is operated by its own executive committee, which apportions the Coordinating Board's appropriation among its various programs.

    Each council's treasurer must complete the budget form shown on the following page for each program. The Council of Doctors has developed a project to evaluate new methods of treatment in a neighboring

```
┌────────────────────────────────────────────────────────────────────────┐
│                                                                          │
│                 State Society of Lawyers and Doctors                     │
│            _____ Council  _____ Project  Year 19_____ │
│                                                                          │
│         Project number: __ - __ - __ - ____                              │
│                         council   project  App/Enc/Exp   category        │
│                                                                          │
│            Category          Year     1st      2nd      3rd      4th     │
│                              Total   Quarter  Quarter  Quarter  Quarter  │
│    Project revenues 6434     _____  _____  _____  _____  _____  │
│                              _____  _____  _____  _____  _____  │
│                              _____  _____  _____  _____  _____  │
│    Total revenue             _____  _____  _____  _____  _____  │
│    Office expenses 5043                                                  │
│       Photocopy/printing     _____  _____  _____  _____  _____  │
│       Postage                _____  _____  _____  _____  _____  │
│       Advertising            _____  _____  _____  _____  _____  │
│       Prof. fees/temp. help  _____  _____  _____  _____  _____  │
│                              _____  _____  _____  _____  _____  │
│                              _____  _____  _____  _____  _____  │
│       Total office expense   _____  _____  _____  _____  _____  │
│    Meetings 2200                                                         │
│       Meals                  _____  _____  _____  _____  _____  │
│       Room/eqpt. rental      _____  _____  _____  _____  _____  │
│       Total meetings         _____  _____  _____  _____  _____  │
│    Telephone 3350            _____  _____  _____  _____  _____  │
│    Travel 1170               _____  _____  _____  _____  _____  │
│    Total Project Budget (  ) _____  _____  _____  _____  _____  │
│    Total Council Budget (  ) _____  _____  _____  _____  _____  │
│                                                                          │
└────────────────────────────────────────────────────────────────────────┘
```

state. No revenue would result from this project. There would be two visits to the neighboring state, in June and August; these visits would cost $2,500 and $3,500 respectively, including $800 for meals on the first visit, and $1,000 on the second visit. The remaining costs of both visits would be for travel. Correspondence and postage are estimated at $800, spread evenly through the months from May to December. The project would require the society to pay a lawyer to evaluate the risk of liability. These fees would be $2,000, payable in October. Supplies and office expenses, primarily for preparation and distribution of the project report, would cost $4,000, spread evenly through September, October, November, and December.

The total budget of the Council of Doctors is $160,000, distributed evenly over the four quarters.

Required:

    (a) Complete a budget form for this project.

    (b) Design a reporting form that will allow for comparison of actual expenses with those budgeted.

    (c) Construct an account coding system for the society and explain how it could be used in the reporting process. (Hint: the coding system is explained briefly at the top of the budget form.)

PART 3

Controls and Accounting

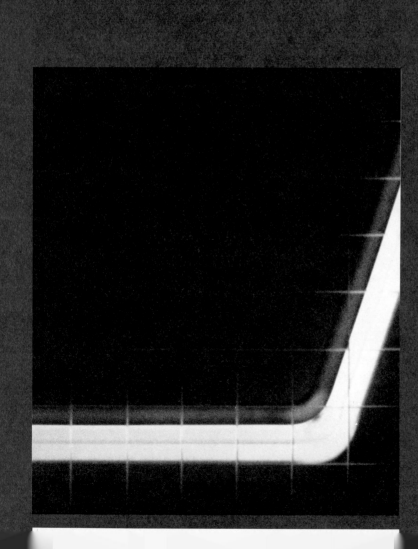

When asked what technical knowledge they put to use with the most effect early in their careers, successful accountants often identify their understanding of accounting and processing controls. Such controls are part of all successful accounting systems. Chapter 11's descriptions of the activities of the data processing function expand your understanding of these controls.

Even though each application has its own accounting controls, applications share many of the common processing controls described in Chapter 12. Processing controls in the data processing function consist of the same elements (objective, preventive, feedback, and comparative) as other controls.

Though controls reduce the risk of many activities, they may not always be cost-effective. Chapter 13 helps you select the controls that promise economic benefit, especially when neutralizing threats to data or property from computer-related fraud, crime, and incompetence. Thwarting crime, in particular, requires a combination of alertness and technical expertise that challenges even the brightest accountants.

Although many computer controls are built into processes and applications, these controls must be examined regularly to see if they are working. EDP auditors carry out this function. EDP auditing differs dramatically from financial auditing—the two have very different objectives and techniques. EDP auditors' special talents and the "secrets" of EDP auditing are discussed in Chapter 14.

Part 3 contains the following chapters:

Managing Data Processing

Learning Objectives

After studying this chapter, you should be able to

- List and describe the specialized missions and operations within data processing, such as technical support, systems development, and operations.

- Compare and contrast processing and accounting controls.

- Describe the function and composition of user advisory groups as a means of communicating with data processing management.

- Explain the major components of the services data processing provides to the organization, including operating user applications, accepting uniform standards for applications, and participating in the upgrade or replacement of an application.

- Explain the issues surrounding the degree of centralization of data processing.

- Distinguish between efficiency in *providing* and in *using* data processing services.

- Explain how to calculate charges to user departments for data processing services, how to apply these charges, and how to use them to estimate data processing efficiency.

- Explain how to use data-processing-cost applications to measure the efficiency of use of data processing services within an organization.

In 218 B.C., Hannibal crossed the Alps with 26,000 soldiers, 6,000 horses, and a few elephants and very nearly conquered Rome. There is no evidence his army had any special data processing ability that helped his conquest attempt. But Hannibal's army did not do business on credit. Today, no organization would dream of undertaking any large-scale endeavor without forethought about its data processing systems.

Over time, data processing has developed into a free-standing service function. Its purpose is to capture and process data—that is, to record data and convert it into information. Like virtually every other aspect of business, data processing proceeds most effectively when it is planned, organized, documented, and controlled. This chapter presents some issues accountants must consider when managing or reviewing an existing data processing system or establishing a new one.

The broad mission of data processing is clear: to provide managers and decision makers with information they can use to control their environment and achieve their objectives. This mission requires descriptive analysis to identify the information executives expect the data processing system to produce for their use, for the archives, and for users outside the organization. Will data processing serve only the accounting, marketing, finance, production, or some other relatively narrow set of functional requirements? Or will its service priorities be set without regard to particular functions and staff purposes, including, for example, engineering design and long-range planning? Will data processing operations be centralized, or distributed near the activities they describe or serve? Who will develop the data processing systems? Who will keep them up-to-date? Who will help users get the most out of them? Who will have priority in using the data processing facilities? Who will have operating and archival custody over the data processing records?

Data Processing's Position in the Business Organization

No two organizations will manage data processing in exactly the same way. The main issue in data processing management is the degree of centralization—how much input and control the users have over data processing policies, procedures, and operations. Any single solution is organization-specific and unlikely to be suitable for other organizations.

When computers first arrived in large organizations in the 1950s, responsibility for data processing was usually assigned to the accounting function, because accounting transaction processing was among the first data processing application areas to be developed. As data processing evolved and its application areas became abundant, it made less sense for the controller to supervise this function. Consequently, data processing has moved toward a more independent position within most organizations.

There are several reasons why an organization should be reluctant to give the accounting function full control over data processing. Nonaccounting users may feel that their data processing needs are slighted, and they may be right. Within accounting, skilled managerial talent and financial resources may be diverted from achieving the accounting objectives to looking after data processing concerns. Top-management control over data processing will be stronger and more direct if data processing is an independent service center, not a component of another department. If data processing is independent, it can remain neutral and free to serve all the needs of the organization. Figure 11.1 illustrates a typical placement of data processing within an organization responsibility chart. The figure emphasizes that all functions and centers within an organization have data processing needs. To help in designing, troubleshooting, maintaining, and operating applications to meet those needs, data processing provides helpful coordination services and procedures.

Management expects data processing to act as an independent specialization uniquely different from manufacturing, finance, or marketing. Yet to record data and report information that users trust, data processing must integrate its activities with the procedures of the other functional areas. The coordinator boxes in Figure 11.1 represent the coordination of data processing applications and services with the operating requirements of the various functions. Within data processing, the coordination responsibility is assumed primarily by the technical support group, which helps users understand data processing and adapts existing data processing to user requirements. The data processing staff must also help other parts of

Figure 11.1   Typical Positioning of Data Processing Within an Organization
Data processing activities are managed independently of the major functional areas to assure that all these areas have equal access to data processing services.

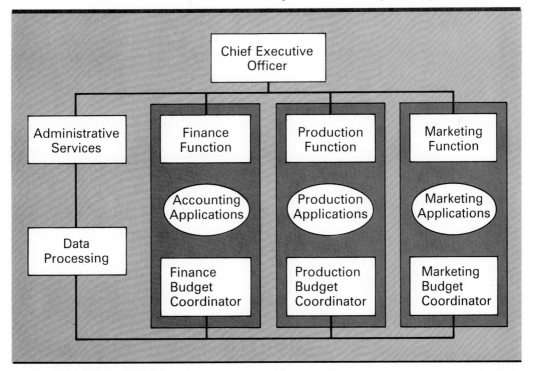

the organization use the available applications and plan for their future data processing needs. Each function should also include one or more staff members who understand how data processing services operate and are coordinated with the operating requirements of that function.

Delivery of data processing services may be either centralized or distributed. Day-to-day operations reflect the data processing strategy selected by the organization. **Centralized data processing** is a strategy that maintains data processing management and operations in one location, and **distributed data processing** carries out data processing management and operations in multiple locations. In distributed processing, all or part of management or operations resides in the functional areas and not in a central office. The data processing budget may also be distributed to the functional areas. Maximum distribution of processing occurs when the functional divisions entirely control the operations part of data processing, with only such technical support as training, consulting, and advisory services being coordinated by the data processing department.

Given reasonable, workable, *enforceable* standards, distributed processing has three distinct advantages. First, data processing is funded in whatever way each responsibility center expects will make the data processing function most efficient. Second, revision or replacement of some system segments will not disrupt the operation of other segments. Third, it should be possible to use simpler and less expensive equipment since smaller quantities of data are processed at each site.

Distributed processing also has disadvantages. It is more difficult to achieve a high level of data integration and standardization in a distributed system. Data gaps, duplication, or discrepancies can occur. To minimize these potential disadvantages, technical support and systems development should not be wholly decentralized, even in the most distributed system. A distributed system should be governed by policies assuring that data from its various sites are consistent and complete and can be exchanged with other sites. Technical support should operate from a single budget under the control of the data processing director. Systems development should be a coordinated effort, and all functions within the organization should participate. Systems development is too costly not to be centrally controlled.

Specialized Capabilities in Data Processing

Figure 11.2 is an overview of the four major parts of the data processing organization—operations, technical support, systems development, and electronic data processing (EDP) audit. Please keep it in mind as you read this section.

Figure 11.2 Internal Structure of the Data Processing Function
The major data processing specializations report to the data processing manager.
EDP auditing reports to top management and has links to all DP centers.

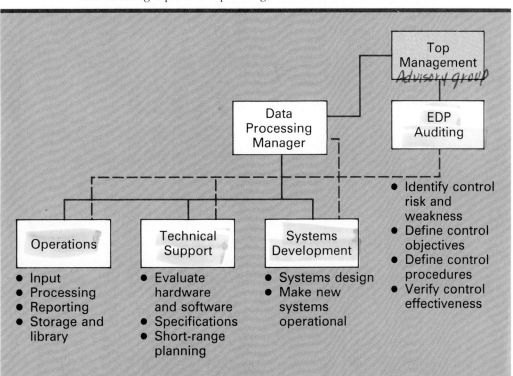

Operations

Data processing operations perform the day-to-day tasks that keep data flowing, process data, and generate and send reports to users. Four separate responsibilities report to the operations supervisor:

1. *Archival storage*, including security and control at an off-site location
2. *Operating program and file library*, located on-site and maintaining control over files and programs for everyday use
3. *Data capture*, including training personnel who prepare and transcribe input data in marketing, manufacturing, and other functional areas
4. *Data processing management*, directing all aspects of data processing, including turning equipment on and off; routine running of programs; scheduling and sequencing short-run activities; loading, check-out, and return of files and programs; routine backup of data; keeping the log of activities; ordering supplies; and maintaining equipment

The operations group specializes in keeping day-to-day data processing running smoothly and on schedule. Because data processing operations are repetitive and predictable, any failures readily attract critical then remedial attention. The level of performance expected of this group requires highly trained staff.

Technical Support

Data processing technical support assists users in taking advantage of existing data processing capabilities. The technical-support group has responsibility for keeping the existing data processing system technically current and in tune with the changing organization. It helps users get the most out of the existing system by explaining its features to them and helping them take advantage of those features. Technical support is also the group that responds to new requirements, sometimes even before they are perceived by users. It compares the capabilities of new hardware and software with emerging specific organizational needs, and it recommends new products that would make the existing system more efficient and productive. Technical support prepares specifications for any proposed expansion or change, such as a new communications link, a revised file structure, a modification to the data dictionary, addition of secondary record keys, installation of enhancements to the system, development of control or access program procedures, or the addition of new users. It also conducts planning studies for the enhancement of existing capacity in the intermediate-range future. Most organizations maintain at least some technical-support capability. Smaller organizations, however, may not be able to afford staff whose sole responsibility is technical support. In such cases, the same personnel may share responsibility for technical support and operations. If this dual-purpose approach is necessary, the organization should take pains to hire personnel qualified for the more demanding job requirements of their combined missions.

Systems Development

Data processing systems development consists of long-term planning and development to meet an organization's data processing requirements. The personnel in this group include programmers, systems designers, and analysts who can translate functional performance requirements into conceptual and detail designs and pursue them through all the stages of systems creation to operational status. This group of employees may also perform reprogramming or other programming chores of a short-run nature. Although systems development is a structured process, most systems designers and analysts regard it as intellectually stimulating, challenging, and therefore fun. Because the useful life of the average system spans six to ten years, only medium-to-large organizations are likely to generate enough systems development work to maintain a separate specialization. As a result, permanent positions in systems development are not available in all organizations. In such cases, minor improvements and upgrades may be handled by technical-support personnel. For more significant changes, smaller organizations are better served by hiring consultants to determine when to design a new system or introduce major enhancements into an existing one.

That the life span of systems results in relatively infrequent installation of new systems does not imply a low priority for systems development. Careful systems development work can save a lot of money by matching organizational needs with efficient, well-designed applications, and it costs little more than superficial work. Often systems development projects extend over a year or more and involve the system users deeply in design and testing. A major development project will produce an operational data processing system that will, throughout its six-to-ten-year lifetime, have a major influence on the efficiency of the organization using it. Savings of up to 40 percent of the annual operating costs of a mediocre system may be realized through reasonable attention to controls, efficiency, capacity, and user requirements. Such savings could pay for the entire system development effort!

We discuss the systems development process in additional detail in Chapters 17 and 18.

EDP Audit   *part of auditing*

EDP controls assure that the use of computers in data processing takes place in accordance with management objectives and policies. Well-chosen and properly implemented EDP controls help data processing attain the performance expected by each user, including the accounting function. These controls differ from accounting controls that describe standards for collecting, classifying, processing, and reporting transaction and other data that will be used to prepare financial statements. Accounting controls ensure that, whether or not computers are involved, financial statements will be consistent with generally accepted accounting principles. The broader scope of EDP controls makes them important throughout the whole organization, wherever computers are used.

The EDP audit group, which may be a part of the organization's internal audit function, ensures that EDP controls are adequate as written and implemented. The controller may train and administer the EDP internal audit group, but this group should be independent enough to audit data processing operations wherever they occur. If a severe control breakdown appears to have occurred, the EDP audit supervisor needs the authority to approach the chief internal auditor directly, without first obtaining the approval of the controller or data processing director. EDP audit is discussed more fully in Chapter 14.

Relations with User Groups

Each part of an organization uses data processing. All centers and functions have whatever access to data processing their objectives and procedures require. In this respect, data processing resembles typing and filing, maintenance, heating and air conditioning, mail service, and performance evaluation, all of which are broad service functions. In other words, data processing is a *management utility.* Like the phone company and other utilities, data processing works best if it responds to what its users want. The data processing department cultivates close contact with the users of its outputs and, by adapting to constraints and goals they propose, can provide really useful assistance.

Data processing management must treat user communications seriously; otherwise, it will probably overlook important user requirements. User input should not be limited to voluntary complaints and compliments; the best way to encourage continuous, significant, responsible user input is to set up a formal structure for generating and considering such input. One common feature of such a structure is a **user advisory group**— a group of users who provide formal feedback and assistance to the data processing function. The user advisory group should be a carefully selected council or committee composed of top managers from the major users or functional divisions. For example, the user advisory group might include the controller, the marketing vice president, the manufacturing vice president, the director of purchasing, the treasurer, and the secretary of the board of directors. This advisory group should meet regularly— monthly, quarterly, or annually. Typical agenda items might be as follows:

Proposals for changes or enhancements. The advisory group should evaluate any change that would affect the way data processing "looks" to users.

Complaints or criticisms about the system. Often the advisory group can help the processing director gain insight into these complaints and offer suggestions for solutions.

Guidance during design of a new or radically revised system. The user advisory group should approve the mission and conceptual design of any new system.

Ordinarily, the supporting staff for this group would come from operations and would refer proposals for changes to technical support. However, when the user group's major concern is systems development, its staff support should come from that area. Proposals for extensive changes would be referred to top management for evaluation.

Managing User Applications

Two important aspects of user applications affect the management of data processing activity: demand for data processing services by each user that data processing serves and use of data processing's own resources to produce reports and other outputs to users. Many resources, including staff time, documents, and computer equipment, are required to perform data processing operations. Reports are produced both regularly and on demand—how efficiently depends on the data processing department. After reports have been produced, the responsibility centers must make effective use of them in determining what goods or services to provide and how to produce and market them. How efficiently reports are so used depends on the responsibility center. Figure 11.3 illustrates these two points.

Management's Use of Data Processing Services

Each management user of data processing services has opportunities to specify the data it will supply to data processing and the information it expects to be reported back. In other words, a management user determines the amount of service it will receive from data processing, much as a user of electricity determines how much and what kind of power the electric company supplies it. A manager outside data processing has four

Figure 11.3 Efficiency of Data Processing and Its Use
Appropriate cost comparisons allow measurement of efficiency in both the data processing department and in the functional operating centers that use data processing services.

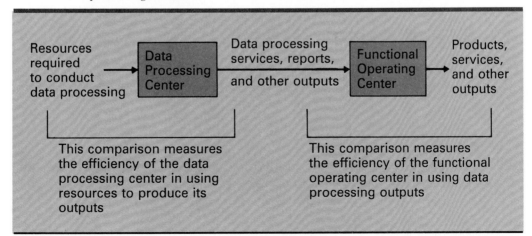

data processing responsibilities, which can be summarized by saying that the manager must use data processing as carefully and as efficiently as he or she uses other material, labor, and service resources. The four responsibilities are preparing inputs, limiting access to the computer, assigning responsibility for use, and using information.

1. **Preparing Inputs.** Probably no single activity has more importance than data capture. Some data, such as incoming shipments, cash sales, or manufacturing, cannot be recorded completely or accurately except at the time the events they describe actually occur. When a system is designed, a manager has a responsibility for determining which data elements to record and what edit and other procedures to use to accomplish accurate recording. When the system operates, the user has the responsibility to follow these procedures faithfully.

2. **Limiting Access.** In many data processing environments, computer access is relatively easy. For example, a terminal may be left on continuously for quick recording of data or searching of records. Such access can easily be abused. Many control measures exist to prevent or discourage abuse of access to the computer or its records. The user should help select and implement appropriate physical-access controls (that limit who can use a computer) and logical-access controls (that limit what data a user can add, delete, view, or modify).

3. **Assigning Responsibility.** Each operating center that uses data processing services should assign responsibility to specific individuals. For example, if the operating center captures credit sales transaction data, specific individuals should be trained to record and enter these data. Reports should be addressed to specific individuals. Modifications that are proposed in applications serving a specific operating center should require approval by an operating center manager before they are put into effect.

4. **Using Information.** Each operating center has an obligation to request all information it requires to conduct its operations and to use all the reports it requests and receives. The operating center should regularly review the value of the reports it has requested and received.

Data Processing's Use of Resources

In many ways, data processing resembles a production operation. It uses resources—human beings, material, equipment, and data—to produce information. As in manufacturing, the production processes should be designed to be efficient. Then data processing management must control operations so that these processes are followed. Three areas in need of controls and policies to help achieve data processing efficiency are user-application priorities, performance standards for applications, and decisions to upgrade or replace an application.

1. **User-Application Priorities.**   Very few data processing departments command sufficient processing capacity to maintain all applications on-line simultaneously. With the cooperation of users, a data processing manager must schedule which applications may be on-line and whether off-line applications will be run at user request; on a fixed schedule and if so, at which hours; or not at all. Once a schedule exists, data processing should be reliable in adhering to it. In addition to computer-time allocation, priorities must be set for other scarce resources, such as technical support and systems development.

2. **Performance Standards for Applications.**   In general, the more standardization of programs, files, hardware, and procedures that exists within a system, the better. Management and clerical personnel who move around in an organization, using different data processing services as they move, benefit from standardization because the different functions operate similarly. They should find that similar files look essentially the same, that report generators use the same commands, and that reports use the same terminology to identify similar revenues, expenses, and variances. Standardization becomes particularly important as distributed processing increases and computers proliferate within the organization.

As an example of the need for standardization, suppose that in a company composed of two units, Unit A wants to use dBASE III on an AT&T microcomputer to create and maintain its files, and Unit B already uses Omnis III on an Apple Macintosh for this purpose. These two systems, although similar in capability, are largely incompatible. Unless each system can read the other's standard file formats, files created on one cannot be used by the other without lengthy and costly intervention by a programmer.

Similar problems can arise even with similar equipment using compatible operating systems. Suppose, for instance, that the Order Entry Unit uses a 30-character name field in a customer record, and the Direct Mail Unit uses a 25-character name field. If Direct Mail wants to print labels for every customer who purchased something during the last year, it may lose the goodwill of some customers by truncating their names on the labels. Such examples illustrate the desirability of standardizing files, applications, and procedures as fully as is possible without compromising efficiency.

3. **Decisions to Upgrade or Replace an Application.**   An existing accounting application is like a language—it has its problems, but everyone is used to them. Introducing a new system without adequate preparation is like forcing people to learn a new language; it creates resistance. System planners should learn from the example of those who tried to introduce Esperanto, which was touted as the perfect language but never caught on. The controller and data processing management can lessen resistance by soliciting user input and concurrence before making changes.

Problems inevitably arise when controls and policies are lacking. Managements typically underestimate how much calendar time and how many work hours are required to introduce a new application. The transition generally has a negative effect on operating efficiency. Additional staff help often becomes necessary to maintain operations without neglecting the systems work. Finally, the structure of the responsibility centers that will use the application may have to change to complete the upgrade or replacement process. The controls and policies must state a clear choice among these alternatives and any others that are available.

Evaluating Data Processing's Performance

Efficiency in the data processing center is measured by whether total costs allocated to users are greater than the costs incurred to provide the data processing services.

To compare these two types of costs, the accounting system design must identify, forecast, and measure both allocated and incurred costs. The accounting system uses this information to identify measures of utilization and the charge rates to users for services provided.

Data processing uses cost classifications, cost pools, and other cost accounting concepts to relate the costs of its inputs to its outputs. Data processing accepts data, human skills, and machine time as inputs and transforms them into outputs in the form of files, information, and reports. This section describes the application of selected cost accounting principles to data processing cost control and performance reporting.

Accounting for the Cost of Data Processing Services

Data processing costs include numerous indirect and direct costs. The indirect costs are either committed costs or costs that arise as a function of time rather than of level of activity. They include expenses for supervisor, programmer, and operator salaries; equipment leasing or depreciation; software leasing or amortization, equipment maintenance; and building overhead, insurance, supplies, and maintenance. Technical consultants and systems development experts who are employed in-house, whether or not they are directly helping a user center, are also an indirect cost.

Direct costs are either discretionary or a direct input component of each service provided. These costs include data entry salaries, outside consultants, and rental of off-site software or hardware for a specific user application.

Performance-Measurement Concepts

Performance measurement requires measuring both data processing *function* efficiency and data processing *user* efficiency. As a service operation, data processing must be certain that its services provide a cost-effective benefit to the responsibility centers using them. If data processing does not accept this obligation, the consequences may be excessive use of the services (as if they cost nothing to provide) or underuse (as if the service were too precious to be used). The best way to encourage cost-effective benefits is to design and use a cost accounting and control system to allocate costs for data processing, and then to use these allocations to measure performance and efficiency of data processing. It is common to use a standard costing approach like that used in manufacturing departments, as described in Chapter 9. Figure 11.4 schematically illustrates this control concept. The figure shows the suspense and distribution accounts

Figure 11.4   Using Costs to Measure Data Processing Performance
Measurement of data processing and user efficiency requires that costs incurred be classified into cost pools, then distributed to user centers.

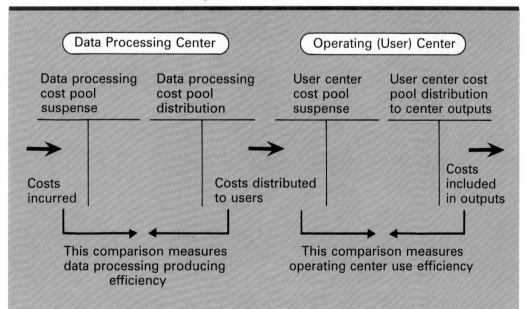

typical of manufacturing cost systems. The arrows at the bottom identify the comparisons that have performance-control significance. The distributions from the data processing and operating centers, made at standard rates and based on their outputs, are matched with their respective actual input quantities at standard costs.

The method of allocation is extremely important, because some methods can actually hinder the measurement of performance. If you can associate the cost of data processing services with users by allocating costs on the basis of each user center's proportionate share of total salaries or total dollar purchases, or both, the accounting system can allocate these costs each time management accounting reports are prepared. Each year, the accounting function can review and update the proportion basis for allocation to reflect recent experience. Users who absorb the costs should participate in the review to make certain the allocation basis remains acceptable. Consider the example in Table 11.1, which allocates costs between two centers at the Menard Company solely on the basis of salaries expense. This fixed allocation plan is simple, but it has a serious flaw. Neither center has a performance-measurement incentive—that is, a cost-related incentive to curtail its demands for use of data processing. Under this plan, some totally unexpected factors can also have strange effects on the apparent performance of centers such as Menard Company's Word Processing and Electronic Assembly. Allocated costs may increase or decrease when the centers' salary shares change. For example, if Electronic Assembly's salary costs decline, Word Processing's relative share of salary expense will rise and its allocated data processing expenses will increase. This will occur whether or not there is a change in data processing use or efficiency at either center.

An improved allocation plan would identify relationships between data processing costs and how much each user has used data processing services. Data processing would define cost pools based on each relationship. The costs in each pool would be charged only to users of the cor-

Table 11.1   Fixed Allocation of Data Processing Expense, Menard Company, January 19XX

At the Menard Company, salaries expense (a direct cost) is the basis for allocating data processing expense (a fixed cost) to the user departments.

	Word Processing	Electronic Assembly	Total
Salaries	$450,000	$550,000	$1,000,000
Share of total	45%	55%	100%
Data processing expense: $30,733			
Allocation	$ 13,830	$ 16,903	$ 30,733

responding service. Given the cost of each unit of computer service, each user could decide individually how much of its total budget to spend for that service.[1]

There are various ways to define a unit of computer service. These nonoverlapping unit definitions must isolate discrete items that can be counted manually or by the computer. Sample units might be a page of printed output, a second or minute of CPU time (computer operating systems can keep track of time spent on each program run), a block of disk or tape storage space (operating systems can count storage space used by each account; ordinarily they do so at preset intervals, such as hourly or daily, and can average the counts to obtain weekly or monthly estimates); an hour of technical support or systems development consulting time (each consultant should keep a record of time spent with each user and report the times regularly). All these units could be used in determining the data processing cost allocation. Under this plan, the user could control its data processing costs by using or not using data processing services.

Performance Measurement Applied

Although no plan is perfect, what follows is a workable outline for using cost allocation to evaluate use of resources. It shows how to use the cost allocation rates associated with units of computer capacity to allocate data processing costs, and how users in turn allocate these costs to their outputs.

Determining Charges per Unit of Service and Calculating User Charges. The first step in charging costs to users on a unit basis is to calculate the allocation rates, or charges per unit of service delivered. These charges, which serve as cost allocation rates, will vary depending on the type of computer equipment and the sophistication of the service. For example, the charge for a page printed by a high-quality laser printer might be $0.25, but only $0.05 might be charged for a page printed on a draft-quality, high-speed dot-matrix printer. The discussion that follows carefully explains the calculation of such charges. Efficient use and control of data processing services depends on allocation rate calculations being defined and carried out competently, and the calculation of such charges merits careful study by everyone concerned.

The easiest way to see how a data processing center converts its incurred costs into specific charge rates to users is to consider a particular case. The specific apportionments made within this example are arbitrary;

---

[1]Economic theory predicts that the user will acquire computer services until the expected benefit (revenue, savings, or value added to product or service) of a given additional expenditure equals the expected benefit of the same expenditure on additional other resources the user needs.

in a real data processing center, a knowledgeable cost accountant could determine them accurately.

First, the data processing center estimates and lists both its indirect and direct expenses for the period. Then, data processing links these expenses to the type of output the user will receive. For example, some staff members' time may be spent on input and output operations; others may concentrate on computer operation. The salary costs of the first category of staff should be recovered through report-page charges, of the latter, through CPU-time-used charges. Each expense must be analyzed to determine how it should be recovered through charges for service delivered. Outputs for which charges to users are made serve as the cost allocation basis.

On-line disk-storage charges deserve special consideration here. The volume of data a user stores probably varies little from month to month. The amount of space required is a measure of the ongoing service commitment that the data processing center must make to each user. Even if a user has a low-activity month, it must maintain its on-line files and keep them accessible. This need is comparable to the data processing center's need to keep its CPU available whether or not it is currently in use. A high proportion of the committed and indirect costs of the data processing center can be recovered through charges to users for on-line storage.

Indirect data processing costs are those that are not proportional to the volume of data processing output; they are about the same each period and are unaffected by the output rate. The distribution of expenses using each type of cost allocation basis for a list of typical indirect costs is presented in Table 11.2. Nine separate indirect costs, shown as rows, are allocated among the four measures of data processing output, shown as columns. For each output measure, the table shows both the percentage of the indirect cost and its dollar amount. Note that these are *estimated* costs, developed as part of the budgeting process.

Direct data processing costs are those that are proportional to the volume of data processing output. Four estimated direct costs of data processing are allocated among the same output allocation bases in Table 11.3. Note that there are no direct costs for on-line storage and consulting hours. The costs identified with these allocation bases are all a function of time, not of the level of demand for data storage and consulting. This situation may be unusual and should not be taken as a generalization that these output measures would never have related direct costs.

Table 11.4 shows total direct and indirect costs and their allocations. Note that on-line storage and consulting hours contain *only* indirect costs in this example and that the other two categories consist *mostly* of direct costs. This separation of direct and indirect costs makes the variations in the allocations more significant and makes comparisons of actual and budgeted costs more meaningful, an objective of our cost classification

Table 11.2   Estimated Indirect Costs Related to Output Measures

Each indirect cost is allocated among four cost pools. The allocated amounts are summed to form the cost pool debits in the bottom row of the table.

Indirect Cost	Total Costs Amount	Report Pages Percent	Report Pages Amount	CPU Minutes Percent	CPU Minutes Amount	On-line Kb Storage Percent	On-line Kb Storage Amount	Consulting Hours Percent	Consulting Hours Amount
Supervisor salaries	$ 46,000	50	$23,000	16.7	$ 7,667	16.7	$ 7,667	16.7	$ 7,667
Programmer salaries	33,000	16.7	5,500	16.7	5,500	16.7	5,500	50	16,500
Operator salaries	42,000	16.7	7,000	33	14,000	33	14,000	16.7	7,000
Systems development fees	23,000							all	23,000
Equipment lease or depreciation	35,000	20	7,000	40	14,000	20	7,000	20	7,000
Software lease or amortization	40,000			80	32,000	10	4,000	10	4,000
Equipment maintenance, annual contract cost	6,000	33	2,000	33	2,000	33	2,000		
Building overhead	20,000	20	4,000	30	6,000	40	8,000	10	2,000
Insurance	7,000	10	700	30	2,100	60	4,200		
Total indirect costs	$252,000		$49,200		$83,267		$52,367		$67,167

Table 11.3   Estimated Direct Costs Related to Output Measures

Each direct cost is divided among the same four cost pools as in Table 11.2.

Direct Cost	Total Costs $Amt	Report Pages $Amt	CPU Minutes $Amt	On-line Kb Storage $Amt	Consulting Hours $Amt
Data input salaries	$60,000		$60,000		
Paper, ribbons, and other supplies	$12,000	$12,000			
Outside consultants	0				
Rental of off-site software or hardware for remote access to data bases	$19,000		$19,000		
Total direct costs	$91,000	$12,000	$79,000	$0	$0

Table 11.4   Estimated Total Costs Related to Output Measures and Calculation of Cost Allocation Rates
Calculate the budgeted cost-pool allocation rates by dividing the total of each cost pool by the expected activity measure for that cost pool.

	Total Costs	Cost Allocation Basis (Cost Pools)			
		Report Pages Amount	*CPU Minutes Amount*	*On-line Kb Storage Amount*	*Consulting Hours Amount*
Total indirect costs	$252,000	$49,200	$ 83,267	$52,367	$67,167
Total direct costs	91,000	12,000	79,000	0	0
Total direct and indirect costs	$343,000	$61,200	$162,267	$52,367	$67,167
Total expected activity for 1988		1,225,000 pages	27,000 minutes	218,000 Kb for users	2,700 hours
Budgeted rates for data processing services		$0.05/page printed	$6.00/minute CPU	$0.24/year per Kb ($0.02/ month)	$25.00/hour

plan. To complete the calculation of the unit charges, the forecasted total costs for each unit must be divided by the forecasted levels of output measures expected to occur throughout 19XX. The final row in Table 11.4 shows the results of dividing cost totals by expected output measures. These are the calculated rates for allocating costs of data processing services to users. The calculated rates shown have been rounded slightly to simplify subsequent calculations. To use the rates in Table 11.4 in controlling data processing costs, you must calculate total costs passed on to users through these rates and compare these allocated costs with the "actual" costs incurred.

Having made the appropriate calculations, the computer center can establish the charges shown in Table 11.4, which are intended to allocate combined direct and indirect costs:

$0.05 per page of printed output
$6.00 per minute of CPU time
$0.02 per kilobyte of on-line disk storage space per month (no charge for back-up storage of data and programs)
$25.00 per hour of technical-support consultant time

Now, consider these cost allocation rates applied to actual January use of data processing by Menard's two users, Word Processing and Electronic Assembly, as shown in Table 11.5.

We see in Table 11.6 that the total allocated in Table 11.5 is $7,268 less than the total actual costs of data processing shown in Table 11.1 (page 394). This difference is called a cost allocation variance, and its negative magnitude here indicates data processing inefficiency. It is inefficient because *the data processing department supplied on-demand services with an allocated value of $23,465 and spent $30,733, or $7,268 more than was budgeted, to supply them.* Thus, data processing services appear to have been provided inefficiently in January, as indicated by the $7,268 cost variance.

The calculations shown illustrate a single allocation rate, which combines both direct and indirect costs. With some added complexity (but also greater accuracy) separate direct and indirect cost allocation rates could be calculated. Thus the indirect costs, which primarily represent the cost of keeping available permanent capacities such as computing, printing, on-line storage, and consulting, could be allocated on the basis of how much of each capacity is kept available for each individual user. Then only the direct costs, which vary with actual activity, would be allocated on the basis of actual use. As a very simple example, if *half* the on-line storage capacity is kept for a particular user, which occasionally stores very large amounts of data on-line for short intervals, then half the indirect on-line storage costs should be borne by that user every month. From month to month, any direct costs of on-line storage would be allocated to that user based on actual use.

Monthly Performance Reports.   Accounting prepares performance reports monthly, or as often as necessary to help data processing managers and users control the production and use of data processing services.

Table 11.5   **Data Processing Cost Allocation by Unit Usage, Menard Company, January 19XX**

Make allocations from the cost pools to Word Processing and Electronic Assembly using the rates calculated in Table 11.4 and the actual observed values of the four cost-allocation bases.

	Word Processing		Electronic Assembly		
	Actual Units	*Allowable Cost*	*Actual Units*	*Allowable Cost*	*Allowable Total*
Reports (pages)	63,000	$3,150	100,000	$ 5,000	$ 8,150
CPU time (minutes)	700	4,200	1,100	6,600	10,800
Disk storage (Kb)	37,000	740	35,000	700	1,440
Consulting (hours)	3	75	120	3,000	3,075
Total		$8,165		$15,300	$23,465

Table 11.6   Data Processing Cost Report, Actual and Accrued Costs, Menard Company, January 19XX
This report utilizes actual January expenses and the calculated allocation rates to produce actual balances in the cost pools. Note the similarity to Tables 11.2 and 11.3, which contain budgeted costs.

		Cost Allocation Basis							
		Report Pages		*CPU Minutes*		*On-line Kb Storage*		*Consulting Hours*	
		Percent	*Amount*	*Percent*	*Amount*	*Percent*	*Amount*	*Percent*	*Amount*
Indirect costs									
Supervisor salaries	$ 3,833	50	$1,917	16.7	$ 639	16.7	$ 639	16.7	$ 638
Programmer salaries	2,750	16.7	458	16.7	458	16.7	458	50	1,376
Operator salaries	3,600	16.7	600	33	1,200	33	1,200	16.7	600
Systems development fees	1,900							all	1,900
Equipment lease or depreciation	2,917	20	583	40	1,167	20	583	20	583
Software lease or amortization	3,333			80	2,667	10	333	10	333
Equipment maintenance	500	33	167	33	167	33	167		
Building overhead	1,667	20	333	30	500	40	667	10	167
Insurance	583	10	58	30	175	60	350		
Total January indirect costs	$21,083		$4,116		$ 6,973		$4,397		$5,597
Direct costs									
Data entry salaries	$ 5,000				$ 5,000				
Paper, ribbons, and other supplies	1,500		$1,500						
Outside consultants	(none)								
Rental of off-site software or hardware for remote access to data bases	3,150				3,150				
Total January direct costs	$ 9,650		$1,500		$ 8,150		$ 0		$ 0
Total actual direct and indirect costs	$30,733		$5,616		$15,123		$4,397		$5,597

These reports list costs *incurred* by data processing, then compares them with costs *allocated* to users of data processing services for the reporting period in the same categories used in the budget. Table 11.6 presents actual costs incurred in January 19XX. These costs are then used in Table 11.7 to calculate performance variances. Variances are favorable if the allocated costs exceed the actual costs; otherwise, they are unfavorable. In Table 11.7, the user-allocated costs are subtracted from actual costs to obtain the

January variances. These variances help the data processing center determine whether its costs are under control relative to demand for its services. In this case, data processing costs seem to be adequately controlled. The flow diagram in Figure 11.5 (page 403) summarizes the cost accumulation and variance-calculation processes discussed above.

Evaluating User Centers.   How efficiently do other centers use the data processing services they receive? Under a usage-cost allocation plan, each center must accept responsibility for its own use of data processing. The accounting system should measure and report on whether a center's consumption of data processing represents efficient use of that resource.

In a well-run organization, each center will have an overall budget that details all of its expected revenues and expenses, of which data processing is only one. The budget should establish a realistic "expected" cost of data processing services based on that center's past usage and the potential efficiency to be gained by expanded usage.

Let us look more closely at Menard's Word Processing Center. Suppose that all data processing costs enter one cost pool at Word Processing. The Word Processing center measures its activity level by the number of reports it delivers. Word Processing's data processing charge is budgeted at $0.10 per page, and this rate is included in the charge it makes to users

Table 11.7   Data Processing Performance Report, Menard Company, January 19XX

This report measures data processing performance based on a comparison of actual data processing costs with costs allocated to users.

	Cost Allocation Basis			
	Report Pages	*CPU Minutes*	*On-line Kb Storage*	*Consulting Hours*
Total actual direct and indirect costs: $30,733	$5,616	$15,123	$ 4,397	$ 5,597
Total actual activity for January 19XX	163,000 pages	1,800 minutes	72,000 Kb for users	123 hours
Budgeted rates for data processing services	$0.05/page printed	$6.00/minute CPU	$0.24/year per Kb ($0.02/ month)	$25.00/hour
January costs allocated to user departments	$8,150	$10,800	$ 1,440	$ 3,075
January variances	$2,534 FAVORABLE	$(4,323) UNFAVORABLE	$(2,957) UNFAVORABLE	$(2,522) UNFAVORABLE

Figure 11.5   Data Processing Cost Flow and Control (facing page)
This diagram shows the progression of costs from incurrence (or accrual) into cost pools and finally to users of data processing services.

for each page of completed report it delivers. In January, Word Processing delivered 85,000 pages of reports to other centers. Its budgeted data processing cost for this level of activity was therefore $8,500. Using the data from Table 11.5, costs allocated to Word Processing were $8,165. The difference between costs allocated and costs budgeted is $335, a favorable efficiency measurement since charges to other centers exceeded allocated data processing costs. This favorable result suggests that Word Processing used data processing services more efficiently than expected, perhaps because it had to make fewer rough drafts or fewer error corrections.

Both rates used for allocation—from data processing to the user center and from the user center to its output—were predetermined "standard" rates. When standard rates are used to determine variances, the user-center variance computed is an efficiency measurement. Word Processing's data processing efficiency measurement shows how efficient the center has been in using data processing inputs to produce its principal output—finished report pages.

Now consider Electronic Assembly. At this center, the rate and mix of production change frequently; however, each product uses a known number of hours of direct labor per unit. Therefore, as the basis for charging allocated data processing costs to production activity, Electronic Assembly uses the number of direct labor hours that should have been required for that period's output.

Electronic Assembly has established the allocation rate at $0.50 per actual or standard direct labor hour. To calculate efficiency variances, production supervisors keep a careful record of the time production workers spend on each product. In January, Electronic Assembly produced a mix of products with a total direct labor content of 30,000 hours, which resulted in a budgeted data processing cost for this department of $15,000 (or 30,000 hours × $0.50/hour). Since the actual cost allocated *to* Electronic Assembly in Table 11.5 was $15,300, there is a difference of $300. It is an unfavorable variance because Electronic Assembly received more allocated costs from data processing than it was able to distribute to its own production activity.

As this example illustrates, the four distinct measures of data processing service use can provide a detailed, objective, and acceptable description of both user and data processing cost efficiency. A favorable data processing variance should mean that the center has used data processing services efficiently. An unfavorable variance should correspond to inefficient use of data processing services.

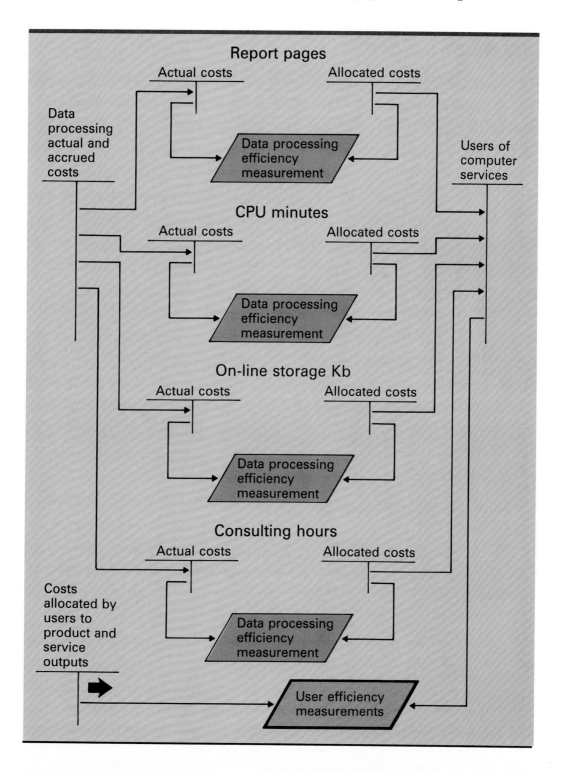

Summary

Data processing conducts day-to-day data processing operations, advises users on how to get the most out of the data processing system, evaluates and designs new systems and applications, and cooperates with EDP auditing to ensure active controls on computer-based activities. Data processing remains independent of its users yet closely integrates its data gathering, processing, and reporting with the user activities it supports. To maintain this sensitive position, data processing encourages regular, continuing feedback from its users.

To evaluate the interface with users, data processing identifies allocation bases, or objective measures of output utilization. It then groups the costs of its inputs into cost pools centered on these allocation basis measures and calculates the cost to be allocated to each user per unit of output consumed. Within data processing, efficiency is measured by comparing actual costs of inputs with the costs allocated to users. Each user measures how efficiently it uses data processing services by comparing the costs allocated to it with the data processing costs it has allocated to its outputs or to other centers.

Key Terms

centralized data processing
data processing operations
data processing systems development
data processing technical support
direct data processing costs

distributed data processing
EDP controls
indirect data processing costs
user advisory group

Review Questions

1. What is the broad mission of data processing?

2. Name the three major specialized capabilities or functions within data processing. What is the relationship of EDP auditing to data processing and to top management?

3. How does technical support differ from systems development? Give at least one example of an activity of each.

4. Name at least four activities that fall within the scope of data processing operations.

5. Define both accounting controls and data processing controls. Explain the difference between the two in terms of the people who are responsible for making them work and the applications they apply to.

6. What is a user advisory group? What does it do? What types of issues

does it consider? Which functions within data processing would you expect to have user advisers? From what groups does data processing draw its user advisers? What risk does data processing run by not having such groups?

7. Who are the users of data processing services? What are their responsibilities?

8. What is distributed data processing? What are some of its advantages and disadvantages?

9. Which costs are compared to measure the efficiency of data processing? Which costs are compared to measure the efficiency of data processing service users?

10. What are some common output measures used in data processing? Are they also output measures for data processing users? If not, name output measures for a maintenance department and for a typing pool.

11. What is a favorable data processing efficiency variance? How is it calculated, and what does it mean?

Discussion Questions

12. The life cycle of a typical data processing system is about seven years. If a new system will be installed only about once every seven years, why not initiate systems development only at the time it is needed and save the money that would be spent on it the rest of the time?

13. Would a small business with only one or two data processing employees need data processing operations, technical support, systems development, and EDP audit capabilities as listed in the text? Specifically, can it "get along" with just operations? If not, what must it do to have a smoothly functioning data processing center?

14. Why should data processing develop, and users adopt, uniform application performance standards? Does this have anything to do with the degree of centralization in the organization? in data processing?

15. What problems can occur when a familiar data processing application is replaced or changed? How may these problems be reduced or prevented?

16. The chapter gives three reasons why the controller should not supervise data processing. The first two are phrased negatively. As an advocate of placing data processing under neutral administrative control, rewrite these arguments in a positive vein.

17. In your own words, state the arguments against allocating data processing costs on the basis of each user's proportional share of some type of common cost. What benefits does an organization lose when it uses a method of this type?

18. Most data processing centers charge for storage space committed to users regardless of its purpose or type of storage. Why do you think that data processing might decide against separately identifiable charges for storage space devoted to back-up by users of their programs and data? Would you agree with this policy?

19. Which of the three diagrams below depicts a distributed system? Which is centralized? And which is a mixture of the two?

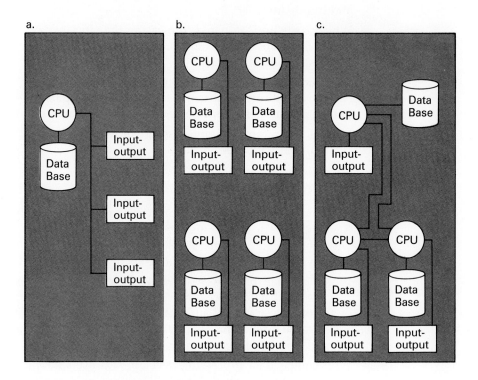

20. Which of the following activities should be performed by operations? which by technical support? and which by systems development? In each case, explain why.
    (a) Attend a trade show exhibiting future computer hardware products
    (b) Back up on-line files every 50 minutes
    (c) Review the organization's long-range plan to assess future data processing needs
    (d) Design a new form for use in analyzing credit risks by marketing
    (e) Train data entry clerks
    (f) Extend existing credit-approval processes to a newly opened site
    (g) Prepare data to test the functioning of the payroll application

(h) Combine data from several smaller files into one larger file, using already developed procedures

(i) Redesign an application that is no longer adequate for the organization's needs

(j) Maintain a library of programs and files in current use

21. Why must users accept some responsibility for the efficient functioning of a data processing center? In light of your answer, determine whether any of the following does *not* contribute to efficient data processing functioning, and explain why:

   (a) Data capture procedures call for a total of transactions submitted to be forwarded to data processing daily for comparison with the computer operating system's tally of transactions processed.

   (b) Users rely on data processing to verify the accuracy of data forwarded to it for entry and processing, including account coding.

   (c) When checks are to be printed, the treasurer brings the blank sequentially prenumbered checks to the data processing center, which runs the cash disbursements application. As soon as the checks have been printed, the treasurer regains custody of any remaining blank checks. The cash disbursements application causes the check number to be printed on each check. This number should correspond to the number already on the check. The checks are immediately placed in envelopes and mailed.

   (d) Owing to a massive backlog of data processing work, the credit manager has not forwarded changes in the approved-credit-customers file to data processing. Instead, he has acquired a small computer and employed a clerk to maintain the approved-credit-customers file under his supervision.

22. Decide whether each of the following user applications should be (1) on line continuously during working hours, (2) on line but able to be suspended, (3) run at user request, (4) run only at certain times, (5) not permitted on the system

   (a) Sales-order-entry process

   (b) Computer games

   (c) Operating system

   (d) Year-end-closing application

   (e) Payroll application

   (f) Cash disbursements application

   (g) Credit-check process

   (h) Programmer tests of programs under development

   (i) Process linking central location to remote sites

   (j) Process preparing financial statements from general ledger

23. The data processing center proposes to acquire expensive new equipment to replace fully depreciated equipment. The new equipment will

perform the same functions as the equipment it replaces. The user advisory committee acknowledges the need for the equipment but is concerned that higher depreciation on the new equipment will result in higher charges to users for data processing services, making it more difficult for them to show favorable performance. Suggest several steps that could be taken to generate more information about the decision, change operating policies, and gain the user advisory committee's support.

Problems

24. The costs that Data Processing, Center X, and Center Y incurred (actual or transferred in) and allocated (distributed or transferred out) over the past six months are shown in the table below.

		Data Processing	**Center X**	**Center Y**
January	incurred	$60,000	$17,000	$42,000
	allocated	59,000	18,000	43,000
February	incurred	62,000	18,500	43,700
	allocated	62,700	18,800	44,000
March	incurred	65,000	19,000	45,000
	allocated	64,000	18,700	46,000
April	incurred	64,000	19,000	43,000
	allocated	63,000	19,200	46,000
May	incurred	66,000	20,000	44,000
	allocated	64,000	19,500	46,000
June	incurred	64,000	20,000	43,000
	allocated	63,000	20,200	45,500

Required:

(a) For each month, indicate whether the variances are favorable or unfavorable

(b) Do you see any indication that the data processing center is inefficient or that the rates it used to allocate costs to users are inaccurate? If so, what is the evidence you see?

25. Navasota Vehicle Service Company has three locations at which it performs maintenance on commercial vehicles. When a vehicle is brought in, the service writer enters information from which a software program makes a vehicle-service-header record. As technicians work on the vehicle, they enter progress information from which the software program creates records linked to the vehicle-service-header record. If a customer inquires about the status of repairs, a service clerk can display the records to determine what has been done, the charges, and whether the work is complete.

The computer is located centrally. Each location is charged monthly for its use according to three factors: (1) the number of terminals at that location; (2) the number of header and linked records created that month; (3) the number of inquiries made that month.

For October, the allocation statistics are as shown in the table below.

	Data Processing Allocable Cost Pool	Location G	Location H	Location I
Terminals	$15,000	3	6	6
Records created	$24,500	9,000	16,000	24,000
Inquiries	$48,000	23,000	26,000	15,000
Vehicles brought in		4,000	6,000	7,000

Required:

(a) If *all* of the costs in each pool must be allocated, what will be the total costs allocated to each location?

(b) Assume that all three locations allocate $5.00 to each vehicle to cover data processing charges. Which locations had favorable data processing use variances?

26. (*This problem requires understanding of net-present-value analysis.*)

The Bryan Service Bureau (BSB) provides comprehensive computer data processing to small businesses in the Bryan area. BSB sends a systems development consultant to each new client company. Together the client and the consultant select the appropriate options for processing the client's data. BSB does not charge for this service. Each client also receives 10 free hours of time annually from a BSB technical-support consultant. If the client needs additional time, the charge is $25.00 per hour. The basic charge to the client for data processing is $0.10 per record processed, plus $10.00 per page for reports.

A competing firm, Kellogg Service Bureau (KSB), charges $25.00 per hour for systems development, $25.00 per hour for technical support (no free time), $0.05 per record processed, and $8.00 per page for reports.

Columbus Company is choosing a service bureau. It estimates that it will require 40 hours of one-time-only systems development time and 40 hours per year of technical support. It expects to process 3,000 records per year, and to receive 500 pages of reports. The company expects to use the same service bureau for three years.

Required:

Ignoring the tax effects and using the net-present-value method of investment evaluation, rank these two firms in order of their cost-effectiveness over the three-year period serving Columbus Company. Columbus's target rate of return is 20 percent (use this as the discount rate).

27. Manchaca Company has the following budgeted and actual data processing costs for the month of September:

Account Title	Budgeted	Actual
Supervisor salaries	$3,000	$3,000
Programmer salaries	4,000	4,000
Operator salaries	1,000	1,500
Technical-support salaries	2,500	2,500
Consultant—technical support	500	1,000
Systems development salaries	2,600	2,800
Equipment depreciation	3,100	3,300
Software amortization	2,300	2,500
Maintenance contract	500	500
Data entry salaries	2,000	1,900
Lease—off-site data storage	500	500
Allocated building overhead	1,800	2,000
Forms and supplies	300	3,600
Insurance	200	200
Outside consultants	500	0

Required:

(a) Could forms and supplies really have exceeded the budget so much? What is a more likely explanation?

(b) Divide these costs into five cost pools: systems development; technical support; operations—data gathering; operations—processing & reporting; and operations—back-up & storage.

(c) Calculate the actual and budgeted costs in each of five cost pools, using the following format:

	Budget	Actual	Variance

1. Systems development
   (list of costs included)
      Systems development total
2. Technical support
   (list of costs included)
      Technical-support total
3. Operations—data gathering
   (list of costs included)
      Data gathering total
4. Operations—processing & reporting
   (list of costs included)
      Processing & reporting total
5. Operations—back-up & storage
   (list of costs included)
      Back-up & storage total

       If you feel that any cost does not belong entirely in one pool, divide it equally among all pools to which you feel it belongs.

(d) Write a paragraph summarizing how you would use these cost pools in controlling data processing costs.

28. Pecos Interstate Company designs products, arranges for manufacturers to produce them, and wholesales them to department stores. It is experiencing serious dissatisfaction with its data processing center. Pecos is organized into the following functions: relations with manufacturers; finance, including the treasurer and controller; and marketing, including department store relations, market analysis, product design, and data processing. These functions report to the president.

    Market analysts prepare product profiles, specifying target-market size, performance, appearance, durability, and cost. Product design prepares the designs, circularizes them to selected manufacturers, and asks manufacturers for proposals to produce a given product in accordance with the product profile. The chosen manufacturer sends its shipment to a bonded warehouse. When Pecos pays for the shipment (in advance), the manufacturer sends Pecos a bill of lading and warehouse receipt. Pecos then invoices the department store. Upon receiving payment, Pecos forwards the warehouse receipt to the department store, which is responsible for claiming the shipment. Pecos implemented its data processing department about ten years ago.

Required:

Pecos proposes to select a data processing user advisory committee to reduce current dissatisfaction. Draw an organization chart for Pecos, showing the functional areas described. Identify the functions that should be represented on the advisory committee and explain why.

29. Hutto Aircraft Company stores, services, and sells airplanes at three airports near northeastern U.S. cities. Because its customers often have tight schedules, the company has a primary objective of meeting its time commitments to them. The company has acquired four microcomputers to meet this objective; one is located at each airport and one at the corporate home office. These computers have scheduling and accounting software and can be used by each office manager to schedule, cost, and bill customer services.

    Customers often make arrangements for a service at one airport, and take delivery of it at another. The following table shows how often this affects the dollar volume of business.

		Service Delivered at Location		
		1	*2*	*3*
Service	1	$600,000	$250,000	$120,000
Arranged	2	50,000	700,000	40,000
at Location	3	90,000	250,000	300,000

At each location, the computer costs, including the links to other locations, are $26,000 annually.

Required:

(a) Which location receives the most referral business?

(b) If each location agrees to allocate computer data processing costs proportionally to the dollars of revenue it arranges, calculate the data processing costs of each location after allocation. Disregard the home office computer costs. Does this result surprise you? Does it seem fair?

(c) Now consider the home office computer. It is used for a variety of applications, including payroll, financial planning, cash management, and systems development, all of which indirectly support Hutto Aircraft's operations. Assume the allocation in *b* came out as follows:

Location 1	$18,000
Location 2	$40,000
Location 3	$20,000

Recommend allocating the home office computer costs on the basis of one of the following, and defend your choice:

(1) No allocation; not relevant

(2) Revenues for services booked at that location

(3) Revenues for services delivered at that location

(4) Location computer costs after allocation as shown in the list of location allocations

Case: **Crystal City Company**

Crystal City Company produces radar detectors and other consumer electronic products for automobiles. Revenues last year were $42 million; the company employs 800 people. The president directly supervises the controller (25 employees), treasurer (10 employees), data processing director (35 employees), production manager (600 employees), purchasing agent (10 employees), sales manager (50 employees), customer relations manager (20 employees), and deliveries manager (50 employees). The company has one factory, supervised by the production manager; it uses on-line computer-controlled assembly and quality-control processes.

The company's products are top quality and carry a five-year unconditional replacement warranty. The sales manager advertises in magazines and via direct mail; customers order by mail, sending cash, check, money order, or credit card number. Orders go to the sales manager who verifies the payment mode with the treasurer and creates a computer record of the order. The deliveries manager maintains inventories for quick delivery of customer orders, reads the computer order records, and ships the orders the same day the record was created. If any unit under warranty becomes defective, the customer notifies the customer relations manager, who sends the customer a box in which to return the defective unit. As soon as the return is received, the deliveries manager sends the customer a replacement.

All the other functions use the data processing system. It consists of a general-purpose computer with 270M bytes of external storage. Production control requires 50 percent of the computer's disk in-use capacity; accounting requires 40 percent. Data processing itself uses the remaining 10 percent of disk in-use capacity. The data processing director supervises the operations and technical-support departments. Terminals for on-line computer use are found in production (seven), the treasurer's office (two), the sales department (three), the deliveries department (four), and in data processing (two). A printer in the controller's department prepares 8,400 pages of reports monthly. A printer in the treasurer's office prints all checks and cash reports, totaling 3,500 pages monthly. A third printer in the deliveries department prints 4,000 customer-related documents monthly, including packing slips, order acknowledgments, and invoices. The total data processing budgeted expenditures, their three bases for allocation to users, and the percentage of each cost allocated on each basis for the current year are shown in the table that follows. This paragraph has given the values for the allocation bases or information from which they can be computed.

Annual Costs		Disk Capacity	Terminals	Pages Printed	Number of Employees
Indirect	$200,000	30%	40%	20%	10%
Direct	$300,000	25%	25%	40%	10%

Required:
   (a) Calculate allocation rates for data processing costs.
   (b) Calculate the total budgeted cost allocated to each user department.
   (c) Call attention to any deficiencies you see in this description of data processing and cost allocation.
   (d) What additional facts would you need to know to prepare performance reports for data processing and the user departments?

Accounting and Processing Controls

After studying this chapter, you should be able to

- Identify four major objectives of processing controls.

- Distinguish between risk and weakness and explain how to respond to each.

- Explain the role of internal audit.

- Explain how processing controls relate to other kinds of controls.

- Name, explain, and use specific types of processing controls such as the length and check-digit tests.

- Describe the objectives of and give examples of entry, processing, and reporting controls.

- Discuss and describe in detail selected processing controls used in the cash receipts, cash disbursements, and retail credit sales applications.

- Review the relationship of selected application controls to the corresponding control objectives for cash receipts, cash disbursements, and retail credit sales.

- Classify controls according to their objective, and select controls that will achieve a given objective.

As we have seen, management and financial controls depend for their success on feedback information, which is based on properly recorded, classified, and posted data. This feedback derives from the entry, listing, sorting, searching, reporting, and other activities of the accounting and data processing functions that place information into management hands.

Internal controls applicable to data processing operations are called **processing controls**. There are several kinds of processing controls. General processing controls apply to all data handled by the data processing center; application processing controls apply to single applications such as manufacturing operations. **Accounting controls** are a type of application control specifically designed to ensure that data collected, processed, and reported by the accounting system are reasonably error free, are complete, and can be used to prepare financial statements. Figure 12.1 shows the "nested" nature of these controls.

Figure 12.1   Relation of Accounting Controls to Other Controls

Accounting controls, consisting of general ledger and application controls, are the part of the control system that ensures the consistency of accounting statements with accounting principles; processing controls have the broader objective of ensuring that information results from data recorded, processed, and reported according to management policies.

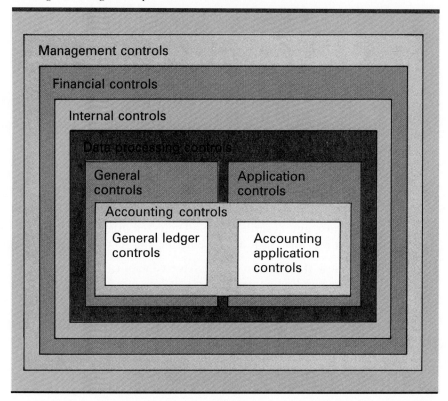

In this chapter we will look at major accounting controls. Knowledge of these controls will enable you to analyze any processing operation and determine the adequacy of the controls applicable to it, as explained in Chapter 14.

Control Risk and Weakness

The need for controls is determined by asking whether the controls would reduce the organization's exposure to net financial loss. Any situation in which the installation of controls would create potential savings is called a control risk. (Of course, accounting and processing controls cannot always create actual savings.) When the implementation of controls would, on the average, create *savings greater than their costs*, then the risk is also a control **weakness.** Thus, a control weakness is any control risk in which the expected savings exceed the expected installation and operating cost of the control, since by definition a weakness is cost-effectively correctable. All control weaknesses should be corrected by implementing controls. If analysis shows that a risk cannot be corrected cost-effectively because the cost of the required procedures would exceed the potential savings, the organization should protect itself by acquiring insurance against risks or by avoiding the situation that causes the risk. Figure 12.2 illustrates these points logically.

Consider this example: The Austin Company's accounting department adds a new employee to the company's payroll each time it receives

Figure 12.2   Management Strategy for Control Risk and Weakness
The basic characteristic of a weakness is that it can be corrected cost-effectively by means of appropriate controls.

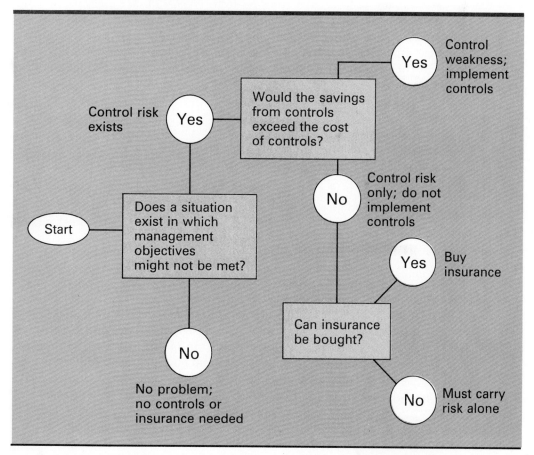

an approved job application from the manufacturing superintendent's office. Since nobody in accounting checks to be certain the employee actually exists, there is a *risk* that someone in the manufacturing superintendent's office could forward an application for a fictitious person, collect the paychecks and effectively embezzle from the company. To protect against this risk, someone from the personnel office could interview each new employee to verify the basic facts shown on the job application and then inform accounting that verification occurred. It is estimated that this procedure would cost Austin Company $4,000 per year. The company estimates that, without such a control, its average annual losses to this type of fraud would be $9,000. This risk is also a *weakness,* because the cost of correcting it is less than the cost of leaving it uncorrected.

Objectives of Controls on Processing

Accounting controls, like other controls, consist of objective, preventive, feedback, and comparative follow-up elements. More specifically, the *objective,* the *expected result* (specified as a preventive measure), the *actual result* (specified as a feedback measure), and the *follow-up* form the backbone of accounting controls. They provide assurance that accounting processing meets four major objectives:

> **Authorization:** approval for a transaction to take place; the control objective is to ensure that all transactions are authorized.
>
> **Recording:** creating a documentary or computer record of the data in a transaction; the control objective is to ensure that all transactions are recorded.
>
> **Access:** the use of assets, including production, processing, and transfer to an outside party; the control objective is to allow access to assets only for authorized purposes and to record access whenever it occurs.
>
> **Asset accountability:** having accounting records that describe the organization's assets; the control objective is to ensure that accounting records describe only real assets and describe all of them.

Specific controls must be designed to achieve each of these objectives. Control success depends on intelligent design and use. Most procedures that serve accounting control objectives can be incorporated into the internal structure of hardware, software, and administrative routines.

A lot of latitude is possible in designing procedures to meet each objective. However, each procedure must be related to one or more objectives by specifying (1) a statement of the planned or expected result; (2) a method for measuring the actual result; and (3) recommended follow-up procedures, including comparison of expected and actual results. Procedures that support the respective objectives include the following:

Objective 1: Authorization   Designate appropriate individuals to—

- Set policies and procedures
- Approve transactions
- Set asset valuations
- Authorize policy exceptions
- Follow up to ensure policies and procedures work as intended
- Follow up reported information that requires a response

Objective 2: Recording   Ensure that all transactions are—

- Real
- Recorded in all appropriate accounting records
- Properly valued and classified
- Recorded in a timely way
- Summarized and posted correctly

Objective 3: Access   Ensure that all tasks involving access to assets or records are—

- Appropriately segregated so that the authorization, the process, and the associated record keeping are performed by different individuals
- Documented to delineate applicable policies and procedures
- Performed by competent, properly trained people
- Recorded pursuant to applicable policy and procedures
- Protected from unauthorized access

Objective 4: Asset accountability   Ensure that all asset records are—

- Prepared according to authorized policies and procedures
- Protected from unauthorized access
- In agreement with supporting records; for example, that the control account agrees with the total of the subsidiary ledger
- Recorded in agreement with recent evidence from other entities (such as accounts receivable confirmations)
- Recorded in agreement with physical examination of assets

Above and beyond these accounting controls, data processing controls should ensure that transaction processing outputs are produced by the budgeted inputs, that is, that data processing is operationally efficient.

Accounting control procedures typically operate over a short time and apply to repetitive activities. Individually, these controls are very simple, as can be seen in the following example: Austin Company receives several dozen sales orders through the mail each day. These sales orders are written on coupons torn from magazine advertisements. One company *objective* is to ensure that all orders are processed and that no order is ignored. The mail clerk opens the mail at 10 A.M. daily, counts the orders and records the result, and then recounts them and records the second result. This verified count is the *preventive* measure; the number of orders that should be processed for that day—the expected result—is reported to the sales supervisor daily. The opened sales orders are passed to the data entry clerk, who enters them into a computerized file of orders to be filled. The computerized sales-order-entry program automatically counts the orders and reports the total in a daily processing report, which is the actual result or *feedback* measure of sales order processing. The report is sent to the sales supervisor, who compares the verified number of orders received with the number processed; this comparison is the *follow-up*. Any discrepancy receives additional attention, with attention to the objective of processing all orders.

Internal Audit

Accounting control systems include many controls harmonized and integrated to achieve the four broad objectives that result in reliable data processing. Internal audit, the examination of operational compliance with internal controls, is itself both a preventive and a follow-up control. **Internal audit** is the part of the accounting system that regularly analyzes or "audits" the workings of the various control systems to determine whether, on an overall basis, they are fulfilling their purposes. Internal audit is preventive in the sense that managers expect the audit to occur, feedback in the sense that it records activities, and follow-up in the sense that it does compare how managers acted with how they were expected to act. A strong internal audit department provides considerable reassurance that the accounting system is working as intended. We will discuss internal audit in detail in Chapter 14.

General Data Processing Controls

Data processing is typically a responsibility center or function within an organization. As such, data processing has its own assets, director, staff, goals and objectives, policies, procedures, and internal structure. It provides data processing services for other parts of the organization and for its own use. These services include running data processing applications, among them the various applications that make up the accounting system. As a major "customer" of the data processing function, the accounting system relies on data processing's controls. Those controls (identified in Figure 12.1), which must implement the four broad control objectives listed on page 418, determine how much reliance users can place on the output of the data processing service.

Data processing's controls can be classified in a manner similar to controls for the entire organization. Its management and financial controls are subdivided as follows:

1. Top-management controls, which specify the internal structure (including position descriptions) and goals for the scope and quality of services
2. Financial controls which include the data processing budget and performance-reporting standards
3. Internal controls, including the controls that describe how day-to-day operations will be conducted and what data about operations will be recorded

Data processing's internal controls can also be subdivided into general controls and application controls. **General data processing controls** apply to all data processing activities and can be classified as follows:

Goals and objectives, which suggest the scope and procedures for systems development
Back-up and security controls for data, programs, and equipment
Scope and procedures for technical support and user assistance
Controls on all data entry, processing, and reporting, regardless of the application in which they occur

Internal **application controls** affect only one application and are specifically designed for the situations encountered in that application. These controls are incorporated into the data entry, processing, and reporting operations for that application.

The remainder of this section describes the general data processing controls that apply to data entry, processing, and reporting.

Data Entry Controls

Data entry controls, also called edit controls, ensure the integrity of data as it is entered into a data processing system's records. The adage "garbage in—garbage out" succinctly states the need for effective input controls. Most managers would rather devote their resources to acquiring correct data initially than to correcting it during or after processing and reporting. Data entry controls achieve most of the objectives of authorization and recording listed on page 419. These controls ensure that input is consistent with management's authorization, is accurately entered, and is complete. Both manual and computerized systems have data entry controls. The examples that follow pertain to a computerized system, in which data are entered to a computer program that edits it into a computer-usable form suitable for processing. These tests are performed by the computer to screen out any errors introduced in the data before or during the input processes.

Alphabetic-or-Numeric Test. The **alphabetic-or-numeric test** asks whether the data entered is all alphabetic or all numeric and compares the result to the specification of the field in which the data are to be placed. Some data *must* be solely numeric, such as a social security number. If numbers *only* are in the field, the results of the test give assurance that the data in question are or resemble a social security number to the extent that they consist of digits only. If the field contains letters or other symbols, the entry is not a correct social security number.

Length Test. The **length test** asks whether the correct number of characters have been entered. Many data variables, such as a social security number, phone number, ZIP code, birth date, product code, or account number, have a specified length—more or fewer characters indicate error.

Value Test. The **value test** asks whether the variable has one of several acceptable values and rejects the variable if it does not. Sometimes a system will establish abbreviations for commonly recurring values, like the 2-character abbreviations of state names. In this case, the 2-character field substitutes for 54 names of variable lengths, all of which the program stores. An entry that does not match one of these abbreviations indicates that an error was made. Other examples of variables used in a value test include credit-status symbols, shipping-priority codes, and job-classification codes.

Range Test. The **range test** asks if the data falls into preset limits, such as between 0 and 1,000, and rejects them if they do not. Hourly pay rates, for example, *must* lie between the highest and lowest rates for the job classification. Sometimes companies also create artificial ranges that must be complied with. To control cash disbursements, the computer could be limited to checks of less than $1,000. Any larger amounts would require additional authorization.

Check-Digit Test. The **check-digit test** asks whether a special addition to a data value, called a *check digit,* is correct. The check digit is a value computed by a formula when data are entered, then recomputed and compared to the original value whenever the field is used; the purpose is to verify correct input or output. Data variables that often include check digits are internal account numbers, employee identification numbers, and the account numbers on credit cards. The value of the check digit depends on the value and positions of the other digits and can also be calculated from them. When the check digit calculated from the rest of the numbers in the field differs from the check digit included in the data number as entered, the latter is probably inaccurate.

There are numerous methods for calculating the check digit. One is called *"modulus-11."* The modulus-11 check digit for the number 52956 is 7, calculated as follows: starting with the rightmost digit, each digit is multiplied by a successively larger weighting number starting with 2 and increasing by 1 each time; then the sum of these products is calculated as shown in Table 12.1. Any error in the entry of the number will change the calculated value of its check digit.

Table 12.1   Modulus-11 Calculation for the Number 52956

Digit	Weighting	Product
6	*2	= 12
5	*3	= 15
9	*4	= 36
2	*5	= 10
5	*6	= 30
	Sum	= 103

This sum is divided by 11 (hence the name *modulus-11*). The quotient is discarded. The remainder, 4, is subtracted from 11. The result is the check digit, 7, which is added to the original number to make 529567.

$$\frac{103}{11} = 9 \text{ remainder } 4$$

The stored number is

$$11 - 4 = 7$$
52956 " +" 7, or 529567

Other check-digit methods use variations on such a procedure. For example, the modulus number may be any prime number, and the weights multiplied by the digits may increase arbitrarily.

Valid-Combinations Test.   The **valid-combinations test** asks whether the *combination* of data entered is correct. Some data combinations should not occur. Looking for them can expose otherwise hidden errors. For example, employees ordinarily cannot earn overtime without first working a minimum number of hours, usually 40, at regular-time rates.

Processing Controls

Processing controls make certain that data storage, classification, combination, movement, and retrieval occur according to management authorization. Many of these tests are based on calculating one sum both before and after processing and comparing the two. Processing controls achieve all four broad control objectives and also enhance operating efficiency. They are usually designed into applications programs and are closely integrated with routine processing. The following are examples of computer-implemented processing controls.

Control-Total Test.   The **control-total test** assures that all items in a given set or batch are processed. The test counts the number of items independently before and after processing and compares the total entered with the total processed. An example of a control-total test appears in the description on pages 419–420 of the Austin Company's sales-order-entry procedure.

Hash-Total Test.   The **hash-total test** determines whether the identity of items in a set remains unchanged throughout processing. More specifically, this test asks whether transactions are posted to the correct accounts. The operator adds together the account numbers that should have been used, and the computer application program adds together the account numbers actually used; the two totals are then compared. A difference in the totals means that some items were not processed, that at least one account number used in the processing was incorrect, or that at least one account number was changed during processing. The hash total has no value or meaning beyond its control significance.

Correct-File Test.   The **correct-file test** is a built-in procedure that asks whether the file copy being processed is the correct copy; for example, the most recent copy. This test can be very important, since it is possible to get hold of an outdated copy of a subsidiary ledger accidentally and begin posting entries to it. To prevent such an error, all files that are backed up should be dated. The journal should be posted only to the subledger copy bearing the same or a later date.

Unprocessable-Transactions Procedure.   An **unprocessable-transactions procedure** is not really a test but a procedure to make certain that only complete transactions are recorded, that all complete transactions are recorded, and that no transactions are lost. This procedure handles transactions that, despite data entry controls, cannot be processed and posted as entered. In an on-line application, the transaction will not be posted at all; the software will prompt the data entry operator (such as a sales clerk) for correct data or display a message rejecting the transaction and explaining why ("customer credit authorization has expired"). In a batch processing application (in which a file of transaction records are all posted in a single run), such transactions are dumped into a special file that returns the transaction data to their origination point. The party who originated the data corrects and resubmits the transactions. To ensure that none of these "dumped" transactions are lost, each transaction has a number. Eventually all these transaction numbers must be accounted for as either processed or officially canceled. Adequate data entry controls can hold the number of unprocessable transactions to a minimum.

Output Controls

Output controls ensure that accounting output consistently reaches those for whom it is intended and no one else. If all entry and processing controls are being applied properly, the content of the output should be, and is assumed to be, correct.

Verification Test.   The **verification test** asks whether accounting controls are being applied during processing. For example, paycheck printing stock should be prenumbered. To print paychecks, the computer payroll program relies on information stored from its last use; it calculates and prints on each paycheck a second number that should be the same as the pre-printed number. If the two numbers are not the same, either paycheck blanks are missing or the computer has been used to print checks without authorization. Although the verification test most often applies to checks, it can also be used to control copies of sensitive reports.

Distribution Test.   The **distribution test** assures that reports go to those for whom they are intended and to no one else. There are several ways to achieve this control's objective. Recipients might have to sign a receipt for each report, or turn in the previous report to get the new one, or pick up the report at a specific place after presenting identification. The output that requires the most extreme distribution controls is the paycheck—a special kind of "report" that must go only to the intended recipient.

Figure 12.3 summarizes the data processing controls that apply to accounting processing.

Figure 12.3   Data Processing Controls Summary
Data processing controls rely heavily on procedures integrated into a system. Such controls require a minimum of human attention to do their work.

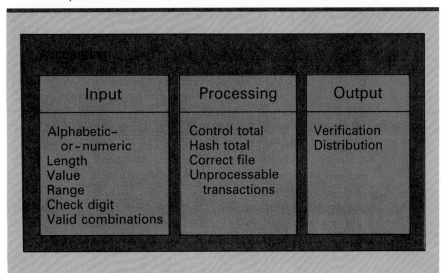

Illustrative Application Controls

Application controls are specific to a particular application; each accounting application has its own unique controls. This section outlines typical accounting system control objectives for three applications: cash received by mail, cash disbursed to pay accounts payable, and retail credit sales. The next section will describe the procedures for accomplishing these control objectives.

Cash Receipts by Mail

Nearly all businesses extend credit and receive cash through the mails. *Cash* includes not only currency but also personal or business checks and other negotiable instruments. Handling cash is inherently risky: the risk of a sudden large loss of assets increases proportionately with the liquidity of the asset. Since cash is the most liquid asset, the controls to protect cash are highly developed.

The Process.   The cash receipts process is simple. The mail arrives and is opened. If the mail contains cash, the organization identifies the sender, reduces the sender's debt by the amount remitted, and deposits the cash received. Control theory requires that the cash received and the **remittance advice**—the documentary evidence accompanying the cash payment and identifying the payer and reason for paying—be processed separately, then reconciled. The expectation is that the payment and remittance advice will agree. This process presents a neat problem because the cash payment and its accompanying remittance advice arrive together in the same envelope! Figure 12.4 depicts the receipt of cash and its subsequent handling.

Control Objectives.   The cash receipts process provides a good illustration of control through separation of duties. Table 12.2 outlines the control procedure in terms of the four major control objectives and some subordinate objectives. Note the similarity to the Austin Company's procedure for handling mail orders, the degree of control, and the attention given to separation of duties. The preventive measure, the feedback measure, the process itself, and the comparative follow-up step should be kept separate. This separation ensures that no one individual can process cash, report the processing results, and interpret those results. Consider, for example, the first control objective listed in Table 12.2 (page 428): that bank accounts be opened and closed only with proper authorization. This objective precludes the closing of a needed bank account by mistake and the opening of a secret unauthorized bank account. (Without such a control, cash receipts could be deposited in an unauthorized account and then transferred to a personal account, and thereby stolen.) As a preventive element of the control designed to achieve this objective, you could establish a procedure that allows only the board of directors to approve or authorize opening or closing bank accounts used for deposits. The secretary to the board would keep a list of these accounts. As a feedback element, you could have the treasurer make a list of bank accounts actually used for deposits. As a comparative follow-up element, the controller could compare the two lists.

Figure 12.4   Handling of Cash Receipts
Although proper cash receipt handling is simple, it is often ignored. Sustained disregard for control over cash receipts virtually guarantees loss of cash.

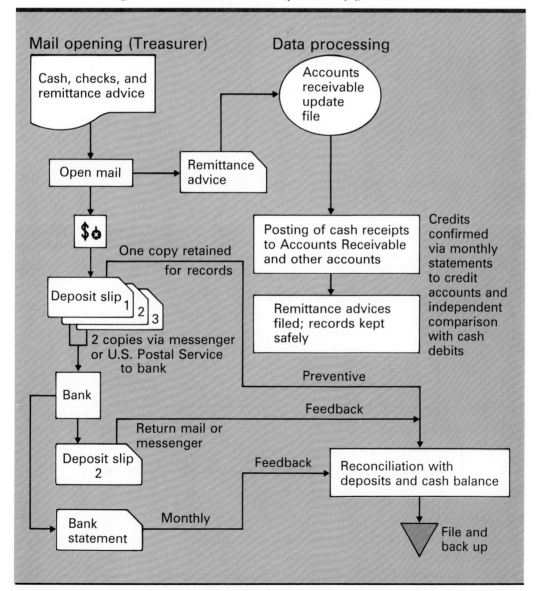

Table 12.2   Control Objectives for Cash Receipts by Mail

Major Objective: Authorization
  Subordinate objectives:
    Opening and closing of bank accounts occurs only with proper
      authorization.
    Mail likely to contain cash is opened only by individuals authorized to do so.
    Only authorized persons make bank deposits.

Major Objective: Recording
  Subordinate objective:
    All cash received is processed and recorded in a timely and accurate
      fashion.

Major Objective: Access
  Subordinate objectives:
    Access to incoming cash is limited to the individuals assigned responsibility
      for processing it.
    Access to cash records is limited to individuals assigned responsibility for
      keeping them.

Major Objective: Asset Accountability
  Subordinate objectives:
    All cash received and deposited satisfies genuine obligations to the
      organization.
    Cash balances stated in the records are correct on their recorded dates. Cash
      receipts stated in the records are correct as to amount and origin.
    Distributions of cash receipts to Accounts Receivable are correctly stated
      in the records.

Control Effectiveness.   Cash controls are highly developed because the risks associated with cash are well understood and defined. The controls described in Table 12.2—supplemented by rotation of duties and enforced vacations to ensure periodic fresh looks at sensitive responsibilities, as well as by bonding of cash-handling employees—should be adequate to protect against hiring mistakes and deliberate evasion of controls. These controls have proved cost-effective for most organizations. For more examples of control procedures, please see the next section.

Cash Disbursements for Credit Purchases

All organizations must disburse cash. Making disbursements by check allows record keeping to be more easily controlled.

The Process.   Most organizations choose to purchase on credit the goods necessary for their operations because credit purchasing allows better control over cash disbursements. The controller or other person who manages the accounts payable application, described at length in Chapter 8, bears the responsibility for authorizing cash disbursements for accounts payable. Before authorizing payment of cash to a vendor, the controller will compare and match three documents:

1. The **purchase order**—a document that records an offer to purchase merchandise or services from a vendor, specifying items and quantities—is prepared by the purchaser and sent to the vendor. On the purchase order, the purchaser identifies the items ordered.

2. The **invoice**—a source document about a sales or purchase transaction containing the information necessary to record that transaction—is prepared by the vendor and sent to the purchaser. Sent after the vendor fills and ships the order, the invoice tells the purchaser how much is owed for the order.

3. The **receiving report**—a record that goods or services purchased have been received by the buyer—is prepared by the purchaser when the shipment arrives in the purchaser's receiving area. The receiving report provides evidence a shipment was received and reports the items and quantities actually found in it.

If these three documents exist and corroborate each other, the controller creates a **voucher**, which authorizes preparation of a check payable to the vendor and organizes all the documentary evidence supporting the payment. The voucher and attached documents are reviewed by the treasurer, who prepares, signs, and mails the check. The treasurer also cancels the voucher so that it cannot be used again as support for a cash payment.

Control Objectives.   Successful control of cash disbursements also depends on separation of duties. Activities (such as purchasing) that create the need for cash disbursements should be separated from authorization of cash disbursements and actual disbursement of cash. The major control objectives and some subordinate objectives are shown in Table 12.3. Procedures for implementing these objectives are described in detail in the next section. These objectives should be implemented by control procedures that separate the preventive, feedback, and follow-up elements.

Control Effectiveness.   If good controls are part of the company's procedures, failures in the control of cash disbursements usually occur because the controls were ignored, either deliberately or out of carelessness. To keep disregard for controls to a minimum, management should establish specific procedures for maintaining a compliance record, and internal auditors should examine the record regularly. For example, suppose the authorization objective is that all payments in excess of $10,000 must be approved by the chief executive officer. As a preventive element, the cash disbursement application places all payments that exceed this amount into

Table 12.3   Control Objectives for Cash Disbursement for Credit Purchases

Major Objective: Authorization
Subordinate objectives:
   Liabilities result from authorized transactions.
   Use of cash to pay liabilities occurs only with management authorization.

Major Objective: Recording
Subordinate objectives:
   Liabilities are reflected properly in the accounts.
   Payment or adjustment of liabilities is reflected properly in the accounts.

Major Objective: Access
Subordinate objective:
   Cash is only paid to satisfy recorded liabilities.

Major Objective: Asset Accountability
Subordinate objective:
   Initial balances of cash, purchases, and accounts payable are all reconciled
      with the transactions affecting them and with their respective subsequent
      balances.

a separate file and reports them to the CEO, who indicates approval to the treasurer. As a feedback element, the treasurer prepares the checks using vouchers received from the controller. As a comparative and follow-up element, the treasurer matches each check over $10,000 with the CEO approvals.

   Multiple purchase and cash disbursement points—such as locations in different countries transacting in different currencies—will complicate the chain of authorization for assembling, approving, and later canceling vouchers. Controls must be developed accordingly.

Retail Credit Sales Using Point-of-Sale Terminals

Chapter 7 describes how the various files and processes of the credit sales application contribute to the security of the buyer's and seller's assets and the accurate capture of sales information. Here, we review this familiar process, giving special attention to the necessary controls.

   Sales transactions consist of an offer to purchase or sell property in exchange for some consideration and of an acceptance of the offer and delivery of the property to the buyer. The buyer's promise of future payment is one form of consideration. The seller's consideration is the delivery of the merchandise or (if the merchandise is in a distant warehouse or not yet ready for delivery) the promise to do so very soon. The buyer is obligated to make the future payment when it is due. The seller's documentation confirms what was purchased, what the price was, where it was delivered, and, eventually, whether it was paid for.

The Process.   Figure 12.5 (page 432) depicts the retail credit sales process. The buyer provides data to the order taker. At a minimum, this data must include the name, billing address, and credit-account number of the buyer and a description of merchandise to be bought. The first three items may be embossed on a credit card, which serves to identify the buyer. Additional information, such as the buyer's credit limit, may be encoded on the magnetic strip on the card's reverse side. Further identification may be required to verify that the credit card bearer is entitled to use the card. The order taker may inquire whether the buyer's name is spelled correctly, whether the address and account number are current, and whether other required data are correct. Seller and buyer sign a credit agreement, of which the buyer gets one copy. The other copies remain with the seller, who uses them for accounting and control purposes.

Control Objectives.   The major objectives and some of the subordinate objectives for retail credit sales using point-of-sale terminals are summarized in Table 12.4. The procedures to achieve these objectives are described in detail in the next section. These objectives should be implemented with procedures that separate the preventive, feedback, and follow-up elements of the control and contribute to operational efficiency.

Table 12.4   Control Objectives for Point-of-Sale Recording

Major Objective: Authorization
  Subordinate objective:
    The organization's conditions for a credit sale are met.

Major Objective: Recording
  Subordinate objectives:
    All information necessary to establish the facts is documented according to the seller's procedures.
    Information unrelated to a sale is not placed in the accounting records.

Major Objective: Access
  Subordinate objectives:
    If a documented sale does occur, the merchandise is distributed.
    In the absence of a documented sale, merchandise cannot be distributed.

Major Objective: Asset Accountability
  Subordinate objectives:
    For any time interval, the physically verified beginning balances of Inventory, Accounts Receivable, and Credit Sales *plus* the recorded additions to these accounts owing to transactions *minus* the recorded reductions owing to transactions *equal* the physically verified ending balances.

Figure 12.5   Credit Sales Process
Careful planning for credit sales allows one to anticipate the different decisions, processes, documents, and files that will be required.

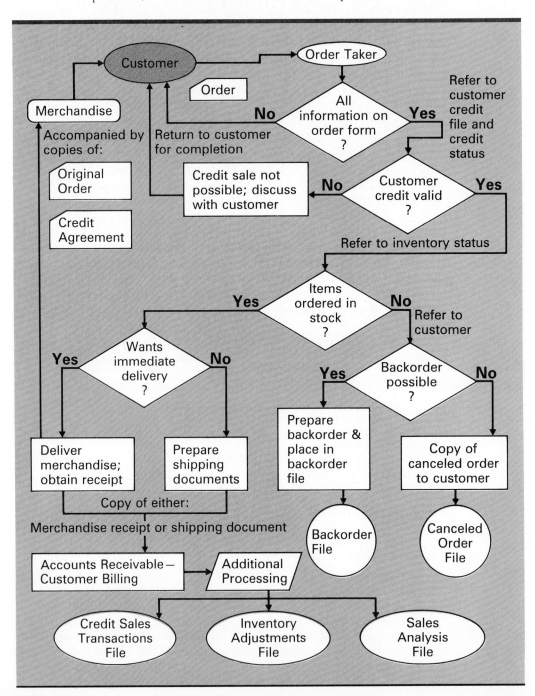

For example, consider the objective that merchandise should not be distributed unless there is a documented sale. Suppose you buy a stereo in a department store. The salesperson gives you two copies of the sales invoice, which is part of the preventive control element. You drive to the package-pickup door and present these copies to the attendant, who has a third copy that was sent to the pickup door. This third copy is the feedback element. The package-pickup attendant assumes that unless all three copies are present, no sale occurred and the stereo cannot be released.

Control Effectiveness.   Specific situations may involve more or fewer controls than those described here. Control objectives are achieved by eliminating all the weaknesses in a specific credit sales process, and only control procedures that eliminate weaknesses should be employed.

Illustrative Control Procedures

This section describes procedures intended to accomplish the control objectives presented in the preceding section. The major objectives are not shown; each subordinate objective is followed by one or more typical control procedures. These descriptions are not detailed enough to serve as checklists for systems design manuals; however, they will orient you toward the type of controls used in each of these applications. They also provide a good foundation for understanding which situations lead to computer crime and why the need for internal audit is strong.

Control Procedures for Cash Receipts by Mail

Opening and Closing of Bank Accounts Occurs Only with Proper Authorization.   *Authority to handle cash* should be explicit. The board of directors or other top-level management authority could designate those employees with cash responsibilities and make certain that company records identify those people, their duties, and when their authority expires. The bank is also told who is empowered to open and close accounts.

Mail Likely to Contain Cash Is Opened Only by Individuals Authorized to Do So.   A *description of cash-related duties* should be explicitly stated in the job description of each person handling cash. Mail distribution procedures should discourage unauthorized people from gaining access to mail. All cash should be deposited.

Only Authorized People Make Bank Deposits.   To be certain a deposit has actually been made, there should be a means of securing *positive evidence* of it from the bank. Deposits are made by an authorized messenger or by mail. If by messenger, the person in charge places the cash deposit into a lockable bank bag, along with a sealed envelope containing two copies of the deposit slip, and locks the bag. The messenger takes the locked bag to the bank teller, who has a key to unlock the bag. The teller opens the bag, segregates and removes the cash, validates one copy of the deposit slip, returns it to the bank bag, and returns the locked bag to the messenger. Mail deposits are placed in an envelope and put in a mailbox. The bank mails back the validated deposit slip, preferably in a pre-addressed envelope provided by the depositor.

All Cash Received Is Processed and Recorded in a Timely and Accurate Fashion.   *Frequent posting* is necessary for timely recording. Cash receipts are posted to accounts as often and as quickly as possible. The amount of each posting, and the number of postings, should agree exactly with the amounts and number of cash receipts deposited during the same time interval.

An incoming envelope containing cash should also contain a remittance advice as a means of accuracy control. To encourage credit customers to use a remittance advice, a business may design an invoice or statement with a removable portion on which the name of the remitter, the date of the bill, and the amount due are preprinted. The customer marks the amount of payment on it and sends it back with the payment in a pre-printed envelope. This type of remittance advice is an example of a **turnaround document**, a document for control purposes designed by one party (in this case the creditor) to be returned by another party (the customer). The turnaround document shown in Figure 12.6 is an example of a remittance advice.

A special cash payment box number is printed on the preaddressed envelopes sent with invoices to ensure that cash is mailed only to that address. Immediate separation of incoming checks from accompanying remittance advices is necessary to control the flow of cash receipts. If the remittance advice is missing, the person who opens the mail prepares a substitute. From this point on, handling the cash, accounting for the cash, and posting credits to Accounts Receivable are separate and independent activities, performed by different employees, with the expectation that they will eventually reconcile.

The person who opens the mail also lists and totals the checks on a deposit slip in triplicate. Two copies of the deposit slip accompany the cash to the bank. The third copy is the company's record of cash received and deposited and is the basis for a debit to a cash account. Later, someone not responsible for opening mail or processing transactions will compare the third copy with the bank-validated copy of the deposit slip.

An *independent record of deposit* provides a back-up control over cash. The independent record of deposit is one of the two deposit slip copies sent to the bank with the deposit. The bank stamps this copy with the time and date of deposit and mails it to the treasurer—not to the employees

Figure 12.6   A Remittance Advice
The remittance advice is a feedback control on cash receipts and a preventive control on posting credits to accounts receivable.

Smith Brothers Hardware **Box 15082** **Smallville, USA**	Remittance advice: Please include this portion of statement with your payment!
TO: Robert Customer 200 East 50th Street Smallville, USA Acct. # 345678	**TO:** Robert Customer 200 East 50th Street Smallville, USA Acct. #345678

DATE OF BILLING:	9-15-84	**Smith Brothers Hardware**
DUE:	9-25-84	**Box 15082**
PREVIOUS BALANCE:	$104.00	**Smallville, USA**
8-24-84 MERCH.	+ 75.00	
8-31-84 MERCH.	+ 50.00	DATE OF BILLING: 9-15-84
9-10-84 PAYMENT	− 104.00	9-15-84 BALANCE DUE $125.00
9-15-84 BALANCE DUE	$125.00	
Please retain this portion for your records.		**AMOUNT THIS PAYMENT:** $_____

who prepared the deposit. It is compared with the deposits reported on the bank statement as part of the monthly bank account reconciliation and audit. No irreconcilable differences are expected.

Access to Incoming Cash Is Limited to Individuals Assigned Responsibility for Processing It.   To ensure that *deposits are mailed to authorized persons,* the special address or box number printed on the envelopes that go to customers is accessible only to the person authorized to open mail likely to contain cash. Such mail is opened in a designated restricted-access area. To minimize the time cash is subject to theft, misuse, or misplacement, *cash should be deposited daily* or more often.

Access to Cash Records Is Limited to Individuals Assigned Responsibility for Keeping Them.   All documents pertaining to cash (such as deposit slips) are *serially numbered;* all numbers are periodically accounted for. Computer routines that access cash records can be used only according to a predetermined *schedule* and/or with a *password* or other authorization.

All Cash Received and Deposited Satisfies Genuine Obligations to the Organization.   Control accounts must be reconciled to subsidiary ledgers and to debits to Cash. Remittance advices go to data processing, which lists and totals them. This list is the basis for credits to various accounts receivable. After the individual credits are posted, the total decrease in accounts receivable should equal the increases in cash and in the control account balance. This reconciliation ensures that all deposits (debits to Cash) have offsetting credits to Accounts Receivable.

The organization must *verify* its right to receive cash. Any cash that appears not to satisfy a genuine obligation to the company is returned if possible, or else deposited. If deposited, it is segregated in the accounts and not authorized for general disbursement.

Procedures are needed for handling *exceptions*. For example, people occasionally mail money to others by mistake, or even without sufficient identification for the recipient to determine by whom or why the cash was sent. A cash remittance in a nonstandard envelope, lacking a proper remittance advice, may be intended for a business with a similar name or address. The money should be returned to the sender if a reasonable search immediately after receipt does not reveal the remitter's obligation. A document should exist for reporting unexplained cash receipts that cannot be regarded as assets belonging to the organization.

Cash Balances Stated in the Records Are Correct on Their Recorded Dates. Cash Receipts Stated in the Records Are Correct as to the Amount and Origin. Distributions of Cash Receipts to Accounts Receivable Are Correctly Stated in the Records.   Cash and cash-equivalent account balances are verified by counting the organization's assets corresponding to the account and comparing results with the balances shown in the accounts. Periodically, physical and recorded Cash and Accounts Receivable balances are compared by people not responsible for transaction processing. This comparison should include counting the cash and directly contacting trade debtors to seek positive confirmation from their records of the amounts they owe and have paid.

The company receives *verification of its account balances directly from customers.* Credit customers are frequently informed of their account status, including previous balance, payments received, purchases, other adjustments, ending balance, and the date the ending balance was determined. The customer verifies this information and notifies the creditor if there is any discrepancy.

Control Procedures for Cash Disbursements (Accounts Payable)

Liabilities Result from Authorized Transactions.   All responsibilities should be assigned. Someone is designated to be responsible for initiating all transactions that might result in liabilities. A different person and a specific location are designated for receiving merchandise. Preprinted, serially numbered forms are used for purchasing and receiving. Established policies and guidelines include a list of vendors from whom purchases are authorized, and this list should be checked before a purchase order is sent. There should also be a list of items approved for purchase, with the normal purchase quantity of each. Policies of this kind tend to control liabilities and pinpoint their sources.

Use of Cash to Pay Liabilities Occurs Only on Management Authorization.   Any claim on cash should be investigated thoroughly. The voucher system described on pages 428–430 will be adequate for most credit purchases. The voucher is assembled by the controller, then examined and accepted as the basis for a check by the treasurer. Of course, both of these positions should be filled by individuals approved by the highest authority in the organization.

In some cases, the voucher system is not appropriate. For very small payments, a petty-cash fund should be established in an amount sufficient to operate the fund for a short time. Small purchases are paid for in cash and the receipts retained. At any time, the remaining cash plus receipted amounts should add up to the initial cash amount. When the fund's cash balance gets low, the receipts are turned in and replaced with cash, restoring the initial total. The receipts are examined to make certain the small purchases they represent were consistent with company policy. Larger purchases should not be handled through a petty-cash account but through normal purchasing procedures.

Liabilities Are Reflected Properly in the Accounts.   All transactions should be recorded. All the copies of purchase orders are accounted for by specific handling procedures and specific filing locations. Someone checks regularly to make certain no orders are missing. In a computerized system, the program should automatically, at regular intervals, perform this check. All incoming shipments are reported. The receiving function is centralized and kept separate from ordering, purchasing, and accounts payable; vendors and shippers receive instructions about where to deliver shipments. The receiving reports go directly to accounts payable as soon as they are completed. The vendor's invoice must be matched with purchase orders and receiving reports to identify a liability. Any vendor claim of an overdue balance is investigated to determine whether payment has gone astray.

Payment or Adjustment of Liabilities Is Reflected Properly in the Accounts.   When matching invoices with purchase orders and receiving reports, verify the consistency of all details, particularly that the quantities and prices match. Indicate on each document that the verification has been performed. To limit the use of documents to only one transaction, use a stamp, mark, punch, or some other means to indicate that they have been processed and clearly identified with one purchase or payment transaction. Account for each paid voucher and reconcile it to the corresponding check issued. Use checks, not cash, to pay liabilities. Examine the endorsements on checks returned with the bank statement to make certain that the appropriate party cashed each check. Examine and account for documents near the end of each reporting period; accrue liabilities, if necessary, to make certain they are recorded in the proper period.

Cash Is Paid Only to Satisfy Recorded Liabilities.   Use a voucher system to control payments. Rely only on approved and complete prenumbered vouchers as the basis for issuing checks. All the numbers should be accounted for regularly.

Keep blank checks physically secure. Do not issue checks to "cash." The party named on the check should be the party named on the voucher. Do not issue checks on the basis of duplicate documents. Mail checks directly to the payee; do not return them to the person who prepared the voucher. A different person, or a computer edit-and-check program, should review the account coding for the debits accompanying all cash disbursements. Checks are serially numbered, and the number of checks used is reconciled with the number of entries in the cash disbursements journal.

Reconcile each bank statement with the cash records to verify that the organization's records jibe with the bank's.

Initial Balances of Cash, Purchases, and Accounts Payable Are All Reconciled with the Transactions Affecting Them and with Their Respective Subsequent Balances.   Bank statements should be mailed directly to someone who does not have responsibility for approving expenditures, making deposits, or issuing checks. That person reconciles every bank statement with the cash records. As part of an annual and more intensive examination, assets are inspected directly. Cash should be counted. Accounts receivable should be confirmed with customers. Accounts payable should be confirmed with creditors and a search performed for hidden or understated liabilities. Any differences between the actual assets and the accounting records should be completely resolved. All cash controls are evaluated by internal audit, both regularly and on a surprise basis.

Control Procedures for Retail Credit Sales Using Point-of-Sale Terminals

The Organization's Conditions for a Credit Sale Are Met.   If the buyer asks for credit privileges with the company, the seller will examine the buyer's identification and credentials to ascertain that they demonstrate the buyer's creditworthiness. The seller compares the identification with an internally maintained file of customer credit histories or with reports from a suitable credit service such as TRW or even Dun & Bradstreet or

Standard & Poor's. If the buyer's information disagrees with that in the credit-information source, the disagreement must be resolved before the buyer's offer can be accepted.

Although oral offers to buy are legally binding, accounting control procedures require that they be put in writing before being recorded, except in the most intimate business situations. To record a sale from the accounting point of view, the seller must possess written documentation—a contract with the buyer, a buyer's or seller's purchase order, a charge or credit sales form, or the sales credit agreement. Prepared forms must be 100-percent complete and the information they contain must be satisfactory to the seller before the buyer's offer can be accepted. In practice, this usually takes very little time in a retail credit sale.

When an approved credit buyer makes a credit purchase, the seller accepts the completed, signed charge slip from the buyer. At some stores, the sales terminal prints the sales data—including the date, the amount, and a unique sales number—on the charge slip. The sales terminal also creates an independent, sequential record of all transactions it performs. If there is any question about whether the charge slip was prepared in an authorized manner, the sales-terminal record confirms it. In any future contacts concerning the merchandise, the copies of the sales documents are used by both the seller and the buyer to confirm that the transaction occurred. The copy given to the buyer establishes that the buyer did acquire the merchandise from the seller. The seller keeps copies of all sales documents as protection against claims by buyers who want service, refund, or exchange when they did not buy the merchandise from the seller.

The seller delivers the merchandise. If the seller has a filled-out credit sale invoice signed by the buyer, and the buyer's copy has been removed, the presumption is that the buyer did receive the merchandise described on the charge slip. A signed statement on the charge slip that the "Buyer acknowledges receiving the merchandise described herein" serves as evidence that the merchandise was delivered.

All Information Necessary to Establish the Transaction Is Documented According to the Seller's Procedures. Prepared forms are used to record transactions. The seller may insist on the use of its own prepared forms or may transcribe the data to its own form from a buyer's purchase order. When the seller's form is completely filled out, all the required data have been collected.

Because every transcription is an opportunity for error, unnecessary data transcriptions should be eliminated. One expects data in processable form to be accurate; many procedures are designed to fulfill this expectation. Methods of reducing the amount of manual transcription include specially printed price tags that can be read by an optical character sensor, magnetic ink characters, punched cards attached to merchandise and torn off for processing, magnetic strips that contain coded information on credit cards, and even simple "menu" forms on which the sales clerk checks off options rather than filling in blanks.

Routine automatic edits and checks are performed by the computer and the staff. If the sales terminals are directly connected to a computer programmed to record sales transactions, the computer program "edits" the data to test it for errors as it is entered. The merchandise identification number and selling price entered through the terminal are compared with the same information in the computer's inventory master files to verify that they agree. Any data that fail the edit tests are rejected. The sales terminal will not complete the sale until the order taker has correctly entered the data required by the computer program. The program may even keep the terminal's cash drawer locked and refuse to print a sales receipt until all the data have been entered correctly, edited, and found acceptable. These powerful features reduce human error that could affect an organization's records.

Information Unrelated to a Sale Is Not Placed in the Accounting Records. On-line editing controls discourage the recording of incomplete, wrong, or fictitious transactions. For example, since a sales terminal accepts only sale data, irrelevant or extraneous information does not get into the files. If an idle order taker enters the name "John Doe" with an address and numerous items supposedly "purchased" on credit by Doe, the transaction cannot be recorded unless a credit-account number is offered.

Three features make it difficult to persuade the computer to accept a fictitious number. First, a long (12-digit) credit number offers 100 billion possible account numbers, of which only about 100,000 to 100 million could be in use. Because the credit-number validation routine will reject more than 999 numbers offered at random for each number accepted, random entry of account numbers is time consuming. Second, repeated attempts by a persistent clerk to enter an invalid number would activate a terminal-locking control. After three or four failures to enter a valid number, the software refuses to accept any more input from that terminal until a supervisor "unlocks" it by entering a code number. Third, it is highly unlikely that numbers entered at random will contain the correct check digit.

If a Documented Sale Does Occur, the Merchandise Is Distributed. An organization is open to breach-of-contract claims if it does not deliver legitimately purchased merchandise. If the buyer does not take delivery of the merchandise at the time of sale, the seller forwards several copies (typically three) of the sales invoice to its inventory supervisor. The sales invoice shows that credit has been accepted and specifies the address where the buyer wants the order to be shipped. These copies constitute an open order and authorize the inventory supervisor to segregate and ship the merchandise in the order. When the merchandise is shipped, one copy goes with the shipment as a packing slip. One copy remains with the inventory supervisor to show the order was shipped. The third copy will go to accounts receivable to be placed with the record of the original order. At any time, the inventory supervisor should be able to identify the orders that have been shipped and those that have not by the number of copies. If insufficient copies are received, the inventory supervisor should not process the order.

When accounts receivable receives its copy of the shipping document, the shipment is included in a billing statement to the buyer.

In a computerized system, physical copies of sales documents are not necessary to control merchandise shipping and billing, but they may be retained as an audit trail outside the computer. The **audit trail** consists of documents and forms that describe the history of a transaction and its processing. The audit trail runs from the original source documents to the transaction's effect as summarized in the accounts. (The audit trail is discussed in Chapter 14.) The accounting system deliberately creates and preserves the audit trail as a feedback control element to compare with the preventive elements of transaction recording and processing. The shipping supervisor enters a receipt number into the transaction record when merchandise is distributed, adding to the audit trail. The shipping supervisor may selectively use the check for an audit trail by means of a terminal displaying sales transactions. For example, if a valid shipping authorization does not appear there, the merchandise is not shipped. For shipments actually made, the shipping advice number entered by the shipping supervisor becomes part of that shipment's audit trail, enabling the accounts receivable function to identify transactions that should be billed.

In the Absence of a Documented Sale, Merchandise Cannot Be Distributed. Positive evidence of the buyer's right to receive merchandise is necessary before it is shipped. If one or more copies of an authorized sales invoice is missing, the shipping supervisor may not ship the order. Nor may the supervisor deliver an order directly to a customer without the copy of the sales invoice given to the customer at the time of the sale.

The Accounts Receivable Subsidiary Ledger Must Be in Balance with Its Control Account. For any time interval, the physically verified beginning balances of Inventory Accounts Receivable, and Credit Sales *plus* the recorded additions to these accounts owing to transactions *minus* the recorded reductions owing to transactions *equal* the physically verified ending balances. Sequential numbering controls the use of sales and credit documents. The number identifies both the transaction and its related documents and allows comparison of documents with processed transactions. The data processing equivalent of sequentially numbered documents is a file containing records that must be processed sequentially. Every document used and every record created will result in a completed transaction or an explanation of why the transaction was not completed. Any number missing in the sequence should be regarded as indicating a possible unrecorded, unauthorized, or incomplete decrease in assets.

Surprise counts and outside confirmations both deter and detect losses and theft. Frequent surprise counts of cash and inventory and reconciliation to the accounts help ensure that other controls are working. This assurance is especially important if inventory is stored in a warehouse owned by others. With a reasonable allowance for shrinkage, count (feedback element) and record (preventive element) should agree. Frequent confirmation of the accounts receivable balances—comparison of the organization's records with records of customers—helps ensure that the recorded accounts receivable balances represent genuine current obligations owed by customers.

Limited access to records and keeping duplicates of records safeguard the information required to allow physical verifications. Restricted access to data processing records, so that unauthorized persons cannot obtain or alter the information in the records, safeguards the accuracy of the information retained. Duplicate records, with fresh copies of files stored at a distance from the data processing site, allow the reconstruction of accounting records in cases of equipment failure or disaster and also maintain accountability.

Summary

Accounting and processing controls manage risks and eliminate weaknesses in accounting data processing. The broad objectives of these controls are authorization, recording, access, and asset accountability. Accounting controls are necessary both to ensure a flow of reliable information to allow the organization to function and to support its management and financial controls. Processing controls fall into two major groups: general controls that apply to accounting data processing generally and application controls that relate only to a specific accounting application. The fundamental mechanism of each control consists of a control objective, preventive and feedback measures, and comparative follow-up.

Application processing controls, in turn, may be subdivided into input, processing, and output controls. Input control procedures include the alphabetic-or-numeric test, length test, value tests, range test, check-digit test, and valid-combinations test. Processing control procedures include the control-total test, hash-total test, correct-file test, and unprocessable-transactions procedures. Output control procedures include the verification and distribution tests.

The chapter illustrates objectives for three representative applications: handling of cash received by mail, cash disbursements for credit purchases, and retail credit sales using point-of-sale terminals. The final sections of the chapter detail control procedures that accomplish the objectives for the three applications.

Key Terms

access

accounting controls

alphabetic-or-numeric test

application controls

asset accountability

audit trail

authorization

check-digit test

control-total test

correct-file test

distribution test

general data processing controls

hash-total test

internal audit

invoice

length test

processing controls

purchase order

range test

receiving report

recording

remittance advice

risk

turnaround document

unprocessable-transactions procedure

valid-combinations test

value test

verification test

voucher

weakness

Review Questions

1. What is the difference between *general data processing controls* and *application controls?* To what class of controls do both belong?

2. What are the four objectives of processing controls?

3. In designing a control procedure, what four elements must the control contain?

4. The data processing function, like other segments of an organization, has unique management and financial controls. Name three types of management and financial controls you would expect to find in the data processing function.

5. The data processing function also has internal controls to regulate its operations. Name four groups of internal general processing controls you would expect to find in the data processing function.

6. Are data entry tests in the category of application controls or general controls? Which broad control objectives do they serve?

7. At Cedar Park Bank, a rear-office data processing clerk noticed that a teller had apparently made an error in handling a deposit transaction. The clerk corrected the error and resumed processing. What should the clerk have done, and why?

8. What are the differences between the check-digit test and the range test? Explain the distinctions in your own words.

9. In Figure 12.4, which diagrams the cash receipts process, how many copies are made of each deposit slip? What is the control purpose of each copy? Do you think more copies are required? Explain your response.

10. Able, Baker, and Charlie all work for Seward Junction Farms. Among them, they perform the following tasks.

Receive mail

Open mail

Collect and total the remittance advices

Collect and count the cash

Prepare a deposit slip in triplicate

Take two copies of the deposit slip and the cash to the bank and secure one validated copy of the deposit slip

Receive the monthly bank statement

Reconcile the bank statement with the deposit slips, the cash balance, and the total debits to accounts receivable

Post cash receipts to accounts receivable

File remittance advices

Outline how these duties should be allocated among Able, Baker, and Charlie to achieve a reasonable separation of responsibilities and to make sure that the preventive and feedback elements of controls are handled separately.

11. What is a voucher? What is its purpose? Who prepares it? Who acts on it?

Discussion Questions

12. Explain what is meant by a control risk. Can a control risk be corrected? When is a control risk also a weakness? Can a control weakness be corrected? Why is it important to identify control weaknesses?

13. Leander Jewelry Company does not have a trained bookkeeper. As a consequence, Alison Leander, the business owner, hires a bookkeeping service that sends in someone twice a week. The bookkeeper sits at a desk whose drawers contain much of the store's jewelry inventory. Typically, a different bookkeeper shows up each week. The bookkeeping service does not bond its employees. In June 1985, one of the bookkeepers stole $20,000 worth of jewelry; in December 1987, another one took $30,000 worth of diamonds. No jewelry recoveries were made in either case, and further losses can be expected. The bookkeeping service costs $200 per week. A full-time bondable bookkeeper would earn $25,000 per year but would bring a net insurance premium reduction of $5,000. Indicate whether there is a control risk here and whether it is also a weakness. Explain your reasoning.

14. What is the relationship between a control objective and a control procedure? What are the four parts of the control objective illustrated in the Austin Company example described in the chapter?

15. In regard to asset-access control, what three functions should be separated as completely as possible? List at least one weakness that exists if separation is not complete.

16. What does the statement *data processing is operationally efficient* mean? Use your own words.

17. What is internal audit? How does internal audit serve as the feedback part of many controls?

18. What does the data processing function do? What is the relationship between it and the accounting function? How do you distinguish, *within* the data processing function, among financial controls, internal controls, and application controls?

19. Consider the following data entry tests: alphabetic or numeric, length, range, check digit, and valid combinations. Which one(s) would be most appropriate in each of the following data entry situations? Why?
    (a) A customer whose credit limit has been exceeded should not be allowed to charge additional merchandise.
    (b) A date field on an employment application must contain exactly six digits.
    (c) Data entry operators are looking for a way to identify incorrectly typed credit card numbers.
    (d) Checks for more than $1,000 must bear two signatures to be valid.
    (e) If library books are returned more than two weeks after they are borrowed, a late-return fine may be imposed on the borrower.
    (f) Telephone numbers must contain exactly ten numeric characters.
    (g) Finished-goods inventory numbers consist of eight characters, of which the first three are letters, the next four are numbers, and the last one is a letter. The first letter must be an *A, B,* or *C;* the last letter must be *B* or *R.*
    (h) The percentage of potash in bulk-shipment fertilizer sales must fall between 5 percent and 20 percent.

20. What is a control total? For what objectives are control totals best suited? Are all control totals also hash totals? Indicate which of the following examples are hash totals and explain why the others are not hash totals.
    (a) Total hours worked in a week by all employees.
    (b) Total of the identification numbers of all employees.
    (c) Total of all customer account numbers to which postings were made.
    (d) Total number of deposits to cash during September.
    (e) Total sales in Texas during September.

21. Suggest a way that the correct-file test could be implemented on a computer-based system.

22. Suggest three ways that report-distribution controls could be implemented. Assume the reports are computer files and not hard copy (printed on paper). If a report is stored in a computer file, as a word-processing document might be, how can data processing ensure that only its intended user can print or read it?

Problems

23. If a transaction must meet the objective of being properly recorded, what five specific attributes must it have? A service-station attendant has the responsibility of creating a computer record of a gasoline credit sale transaction. For each of the five attributes you listed in (a), suggest a weakness that could arise if the attribute did not exist. For example, if the transaction is not real, a risk arises that the imaginary transaction will distort sales and accounts receivable balances.

24. List the four elements of the fundamental control mechanism. Then describe how the four parts of this mechanism pertain to the control objective of ensuring, by means of a bank-validated deposit slip, that all cash sent to the bank is actually delivered to the bank.

25. Refer to the modulus-11 method of calculating check digits. Determine which of the following numbers are valid, assuming the check digit is the seventh digit, on the extreme right.

    7265484   4209761
    1134528   6377700
    9984526   3125255

26. Thorndale Research Company is a major project manager for construction of chemical and utility plants. It has a chart of accounts with well over one million separate 36-digit account numbers. A typical number looks like this:

    101011
    001000
    211232
    001100
    786771
    001999

    The long number lets the company categorize expenses very precisely and contributes to control of costs on its various projects and to justifying their recovery to the project and contract sponsors. When an expense is incurred, it is extremely important that it be charged to the correct account number; an error may mean that the expense cannot be identified with work being done for a given sponsor and therefore cannot be recovered. Such errors now result in about $900,000 per month in nonrecoverable costs. The company has never used check digits before and is not certain whether it could add a check digit to each authorized account number to ensure correct entry of the account number.

    The following facts have been determined: the modulus-11 check-digit test would require that one digit be added to the account number, making it 37 digits long; implementation would require a one-time cost of $300,000 to modify the accounting system to compute the check digits and use the longer number, to revise documents and forms, and to train employees to use the procedure. Additional costs would be associated with the extra calculation required to compute and verify the check digits. This extra cost is estimated at $0.005 per account posted. The company normally processes about 100,000 transactions per month, each requiring postings to an average of 2.4 accounts using the check-digit test. If used, the check-digit test would save 90 percent of the present amounts lost due to incorrect postings.

Required:

(a) Calculate the check digit for the account number shown.
(b) Analyze the cost-effectiveness of the check-digit test on account numbers for Thorndale Research. Would you recommend that the company adopt this test? Support your recommendation.

27. Read the following description of a cash-by-mail operation, looking carefully for control weaknesses: The Evans Company handles mail-order sales for a number of smaller companies and advertises client companies' merchandise in a number of popular magazines. When Evans receives customer orders accompanied by checks, cash, and money orders, the receptionist at the front desk opens the mail and places the money in her left top drawer. All the accompanying orders are sent to the marketing relations department for forwarding to the client companies. During her spare moments, the receptionist makes a list of the orders and accompanying cash receipts, noting who they are from and the dates received. The receptionist also makes out a deposit slip. When the amount to be deposited reaches $5,000 or more, the receptionist mails it to the bank. Deposit confirmation is the monthly bank statement. While the deposit is growing, any cash received is used to buy lunches, office supplies, and other items. The receptionist writes down the amount, user, and use. Once a month the bookkeeping department picks up the list of checks. Although the bank statement usually comes to the bookkeeping department, they allow the receptionist to reconcile it. The receptionist was hired six months ago as an emergency temporary employee and has never completed an employment application.

Required:

Identify at least seven of the nine or more weaknesses in the procedures above. Identify control objectives that would eliminate each weakness. In addition, for each control objective, suggest a procedure that would at least partially implement it. Identify the preventive, feedback, and comparative follow-up elements in the procedure.

28. The diagram on the next page represents cash disbursements for accounts payable as described on pages 428–430.

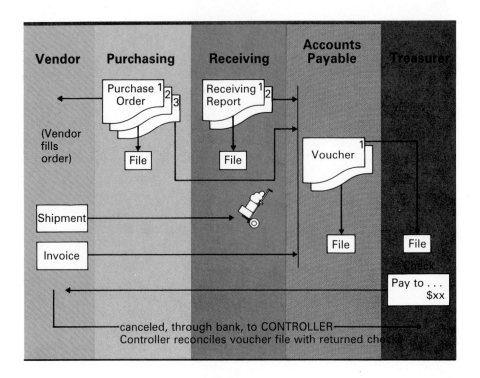

Required:

(a) List the documents in the diagram.

(b) List the processes shown in the diagram.

(c) Identify and describe the controls that apply to the various elements in the diagram.

29. Read the following description of a cash disbursements operation, looking for control weaknesses: Epco Awning Company makes custom awnings to the specifications of its customers. It buys awning fabric, framing, assembly supplies, paint, packing material, and tools from a number of vendors. The company prides itself on its tradition of quality and allows its six master craftspeople to buy their own materials, supplies, and tools. Usually, the craftspeople order these items by telephone. All incoming shipments are delivered to the shop. The craftspeople review each day's shipments received, pick out the ones they ordered, and take them into their work areas. Vendors ship and invoice each order separately. The invoices come to the treasurer, who schedules monthly sessions with the craftspeople to decide which invoices should be paid and whether any adjustments are necessary for returns. The treasurer writes checks as directed by the craftspeople and gives them to the craftspeople for delivery to the vendors' sales representatives, who call on them frequently. For convenience, the

checks are kept out in the open. The treasurer keeps the bank statements but does not reconcile them or examine the individual checks returned with the bank statements.

Required:

Identify at least five of the eight or more weaknesses in the procedure described. Identify the control objectives that could eliminate each weakness. For each control objective, suggest a procedure that would at least partially implement it. Identify the preventive, feedback, and comparative follow-up elements in the procedure.

Case: **Bastrop Computer Company**

Bastrop Computer Company produces and sells software for popular microcomputers. Each employee is allowed to choose one free software program per year. An employee who requests a software package under this policy completes a software request form and takes it to the personnel manager. After verifying that the person is actually an employee and has not yet received any software that year, the personnel manager signs the form. The employee gives the signed form to the inventory manager and receives the software. The inventory manager notes on the form that the software was delivered and returns the form to the personnel manager, who places it in the employee's file for future reference.

Required:

Identify the control objective and other components of control present in this description.

Case: **Whitetail Computers, Inc.**

Whitetail Computers, Inc., is a retailer of commercial computers and software. Some customers buy from the store floor, but the majority of sales occurs as follows: A salesperson visits Antler, a potential customer. After several visits, the salesperson suggests equipment and software that would help achieve Antler's business goals. If Antler agrees, the salesperson has the equipment and software delivered to the customer. Often the salesperson spends several hours helping to set up the system and showing the customer how to operate it. If Antler wishes, all or part of this trial system can be exchanged for other types of equipment. When, after several days or weeks, Antler is satisfied, the salesperson asks the customer to sign a sales order listing the items sold. If Antler is unsure about any of the items, they remain on an informal trial basis and are not included in the sales order. Later, when Antler is sure that these items are suitable, they will appear on an invoice. The salesperson takes the sales order to the floor manager, who gives it to the treasurer. The treasurer places the sales order in a file of accounts receivable.

As a condition for a bank loan, Whitetail Computers engaged Buck & Doe, auditors, to examine its financial statements. The auditors made the following comments about internal control:

> Our examination included a review of accounting controls. We note the following situations and propose corresponding control objectives that are not presently achieved:
>
> No documentation prepared showing where salesperson has placed equipment.
>
> **Objective**   Inventory location and amounts correspond to accounting records.
>
> No receipt obtained from customer for equipment on trial.
>
> **Objective**   Customers with inventory on free trial should acknowledge that they have it and are aware of its trial status.
>
> No agreement reached with customer governing terms of equipment trial use.
>
> **Objective**   Customer acknowledges responsibilities toward equipment on free trial, such as maximum period it can be kept and liability if damaged or lost.
>
> No customer credit check performed prior to equipment delivery.
>
> **Objective**   Inventory is released on credit only to customers with approved credit.
>
> No record kept of equipment exchanges prior to purchase or return.
>
> **Objective**   Inventory location and amounts corresponding to accounting records.

Required:

(a) For each control risk and proposed objective, state the other three elements of the control needed to correct the situation. Then evaluate the control as a whole and state whether the situation as described by the auditors is (1) not a control issue, (2) a control risk only, or (3) a control risk that is also a weakness. Give the reasoning behind your response.

(b) Assume that the process, as described, results in a high level of sales but also in a high level of bad debts and lost inventory. How would you modify it to retain its desirable features while eliminating the two undesirable ones?

CHAPTER 13

Controlling Computer Crime, Incompetence, and Carelessness

Learning Objectives

After studying this chapter, you should be able to

- Understand and explain crime-relevant terminology, such as hearsay evidence.

- Recognize the roles of *intent* and *control* in the risk of computer crime.

- Recognize and call attention to common types of computer crime and criminal techniques.

- Compare and contrast computer crime to other causes of loss, such as carelessness and incompetence.

- Explain and apply four successful anticrime strategies and procedures.

- Use anticrime procedures that are economically sensible.

- Spot and protect against lapping and kiting—two common crimes of which everyone should be aware.

━━━━━━━━━━

Ever since the dawn of commerce and private property, certain people have tried—often successfully—to deprive others of their property without appropriate compensation or without the consent of the rightful owner. The laws of contracts, bailments, property, sales, and rules of evidence are intended to provide victims of property crimes with remedies and to enable the state to prosecute perpetrators. Carelessness and incompetence can also cause loss, against which laws cannot protect. Only vigilance and control of financial, accounting, and internal operations stand between an organization and careless and incompetent acts on the part of its employees and the public.

Techniques and Examples of Computer Crime

In the past quarter-century, the attractiveness of computers as objects or means of business crime has emerged as a growing business risk. A few examples of computer crime will quickly acquaint you with its variety and methodology. You will notice that most of these crimes were made possible by nonexistent or unenforced controls. Many of these examples are based on material from *Crimes by Computer*, by Donn B. Parker.[1]

- A frustrated computer operator fired a pistol at a computer.
- All copies of a computer program were kidnapped and held for ransom.
- An accounts receivable file was used to identify purchasers of valuable items, which were then stolen from them.
- A trade school advertised a computer-use course, complete with pictures of students using computer terminals, but did not provide access to computers.
- A man used wrongfully obtained passwords and parts numbers to cause a computerized delivery system to send merchandise to him.
- An employee gave authorized-vendor status to a dummy company and arranged for his employer to pay the dummy company for imaginary services.
- A man set fire to a computer to destroy evidence of his crimes.
- A kidnapper tried to collect a ransom safely by insisting that it be deposited in a bank and then withdrawing it from an automatic cash-dispensing machine. (He was caught when a quick-thinking programmer instructed the bank's computer to locate the machine while the kidnapper was in the act of using it.)
- A ring of computer personnel at several large data processing centers fed false reports and credit ratings into computers, creating false references that appeared to corroborate each other. These references were used to order (but not pay for) merchandise on credit.
- A computer network's valuable graphics-plotting program was copied from storage by an employee of a competing network, using techniques learned when he worked for the victimized network.
- A programmer placed unauthorized instructions in the operating system, allowing him access to the highest level of information stored by the computer. He sold the information he obtained. This method is known as a **Trojan Horse technique** because, like the horse, the instructions allowed access to the system by a person the managers really wanted to exclude.
- A bank's programmer altered the computer's method of calculating interest to round down to the nearest cent, accumulated the fractional overages, and credited them all to his own savings account. (This classic technique, called **rounding**, was used by Gus, the character played by Richard Pryor in the 1983 movie *Superman III*).

---

[1]Reprinted with permission from *Crimes by Computer*. Copyright © 1986 Warren, Gorham & Lamont Inc., 210 South Street, Boston, MA 02111. All rights reserved.

- A Social Security clerk whose job it was to discontinue sending benefit checks to deceased individuals instead changed their addresses and received and cashed the checks personally.

- Federal prisoners in Leavenworth prison who received vocational computer training used the training to file fraudulent tax-refund claims with the IRS.

- An unhappy clerk brought a powerful magnet to work and made certain all tapes were exposed to it, damaging at least some data on every one of them.

- Upon being dismissed, a computer operator disabled the alarm that would warn of a failure in the facility's air-conditioning system. No failure occurred before the disconnected alarm was found in a routine inspection a few weeks later, but if one had, the resulting high temperatures might have shortened the lives of many computer components or even caused some of them to fail immediately.

- A computer program was used to generate phony accounts receivable and to render them invisible to the auditor, who selected accounts at random for confirmation directly by the customer. The phony receivables replaced cash the criminals had stolen.

- A programmer inserted a short section of machine-language code into an otherwise normal program. When the program ran under certain conditions, this code copied itself onto the inventory file, ruining it. Machine-language code that replaces software or data with a copy of itself, without authorization, is called a **virus.**

- A programmer inserted into an otherwise normal program a short section of machine-language code that, under certain conditions, erased parts of internal memory and even of disk-stored files in use. Machine-language code that deletes software or data, without authorization, is called **worm code.**

- A bank teller who knew the dates when interest calculations were made on different types of savings instruments temporarily replaced, on those dates, money he had stolen, making the interest calculations appear to be correct.

As these examples illustrate, the term *computer crime* applies to a broad array of illegal incidents, most of which draw on knowledge of how a computer functions. The criminal may steal or damage the computer records, use the computer without permission, or make it an accessory in a theft of noncomputer property or services. More formally, ***computer crime** is any deliberate act, requiring knowledge of how a specific computer works, that deprives the rightful owner of a benefit such as compensation for the use of the computer or of computer-produced information, or the exclusive use of information or other property.*

For example, an employee could deprive an owner of compensation for computer use by calculating stock and bond yields for an investment club without authorization. A worm program deleting important files deprives their owner of the information contained in them. Some information derives much of its value from the owner's right to its *exclusive* use. Accessing someone else's private on-line data base to copy mailing lists, credit ratings, or other information deprives the owner of the exclusive right to that information and thus reduces its value. In accounting, most computer crime involves the misprocessing or misuse of computer-produced information, including computer-aided embezzlement.

Limits of Legal Deterrence

The law offers some protection against computer crime, but there are limits to what legal prosecution can accomplish. These limits arise largely from the level of proof required to convict someone of a crime, the type of evidence required to achieve this level of proof, and the reluctance of many victims to prosecute and thereby publicly admit that they have been victimized. In practice, these circumstances make certain types of crime, including deprivation of information and deprivation of exclusive use of information, especially difficult to prosecute.

Any crime, including fraud or embezzlement, is difficult to prosecute unless there are eyewitnesses who can give firsthand verbal evidence of it (direct testimony) or a confession. The involvement of a computer in these two crimes simply introduces another complicating factor. Since most computer criminals work alone, no one sees them committing the crime. To the casual observer, criminal activity at a computer terminal might be indistinguishable from normal attention to assigned duties. The Fifth Amendment, of course, protects the accused from any requirement to give self-incriminating testimony. If someone brags about committing a crime, others can only testify that the person *admitted* the crime, not that he or she committed it. Such indirect verbal evidence of an incident where, for example, *B* testifies that *A* confessed the incident to *B*, is **hearsay evidence**. Even if the accused corroborates that he or she said what was heard, it still does not prove the accused actually committed a crime.[2]

If disks or tapes are stolen and recovered, they constitute physical evidence of the crime in the same sense as any other stolen goods. But the records created by the criminal and placed in RAM or external storage cannot be introduced directly as evidence, because their physical appearance gives no indication of their contents. Only printouts—the computer-generated printed representations of the records—are readable. Such printouts must be qualified by testimony that they were actually derived from the allegedly copied, damaged, used, or stolen file. Otherwise, they too constitute hearsay evidence, since the computer cannot be called to

---

[2]Normally, hearsay evidence alone cannot produce a conviction; it must be corroborated by other types of evidence. The need for corroborating evidence may be lessened if the accused is tried before a jury, because the jury is empowered to decide whether the accused actually committed the acts necessary to constitute the crime.

the stand and cross-examined about them. A related difficulty is that some organizations routinely destroy computer-generated records before anyone realizes their potential significance as evidence. Even if the prosecutor finds persuasive admissible evidence, it is no easy task to familiarize a jury with such concepts as computer operating systems and magnetic storage to demonstrate to them *what* was done, *how* it was done, and *why* it was wrong.

The National Association of State Information Systems has drafted proposed legislation that makes it a crime to access, modify, damage, or destroy a computer or its contents without permission or to use a computer in committing a crime. Laws based on this proposal have been passed in several states, but their effectiveness appears to be low. Because of all these complicating factors, it is apparent that the first and foremost defense against computer crime is not prosecution after the fact, or fear of detection, but prevention through proper controls. The primary responsibility for preventing and detecting computer crime still rests with management. Generally speaking, management seems reluctant to accept this responsibility; even when ample evidence would support a successful prosecution, management is typically reluctant to prosecute a white-collar employee. In practice, this reluctance often means that the criminal faces only dismissal and an unfavorable reference from the employer.

Common Types of Financial Fraud

The three types of fraud discussed in this section are classics and every student of systems and controls should be familiar with them. They are classics because they are simple and have been used often and successfully even though they can easily be prevented.

Lapping

Lapping is a means of stealing money and concealing the theft. Specifically, **lapping** is the unauthorized use of current cash receipts to replace earlier receipts used for unauthorized (usually personal) purposes. Although not computer dependent, lappers can use computer records to hide their work. Anyone who works with accounting systems should know how lapping occurs and what controls prevent it.

A lapping fraud is perpetrated by an employee of a firm that extends credit to its customers. The lapper's duties normally include opening mail containing cash or checks sent as payments on customers' outstanding balances. The lapper's crime is diverting a part of these payments for personal use.

Suppose, for example, that two days ago the mail included the following remittances:

Date	Name of Remitter	Amount Remitted
Day 1	Holiday	$500
	Heard	300
	Marrola	700
	Singh	400

The lapper takes Heard's $300 check, endorses it fraudulently, and deposits it to his personal account. He treats the other three checks as required by orthodox cash receipts processing. The next day's mail includes the following checks:

Date	Name of Remitter	Amount Remitted
Day 2	Samuelson	$300
	Rodriguez	600
	Mueller	200
	Kelner	400

In the cash receipts credit distribution report, the lapper now lists Samuelson's check as received from Heard, and at the same time, alters Mueller's check and deposits it to his personal account. The day 2 credit distributions now show correct amounts for Rodriguez and Kelner, a correct but late credit (with false origin) for Heard, and no credits for Samuelson or Mueller. Samuelson's check is "lapped" on Heard's account to create a credit. On day 3, the mail brings these checks:

Date	Name of Remitter	Amount Remitted
Day 3	Anthony	$900
	Karima	200
	Short	300
	Murphy	400

Now the lapper uses the cash receipts credit distribution report to lap (credit) Karima's check to Mueller's account and lap Short's check to Samuelson's account. He alters Murphy's $400 check for deposit to his personal account. Soon he has trouble remembering to whose account each check has been credited, and he begins keeping a separate record of these adjustments and the thefts they conceal. If this record is discovered, it can be used as evidence against him.

As the amount of money stolen increases, the time lag between receipt of a remittance and its credit to a customer's account is likely to increase. If the lapper persists, this lag time grows until some credit customers notice—and report—that their remittances are not reflected on their most recent monthly statements, despite the return of their own peculiarly endorsed and canceled remittance checks. The ensuing investigation usually nets the lapper and plenty of incriminating evidence.

Notice that the lapper was able to succeed, for a time, because his duties combined functions that good control procedures require to be separated: receipt of cash, deposit of cash, and distribution of accounts receivable credits. If these functions were kept separate, inconsistencies would be discovered and reported long before the fraud could gather momentum. Realizing this, many potential lappers never attempt to circumvent good controls.

Kiting

An elegant and vicious crime, **kiting** consists of taking advantage of normal delays in processing financial transactions to create the appearance of assets that do not exist. Although usually done with cash in checking accounts, it also can be done with warehouse receipts, bearer bonds, or even physical goods.

The rules under which financial institutions normally operate, which put a "hold" on a deposited check until the funds backing it are received from the institution on which the check is drawn, can prevent kiting. However, these rules may be waived for familiar and trusted customers. Many organizations and individuals take advantage of these waivers to pursue aggressive cash management policies, moving cash into an account to cover checks at the last minute. This practice often results in a technical overdraft, which corrects itself when the deposited funds arrive from another bank. The difference between aggressive cash management and kiting is that kiting involves the supposed transfer of assets that never in fact existed.

In brief, the kiter deposits in bank *A* a check drawn on bank *B*. Funds do not really exist in bank *B* to cover the check. The kiter then presents to bank *C* a check drawn on bank *A*, and deposits these funds in bank *B* in time to cover the check on its way from bank *A*.

As a more detailed example, the kiter, typically an individual with more cleverness than common sense, has printed some personalized checks from bank *B*, for example, the West Bank of the Mississippi. (Actually, the checks would name a real bank in a distant location.) The kiter uses one of these checks to obtain $1,000 and deposits it in bank *A*. Bank *A* sends the check into the clearing-house network. In a few days, the check will come back marked "no such account." Before that time, the kiter will have withdrawn $900 from bank *A* and deposited it in bank *C*, perhaps along with another check for $1,000 from bank *B*. If bank *A* contacts the kiter about the rubber check he gave them, he covers it with another check drawn on bank *B*. At some point, the kiter obtains some part of his kitings in cash or negotiable securities and travels to a country from which extradition to the United States is unlikely.

Kiting requires frequent transactions and many banks if it is to pay off for the kiter. The kiter garners a payoff in one or both of two ways: first, by keeping some of the money he or she withdraws, instead of redepositing it in other banks; and second, by earning interest on his or her "deposits." To any given bank, the kiter merely appears to have a very active account and some difficulty avoiding overdrafts. However, if the kiter gets the flu and cannot keep up the flow of phony paper, there will be overdrafts in all the banks involved.

Kiting can result in very large losses. In 1985 a major brokerage firm confessed to a kiting scheme involving millions of dollars and over 400 banks. The brokerage firm did not engage in kiting to create fictitious cash; it did so to convince individual banks that it had larger deposits with them, for longer periods of time, than was actually the case. The brokerage firm argued that these large, long-lived deposits entitled it to higher interest earnings from the banks—approximately $8 million more than it should have earned. The firm used its own computers to plot, coordinate, and schedule the transactions that moved its cash around. Thus, although kiting predates the computer age, computers compound the risk it poses to financial institutions and make the controls needed to contain the risk more complex—and more necessary.

Controls against kiting are totally effective if they are followed. The principal control is to freeze deposits by check until the check clears. Some banks are reluctant to do this because it is unpopular with customers, who do not want their cash languishing in non-interest-bearing accounts. Another control is to inquire into the character and reputation of new depositors. A third approach is to program into the accounting system a means of identifying activity levels and patterns that signal kiting may be in progress; these patterns include a high volume of deposits and withdrawals that involve many different financial institutions, and huge swings in account balances. A fourth control is to communicate to other banks the identities of depositors with suspicious activity patterns. If the same depositor appears on the suspicion lists of several banks, an investigation is urgently needed.

Laundering

Laundering is a set of practices intended to obscure the true sources of funds. Many crimes, computer dependent and otherwise, generate profits that call for some sort of cover story. This is the case, for example, when a lapper steals a sum of money too large to be explained by his or her known and legitimate means of support. These funds may be cash, negotiable securities, or checks. If the funds are in the form of checks made out to other parties, the criminal must somehow alter them so they can be cashed or deposited. This is risky but, all too unfortunately, can often be done successfully. Negotiable securities may only require filling in the transfer information. These and other means of laundering money may be handled by underworld elements, who take a cut of the funds as their "compensation."

One means of laundering is to deposit the money in several financial institutions successively, creating a trail that can be followed only with difficulty and persistence. Another is to pay legitimate but inflated "fees" or "investments" to others, who rebate some of the money back to the criminal. Here is an illustration showing how each of these means could be used to launder $10,000 in cash.

Because a cash deposit so large must be reported to the banking authorities, it must be laundered in small quantities. It could be converted to a number of odd-amount money orders, which could then be deposited in several bank accounts and either used individually or consolidated. The money could be withdrawn and redeposited a number of times, or even sent to banks in foreign countries. If the thief uses several identities in these transactions, only a very persistent investigator could link the trail to the thief. This type of laundering precludes reporting the laundered funds as income and leaves the thief open to an IRS investigation and penalties for not paying taxes, in addition to the penalties for originally stealing the money.

In the second type of laundering, the thief wants to avoid trouble with the IRS by showing the funds as legitimate income. To do so usually requires collaboration with another party. For example, suppose the thief hands over the $10,000 to Blackheart, who owns a restaurant and a stationery store. Blackheart then employs the thief as a "consultant" and pays him a fee of $6,000. Blackheart retains the remainder of the money as a fee for the laundering. Blackheart may report the $10,000 as cash sales in his businesses. He furnishes a 1099 form to the thief to show the IRS. Of course, both the thief and Blackheart can be prosecuted if and when the original theft is discovered.

Laundering may be facilitated by computers—either those at financial institutions performing legitimate functions that inadvertently help the launderer, or those used by laundering participants—like Blackheart, for instance—to deliberately obscure the sources of funds.

Causes of Computer Crime

Two main factors that contribute to computer crime are the presence of individuals who perceive reasons—real or otherwise—to deliberately and intentionally plan and commit crimes and management incompetence and ignorance of the controls needed to prevent crime, which lulls managers into maintaining inadequate system controls.

Deliberate Intent

Intentional crimes may be committed by anyone with the requisite technical knowledge—typically by current or former accounting, data processing, programming, or operating personnel. Numerous reasons exist for employees to create and take advantage of opportunities to serve their own personal interests rather than those of the organization. If senior officials in a firm have little or no contact with other employees, the employees may feel that their contributions have not been noticed or appreciated. They may feel that they have complied with the organization's expectations, but that it has not met their expectations. For example, employees may feel slighted if their best efforts to promote the organization are not compensated fairly or rewarded by bonuses or promotion.

If salaries and working conditions deteriorate rapidly, relative to the past or to those in comparable organizations, some employees may feel the company "owes" them and may seek to extract compensation or even revenge. For example, between Thanksgiving and Christmas suppose that one year at Bateman Airlines, all employees below the level of assistant manager were assigned a 20-percent salary rollback. Over the next three months, employee absenteeism, turnover, tardiness, and sickness increased. In addition, someone awarded twenty-four coworkers bonuses of up to $2,500 which, according to the auditor's report, were not approved. One of the twenty-four, an accounting employee with technical-support responsibilities, resigned shortly after the report appeared and may have been responsible for the bonuses; no conclusive evidence was ever found.

Managerial Ignorance

Managerial ignorance of and indifference toward computers may encourage employees to feel that their own lack of computer expertise is excusable. Management fosters such an attitude when it fails to schedule proper training, hire qualified computer personnel, or enforce reasonable controls. Such failures undermine management's control and reinforce employee indifference. Even if no actual ill will exists, an organization whose value system does not reward computer competence or excellence will, sooner or later, experience lapses that seriously hurt the organization. Such a value system does little to discourage a criminal opportunist from seizing an opportunity to commit a major crime.

Inadequate Controls

If the control system deteriorates, criminal opportunists may take advantage of the lack of adequate deterrents in the system. For example, if management ignores the recommendations of a review of its controls, its laxity may prompt individuals to plan and carry out crimes. Or the organization may have changed significantly since the last review, leaving clear-cut gaps in system controls. For example, an organization may acquire the ability to prepare checks by computer, and leave the blank check stock where anyone can take it. Another example is a new computer system that the data processing director doesn't understand, leaving employees well aware of how loosely they are being supervised. Even if controls are good, a determined and skilled person may be able to defeat them.

Causes of Carelessness and Incompetence

Crime is not the only cause of unnecessary financial losses involving computers. Business losses owing to computer carelessness and incompetence may exceed losses resulting from computer crime. Table 13.1 lists the types of losses that can result from carelessness and incompetence. Here are examples of each type:

- *Lost discounts on quantity purchases*
  Example: An inexperienced manager was assigned to supervise development of a purchasing application. The application failed to provide for recording available quantity discounts. As a result, invoices from vendors were paid on a regular schedule—without regard to discounts—and the organization missed thousands of dollars' worth of such discounts annually.

- *Unsupervised and unqualified programmers*
  Example: Two programmers were hired to program a certain type of computer on a rush basis. No one verified the programmers' qualifications. One of them was unqualified. Because the rush project was better funded than supervised, six months passed without either progress or personnel reassignment. Large losses ensued.

- *Careless program preparation and testing*
  Example: A competent personnel executive with a personal computer, a spreadsheet/data base software package, and more enthusiasm than experience attempted to create on his own a spreadsheet for evaluating middle-management performance. Nearly a dozen logical errors, individually minor, made for final performance scores that meant virtually the opposite of what the executive intended. All the top managers used this application to evaluate about a hundred supervisors, eleven of whom quit after hearing their evaluations. After the errors had been found and corrected, a curious controller reevaluated the scores. The eleven who quit would all have scored in the top twenty!

- *Inattention to data file back-up*
  Example: A small business, using a personal computer satisfactorily to maintain its accounts receivable, added its first hard disk to the system. Although the computer operator knew that back-up on floppies was important, this was not done after the first few weeks of operation. Unfortunately, a few months later the disk suffered a catastrophic failure and nine weeks of accounts receivable activity was lost. The company estimated its losses in unbillable accounts at about $34,000.

Table 13.1   **Losses from Computer Carelessness and Incompetence**
This table shows just four of the many ways an organization can suffer from
inadequate computer competence.

Type of Loss	Effect of the Organization
Lost discounts on quantity purchases	Steady loss owing to higher costs of materials and supplies
Unsupervised and unqualified programmers	Slower and costlier production of programs
Careless program preparation	Programs that are larger, slower, and more abundantly "bugged" than necessary
Inattention to data file back-up	Annoying and excessively large losses of data to relatively trivial causes

Lack of control may be the largest single cause of carelessness and incompetence. For example, the procedural elements necessary to carry out an important control objective, such as making certain that data processing personnel have the skills and training required to operate the system, may be lacking. In this instance, the control objective would be concisely stated in the form of job descriptions for each position in data processing. The preventive elements would include the qualifications and performance expected of each person who fills such a position and hiring procedures and training programs to produce this performance. The feedback element would be training and job-performance evaluations. The comparison and follow-up element would compare expected and actual performance and follow up with responses ranging from employee counseling, additional training, and promotion to reprimand and dismissal.

A well-meaning management may leave employees to develop skills on the job, without formal supervision. The employees may indeed learn these skills, but they may do so on a trial-and-error basis in which the trials are lengthy and the errors costly. The employees may try to cover up their errors. High turnover, lack of dedication, and lack of respect for management are among the possible effects of managerial neglect of employees who are under pressure—especially if performance reviews are irregular and concrete rewards are lacking or scarce.

Lack of control may also result from managerial insensitivity to carelessness and incompetence. Or it may arise from managerial emphasis on information from external and informal sources, in contrast to which the computerized accounting system lacks attention and appears to have low status.

Although the causes of crime, carelessness, and incompetence are not identical, all the losses they cause may be contained using the same strategy, namely, to purge away the control weaknesses that make computer crime, incompetence, and carelessness possible.

Data Processing Strategies to Control Losses

The general strategy to control losses from crime, incompetence, and carelessness is to use the normally applicable controls to find and eliminate the weaknesses that make them possible. This strategy has three elements:

- *Control objectives,* which are put in writing and designed to ensure that data and information processing supports accurate, reliable, authorized, and accountable asset use and custody

- *Control procedures,* also written, which are known and understood by employees and fully implemented, and which include insurance against risks where cost-effective control procedures don't exist

- *Control review,* on a regular basis, of both objectives and procedures to ensure that they continue to be adequate and operational

Some controls aim to discourage the temptation to break rules or commit crimes. Someone who is prone to commit crimes like fraud, embezzlement, or vandalism may choose not to do so if visible and effective barriers promise to make such actions difficult or readily apparent to supervisors. Any review of controls whose scope includes preventing computer crime should make certain that the controls described in this section either exist or aren't needed.

The same controls will limit losses owing to carelessness and incompetence. The real difference between these phenomena and crime is not in the outcome but in the sphere of motive and personal gain. In terms of the losses they produce, the three are virtually alike. A paycheck for an unauthorized employee generates the same loss to the company whether the employee is listed by design or by accident. Put another way, comparison of the payroll with the properly maintained master list of current employees will pinpoint both the terminated employee still mistakenly listed on the payroll and a deliberately added nonexistent person.

Note that the first three of the following controls restrict physical and/or logical access to computer files, hardware, and software, while the last three limit the discretion of personnel and the extent of possible loss.

Physical and Logical Access Security

It is extremely important to establish access security for an information system, to limit opportunities to see, use, or abuse computers, programs, and records. **Physical access security** includes measures to make a data processing site less subject to disruption due to natural disasters or mechanical failure (such as air conditioning or power failure), or to unauthorized intrusion. Even when physical security exists, management must also provide **logical access security**—assurance that electronic access to data and software will be for authorized purposes only.

Physical Access Security.   The computer facility is situated in its own dedicated space, with separate spaces for records storage, the CPU, data processing specialists, and users. The CPU area or room is protected from microwaves with strong, fire-resistant walls that contain little glass or wood. The area is air conditioned and not subject to flooding. The protected power supply has remote surveillance and alarms, and trained security personnel are either present or on call. In addition, personnel access is limited by monitoring all entrances and requiring identification to enter the facility. It is important to schedule and record all access to any part of the system—equipment, data, programs, personnel on duty.

Logical Access Security.   Logical access security helps to assure that data may be created, deleted, or altered only in authorized fashion. To protect data files, they are named, dated, catalogued, inventoried, and copied. Copies are stored in a completely secure remote location. Extensive editing is performed at data entry to limit errors.

Controls should limit use of programs and files to people with a verifiable need. The controls should require specific authorization for each type of entry, file, and execution of responsibility. They should limit opportunities to learn how the system operates by restricting access to program documentation, require all users to give passwords for remote access, and rule out access by people whose need has expired. Organizations should renew authorizations and change passwords frequently and equip computers so that they accept a password, disconnect, look up the password internally, and—if the password is valid—reconnect with a location or phone number authorized for that password. Figure 13.1 is a password application form used to apply for authorization to use the computer. Someone in data processing should randomly monitor and log data communications and computer use to see which terminals and account numbers are in use and which programs they are using. Someone should then confirm the resulting log with the individuals whose account numbers reflect recent activity. *Encryption*—coding data to make it unintelligible—should be considered if the information is sensitive enough to warrant it. Only three copies of a program should exist: the one in use, the one in secure back-up storage, and one for the system developers to work with. If an unauthorized program or file appears, the system managers should find and correct the cause of its appearance.

Human-Resources Management

Information management employees should have the appropriate qualifications to carry out their responsibilities, including the maturity to accept ethical obligations. They should be assigned clear-cut and distinct responsibilities. They should be trained and properly supervised, and their competence should be periodically checked. Employees should not swap jobs or trade duties except in accordance with organizational procedures.

Figure 13.1   Password Application Form
A computer-use application like the one below is used to keep records of persons
with computer access and limit access to persons with a legitimate need for it.

Marlin Title & Guaranty Company   form revised 9-1-86
              Computer-Use Application   NO. 00987345

This part for computer center use only: Account number _____

Date: _____ Expires: _____   │ Password _____

Authorized by _____   Title _____

Name: _____   Phone: _____

Office: _____   Department: _____

Computer ID: _____   Location: _____

Files: (1) _____   (2) _____   (3) _____

Number of disk sectors requested: _____   Workspace size: _____

Please explain why you are requesting to use the computer:

Account for CPU time: ____-____-_____   Account for supplies: ____-____-_____

Supervisor approval: _____   Phone _____   Date _____

When management has found and trained suitable employees, it
should provide a suitable work environment and reasonable compensation
and working conditions. Employee morale should be important to management, and employees should know it is.

Before making assignments to highly sensitive positions, high-risk
employers may wish to review especially closely those candidates with
computer-crime-prone profiles. This profile is based on the observation
that a high proportion of persons found to be involved in computer crimes
are male, young, white, well educated, intelligent, self-confident, and self-
motivated. Its value when used alone is open to question, however. For
one thing, it also describes many promising managers; and the over-
whelming majority of persons it describes will never commit a computer
crime. Therefore, additional investigation—a search for a possible criminal
record, for example—should be conducted on persons fitting the profile.
The profile reduces the number of candidates for which such costly investigation must be conducted.

Audit

Regular periodic review of computer-related control objectives, procedures, and compliance is performed by both internal and external audit. Data and program integrity are verified physically. Particular emphasis is placed on who authorizes access and programming, whether authorization has been granted properly, and whether unauthorized access has occurred or may occur. If management has recently approved changes in procedures or security, the auditors should verify that the changes were implemented as anticipated. A complete financial or operational audit would also review efficiency, compliance with accounting principles, and consistency. These audit objectives are aimed only at protecting against crime, incompetence, and carelessness and do not include objectives aimed at promoting accurate processing or managerial efficiency, for example.

Insurance

When loss-prevention efforts are not cost-effective, business insurance is the best protection against large but unlikely or infrequent losses. Insurance is not available as a protection against ordinary operating weaknesses for which controls are a cost-effective remedy. But, it can protect against physical damage to the computer by terrorists, vandals, fire, or natural disaster; theft of programs or embezzlement or fraud by employees with access to the computer; and loss of income from interruptions in business while deprived of a computer or data. An example of the latter is a consumer credit-information service that loses the use of its computerized files and is therefore unable to respond to credit inquiries.

The amount of coverage purchased and size of the deductible depend on what premium managers are comfortable with and on the amount of loss from any one crime that the business could withstand.

Extra Measures

Consultants often recommend that controls for existing computer systems be strengthened. They also urge designing controls into a new system that make crime prevention part of its automatic functioning. Organizations that are exceptionally sensitive to computer crime may well go beyond the measures just described. Such firms may hire consultant specialists to review and test security measures against computer crime. These specialists sometimes test security by devising schemes to defeat it. Two examples follow:

1. The computer-security consultant hired by a mailing-list marketing firm acquired a printed copy of a valuable mailing list. He was able to do so because several of the firm's managers used the computer from home terminals; the firm had a password access-protection system, but the

passwords were common knowledge among all employees. While waiting to see the manager, the consultant asked a secretary what the manager's password was. The secretary, happy to be helpful, told him. The consultant used the password from his own remote office to extract the mailing list, which he showed to management as evidence of the risk. This case resembles most illegal access to computers in that the enabling information was provided voluntarily, not extracted by cleverly defeating security and encryption schemes.

2. A consultant who was testing physical security walked unchallenged into a room filled with disk and tape magnetic media. He waved a small briefcase around as if it were a tennis racket for the better part of 4 minutes before he was asked to explain himself. He refused to give identification and volunteered to leave the room—saying he was "lost." Had his briefcase contained a powerful, portable magnet, his antics would have made much of the stored data useless. No one attempted to detain him or call a security officer. A day or two later, the employees who had encountered him barely recalled the incident! On his way out, the consultant pocketed loose copies of recent sales reports about to be distributed to top executives—evidence of yet another lapse.

Economics and Deterrence of Computer Crime

A computer criminal must have both **opportunity**—a chance to commit a crime—and **motive**—an objective or incentive to do so. The controls described in the preceding section are designed to restrict opportunities for criminal activities. Now, let us turn our attention to the other aspect of the crime—the motive.

Some motives are very difficult to defend against. Consider, for example, an anarchist's motive of sabotage, or a teen-age computer hacker's desire to break a bank code for the fun of it. A common motive is financial need accompanied by a sense of having a "right" to gratify that need without regard to the rules accepted by the rest of society. Other rationalizations are frustration, desire for recognition, revenge, or even a Robin Hood complex. Since financial need or greed is probably the most common motive, let us approach computer crime deterrence with the goal of denying the criminal opportunities to satisfy avarice.

Criminal Gain and the Payoff Threshold

It is difficult to anticipate how a potential wrongdoer would analyze any particular situation. However, if a "logical" criminal perceives the potential gain as highly attractive compared with the risk of failing or being caught, there is no deterrence. Thus, system developers consider it important to create risks that appear, to a rational person, to outweigh any potential gain from tampering with the system. Another way to say this is that the potential gain must be less than the criminal's payoff threshold—the minimum payoff expected value that would make the criminal consider committing a computer crime.

To illustrate, we'll use an expected-value model of the criminal's alternatives. Suppose that Robert, the would-be criminal, is willing to consider only those criminal acts that offer an actual payoff of over $20,000 and for which the probability of being apprehended is less than 5 percent. Robert's payoff threshold may be a function of his annual salary. Robert rejects any criminal acts whose payoff is smaller or risk greater. For Robert to remain a "safe" employee, his employer needs only to make certain (cost-effectively) that at least one of these conditions is lacking. Reality is seldom so simple.

To make the situation slightly more complex, let us say Robert is willing to pursue a payoff with an expected value in excess of his payoff threshold of $20,000. The simple decision model in Table 13.2 depicts Robert's thinking about committing a crime, in a company with poor controls, with three possible outcomes. The probability figures are merely hypothetical and ignore the effect of taxes.

Table 13.2   Computer Crime Decision Model (Firm with Poor Controls)
This table organizes the criminal's decision in the format of a statistical decision model. Note the low probability the criminal perceives of being caught; this is all too typical and realistic.

	Possible Outcomes		
	Crime Succeeds but Robert Caught	*Crime Succeeds and Robert Escapes*	*Crime Fails and Robert Escapes*
Probability of outcomes: (total = 1.0)	p(caught) 0.05	p(success) 0.25	p(failure) 0.70
Robert's options:			
Commit crime	Lost income of −$25,000, disgrace, criminal conviction	Gratification, +$100,000, self-esteem and "accomplishment"	Wasted effort, $0, and wasted time
Don't commit crime	nothing $0	nothing $0	nothing $0

The expected value to Robert of committing the crime is

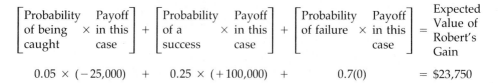

$$\begin{bmatrix} \text{Probability} & \text{Payoff} \\ \text{of being} & \times \text{ in this} \\ \text{caught} & \text{case} \end{bmatrix} + \begin{bmatrix} \text{Probability} & \text{Payoff} \\ \text{of a} & \times \text{ in this} \\ \text{success} & \text{case} \end{bmatrix} + \begin{bmatrix} \text{Probability} & \text{Payoff} \\ \text{of failure} & \times \text{ in this} \\ & \text{case} \end{bmatrix} = \begin{matrix} \text{Expected} \\ \text{Value of} \\ \text{Robert's} \\ \text{Gain} \end{matrix}$$

$$0.05 \times (-25,000) \quad + \quad 0.25 \times (+100,000) \quad + \quad 0.7(0) \quad = \$23,750$$

If Robert's payoff threshold is $20,000, this formula suggests that the crime in question would be attractive to Robert, and his employer is at risk. Since the crime is attractive to Robert, sooner or later he is likely to commit it.

Few criminals would apply this formula literally, but some might do a more informal and roughly equivalent calculation.

Loss to the Employer

Although there is a 70-percent chance the crime will be unsuccessful, there is a 30-percent chance that, *whether or not Robert is caught*, the crime will succeed and the employer will lose $100,000. Using the above probabilities, the employer's expected loss is calculated as

$$\begin{bmatrix} \text{Probability of a} \\ \text{successful crime} \\ \text{by Robert} \end{bmatrix} \times \begin{bmatrix} \text{Loss if} \\ \text{crime} \\ \text{succeeds} \end{bmatrix} = \text{Value of employer's expected loss}$$

$$(0.05 + 0.25) \quad \times \quad -\$100,000 = -\$30,000$$

The prevention of the crime depends on creating a deterrent—a control, barrier, or condition that tends to make commission of a crime more difficult or less attractive. The employer can, at some expense, increase the risk Robert perceives, or reduce the potential payoff, by analyzing the existing controls, identifying their weaknesses, and correcting them. These controls could be designed to reduce the likelihood that the crime will be successful, increase the penalty if Robert is caught, or decrease the employer's maximum loss. If the analysis and new controls cost less than the probable loss, the employer is likely to implement them. Suppose the employer chooses to reduce the maximum loss to $50,000. The expected value to Robert of committing the crime has changed to

$$\begin{bmatrix} \text{Probability} & \text{Payoff} \\ \text{of being} & \times \text{ in this} \\ \text{caught} & \text{case} \end{bmatrix} + \begin{bmatrix} \text{Probability} & \text{Payoff} \\ \text{of a} & \times \text{ in this} \\ \text{success} & \text{case} \end{bmatrix} + \begin{bmatrix} \text{Probability} & \text{Payoff} \\ \text{of failure} & \times \text{ in this} \\ & \text{case} \end{bmatrix} = \begin{matrix} \text{Expected} \\ \text{Value} \end{matrix}$$

$$0.05 \times (-25,000) \quad + \quad 0.25 \times (+50,000) \quad + \quad 0.70 \times (0) \quad = +\$11,250$$

Although the expected value of the crime is still positive, it is less than Robert's payoff threshold to make the crime worth committing. Robert would probably pass this one up and keep looking. Thus the employer has obtained protection from an original expected loss of $30,000; the difference between this amount and the amount spent on controls is savings to the employer. For example, if the controls analysis and implementation cost $10,000, the expected savings are $30,000 − $10,000 = $20,000.

While criminals may not think solely in terms of expected value, the controls and preventive measures the prospective criminal perceives must have adequate deterrent effect. The point is that the crime should not look attractive. The method of analysis outlined is one means of identifying and evaluating potential weaknesses in the organization.

Deterrent Strategies

Once weaknesses are identified, the analyst should consider four strategies for giving controls an economic-deterrent effect:

- *Deterrent strategy 1* is to increase the apparent or actual probability of getting caught or failing in the commission of a crime. Two representative methods to implement this strategy are surprise counts and verifications and rotation of responsibilities. For example, in Table 13.2 the probability of being caught was only 0.05. If the probability were 0.95, the criminal would probably not commit the crime.

- *Deterrent strategy 2* is to increase the penalty for committing a crime. A well-publicized company policy of vigorously prosecuting all detected crimes would increase the expected penalty. Overt implementation of this policy and employee awareness of it would further reinforce the expectation of penalties. If Robert's employer used this strategy, Robert might perceive the cost of being caught as higher than his threshold amount.

- *Deterrent strategy 3* is to reduce the amount of gain a criminal would expect if the crime were successful. Two typical means of implementing this strategy are to make more frequent deposits and to reduce the amount of cash or other resources employees may handle without the cooperation and authorization of others.

- *Deterrent strategy 4* is to increase the difficulty of committing a crime. The controls that can be implemented to do so tend to be specific to particular crimes and settings. For example, if Robert were thinking of modifying a computer program to deposit funds in his own account, he would find this more difficult to accomplish if he only had access to machine language versions of that program.

SLIP IN DUMMY TRANSACTIONS - LOOKING FOR IT TO BE HANDLED UNUSUALLY

These four strategies are a useful frame of reference in the control-design process. Within this framework, a thorough review of policies and procedures will result in an adequate combination of controls and insurance.

Files that contain descriptions of volatile assets and are accessible from remote locations by many individuals are a temptation to computer criminals. Potential deterrents applicable to file protection include making frequent copies of files and retaining them in a location remote from the data processing center. The passwords required to enter these files should be changed often. Additions to the list of people with passwords should be reviewed carefully. Physical inventory counts should occasionally be performed by surprise. Sequentially numbered purchase orders should be accounted for regularly. Every bank account statement should be reconciled with the cash control account when received.

Figure 13.2   Controlling Program Changes
This serially prenumbered form will provide a record of program changes. It also gives management a way of reviewing and evaluating proposed changes; some will probably be rejected.

Lake Victor Collections, Inc.   no.   00128742
AUTHORIZATION OF PROGRAM CHANGE

NAME OF PROGRAM _____ NUMBER _____
Description of proposed change (attach all necessary documents)
(Approved) (Not approved) by _____ Date _____

Programmer assigned: Application supervisor
                            _____ Date _____
                            Data processing director

SCHEDULE:

Step	Proposed date	Actual date	Checked by	Checked by
Programming	_____	_____	_____	_____
Segment test	_____	_____	_____	_____
Integrated test	_____	_____	_____	_____
Conversion	_____	_____	_____	_____
30-day review	_____	_____	_____	_____
180-day review	_____	_____	_____	_____

Programs and files developed by the organization's own employees are another tempting target. The deterrents to criminal use include maintaining duplicate master copies of programs in secure locations. The master and operating copies of each program and file should be compared often and on a surprise basis. Programmer access to the computer should be restricted to scheduled use by authorized programmers. Documented authorization should be required for any changes made in programs. Figure 13.2 shows a form for recording and controlling the authorization, approval, and implementation of a change in a computer program.

Another volatile area consists of situations in which the organization must trust employees not to use or transfer knowledge that would enable them to commit or abet computer crime. Some effective deterrents to such crimes include bonding employees who handle assets that can be misappropriated or stolen, separating duties to ensure independent feedback and preventive control elements, and rotating responsibilities at frequent intervals. (Rotation is a good preventive control element because it deprives would-be criminals of the extended time they typically need to plan the complex operations that lead to major losses.)

Summary

Computer crime, incompetence, and carelessness all represent challenges to an organization's financial and processing controls. They can deprive an organization of its computer and its records or of their exclusive use and of the confidentiality of its information. While computer crime is newsworthy, losses from incompetence and carelessness may be more pervasive and extensive. Controls that are effective against all three include physical and electronic security, data security, access security, human-resources management, audits, insurance, and use of qualified consultants. Where crime is concerned, all of these controls share the purpose of deterring crime physically and economically by limiting opportunities and making detection more likely. Other deterrent controls are increasing the penalty if detected, reducing the reward incentive, and making the crime more difficult.

Key Terms

computer crime	logical access security	Trojan Horse technique
hearsay evidence	motive	virus
kiting	opportunity	worm code
lapping	physical access security	
laundering	rounding	

Review Questions

1. As computers have proliferated, crimes involving them have also increased. Name two control-related conditions that contribute to the rise in computer crime.

2. Give a working definition of computer crime that differentiates it from other kinds of theft, fraud, or vandalism.

3. Give at least two reasons why it is difficult to prosecute a computer crime.

4. The text describes two contributing "causes" of computer crime. What are they?

5. Often, management's own behavior and policies foster negative attitudes in employees. What specific failures of management may convince employees that their own lack of expertise is inconsequential? For each failure, what is the remedy?

6. What are the three elements of a successful data-processing strategy to combat crime, incompetence, and carelessness? Do these elements fit into a set of internal controls? What personality tendencies are controls intended to discourage? How do they do so?

7. Name and discuss at least three types of controls aimed at computer crime. Describe the objective, preventive, feedback, and follow-up elements of one of them.

8. What four deterrent strategies can an organization employ to reduce the likelihood of crime by "rational" criminals? In your answer, use the term *payoff threshold* and explain its meaning.

Discussion Questions

9. Helen Abstract works in the legal-abstract office of the administration department at Marlin Title & Guarantee Company. She will be selecting and down-loading case precedents from a national computerized legal network. This network also offers computer shopping, stock market and commodities investments, and much other useful information on line. Abstract will use the accounting department's Tandy 4000 personal computer with a modem and a direct phone line. She will require 1M byte of disk space; each disk sector holds 4K bytes. Her CPU time charges will be allocated to account 0193284756. Her supervisor, L. D. Praha, approved her request on November 1, 19XX. Using this information, complete as much as you can of the password application form shown in Figure 13.1. Explain why some parts of the form cannot be completed. Do the other services available on the network present any crime opportunities? If so, name at least one.

10. The text describes several cases of computer crime. If you are familiar with a computer-related crime, describe it. If not, select one of the examples from the chapter. Name control objectives and procedures that you believe would have prevented the incident or made it more difficult to commit.

11. Define *hearsay evidence*. Is it possible to conduct essential managerial business without reliance on hearsay? If not, why is hearsay a weak form of evidence in a criminal proceeding? Why is hearsay often the only evidence that a computer crime was committed?

12. How do carelessness and incompetence resemble crime? How do they differ? Why do controls that deter crime also deter carelessness and incompetence?

13. Does insurance prevent crime? What economic purpose does insurance serve? Would insurance covering the replacement value of the computer and its programs be sufficient for most businesses?

14. Six months ago, Lockhart Company hired a new controller. The company is not presently profitable, and to save on costs the new controller has suggested the following actions. Discuss the control significance of each proposal, noting the weakness each proposal would create.
    (a) Discontinue off-site storage of duplicate copies of computerized accounting journals and ledgers.
    (b) Discontinue bonding employees in the treasurer's department.
    (c) Terminate the programmer and let the computer operator, who has considerable programming skill, develop new computer applications and improve existing ones.
    (d) Terminate the office messenger and allow managers to pick up their own periodic accounting reports.

15. At McNeil Corporation, a marketing manager wandered into the data processing department at 7:30 P.M. one day in search of some old floppy disks for his children to use to save games and files from a public-access computer network. Since no one was around, he simply picked up the most beat-up disks in sight; they turned out to be the primary copy of unposted accounts receivable debits. To prevent this from happening again, McNeil hired a consultant who recommended the following:

    (a) An unarmed 24-hour guard at the doorway to the data processing department.
    (b) Bonding of all data processing employees.
    (c) Firing of the data processing assistant, who had gone home without placing the floppy disks in the lockable safe provided for that purpose.
    (d) A separate library for all programs and tapes, with a log book for entering all uses of materials.

(e) Business-interruption insurance for loss of records, equal to one week's average net sales.

(f) Preparation of a run schedule, and training of data processing personnel in how to follow it.

(g) Surprise inspections to determine whether data processing's operations conform to the established rules and procedures.

Required:

Explain whether each of these recommendations is reasonable or unreasonable, and why.

16. At a major university's computer center a few years ago, a night attendant got chilly and turned up the thermostat. When alarms began to sound, warning of potentially damaging heat build-up, the night attendant thought they were malfunctioning and turned them off. The computer was severely damaged. Describe at least two controls that would have prevented this disaster.

17. Cypress Creek County contracted with Fastcomp to install in the courthouse a computer system for keeping track of state sales taxes due and remitted from the state treasurer. By state law, these remittances were supposed to be 20 percent of all state sales tax revenues collected within the county limits. The county used its computer to peruse state records and compute an independent estimate of the remittance it would receive from the state. Because these estimates seemed to be consistently in excess of the amounts actually received, the county hired Fastcomp to study the situation. Fastcomp's compensation was 30 percent of all additional revenues the firm could help the county collect from the state. Fastcomp's study found that many sales recorded by the state as taking place in other counties actually occurred in Cypress Creek County. A Fastcomp staff person was constantly at a terminal in the courthouse identifying these misclassified transactions.

Required:

Propose controls that would make it difficult for Fastcomp to alter state records in favor of the county purely to increase its own billable compensation.

Problems

18. You have been hired as a security consultant to evaluate Smith Company's computer installation. You notice the following:

(a) Employees must sign in and out of the computer facility in front of a receptionist.

(b) All files are copied at the end of the day, and the copies are locked in a large safe.

(c) Disk drives have been pushed together to serve as a table at which employees eat lunch.
(d) Whenever they wish, system programmers store and test new programs at the main console.
(e) The temperature in the computer room is 65 degrees.
(f) A number of master copies of programs are missing.
(g) Reports are piled on a table next to the console for managers to pick up.

Required:

Indicate which of these conditions represent control lapses conducive to crime or carelessness, and suggest how they could be corrected.

19. Austin Chalk Sands Company is an oil-exploration firm. Its field agents can gain access to data in the company computer from any location simply by dialing a phone number.

Required:

Identify the major weakness of this situation and suggest three examples of control procedures the company could adopt to eliminate this weakness. Describe all four elements of each control.

20. Douglass Company is considering acquiring a new payroll application software program. It could ask its own skilled programmer to write this program, or it could purchase a program available from Mountain Home Corporation.

Required:

Describe a crime that could occur if the firm develops its own payroll software. Specify at least two controls that would tend to deter this crime, and explain *how* they would do so. Give all four elements of each control.

21. Clyde Pocket is a ticket agent at a movie theater. The theater's ticket office has a computer that simultaneously prints an admission ticket and records that an admission has been sold. Every night after closing, the number of tickets issued is compared with the amount of cash collected (at $5 per ticket) and the number of ticket stubs collected by the usher. Pocket is determined to steal some cash but until now has been frustrated by the controls described. Now, however, he believes he has a workable plan. He will tell the usher that because the computer is acting up, it will not print tickets; he will ask the usher to save tickets from the previous performance so they can be reused. Of course, Pocket will take some of the admission money, not record the sale on the computer, hand the customer a "used" ticket, and wave him on to the usher.

Required:

Explain why Pocket's plan probably won't work.

22. Polly Sorbate, security manager for Disk Chemicals, has developed a computer-criminal profile. According to this profile, employees at Disk Chemical would be inclined to disregard existing controls whenever they perceived that the expected value of doing so was $30,000 or more. Sorbate has identified three situations that appear to pose some risk. She has estimated the probability of each possible outcome, and the actual payoff to the employee if that outcome were to occur. She has also identified the controls to eliminate each risk, and estimated the cost of installing the controls, should it appear to be economically justifiable. This information appears below:

	Crime Succeeds but Criminal Caught	Crime Succeeds and Criminal Escapes	Crime Fails and Criminal Escapes
Case A			
Probability	0.50	0.30	0.20
Loss to Disk	–$200,000	–$200,000	$ 0
Payoff to criminal	–$25,000	$200,000	$ 0
Control cost: $40,000			
Case B			
Probability	0.30	0.40	0.30
Loss to Disk	–$100,000	–$100,000	$ 0
Payoff to criminal	–$25,000	$100,000	$ 0
Control cost: $40,000			
Case C			
Probability	0.10	0.80	0.10
Loss to Disk	–$50,000	–$50,000	$ 0
Payoff to criminal	–$25,000	$40,000	$ 0
Control cost: $40,000			

Required:

Analyze each case and explain why Disk Chemicals should or should not implement the corresponding controls.

23. Ron Ray works at a lumberyard. When a contractor places an order, it is entered into a computer terminal by a clerk. The clerk prints a copy of the order on a printer next to the terminal. This copy is the yard boss' authorization to load the order into the contractor's truck. The clerk then saves the order information as a computer record, which is later used to generate an invoice to the contractor. When the contractor's truck leaves the yard, a gate attendant verifies that its contents match the items on the printed order copy.

Ron Ray's brother is in the contracting business and buys lumber at this yard almost every week. Last week, Ron's brother came in and ordered materials in the usual way. After the order was printed but before the record was made, Ron Ray paged the clerk to answer an urgent phone call. When the clerk left the terminal, Ron deleted five items his brother had ordered, with total value of $2,500, and saved the record. The clerk never noticed that the items were missing. At the gate, the contents of the brother's truck exactly matched the sales order copy. The lumber company's invoice did not list the items Ron had deleted. The brothers enjoyed reliving this incident and agreed to repeat it regularly once a month.

Required:

Analyze this situation carefully; then propose a control that would prevent this type of computer crime.

24. Ace Insurance Agency maintains offices in six major cities. The company has a large computer it uses to store information about policyholders, including names, addresses, and dates their policies come up for renewal. Information in this file can be displayed or printed. All six offices have terminals and modems and can dial in to the computer any time they need information about a customer or a policy. When an agent dials a telephone number at the home office, the main computer's modem answers the call and requests the agent's password. If the agent does not give the correct password in three tries, the computer hangs up.

Todd Lee was an agent for the St. Louis office of Ace Insurance, until he was dismissed for a variety of causes. Since his dismissal, the percentage of Ace's Denver policyholders who renewed their policies has dropped significantly. Meanwhile, the insurance office Lee opened in Denver has prospered. At the time he left Ace, Lee did not know any of the firm's Denver policyholders.

Required:

Explain in detail what is probably happening and what Ace can do to put a stop to it and prevent it from recurring.

25. At Equity Funding, management compiled a list of customers who were supposed to own term life insurance policies. In fact, about 80 percent of the names on the list were fictitious. Each fictitious name was identified as such by a secret code. Because of the cash flow associated with life insurance policies, these fictitious policies represented a substantial apparent asset for the company, which was likely to be examined and confirmed by the independent auditors. When the auditors signaled their intention to do so, Equity's managers volunteered to select a sample of policyholders, according to the auditors' specifications, for direct confirmation. The auditors accepted this offer. Equity's managers then constructed a printout of real policyholders, which they presented to the auditors.

Required:

Explain how the auditors should have proceeded, in order to detect the presence of fictitious policyholders.

26. Robert Cube, a programmer, has written an accounts receivable application program for his employer. His program includes a segment that counts the number of times the program is run; when the 500th run occurs, the program will delete every accounts receivable account, including the name and address of the customer and the amount of the outstanding balance. The code for this segment is very compact and is tucked away in an obscure part of the program. Cube considers his act is justified for obscure personal reasons and is very pleased with himself. The program is running today for the 420th time.

Required:

(a) What controls, if they exist, would render this vandalous act virtually ineffective when it does occur?

(b) Can you think of a control that might prevent Mr. Cube's software time bomb from ever exploding? (This is a difficult question.)

27. A bank trust fund manager who is unsatisfied with her salary knows the trust portfolio includes state bonds with a face value of $1 million and a rate of return of 6 percent. She alters computer records to show that these bonds were sold under a six-month repurchase agreement to EST Securities, and that EST will retain and invest the cash proceeds of the sale. She then sells them privately to investors for $500,000. Part of this sum supplements her salary; the rest is used to make regular investment-income "payments" to the bank from EST Securities.

Required:

(a) Assuming that no one in the bank becomes aware of the fraud, what is the trust fund manager likely to do in six months when the nonexistent repurchase agreement expires?

(b) What should the bank be doing to prevent or deter this sort of fraud? Name at least two controls.

28. Anthony Flight, a programmer for Mighty Financial Services, has been working on the coding of a new cash disbursements application being written in COBOL for a GBM System 66. The module he is writing will print a check to the party named in a computer record in the approved-voucher file. When the program module is complete, it is tested by the data processing director and found satisfactory. The module is compiled, and the machine language version of the program placed on disk to await merging with other modules still under preparation.

Two days later, Flight, who can program in System 66 machine language, recovers the segment, places eleven lines of machine language code in the middle of it, and saves it back on an on-line disk under the same name. The eleven lines of code instruct the computer to look for a certain small file on another disk named SCRATCHDT. If the file does not exist, the module will resume. If it does exist, the module reads the sixth record in the file and prints a check whose amount and recipient are named in the record. It then alters the next record in the approved-voucher file to appear as if it authorized this check. Next, the added lines of code will delete the file SCRATCHDT. Then the application will resume.

Required:

    (a) Explain what this program modification would allow the programmer to do, and decide whether this would be a computer crime.

    (b) What controls might exist that would help deter or prevent this sort of thing. *How* would the controls work?

Case: Downstate Agriculture Service

The Downstate Agriculture Service (DAS) serves about 15,000 farmers in five southern counties. It offers numerous consultative programs and administers a system of price supports, payments, and subsidies for a variety of crops. The farmers agree to abide by DAS rules and regulations, including what crops they plant, when, in what acreages, and how they sell them. The farmers elect an advisory board, which assists in setting policies and adjudicating disputes and misunderstandings. Such disagreements historically have occurred in about 6 percent of all payment cases in the downstate area.

In recent years a resurgent interest in farming has caused farms to be divided and sold to a growing number of small-acreage farmers unfamiliar with DAS rules, which has generated an enormous work overload for the DAS in field offices. The field offices use terminals connected by phone lines to a computer in the state capital, which maintains a record for each farmer. The payment programs depend upon the presence of a record in the computer for each farmer, and the DAS has fallen behind—it has not yet entered some 1,200 new-farmer records. There are also over 12,000 farmer-update entries not yet posted to farmer records. As a result, farmers are experiencing delays establishing their eligibility for programs and getting their payments. Last year, such delays occurred in 27 percent of all payment cases.

The State Consulting Company (SCC), a private firm, has proposed to provide auxiliary help in an effort to bring the records up-to-date. It has done so for other state agencies without incident—except once five years ago, when an employee of the SCC was accused of using information from state records to extract bribes from citizens as a condition for expediting their business with the state government. The DAS director, a career public servant, has decided to engage the SCC in order to help bring the records up-to-date, provided the following questions can be answered to her satisfaction:

(a) Assuming the DAS data entry controls are adequate for its own employees, what additional programs and controls will be necessary when SCC employees are on the premises entering data?

(b) What requirements should DAS insist that SCC employees meet?

(c) What changes in procedures and controls would make it unnecessary to rehire temporary data entry help again, once SCC brings DAS records up-to-date?

Required:

Address the Director's concerns.

Case: Hometown Bank

At Hometown Bank, the vice-president of development wrote the following memo to the bank's president:

> To the President:
>
> This is to bring you up to date on our negotiations with Real Estate, Inc., the national firm we have approached about moving their regional cash-collection and payment operation to our bank. As you recall, we have projected that this firm would maintain a $4-million average balance in their special savings account. The savings account would receive $10 million in remittances between the first and fifth of each calendar month. Each month, all receipts in excess of $4 million in their savings account would be wired to their corporate headquarters for deposit in their national bank. In any event, this remittance must be no less than $9 million regardless of the balance in the savings account or actual remittances to Real Estate's account. This means that in some months, we may remit to them more funds than we receive for their account. They require that, if this happens, they earn interest as if the balance in the savings account were $4 million, that the interest rate be equal to the current prime rate, and that this interest be remitted at the end of each month to their corporate headquarters.
>
> Although these conditions seem somewhat complex, please keep in mind that they should mean an additional $4 million in deposits, which can be loaned for short term at rates 2 to 6 percent above prime APR.

The president referred this memo to the internal audit department with the request, "Tell me everything you can about the actual risk to us if we accept this proposal, and what control objectives we will have to add to reduce our risk. Assume that the prime rate will be 6 percent annually, that Real Estate will deposit $4 million initially, and that monthly receipts the first year will be as follows:

January	10 million	July	$11 million
February	9 million	August	$10 million
March	8 million	September	$ 9 million
April	7 million	October	$10 million
May	6 million	November	$ 9 million
June	8 million	December	$12 million

Please reply as soon as possible."

Required:

Respond to the president's request as if you were the head of the internal audit department.

CHAPTER 14

Auditing Computer-based Accounting System Controls

Learning Objectives

By studying the information in this chapter, you should be able to

- Describe operational auditing, and explain how its objectives differ from those of independent auditing, especially when computers are used for accounting processing.

- Explain how internal and independent auditors differ in their mission and responsibilities to various groups.

- Understand the basic auditing steps and apply them to computer-based information systems in an organization.

- Distinguish between two different types of evidence collected by auditors.

- Understand how to analyze the cost-effectiveness of additional computer audit procedures as measured against their ability to reduce control weaknesses.

Historically, the first auditors read accounts aloud. Their objectives were to understand a company's activities, as implemented by its managers, and to explain the cumulative financial significance of those activities—that is, the bottom line on management performance—orally to the financial backers. Auditors were an important element in the evolution of capitalism, assisting in the separation of capital and management and the development of industry, trade, and specialization. Today, **auditing** includes methodologies for collecting and analyzing evidence on consistency and other attributes of business information, including financial reporting, as well as for diagnosing operational problems, for assessing managerial efficiency, and for identifying or preventing conditions that could permit crime, incompetence, or carelessness. These methodologies operate in part by examining the systems that prepare the information, through intensive study of the system records and other evidence. Before considering the special aspects of auditing that pertain to computer-based accounting systems, let us review its general structure.

Independent and internal auditing are separate functions. An **independent auditor** is not controlled or supervised by the entity being audited. Independent auditors attest to the fairness of management's financial statements to a broad spectrum of financial statement users and readers: equity holders, regulators, lawmakers, various guardians of the public interest, customers, and the public at large. An **internal auditor** is employed by the entity being audited. Any but the smallest organization should establish an internal audit staff. The internal audit staff reviews operational compliance with management, financial, accounting, and internal controls and serves as a source of information for management about its effectiveness. For example consider a corporation that experiences financial reverses. The *independent auditors* must assure that management gives a fair report of these reverses in the corporation's financial statements and, perhaps, question whether the corporation remains a going concern. The *internal auditors* must try to associate the reverses with omissions or failures of established controls and should recommend control changes to prevent recurrences of these or similar reverses. In making recommendations, the auditors keep in mind that management's expectation that audits will occur acts as a preventive element, and the audit results as a feedback element, of many controls.

This chapter discusses both independent and internal auditing. Independent auditors are legally obligated to express an opinion regarding

Figure 14.1   Short-Form Standard (Unqualified) Audit Opinion
The accounting profession has evolved and refined the short-form standard audit opinion for more than a half century. It serves both to reassure third parties that a real audit has occurred and to protect the auditor from unnecessary liability.

We have audited the accompanying balance sheet of X Company as of December 31, 19XX and the related statements of income, retained earnings and cash flows for the year then ended. These financial statements are the responsibility of the Company's management. Our responsibility is to express an opinion on these financial statements based on our audit.

We conducted our audit in accordance with generally accepted auditing standards. Those standards require that we plan and perform the audit to obtain reasonable assurance about whether the financial statements are free of material misstatement. An audit includes examining, on a test basis, evidence supporting the amounts and disclosures in the financial statements. An audit also includes assessing the accounting principles used and significant estimates made by management, as well as evaluating the overall financial statement presentation. We believe that our audit provides a reasonable basis for our opinion.

In our opinion, the financial statements referred to above present fairly, in all material respects, the financial position of X Company as of [at] December 31, 19XX, and the results of its operations and its cash flows for the year then ended in conformity with generally accepted accounting principles.

Reprinted from *SAS no. 58, Reports on Audited Financial Statements* by permission of the American Institute of Certified Public Accountants, Inc. Copyright American Institute of Certified Public Accountants.

the fairness and consistency of the client organization's financial statements. The short-form auditor's opinion shown in Figure 14.1 is an example. The entity to whom the statements belong may show this opinion to third parties, who interpret it as meaning that the statements derive from actual transactions, compiled and processed according to generally accepted accounting principles. Internal, or operational, auditing has a broader scope of objectives. To internal auditors, the financial statements are only one of several concerns. The additional responsibilities of internal auditors involve reporting to management on business operations' efficiency and success in achieving management objectives. In addition to understanding the process of defining audit objectives and gathering and interpreting audit evidence, the internal auditor must also understand the organization, its objectives, how these objectives are pursued through operations, the methods for controlling business processes at all levels, and the indicators necessary to discriminate between different levels of operational efficiency.

Independent Financial Auditing

Mission

Independent auditors collect evidence to determine, in part, whether a firm's accounting systems are functioning well enough to produce financial statements that are fair, consistent, and in accordance with generally accepted accounting principles. If the accounting systems are not sufficiently reliable, the auditors determine whether the financial statements must be corrected and if so, how. As a by-product, they may make recommendations to correct deficiencies in the accounting system.

An independent auditor must be a **Certified Public Accountant (CPA)**, a designation of accounting professionals who meet certain legal standards. To become a CPA, one must pass a three-day national written examination and meet the education and experience requirements of one of the 54 licensing jurisdictions—the 50 states, Puerto Rico, Virgin Islands, Washington, D.C., and Guam. In many jurisdictions, CPAs must meet continuing-education requirements intended to keep their skills up-to-date. CPAs are the only persons licensed to express an independent opinion on financial statements.

Methodology

The methodology used by independent auditors consists essentially of analytic review, followed by field work. Figure 14.2 illustrates this strategy. The auditor's analytic review typically focuses on client-prepared financial statements, internal control objectives and procedures, interviews with management personnel, and certain summaries that the auditor requests.

Figure 14.2   Auditor Strategy
Auditor strategy begins with deciding the audit objectives and includes the extent of work to collect analytic and test evidence.

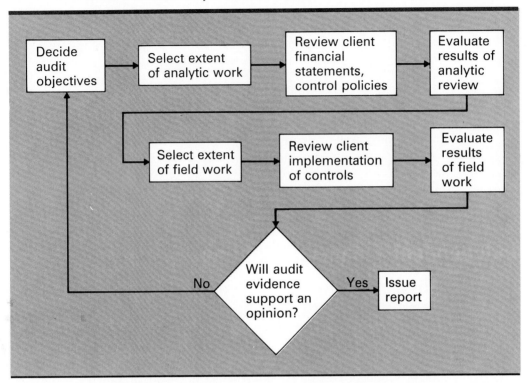

Field tests of controls are selected in light of the results of this review. Testing controls by field work usually entails verifying that the data recording, processing, and reporting controls function as the analytic review led the auditors to expect. When the accounting system is computer based, tests of controls must include procedures specific to computer-based systems.

Levels of Service

Independent auditors may provide any of three different levels of service: audit, review, or compilation. These levels differ in the scope of the opinion and the amount of evidence developed to support it. Before doing any work, the auditor contracts with management for the type of service to be performed. An **audit** is the most comprehensive examination conducted with third parties in mind; the auditor evaluates control objectives, adequacy, and effectiveness through a well-planned program of work and records all evidence collected. At the conclusion of the audit, the auditor provides a formal, broad-scope opinion (such as the one in Figure 14.1), possibly with qualifications, based on the evidence collected and intended for third-party reliance. In rare instances, an audit may fail to produce sufficient evidence to support an opinion, and so no opinion can be expressed. A **review** is a more limited examination than an audit, and the more limited opinion that results from it must include a disclaimer that an audit was conducted. It is understood that in a review the CPA need not include in the work program a search for evidence of material financial statement misrepresentations, control lapses, or misstatements. However, if any of these are encountered, the review work must follow up to ascertain their effect on the financial statements. In practice, a review involves less work than an audit and omits the audit report's sweeping assertions regarding the fairness and consistency of accompanying financial statements. The **compilation** is the assembly of information provided by management into financial statement form. The CPA gives no opinion and makes no guarantee of any kind regarding a compilation.

Internal or Operational Auditing

An **operational audit**, a type of audit performed by internal auditors, aims to enhance operating management's success in achieving top management's objectives. Thus an operational audit has a much broader objective than the financial audits performed by independent auditors. Figure 14.3 shows the stages of operational auditing, which are discussed in the remainder of this section.

Figure 14.3   Stages of Operational Auditing
The operational auditor's work is neither as structured nor as evidence-oriented as that of the independent auditor, and it may have a much different scope.

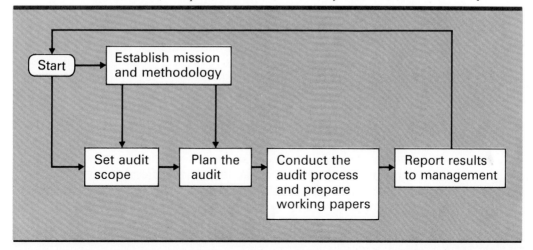

Establish Mission and Methodology

The operational audit concerns itself with all of management's objectives and the corresponding controls, not just with financial objectives and controls. Of course, the scope of any given operational audit may be less comprehensive. For example, internal auditors may examine the multifaceted effectiveness of a single segment of an organization or one facet of effectiveness for the entire organization, such as its selection of capital investments. The operational auditors' flexibility of scope makes them valuable in the control process, from verification of accounting controls to review of management and financial controls at all levels.

Before auditors can function effectively in an organization, they must study and understand it. This study may continue virtually throughout the audit, but it is concentrated in the scope-setting and audit-planning stages. Study methodologies include review of objectives, strategies, organization charts, position descriptions, policies, and procedures; interviews with managers and other employees; comparison of the organization with others in the same industry; and study of the environment in which the organization operates.

Activities Subject to Internal Audit. Many management activities may be subject to audit. Understanding all these activities is one purpose of studying the organization. For example, an organization with the objective of becoming profitable in development of real estate has strategic choices to make: urban or rural, commercial or residential, industrial or retail, apartments or condominiums, limited partnerships or bank capital, and the like. Management chooses a set of guiding principles, which it expects, if followed, to result in progress toward the objective. Operational auditors try to reconstruct the logic that led to the selection of the prevailing strategies and to develop a critique of the strategic planning process, pointing out errors and omissions. The operational auditors continually ask, *"How likely are management's strategies and procedures to be implemented? If implemented, how likely are they to achieve the approved objectives?"*

For example, to implement its selected strategy, management develops programs—sequences of activities, usually extending over several reporting periods, that are coordinated to achieve selected management objectives. Management programs require detailed financial and technical planning, not unlike what is required to develop and implement an accounting system. Like an accounting system, a program must possess organizational, technical, time-frame, and financial feasibility. The operational auditor will be expected to determine whether a management program is consistent with management's stated objectives and strategies, whether it has achievable goals and is feasible, whether implementation is proceeding acceptably, and whether results to date are within tolerable limits.

Strategies, Budgets, and Operations.   Auditors should understand the distinction between evaluation of a manager's performance and evaluation of management's strategies and procedures. A manager accepts (and should help develop) defined objectives and responsibilities, a budget, time frame, and human resources for deployment in pursuit of the objectives. The manager works within the context of existing strategies and procedures by setting short-term objectives, organizing, motivating, communicating, and modifying and evaluating performance. The budget becomes the manager's basic instrument of financial and scheduling control over operations. The budget details each manager's expected inflows and expenses by time periods, plus the charges for supporting services such as accounting, purchasing, and top management activity. Each manager receives regular reports comparing actual operations with this budget and has the opportunity to adjust operations as necessary to sustain progress toward the objectives. How well the manager uses such reports and achieves objectives will be reflected in the manager's performance, merit evaluation, promotion, and compensation.

To evaluate operating strategies and procedures, top management must ask questions such as: Have the most appropriate objectives been selected? Have managerial responsibilities been properly distributed? Are performance reports timely, correctly prepared, and used? Top management depends on the internal auditors to collect the evidence that answers these questions.

Thus, management does not depend on the operational auditors to collect or report information that describes day-to-day operational performance in the organization, but they do rely on the auditors to help them improve the management control system. The operational auditors may follow up the actions taken based on comparison reports of budgeted versus actual performance during a period. Or, they may compare results of several periods of operation or of several managers. The auditors' interests are (1) whether signals of extremely good or poor performance were reported to managers, understood, and used in the ongoing management process; (2) whether the organization as a whole complied with its performance goals, budget constraints, and internal controls; and (3) whether specific programs complied with their performance goals, budget constraints, and internal controls.

Accounting Systems.   Operational auditors must have detailed understanding of accounting systems. Independent auditors rely on operational audits to monitor accounting and data processing controls and to maintain them at a level of quality sufficient for the independent auditor to rely on them in collecting evidence for the opinion on financial statements. To make this possible, operational auditors work closely with the accounting and data processing staffs. For example, to describe and understand an accounting transaction system, the auditors may separate it into transaction data capture, transaction data processing, and activity and responsibility reporting segments. Then they design audit objectives and steps for each segment.

Set Audit Scope

When the auditor selects objectives, these objectives define the scope of the audit. Audit scope is broadly determined by the need to find out whether operations are progressing toward management objectives. It is further determined by possible opinions or recommendations the auditor could express and the types of controls the auditor must examine to gather evidence in support of those opinions. An audit may have a narrow scope, such as an opinion on the amount of inventory or other assets on hand at a certain date, or a broad scope, such as the extent to which a government program fulfilled the broad social purposes set for it.

An audit's scope should be selected with an eye toward its cost-effectiveness. Audits are labor-intensive undertakings and must be managed as carefully as other complex and difficult projects. Auditors perform part of this management function by defining the questions they expect the audit to answer; by identifying in advance the evidence that would support an answer to each question; and by developing careful audit plans that will produce the evidence if it exists. Clearly, the broader the audit scope, the more complex the audit plan and the more evidence and resources are required.

The audit scope may encompass a review of management's choice of objectives. While this sounds presumptuous, it serves as an independent in-depth review of the objectives, with attention to real resource constraints, by qualified consultants. The operational auditor also considers whether the prevailing management strategy and programs are the best possible choices to achieve the objectives and whether the method of implementation is the most effective one available. Finally, the internal auditor evaluates organizational controls at all levels—management, financial, and internal—including data processing and accounting controls. The internal auditor reports on the information system's ability to generate appropriate signals and on management's ability to act effectively on the signals.

If computers are used in the accounting system, the audit must look into the proper functioning of the system's computer-based segments. In this sense, computer-based accounting and control systems require broader-scoped audits and auditors more skilled in EDP than systems without computers. Among the problems that computers might introduce into an audit are the possibility of reproducing the same logical error throughout a set of records, short-term inflexibility in responding to quickly changing user needs, the possible loss of connection between the documented audit trail and the computer records, lack of management or effectiveness in the data processing center, the possibility of breaking down without warning, loss of data confidentiality if communications are misdirected, and the risks of deliberate crime. Audit objectives take these possibilities into account and establish an audit scope pertinent to them.

The scope of an audit influences the audit plan and the resources required to collect evidence to support an opinion. The scope of an audit should be such that by establishing the expectation that it will occur, the audit serves as a preventive control element. Then, the results of actual audit reviews act as a feedback element. The function of an operational audit is to make possible comparisons above and beyond those generated through financial controls and comparisons of accounting results.

Scope and Evidence.   The *basic* audit plan is always the same: to collect evidence that establishes the reliability of system controls and the suitability of system information outputs for use by management. Such evidence may be classified as either "analytic" or "testing" in origin; both types of evidence are collected throughout an audit. The evidence collected allows the auditor to answer these questions: What system controls are designed well enough that, if they function as expected, the auditor (and management and third parties) may rely on the information the system produces? Of these controls, which ones actually function as designed? In which operational areas are system controls not well designed or not functioning as designed, so that the auditors must collect their own evidence of system reliability by examining individual transactions, processes, and assets? And finally, once the reliance that may be placed on system-generated information has been established, how suitable is this information for use by management in formulating and pursuing its strategies and carrying out its procedures?

In general, **analytic evidence** tells the auditor whether the system controls, if they work properly, are of adequate *design*. Analytic evidence tends to be collected early in the audit from sources such as organization records and personnel interviews. The auditor analyzes the evidence to determine how the organization's procedures and controls should operate. For example, an operational auditor, concerned because customers are returning defective disk-drive controllers, might conduct an audit with the limited scope of determining whether manufacturing quality standards for disk-drive controllers are being met. The auditor should gather analytic evidence by obtaining copies of the existing manufacturing quality standards, testing procedures, and the internal controls that cover quality testing and assurance. The auditor should analyze the internal controls to determine whether, if adhered to, they are likely to reveal departures from manufacturing quality standards. From the analytic evidence, the auditor makes a judgment about how much testing to do. Continual testing is necessary because audit judgment is being formed continuously and may be modified during the audit in light of the results of subsequent analysis and testing. If the auditor concludes that the quality-testing procedures and controls, properly performed, would reveal failure to meet quality standards, subsequent auditor testing would seek to determine whether actual testing complied with the written procedures and controls. A positive finding might lead the auditor to conclude that the product returns had some other cause. Evidence that quality procedures were being ignored or implemented incorrectly might lead the auditor to name these control failures as at least a contributing cause to the problem of controller returns.

The auditor also looks for specific general and application controls in the data processing department. These controls include separation of the data processing department from other organization functions, separation of functions within data processing, input from users on what services data processing should offer, written policies and procedures, limited access to computer hardware and software, consistent transaction documentation, and a process for approving and documenting all system changes. The more of these controls the auditor finds, the stronger and more supportive the analytic evidence that the computer controls, as designed, are adequate.

Test evidence tells the auditor whether system controls work as intended. Test evidence reveals whether steps have been taken to make the controls reliable and, when controls cannot be relied on, whether the system did produce information that could be used as intended. Test evidence may be gathered primarily in the later stages of the audit, from planned procedures or tests conducted by the auditor under controlled conditions. The results of each test become an input to the audit-judgment process. An auditor might perform tests of data input controls, observe the day-to-day separation of functions in data processing, ask employees to describe their daily routine to see if it corresponds to the written policies and procedures, observe control of access to hardware and software, examine selected transaction documentation, and compare the in-use copies of software programs with their archive copies to see if all authorized changes have been made. The auditor must continue accumulating test evidence until it is sufficient to support an opinion that the controls *do* function substantially as described, or that they *do not* function substantially as described, or that no opinion is possible. In addition, the opinion in an independent financial audit must apply to the information in the financial statements as a whole, whereas an operational audit may render an opinion on each individual control or procedure tested.

As an audit proceeds, the test evidence is linked and evaluated with the related analytic evidence. At checkpoints during the audit, the auditor decides what to do next: form an opinion, decline to give an opinion, or continue collecting evidence. If the decision is to continue collecting evidence, the auditor decides what kind of evidence. In the early part of an

Figure 14.4   Distribution of Effort Over Evidence-gathering Activities During an Audit
In general, the amount of analytic work declines as an audit progresses. This diagram does not show the effort devoted to review and interpretation of evidence, including writing and presenting the audit report.

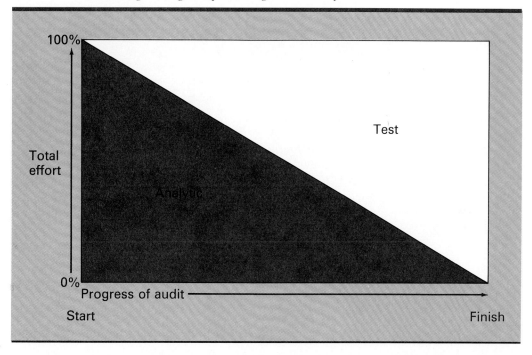

audit, the evidence is mostly analytic; later, it is mostly test. Figure 14.4 illustrates the shift in audit effort from analytic to test evidence as the audit proceeds.

Plan the Audit

After the scope of an audit has been established, the auditor prepares an audit plan. It describes the steps required, the sequence in which they should occur, and the time and staff resources likely to be needed. Most of the steps will fall into one of the six sequential stages shown in Figure 14.5. These stages may be repeated for each objective that is within the scope of the audit. The audit plan will contain many such parts. Although the stages tend to be the same for each objective, the steps within each stage will be customized for a particular objective.

Figure 14.5 Stages Covered in Audit Implementation
Each box represents a major segment of audit implementation. The audit program would be developed by deciding what steps would be necessary in each segment.

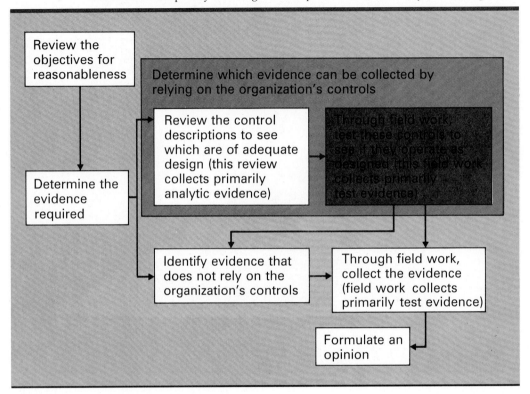

The auditor develops an audit plan tailored to the specific unit being audited. The plan provides for protecting the collection and analysis of evidence from client influence. The auditor also seeks to produce sufficient evidence at less cost than the economic value of the opinion. Auditors usually do not find it necessary to examine an entire system before forming an opinion; they examine parts of the system, selected for their importance. Depending on the results of this partial examination, they may not audit other parts of the system. In verifying that 16,350 accounts receivable balances represent actual obligations totaling $751,705 by credit customers, the auditor may correspond directly with the 350 credit customers with balances over $1,000 and with 1,000 others selected at random. If there are no discrepancies, or very few, that lack reasonable explanations, the auditor may conclude that the remaining 15,000 account balances are unlikely to contain significant discrepancies and need not be directly confirmed.

Similarly, if an examination of 300 purchase transactions selected at random reveals only evidence of satisfactory control functioning, further examinations of purchase transactions may be judged unnecessary.

Review Objectives for Reasonableness. Reviewing each objective for reasonableness allows the auditor to accept or modify each, based on the objective's importance to the audit as a whole. For example, a typical audit objective is to ascertain that all liabilities incurred and paid were valid obligations. Suppose that the objective applies to operations of a branch office of a company with centralized purchasing and payroll applications, and the branch office is responsible only for petty cash and minor liabilities. The auditor may review this objective, decide it is relatively unimportant, and omit it from the operational audit of that branch. On the other hand, if the branch purchases its own supplies and inventory, the auditor may include the objective in the audit.

Determine the Evidence Required. For each objective, the auditor must specify what evidence will define an acceptable result. That evidence becomes the target of the evidence-gathering activities. If the acceptable evidence is not defined ahead of time, there is a *large* risk that whatever evidence exists will be accumulated without evaluating its adequacy. Evidence that liabilities incurred and paid are valid obligations would be planned to include evidence that purchase orders were approved by authorized personnel; that liabilities are supported by vendors' original invoices reconciled back to authorized purchase orders, receiving reports, returns and allowances, and backorders; and that all prenumbered purchase orders have been accounted for.

Identify Evidence to Be Collected Relying on the Organization's Controls. Much of the required evidence may be available through the organization's information system. If the system's controls are complete and well designed, and perform as designed, this evidence may be accepted by the auditor. For example, as evidence that liabilities are supported by vendors' invoices, the auditor may determine that the following control objectives would, if adhered to, be sufficient to allow the auditor to accept the vendors' invoices as evidence of genuine liabilities to outside parties:

1. All invoices received during the period under audit are identified, and no other invoices for other periods are included.
2. All merchandise invoiced is referenced to a receiving report, and all receiving report numbers have been accounted for.
3. Each invoice is associated with a uniquely numbered payment voucher.
4. All such voucher numbers for the audit period are accounted for.

5. All payment vouchers for the audit period have attached to them an original vendors' invoice not previously canceled by punching holes in the physical documents or affixing an indelible mark in a specified field in the computer records.

A further level of detail would show the tests of these controls. These would be mostly tests of transactions: the examination of actual transactions to find evidence about how data entry and processing controls operate. For example, objective 1 might be tested by examining all invoices processed for several days centered on the start and on the end dates of the audit period and accounting for all the invoice numbers between the first and last invoices of the period. One test of objective 2 would be to examine a sample of invoices and then look up the corresponding receiving reports to make certain they reflect the merchandise being invoiced. A test for objective 3 would be to select a few invoices and then look up the corresponding voucher numbers to make certain they include those invoices. For objective 4, the auditor would examine all vouchers apparently processed during that period to make certain they all exist; the auditor should also look up the invoices referenced on a few vouchers to make certain they were processed during that period and reference the voucher on which they were found. Finally, for objective 5, the auditor should select a few vouchers and look carefully for any evidence that the invoices associated with them have been paid more than once.

The final level of detail will be single steps or procedures that may be assigned to one or two persons to perform. The plan must be complete at this level of detail to ensure thorough review of the controls that affect a particular audit conclusion.

Identify Evidence That Does Not Rely on the Organization's Controls. When the auditor cannot rely on the organization's controls, the audit plan must provide for more extensive review. For example, if tests of controls reveal that several invoices have been paid twice or that receiving reports are unreliably prepared, the auditor cannot accept that all liabilities incurred and paid were valid obligations without further examining the liabilities as recorded by the organization to see if they are in fact valid and, if they are not valid, correcting them until they are. Some work of this sort will be necessary in most audits. Planning of these tests may await some analytic review and tests of controls.

Collect the Evidence Through Field Work.   After the audit plan is completed, a schedule is made detailing who is to perform each task in it and when, and how many hours each task will require. To translate the audit plan into a work plan, each step or procedure is listed, leaving space to describe what actually happened when it was performed, conclusions about the evidence thus produced, and the date, time, place, and other particulars. Both operational and independent auditors do this. Independent auditors do it knowing they may ultimately have to defend the integrity of their evidence under adverse circumstances in court. Operational auditors do not usually have this concern; they keep careful records to demonstrate to the independent auditors the quality of the organization's internal controls—which can reduce the extent and therefore the cost of the independent audit—and as supporting evidence for their recommendations to management.

Formulate an Opinion.   The exact opinion, of course, cannot be planned. However, the audit plan should anticipate the use of time and resources to reach an opinion about every item in the audit scope. The conclusion for a given objective may be very specific; for example, with respect to the opinion, "All liabilities incurred and paid were valid obligations," the auditor may concur provided that specific adjustments are made increasing the liabilities by $73,500. The auditor may also plan to recommend that additional control objectives be adopted or that existing control objectives be better implemented, so that the system henceforth produces information that meets the objective *without* such adjustments.

The auditor will also plan to express overall opinions that rest on the specific conclusions reached during an audit. In the case of the example we have used throughout this section, these conclusions might lead to opinions or recommendations that affect purchasing, accounts payable, and cash disbursements activities.

Conduct the Audit Process and Prepare Working Papers

After the scope has been set and an audit plan developed, an effective audit will result from competent implementation by skilled auditors who document in their working papers all the work they perform. Since the major output of an audit is conclusions based on *relevant evidence*, the auditors plan the gathering and organization of such evidence. Carrying out the audit process consists of the six stages detailed in Figure 14.6: (1) review the audit implementation plan, (2) staff the audit, (3) establish working relationships, (4) carry out audit plan, (5) interpret audit results, and (6) report to management.

Review the Audit Implementation Plan.   This step gives those responsible for implementing the audit an opportunity to review its plan and to make changes they consider essential. Such changes might be made necessary by changes in organizational structure and responsibilities or in the information system processes that will be audited. An internal auditor may

Figure 14.6 Managing the Audit Process
Implementing an audit strategy requires managerial and communication skills. The boxes below show the major audit activities in which such skills are needed.

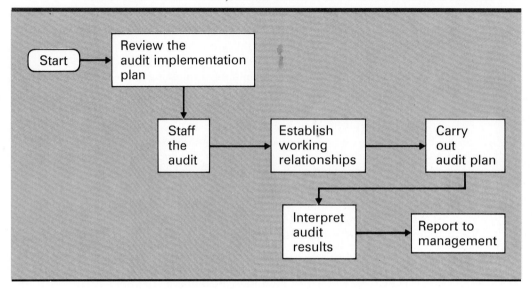

review certain parts of the plan with the managers of the organization segments being audited. Further review occurs at checkpoints during the audit as audit evidence becomes available.

Staff the Audit.   The audit plan specifies the time and staff requirements. As many audit activities as possible should be performed by regular staff people with the skills and system familiarity to perform them. The remaining activities, including all those requiring an auditor's judgment and interpretation, should be performed by auditors. One auditor may be sufficient to staff many audits; other cases call for two, three, or more auditors. Where several auditors work together, one should be in charge and the distribution of authority should be well understood.

Establish Working Relationships.   Since auditors intrude into parts of the organization where they are not ordinarily present and consume resources by asking questions and looking into records, they should take pains to establish good relations with the management and staff they will be auditing. Before auditors enter a work center, top management should ask employees in the unit to cooperate with the auditors. The person in charge of the audit should explain the authority and need for the audit, and ask for cooperation and assistance. All those on the audit assignment must respect the rules and authority structure of the unit being audited;

for example, an auditor cannot give orders to nonmembers of the auditing staff and cannot use records for routine nonsurprise tests when the records are needed for operations. If cooperation is withheld, the auditors should utilize their access to top management to resolve the conflict constructively and with a minimum of confrontation.

Carry Out Audit Plan.   The audit plan being explained contains many steps, some of which will be described in more detail later in this chapter. To help keep track of these steps, the auditors will use **working papers**, records of audit procedures, evidence that resulted from them, and the conclusions drawn therefrom. An example of working paper design appears in Figure 14.7. The working papers provide an orderly framework for conducting the audit thoroughly and keeping track of all its steps and their results. Note that the working papers provide for review of all the work done, and for the auditors to specify additional work and then to conduct and review it. Working papers may be handwritten, typed, or generated by a special computer application that will select steps and print

Figure 14.7   Example of Working Paper Design
The audit implementation plan is documented to allow reconstruction of the evidence collected, how it was collected, and how it was interpreted. Working papers such as this one establish accountability over audit implementation. The description of each step, omitted from this illustration, would show the step's objective, auditor procedure, and expected result.

Title of Working Paper						Page ___ of ___		
Description of audit step and hours budgeted	Name of person conducting audit step	Actual hours	Date work done	Results of doing audit step	Name of person reviewing audit step	Follow-up work proposed, if any	Results of follow-up work and review
Step X Budgeted Hours: ____								
Step Y Budgeted Hours: ____								
Step Z Budgeted Hours: ____								continued. . .

descriptions of them based on the audit objectives and audit plan. As the audit proceeds, it is not unusual for additional working papers to be designed and used. The working papers are kept for a specified period after the audit, usually for several years.

Interpret Audit Results.   The audit plan provides for the auditors to interpret the meaning of the evidence they have accumulated. In an operational audit, this evaluation is often done in collaboration with management. Such interpretations can be extremely difficult when they deal with apparently subjective matters like management judgment and controls. The auditors may check and recheck their conclusions, and change them as more evidence accumulates and their perspective changes.

Report to Management

In most audits, this step is the most time consuming and tedious. Much of the preparation for reporting to management is spread out over the course of the audit in the form of ongoing interpretations of the evidence. When all analytic and field work has been completed, the auditor can consolidate and integrate these interpretations relatively quickly.

The prepared report will contain both facts, supported by audit evidence, and recommendations, supported by interpretation of the evidence. It goes first to management of the unit that was audited and then to top management. The auditor will ask management of the unit to concur with the facts and recommendations, so that the audit report will represent joint agreement. The report is subject to top-management acceptance if implementation requires additional resources or affects how the audited unit relates to other units in the organization.

If there are any disagreements as to the facts, they should be resolved. The unit's management has the option of agreeing to carry out the recommended improvements and changes, or taking exception. If the auditors and unit management cannot reach agreement—differing, for example, over whether what the auditors collected is actually evidence or over how the evidence should be interpreted—they may submit separate reports.

Both independent and operational auditors seek management concurrence—the independent auditors as representatives of the equityholders, the internal auditors as members of the management team. In most businesses, the pressure to respect established channels and structure helps limit disagreement to cases of serious differences over interpretation of the facts discovered during the audit. In an open dispute, either unit management or the auditors will lose some credibility. If top management upholds the unit management's interpretation, other audited units may threaten to seek top-management reversals of adverse audit findings. If the auditors are upheld, management of the audited unit may lose respect and face a burden of proving its competence. Thus, there is some rough parity in the pressures on the auditors and on unit management to reach agreement on the audit results and to present results jointly to top management for review and approval prior to implementation.

Computer Auditing

The introduction of computers into accounting and control systems has changed the scope of virtually all independent and internal audits and has therefore affected the strategies and procedures that characterize these audits. At one time, auditing was essentially an intensive review of transactions occurring during a given period. Multiple manual recording of these transactions made transcription errors a primary source of discrepancies in the records. Many control procedures were aimed at minimizing and detecting transcription errors. When computers began to replace manual and unit-record data processing, several changes occurred in the accounting system environment:

- Computer processing is impossible to observe, since it takes place within a box. By contrast, manual data processing occurs in plain sight and may be simply observed.
- Most computers and computer programs are too complex, even at their most fundamental level of operation, for anyone but specialists to understand. In contrast, most people in a manual data processing facility can understand what is happening.
- Much computer output is in the form of magnetic storage, impossible to inspect unless it is converted to paper or video display. In contrast, manual data processing produces a readable record.

The effect of these changes on auditors was (a) to remove the well-understood manual data processing environment and (b) to take away the **audit trail**—the documentation that describes a transaction's history. Computerization replaces the paper audit trail with a new type of magnetic-media documentation, out of reach within the computer. The computer performs multiple recording free of transcription errors. The primary sources of errors are incorrect input and procedures within the computer that do not function as expected. To accommodate these changes, the recent trend in auditing has been to replace transaction testing with controls testing and to regard the latter as the primary means of confirming conclusions about controls reached through analytical review and preliminary field work.

Computer Audit Strategies

The audit tests developed to cope with the changes accompanying computerization can be classified as auditing "with," "around," and "through" the computer. All of these classifications help achieve the purpose of testing the reliability of the computer's processing. **Auditing around the computer** means testing to verify that the results of specific routine processing, already done on a computer, can be duplicated by manual processing. **Auditing through the computer** means using test data to probe how the computer would process actual data. The test data are selected so that outputs will be correct if proper controls are in place, but distorted if they are not. Most audits must draw appropriate tests from all three categories.

With the Computer. It has become fairly common to use a computer for the clerical work in the audit process, although the auditor continues to exercise the expert judgment. **Auditing with the computer** includes testing calculations performed during transaction processing, selecting accounts to be confirmed directly with credit customers, and comparing data from different files that should be identical. For quick access and review, electronic spreadsheet software can be used to record the results of tests and proposed adjustments, and project-management software can be used to sequence, schedule, and administer audit steps. The following paragraphs describe one more advanced example of computer-assisted auditing, the use of a computer-based sample design plan.

When using a computer-designed sampling plan, the auditor selects the variable to estimate—like the dollar amount of accounts receivable over one year old—and the degree of certainty the estimate must display. A computer program, written by the auditor in a special audit-programming language such as STRATA, AUDITAPE, or S/2170, selects the sample plan and (given information about the file containing the variable) may select the items for the sample, create a work file to contain them, carry out all calculations, and present a report to the auditor. This audit tool neatly distinguishes the intellectual work (selecting the audit objective, the key variable, and the level of confidence, then interpreting the results) from the mechanical work (designing the sample, analyzing sample statistics, and calculating the results).

A random sample is a test of a portion of total transactions, from which inferences can be made about all transactions. A properly designed random sample reduces the audit effort while retaining confidence that the inferences are correct.

As an example of simple random sampling, suppose the unit uses the purchase order system to control purchasing, and it made 20,000 purchases during the past period. The auditor wishes to know the probability that the number of purchase orders that were *not* properly authorized is less than 400, or 2 percent of this population. The auditor wants to have a 95.5-percent or "two standard errors of estimate" confidence that the estimate will be plus or minus 100 units of the actual number. Thus the standard error of estimate = 50. The approximate sample size that gives this value is 3,100. Using a portable computer and audit software, the auditor selects and reads into a separate file 3,100 purchase order records. A sequential computer examination of the "approval" field in each record shows that of these 3,100 sampled purchase orders, 70 are without proper authorization. The estimate of the number of such orders in the population is $(20,000/3,100) \times 70 = 452$, and the probability that the true value lies in an interval of 352 to 552 is 95.5 percent. The auditor, using a table of areas under the normal curve, calculates that there is a p (unauthorized purchase orders < 400) = 0.15. Because this probability is much lower than the auditor expected, the auditor concludes that purchase approval controls are unreliable and that a more extensive examination of purchase orders must occur.

Many auditors rely on their own partially computerized models of computer processing as it is supposed to be taking place. These reconstructions are built using computer languages designed for that purpose. If the reconstruction's calculations match those of the operational application, the auditor gains confidence in the application.

Around the Computer.   Although the auditors cannot directly observe the computer at work, they can test its logic. If they select actual input transactions, calculate what the results of processing should be, and then actually observe those same results from the computer processing, the auditors will have established a strong presumption that the internal logic of the application produces acceptable results. Conversely, the auditors could select computer output, such as an account payable, and reconstruct it from its source documents.

The advantages of this strategy, when it is appropriate, are that it is easy to understand, inexpensive to implement, and simple to carry out. However, it has three serious disadvantages. First, auditing around the computer depends on analysis of a random sample of actual transactions, which may not include those processed incorrectly and may not include features that would reveal processing errors or lack of controls. Second, auditing around the computer looks back at processing that has already occurred, rather than at prevention of problems in future processing. The only possible future benefit is to find a logical error in completed processing that can be prevented from affecting future processing. However, examining randomly selected transactions is an inefficient way to search for logical processing errors. Third, auditing around the computer is essentially a time-consuming *manual* process that makes little use of the computer itself as an audit helper. Figure 14.8 illustrates auditing around the computer.

Through the Computer.   Auditors have been quick to see the advantages of observing the computer's logic in operation and of following the audit trail as developed within the computer programs and files, but they have not been quick to develop the ability to do so. Indeed, to some extent, processing technology still exceeds auditing technology.

Auditing through the computer proceeds on the assumption that specific data should, if processed by a designated application, produce certain predictable output. It uses tests of *how* data are processed. The data are not real—auditors construct **test data** (called a *test deck* when computer data input was mostly by means of punched paper cards)—simulated transactions expressly designed by auditors to probe for critical weaknesses and control features. This probing cannot be accomplished reliably

Figure 14.8   Example of Auditing Around the Computer
An audit around the computer only rechecks calculations and processing already performed. As shown here, the auditor manually calculates the amount that should appear on the voucher, then compares the calculation result with the voucher.

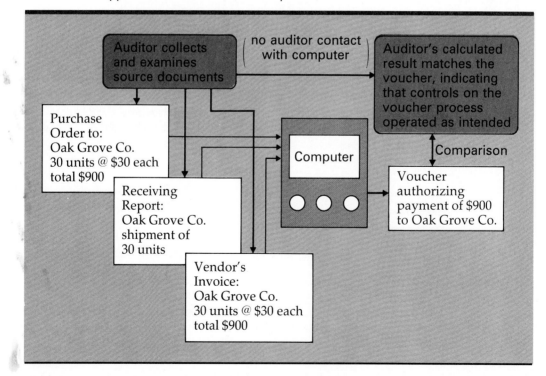

Figure 14.9   Use of Test Data in Auditing Through the Computer
These are not real source documents. They have been designed so that processing them will test for the possibility of a critical control weakness. The resulting voucher is invalidated without being paid, since it results from a test and not from a real transaction.

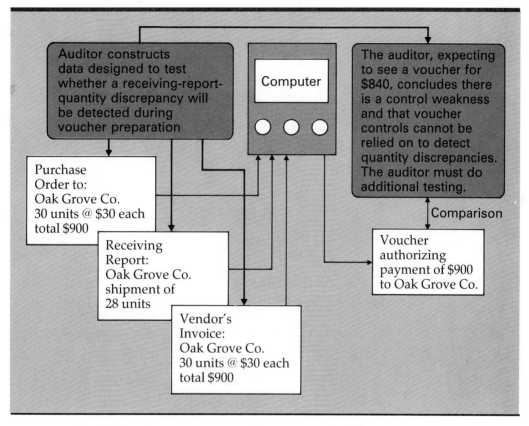

with randomly selected actual transaction data. The auditors know in advance what output corresponds to acceptable controls. If this output results, the application passes the audit test. Figure 14.9 illustrates the use of test data. Compare this figure with Figure 14.8 to see how this strategy differs from auditing around the computer.

Auditing through the computer starts with the computer programs themselves. Management controls the adoption and use of programs; auditors seek to verify that the programs used to process data are exactly those programs authorized by management, unchanged. They seek to verify that these programs access, process, and produce the proper files. Finally, the auditors perform real-time testing under actual processing conditions by inserting simulated transactions into the stream of real transactions to see if the features they contain will trigger controls properly. This feature, called an **integrated test facility (ITF)**, enables the auditor to approach transaction processing as a quality-control inspector approaches product testing; by testing actual output as it is produced.

Auditing through the computer gives credible and comprehensive evidence about accounting data processing as it actually occurs. However, its complexity makes it costly, and it disrupts normal processing.

Specific Computer Audit Tests

This section discusses other basic computer-related tests that auditors use. Instead of listing all the tests an auditor would perform, we discuss only a few selected tests that assess the integrity of the computer in accounting data processing. The auditor selects procedures consistent with the type of audit being performed and tests the specific controls being evaluated.

Transactions

If an objective is to determine how well the controls on transaction processing operate, then selected transactions may be examined. The auditor decides in advance how many transactions to test in order to make an accurate assessment of the system, selects transactions at random, and ascertains that they have been processed correctly. To determine that the payroll application is being processed correctly, an employee's time card may be subject to numerous tests such as these:

- The number of hours worked may be calculated.
- The employee's permanent personnel file may be inspected.
- Gross pay, deductions, and net pay may be calculated, using information from the employee's permanent personnel file.
- The results of these calculations may be compared with the payroll journal to determine that the computer generated and posted the same amounts to the correct accounts.
- Finally, the canceled pay checks may be inspected to determine whether the employee received the proper amount.

Another type of transaction test accumulates transaction processing information that may point to abuse or carelessness. For example, if the computer system uses account numbers and passwords, the operating system could record unsuccessful attempts to use an account number by entering incorrect passwords. It could record all uses of sensitive files, such as the ITF files. And it could record the unauthorized use of very powerful programs, called *zappers*, which are sometimes used to unscramble or recover data after a system crash. A zapper program also could be used to *zap*, or change, data that should not be changed. When the accumulated information is examined, the auditor may wish to conduct specific audit tests to confirm or refute suspicions aroused by it.

Program Authorization

If an objective is to evaluate the controls governing which application programs are being used, then selected tests of program authorization will be performed to see if the operating version of software is authorized. It should be an objective of the organization that *only* authorized programs may run on its computer. To assure this objective, the data processing department should follow control procedures such as the following, which the auditor will verify.

The master copies of authorized programs and files are kept in a secure location, inaccessible to anyone routinely involved with data processing and available to others only after authorization by top management. Since such access could occur frequently during a period of intensive systems development, there is particular reason to control it very tightly at such times. An authorized person must approve insertion of any new program or category of file in the accounting system inventory. Similarly, an authorized person must approve any change, amendment, enhancement, or deletion of an authorized program or category of file. Computer time for systems development should be scheduled when operating programs are not being run. Programmers should have access only to "development" or test versions of programs used in accounting applications; they should never have access to the operating versions. An authorized person must approve the "run schedule," the calendar of programs to be run on line at particular hours during the day. The "run log," which records the programs that were actually on line and the files that were actually open, must be regularly compared with the run schedule.

Only authorized persons may have access to computer terminals to load programs and open files. To minimize the likelihood that anyone can alter the application programs, only the machine-language versions should be available to data processing operators for daily processing. (Only highly skilled computer programmers can alter these, but clever nonprogrammers might be able to tamper with the simpler-to-understand source versions written in computer programming languages.) Systems development and technical-support work must be done only by programmers and development staff.

The tests of controls described in the remainder of this section determine whether these procedures are followed, and have the desired effect, under actual operating conditions.

The Element of Surprise.   Tests that are scheduled may be performed on a surprise basis, without prior warning to the audited unit. In some cases, the element of surprise can be critical to their effectiveness. In the famous Equity Funding fraud, the auditors were fooled partly because their *scheduled* computer tests gave management time to hide incriminating records and create reassuring but false evidence of normalcy. The byte-count test, the program-logic test, and the use of prepared test data all require the element of *real* surprise. The auditors must literally sweep in unexpectedly, briefly take control of data processing, and conduct their tests.

A **byte-count test** is a comparison of the length of the in-use and back-up copies of a program. For the *surprise byte-count test*, the auditors enter the computer facility just as the programs and files they want to check are about to be removed from the computer memory. The auditors will make a copy of these programs or files and take it into their possession immediately. Then, using a program that counts the number of bytes in a file, they will compare the number of bytes in the operating version of the program with the number in the master (authorized) copy. This test is revealing because it is difficult to change the logic of a program without affecting its length. If a length difference exists, the auditor must determine exactly what caused it. The causes of a length difference include unauthorized tampering and outright fraud, although a more likely explanation is that authorized changes have not yet been added to the operating program. The major transaction recording applications, on-line back-up copies of asset files, and report generators are good candidates for this test.

A **program-logic test** is a comparison to see if the operating version of a program is identical to the archival version. *Surprise comparison of program logic* is more sophisticated than the byte-count test but has the same objective. A special logic analysis program developed by the auditors compares the operating and master versions of the program byte by byte, command by command. Alternatively, a "trace program" can identify the path taken through each copy of the program to process selected data. This is a time-consuming test: it is used when the auditor thinks parts of one copy of a program have been changed. Assuming the master copy is authentic, this test is conclusive evidence that the operating copy is or is not one that is authorized. Figure 14.10 illustrates the use of a trace program.

The auditor may also choose *surprise use with prepared data* when there is strong suspicion of a specific misdeed or control flaw. The auditor devises a relatively small set of transactions or other inputs that will produce computer responses capable of proving or disproving the suspicion. The need for fidelity to true operating conditions determines the exact method of presenting test data to the computer, whether on a floppy disk or a tape or keyed in by hand. In the case of a remote-access computer, the auditor might use a modem and remote computer terminal.

Figure 14.10   Use of a Trace Program
A trace program's output, shown in simplified form below, allows an auditor to compare the logic of two supposedly identical programs processing the same data.

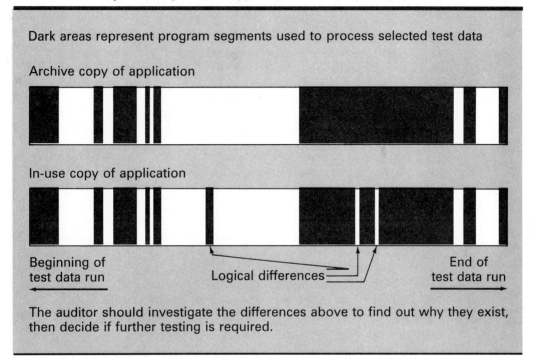

Dark areas represent program segments used to process selected test data

Archive copy of application

In-use copy of application

Beginning of test data run   Logical differences   End of test data run

The auditor should investigate the differences above to find out why they exist, then decide if further testing is required.

If a file, rather than a program, is the object of testing, it may be more convenient—especially in the case of long, sequentially organized files—to remove a copy from the client's site either physically or by modem. The copy can then be analyzed at leisure, under complete auditor control, using the auditor's own computer and analytical programs.

More Comprehensive Tests.   A *test of controls with prepared data* is potentially much more comprehensive if it is not performed on a surprise basis. The auditor, having examined and analyzed the controls that should exist, decides which ones to verify and creates an exclusive series of computer inputs to do so. The prepared data may require several days, or even weeks, to design and create. When it is run, the auditor uses existing operating programs and data files but controls all system inputs and outputs. The auditor also keeps a copy of the system run log, showing all accesses by the computer to programs and files. This test is very powerful. Its principal shortcoming is that it uses artificial data and does not occur under actual operating conditions. These disadvantages make possible its major strength—the auditor can test what he or she believes needs testing. This test and the next one are more complex and probably less common than the ones described in the preceding paragraphs. However, their effectiveness justifies their use in appropriate situations.

The *installation of an integrated test facility* enables the auditor to insert simulated transactions into processing at random intervals, without the knowledge of the system operators. The basic premise of ITF is that the best way to study an operating accounting system is under actual operating conditions. In practice, the auditor works with programmers to embed audit routines in the client's operating system and applications. These routines inject simulated transactions into the normal transaction flow at irregular and unpredictable intervals and recover them after processing. As far as the system operators are concerned, these transactions are real and must be processed like all others. By comparing the results of processing the simulated transactions with the expected results, the auditor can see which controls were effective at the time of processing. The results are stored in a secure file reserved only for auditor access.

An example of ITF in the voucher-preparation process may clarify its operation. Several fictitious vendors are inserted into the authorized-vendors file. Several times a week, the auditor submits purchase orders addressed to these vendors, adds fictitious vendor-invoice records, and creates fictitious receiving reports. Some of these documents, which are to be processed normally along with other data, will be completely in order and others will contain discrepancies. Any control lapses or abuses that affect other data have a good chance of affecting the simulated data too; an example is preparation of a voucher without a purchase order. Downstream from processing, the ITF includes programs that recover the outputs, such as approved vouchers, and examine them for control lapses or abuses, before removing them from the accounting records. One objective is to see if any of the invoices result in an approved voucher or are paid—violating the control objective that no invoice can be approved for payment without a matching purchase order and receiving report. Removing records also presents difficulties—for example, if vouchers are sequentially numbered then the ITF voucher received a number and, if eliminated, will make it appear as if there is a missing voucher. Someone could spend time searching for this voucher, or find it and reinstate it, if removal is not handled properly.

An integrated test facility is the most complex, difficult to use, and expensive of all auditor tools, which helps explain why very few actual applications of integrated test facilities yet exist. The ITF consumes significant amounts of CPU time and internal memory. Designing its parts requires an additional set of steps above and beyond those required to design the system itself, and it needs its own controls to be certain operators do not disable it. Another reason for its rarity is that the ITF's controls could be defeated by a knowledgeable operator. For example, the operator might be able to direct all payments on ITF-generated checks to another vendor or address and eventually recover and cash them. The ITF files containing the results of processing the test transactions might also be deleted or tampered with. Nevertheless, the ITF is still the best means of testing the performance of a computerized accounting system.

Cost-Effectiveness of Additional Auditing

Deciding how extensive auditing should be as a form of control is subject to considerations of cost-effectiveness. An audit, to be cost effective, should produce benefits in excess of its cost. Conceptually, the operational auditor should probably decide to audit until the additional costs of auditing would produce less than the minimum return on investment from other uses of the same funds. This principle is easy to state but difficult to apply. Simple examples illustrate the principle; dozens of rules guide its application in specific situations. Most auditors rely on intuition or on simple cost-benefit models in deciding how much auditing to do.

To determine whether an ITF program would be the most cost-effective method available, the auditor compares both the capacity and cost of the ITF with alternative audit and control methods available. Consider this simple example of a pay-back comparison for one ITF application and one alternative control. The organization's five-year-old, on-line, real-time accounts receivable application includes a control program, to be run before customer statements are prepared. The control program finds and reports unauthorized returns of merchandise. Unauthorized returns and allowances currently amount to $8,000 per year. The auditor wants to be certain that this program is run prior to customer-statement preparation. Using an integrated test facility, the auditor can insert occasional fictitious reports from the receiving department that a credit customer has returned certain goods. The ITF will recognize any of the fictitious transactions that are not found and reported by the data processing staff; finding such transactions is evidence that the staff failed to run the finder program. If this ITF program costs $9,000 to develop and $4,000 annually to operate, and if it annually disallows returns of $7,000, it will save the company $3,000 annually: the savings from disallowed returns of $7,000 less the annual operating cost of $4,000. The time required to pay back the original cost of $9,000 will be three years: the original cost divided by the annual savings of $3,000.

The alternative is to modify the application itself so that when the shipper tries to deliver the returns, the receiving department must reconcile incoming shipments with acceptance authorizations on an on-line basis. This feature would make it easier for the receiving department to determine whether a return was authorized. If this feature cost $5,000 to implement and $1,000 a year to operate, and reduced unauthorized returns by $5,000 annually, it would produce a net annual saving of $4,000 annually: the savings from disallowed returns of $5,000 less the operating costs of $1,000. The time required to pay back its original cost would be 5,000/4,000 = 1.2 years. The company must consider the ITF's longer payback period and its greater efficiency in reducing returns to determine whether it is more economical than the return-control alternative. In this case, due to rapid changes in computer technology and the likelihood of system development changes, the ITF is probably not economically justifiable relative to the simpler control. This example illustrates the importance of considering not only the effectiveness but also the cost of an audit tool in a control context. Do *not* interpret it as a rejection of ITFs in other circumstances, where they may have an economic advantage.

One very effective approach to audit cost-effectiveness starts in the planning stages of system development. If allowed to participate in systems development, the auditor should do the following:

1. Participate in establishing the control objectives for the system.
2. For each control objective, develop alternate combinations of built-in controls and audit procedures.
3. For each alternative, estimate the sum of losses due to not achieving the objective; cost of insurance, if available; cost of the built-in controls; and cost of the audit procedures.
4. Search for and recommend the combinations of insurance, built-in controls, and audit procedures that, for the application as a whole, promises to be the most cost-effective.

Using this process to develop cost-effective audit programs typically means examining and reexamining a series of combinations; the final result may be a compromise between the most effective solution for each objective and the solution that is most effective for the application as a whole.

In an existing system, especially one that has evolved or been changed a great deal since its original installation, the auditor cannot rely on the system design's integrity. This is especially true in operational auditing. Consequently, for the unit under examination (or, in a large unit, for each subsystem of the unit) the auditor answers the following five questions:

1. What possible combinations of control failure could significantly impair the system's effectiveness?
2. What is the estimated cost of each significant impairment?

3. What are the possible combinations of audit objectives, evidence, and procedures that would detect and halt or minimize each impairment?
4. What is the cost of each control combination?
5. Which combination of controls offers the greatest savings, defined as the expected benefits of prevented control impairments less the cost of implementing and maintaining the controls?

The considerations are the same for both new and existing systems, but the perspective is different. With new systems, the designers (including the auditors) are responsible for the entire system; in modifying an existing system, they are dealing with many more uncontrollable variables. In both cases, of course, the objective is to develop cost-effective controls for every weakness. Any reader who has played chess or computer adventure games will recognize that the cost-effectiveness dimension of audit planning resembles the strategy of these games: pursuing an objective while complying with constraints. Achieving cost-effective audits requires consideration of complex alternatives, contingencies, restrictions, limitations, and uncertainties.

Summary

Auditors report to management and third parties about whether an organization's controls, including its financial reporting system, are operating as they should. Internal auditors also study the overall effectiveness of management; operational auditing looks into management objectives and structure, strategy, programs, budgets, and performance reporting. Both types of auditors analyze the appropriateness of system controls. Then they study (or "test") the organization's activities, including activities that implement controls and handle and record transactions to determine whether the controls actually exist and are functioning effectively.

The auditor depends on the existence and preservation of an audit trail. The nature of the audit trail has been changed by the introduction of computers into data processing. To maintain their effectiveness, auditors have developed techniques for auditing with, around, and through computers. These techniques help determine whether approved programs are in use, whether approved procedures are followed, and whether data processing results are consistent with data inputs. In many audit tests, auditors rely on the element of surprise.

To support their opinions and recommendations, auditors plan their work carefully and organize and document the evidence their audit discovers. They take into account the cost of additional audit work and the relative costs of implementing alternative recommendations they might make.

Key Terms

analytic evidence
audit
auditing
auditing around the computer
auditing through the computer
auditing with the computer
audit trail
byte-count test
Certified Public Accountant (CPA)
compilation

independent auditor
integrated test facility (ITF)
internal auditor
operational audit
program-logic test
review
test data
test evidence
working papers

Review Questions

1. What is auditing? How did auditing originate? What purpose does it serve today? Why do you think there are both independent and internal auditing functions?

2. What is a CPA? How does one become a CPA? Must an internal auditor be a CPA?

3. What is the difference between analytic evidence and test evidence? Should an audit be based exclusively on one kind of evidence?

4. To what extent must auditors study or examine an accounting system before expressing an opinion on its accounting statements?

5. Explain the difference between audit, review, and compilation. Specify the differences in the product or result and in the type and quantity of work the auditor must perform.

6. Name some of the management activities that are subject to internal audit. What question does the operational auditor seek to answer when evaluating the implementation of management objectives in these activities? What service or function is the operational auditor thereby performing?

7. Explain the relationships among audit scope, audit evidence, and audit conclusions.

8. How does the auditor determine whether an organization's controls can be relied upon? If they cannot, how does the auditor obtain enough evidence to achieve the objectives of the audit?

Discussion Questions

9. If the scope of an audit is decided before beginning the audit, is there a risk that it will inadvertently exclude problem areas and thus not reveal control lapses that should be corrected? Is there anything that

management and the auditor should do to reduce the risk of letting problem areas go undiscovered, without having to conduct every audit with the broadest possible scope?

10. What are the five stages in an operational audit? Why does one of these stages have input to two of the other stages? Why does Figure 14.3, which describes these stages, show the process as cyclical?

11. What are the six stages in an audit plan? What economic criterion must the plan satisfy? To what extent is the audit plan the same for most audit objectives? To what extent does it differ?

12. Explain the advantages and disadvantages of (a) auditing around the computer and (b) auditing through the computer. Can you envision any situations in which auditing around the computer could by itself produce sufficient evidence for an audit opinion?

13. What is the distribution of effort in the auditing process between effort to develop test evidence and effort to develop analytic evidence? Explain why internal and independent auditors might differ in their handling of working relationships before and during the audit. What is the purpose of using the computer to assist in the auditing process?

14. What organizational pressures do the internal auditor and the audited unit feel to reach agreement on the final audit report? Contrast these pressures with those on the independent auditor and management in a case in which the auditor proposes changes in the financial statements and management disagrees that the changes are necessary.

15. The text suggests different ways to classify audit steps: for which audit objective they produce evidence, whether they are analytic or test, whether they depend on surprise or are scheduled, and whether they require computer use and knowledge to carry out and interpret. How do these different classifications contribute to understanding computer auditing?

16. How does verification that selected actual transactions were handled correctly by the computer differ from the use of test data to verify that selected features of the information system were operating as expected? Answer in terms of the following questions: Which is the more powerful audit step? Which would require the least skill to implement? Which would be the least costly to implement?

Problems

17. The Wharton Railroad Company's internal auditors were puzzled by their inability to locate twenty-two tank cars that the company had purchased. The location of all tank cars was tracked by a computer application. The manager of the tank-car division maintained that unless the computer application had been modified, the cars could not

have been lost. The auditor considered it possible that controls in the tank-car division had become lax.

Required:

Comment on these two possibilities and recommend how the auditor should proceed next.

18. Refer to the procedures for a test of payroll transactions on page 508. Develop and write a similar series of procedures to test for the correct processing of a previously completed merchandise receiving report. Assume that the receiving report contains the following information:

- a unique serial identifying number of receiving report
- purchase order number(s) referenced
- name of vendor
- name of shipper
- date of delivery
- description of item(s) accepted unconditionally
- description of item(s) rejected or accepted subject to claims

19. The Waco Bottling Company has a small computer system. The auditor is conducting a review of the authorization of a program that tracks inventories of bottles, bottle caps, and bottling supplies. The audit produces the following evidence:

The program was acquired and placed in service on June 1, 19XX. It is written in BASIC and was acquired by the data processing director. The system operator has modified the program to make it easier to interrupt if a program with higher priority must be run. Two copies of the program are kept by the system operator, two copies by the controller's office, and one copy by the programmer, who tinkers with it and occasionally modifies the system operator's copies to include her changes. The program is run according to a schedule approved by the data processing director. The schedule is made out two weeks in advance and must be initialed by the system operator when the run occurs. However, the system operator will run the program whenever a company manager needs information from it. The system operator usually records these extra runs in the margin of the current schedule.

Required:

Point out exceptions to good practice in this description.

20. Anaheim Company provides communications consulting and planning services to clients nationwide. One of its programs keeps track of consultants' appointments and schedules, how they actually spent their time, and how clients should be billed for consulting services. Audit evidence in regard to this program shows the following:

The program was acquired and placed in service in March 19XX. At that time its length was recorded as 442,890 bytes. Its acquisition was approved by the controller, the data processing director, and the director of consultant operations. The program is written in COBOL. Only the machine-language version is kept on-site. On six occasions, modifications were proposed, approved by the three managers listed, and given to the system operator for incorporation into the program. These modifications changed the program's length as follows:

1. + 990 bytes
2. − 75 bytes
3. + 1,064 bytes
4. + 256 bytes
5. + 751 bytes
6. + 12,380 bytes

The system log shows that the changes were made. A master copy of the program and current copies of the files it uses reside in an off-site vault. The master copy is 456,754 bytes long. The in-use program is continually on line. The auditors measured the length of the on-line copy at 456,754 bytes.

Required:

Do you see any indication that this program's authorization should be questioned? If so, what is it and what should the additional audit work attempt to establish?

21. At the Wichita Company's home office, the following events occurred recently:

Ira Smith, the auditor, and his assistant appeared in the office of the data processing supervisor and stated their intention to conduct a surprise test of the purchasing and accounts payable application using specially prepared test data. The supervisor replied that it was unnecessary to perform such a test on a surprise basis, arguing that it would disrupt normal processing, confuse the operators, and possibly damage existing files; the supervisor would not allow the surprise test to be performed. The auditors were taken aback by this negative reaction and withdrew. Two days later, the data processing supervisor received a memo from the president, asking for cooperation in scheduling the test for the next day. The test was performed, and its results indicated that the logic of the program in use was identical with that of the master copy.

Required:

Explain why the auditors tried to run a surprise test, whether they acted properly in withdrawing, and what significance the results of the scheduled test should have in the audit. What might the auditors have done differently, and would that have changed the significance of the test results?

22. The Borger Credit Union has grown to the point that its managers believe it should hire an internal auditor. The credit union accepts deposits, makes loans, issues certificates of deposit, processes share drafts (similar to checks), and sells travelers checks. The credit union has a computer that processes all its transactions with members and other parties. The computer creates transaction files and posts them after each day's working hours. All of the accounting software programs were purchased from Credit Union Software, Inc., which issues updated versions once a year.

Required:

Write a memo from the credit union's chief accountant to its president explaining what the objectives of internal auditing should be in this organization.

23. The internal auditor at Periwinkle Company has observed that accounts shown as six months overdue on one computer-generated aging of accounts receivable occasionally disappear from the aging shown on the next report. The auditor cannot find any evidence that the amounts due were ever written off or paid. The accounts receivable subsidiary ledger is in balance with its control account. The auditor suspects that someone—perhaps an accounting clerk, salesperson, or computer operator—is entering unauthorized instructions between the reports to reverse the original sale that resulted in the receivable, thus causing it to disappear.

Required:

What audit steps might the auditor perform to determine whether this hypothesis is correct? List the steps and tell what each one does.

24. Langtry Asphalt Company maintains a depot at which asphalt is mixed and sold to contractors who pick it up for their projects. Typical volume is about 2,000 loads per month. Because the asphalt begins to cure as soon as it is mixed, it must be used almost immediately. Depending on the mix of ingredients, curing time can vary anywhere from 1 to 8 hours. If the asphalt cures before the requested delivery time, as measured from the time the truck leaves the depot, Langtry Asphalt will furnish a properly cured second—or third—load free. In the past year, about 10 percent of the loads have been returned to Langtry, at a cost of $300 per load. The company auditor hypothesizes that this is caused by inaccurate weighing scales and careless workers who are not following the mixing instructions. The auditor wants to

calibrate the scales daily and verify the ingredients of approximately every fourth load. This approach would cost $12,000 per month and would reduce the percentage of returned loads to 1 percent. The mixing department agrees with the auditor about the causes of returns and the effectiveness of these proposed controls but wishes to buy a computerized mixing machine that would measure and mix ingredients automatically for any given curing time. This machine would cost $360,000, have a three-year useful life span, and have the same operating costs as the present technology. It would reduce the percentage of returned loads to 3 percent.

Required:

Assuming that only one of these alternatives can be accepted, which do you recommend as most cost-effective? Justify your choice.

25. Green Publishing Company ships to bookstores all over the United States. It has a computerized inventory and shipping system. The following facts apply to it:

When an order is received, an operator enters the information into a computer file of orders pending. The computer automatically verifies the credit standing of each purchaser; if the customer's credit is good, the order is added to a file of orders for shipment. Warehouse personnel, using a terminal, fill these orders by collecting and boxing the items required, then placing them on a shipping dock with a computer-printed copy of the order and computer-generated shipping papers. If an item is out of stock, the warehouse personnel enter that on the computer. The same program that prints the shipping papers transfers the order to a file for posting to accounts receivable and invoicing. Twice daily, a shipper picks up ready orders. At the yard gate, a guard verifies that each box is accompanied by documentation.

The internal auditor has noted that requests for credit memos for items ordered and billed but omitted from the shipment are averaging $10,000 per month; she suggests carelessness by shipping employees and possibly even theft of items destined for customers. The warehouse personnel insist that pilferage and loss by customers explain the shortages. The internal auditor has suggested that an integrated test facility be programmed into the computer to generate phony orders at the rate of one per day. These orders would be shipped to locations controlled by Green Publishing Company and opened and inspected by Green personnel. Any differences between order and shipment quantities could be traced directly to the warehouse employees responsible. This plan would cost $2,000 per month, and is expected to reduce credits from warehouse error to $1,000 per month. The warehouse proposes that before shipping boxes are sealed, an independent warehouse checker completely verify each shipment; this plan would require an additional employee at $1,800 per month, and the warehouse believes it would completely eliminate all credits due to warehouse error.

Required:

(a) To the extent possible, determine the relative cost-effectiveness of each of these two proposals.

(b) Which proposal do you think is most likely to work in practice? Why?

26. The chief auditor of a certain state government is responsible for auditing 36 state agencies and offices annually. These units were all established at different times, and no two have the same accounting system. As a result, the chief auditor has been obliged to develop a unique audit plan for each one. He believes audit costs would be greatly reduced if the agencies all shared a common accounting system, and he estimates the cost of replacing the present 36 diverse systems with one unified system at about $12.5 million to implement it initially, plus $1.5 million annually to maintain it. Direct audit costs per agency would then average $200,000, which is 60 percent of the average current direct cost of audits.

Required:

(a) What is the current average direct cost of a state agency audit?

(b) What is the total annual direct cost of auditing all the state agencies? What would be the total annual direct cost if the agencies shared an integrated accounting system?

(c) How many years would it take to recover the initial cost of the integrated accounting system?

(d) Would you recommend that the state adopt its chief auditor's recommendation?

27. Payroll Data, Inc., prepares payrolls for many different companies. Most choose to transmit their payroll data via phone link from their computers to Payroll Data's computer. Because of the sensitivity of payroll information, Payroll Data goes to extraordinary lengths to provide security. The password procedure is as follows:

- The client dials Payroll Data's phone number and their computer responds, asking for a password.
- The client gives an 8-character password.
- The Payroll Data computer requests the phone number of the client's computer.
- The client gives its phone number.
- The Payroll Data computer breaks the connection with the client,

verifies that the phone number is on a list of approved numbers, and dials it.

- The Payroll Data computer, once recognized by the client computer, transfers control to it and awaits the command to transfer or receive payroll data.

Required:

(a) Consider the above procedure as a control; identify its objective, preventive, feedback, and follow-up elements.

(b) What are the objectives of the Payroll Data auditor in determining whether this control is working as intended? Suggest steps in an audit plan to accomplish these objectives.

(c) Do you see any possible weaknesses in this control? If so, list them.

(d) Suggest how Payroll Data should control the phone-number list so that only valid numbers appear on it.

Case: Harlingen Vineyards

Harlingen Vineyards was established by Mr. Founder, a retired investor. Four years ago the firm achieved sales of $90 million annually. Since then, sales have remained stable; the firm is profitable. The vineyards are managed through a series of computer programs, which calculate yields, harvest times, storage-space requirements, wine availability, and other information. Last year Mr. Founder sold the vineyards to a syndicate. An investigation by the new owner's internal auditor revealed the following:

Management has an excellent set of computer programs that produce a great variety of information and estimates of current significance. All long-run and many short-run decisions were made by Mr. Founder using this computer-generated information. We have located no statement of long-term objectives or strategy made by Mr. Founder. He met with his managers in small groups to discuss specific issues, then expressed his decisions as opinions about what should be done. No pattern emerges from his decisions, except that the company has grown and remained profitable in a competitive industry. All the current managers were hired by Mr. Founder. They got along well with him and with each other. They are a well-qualified and experienced team. They seem to be waiting, however, for the next meeting with Mr. Founder—which, of course, will never occur.

Required:

(a) Describe and analyze the process that produced the objectives, strategies, and programs of Harlingen Vineyards.

(b) How should the new owners alter this process? With what should they replace it? What should be the objective of their work? What will be the role of the internal auditor in this process?

Case: Beaumont Orange

Beaumont Orange is a new auditor on the staff of a public accounting firm. He has been asked to prepare an audit plan to verify that a computer-kept fixed asset subsidiary ledger is in agreement with actual fixed assets.

The client is a construction-equipment rental business. The business owns 39 pieces of equipment used in operations and 227 pieces of rental equipment ranging from bulldozers and dumpsters to power saws to transit levels, all rented for a few days at a time by various contractors. The equipment is kept on a 4-acre lot about a mile south of the city limits in a metropolitan area of about 300,000 persons. The lot is surrounded by a 10-foot-high woven-mesh fence with three strands of barbed wire on top. The gates are heavy-duty and secured by hardened steel chains and locks. Contractors must reserve equipment in advance and either establish credit or make a cash deposit equal to the equipment's value before renting it. The business office is located in a transportable building on the rental lot, set on concrete piers. The building houses the computer and its applications and files. Only the operating copies and their immediate backup copies of software are kept on the premises; master copies of applications are kept at the business owner's home, where daily back-up file copies are taken every evening. The owner buys all equipment to be used in the business. When the business acquires an asset, a computer record of it is created by the office manager, who is also one of two computer operators. This record provides space for the equipment's unique identification number, a short description, acquisition cost, date of acquisition, date placed in service, predicted salvage value, depreciation calculation method, accumulated depreciation expense taken, major maintenance schedule, major additions and overhauls, and date removed from service. Equipment can only be removed from service or sold with the business owner's consent. Every month, the owner reviews a computer printout prepared by the manager showing the fixed asset subledger and the record of rentals. The owner makes this review to determine which equipment should be removed from service, put back into service, or sold and to predict needed equipment that should be acquired. The office manager does not record rentals of equipment; this is done by the other computer operator, based on information supplied by the rentals department.

A partial excerpt of Beaumont's plan follows:

1. On a surprise basis, secure a copy of the operating version of the program used to maintain the fixed asset subsidiary ledger.
2. Compare the length of this version and the master version.
3. Secure from data processing administration a list of all approved changes and modifications in this program since the previous audit.
4. Examine the computer run log for positive evidence that these changes and modifications all were made.

5. Develop a set of test transactions to test the following features:
   (a) Add an asset.
   (b) Change location of an existing asset.
   (c) Change depreciation method of an existing asset.
   (d) Retire an asset.
   (e) Calculate annual depreciation expense on four different types of assets in each year of their lives.
   (f) Sell an asset.
   (g) Make major improvements in an asset, resulting in changes in its book value, service life, and depreciation method.

6. Obtain a printout of all assets at the end of the fiscal year and physically inspect each one to verify its existence, location, and condition as described in the printout.

7. Review all audit evidence and recommend changes in current procedures and programs.

Required:

   (a) Is the degree of detail in this plan responsive to the request made to Mr. Orange? Explain your answer.
   (b) Find at least four major errors or omissions in this plan that will impair its effectiveness. For example, are its provisions for analytic review adequate?

PART 4

New Developments Affecting Accounting Information Systems

Although many aspects of accounting systems remain the same or change very slowly, in other areas new ideas and innovations are constantly making accounting systems more effective. The two chapters in Part 4 introduce two such areas.

As human expertise becomes more costly and must handle more problems and more data, management interest in artificial intelligence has increased. Computer systems that incorporate artificial-intelligence applications have been called the "fifth generation" of computers and will begin to appear in the 1990s. Chapter 15 introduces the accounting applications of artificial intelligence by describing the structure of expert systems designed to evaluate controls and computer performance. Other successful expert systems applications emerging in tax planning, auditing, and systems design are sure to affect how accountants do their work.

As computer technology has developed, so have communications economy, capacity, and ease of use. The combination of high-tech computers and data base structure with space-age communication is creating versatile new information systems. The communications technology described in Chapter 16 allows all parts of an organization to be in touch with each other, and with other organizations, on every level of data and information exchange. Even small or one-office organizations can now link with large national data bases maintained by industry trade groups, financial networks, suppliers, and customers. And, large organizations are utilizing communications technology to compile data and produce performance reports as quickly as smaller ones.

Part 4 contains the following chapters:

Decision Support and Expert Systems

Learning Objectives

After studying this chapter, you should be able to

- Describe and recognize basic applications of artificial intelligence.

- Rank the uses of computers to support decision making in the order of how well those uses can be substituted for human information processing.

- Distinguish between expert systems and decision support systems.

- Name at least one commercial expert system, describe its field of applications, and explain why it is successful.

- Describe the prime uses of expert systems in accounting.

- Describe how an expert system examines premises.

- Specify the advantages and disadvantages of an expert system in any given situation, and conduct a feasibility analysis for a proposed implementation of an expert system.

In Chapter 1 of this book, we distinguish between *data* processing—computer conversion of data into information—and *information* processing—managerial conversion of information into decisions. A third kind of processing has recently become an area of intense research and development.

Knowledge processing is the use in the management process of expert knowledge, judgment, experience, computer-processed information, decision structure, and management objectives. Managers exercise knowledge processing when they pursue sound policies and decisions by sharing and analyzing their data, information, ideas, and intuition. When a computer system performs these tasks, which are normally associated with human intellectual capacity, it is called **artificial intelligence**, a term applied generally to any ability of a computer system to perform tasks normally associated with human intelligence.

Artificial intelligence is a tantalizing area for managers involved in decision making. Most individuals, no matter how creative, occasionally yearn to make complex decisions and judgments without paying the usual price in effort and time. This yearning has been caricatured in science-fiction movies like *Forbidden Planet,* in which curious scientists program a computer to respond to difficult questions and receive unexpected answers. What those celluloid protagonists were attempting is something many scientists, engineers, accountants, and managers now accomplish regularly: building an **expert system**, which is a computer program capable of selecting conclusions based on situation-specific input data, processed according to previously learned rules.

For decades executives have sought easy, rapid access to decision-specific information. The **decision support system (DSS)**, a collection of data, information, and processes specifically intended to provide relevant information to managers, fulfills this need. A DSS is possible thanks to data base processing using computers and is economical because it cuts the time and cost of organizing and reviewing all stored information related to specific decisions. In fact, many decision support system features can be incorporated into state-of-the-art management information systems.

In the United States, Europe, and Japan, researchers have been working with artificial intelligence, including expert systems, over the past three decades. This work is known as fifth-generation computer design (first generation: vacuum tubes; second generation: transistors; third generation: integrated circuits; fourth generation: very large scale integrated circuits, for example, microprocessors). **Fifth-generation computers** under development are especially intended for artificial intelligence applications. They will have the speed, capacity, and internal circuitry to run artificial-intelligence software. Recently fifth-generation work has begun to appear in applications in tax accounting, auditing, and financial control. It makes possible substantial enhancement of accounting and management information systems beyond mere transaction processing and minimal financial reporting.

This chapter will introduce you to decision support and expert systems and should enable you to identify valid applications for such systems within your future areas of responsibility. The chapter initially relates some of the abstract concepts that comprise computerized knowledge processing, or artificial intelligence. Within the field of artificial intelligence, we concentrate on expert systems and the ways they can offer support to those responsible for accounting information systems. Then, because it is a useful example of the way expert systems can support professional decision making, we look closely at MYCIN, a system that is already at work helping medical doctors diagnose bacterial infections. The chapter concludes with a sample (not-for-use) accounting application, a discussion of the relevance of expert systems in the areas of financial and auditing control, and a look at what accountants can hope for in the near future.

Knowledge Processing and Artificial Intelligence

Recently, creative systems analysts have developed computer programs capable of a limited version of knowledge processing. Specifically, these programs replicate the informed logical analysis that characterizes professional activities like medical diagnosis and production scheduling. Of course, the objective is ultimately to produce versatile computer programs with useful knowledge processing ability in many specialized fields, that is, to produce artificial intelligence.

Knowledge Processing

A generalized knowledge processing program would make expert judgment available to anyone with a computer. Such a program would operate by accepting two kinds of input: (1) fact situations or premises, and (2) rules.

Initially, such a program would receive premises and would process a set of judgmental rules. **Premises** are the values of variables that describe specific fact situations in which the knowledge processing program must perform. **Rules** relate these values to specific elements in the set of possible conclusions. For example, a variable may be the credit status of a customer. This variable may have the values "credit OK" or "credit not OK." The rules that use these premises are, "If credit is OK, continue with sale" and "If credit is not OK, sale may only be for cash." Through its built-in knowledge processing structure, the program would apply these rules to the credit-status input data that describe a specific customer and sale. Next, the program would express judgments or recommendations about that situation. Finally, if requested to, the program could provide additional output relating its judgment and recommendation outputs to the original premises and rules, producing a kind of audit trail.

The development of such programs includes a learning phase. For example, a program to monitor production quantities for various products might be developed in the following manner. As sales transactions occur, a computer application records them (data processing). Product-line managers then receive and study computer-produced sales summaries, which they examine to identify product-preference trends apparent in the transactions (information processing). At weekly meetings, the product line managers discuss how to modify production schedules to maintain the proper relationships among sales, inventories, and production (knowledge processing).

The product-line managers could "teach" the computer how they analyze sales, inventory, and production to make their decisions. Then, they could use the computer program to produce recommendations as starting points for their own analyses. Eventually, as the computer program learns more rules and becomes smarter, the product-line managers might be willing to assign this aspect of decision making to the program, if it were implemented with appropriate controls such as periodic review.

The design of most accounting transaction processing systems is not intended to support ongoing managerial decision-making processes. Such systems are designed to record the basic activities of an organization in a way that allows auditable financial statements to be easily prepared. Where no thought has been given to information support for management, the existence of a basic accounting system gives no assurance that managers will be provided with adequate information to make appropriate or acceptable decisions. Of course, many managers develop their own sources of information, unsupported by a computer-based system; naturally, some will do a better job of this than others. Computer-based knowledge processing, though, potentially makes available to all executives a supply of consistent, high-quality information support for managerial decision making and control processes—through a decision support system.

Artificial Intelligence

Artificial-intelligence researchers have developed, or expect to develop, successful applications in three major areas: natural languages, robotics, and expert systems. Since the first two areas, natural language and robotics, are less directly relevant to managerial decision making than is the area of expert systems, we will discuss them only briefly here.

Natural languages are those that people use in speaking to each other, in contrast with the artificial languages employed in computer programming. If computers could accept instructions in natural languages, the programming phase of applications development would be much easier. Communication with computers in natural languages would also enhance the use of computers in situations that require the interactive exchange of data between managers and computers, such as long-range planning, strategy development, and short-term "what-if" analysis of decision alternatives. Natural languages would simplify data base interrogation and might even allow managerial users to forgo most of the technical support they receive from applications programmers.

Robotics is the technology of designing, building, and using robots. Robots, combinations of machine and computer, can be programmed to carry out and repeat complex sequences of movements. The use of robots is well established in certain industrial and medical situations. They routinely handle radioactive and toxic materials, assemble automobiles, and perform such medical procedures as scanning organs. The advantages of robots in such situations are that they can't be distracted, aren't harmed by their environment, operate with precision and consistency, and if irreparably damaged on the job—well, it was only a machine.

In most cases, robots lack the ability to modify their performance in response to changing conditions they encounter as they work. One of the goals of robotics research is to produce robots with the ability to adapt their own programs and procedures to variable conditions. For example, a human needs strength, dexterity, and years of experience to recognize and align the two pieces of metal to be welded, reject them if they cannot be aligned, select the right position for the seam within manufacturing tolerances, make certain the surfaces are smooth and properly prepared, make the weld, and inspect it for flaws. The "intelligent" robot would have x-ray or tomographic sensors, precisely controllable arms, and a programmable computer connected to the sensors and arms. Properly written programs would enable the robot to do everything the human welder would do, more consistently and precisely.

Eventually, robots could move out of factories and laboratories into order entry, transaction recording, and other office chores; already, mail-distribution and snack-selling robots roll through some offices. Robots could also work in conditions that human beings would find intolerable, such as extreme heat and cold, radiation, and outer space.

Unlike natural language programs and robotics, expert systems are computer programs designed to analyze *information* according to rules and to draw conclusions consistent with those a human expert would draw from the same facts. The type of judgments an expert system can be expected to make are comparable in complexity to those humans would have to make in similar circumstances. Expert systems currently in use identify diseases, design and configure computer systems and elevator systems, and identify and recommend remedies for problems in complex communications systems, diesel-engine design, oil-well drilling, job scheduling, and production management.

But most important, expert systems seem to have the potential to perform functions in financial control systems, thus changing the way accountants operate in organizations. We will therefore discuss them at length in this chapter.

A Hierarchy of Systems Support

The expert system has a distinct place in the hierarchy of information systems and computer-assisted aids to management decision making and control. This hierarchy consists of four categories, distinguished by the extent to which each can be substituted for human processing of information and knowledge. The lowest category, file-oriented data processing, offers only limited and passive access to information. The two intermediate categories—data base processing and decision support systems—offer active access to limited information and information processing, applicable to many different managerial situations. The highest category, expert systems, offers extensive information and knowledge processing, applicable to very specific managerial situations.

File-Oriented Data Processing

As you will recall from Chapter 5, file-oriented data processing systems organize information into records, which in turn are organized into files. Each record in a file may have one, two, or more indexed key fields. An analyst who knows the value of at least one of the key fields can quickly find and process a particular record. Otherwise, a time-consuming sequential search or reindexing of the entire file is necessary to locate the record.

File-processing systems have two unique advantages. First, file processing can provide a rapid flow of ordered but undifferentiated information. If two or more managers share the decision-making style to which the system was originally adapted, a file-processing system excels at providing lots of predetermined reports that support that style. Second, file processing is inexpensive: acquisition, maintenance, and operation costs are all low, although major modification is costly. File processing is probably the most cost-effective use of computers for simple, repetitive decision situations. However, its information output generally cannot be adapted or changed except by changing the system itself, often a tedious, resource-intensive, and time-consuming procedure. Managers must adapt to file-processing systems by learning (through training, experience, and trial and error) what information to get elsewhere and what information to overlook. An organization that encourages its managers to develop unique decision-making styles that may change frequently should not make file processing its first choice for a system design.

Data Base Processing

For those whose responsibilities do not allow them to anticipate their information needs far enough into the future to specify record layouts and report formats in a file-processing environment, data base processing may be the answer. Data base processing represents an advance over file processing because it can be more flexible in the way it responds to users. It uses pointers, invisible to users, to link together records containing potentially related information. Application programs employ pointers to move from one record to another in whatever order is required to obtain the needed information and to present it in report format. These application programs depend on a data base environment. Since a good data base environment allows virtually unrestricted access to the data and information it stores, your problem-solving behavior includes the option of specifying the information the data base will provide *in the short run* (that is, while the problem is being solved). In contrast to a file-processing system, you need not wade through quantities of output and learn to ignore the irrelevant items while making decisions.

A data base system initially costs more to develop than does a file-processing system; it requires more programming and more computer power. However, its far greater responsiveness to managerial needs usually gives it a longer useful life over which to spread the initial cost. The data base approach is most cost-feasible for applications involving diverse decisions based on the same storehouse of information. But because of the additional resource requirements, management may initially define a data base system to service fewer needs than the same management would define for a file-processing system of comparable cost. Doing so can be shortsighted. Although a data base can be extremely user-friendly, it remains basically a passive mechanism—accepting what it is programmed to accept, providing what it is programmed to provide. Valuable facts can lie sealed in it forever if its users do not ask for them.

Decision Support Systems

The objective of a DSS is to make it difficult for a manager to overlook relevant information. The systematic assistance and augmentation that a DSS provides the decision maker include files, consultants, controls, decision or planning models, training, and communication. This chapter, however, limits discussion of DSS to those systems that include computer-maintained information and models specifically intended for decision support.

In practice, the performance requirements for an accounting decision support system determine the data collected, the rules and models used in processing, and the data base or file structure used by transaction processing applications. Such systems are expensive but widely applicable to managerial responsibilities. To be useful to managers who have limited understanding of computers and of how the DSS actually works, the DSS must assume no special skills on the part of the user. To simplify the pulling together of information related to a specific decision, the DSS must be able to retrieve information from forecasts, projections, time series, risk analyses, budgets, and models, as well as from transaction processing. To "back up" the manager, the DSS should be programmed to present potentially pertinent information even if it isn't specifically requested.

The DSS separates the managerial user from transaction processing even though, like data base processing, it can combine data elements however the user wishes. The DSS can also access needed information from external sources, such as sales and foreign-currency trend forecasts, economic statistics, budget projections, and even engineering product designs and specifications. To help a manager use all this information in reaching a decision, the DSS should prompt him or her about its availability, the decisions in which it could be beneficial, and the process for making complex decisions. Experienced managers performing well might not require such extensive support, but the DSS will help good managers perform more consistently and average managers perform better than they could without the system. You could consider the DSS as a very sophisticated data base, limited in its scope to specialized decisions and functions conceived by users.

Figure 15.1 illustrates the components of file-based processing, data base processing, and decision support systems and the relationships between them.

As an example of a DSS, let us use the Rosharon Bolt & Supply Company's inventory-management and purchasing function. The company maintains in stock nearly 65,000 different items required by builders, suppliers, and manufacturers. The system inputs, which it regularly records or calculates for each item from transaction files and other sources, include the following:

- Average daily unit sales of each item since last reorder
- Standard deviation of average daily unit sales of each item in same period
- Preferred supplier
- Average delay from time of order until shipment arrives

The DSS processes these inputs to calculate a reorder point for each item. The reorder point varies with the average rate of sales and the variability of that rate according to this formula.

$$\text{Reorder point} = \left[\begin{array}{c} \text{Average} \\ \text{daily unit} \\ \text{sales} \end{array} + \begin{array}{c} 2 \\ \text{standard} \\ \text{deviations} \end{array} \right] * \begin{array}{c} \text{Average days} \\ \text{delivery} \\ \text{delay} \end{array}$$

The DSS also calculates the order quantity, based on the demand level plus cost information stored in other files.

For each item, the DSS compares the computed reorder point with the quantity in stock. If the reorder point is greater than the quantity in stock, the DSS lists that item and the proposed order quantity in an "order priority" report, which the purchasing manager receives. The purchasing manager reviews all such items, since whether and how much to reorder may depend on factors other than those considered by the DSS. If the purchasing manager approves the orders, the DSS will link all items to be ordered from the same supplier and print the purchase orders.

This DSS separates decision makers from transaction data, makes relevant information readily available, and has an easy-to-understand user

Figure 15.1   Types of Support Systems
File and data base processing are relatively involved in data capture; DSS is relatively active in processing information for decision-making. DSS includes features to assure that the decision maker receives and acknowledges the information. Note the link between DSS and the data base produced by data base processing.

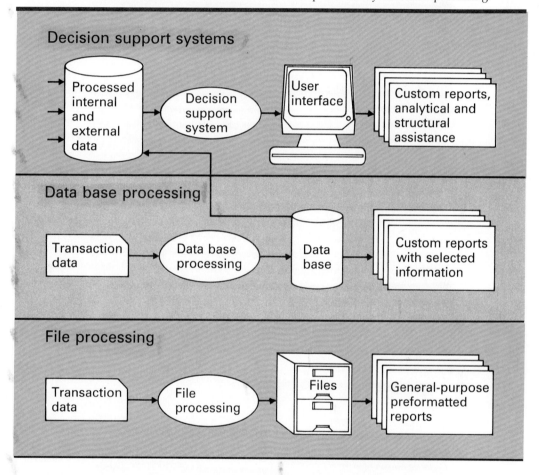

interface. It does not require special information systems skills on the part of the purchasing manager. It relies on data created through transaction processing, but not exclusively, and uses other information and rules and models based on cost and profit objectives. Finally, it presents unsolicited but related information that will help the purchasing manager to maintain sufficient stocks of all items. Because every decision support system is tailor-made to meet unique requirements, even others that support inventory and purchasing management in similar firms might be quite dissimilar to the one described.

Auditors have access to a nationwide DSS. The **National Accounting and Auditing Retrieval System (NAARS)** is a data base of comparative information for use in the latter stages of an audit. It was also one of the first major on-line applications of relational data base technology. After compiling their audit results, auditors can consult NAARS for similar fact situations and guidance on how to structure an audit opinion for the client.

Expert Systems

An expert system is a different species from DSS. An expert system *makes judgments and gives advice based on information provided by the files, the data bases, and the system's managerial users.* An expert system makes recommendations about decisions with a high logical content. It requests additional data, draws conclusions using logical or judgmental decision rules, infers rules or conclusions, states the reasons for its conclusions, and provides an audit trail in support of those reasons. An expert system also draws its strength from a very narrow scope of applicability and the number-crunching ability of fast computers.

Expert systems may even intervene in decisions and second-guess the managers. Once implemented, an expert system functions as an active adviser to the manager. It supplies additional detail or summary as requested. Along with the manager, it learns and applies new rules. The expert system should be able to do two things no other form of managerial aid can:

1. *Request* specific additional information required to complete a file or perform a function.
2. *Learn*, store, and apply externally imposed rules, some of which lead to other rules at different levels.

Expert systems also offer a third major benefit—greater depth of assistance in selected applications. An expert system may sound like a manager's dream, but as usual, there is a trade-off—its major drawback is the expense of its development. It requires time-consuming and expensive "prompting" and "training" to build a logical processing structure for dealing with the facts of specific consultations.

By 1990, some expert-system applications may achieve parity in cost-effectiveness with human expert consultation. Already, systems have been programmed for microcomputers. One intended for use in designing information systems is available from the accounting firm of Arthur Young at a cost of $7,500 for the software alone (not including the cost of preparing each application of the system). Another, which provides tax-planning suggestions to clients, incorporates the expertise of forty tax experts and is used by another accounting firm, Coopers & Lybrand.

Expert Systems: Advisers to Management

The structure that makes an expert-system application effective for specific uses also imposes limitations on its use. This structure consists of a user interface and two data bases—a static data base and a dynamic data base. The **user interface**—that is, the boundary between the human user and the computer, through which the two communicate—allows the user to supply data, receive conclusions, and if necessary, document the reasoning that led to those conclusions. The **static data base** is permanent; it includes the premises, rules, and expert knowledge used to analyze each situation. The rules need not be scientifically verifiable in the same sense as the law of gravity, but they must relate premises to the conclusions in a way that experts would agree is meaningful. The **dynamic data base** consists of the facts associated with an individual application of the expert system and the conclusions it reaches based on these facts and on the static data base. An expert system will be very effective in analyzing situations like the one for which its static data base was designed. But because this static data base cannot be changed, the system cannot understand or relate to situations that do not match it.

Favorable Environments

Operational expert systems work best in well-defined decision-making environments that share certain characteristics. An environment favorable to expert systems is one in which known experts give advice to clients on complex matters. These experts rely on logic and, to a lesser extent, experience and intuition to analyze fact situations and to formulate their judgments and recommendations. The experts should be able to explain how they reach their conclusions and to transfer their expertise to others, or to the expert system. The amount of time an expert devotes to a typical decision should not exceed several hours. This criterion helps assure that the benefits of a consultation, which involves a human interface with the expert system, will exceed the cost of using the expert system. Finally, there should be enough demand for the type of knowledge the expert system will incorporate to make it economically attractive to develop.

The current generation of expert systems, although remarkable, has shortcomings that restrict the environments in which the systems can be useful. They cannot draw on general knowledge, such as familiarity with human language or social structure. Thus they cannot be used by people unfamiliar with computers. Nor can they analyze or resolve behavioral problems, such as staffing a management structure, very well. They cannot extend their conclusions beyond the scope of their expertise, which is programmed in or implicit in the static data base. For instance, an expert system that identifies bacterial infections will always try to identify a bacterial infection, even if a virus is clearly responsible for the symptoms reported in the dynamic data base. Since expert systems cannot measure and probe for themselves, they have no access to the real system about which they are "expert." This limitation is called the "frame" problem by AI researchers, who report very little progress in solving it. This makes the expert system utterly dependent on human beings for its learning and development. Thus expert systems are likely to exhibit all the weaknesses of human beings, but without the human ability to learn from mistakes. Anyone who uses an expert system must keep all of these limitations in mind when relying on the conclusions it produces.

MYCIN: A Working Example from Medicine

Medicine is a fertile field for designers of expert systems. Diagnosis, in particular, with its inherent logic and extremely high volume of relevant technical information, is a receptive environment for an expert system. Indeed, an expert system called MYCIN[1] has been developed to diagnose bacterial infections. MYCIN requests information about a patient's illness and then analyzes it using approximately 400 IF/THEN rules. These rules consist of a list of attributes that result in a given conclusion. The format is as follows:

> IF (premises)
>   (1) Attribute 1 exists
>   (2) Attribute 2 exists
>   (3) Attribute 3 exists
>   (4) Attribute 4 exists
> THEN (conclusions)

For example,

> IF
>   (1) Patient has spasms of the jaw and neck muscles
>   (2) Patient has a deep wound
>   (3) Patient has not received DPT immunization
> THEN
>   Patient probably has a significant infection
>   The infection is probably tetanus
>   Both antibiotics and sedatives should be administered

Other possible conclusions might be that:

> The infecting organism is _____
> Drugs _____ , _____, and _____ will be effective
> Drug _____ would be best for this patient

---

[1]MYCIN was developed by Edward Shortliffe and others at the Stanford Heuristic Programming Project with assistance from the Stanford Medical School.

Each conclusion may have a certainty factor. The certainty factor quantifies the degree of confidence the physician should place on the conclusion if the premises are true.

When confronted by illness in a patient, a physician observes and interviews the patient to collect information, diagnoses the illness, and then selects and applies a treatment. This procedure works with varying degress of success, depending on the specificity of the causes and symptoms of the illness. For example, meningitis can be caused by several different types of bacteria. Physicians try to identify the bacterium responsible for a specific case of meningitis through laboratory tests. The treatment will depend on the type of bacteria indicated by the tests and the condition of the patient. Because laboratory tests are not always 100-percent specific, there is usually some uncertainty about a diagnosis. The available treatments are not 100-percent effective either. For this reason, a physician will often combine several treatments. Thus, there are many factors to consider when diagnosing and treating a bacterial infection that looks like meningitis. With diseases of this complexity, an expert system can be a valuable aid.

Once the factual symptoms have been transmitted to MYCIN, the expert system determines whether an infection exists, identifies the probable cause, recommends treatment, and gives its reasons. If more than one possible cause or treatment exists, MYCIN names all of them. Because the diagnosis and treatment of bacterial infections requires *very* extensive and detailed medical knowledge—more than most physicians can keep constantly at their fingertips—MYCIN fills a need. In tests, the accuracy of its performance has proved comparable to that of the best medical experts.

A Sample Consultation.   A consultation with MYCIN begins with the physician or medical technician "logging on" the computer, giving a password, and requesting the operating system to run the MYCIN program. MYCIN's user interface asks the patient's name, age, sex, race, whether a positive culture report exists on the patient and when it was received from the laboratory, and from what sites the cultures were taken. From this point on, the direction of questioning depends on the program's interpretation of all the information previously supplied. After it has gathered sufficient information, MYCIN makes its diagnosis and recommends treatment.

In the abridged MYCIN session that follows, M is the expert system and P is the physician:

M: Let's call the most recent positive culture CULTURE-1. Let's call the first significant organism from this culture ORGANISM-1. Do you know the identity of ORGANISM-1?

P: No.

M: Is ORGANISM-1 a rod or coccus or something else?

P: Rod.

M: What is the gram-stain of ORGANISM-1?

P: Gramnegative.

M: Did ORGANISM-1 grow aerobically?

P: Yes.

M: Did ORGANISM-1 grow anaerobically?

P: Yes.

M: Is the patient's illness with ORGANISM-1 a hospital-acquired infection?

P: Why?

M: This will aid in determining the identity of ORGANISM-1. It already has been established that ORGANISM-1 is

—rod

—gramneg

—facul

Therefore if the infection with ORGANISM-1 was acquired while the patient was hospitalized

Then there is p = 0.2 that the identity of ORGANISM-1 is pseudomonas.

P: (Answering the original question) Yes.

M: My recommendation will be based on the opinion that the identity of ORGANISM-1 may be 1 Klebsiella pneumoniae (0.6) or 2 Bacteriodes fragilis (0.4). On a scale of 0 to 4 how would you rate the patient's degree of sickness?

P: 3.

M: How much does the patient weigh?

P: 80 kg.

M: My first recommendation is as follows: In order to cover for item 1, give Gentamycin using a dose of 145 mg every 8 hours for 10 days. And in order to cover for item 2, give Clindamycin using a dose of 660 mg every 6 hours for 14 days.

P: Why didn't you think that ORGANISM-1 was Neisseria?

M: The following rules could have been used to determine that the identity of ORGANISM-1 is Neisseria: 9

However, none of these succeeded in the context of ORGANISM-1.

If you would like an explanation for why any of these rules failed, please enter their numbers:

P: 9.

M: Clause 2 of rule 9 ["the morphology of the organism is coccus"] was already known to be false for ORGANISM-1, so the rule was never tried.[2]

---

[2]Excerpt from Chapter 15, in "Inside an Expert System: A Rational Reconstruction of the Mycin Consultation System" by Jadzia Cendrowska and Max Bramer in *Artificial Intelligence: Tools, Techniques, and Applications*, edited by Tim O'Shea and Marc Eisenstadt. Copyright © 1984 by Harper & Row, Publishers, Inc. Reprinted by permission of Harper & Row, Publishers, Inc.

This dialogue should give you a sense of how the program gathers information, and how it explains its reasoning. Of course, M's informal yet precise conversational style is actually the product of clever data output formatting by M's programmers.

The program also contains instructions that govern the flow of control and the flow of information during the consultation. Figure 15.2 maps these flows of control and information within MYCIN. In this diagram, the colored arrows represent flow of control; the black arrows indicate flow of information. As the colored arrows indicate, the user interface is part of the "consultation program," which draws data from both the static and dynamic data bases. After MYCIN makes its diagnosis and recommends treatment, the "explanation program" is available to answer ques-

Figure 15.2　Flow of Information and Control Within MYCIN
MYCIN is typical of expert systems in that it separates the dynamic and static data bases and separates logical control from information flow.

Source: Jadzia Cendrowska and Max Bramer, "Inside an Expert System: A Rational Reconstruction of the MYCIN Consultation System," in *Artificial Intelligence: Tools, Techniques, and Applications*, eds. Tim O'Shea and Marc Eisenstadt. (New York: Harper & Row, 1984), pp. 453–497, Fig. 15.1, adapted from E. H. Shortliffe, *Computer-based Medical Consultation: Mycin* (New York: American Elsevier, 1976), p. 46.

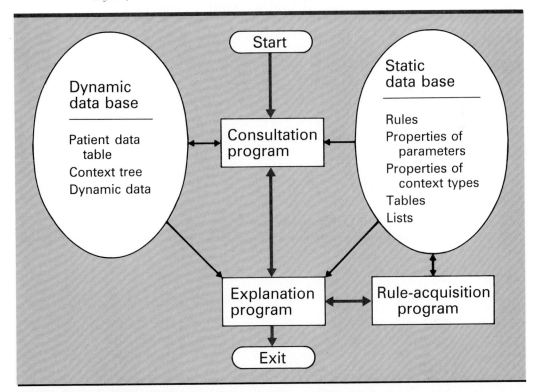

tions and explain how MYCIN reached its conclusions. The "rule-acquisition program" is not normally used during a consultation. It is used at the design stage to develop the rules in the static data base and may be used later to add to or amend these rules.

An Accounting Example:
Building a Systems Watchdog

Before considering more complex applications, let's look at a very simple expert system not really intended for real-world tasks. The example will illustrate how such a system is developed or trained and what its basic components look and act like. This very simple expert system is designed to conclude whether current computer capacity is adequate to support the current accounting system or if accounting system planning is required. The eight possible conclusions will be accepted or rejected based on premise values unique to an individual consultation and supplied in response to four questions. The static data base consists of the relationships linking the premises and conclusions; the dynamic data base consists of the premise values. As illustrated in the MYCIN example, the initial procedure would be to identify the patient (or in this case, the accounting system) and determine the premise values on which the expert system bases its opinion. As values are entered, the expert system reviews them and relates them to conclusions they support, eliminates rules it need not pursue further, and maintains a tentative set of rules that forthcoming information might satisfy.

Conclusions.   The expert-system developer wants the completed system to validate up to three of eight possible conclusions, based on the premises developed in a specific consultation. The conclusions are listed in Table 15.1. Each will be included in a rule that relates it to one or more premises.

Dynamic and Static Data Bases.   In this illustration, the dynamic data base consists of the answers to four basic questions. The answers to these

Table 15.1   Illustrative Expert-System Conclusions

C0: No recommendations possible
C1: The accounting processing system is adequate
C2: Accounting system planning is required
C3: The accounting processing system is inadequate
C4: Disk capacity is adequate for the time being
C5: Disk capacity is now inadequate or soon will be
C6: It is not necessary to do accounting system planning now
C7: Please recheck premises, as they may be internally inconsistent

Table 15.2 Illustrative Expert-System Premises

P1: What percentage of on-line disk storage capacity is actually in use?
    P1.1 <30%   P1.2 30–70%   P1.3 >70%   P1.4 Do not know

P2: How old is the system?
    P2.1 <5 years   P2.2 >5 years   P2.3 Do not know

P3: What percentage of CPU operating time is spent accessing existing data?
    P3.1 <40%   P3.2 >40%   P3.3 Do not know

P4: What is the average annual rate of growth in accounting processing activity?
    P4.1 <5%   P4.2 >5%   P4.3 Do not know

questions form the premises of a specific consultation. The questions and their possible answers are given in Table 15.2.

The expert system's knowledge, or static data base, is stored in the form of rules. These rules must be "learned" from human experts. In general, a system's static data base will be built in one intensive effort, then modified as needed in response to experiences and changes in the underlying body of knowledge. Each rule relates certain premise values to certain conclusions. Links between rules may make it possible, if one rule proves valid, to immediately test other rules with a significant probability of also being valid.

As its static data base is being built, an expert system should prompt its human trainers to enter rules and should then (1) verify that new rules are consistent with existing rules, (2) seek links between rules, and (3) ensure that the data necessary to apply a new rule are available. Meanwhile, the experts convey to the system their knowledge of how premises should be linked to conclusions, doing so either directly or by providing actual situations the program must analyze to discover the linkages.

Table 15.3 shows the rules for our sample-system. These rules can be phrased verbally. For example, the first rule means that

    IF
        (P1.1) Less than 30 percent of on-line storage capacity is in use
        (P2.1) The system is less than 5 years old
        (P3.1) Less than 40 percent of CPU operating time is spent accessing existing data
        (P4.1) The average annual rate of growth in accounting processing is less than 5 percent
    THEN
        (C1) The accounting processing system is adequate
        (C4) Disk capacity is adequate for the time being
        (C6) It is not necessary to do accounting system planning now

Table 15.3   Illustrative Expert-System Rules (See Table 15.2 for Premise Values)
This table shows how the illustrative expert system responds to each combination of input data.

Combinations of premise values	Disk cap used				Age of system			Access time			Growth rate		
	P1.1 <30%	P1.2 30–70%	P1.3 >70%	P1.4 Don't know	P2.1 <5yr	P2.2 >5yr	P2.3 Don't know	P3.1 <40%	P3.2 >40%	P3.3 Don't know	P4.1 <5%	P4.2 >5%	P4.3 Don't know
C1, C4, C6	Y				Y			Y			Y		
C1, C4, C6	Y				Y			Y				Y	
C1, C2, C4	Y				Y			Y					Y
C1, C2, C4	Y				Y				Y		Y		
C1, C2, C4	Y				Y				Y			Y	
C0	Y				Y				Y				Y
C1, C4, C6	Y					Y		Y			Y		
C1, C2, C4	Y					Y		Y				Y	
C0	Y					Y		Y					Y
C1, C2, C4	Y					Y			Y		Y		
C1, C2, C4	Y					Y			Y			Y	
C0	Y					Y			Y				Y
C1, C4, C6		Y			Y			Y			Y		
C1, C2, C4		Y			Y			Y				Y	
C1, C2, C4		Y			Y			Y					Y
C1, C4, C6		Y			Y				Y		Y		
C1, C2, C4		Y			Y				Y			Y	
C0		Y			Y				Y				Y
C1, C4, C6		Y				Y		Y			Y		
C1, C2, C4		Y				Y		Y				Y	
C0		Y				Y		Y					Y
C1, C2, C4		Y				Y			Y		Y		
C1, C2, C5		Y				Y			Y			Y	
C0		Y				Y			Y				Y
C1, C2, C4			Y		Y			Y			Y		
C1, C2, C4			Y		Y			Y				Y	
C0			Y		Y			Y					Y
C7			Y		Y				Y		Y		
C2, C3, C5			Y		Y				Y			Y	
C0			Y		Y				Y				Y
C1, C2, C4			Y			Y		Y			Y		
C2, C3, C5			Y			Y		Y				Y	
C2, C3, C5			Y			Y		Y					Y
C1, C2, C5			Y			Y			Y		Y		
C2, C3, C5			Y			Y			Y			Y	
C2, C3, C5			Y			Y			Y				Y

Training the System. The expert system's training consists of preparing the computer equivalent to the matrix in Table 15.3, which relates the conclusions to premise values. In the matrix, every possible combination of premise values is related to one or more conclusions.

To keep the illustration simple, assume that P1, P2, and P3 will never be answered "do not know." Table 15.3 shows the thirty-six combinations of premises and conclusions that are possible given this limitation. The matrix lists the premises across the top of the figure and provides a column for a yes or no response to each possible value. By reading the "Y" responses across a row, you can determine which premise values apply. The left-hand column lists the reference numbers of the conclusions related to the premises specified in each row. For many of the combinations of premises, the potential conclusions are identical. In fact, only six unique combinations appear in the thirty-six premise sets:

1. C1, C4, C6
2. C1, C2, C4
3. C0
4. C1, C2, C5
5. C7
6. C2, C3, C5

A Consultation. Imagine that you've just decided to consult with this expert system. You report that over 70 percent of the task system's disk capacity is filled (P1.3). At this point, five out of the six possible conclusion sets are still open: {C1, C2, C4}, {C0}, {C1, C2, C5}, {C7}, and {C2, C3, C5}. The expert system, seeking to eliminate some of these combinations, asks for the average annual growth rate of data processing, which you report as more than 5 percent annually. The possible conclusion sets are now reduced to only two: {C1, C2, C4} and {C2, C3, C5}.

You may need to answer only one of the two remaining premise generating questions to eliminate one set. The expert system selects premise question 3 and asks how much time is spent by the CPU in data access (See the Access Time column in Table 15.3). You respond that the computer system devotes more than 40 percent of its time to such activities. This eliminates {C1, C2, C4}, leaving only {C2, C3, C5}. The expert system thus reports that accounting system planning is required; the accounting processing system is inadequate; and disk capacity is now inadequate or soon will be.

Introducing More Premises. So far, you could review the alternatives about as rapidly as a computer could. So let's make the decision more complicated. If all 4 premise-generating questions could be answered "Do not know," there would be 108 possible premise combinations. If 4 more premise-generating questions, each with 4 possible answers, were added to the existing 4, the number of premise combinations would increase to 27,648. (One such question might be, "Is the major user of this system private-sector services, private-sector industry, government, or not for profit?"). And 100 possible questions, with 4 possible answers each, would bring the number of premise combinations to $4^{100} = 1.6 \times 10^{60}$. The power of the computerized expert system now becomes very clear. *The expert system can move quickly through all these details without missing the significance of any one of them.*

A well-programmed expert system need not be, as our illustration is, limited to completing a premise set and inspecting the possible conclusions. It may also scan premise sets and ask for additional information that might eliminate some conclusion sets.

Some Suitable Auditing Applications

Many audit tasks have the attributes that make them suitable for decision support and expert system applications. Figure 15.3 spells out the major steps in a typical audit. Those shown in color represent potential major decision support and expert-system applications. The steps not highlighted in color lend themselves to computerized data *capture* by auditors.

The prime auditing application for expert systems may be evaluating the results of the analytic review of internal control. Insofar as the audit

Figure 15.3   Steps in a Typical Audit
Audits include many opportunities for expert-system applications.

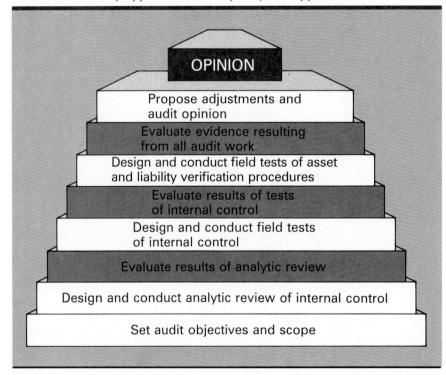

program calls for quantitative or yes-or-no responses to specific questions, the auditor can enter the response directly onto a screen form for review, edit, or addition to a data base or spreadsheet template. Later, the auditor can activate either a report generator (to summarize the aggregate audit evidence) or an expert system (to interpret the significance of the evidence).

Analytic Review.   As you will recall from Chapter 14, the audit's analytic review of internal control consists of (a) putting together a description of the internal controls as they are designed to function and (b) evaluating how well these controls will meet their objectives if they actually operate as designed by management. The audit field tests of internal control probe whether the internal controls function as described and, if not, what control elements need to be enhanced and what objectives and elements need to be added.

If one audit objective is to determine whether all purchases recorded were authorized, an expert system's software program might include the following logic:

IF
- P1   Client uses purchase requisitions
- P2   Client uses only authorized vendors
- P3   All purchases must be through client's purchasing department
- P4   All purchase orders must be approved by purchasing department
- P5   No payment for purchases are made without matching receiving report and vendors' invoice

THEN
- C1   The control procedures to assure that all purchases are authorized appear to be adequate

In light of such expert system output, an auditor might schedule relatively light field work to test compliance with the purchasing controls. If the expert system concluded instead that purchase-control procedures appeared inadequate, the auditor would schedule sufficient audit field work to determine the extent of unauthorized purchases, if any. Managers and auditors alike should note that the high cost of extended audit field work argues in favor of using an audit expert system to hold field work to the required minimum.

Field-Work Specification.   One natural outgrowth of evaluating audit evidence collected at the preceding stage is audit field work specification. The expert system applies rules that relate field work (conclusions) to the results of analytical review (premises). Let us look at two variations on the purchasing example above to illustrate how the logic changes with each change in premises.

IF
- P1 Client *does not* use purchase requisitions
- P2 Client uses only authorized vendors
- P3 All purchases must be made through the purchasing department
- P4 All purchase orders must be approved by purchasing department
- P5 No payment for purchases is made without matching receiving report and vendors' invoice

THEN

Select a simple random sample of 50 receiving reports to examine for proper authorizations; more than 1 negative finding requires additional work.

IF
- P1 Client *does not* use purchase requisitions
- P2 Client uses only authorized vendors
- P3 Purchases are *made individually* by each department
- P4 Purchase orders are approved by *each department manager*
- P5 Payment for purchases is made upon presentation of vendors' invoice *without matching to receiving report*

THEN

Select a sample of 50 vendors' invoices over $1,000 and 100 vendors' invoices under $1,000 *from each department's purchases* to examine for proper authorizations; more than 2 negative findings in one department requires additional work in that department.

Other Uses.   Two other productive spheres for expert systems are (1) comparatively evaluating staff and supervisors who work on different audit engagements and (2) evaluating audit evidence, client risk of bankruptcy, and fraud and the like by comparing them with norms for similar clients in the same industry. This second comparison can apply when considering audit adjustments, opinion qualifications, or even fee adjustments for an audit client that seems to pose exceptional risks.

Implementation: The Accountant's Role

Management should think carefully before implementing any expert system—in accounting, internal auditing, financial planning, manufacturing, marketing, or elsewhere. Accounting management is often asked to express an opinion on the proposed implementation of an expert system in another sphere of business. This opinion will often be guided by whether data to make the expert system work are available through the accounting system. Accounting management should also call to top management's attention the suitability of the proposed application, the cost and other resources required to implement it, and the detailed planning necessary to make it successful.

Management must be certain that suitable conditions and incentives exist before it attempts to create an expert system. Tasks that do not meet the conditions outlined on page 539—a consultation on complex matters requiring transferable expertise consisting primarily of logical analysis—will probably not succeed. Managerial situations that are not suited to expert systems (at the present state of the art) include long-range planning, organizational design, product design, writing job descriptions, budgeting, general performance analysis, structuring multistage problems, production scheduling, and optimizing the use of scarce resources.

Proper implementation requires extensive resources: not just computer power and capacity, but also a large-scale investment in human resources. The current rule is that it takes four to six people working virtually full-time for two or three years to implement an expert system successfully. This group will include a manager, a designer, a programmer, and experts willing to convey their special knowledge to the expert system.

Although it is possible to write an expert system from scratch using a conventional computer language or the artificial-intelligence language LISP, more than a dozen packaged expert systems are on the market for use on large and specially configured models of Digital Equipment Corporation, Texas Instruments, Xerox, IBM, and Symbolics computers. These packaged systems can make expert-system development less dependent on programmers. Applications of expert systems do exist on microcomputers that have been modified to include 3 to 6 megabytes of RAM memory. These applications have the advantage of physical and logical portability. A good use of unmodified microcomputers in expert-systems implementation is as terminals that communicate with a larger mainframe that actually runs the expert system. If major programmer resources are devoted to developing expert systems for high-capacity microcomputers when they become widely available, the popularity of expert systems could increase as dramatically as has that of relational data bases. In the meantime, do *not* underestimate the resources required to achieve success.

Before implementation, an expert system passes through a multiphase planning process. In the first phase, the intended users define the problem or decision that the expert system is expected to solve. The designers and programmers then develop a structure for the system. The structure connects the tasks, the knowledge areas to be covered, and the intended users. Typically, the phases of development might proceed as follows:

1. Specify the system's mission, knowledge areas, scope, tasks, and intended users.
2. Develop a conceptual design of the system's processing.
3. Produce a prototype that includes a few representative premises, conclusions, and expert knowledge linkages to determine whether in a few

typical cases the system can capture a dynamic data base and whether users can extract useful results from the system in trials.

4. Scale up the system and develop user interfaces from the prototype.

5. Have experts "teach" the system its static data base (how to process information).

6. Validate the expert system's effectiveness in increasingly challenging situations until it is operationally acceptable.

Recently, programs capable of *generating* expert systems have appeared. For example, a program named EMYCIN, based on the logic of MYCIN, is designed to produce rule-based expert systems. Texas Instruments offers an expert-system generator, called EXPLORER, consisting of integrated hardware and software. **PROLOG**, an artificial intelligence programming language available for computers as small as the Commodore 64 and Apple II family, is the most successful declarative language developed to date. PROLOG has been found useful in writing expert systems in both the United States and Japan. A **declarative language** allows the programmer to describe the structure of a problem, which the program then solves using logical analysis; a declarative language contrasts with an **imperative language,** which gives the computer instructions for solving a problem. Electronic spreadsheets are another familiar example of declarative languages; FORTRAN and BASIC are examples of imperative languages. Most accounting applications are written in COBOL, an imperative language. **Object oriented languages** are yet a third category; developed in 1981, they treat data as objects to which various routines may be applied. Object-oriented languages may someday have significant applications in many system-related areas, including artificial intelligence. Although development of a system will still be labor intensive, the use of an expert-system generator could reduce resources devoted to conceptual design, detail design, and programming. The developers could concentrate on the performance objectives, controls, expert knowledge, and applications.

Summary

In the hierarchy of information systems, the first type of system records and summarizes transactions, placing them into files. The second type places the same information into data bases. The third type, decision support systems, finds and reports the information in files or data bases to managers. The fourth type, expert systems, makes judgments and gives advice based on the information provided by the files, data bases, and system users.

Decision support systems and data base and file-processing systems merely provide information to a human decision maker; they perform little or no logical analysis of the information. In contrast, knowledge processing—also called artificial intelligence when done by a computerized system—is the use of logic and inference to extract judgments, policies, and decisions from information. Artificial intelligence contains within it three major specializations: robotics, natural languages, and—the concern of this chapter—expert systems. Once an expert system's structure has been established, human experts transfer to it the specialized premises and rules it will use. They then provide the system with a fact situation. The expert system should be able to make recommendations and explain the "reasoning" that supports those recommendations, and its decisions should be comparable in quality to those of human experts. Expert systems are suitable for applications characterized by a well-defined problem and well-defined knowledge and by the potential to be cost-competitive with human expert consultants.

The most promising applications of expert systems in accounting involve interpretation of auditing evidence and evaluation of controls. As these applications mature, they hold out the prospect of streamlining audit field work. The keys to success with an expert system are to select a promising application, commit adequate resources to its development, and pursue a planned and orderly development process.

Key Terms

artificial intelligence
decision support system
  (DSS)
declarative language
dynamic data base
expert system
fifth-generation computers
imperative language
knowledge processing
MYCIN

National Accounting and Auditing
  Retrieval System (NAARS)
natural languages
object-oriented language
premises
PROLOG
robotics
rules
static data base
user interface

Review Questions

1. What is artificial intelligence and what relationship does it have to fifth-generation computers?

2. Write a paragraph that distinguishes among data processing, information processing, and knowledge processing. Which of these terms is more or less synonymous with artificial intelligence?

3. What are the two categories of user input to an expert system, and how do they differ?

4. What are the three main applications of artificial intelligence?

5. Construct a table comparing file processing, data base processing, decision support systems, and expert systems in terms of the factors that follow. Fill in the grid with short descriptive phrases. For example, to describe the complexity of file processing, you could say "relatively less complex."
   (a) Complexity
   (b) Cost
   (c) Availability to user during decision making
   (d) Diversity of decisions to which its outputs may be relevant
   (e) Sources of information content

6. How is an expert system "trained"? What human and situational resources are needed in this training?

7. What is the difference between an expert system's static data base and its dynamic data base? What is the origin of the dynamic data base?

8. What are the attributes of situations in which an expert system can function successfully. What situations can you think of in management and accounting that possess these attributes?

9. What is MYCIN? What does MYCIN do? Why is it useful?

10. Which steps in an audit are potentially suited to the use of expert systems? Why are these steps more hospitable than others to expert systems?

11. What is the difference between an imperative and a declarative artificial language? In which type of language are most accounting-application programs written?

12. Name at least three limitations or drawbacks of expert systems.

13. Give three general rules for developing an expert system.

Discussion Questions

14. Indicate whether data processing, information processing, or knowledge processing is best suited to each of the following situations.
    (a) Recording of purchases
    (b) Selection of audit steps for a field work program
    (c) Portfolio management
    (d) Comparison of several alternative capital investments
    (e) Preparation of a voucher for payment of vendor invoices
    (f) Calculating an aged accounts receivable balance
    (g) Calculating manufacturing direct labor variances
    (h) Design of a new accounting system
    (i) Cash control

15. The manager of Desktop Awning Co. says, "Because we experienced such a large gain in information usefulness when we moved from file processing to data base processing, I recommend that we go straight

to expert systems now. Then we should *really* get a boost in usefulness!" What does this statement reveal about the manager's understanding of expert systems?

16. Dalhart and Texline are partners in a financial planning firm. For years
they have advised pension funds, foundations, and trusts on investment strategies; now they want to expand their business and give
financial planning advice to individuals. They are considering acquiring a $50,000 software package called Eazi-Plan Intelligent developed
by Expert Systems of Topeka, Kansas. This program uses over 6,000
rules to form its conclusions. Identify at least ten factors that Dalhart
and Texline should consider when they evaluate this strategy and explain how each should bear on their decision.

17. You are a physician with a patient who has a baffling bacterial infection. You want to consult an expert. Would you prefer to consult a
human expert or an expert system? Why?

18. You are the auditor of Post Air Promotions, Inc., a company that sells
franchises for local air charter companies. Since it was founded five
years ago, the firm has enjoyed an average annual growth rate of 48
percent. It went public last year, and the per-share price of its stock
has fluctuated from 21 to 134.

   Two former members of management are suing Post Air. One of its
five planes has been grounded for lack of proper maintenance. Three
companies are competing to acquire Post Air, yet one of the three
banks that provide its short-term financing has threatened to initiate
bankruptcy proceedings if Post Air does not pay $300,000 in principal
and interest, which the bank claims is past due. Finally, management
is considering making an offer for a controlling interest in one of the
companies competing to acquire it. Post Air expects to declare a $.50
per share cash dividend for the quarter just ended. Would you benefit
from consulting an expert or decision support system about the effect
of each of these factors on your audit opinion? Why or why not?

19. Would expert systems be possible without computers? Are microcomputers widely used to prepare and run expert systems? Why or why
not?

20. Nederland Video Film Rental Company has been thinking about using
an expert system to help decide which video cassettes to carry in each
of its forty-four locations. Currently, individual store managers make
these decisions. The firm has a 23-percent return on equity, well above
average in an industry characterized by a rapid turnover of companies.
Management wants an expert system in part because it hasn't been
able to locate a sufficiently competent consultant. Although no expert
systems now exist for this type of decision-making process, management envisions adapting a system that predicts the locations of mineral
deposits using satellite survey data. Discuss whether Nederland
should proceed, and why.

21. A friend asks you to evaluate a new expert system technique he has developed. As a simple example, the system will identify an animal by asking you questions until it has enough information to guess and by learning from its mistakes. The session goes like this:

You:	Ready.
Expert system:	*Is it an elephant?*
Y:	No.
ES:	*Tell me what animal it is.*
Y:	Tiger.
ES:	*Please tell me a characteristic of a tiger that an elephant does not have.*
Y:	Stripes.
ES:	*Want to try again?*
Y:	Ready.
ES:	*Does it have stripes?*
Y:	Yes.
ES:	*Is it a tiger?*
Y:	No.
ES:	*Please tell me what it is.*
Y:	Zebra.
ES:	*Please tell me a characteristic of a zebra that a tiger does not have.*
Y:	Hooves.
ES:	*Want to try again?*
Y:	Ready.
ES:	*Does it have hooves?*
Y:	No.
ES:	*Does it have stripes?*
Y:	No.
ES:	*Is it an elephant?*
Y:	No.
ES:	*Please tell me what it is.*
Y:	Eagle
ES:	*Please tell me a characteristic of an eagle which a elephant, tiger, and zebra do not have.*
Y:	Wings.
ES:	*Want to try again?*

Required:

(a) Is this an expert system?

(b) If you said yes, think of a real-world application and give an example of how it would work. If you said no, explain why not.

22. Describe the typical sequence of events in expert-systems development. What sort of otherwise suitable task situations are disqualified by the length of time it takes to design an expert system?

23. The expert system CREDIT helps a business decide whether to accept

another business as a credit customer. Suggest six to twelve premises for such a system, each framed as a yes-or-no question about the customer. If the only admissible conclusions are "reject" and "accept with credit limit of $10,000," how might these two conclusions be related by rules to the premises.

24. A type of expert system not discussed in this chapter follows a "tree" pattern to search for a recommendation. In other words, each question answered leads to a new question and excludes the need to ask some other questions. For example, once the expert system has established that the accounting application it is helping to design does not include payroll, it will ask no additional questions about payroll.

    In considering a decision on whether to extend credit to an applicant, any of the following will automatically signal you to refuse credit: bankruptcy within the past three years, unemployment for more than one year, or a negative rating from the Merchants Association. Explain how an expert system could use this information to speed up the consultation. Draw a diagram showing which questions you would ask and the order in which you'd ask them. (Before making any evaluation, the expert system requests information on name, address, employer, annual income level, and amount of installment debt.)

Problems

25. As an auditor, Rod Malone is concerned that the growing volume of financial reporting rules and regulations make it hard for him to know when financial statements are not in compliance. He wants an expert system to make this judgment for him. However, he doesn't want to create such an expert system unless it has a reasonable likelihood of profitability. Rod investigates the available resources and learns that he can lease a suitable expert system for $50,000 annually. At the end of three years, he can buy the system outright for an additional $10,000. To coordinate the technical dimension of training, he should hire an expert systems consultant for 300 hours at $50 per hour. He must also engage four financial reporting experts for 600 hours each, at $60 per hour, to provide the expert knowledge. Finally, he needs to hire a full-time system operator at an annual salary of $35,000. Additional indirect out-of-pocket costs would amount to about $14,000 a year. Development would take six months from the date of leasing the expert system.

    Rod proposes to make the expert system available for consultations. He estimates a total of 1,000 consultations the first year, and plans to charge $120 per consultation. Each consultation would incur direct out-of-pocket costs of about $10 for phone-line charges, paper, and follow-up. Rod hopes that consultations will increase at a rate of 50 percent annually. To encourage this, he will lower the price of subsequent consultations by $15 per year until it reaches $60.

Required:

Based on Rod's estimates and proposed charges, analyze the economics of this proposed venture for five years after startup. Without considering payback period or net present value analysis, does it appear attractive to you? What do you believe to be the weakest assumption about the venture? Why?

26. Refer to Table 15.3. Which combination of premise values would the system report in each of the following situations?
    (a) The system uses less than 30 percent of disk capacity, is more than five years old, spends more than 40 percent of its time in disk access, and has a growth rate of more than 5 percent.
    (b) The system uses more than 70 percent of disk capacity, is more than five years old, spends more than 40 percent of its time on disk access, and has an unknown growth rate.
    (c) The system uses more than 70 percent of disk capacity, is not yet five years old, spends less than 40 percent of its time in disk access, and has a growth rate of less than 5 percent.

27. Cecil Rhodes, a tax counselor, has decided to create an expert system to help him do tax planning. The system will ask three questions:
    (a) What was your taxable income last year?
        (1) Under $50,000
        (2) Between $50,000 and $120,000
        (3) Over $120,000
    (b) What is your age?
        (1) Under 30
        (2) Between 30 and 55
        (3) Over 55
    (c) Is your taxable income increasing or decreasing?
        (1) Increasing more than 8 percent annually
        (2) Changes less than 8 percent either way annually
        (3) Decreasing more than 8 percent annually

    The alternative recommendations Mr. Rhodes has chosen are
        C1: Needs personalized intensive tax planning
        C2: Can manage with computerized tax planning
        C3: No need for tax planning but stay in touch
        C4: No need for tax planning; no need to stay in touch

Required:

(a) Arrange these premises and recommendations in a table like Table 15.3, showing the appropriate recommendation for each possible set of answers to the three questions. Relate the recommendations to the answers in the manner that seems most logical to you and that reflects *your* expertise.
(b) A client answers the questions as follows: a(1), b(1), c(1). Which recommendation does your system select?

28. Jan Gillespie establishes a personal financial planning service and decides to install an expert system to help her advise clients. The system asks three questions:

    (a) What is your annual income after taxes?
        (1) Under $50,000
        (2) Between $50,000 and $100,000
        (3) Over $100,000
    (b) What would you like your net worth to be in 10 years?
        (1) Not interested in net worth
        (2) 5 to 10 times present annual income
        (3) 11 to 20 or more times present annual income
    (c) How much risk can you tolerate comfortably?
        (1) As little as possible
        (2) Moderate risks are OK
        (3) Any risk for a proportionate payoff!

The alternative recommendations to clients about their investments are

    C1: Commercial real estate, puts & calls, oil & gas, futures
    C2: Mutual funds, NYSE stocks, repurchase agreements
    C3: Reduce living standard to save more money for investment
    C4: Review your goals; they may be unrealistic
    C5: Federally guaranteed bank accounts, government bonds, certificates of deposit

Required:

    (a) Arrange the premises and recommendations in a table like Table 15.3, showing the appropriate recommendations for each possible set of answers to the three questions. Relate the recommendations to answers in the manner that seems most logical to you.
    (b) A client answers the questions as follows: a1, b3, c3. Which recommendation(s) does your system select?

Case: Career Placement at Paris College

Dan Stone, director of career placement at Paris College, wants to develop three expert-system applications. The first one would help students schedule interviews with potential employers. The second system would advise them what type of career to seek. The third would act as a consultant to students, helping them choose which of several employment offers to accept. (Mr. Stone feels it would be unethical for him to do this type of advising, but sees no problem with an expert system doing so.) A student could use the system as often as necessary.

    Mr. Stone knows nothing about expert systems and has hired you. You will help him by (1) determining whether each proposal is actually appropriate for expert-system applications. If not, identify the unsuitable one(s) and explain why. (2) For each of the remaining application(s), write the first four questions for the set that will establish the premises or dynamic data base; give each question no more than three possible responses. (3) List eight possible career recommendations in the set of conclusions. (4) State at least one rule linking premises and conclusions. How much confidence do you have that such applications could be built and would be useful within reasonable limitations?

Case: The Hondo Company

The Hondo Company operates with the management structure and information system illustrated in the figure below. In this diagram, the color lines indicate authority and the black lines indicate information flow.

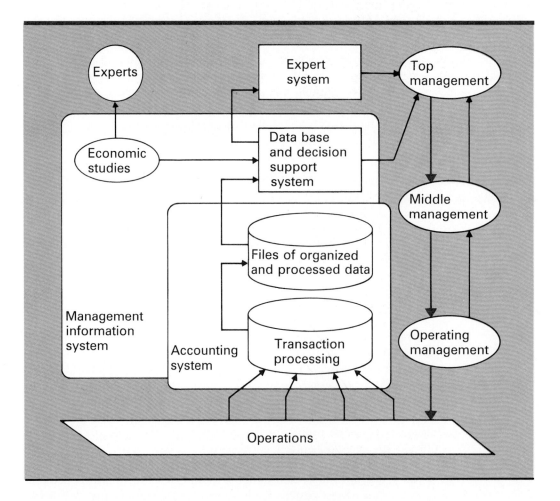

Required:

    (a) Identify two information-flow channels that are not pictured.

    (b) If the two missing information channels were present, describe how this system would translate transaction information into top-management plans and instructions to other management levels.

    (c) Regardless of your answer to *a*, discuss the value of the following information links:

        (1) Experts directly to top and middle management

        (2) Top management to expert systems

        (3) Operating management directly to top management

    (d) The two rectangular boxes with rounded corners represent the boundaries of, respectively, the management information system and the accounting system. What argument could be made that the two should have the same boundaries?

CHAPTER 16

Communications and Computer Networks

Learning Objectives

After studying this chapter, you should be able to

- Recognize and understand communications options available to the accounting manager.

- Evaluate the design of communications systems and their controls.

- Formulate conceptual designs incorporating choices appropriate to a specific situation.

- Identify functions suitable for use with local-area networks.

- Select values for the communications variables that customize the network for specific users.

A communications network combines equipment and procedures to move data and information from collection, processing, or storage points to user destinations. One of the main reasons organizations need networks is to provide management with the most up-to-date information to ensure timely and relevant decisions. All organizations have communications networks because all have some operations that originate data; others that provide channels for moving, transforming, and reporting data; and still others that use data. Networks differ in their formality and data sources, and in the users of their reports.

Often, an organization will contain more than one communications network. These internal communications networks are not necessarily coordinated with each other and some of them are quite informal. Reports from one network may contradict those from another; a marketing network, for example, may report excessive inventories at the same time the manufacturing network reports insufficient inventories. These contradictions often cannot be entirely eliminated, and may indeed play a positive role in decision making and control by enforcing close managerial attention to the premises that cause such differences. Nevertheless, there is a strong trend toward consolidation of information and communication networks. This trend is fueled by the following recent developments: the need to communicate *large volumes of information* quickly and reliably, the availability of computer and communications *technology* to satisfy this need, and the formidable human and capital *investments* that are required to use this technology.

Figure 16.1   Pre-EDP Processing and Communication
Before the advent of computers, top management's access to data and information about business activity were severely limited.

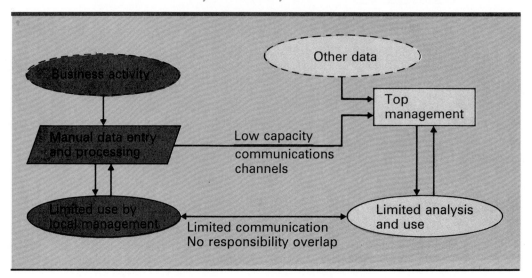

Figure 16.2   Contemporary Processing and Communication
Not only has computer-based processing made more data on more functions available to top management, it has also increased the responsibilities and related information available at lower levels of management.

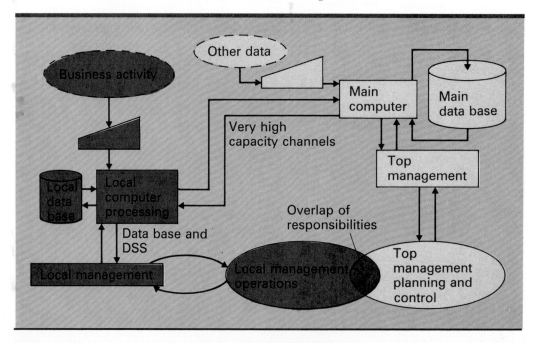

Figures 16.1 and 16.2 illustrate the changes that communications technology has made possible in organizational communications over the past decade. Figure 16.1 shows a typical pre-EDP communications system, based on printed-paper data collection and reporting ability. Most data were used locally or were wasted. Relatively little data—usually only summaries—reached top management. Some organizations still use these methods. Figure 16.2 shows how local and centralized computer processing and electronic communications can support a high degree of processing and communication among all levels of management. There is considerable overlap from one level to the next in managerial responsibility for planning, controls, and operations responsibilities. One implication of Figure 16.2 is that management at all levels must possess sufficient talent and ability to use the information it receives. Another is that planning and administering the movement of all that data is not a trivial task.

The Need for Data Communications

What should a manager or accountant know about communications? Don't managers make decisions on the basis of information they already have? Don't accountants simply prepare statements and let them speak for themselves? Not quite. In this section we shall describe some situations in which data communications is the link between data collection and the availability of data for use by managers. Reliance on communications technology binds accounting transaction recording and information analysis to management's everyday conduct of business.

Participatory Decision Making

Decision making frequently involves people who are in different locations but who work together intermittently over an extended period of time. This demands reliable communication of thousands or even millions of bytes, often over long distances, more or less simultaneously among all the parties. Such information interchange is part of the decision-making process. Many examples of participatory decision making could be cited. In one such case, seven district managers in the New York metropolitan area need rapid access to on-line real-time inventory-availability records when making commitments to potential sales customers about quantities and delivery schedules. The normal daily snarl of traffic makes physical delivery of this information impractical, so an electronic network is adopted. In another case, an airline reservations system accepts seat requests from thousands of travel agents through its electronic reservations system. This system stores and modifies reservations on most airlines and helps agents and travelers find available flights to their destinations. As a third example, a mail-order company is able to print special-sale catalogs quickly to move slow-selling merchandise, based on electronically transmitted reports of shipments from its warehouses to customers.

Decentralized Processing

Often, the transfers associated with the kind of participatory decision making in the examples just given involve some processing of data before or after sharing it. Distributed data processing—data processing at multiple locations within the same organization—has become very common. Many organizations do accounting processing (sales, deposits, payroll, and inventory, for example) in two or more locations. For example, laser printers in an organization's seven North American locations simultaneously create payroll checks from a payroll application program running in a central location. In the same organization, nine locations process worldwide records of inventory, analyzing demand and moving inventory where trends indicate it will be needed. Meanwhile, budget-preparation instructions are transmitted electronically to all locations simultaneously. Ultimately, the various processes must converge in order to accurately update an integrated general ledger of accounts, often within severe time constraints.

The Complexity of Information Transfer

The *rapid* transfer of information between individuals, organizations, and data bases has become both necessary and complex. On a typical day at one company, for example, the division manager may expect to see on her desk every morning a performance report for the division's activities as of the closing of operations on the previous day. In a London-based firm, the sales branch in Singapore may want to update the accounts receivable subledger prior to year end, which occurs in only three hours. A third business made a last-minute decision to send three managers to the tax-update program sponsored by the State Training Institute. The three managers will have no trouble attending because the institute accepts registrations up to one hour before a program begins, simultaneously preparing billing invoices.

Methods of Communication

Data communication between different locations requires special systems in addition to those required for normal data processing. The first choice management must make is between physical and electronic data communications. Physical media include, for instance, documents, tape, and floppy disks, which can be physically transferred from one location to another. Electronic media like wires and microwaves can propel signals from point to point at the speed of light. Each type of media has advantages and disadvantages; the choice depends on an organization's needs and constraints.

Physical Media for Communication

Physical media have definite advantages under one or more of the following conditions: (1) small offices; (2) offices that lack urgency about data transfer; and (3) extreme need for security. Many offices still rely heavily on physical documents for communication and maintenance of the audit trail. It is not practical, though, to print large volumes of data from computer storage for transfer to another location; the receiving location must transcribe the data back into computer-usable form. To avoid this inconvenience, data can be transported on floppy disks and tape. Since these media rely on magnetic patterns for storage, human beings need not participate in the processes of creating or reading them, and they have high rates of data transfer from and to computers.

Although programs and data can sometimes travel adequately between processing centers on tape and floppy disks, this method of transfer has significant disadvantages. Sending data by disk is slow; it is also risky and inconvenient. Floppy disks must be copied, backed up, packed, sent, received, and unpacked. This process is time consuming and can generate delays, loss, or damage. Effective use of much data and information cannot withstand the delays inherent in copying to floppy disks, overnight delivery, and reentry at another location. Managers want—and indeed, their decision responsibilities require—more rapid information access. They want to send and receive files, programs, documents, and messages easily and quickly. Their ultimate objective is to make data and information conveniently available to other managers for direct use and further processing.

Network Topologies

The management needs we have just described can be met when organizations form a communications **network** consisting of nodes that collect, store, process, or use data or information, linked by data-carrying channels. The **nodes** process data and are the "logical devices" in a network; the **channels** move data between the nodes. The conceptual advantage of a network is that it moves data directly without resort to paper or magnetic media. Network designs vary, and the topologies for linking nodes depend on their proximity to each other and the degree to which speed and budget are constraints.

When an organization's computing needs are confined to a relatively small area, the logical devices serving these needs—the nodes, which include computers, printers, terminals, and on-line storage devices—can be permanently linked by cable. Any node that provides a service, such as providing or allocating a shared network resource, to other nodes is called a **server.** Examples of servers are a printer, a modem, an external storage device, and the computer used to manage the messages moving through the network. The servers and stored data that all nodes use are called the *shared resources,* because all the other nodes have access to (share) them. Thus, a user at one node can quickly receive and process data placed in the external storage server by another node. Without the servers, only nodes with a direct link to the shared resources could use them. Networks come in all sizes, from two nodes to hundreds, and may serve one or several organizations, or only a portion of an organization.

The same design principles apply to all systems, but design priorities depend on a system's size and the performance expected of it. The International Standards Organization has published a model for network description called the Open Systems Interconnect Model. While precise standards for this model are still evolving, the model itself is widely accepted. It consists of the following seven components:

1. The physical hardware that comprises the tangible network
2. Data-link software, which enters information into the network and detects errors in data transmission
3. Network routing and relaying between nodes and between networks
4. Transport of messages and handling of errors detected by data-link software
5. Session control, which allows nodes to connect and exchange messages in an orderly fashion
6. Message presentation at the receiving node, including conversion into the proper display format
7. The interface with software application programs that run through the network.

An office network serves the processing needs of a specific office, such as headquarters or district office. Its design typically places a high priority on convenient local access to inexpensive, centralized mass data storage and on concurrent use of nodes by multiple users, each running their own programs with their own data entry and edit, analysis, and off-line storage of sensitive information. An office network typically consists of from one to six micro- or minicomputers, but may include any size central processing unit right up to a mainframe. To keep order and manage the shared resources, one of the smaller CPUs acts as a server.

Design topologies for computer communications networks are of three types: star, ring, and bus. In each case, the nodes share some resources but may retain exclusive use of other resources, for example, of a draft printer or local disk storage. Each topology may stand alone or serve as a building block in a larger network. To visualize these large hybrid systems, imagine replacing one or more of the nodes in a network with an interface connecting it to another network.

Star Networks. The **star network,** shown in Figure 16.3, has a central point, which must be a server, where all the other device connections converge. The star may accommodate a multiuser system in which all

Figure 16.3   A Star Network

A star network gives each node a direct connection to a central server, which is a CPU.

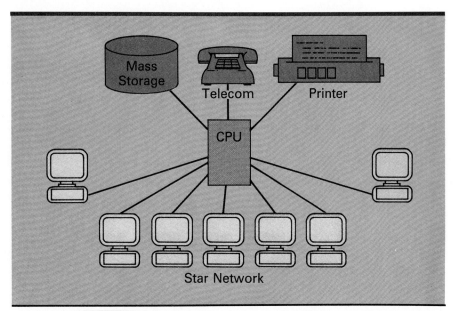

Star Network

processing takes place in a central CPU, or it may be the core of a true distributed processing system that contains computers of different sizes. In a multiuser system, the star responds faster than an equivalent-sized network of another design, and it may cost less if the network is small and confined to a small area. Because each wire in a star network connects only two nodes, inexpensive twisted-pair cable can be used rather than an expensive type of connection designed to carry multiple messages simultaneously.

A star network is used whenever the work stations are far apart. If the main computer and storage are in Memphis and the work stations are in Knoxville, Chattanooga, and Cincinnati, a star is the best design choice. Because the star costs relatively more than the other designs, a higher volume of message traffic or a requirement for high-speed transmission is necessary to justify it where stations are closer together. The star has a higher cost because the server must be more sophisticated and because the network will, in most cases, require more cabling than other types do (each node must be connected to the server instead of to a main cable line or to the next node).

Ring and Bus Networks.   The **ring network**, illustrated in Figure 16.4, has no central clearing point but connects all nodes in a "ring." A message originating anywhere on the ring proceeds in one direction around the

Figure 16.4   A Ring Network
In a ring network there need not be a central server.

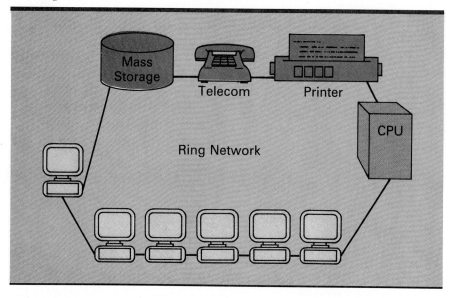

ring as an addressed "packet" until the unit for which the message is intended recognizes and intercepts it. The ring is simpler than the star and, in large networks, less expensive to install. The connecting cable must be able to handle many different messages at once, since more than two nodes may be active, and a node must be able to pick out the messages meant for it. The necessity for "completing" the ring makes this type of network suitable only for small-area communication—for example, an office network. As the area served increases in size, the ring network design becomes less suitable.

A **bus network** is an incomplete ring where all nodes are connected to the bus—a length of cable that transports signals, in the form of packets, between nodes. An addressed packet from any node on the cable can travel in both directions and is examined by every device until it is intercepted by the node for which it is intended. Figure 16.5 illustrates a bus network. The bus network is the simplest, least expensive, and most common type. There are many more commercially available bus-based network products to choose from than there are of other designs.

Organization of Access.   Because the ring and bus networks permit multiple messages in the connecting links, each node must have a way of sorting out messages, passing on those not meant for it and accepting those that are. Two protocols have emerged to handle this problem: token-passing and carrier sense multiple access/collision detection.

In **token-passing**, a special signal, the "token," is inserted at the end of a string of messages by the currently active node. The token signals the next active node to insert a new message if it has one and then to retransmit all other messages *except* those it originated or that were addressed to it, which it does not retransmit. Token-passing gives all nodes a chance to send and receive messages and permits heavy use of the network.

The **carrier sense multiple access/collision detection (CSMA/CD)** protocol, as its name implies, requires each node to monitor the network for impending collisions between messages. Each node then transmits only when the links between them are not carrying any messages. When two nodes try to transmit at the same time, each will become aware of the other's transmission and will retransmit after waiting a short randomly selected interval. CSMA/CD is reliable but slows down under heavy use.

In both systems, each node has a unique name that it knows and recognizes. This name is the node's network address. A message meant for a node must bear this name or that node will not retain it.

All these networks can share mass storage devices, printers, plotters, and other equipment. Sharing obviously means that fewer devices are required than if each user's work station were fully equipped with all devices that would ever be required by that user's work. For example, if mass storage maintains files and programs for all users, a user need not

Figure 16.5   Bus Network
The bus network is the simplest, least expensive, and—all other factors being equal—the slowest of the three major designs.

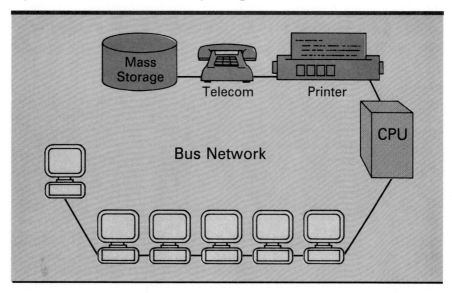

keep his or her files and applications in the limited storage of a small computer disk system. With passwords, users may protect their personal files and programs from other users.

On any network, several users may want access to the same program and data at the same time. This is no problem if they only want to run the program or display the data. In an all-paper system, this would be equivalent to distributing carbon copies of a memo for read-only purposes. However, if several users try to edit (alter) the same memo at the same time, confusion will result. Similarly, if multiple users try to alter the same program or data at the same time, accidental deletion of information or creation of multiple versions of the same record may result. The network design should include controls to prevent one user from altering data that someone else is using. Such controls, called **resource locking**, may take any of several forms. A complete absence of resource locking would allow all users to access and edit a record simultaneously. The strongest form allows access to the file by only one user at a time. A weaker form allows multiple users simultaneous access to a file, but gives only one user at a time edit access to any given record. The weaker form of resource locking is normally the most desirable. Suppose, for example, that one of a credit union's files contains members' current balances in share draft accounts. While the account processing program is posting drafts previously presented by other depositors and financial institutions, a member wishes to cash a draft for $500. If the stronger version of resource locking were adopted, the customer would have to wait until the entire *file* had been processed. If the weaker resource-locking solution were implemented, the customer would have to wait to cash the draft only until the computer released the *record* of his or her account. To reduce the customer's waiting time even more, the system could have a feature that allows the cashier to interrupt the posting program long enough for the member's draft to be processed.

Network Linking

Electronic signals must be transmitted in accordance with standardized patterns governing signal changes, directional capacity, and error detection. One change per second in an electronic signal, equivalent to one bit, is called a **baud**. Each component of a message—each letter, number, unit of punctuation, message start and stop, and nondata message component—represents a signal change, as do fluctuations in voltage and the like. The number of signal changes transmitted each second is called the **baud rate**.

How data communication occurs—such as through full duplex, half duplex, or simplex—is called the **transmission mode** and governs directional capacity. **Simplex** is pure one-way transmission. Your car radio is a familiar example of the simplex mode; it talks to you; you do not have any way to respond to the message you receive. Simplex is inappropriate for computer communications, which require two-way signal flows. **Half duplex** allows two-way transmission, but only in one direction at a time. If one party tries to interrupt while the other is transmitting, the attempt will fail. CB radios and ship-to-shore telephones use the half-duplex transmission mode. **Full duplex** provides simultaneous two-way communication; both parties can transmit and receive at once. An example is a telephone. The full-duplex mode is faster and allows better error detection; for these reasons it is preferred for computer communication. Users of full duplex can take advantage of an error-detection procedure called **echo**, whereby the receiving computer returns the received data to the sending computer for comparison with the transmitted data.

Communications rules also format lines and paragraphs. In some networks, before the receiving node can move to a new line, it requires an instruction from the sending computer. Other receiving nodes can perform this function themselves. Modern practice allows the user to specify whether a certain character indicates a line or paragraph break. Older and smaller computers may require a pause signal inserted at the end of each line to allow them time to catch up before the next line comes in.

Other communications rules define the number of bits used for each character. Some older networks used a reduced character set in which no character used more than 7 bits. The original Apple II computer utilized a 7-bit character set. Most communications links still require the user to specify whether data transmission will use the 7- or 8-bit character set. A **parity check** is an error-detection procedure that adds one extra "on" bit to characters as necessary to make them all contain an odd (or, for some systems, all contain an even) number of "on" bits. "None" parity means that this error-detection procedure is not used. To illustrate parity checking, suppose the communicating computers use the convention that every byte must have an even number of bits "on." In other words, the added bit will be "off" if the byte already has 0,2,4, or 6 bits "on" and will be "on" if the byte already has 1,3,5, or 7 bits "on." This form of parity check is called *even parity*. A communication error involving just one bit will be recognized at the receiving computer as a byte with an odd number of bits on. The receiving computer will signal the sending computer to retransmit that block of data.

Data Communication Using Telephones

Telephone data communication is approaching the same status as telephone voice communication. Most people never think about how remarkable the telephone system is. Of the hundreds of millions of phones around the planet, virtually any two can be in contact within minutes, exchanging messages between individuals or machines. Today, businesses use the telephone system to connect computers to each other, and to terminals, for purposes of data communication. This expansion of use makes the telephone all the more remarkable.

Modems

With appropriate auxiliary equipment, computers can use phone lines to transfer digital data from one location to another and to exchange digital signals between locations. If a signal must be sent between two computers, each computer must have access to a modem, a phone line, and a communications program.

A **modem** is an interface device between a computer and a phone line that converts signals from digital to analog and then back to digital on the receiving end. It was first developed by AT&T and its name is an abbreviation of *mo*dulator-*dem*odulator. *Modulation* means change, and a modem changes computer-generated signals into signals a phone system can handle. The modem is necessary because of the difference between the data-carrying signals produced by a computer and the signals a phone line can transmit. The phone line conveys an **analog** signal, which is an electrical current with continuously modulating frequency and amplitude. Network nodes such as computers, however, only transmit or accept **digital** signals, which consist of discrete changes in voltage that can be assigned the value of either 1 or 0. Thus, the modem modulates the transmitting node's digital signal into an analog signal to be sent through the phone line; a second modem demodulates the incoming analog signal into a digital format the receiving node understands as data. The analog signal can consist of short, sharp changes in the frequency or amplitude of a transmitted tone. Each change corresponds to a baud.

Since the original development of modems, both direct-connect and acoustic modems have become available. **Acoustic modems** emit and receive sounds via the phone handset, converting electrical signals into sound and vice versa. **Direct-connect modems** do not convert electric signals into sound but send them directly to the terminal, printer, or computer for which they are intended. Direct-connect modems were used with teletype and similar machines before the invention of computers.[1] Modern modem designers favor the direct-connect approach because it handles data faster and is less error prone; even so, most modems are compatible with other modems. The data transmission rate of a modem is measured

---

[1]Historically, AT&T had a monopoly on both telephone service and on direct-connect modems. When the acoustic modem was developed by independent businesses in an effort to break the monopoly, the phone company tried to prevent its use. The courts decided in favor of the acoustic modem developers. Today, phone companies have no control over the use of any modem, so long as it meets certain standard requirements. These requirements only assure that modems in use will not disrupt service to other customers.

in baud (one baud is equivalent to one signal modulation or demodulation). Since each baud represents one bit, a rate of 300 baud corresponds to about 30 bytes or characters per second, including such necessary nondata signals as stop bits. Early modems could send/receive at 120 baud, or about 10 characters per second. Because speed is the essence of a computer's value to management, technical improvements have successively produced modems that work acceptably at 300, 1,200, 2,400, and 9,600 baud. A special type of modem even gives the effect of operating at up to double 9,600 baud by abbreviating data before sending it, then reconstructing the abbreviations into full text at the receiving end. Although for small businesses the 1,200-baud modem is standard now, 2,400-baud modems will become standard in the near future. Although most modems are outside the CPU and connected to it by cable, some computers are designed and built with small, compact internal modems as part of the CPU.

System developers may use either synchronous or asynchronous communications devices with phone lines. **Synchronous** devices transmit a fixed number of characters per time interval, measuring short time intervals (thousandths of a second) precisely and interpreting the number of signal changes in each interval as a constant number of characters. **Asynchronous** devices distinguish between transmitted characters by using start and stop bits; the rate of transmission is not a function of time. Asynchronous devices are useful with keyboard input, because keyboard operators' typing speeds are irregular. Synchronous devices are more expensive and offer faster baud rates. Whichever option is selected, the system developer must make certain that the modems and software at each end of the phone line are mutually compatible in both speed and other variables.

Communications Software

Communications programs enable computers linked via modems and a phone line to interpret the arriving signals and to respond with appropriate signals of their own. A good communications program will allow all the parameters described—such as stop bits and baud rate—to be set individually. Problems may arise, however, because not all communications software programs are compatible with each other. For example, if a receiving program does not suppress (disregard) an incoming echo, every character will be printed twice.

The simplest communications programs allow exchange of data files; access to electronic bulletin boards; and delivery of **electronic mail**, a system in which each user has a private file in which other users can place messages, and only the user with the proper password (or address) can read the messages. The more sophisticated communications programs are actually operating systems that allow multiple users. A computer running one of these advanced multiuser programs is acting as a network central controller or network server and is called the **host**. The software that allows one node to control software being run by another node acting as the host is called the **host program**. In a phone-line-based network, this type of program is called a **host environment**; it enables the controller to receive signals, run programs, and deliver data to active nodes. Each active node will require a **terminal emulator**—software that enables a computer to transmit signals identical to those usable by a certain kind of terminal—to accommodate different types of computer equipment. For example, let us say that you are operating a computer that is a node in such a network. The host computer in the network may be a DEC (Digital Equipment Corporation) computer and it expects your computer to have the keyboard layout and function keys of a DEC VT-100 terminal. However, you have an Apple Macintosh, which has a different keyboard layout. The terminal emulator can translate the signals generated when you use certain keys on your Macintosh into the signals sent by another key on a VT-100 terminal. For example, whenever you press the [clear] key on the Macintosh keyboard, the communications program will transmit the VT-100 [PF1] key signal to the host.

Once connected, the host environment program allows the receiver to use the operating system of the host computer to manage files, run programs, and perform other functions. It may also keep track of your usage for purposes of charging you for it.

To coordinate sending and receiving by asynchronous serial interfaces, a protocol called **handshake** has been developed. Without handshake, portions of data might not be received. The handshake involves instructions by the receiving computer to the sending computer to pause, then resume sending data. Handshake is especially important if the receiving computer is saving the transmitted data on a floppy disk or small hard disk, because saving and printing functions are slower processes that cannot accept signals as fast as they can be transmitted. Two common handshake conventions are: **clear to send/none** and **Xon-Xoff**, pronounced "ex-on, ex-off". The latter is more common and is used with rates less than 1200 baud.

A receiving computer may be connected to more than one other computer through a **multiplexer**—an interface device that combines input from two or more communications channels into one channel, or splits messages on one channel into messages for two or more channels. A typical multiplexer for a public-access data base computer (the host computer) might have ten to sixty incoming lines. Each phone line can connect one computer to the multiplexer; sixty units could be connected simultaneously. The multiplexer scans the incoming lines and sends their signals to the host computer so that it only deals with one user at a time.

Figure 16.6 shows a wide-area network incorporating all the main hardware and software elements discussed, in their proper relationships.

Figure 16.6   Wide-Area Network Using Phone Lines
Use of phone lines allows maximum flexibility in locating terminals and other nodes.

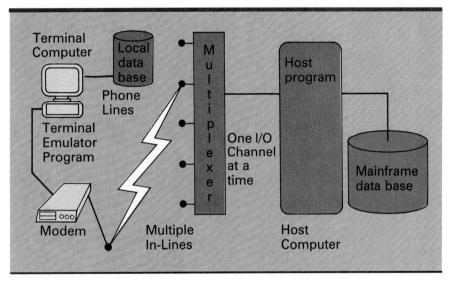

Disadvantages of Phone-Based Networks

Thousands of modem-to-modem computer communications events take place daily. Some people think computer communication via modems is like the flight of the bumblebees; the wonder is that it occurs at all, not that it occurs gracefully (it does not). Modem communication is inconvenient, costly, slow, subject to error, and potentially risky from a security standpoint. Any of these shortcomings would discourage the use of modems if there were a better alternative. Modems are useful just because no other alternative can be used in many situations—for example, when small computers are located many miles from each other and from the main office. Let us look at each of these disadvantages in more detail.

Inconvenience.   Communication by modem is not very flexible. A modem's connection must be technically correct or it will not work at all. Often the telephone line must be installed and devoted to computer communication. Direct-connect modems, which plug into a phone line, rarely work with permanently installed hotel and residence phones. Acoustic modems, which may be used with any phone except a party line, do not fit all phone handsets. To make a computer-to-computer connection via modem over a phone line, both modems must use the same baud rate, be connected, and be turned on. You may need an operator's assistance to help your phone-bound computers link with each other. You may also need to use a second phone line (talking to the person overseeing the other computer) to make the link. When dialing from within a company's private branch exchange (PBX), you may need to follow a detailed lengthy procedure. For instance, you may need to dial a particular phone number to access an outside long-distance service, a second number to reach the computer you want, and a third number to establish your credit, and between these numbers insert required pauses of 2 to 8 seconds! If you make the connection and cannot present an acceptable password, the receiving computer will soon break the connection, and you will have to repeat this long process to reconnect.

High Cost.   Using modems is costly for two reasons: the initial cost of the modem and the cost of long-distance transmission. In 1987, a 1,200-baud modem and communications software program cost about $300 at each end of the connection. Regular long-distance telephone rates ranged from $18 to $50 per hour, although off-hours use and leased lines could have cut the costs.

Lack of Speed.   At 300 baud, the most common modem rate for individual use, the contents of a typical monitor screen (80 columns by 24 lines) could take as long as 60 seconds to transmit. At the most common small-business modem rate of 1,200 baud, transmission of the same information might require up to 15 seconds. At 1,200 baud, transmitting a 4,500-word report (about 15 pages) would take almost 6 minutes, plus nearly as much time for handshake, echo, disk access, and retransmission of passages with errors—not counting time to make and break the connection. A test run under these conditions required 11 minutes to complete such a transmission.

Tendency Toward Error.   Even at slow transmission rates, static and noise on a phone line sound just like a signal to a modem. Some non-AT&T long-distance lines may not carry data at 1,200 baud without intolerable error rates, although this problem may be declining. At heavy-use times, more static and interference are likely. To detect these errors, communications programs use parity checking.

Security Risk.   In addition to these unintentional errors, a computer equipped with an open dial-up phone connection is at risk from unauthorized people who may discover the computer phone number and, with mischievous persistence, copy, change, or delete its files and applications! People who "hack" away at barriers to unauthorized logical access to computer systems via phone-line connections are called **hackers**

Network Choices

A **proprietary network**—a network completely under the control of, and for the exclusive use of, private parties—eliminates many of the disadvantages of public telephone lines for intercomputer communication. Proprietary networks may process a single type of data exclusively, such as accounting data, or they may service other computer applications as well. The network usually has one or more shared resources, such as hard disk storage or a high-speed printer or plotter. The nature of the linkage will depend on how widely separated the nodes are. Networks whose nodes are relatively close to each other typically use direct-connection devices. Such networks are called **local-area networks (LANs)**; you may also see LANs called *local-access* or *cabled* networks.

The larger and more geographically scattered a processing system, the less suitable are LAN design principles. For networks scattered over a wide geographical area, called **wide-area networks**, telephone, microwave, or satellite connections have proved their practicality. In reality, many networks combine these two types, and **gateway** connections bridge the component networks together. A proprietary network can be assembled from either LAN or wide-area network connections. If proprietary networks can be seen as one extreme in the question of using public telephone lines, the other extreme is the choice of using only a public carrier. The organization may acquire only certain logical devices, then may lease the connecting channels and processing capacity from a communications company that specializes in providing them. Between these extremes are many combinations of proprietary and public-carrier arrangements.

LAN Attributes

Most local-area networks fit into one of the six classifications shown in Table 16.1. In general, well-designed networks with a large CPU (A,C,D,F) tend to be more expensive, faster, and more responsive. However, unless they utilize data base processing structures, such networks may be flexible only within the scope of their original design. Networks that consist of small CPUs (even with shared mass storage) tend to be less expensive, faster on tasks involving only local memory or processing, and extremely flexible for an individual user's applications.

Fortunately, the ordinary needs of a given application may be met by several workable designs; the performance differences between designs are becoming less striking as small computers grow faster and cheaper. The user has many "good" design choices. General descriptions and examples of applications for each of the six classifications in Table 16.1 follow.

Table 16.1   LAN Classifications

	One Relatively Large CPU	Many Relatively Small CPUs	Mixture of Large and Small CPUs
Primarily used for transaction processing and file creation	A	B	C
Primarily used for data access and decision analysis	D	E	F

A. One Large CPU for Transaction Processing and File Creation.   This network is a star design. It consists of a powerful mainframe CPU with attached disk storage, printer, and multiplexer with ports to which many terminal input/output devices may be connected. This type of network makes efficient use of available resources but also tends to become intolerably slow as the number of users approaches its maximum. In Figure 16.7, a retail store with many sales points is using this design. Other applications that might be appropriate for the type A LAN include an airline reservations system, a credit card verification system, and a college mini-computer system for student and faculty use.

B. Many Small CPUs for Transaction Processing and File Creation.   The type B network consists of a ring or bus linking together two to ten personal computers or minicomputers and various peripherals—disk drives, printers, and a number of input/output terminals. The software for such a network, and for others that contain more than one computer, would include an operating system intended for network use (such as MS-DOS 3.1). At present, type B networks cannot handle large computing jobs cost-efficiently.[2]

Such a network would be appropriate for a chain of small warehouses, located close to one another and each having its own accounting subledger; an office of tax planners; a network of branch libraries; or a diversified company that must integrate its local and centralized computing requirements. In a type B warehouse network, for example, each node can record transactions in a common format and each can read the others' stock records to determine item availability. A word-processing network

---

[2]Soon, however, it will be possible for a network to break up some large computing jobs so several CPUs in the network can work on them simultaneously. When it occurs, this remarkable development will allow a network to behave like a mainframe or minicomputer when it solves large problems and like a collection of microcomputers when handling its users' individual computing requirements.

Figure 16.7 Classification A: One Large CPU
One large CPU can process a large volume of transactions originating at many different nodes.

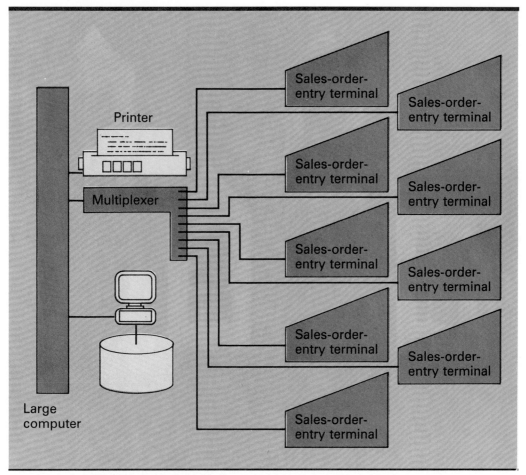

in this format might have a printer as a shared resource. Figure 16.8 shows the warehouse example as a bus network. This network should be connected to a computer elsewhere (not shown in the figure) that would accept transaction records into the general ledger application.

C. Mixture of Large and Small CPUs Used Primarily for Transaction Processing and File Creation.   The type C network can be a star, ring, or bus design. It can be very fast, especially if otherwise idle small computers can be assigned tasks by the larger computer. The large computers serve the same purposes as the smaller ones in the preceding category except

Figure 16.8   Classification B: Many Small CPUs
This design works well where links are necessary but most processing requirements are local ones.

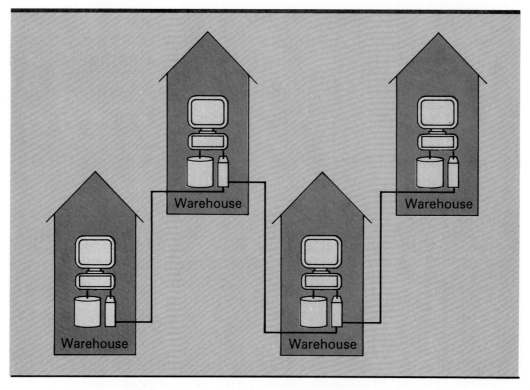

that their higher capacity is justified by greater processing requirements
where they are located. Applications where a type C network would be
appropriate include a large professional office (such as an accounting, legal, or medical practice office) with needs for both local and centralized
record keeping; customer record keeping in a stock brokerage; and an
auditing firm that uses small computers to record data and a few larger
computers to process it. Figure 16.9 shows a stock brokerage, in which
each account executive's personal computer is linked via a star network to
the firm's mainframe.

**D. One Large CPU Used Primarily for Data Access and Decision Anal-
ysis.**   The type D system could be a star, ring, or bus. It would include a
CPU with large RAM and would be equipped for rapid calculations. Examples include a computer-assisted design and manufacturing (CAD/
CAM) facility; manufacturing control and reporting with multiple work

centers to be coordinated; and various stations using one or more expert systems that rely for their static data bases upon large storage maintained through the mainframe computer. Figure 16.10 (page 584) shows a CAD/CAM facility with relatively few terminals, high processing and storage capacity, and sophisticated attached peripherals.

E. Many Small CPUs Used Primarily for Data Access and Decision Analysis. The type E network employs hardware similar to type B's, but its software has different purposes, such as meeting the dispersed data-access needs of a number of smaller-volume users. Like B, it is a popular network concept. A suitable application might be a contractor whose project managers prepare bids, proposals, budgets, and analyses from shared and personalized data bases, as shown as Figure 16.11 (page 585). This system

Figure 16.9   Classification C: One Large and Many Small CPUs
This design results in the flexibility to meet many different needs. It is very similar to design F (Figure 16.12).

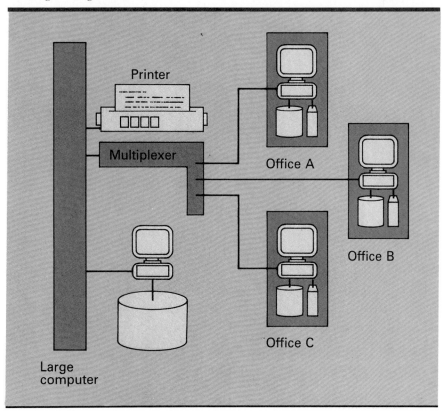

Figure 16.10   Classification D: One Large CPU for Decision Analysis
This design lends itself to highly integrated data bases and rapid incorporation of
new data into a variety of different decisions.

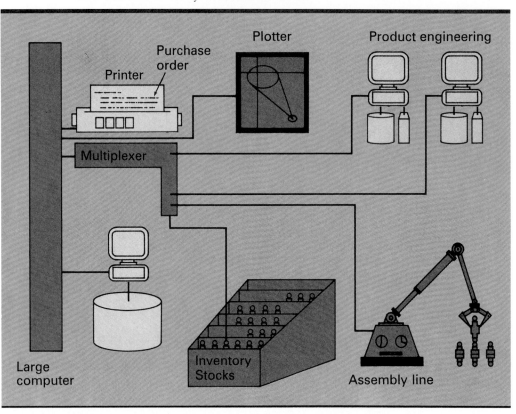

could be a ring or bus, but it is shown as a star design that uses phone
lines, because the contractors move among remote job sites.

**F. One or More Large and Many Small CPUs Used Both for Data Access
and Decision Analysis.**   Type F networks are the most complex, because
they combine different-sized computers with the greatest variety of software. A suitable application would be a real-time accounting and control
system operating in conjunction with multiple subsidiaries and departments, each of which does product design, order entry, and manufacturing scheduling. Other potential users are any diversified company, a government agency with major planning and forecasting responsibilities, and
perhaps the Library of Congress. Figure 16.12 (page 586) shows a simplified version of such a system, combining the ring and bus designs. A close
examination raises some interesting questions about the host organization.

Figure 16.11   Classification E: Small CPUs for Decision Analysis
Organizations that maintain control finance and planning functions coupled with
decentralized operations find this design attractive.

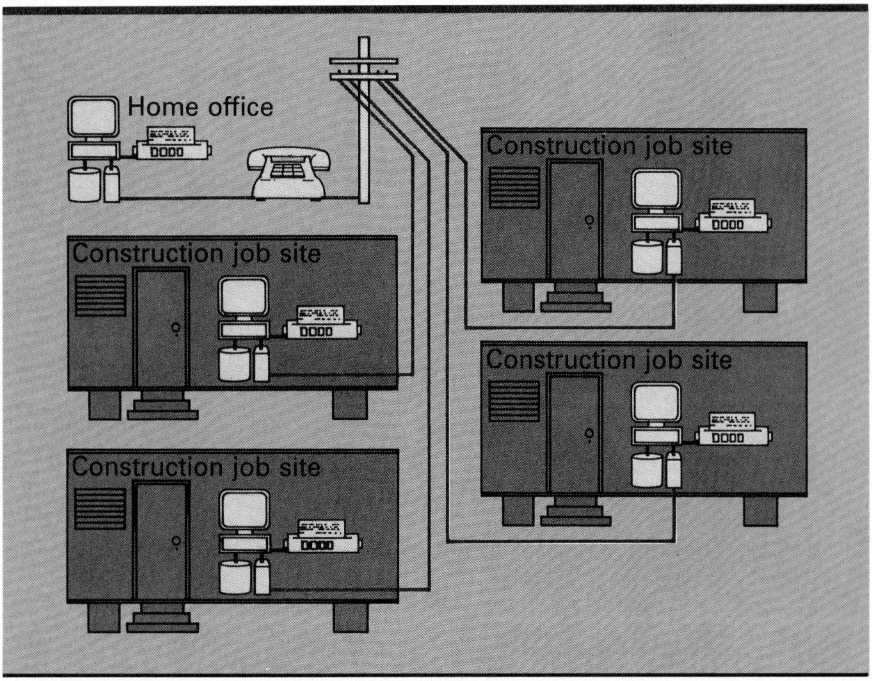

What are the links between marketing, manufacturing, and finance? How
are these functions going to develop integrated computer-based information and decision support systems? Such questions reveal the system in
the figure to be completely inadequate, because the links which would
allow data to be integrated are absent. Properly designed, however, such
a system could be very effective in meeting processing requirements.

Satellite, Microwave, and Optical Fiber

Three recent new communications technologies are promising some break-
throughs in data communications. *Satellites* are now widely used over long
distances by telephone companies, large private firms, and governments.
Microwave transmission is already being used over intermediate distances
by the same types of organizations. And finally, *optical fiber*, although
initially more expensive, is replacing copper wire in many local applications because of its low operating costs, high transmission speed, and
immunity to disruption.

Figure 16.12   Classification F: Mixture of Large and Small Computers for Data Access and Decision Analysis

Large diversified firms often resort to complex networks based on this type of design. It is the most difficult to create successfully.

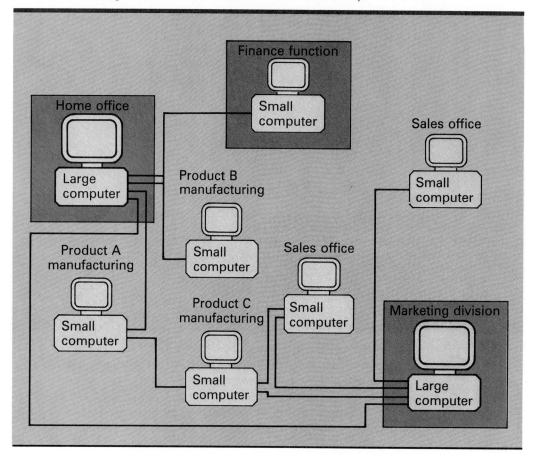

Satellite Transmission

Satellite transmission makes it possible to move vast quantities of data around the world. Communications satellites can be either passive or active. Passive satellites simply provide a reflecting surface off which signals can be bounced and received at another location. Because they cannot amplify signals, switch them from one channel to another, or hold them for retransmission later, passive satellites are no longer used for data communications.

Active satellites receive the incoming signal and retransmit it. An active satellite carries receivers, transmitters, computers, and solar or atomic power resources. These devices enable it to enhance or amplify the signal, speed it up or slow it down, retransmit it at a later time, retransmit it over one or more channels, or even combine it with other signals and retransmit it as a single signal.

A communications satellite is placed in an orbit appropriate for its mission. Early communications satellites could be used by one location for only a few minutes at a time as they passed over. Many recent satellites have been placed in higher orbits, making a given one continuously usable by all points from which it can be "seen," or about one-third of the earth's surface. In addition, though, these satellites can "see" and transmit signals to each other, making their combined range the earth's entire surface.

Cost dictates that governments and communications companies own most satellites. By renting and leasing fractions of satellite capacity, however, they make satellites available via microwave or telephone link even to small businesses and individuals. The price of satellite time to end users has not yet stabilized; it also depends on the volume and duration of communication the user wishes to conduct. An all-day teleconferencing event employing one full-duplex channel might cost around $5,000 (the earthbound sending and receiving equipment for the conference would cost extra, of course).

Microwave Transmission

Microwave transmission, a form of radio communication, uses very short wavelengths (high frequencies). They are not reflected by the earth's ionosphere (as are lower frequencies, such as AM radio broadcasts). Microwaves have a basic 50-to-100-mile range. This range can be extended via relay towers, which amplify and retransmit the signal. Microwaves can be focused so that the outgoing signal is a concentrated beam, similar to the beam a flashlight might project. The short wavelength allows microwave transmission of large amounts of data over hundreds of thousands of square miles, which is especially attractive if the data-transmission sites are remote from telephones or mobile installations. This capability would be important, for example, to a timber company with production units spread across several states. The company could use microwave technology to receive detailed data on board feet cut and delivered to sawmills by its cutting crews. Or an oil-production company might use microwave channels to gather data from robot-operated transmitting stations at remote, unmanned wells.

Optical-Fiber Transmission

Optical-fiber transmission involves sending an intense wavelength of light through a solid glass strand, which corresponds to the copper cable used in electrical communication. The fiber carries the light around corners and for long distances—hundreds, even thousands of yards. To generate a signal, the beam of light varies in intensity. One fiber can carry many different signals if each uses a different light wavelength (color). The signals can be amplified to extend the range of transmission and can travel in both directions simultaneously. Optical-fiber transmission systems require very little energy. They can transmit either analog or digital signals, and they are not subject to interference. Optical-fiber systems are currently being used in underwater cables, local phone systems, and video cable networks. A typical application would be a high-capacity communications network with telephone and computer nodes for occupants of a large office building. Optical-fiber systems cannot transmit over ranges greater than a few miles, and they are expensive to install. However, they promise extremely high reliability, high capacity, and low operating costs.

Telephone- and wire-based data communications systems continue to be the best choice for most smaller businesses, but larger organizations should consider satellite, microwave, and optical fiber, as well as other emerging technologies.

Office-Network Software Applications

Use requirements for specific network capabilities help determine the types of nodes, the methods of linking them, and the software that will be used with the network. It is through software that the network becomes useful within the organization. The choice of application software must be made as early as possible in the network design process, because of the differing capacity requirements of various applications.

One popular application is the **office network**, which provides information support for a group of people performing diverse tasks in close proximity—on the same floor, for example, or in the same building. Most office networks are built from standard components, fitted together according to a proprietary custom design to fit the needs of their users. Often such a system allows a group of people to share an expensive piece of equipment like a laser printer. Office networks are not usually designed to handle transaction recording and processing functions. However, they may offer access to certain accounting or other information files for purposes of updating them—recalling and altering an existing record in the approved-credit-customers file, or making noncash adjustments to an accounts receivable master file.

Office networks can offer a variety of services, including electronic mail and messaging, electronic bulletin boards, information retrieval, and analytic tools.

Electronic Mail. Perhaps you've played telephone tag: you call someone, leave a message, go to a meeting, and return, only to find that the person has called and left a message, then you return *that* call. Or maybe you've had the frustrating experience of dictating several paragraphs over the phone while someone else painstakingly wrote them down; if so, you are probably ready for computer communications. As we noted earlier, electronic mail lets you transmit your message into a special file that the target person's computer can read. The next time he or she uses the computer, it will display your message. If you want to know when the message has been received, the target person's node can be instructed to send a computerized "delivery receipt" to your terminal as soon as the target person next uses the computer. This method of communication avoids the frustration of missed calls but is less formal than a letter or memo since the transmission and delivery process are combined. It has the advantage over telephone communication that a printed hard copy can be obtained by both the sender and the receiver. Electronic mail is not just for communicating at a distance; it is especially effective for use within a single building or suite of offices.

Electronic Bulletin Board. An electronic bulletin board is similar to electronic mail to some extent, but it lets users place messages in a file that any other user can read. Some systems divide the bulletin board into several categories. One category might be announcements that flash onto every screen as soon as they are written—emergency messages or notices of required meetings. Other categories could serve special interests or groups; and users would have to ask to view those messages. One major computer company has even used an electronic bulletin board to transmit to its customers system software upgrades and revisions. Like paper memos and traditional bulletin boards, electronic bulletin boards work only if users check them regularly.

Information Retrieval (Data Base Access). Most executives make constant reference to a set of changing data stored in personal files, workgroup files, and company records. Local-area networks make these data easier to use by providing a user-friendly interface. Users can have access to details and descriptions of specific events and agreements and can add, change, and if the system permits, delete information.

Analytic Tools. Managers can also profit from statistical analysis, graphics, and spreadsheet software made available through a network. The manager may create a personalized set of decision support analytic programs. Such electronic spreadsheets as Excel, Supercalc, 1-2-3, and Multiplan allow the user to define a structured algorithm into which many different sets of data can be inserted for analysis. Programming languages such as

BASIC, PASCAL, and APL accomplish the same purpose in more calcu-lation-intensive analytic applications. Networked tools allow managers to do specific customized analyses of data *as they become available in computer form.* These tools also assist in analyses of one-of-a-kind (as well as difficult but recurring) decisions.

A graphics program lets managers display the results of their calcu-lations in easily understood form, including pie charts, bar charts, broken-line graphs, solid-area graphs, and variations of these four formats. Figure 16.13 shows the same data in graph and tabular form; decide for yourself which presentation is easier to grasp.

Although graphics presentations have a nearly unlimited number of potential uses, managers probably use them most often to display reve-nues, costs, and contribution margins that are a function of time; compare cost and profit results of several companies and divisions; and make pro-jections and productivity comparisons.

Text Preparation.   Word processing software is an extraordinary boon to anyone who must prepare perfect letters, papers, resumés, memos, or essays. Perhaps more people are familiar with word processing software than with any other type, and even students learn how to use it today. Word processing is a form of file management in which each document is a file. The software lets the user type, view, and edit the document a screenful at a time; without retyping the entire document, the user may change the content, order, and presentation as much and as often as necessary.

Figure 16.13   Graphical Versus Tabular Presentation
Computer software makes it possible, from the same data, to generate a variety of tabular and graphical presentations from which to choose.

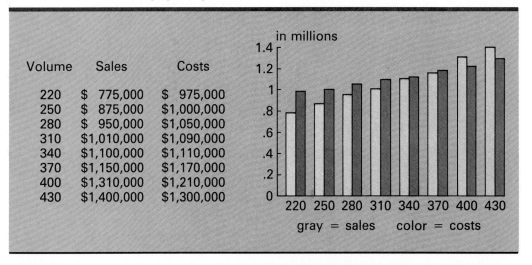

Volume	Sales	Costs
220	$ 775,000	$ 975,000
250	$ 875,000	$1,000,000
280	$ 950,000	$1,050,000
310	$1,010,000	$1,090,000
340	$1,100,000	$1,110,000
370	$1,150,000	$1,170,000
400	$1,310,000	$1,210,000
430	$1,400,000	$1,300,000

in millions

gray = sales   color = costs

It is possible to move chunks of text from one document to another; to change a spelling every time it occurs throughout a manuscript (with a single command); to alter type styles, margins, indentations, or footnotes; and generally to be as creative as the situation demands. Each of these changes takes only a minute or so, leaving the writer free to concentrate on clear communication. Managerial styles differ as to whether a manager should directly use word processing software. Some managers feel that they are more efficient using a computer keyboard; others do their creative revision on a printed document copy to be keyboarded by someone else.

Personal-Support Tools.   The final category of commonly used office network software is short utility-type programs that do limited specialized tasks. Examples are calendars, directories, and timers. The calendar keeps the manager up-to-date on commitments; on a network, others may be able to add appointments to slots open on the calendar or to insert announcements of meetings in the proper date file. The directory contains addresses and phone numbers, which the manager can display on a CRT screen or print out. The timer is an appointment reminder; it can also monitor the length of long-distance calls. Sometimes other tools, called *desk accessories* or *electronic desktops*—an on-screen calculator, a print spooler, a small spreadsheet, or a graphics program—are also included in this category.

Customizing the Network for Users

Implementing a network begins with the applications, the system software, the work stations, the servers, and the connections the network must include. It continues with customizing these features to meet specific everyday user requirements. These requirements may be determined from the following questions:

- Which applications will each user run?
- To which files will users have access?
- Which servers will each user require?

The sections that follow describe some access and control considerations that must be kept in mind when studying the answers to these questions.

Access Control

An accountant should pay particular attention to how access to the network is controlled. When considering a wide-area proprietary network, for example, remember that the dispersal of work can also reduce control over access and processing of data. And if, for example, businesses that are tenants in the same building were to set up a shared local-area office network, the designers would have to build in adequate security so that the tenants would share only network functions and not each other's sensitive applications and data.

Access control can vary significantly, depending on the type of system involved. In the local-area network, physical and logical access are nearly synonymous. Physical control can be accomplished by such measures as locating work stations in easy-to-see places. If access to work stations can be physically controlled, overall security becomes less difficult.

More sophisticated controls are necessary in the area of logical access. Access control is not so problematic with proprietary networks as with phone-connected computers, which may be accessed logically from many locations and even by strangers. Protection against logical access requires a user to enter a password. A two-part password—one part designated by the system manager and the other part chosen by the authorized user—is very effective and can be used to control access to all or part of the system. Options include protecting entire volumes or files, only certain records within files, or only certain fields from individuals who may have system clearance but should not see certain data. Needless to say, security should not restrict access to information that users need to do their work. Order entry clerks, for example, must have read-only access to customer credit ratings, although that information is generally off-limits to other network users.

Physical Installation

Making a computer network operational is a tedious task requiring painstaking attention to detail. Usually the most efficient and economical way to proceed is to let professionals plan and install a system to your specifications. This is not a do-it-yourself project! The cables are bulky and should be installed by technicians who, for reasons of safety as well as aesthetics, will pull them through walls, ceilings, and floors rather than laying them on top of the carpet. If the system cables can be pulled while the building is under construction, it is much like installing electrical wiring. If installation is in an older building, it can be complicated and time consuming. Once the cable has been pulled, all the devices ever to be connected to it must reside near the existing wall outlets. Allowing twice as many outlets as you expect ever to need is likely to add to the usefulness and longevity of the system.

On-line Storage (Server)

Another system characteristic that can have an important effect on how the network appears to users is the way space on the system is allocated. Every network should have a server that reserves some disk data storage space for each user; however, networks vary in how well they do this. Less desirable systems create fixed-size folders or "volumes" on the disk and allocate them to users; the user is allowed to manage sectors within the assigned volumes. The disadvantage of this technique is that an active user can run out of space while an infrequent user has empty volumes. Other systems avoid this wasted space by creating variable-size volumes and dynamically assigning disk space by sectors only. Each user gets control only over space in use. Office local-area networks typically have limited on-line storage relative to a mainframe computer, so the system designer should try to predict whether the volume allocation will be satisfactory. In local-area networks with large CPUs and massive on-line storage, this problem may not arise.

Configuration and Cost

The configuration and cost of a local-area network are closely related. The larger the main processing unit and storage capacity, the more expensive the system will be. For smaller systems, costs also vary depending on features, size, sophistication, and software. A bare-bones installed cost for server and cabling was about $1,500 to $4,000 per work-station outlet in 1987, *plus* the cost of the work station itself and the applications software.

Table 16.2 (page 594) lists typical network components, their desirability, and their cost.

Management of a Network

If management has studied network design, determined organization needs, adopted and installed a suitable design, and customized it, then everyone can relax, right? Almost, but not quite. The typical network containing three to ten nodes will require more systematic attention and more resources to operate than would the same number of unlinked personal computers. One person should be responsible for the network. The qualifications for this slot should include computer expertise and experience in providing services and staff for line management. If management is designing the network, the network manager should be appointed early enough to participate in development and to get to know the managers who will use the network. After the network is operational, the network manager will identify users and assign their passwords and disk volumes; make certain back-up of shared files occurs regularly; document the system's programs and procedures; add and remove network nodes; and oversee network maintenance, technical support, and relations with the vendors that supply and maintain the network components. A network that contains a phone link may from time to time function as part of other networks, and the network manager should also be familiar with those systems.

Table 16.2   Network Components and Their Cost Ranges

Feature	Desirability	Cost Range
Back-up (usually on tape or floppy disks)	mandatory	$1,000–$2,000
Desktop computers (for use as terminals)	optional	$1,000–$8,000 each
Interface board (one in each node)	mandatory	$400–$1,000 each
Modem and terminal emulator	optional	$300 (1,200 baud) to $2,000 (9,600 baud)
Operating system (usually included in cost of hardware; price is if bought separately)	mandatory	$100–$1,000
Network controller (some networks use a microcomputer like the ones at work stations)	mandatory	$2,000–$13,000
Hard disk	mandatory	$1,200 (20 Mb)– $3,000 (60 Mb)
Repeater (boosts signal over a long distance)	mandatory if a long distance requires it	$400–$2,000
Printer or plotter (a shared resource)	mandatory if printed output required	$1,000–$6,000
Laser printer	optional	$2,000–$6,000
Application software: Word processing Accounting Spreadsheet Data base Office productivity	mandatory or desirable	$400–$1,500 per application

Summary

The requirement for networks arises out of management's need for shared information and wide participation in decision making. The purpose of a data communications network is to send data where and when it is wanted. Different designs, such as ring, star, and bus, have been developed to reduce the need for paper records and summaries and the reliance on a large mainframe computer. The star configuration is the most expensive and the fastest. The bus is least costly, most flexible, and slowest. All networks should provide such basic features as a server, shared resources, resource locking, access control, and on-line storage.

The network manager may choose a telephone-based or a proprietary network; the latter may use wire, optical fiber, microwave, and/or satellite technologies. The advantages of telephone-based data communications are low initial investment, flexibility, and access to public data bases. However, phone-based networks also have disadvantages; they are slow, expensive to operate, and open to interference by hackers. The most common alternative to a phone-based network is a proprietary office network, with cable-linked nodes consisting of individual terminals, small computers, disk storage, and printers. One of the nodes will be a server to allocate network resources among the other nodes.

A good network should be easy to use, and flexible enough to meet many different requirements as soon as it becomes operational. It should also be expandable. Some networks eventually cover large geographical areas and include dozens or even hundreds of nodes.

Establishing even a simple network requires planning, including selecting a network manager, paying close attention to back-up, assuring the security of data on the network, and making sure everyone who uses the network understands how it works.

Key Terms

acoustic modems	echo	office network
analog	electronic mail	parity check
asynchronous	full duplex	proprietary network
baud	gateway	resource locking
baud rate	hackers	ring network
bus network	half duplex	server
carrier sense multiple	handshake	simplex
access/collision	host	star network
detection	host environment	synchronous
(CSMA/CD)	host program	terminal emulator
channels	local-area networks	token passing
clear to send/none	modem	transmission mode
digital	multiplexer	wide-area networks
direct-connect	network	Xon-Xoff
modems	nodes	

Review Questions

1. Name three developments that support the trend toward consolidation of intraorganization communications.

2. Describe three situations that call for communication links between data collection and user destinations.

3. What is a terminal emulator program? Can it be used in place of a modem?

4. What is a server? What does it do in a network? What kind of device usually functions as a server?

5. Explain the difference between synchronous and asynchronous transmission, and give an example of a situation in which the latter is more useful.

6. What is resource locking? Why is it necessary? How might it inconvenience users of a local area network?

7. Name at least three features that any local-area network should possess, and explain why they are necessary.

8. Why would it be difficult to create a proprietary star network among offices spread across the eastern United States?

9. Name nine parameters that must be set to establish communication between computers.

10. What is electronic mail? How does it differ from an electronic bulletin board? Does the distance between stations have any effect on the usefulness of electronic mail? What advantages does electronic mail have over (a) voice telephone communications and (b) regular mail?

11. Under what circumstances would an organization send data by telephone instead of direct connection? What alternatives are there to the telephone? What are the advantages or disadvantages of data transfer by telephone?

12. What is a modem? What is the difference between direct-connect and acoustic-connect modems?

13. What is optical-fiber transmission? Can two or more messages be sent simultaneously on the same optical fiber?

Discussion Questions

14. Has communications technology led to stronger or weaker communication between different levels of management? In your opinion, has this development improved or weakened organizational efficiency?

15. If an organization must send data in electronic form from one computer to another, why are floppy disks not completely suitable for this purpose?

16. Explain the difference between digital and analog signals. Which has the potential for greater accuracy? Greater speed? What home entertainment device utilizes digital signals? Which of the signals illustrated on the next page are digital and which are analog?

a.   b.

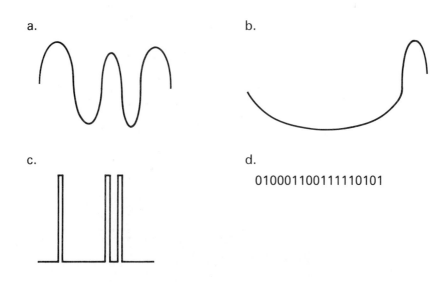

c.   d.

010001100111110101

17. What factors woud prompt an organization to choose a proprietary network? What advantages does an organization look for in a network? Why might a network be superior to an unlinked system using the same number of unlinked computers?

18. Becky sat down at a Compaq XT computer with a direct-connection modem and dialed the number of a popular public data base. The data base computer requested an account number and password. Becky provided them. She received access to the system, located certain information, and asked that it be transferred to her computer's memory. As the transfer began, the message "Parity error. Continue? Y N" appeared. Becky pressed "Y," and the data transfer was completed.

Required:

What risk was Becky taking? In general, would you consider such a risk worthwhile?

19. On December 20, Diego needed to review some unprocessed credit sales transactions. He sat down at a microcomputer linked to a bus network. When he turned on the computer, it automatically loaded and began to run a program directly from an internal hard disk. The screen displayed the message "Give password:" and Diego typed "Maximum." Diego did the work he had planned. Then he decided to try to find out what salary adjustment he would receive in the coming year. He opened a file called "Employee Master File" and typed his social security number. When his record appeared, he saw that he had been specified for a 5-percent increase. Noticing that his address was wrong, he corrected it and saved the record before closing the file and turning to other work.

Required:

Criticize the level of control in this network, and list steps that would improve it.

20. Label each of the network diagrams below on each of the following three design features:
    (a) ring, star, or bus;
    (b) centralized, decentralized, or can't tell;
    (c) likely to work or likely to generate difficulties.

Alternative Top
              Management Marketing Finance Production Research

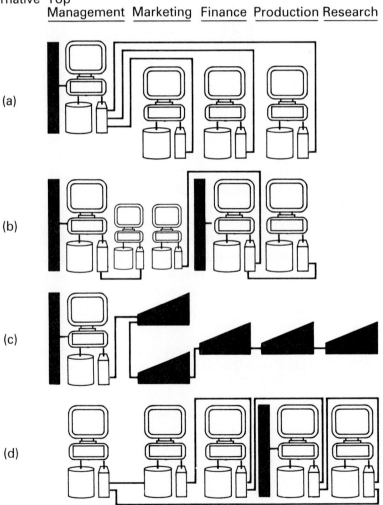

(a)

(b)

(c)

(d)

21. Diagram and explain the differences between star, ring, and bus local-area networks. Compare the three types of network on the basis of

speed, cost, ease of connecting another station, and ease of serving widespread stations.

22. Some possible applications of local-area networks follow. For each one, recommend the design classification, from Table 16.1, that you believe is most suitable.
    (a) A builders-supply store with a sales desk in each department
    (b) A university with teaching, research, and data processing applications
    (c) A law office employing lawyers, secretaries, and clerks
    (d) A tax-return preparation firm
    (e) An automated computer-assembly plant
    (f) A chain of pizza restaurants that takes carry-out orders at a central phone number and transmits them to the restaurant nearest the customer
    (g) An auto dealership with customer-pickup, body, engine, transmission, interior, glass, electronics, and brake-repair centers
    (h) A large home builder with multiple construction sites that deal with local contractors

Problems

23. Fort Davis Brokers, Inc., is a nationwide brokerage firm with twenty-four offices. About 300,000 customers buy and sell stocks through its local offices. The broker accepts instructions and transmits them immediately to the appropriate securities exchange for execution. As soon as the transaction occurs, the broker receives a confirmation. The broker calculates the fee for the transaction and transmits a record of it to the firm's central billing and credit location. The local office also updates its record of the customer's portfolio to reflect the effects of each transaction. Fort Davis Brokers maintains a dial-in phone number that customers can call to give instructions to a computer, which will forward them to both the local office and the broker representative at the securities exchange.

Required:

Outline, in as much detail as you can, a data communications system capable of serving each need described.

24. Two small accounting firms, one in Dallas and one in Cedar City, Iowa, decide to establish a computer link. One firm uses IBM PC-AT microcomputers; the other has a single IBM System 36 minicomputer. The link should be able to transmit electronic mail and standard data files.

Required:

(a) Describe in as much detail as you can a system that would establish the link.

(b) A third firm in Sacramento, California, wishes to join this link. Given the system you designed in *a*, is this possible? Why or why not?

25. Schulenberg & Company, a partnership of 22 veterinarians, has a large office in which management would like to install computers. It is proposed that the computers be connected via a bus network, which will include a server, a 60 M byte hard disk, a draft printer, and a letter-quality printer. The office houses 32 veterinarians and staff members. Only the staff would receive a computer; however, three terminals would be in the treatment area for use by the veterinarians. Each veterinarian will see 20 animals a day. The average visit is 15 minutes long. Before a visit to an animal's home or farm, the vet may review the animal's medical history to take along. During an office visit, the vet may review the animal's medical history on a monitor in the treatment area. After each visit, the vet will complete a card listing the animal's unique identifying number, diagnosis, treatment, and fee. A staff person uses a computer to enter the data on the card into records averaging 200 bytes in length, which are stored on the hard disk. It will take approximately 3 minutes to enter one card's data. Late each day, the administrative director will link all the records in that day's file with appropriate records in the animal owner's master file; this activity will require 10 seconds per treatment record. Once a week, the same person will run a program that sorts the files, adds up the week's visits, and prepares a report to the veterinarians showing the total treatments and billings for which each of them is responsible. No other use will be made of the proposed network. Other programs prepare invoices and record payments.

Required:

How many records will the veterinarians create each day? How long will it take to transfer these records to the hard disk? How many bytes per day will the treatment cards add to the files on the hard disk? If the office is open 300 days each year, how many bytes will be used up by the treatment records in a year? What is your opinion of this system? How would you improve it if you could?

26. The Marfa Company has a small office, currently equipped with three microcomputers. These microcomputers are linked, and the managers have gotten into the habit of leaving messages, memos, and technical information for each other to read by using electronic mail and the hard disk.

    Next year the company expects to add 2 new managers and the same number of computers. In succeeding years, it will add 2, 3, 3, and 5 managers and computers respectively, for a total of 18 computers. Management wants to continue its practice of connecting each computer to the others. Each such connection will cost $300 initially, with no annual maintenance costs. Assuming this cost is constant, calculate the total cost over the next five years of connecting each computer to the other 17. What will be the cost of connecting the 18th computer? If the only multiplexer available for this connection is a five-into-one, what decision will this firm face when it adds the 7th manager? What design network would you suggest the firm adopt instead? *Hint:* The total number of connections is calculated from the formula

$$\sum_{i=2}^{i=n} (i\text{-}1) \qquad \text{where } n = \text{number of computers and is} \geq 2$$

For example, the number of connectors for 4 computers is $(4-1) + (3-1) + (2-1) = 6$.

27. The New Sweden Brokerage Company has five branch offices, each of which executes about 500 trades a day. At present, each office operates its own local-area network. These networks are not linked together. The home office would like to link these networks for real-time access to transaction data as a means of managing cash flow and predicting income. The actual and proposed configurations are as follows:

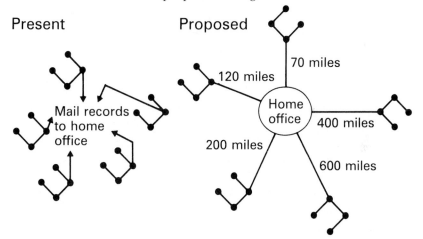

Present

Proposed

Mail records to home office

70 miles
120 miles
Home office
400 miles
200 miles
600 miles

Each transaction requires 20 seconds to transmit to the home office. The company proposes to lease phone lines. The local phone company will lease a line for $0.03 per hour per mile, based on the distances shown, provided New Sweden will lease each line for at least six hours per day. The home-office multiplexer will cost $2,000 and modems (two for each line) will cost $300 each. The consultant the company uses will train one operator per node, including the home office, for $300 each, and will write a users' manual for $3,000.

Required:

    (a) What will be the total cost of equipment and the annual phone-line lease cost of this system, based on 280 trading days a year?

    (b) The two southernmost stations are only 200 miles apart. What would be the annual savings of connecting them and letting the least distant one forward both stations' transactions to the home office 400 miles away?

    (c) Assuming the necessary equipment for *b* is available for $900, how long will it take for savings to pay back this investment?

28. Prices of communications equipment drop about 25 percent annually, if performance is held constant. Installation costs rise about 8 percent per year. In 1985, Friendswood Company designed and priced a network that would have cost $150,000. Of this amount, $120,000 was for equipment and $30,000 was for installation. If a network of equivalent performance were installed in 1993, what would you estimate as its cost? Estimate equipment and installation separately, and then total them.

Case: Sure Refund Tax Preparers

Sure Refund has 675 small offices around the country, at which taxpayers may meet with trained interviewers between 9:00 A.M. and 5:00 P.M. The company has a Wang VS 100 minicomputer, with a tax-return preparation program, in New York. Between 6:00 P.M. and 12:00 midnight, the company hopes to create files of tax information on Apple Macintosh computers and to transmit them to New York starting about 12:30 A.M. The computer would process the tax returns on a first-in, first-out basis, then transmit them back to the local offices between 2:00 A.M. and 8:00 A.M. As each return is transmitted, it would be saved on the computer's disk. From these disk files, the local office's computers would print tax returns during normal working hours. Taxpayers could pick them up two days after submitting their tax information.

Required:

    (a) Identify all opportunities for data communication technology to be applied in this case.

    (b) For each opportunity, identify the choices available and indicate which one you would recommend.

Case: Capitan Reef Bank

Capitan Reef Bank offers "Money Card," with which customers transact 300,000 inquiries, deposits, and cash withdrawals annually. The network consists of three teller machines at the bank and five others in supermarkets within a mile of the bank. These machines are permanently connected in a star network to the bank. The bank directors are worried that they may lose customers unless they link up with a national money-card network. If the bank's network were linked to a regional network, bank customers anywhere in the region could initiate transactions via the network connection for the bank's computer to process. Also, customers of other banks in the network could enter transactions into the Capitan Reef Bank machines for its computer to transmit to the regional network for transfer to the customer's bank.

Required:

Discuss the issues of control, hardware, software, and data structure that the bank may face if it links up with another network.

PART 5

System Design and Implementation

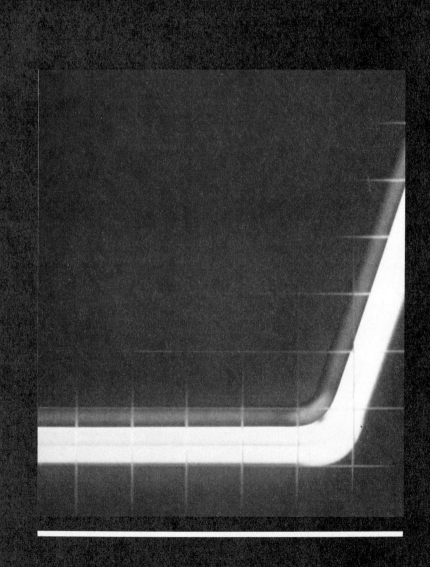

If you have read all 16 chapters in the preceding four sections, then you know what an accounting system looks like. In this section, we explain how one brings an accounting system into being. The process is complex; yet, done correctly, it can produce the accounting system management envisioned.

Chapter 17 discusses the system lifecycle and the first three steps of the "creation" period in the lifecycle. These are the steps in which management decides what requirements a new system should meet, roughs out a design to meet these requirements, and evaluates the design to see if it is satisfactory. Consultants are often used on these activities as well as on those described in Chapter 18: the complete, detailed system design; the startup of the new system; and the post-startup review of the new system in operation to see if it really performs as expected.

Although information engineering is automating system design, human judgment and expertise remain absolutely critical to successful accounting system creation. And make no mistake: just as a good accounting system enhances management's competence, a bungled systems-creation attempt can mortally wound an organization. That is why the material in this section was saved until last. Not only do you now understand what an accounting information system is supposed to accomplish, you also appreciate the importance of the concepts presented in these chapters to anyone who expects to take a management role in creating an accounting information system.

Part 5 contains the following chapters:

17 Developing the Design for an Accounting System
18 Implementing an Accounting System Design

CHAPTER 17

Developing the Design for an Accounting System

Learning Objectives

After studying this chapter, you should be able to

- Explain long-term and operating reasons why an organization would undertake system change or replacement.

- Explain such aspects of systems development as the system life cycle, development process, costs, and the expectations-performance gap.

- Describe the six phases of systems development and the order in which they occur.

- Identify the systems development responsibilities of management, systems developers, and vendors.

- Express in both narrative and performance requirement form the objectives for a given system; categorize performance requirements into user's requirements, accountability requirements, and top-management-control requirements; and explain how to discover these requirements.

- Explain what a conceptual design is, and list and define its component parts.

- Describe and illustrate various graphic aids used in designing a system, such as a data flow diagram, process diagram, system flowchart, and document flowchart.

- Define what is meant by *systems design feasibility* and describe how to evaluate financial, technical, time-frame, and organizational feasibility.

Now that we have looked at the fundamental features of information systems—controls, information structures, communications, decision support, and the details of selected processing applications—we will see how to create information systems that meet the needs of specific organizations.

Accounting systems are simple and elegant in concept, but their smooth operation depends on coordination of many details and related procedures. These details and procedures must be selected and assembled carefully. It is not unusual for the team responsible for system creation to take a year or more to complete the work. Systems experts think of the system-creation period as consisting of a design phase (requirements definition, conceptual design, and feasibility analysis) and an implemention phase (vendor selection, detail design, conversion, and postconversion review). This chapter describes the design phase; Chapter 18 is devoted to implementation. The two chapters together are intended to enable you to participate in the creation of an information system, to recognize the important steps in the project, and to appraise whether they are being done effectively and competently. With experience, you should be able to grasp the design principles inherent in accounting systems and to lead projects that implement them.

Objectives in Creating a New Accounting System

How difficult is it to create a new accounting system? Why would an organization want to replace an old but still serviceable accounting system with a new one? The general answer is that a firm undertakes this major commitment to foster its long-range and operating (or short-range) objectives. Broadly speaking, these objectives include maintaining flows of sufficient and relevant information to the organization's managers, investors, customers, and suppliers. When—owing to changing organizational structure, technology, product design, staffing, or competitive conditions—the accounting system cannot produce these flows, then the time has come to replace it. Sometimes it is difficult for management to see how inadequate a smoothly operating and well-understood system has become, and the decision to replace it is postponed. More often, information users will make plain their dissatisfaction, and management will move unhesitatingly to the replacement decision.

Long-Range Objectives

Systems are designed and redesigned for many different reasons; without fail, however, the systems are intended to relieve certain problems or to assist management in accomplishing objectives. Whether many, few, or none of these objectives are long-range will depend on the specific system under study, but very often, systems designers are called upon to incorporate one of the following long-range objectives into a system design:

- *Organizational change:* The system design may be intended to coordinate operating procedures with changes occurring in the organization. For example, an organization may experience growth through merger, acquisition, or expansion from within. Or it may implement a new organizational structure that would work best with a redesigned information system.

- *New technological developments:* A design may make it possible for an organization to take advantage of new accounting processing technology. The introduction of local-area networks and powerful work stations may enable the organization to move toward distributed processing and reap the rewards of quicker data capture and processing.

- *Commitment to new services:* If an organization wants to offer new services, incorporating additional or unfamiliar new procedures may become an important objective. For example, a bank that anticipates offering debit and credit cards will have to revise its accounting system to record transactions using these cards.

- *Growth beyond system capacity:* A very common long-range process that generates a need for a new system design is plain, healthy growth. Even if an organization's accounting system works well, it may need to increase its capacity to keep pace with the growth of files and requests for access to them. Acquiring this extra capacity often becomes a design objective.

- *New conceptual approach:* Management may adopt a different conceptual approach to accounting processing. To increase its flexibility and speed of response, an organization may want to convert from file to data base processing, or from sequential files to direct-access files, or to an on-line, real-time or local-area system.

Short-Range Objectives

In addition to the long-range objectives that guide a design team's approach to a new system, other forces will shape the system's development. The team's work often acquires its momentum and its sense of urgency from forces exerted by short-term operating needs. Fulfilling these needs then becomes a short-range objective within the system-creation process. Some of the most common of these objectives include the following:

- *Eliminating time lags:* Management may decide that the time between operating events and their appearance in accounting reports has become too long. For example, a manager who currently receives weekly reports prepared from a batch-processing system may decide it is urgent to receive the reports daily or even to have immediate access through an on-line system to information as it becomes available.

- *Increasing control:* Management may feel that processing conditions require it to maintain or improve control over accounting processing; this drive toward control could become a very important short-term objective. For example, if file back-up procedures are inadequate at certain locations, management will want a good back-up procedure to be incorporated in the new system. Other short-term objectives that would improve control include enhanced data entry editing and limited distribution of reports.

- *Using resources more efficiently:* An older information system is likely to use its resources less efficiently than a system of newer design will. Newer designs benefit from automation, faster operating speeds, simpler procedures for users, and fuller integration of their various applications.

- *Minimizing the need for technical support:* Users invariably hope that a new system will have simpler user interfaces than the system it replaces. This will also help reduce demand for technical support. Management should assure that simple and easily learned user interfaces are specified, especially for information search and communications.

Overview of the Systems Development Process

Systems development is the process of planning and preparing a new or improved system and making it operational. Because systems development can be a lengthy process, it must begin while the old system it will replace is still useful. Unlike most processes for which management takes responsibility, the replacement of a major management system such as an accounting application occurs infrequently and requires resources not usually found in small or medium-sized organizations. Partial system replacement and system enhancement, which may occur more often, require the same skills and procedures on a lesser scale. Thus, to avoid wasting resources on an inadequate system design or unsuccessful system implementation, all organizations should choose either to maintain competency in these skills and procedures or to have access to reliable consultants.

This section describes four aspects of systems development: the system life cycle, the steps in the systems development process, accounting system costs, and the potential gap between what the organization expects and what it gets when it implements a new system.

The System Life Cycle

The life cycle of an accounting system passes through four distinct periods—creation, startup, maturity, and decline—collectively extending over a five-to-ten-year period. Many organizations devote the most attention to the system development activities that take place in the first period. Figure 17.1 shows these periods.

Figure 17.1   System Life Cycle
The size of the slice roughly corresponds to the relative duration of the period.

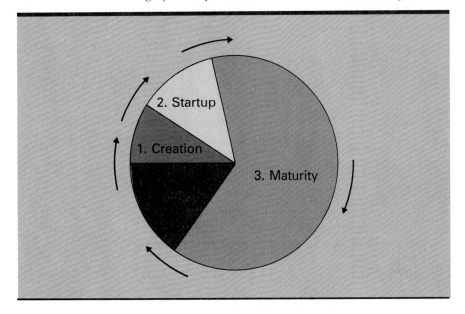

Period 1.   Creation is the process of designing and implementing a new system, to the point that it can meet a satisfactory number of its performance requirements once it is operating normally. The creation period may last from six months to two years, and it includes the first few weeks of operation, in which major problems are caught and corrected.

If resources for systems design are limited, deliberate compromises may have to be made to remain within the budget. If the performance capabilities originally specified cannot all be accommodated, the systems designers focus their efforts on the most critical requirements. For example, a certain system may have as a critical requirement the establishment of a 24-character account code. A lesser but desirable requirement may be that it estimate income tax expense. If these two requirements come into conflict, the designers will opt for the account code even if it means dropping or deferring the income-tax-expense requirement.

Period 2.   In startup, the system experiences rapid gains in productivity and efficiency. Rapid initial progress toward increased internal efficiency is a behavioral phenomenon called the **learning effect;** it might last a few weeks to a year.

A common model of the learning effect uses an exponential function. In this model, the average time to produce one unit of output (such as a report or processed transaction) declines by a fixed proportion—typically 20 percent—each time the quantity of total output doubles. The fixed proportion of decline in the time required to produce a unit of output is called the **learning constant**. A simple expression follows of the general formula for the total time C of processing the total number of units N, given the total time C_0 of processing the first N_0 units:

$$C = \left[1.00 - \left(\frac{\text{learning}}{\text{constant}} \right) \right]^{\log_2\left(\frac{N}{N_0}\right)} * \left(\frac{C_0}{N_0} \right) * N$$

The logarithmic expression is easy to evaluate if (N/N_0) is one of the powers of 2, as the following short table shows, and it can be found easily on a pocket calculator for other values.

N/N_0	$\log_2(N/N_0)$
1	0
2	1
4	2
8	3
16	4
32	5 and so on

To use a simple numerical example, suppose that processing the first 20 transactions requires 30 minutes. Then to calculate the time required to process the first 40 transactions ($N = 40$), $N/N_0 = 2$; $\log_2 2 = 1$; and $C_0/N_0 = 1.5$. Processing the first 40 transactions (including that first 20) would require $(1.00 - 0.20)^1 \times (1.5 \text{ minutes/transaction}) \times 40$ transactions $= 48$ minutes. Processing the first 80 transactions (including now the first 40) would require $(1.00 - 0.20)^2 \times (1.5 \text{ minutes/transaction}) \times 80$ transactions $= 76.8$ minutes.

The learning effect will eventually dwindle and be overwhelmed by such other factors as procedure changes and turnover of experienced personnel. When this drop-off happens, the system will appear to have reached a steady state of efficiency. Additional productivity gains will come much more slowly, if at all, and the startup period will have ended.

Period 3.   During the three to eight years of **maturity**, the system typically operates reliably with only minor deterioration or enhancement. When the learning effect diminishes, advances in systems technology and higher performance expectations on the part of users become the most influential constraints on the life span of an otherwise healthy system. In its maturity, the system should be both productive and satisfying to use. Toward the end of this period, the system—although working well—progressively manifests technological obsolescence and functional inflexibility, setting the stage for less and less relevance to the changing expectations of its users. One example of this process might be an inventory system based on centralized sequential processing of record updates. Although the system has always performed at the level expected of it, management has become better informed about inventory and production management techniques and wishes to implement a just-in-time system. Since the old system cannot support just-in-time, it will have to be replaced.

Period 4. Finally, when everyone can see that the old system has a limited future, its performance may begin to **decline**, and management will become unwilling to devote additional resources to it. Thereafter, the greater utility of a new system may more than offset the investment and effort to acquire it. A forward-looking management could avoid most or all of period 4 by having the replacement system ready.

The Systems Development Process

Systems development is inherently costly. Older and less organized development methods have given way to newer ones that produce superior results at less cost. One such approach, structured design, reduces complexity by dividing the system tasks among a set of modules that have internal cohesiveness and appropriate coupling with other modules. The division process continues until each module is simple and easily understood. Structured design concepts have been incorporated into computer-aided tools that allow a systems designer to add detail progressively to a graphic representation of the new system. As the description becomes more detailed, it eventually contains all the information necessary to generate run-ready computer software. The graphic representation begins with the organization chart. It then accepts descriptions of information collected and received at each organization point, as well as reports, relations, process details, hardware specifications, and other variables. Computer-assisted structured design methodologies (CASDM) are certain to grow in importance in the next few years. They promise to streamline the developing and testing of a system, especially the stages that have to do with manual programming and testing.

Modern systems development—the creation period in the system life cycle—proceeds in six well-defined steps, as shown in Figure 17.2 and briefly described here. You will recall from the chapter introduction that the first three steps comprise the design phase and the last three steps are the implementation phase.

1. **Requirements definition:** determining system scope and performance requirements
2. **Conceptual design:** laying out the broad design principles

3. **Feasibility analysis:** determining whether and to what degree the proposed conceptual designs are acceptable

4. **Vendor selection:** selecting the consultants, suppliers, and programmers who will assist in the remaining steps

5. **Detail design:** programming (if required), documentation, and training

6. **Conversion:** implementation, including putting the system into operation, evaluating its performance, and making changes to achieve the performance envisioned in the requirements definition

We will return to a discussion of requirements definition, conceptual design, and feasibility analysis later in this chapter. Vendor selection, detail design and conversion are the subject of Chaper 18. The first three steps, the design process, lead to selection of a feasible conceptual design for implementation.

Figure 17.2. Systems Creation Steps
The vertical axis shows relative effort; the horizontal scale shows the passage of time. Some steps overlap others. For example, requirements for the inventory application may be complete 30 days after the design phase begins; the team begins work on conceptual designs to meet these requirements while also preparing requirements for the purchasing application.

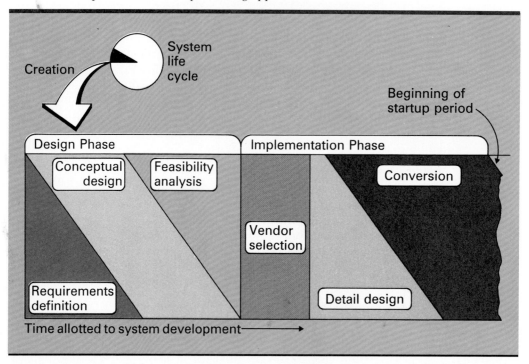

How Much Will a New Accounting System Cost?

The resources required to create a new operational accounting system will depend, of course, upon the organization's size and structure and the nature of its accounting information requirements. Managements tend to underestimate the total effort required. The monetary cost will rank as a major investment in any firm whose management considers accounting information a significant factor in successful operations. The magnitude of time and talent required may surprise management if it has not anticipated these demands realistically.

Rule of Thumb for Estimating Cost.   There is no precise way to estimate how much to spend on system development. Various rules of thumb will, however, offer a starting point for those who need to estimate costs. The following simple example offers a first approximation of cost magnitudes. For a small business with annual gross revenues of $20 million or less, the total investment in a new information system may approximate 7 to 15 percent of one year's gross revenues. It is reasonable to expect one-third of this amount to be spent on hardware and the remaining two-thirds on all other system components including system and applications software, forms design, file conversion, staff training, consultant fees, and the like. The larger the accounting system, the smaller the hardware costs will be as a proportion of the total investment.

The hours expended by managerial, consulting, and supplier personnel on system design may be estimated as follows:

$$\text{Total hours (upper limit)} = \frac{\text{Estimated system expenditure}}{50}$$

$$\text{Total hours (lower limit)} = \frac{\text{Estimated system expenditure}}{150}$$

To gain experience with the system, to maintain control over its development, and to control costs, management should do as much of the system work as possible. Even under these conditions, consultants will put in one-sixth to one-third of the total hours and will charge fees of $40 to $60 per hour; these hours will be divided among the six steps. In general, one-fourth of the total hours will be devoted to the first three steps and three-fourths of the hours to the final three steps (see Figure 17.2).

The following two examples will illustrate the rule of thumb applied to specific situations.

A Larger Organization.   Alice Distributors has $10 million in annual revenues and a *serious* need for an information system that would incorporate inventory, purchasing, and credit sales applications. The company initially expected to spend $700,000 to $1.5 million on design and implementation. Management knew it would have to study carefully any estimate outside this range (or within but near its limits) to make certain the estimate was neither extravagant or inadequate. After some investigation, Alice Distributors decided on $900,000 as the appropriate budget cost figure. It estimated the time required to design and implement all of the system's features as a range of from 6,000 to 18,000 hours. This time would be spent not just on new-system conceptual design but also on implementation, including detail design, hardware and software selection, training, documentation, conversion, and postconversion review. From two-thirds to five-sixths of this time would be spent by its own management, and the remainder by vendors, consultants, and programmers. Alice Distributors finally estimated a time budget of 10,000 hours; hence management expected to spend 6,600 to 8,300 hours in systems development. Note that 6,600 hours is 3.3 work-years of 40-hour work weeks. The time budget in Table 17.1 shows how management planned to distribute 6,600 hours of its time among the major organizational responsibilities and phases of a systems project.

The estimated total of $900,000 may be accounted for as follows:

Consultants at average $50 per hour		
(10,000 − 6,600) hours × $50/hour	$170,000	
Hardware		
one-fourth of $900,000	225,000	
All other costs	505,000	
Total	$900,000	

Table 17.1   Management Time Allocation to Systems Development
Although these allocations are only estimates, they help management anticipate the extra demands on managers made during various phases in the systems development process.

	Hours Spent in					
Organizational Responsibility	Require-ments Definition	Conceptual Design	Feasibility Analysis	Vendor Selection	Detail Design, Programming, Documentation, & Training	Conversion, Postcon-version Review
Controller's office	200	200	60	80	700	700
Treasurer's office	100	70	50	50	200	340
Data processing department	200	200	80	60	500	900
Functional managers & staffs	300	140	50	20	500	900
Total hours	800	610	240	210	1,900	2,840

Additional details about the firm's growth rate, geographical dispersion, organization structure, and need for accounting information would of course narrow or expand these estimates. Remember, above all, the basic uncertainty of these estimates and that the organization should expect some variation from them.

A Smaller Organization. The Rosebud Kitchen, a specialty store in a large shopping mall, has gross revenues of $250,000 annually. It employs a manager and two clerks. The store has one sales desk and a small work area in the back of the store. None of the employees has systems expertise, so the manager engages a consultant who uses the rules of thumb described earlier to estimate that Rosebud Kitchen should spend between $17,500 and $37,500 on its system. Table 17.2 contains specifications for a system that falls within these limits. In terms of time, the $20,000 given as the total system cost would imply from 133 hours ($20,000/150) to 400 hours ($20,000/50), and consultants would put in one-third of this time, including 100 hours to develop and document applications. A reasonable time budget that falls within these limits appears in Table 17.3.

Table 17.2 Small-System Costs
As this table shows, even small-system costs include a high proportion of costs for software, training, and other nonhardware items.

Item	Hardware	Other	Total
16-bit microcomputer with 0.5Mb RAM	$ 4,000		$ 4,000
Floppy-disk drive, hard-disk drive, and tape back-up unit	3,000		3,000
Point-of-sale terminal	3,000		3,000
Cabling and connections	600		600
Letter-quality printer	1,000		1,000
Operating system		$ 200	200
Relational data base application-development environment		1,000	1,000
Programmer to develop and document accounting software applications, 100 hours @ $35/hour		3,500	3,500
Word processor and spreadsheet		500	500
Training and familiarization, all staff		1,200	1,200
Inefficiency and time correcting errors during startup		1,000	1,000
Postconversion review and modifications		1,000	1,000
Total	$11,600	$8,400	$20,000

Table 17.3   **Small-System Development Time Budget**
Consultants are required in small-system development because management generally has neither the expertise nor the time to guide the development process efficiently.

Activity	Management	Consultants	Total
Determine performance requirements	40	24	64
Compare systems and select components	24	12	36
Programmer and documentation		100	100
Training	40	10	50
Hands-on learning	80		80
Postevaluation review	16	10	26
Total	200	156	356

As you may be aware, computers and software with specifications similar to those in Table 17.2 may be obtained for much less than the costs shown. These lower-cost alternatives, known as "discount," "gray market," "look-alike," "clone," or "compatible" products, are often of good quality. A truly knowledgeable systems buyer (in small-business management) could probably distinguish good price-performance combinations and assemble a lower-cost system than the one shown. But most organizations should opt for known top-quality equipment and the consulting expertise to put it together and train staff in its use. They can take comfort in knowing they have avoided the breakdowns, waste, poor performance, and sometimes even business failure that can result from low-quality information systems.

The Expectations-Performance Gap

When management has paid for and completed a systems development process, the question to which everyone wants to know the answer is, does the system live up to expectations? Usually, the answer is "yes," but often a systems project will produce results that disappoint the organization. Inexperienced managements may expect a project to deliver only desirable outcomes and improved performance. In real life, however, even a well-run systems project will have both desirable and undesirable consequences. Common undesirable outcomes include managerial resistance, confusion about the use of newly reported information, uncertainty about planning the extent of continuing systems development and technical support, and frustration with compromises made in pursuit of a favorable performance-to-cost ratio.

In one case, a chain of drug stores in a medium-sized city successfully implemented an on-line accounting system. It expected this system to shorten the lag between transactions at its various stores and the appearance of consolidated accounting reports reflecting operations at all the stores. However, management, which was very decentralized, found that it actually had little use for this feature. Uncertain about why the new system failed to enhance profitability, they tended to believe that the system had failed to perform as expected. The "failure" was blamed on the project team, which lost the respect of other executives, causing an unexpected overall decline in data processing efficiency. Instead of incorrectly blaming the system and the system team, management should have realized that careful consideration at an earlier point might have determined that shortening this lag was a low-priority design feature (or even an unnecessary one).

An alert management can prevent or minimize the negative effects of systems creation. Resistance to implementation arises because some users and managers will misunderstand or fail to cooperate with the systems process. This lack of cooperation may even turn into outright obstruction by those who feel that the system will threaten their jobs. Resistance to implementation can be reduced by involving employees in setting system-performance requirements and by employee training and advance publicity. Incentives for positive cooperation can also help soften resistance to implementation.

Another way to minimize conflict is to anticipate that changes in format, content, frequency, or other features of reports may generate confusion in managers who receive them—or no longer receive them. Such confusion, although understandable and inevitable, can be almost completely avoided if managers are encouraged to help decide what information they will receive. A system's planner should also go over proposed report formats and content with managers to be certain they know what to expect. Technical-support consultants should follow up after the system becomes operational to make certain the managers haven't become confused and dissatisfied. Training system operators to help them respond to routine minor questions may also reduce the confusion.

Occasionally, the demand for systems development and technical support does not taper off as it should after startup. If demand for technical support remains high, some systems development efforts should be directed at modifying the system features that occasion the excessive support requirements.

Keep in mind that new systems rarely reach a state of 100-percent completion. In fact, 100-percent completion is an unachievable and frustrating goal in light of changing or unexpected performance requirements and constant adaptation of the system to a changing organization; these factors keep the system in a state of near completion. Most organizations maintain ongoing development to keep the system responsive to organizational requirements.

Some managers find it hard to accept performance-cost compromises during systems creation. They may be frustrated if the features and goals they valued highly are omitted and, because money and time are limited, some goals remain unachieved. Frequent coordinating-group meetings, at which everyone can advocate their favorite performance features, may help temper negative emotions and disappointment when desirable features must be excluded.

Responsibilities in Systems Creation

Management's role is to provide leadership and to seek outside assistance from consultants and vendors, delegating to them many of the technical responsibilities of bringing a system to successful completion. Because of the resource-intensive nature of information systems design in any single organization, it is rarely cost-effective to maintain on permanent staff sufficient expertise for a major systems project.

Management Leadership: Planning, Staffing, Funding, Approving

Top management must take the leadership role in initiating and planning the systems process—that is, defining its scope, assigning responsibilities, planning and scheduling the various steps, and making the resources available. Management need not have technical skills, perform every step, or even understand every step itself. However, management must be able to *administer* and *evaluate* the systems process. And, ultimately, when the system meets its performance requirements, management must approve the implemented system.

Consultant Services: Design, Program, Training

A **consultant** is an independent professional with specific expertise who applies that expertise by advising clients. Management should consider only those consultants who have specialized in information systems design and implementation. Management should give preference to consultants who present and substantiate their experience, education, and training qualifications and are willing to furnish references. Many consultants maintain membership in one or more professional associations that require adherence to a code of ethics, a desirable assurance of the consultant's responsibility. These organizations include those whose memberships is limited to CPAs, such as the American Institute for Certified Public Accountants and the state CPA societies, and others whose members are not CPAs but meet other tough standards, such as those of the Institute of Management Consultants (Certified Management Consultant) and the Data Processing Management Association (Certificate in Data Processing). Reputable consultants will enter into—even insist upon—a written contract that defines their responsibilities and compensation. And reputable consultants will not make specific promises or guarantees about the economy or performance of the new system. Management should beware of those who make such statements as, "I'll save you 50 percent based on your current operating costs."

The relationship between a consultant and management is called an **engagement**, and it imposes obligations on both parties. Management must specify the matters on which it wishes the consultant's advice. These matters are the **scope** of the engagement, and identifying them is called setting the engagement's scope. Consultants agree to give competent advice on these matters and to keep confidential any information that they learn if public knowledge of it could harm or embarrass the company. Management accepts responsibility for implementing the consultants' advice. To coordinate the consultants' work, management should appoint a steering committee consisting of users and data processing managers involved in the systems process. The steering committee should meet regularly to review progress, resolve disputes, and expedite work; it may refer major problems to higher levels of management. It recommends whether the work of consultants and other participants in systems development should be accepted. So far as the steering committee is concerned, the consultants are members of the system development team, with defined tasks and responsibilities like the other members.

Although the majority of consultants charge by the hour or the day, some consultants charge on a "value-added" basis, meaning that they charge a percentage of what they believe to be the benefits they have provided to management. To avoid value-added billing, management should make a clear statement of the terms of compensation at the start of the engagement. If the consultants charge by the hour or the day, they should be willing to furnish an advance estimate of the total hours in the engagement and should inform management when or if the actual total threatens to exceed that figure. These practices help build management's trust.

Well-selected and supervised outside consultants can bring both technical skill and a sense of momentum and direction to a systems project.

Table 17.4   Representative Consultant/Management Responsibilities
Consultants and managers should agree to a sharing of responsibilities so that all
parties know what they—and each other—will do.

Step	Consultants' Responsibility	Management Responsibility
1. Requirements definition	Describe the existing system. Evaluate operational information requirements and controls.	Make system data available. Describe the desired features to consultants. Review requirements for acceptability.
2. Conceptual design	Select appropriate design concepts. Relate information requirements to systems design concepts and capacities.	Provide data to consultants. Expose design concept to managers affected by it. Decide on a design concept.
3. Feasibility analysis	Do economic analysis and comparison of old and proposed designs.	Review the feasibility analysis and accept it if it reflects actual management capabilities and priorities.
4. Vendor selection	Help management prepare requests for vendor proposals if necessary. Identify qualified vendors. Analyze vendor proposals and identify acceptable one(s).	Approve and send out request for vendor proposals. Select a vendor. Approve contract based on requirements definition.
5. Detail design	Deal with vendors (to the vendor, the satisfied consultant represents repeat business). Direct and control an extended development process. Document the new system so that clients understand it. Train staff to use the new system.	Cooperate with vendor efforts. "Back up" consultant in vendor relations. Compensate the vendor. Accept vendor products if they meet agreed-upon requirements.
6. Conversion	Assist with the adjustments to tailor the new system and the organization to each other. Evaluate the performance of the new system in light of management's expectations.	Learn to use the new system. Communicate unsatisfactory aspects of the system to the vendor and the consultant.

Table 17.4 outlines the consultants' role in each of the six steps of a systems development project.

Vendor Delivery of Requested Products

Responsible manufacturers, suppliers, and vendors can be reliable sources of information about their products. The information they provide will lend some understanding of the products' features, limitations, and costs. Be aware, however, that far too many vendors—especially those who deal primarily with individuals and smaller businesses—have little grasp of what certain products can or can't do or of how reliable the products are. Their knowledge may be limited to how much a product costs. Complete information about each system component will help designers and users select the right products and use them most productively.

Management and consultants should solicit from responsible suppliers full descriptions of all their pertinent products; in turn, they should also provide suppliers complete details of the performance they want from the system. The **request for proposal (RFP)** is a document that summarizes the conceptual design, including performance requirements, for the use of suppliers, consultants, and programmers who may be invited to submit proposals for use of their equipment, software, and development assistance to help meet the performance requirements. An RFP is prepared by management, usually with a consultant's assistance. A vendor's response to an RFP should contain detailed descriptions of its products and services as well as a detailed explanation of how the vendor will meet the client's requirements. Management (assisted by the consultant) should examine these responses very carefully.

Any vendor selected by management should demonstrate willingness and ability to participate in system implementation. The best evidence of this orientation consists of a vendor's commitment to describe the kind of environment where its product works best, to visit the site and install the product, and to test the installed product to make certain it performs as designed. A software supplier, for example, might offer to install its product on the system computer, make any needed programming changes, verify that the software operates as promised, and provide minimum training in the software's use.

Steps in Developing the Design for an Accounting System

Now let us look at the first three steps in the development process— requirements definition, conceptual design, and feasibility analysis—in more detail.

Requirements Definition

Requirements are management's expectations about what the system will do. If the system can meet these requirements, management may justifiably regard the systems development process as successful. *Requirements definition* must be sufficiently complete to articulate and quantify every ability the system must have if management's expectations are to be fulfilled. Another term for these discrete "abilities" is *performance requirements*. Systems developers find it important to define and record requirements clearly to determine later whether the system is functioning as it should.

Requirements Classifications. There are actually two kinds of performance requirements: (a) *requirements that apply to the objectives and scope of the completed system* (**system scope requirements**) and (b) *tasks within this scope that the completed system will be expected to perform* (**system performance requirements**). An example of the former would be a requirement that the new system be an accounts receivable application. An example of the latter would be a requirement that the accounts receivable application be able to prepare an aging analysis of current balances.

System Scope Requirements. The system objectives and scope provide the boundaries of the systems effort and state broadly what is to be accomplished within those boundaries. For example, a systems project could be an enhancement of one application or of several applications or of the entire system, or even a completely new design. A representative statement on objectives and scope, prepared and issued by the chief financial officer at the start of the systems development process, might read as follows:

> This project should produce a payroll application compatible with the existing general ledger, inventory, and cost accounting systems. It should be usable by all our locations and compatible with our Hewlett-Packard computer equipment. The system should distinguish between our different categories of labor and management payroll. It should be able to
>
> 1. Issue the payroll voucher soon enough after the close of a pay period for pay checks or direct-deposit tapes to be ready on the next business day.
> 2. Meet federal, state, and insurance-carrier requirements for remittance of withholding amounts.
> 3. Operate without any increase in operating staff of the data processing or controller departments.
> 4. Provide weekly, monthly, and quarterly updates to the general ledger, weekly summaries of payroll expense, and such other reports as management finds desirable.
>
> This project should begin immediately. Mr. Benitez will be in charge. He will call the first meeting of the steering committee, which will consist of

himself, the Payroll Coordinator, the Data Processing Director, and the Director of Personnel. The steering committee may hire consultants if it deems that necessary. The steering committee should define system performance requirements, develop a conceptual design, and conduct a feasibility analysis, then prepare its interim report. The budget for this part of the project will be $85,000, and completion should occur before October 1.

Failure to specify objectives and scope is the most severe blunder that systems designers can commit. Managing the process will be problematic because no one will know what the process is supposed to accomplish. Other consequences will be extra costs, repetitive design efforts, or failure to achieve normal efficiency. Too broad a scope may also generate excessive costs; too narrow a scope or poorly expressed objectives may produce an application too limited to be of much value.

System Performance Requirements. Performance requirements are usually, but not always, expressed as an output or product that must emerge from the system, such as the ability to prepare a weekly report showing new credit customers sorted by state. All performance requirements must fall within the project's scope. If, for example, a scope requirement is expressed as limited enhancement of the purchasing application, performance requirements that would modify the payroll or cash receipts applications cannot be allowed because they exceed the scope of the project. The methodologies for identifying performance requirements all include much study of the organization's objectives, controls, and policies.

Examples of Nature and Content of Performance Requirements. The best way to introduce performance requirements may be to show you authentic examples. Here are some performance requirements taken from actual systems development situations and requests for proposals:

- Ability to maintain five years of transaction history on line
- Automated listing of inventory items where stock is low
- Automatic printing of report showing additions, deletions, and changes in file of approved credit customers
- Ability to accept user-defined 24-digit account numbers
- At least three levels of password: (1) access to all files, (2) read-only access to certain files, (3) blank-out of certain records and/or fields
- Ability to maintain at least three levels of subledgers within one control account
- Ability to add, change, or delete vendors from the approved-vendors file
- Ability to add, change, or delete any product from the product-description file

- Software controls to prevent initiating the closing process if any subledger remains open
- Hardware or software controls to restrict use of certain applications and files from specific locations
- At least 50 category codes available for use in describing credit customers
- Ability to provide an audit trail of any changes to a general ledger account

Well-written performance requirements should be short and clear. The system designers should choose precise phrases that will let them decide at some later time whether a given performance requirement was actually fulfilled. Thus a requirement such as "System must be fast" is less satisfactory than "System response to an inventory stock status request must be less than 5 seconds, nine out of ten times." Such statements will allow the systems staff to relate requirements to the variables and processes that will implement them.

Categories of Performance Requirements.   Most performance requirements fall into the categories of data processing requirements, operations requirements, and management-control requirements.

Data processing requirements describe abilities to collect, store, protect, process, and report data. Examples might include a statement that "The system must be able to handle a 30-digit account number," or that "The system must be able to store 10 years' sales history on line."

Operations requirements define what managers must know about the organization—its activities, its customers, and its environment—in order to make decisions and discharge their responsibilities. Examples of this type of requirement might include statements that "The payroll application should provide summaries of wage and salary expenses for use in product costing," or "Credit Sales by Product report must appear weekly." Another requirement might be that the daily cash balance reports would show details of short-term cash management, establishing that the cash existed and showing how it was invested. A manufacturing-operations control could show the results of quality-control tests.

Top-management control requirements include the capability to compare actual operations with a budget and to project trends to determine whether current operations are likely to meet future operating targets. For example, a national auto-repair franchise has built into its new system the ability to analyze local economies. This ability will help the firm develop bench marks for measuring the performance of its franchises in those markets. As you can see, the new system is more than a convenient means for recording transactions; it produces information that allows managers to measure progress of organizational units and programs.

Fact-Finding Steps and Procedures.   The system scope and performance requirements described do not spring full grown from the mind of the systems designer. Rather, they are the end product of a thorough fact-finding process that produces a complete description of how management systems do and should operate. Every organization will have management systems and procedures into which an information system's accounting and other data collection, processing, and reporting are integrated. Management's very familiarity with its own processes may make it difficult to produce a complete description of them. Part of the requirements definition process is to produce as complete as possible a description of all management processes, their information requirements, and the ways these requirements are met. One popular means of conducting fact finding is to place a large sheet of brown wrapping paper—the larger the better—across one wall of a work room. The systems developers tape forms, documents, reports—anything that represents an input or output of the system—to this paper. They and management draw lines showing how these documents relate to the system. As the existing system's outlines emerge the body of facts describing it becomes apparent on the brown paper.

The brown-paper approach may also make it possible to use a simple and widely accepted three-step process to identify accounting information system performance requirements. First, a systems analyst must develop a complete list of management responsibilities and describe each responsibility in enough detail to produce a clear image of what that responsibility is. Second, the consultant determines the data processing, operating, and control information that would be used to fulfill each responsibility. Finally, the consultant identifies the controls associated with security and access to that information.

The system performance requirements emerge from the second and third steps. For example, let us say you first identify a management responsibility to approve purchase of merchandise by customers on credit. Second, you would determine that the person who gives approval needs quick access to the contents of the file of customers approved for credit, and that this file is manually maintained by the credit manager. You feel that if adequate controls are to exist (third), sales personnel should be able to access these records only by account number, should be able to view only the credit status, and should not be able to change any information in a customer record. Your performance requirements are becoming evident.

In the interests of completeness and to cross-check information from different sources, the fact-finding study should look at many sources of information. For example, administrative position descriptions are a useful source of facts for systems design. (An administrative position description, APD, is a list of the responsibilities and authority that characterize a particular managerial job.) Most organizations put APDs in writing. Unless reviewed regularly, APDs may become incomplete and fail to describe actual managerial positions. Before relying on APDs, the systems designer should review them with executives holding and supervising the positions.

Much of the expertise and know-how managers and clerical personnel use routinely every day is not written down. The only way this information can be captured is through interviews. Because this type of information is indeed very important, system designers make it a point to acquire good interview skills. There is a right way to conduct interviews. Interviewers should plan in advance the information sought and the questions to ask, and they should initiate the interview in such a way as to gain the respect and cooperation of the interviewee. Specifically, this means setting up an appointment and making certain that the interviewee understands that management endorses the interview. It is important for the interviewer to stick to the interview plan, take notes, and stop before the interviewee becomes tired or bored. Later, the interviewer rechecks important points with the interviewees or other knowledgeable people.

The old system's documentation may be another important source of information about operations. It may describe the data structures used by the old system or procedures that are being ignored but never were formally discarded. System deficiencies often turn out to be inadequacies resulting from noncompliance with existing procedures!

Organizations in the same industry tend to be about the same size, to serve similar customers, and to share other traits. Because they are also very likely to have similar systems requirements, a consultant who has worked with several firms in the same industry will have a fairly good grasp of what the content of an accounting information and control system for such an organization should include. Consultants value this "industry knowledge," and management should seek out consultants with experience in similar firms. Direct transfers of systems and procedures among clients are unethical. But experienced consultants will understand what the firm should expect of its accounting system, and will protect the firm from unintentionally adopting inadequate performance expectations.

Figure 17.3 summarizes the requirements definition processes.

Conceptual Design

Management, the systems staff, and the consultants should review the final version of the performance requirements for the purpose of creating a conceptual design for the future system. The conceptual design sets the directions for systems design and implementation. Its general principles will later be used as a guide to resolve *consistently* all the issues that arise during detail design and subsequent work.

Conceptual Design Content.   No one has established a standard content for conceptual design. Nevertheless, an adequate and complete conceptual

Figure 17.3   Requirements Definition
Requirements definition is the first phase of systems development. Its five steps produce the scope and performance requirements. Unless this first phase is done properly, the remaining development phases are jeopardized.

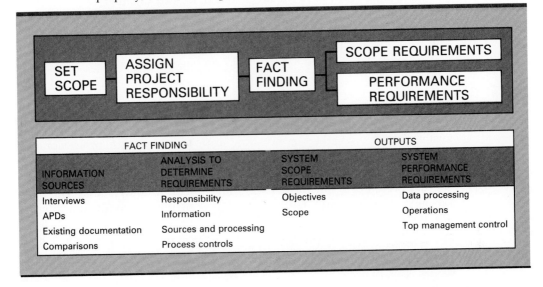

FACT FINDING		OUTPUTS	
INFORMATION SOURCES	ANALYSIS TO DETERMINE REQUIREMENTS	SYSTEM SCOPE REQUIREMENTS	SYSTEM PERFORMANCE REQUIREMENTS
Interviews	Responsibility	Objectives	Data processing
APDs	Information	Scope	Operations
Existing documentation	Sources and processing		Top management control
Comparisons	Process controls		

design must meet certain requirements. It must be consistent with the scope of the system design, including all applications, enhancements, data elements, reports, files, and other components. The conceptual design links, coordinates, and unifies all these elements, creating a system blueprint. The conceptual design must also provide sufficient information and detail to allow its evaluation. Finally, this design should resolve all major issues about the system—processing concept, update frequency, record access, location of files, processing strategy, data elements, names and attributes of files or relations, and names and performance of processes. Additional details in the conceptual design include the data elements and their groupings; the reports to be prepared, their contents, and the processes that will prepare them; the basic processing concept—sequential file, direct-access file, or data base—that each group of related data will use; the data that will be collected and the method of data entry (batch, on-line, or point-of-sale); the configurations of centralized and distributed processing each application will use; and, in some cases, whether applications and the files and relations they use will be an internal-memory-based, external-disk-based, or external-tape-based system.

The *process* of creating a conceptual design should start with review and acceptance (with modifications, if necessary) of the performance requirements. Next, the designers should group the performance requirements according to the process most likely to satisfy them. They identify all the data elements required and select an appropriate data management concept. They specify reports and, tentatively, their content. They prepare descriptive diagrams showing the relationships they envision. These diagrams, reports, and data elements, when viewed together, create a narrative description of the system. Using this overall view as a guide, the designers will decide what system specifications are necessary if their system is to operate. Finally, they review all their work, checking its internal consistency. (Look ahead to Figure 17.7 on page 635 for a diagram of these components.)

Conceptual Design Components.   A conceptual design has well-defined components. Every part should be understandable by people who are system-literate, whether or not they are systems design professionals. Thus, if you participate as an accountant in the conceptual design of a system, you should seriously question and attempt to simplify any conceptual design component that you find difficult to understand. The performance requirements definitions are one of these components; others are described here.

One of the most important components is the **data dictionary**, a listing of all the names and other attributes of all data elements found in the system. The description will include details such as data type (numeric, date, phone number, or other type), length (number of characters), and the files or relations in which the data are found. The data dictionary serves for data the same purpose that the system specifications serve for hardware and software; that is, it identifies the data that will be used to meet system performance specifications. The data dictionary entries also act as a control to ensure that no vital data elements are omitted from the system and no irrelevant elements are included. A typical, fully detailed data dictionary entry would resemble the following:

> *Purchase Order Number.* 10 digits, numeric, appears in purchasing and accounts payable application, originates on source document purchase order, recorded at time of purchase order preparation, may not be deleted, indexed field in purchase order master relation. Also an indexed field in purchase requisition, receiving report, and payment voucher.

A larger system's conceptual design may also include an entity dictionary, which lists and defines processes, forms, hardware, and all other system entities or components. The entity dictionary becomes a common point of reference in large projects, helping to keep track of system components as their numbers grow and many different analysts work on the system.

The **system diagram** shows the general relationships among major components of the proposed system. Major components include the applications programs, files or data bases, source documents, and reports. This flowchart requires only a few symbols and rules and is easy to construct and understand. Optionally, it may show the functional area with responsibility for each data capture, processing, and reporting activity. The chart, if properly constructed, will ensure that all major system components or relationships are included in the system. Figure 17.4 shows a system diagram.

In larger systems projects, there may be a set of multilevel entity diagrams. The highest-level entity diagram would be the organization chart; the next level would show the flow of reports to positions on the chart. Successively lower levels would show the flow of data in the reports, the relations containing the data, the processes that create and update relations and reports, and the logic of the processes.

The **data flow diagram** is the design component that shows the data groupings and process relationships that create, modify, and use data in an application. Its purpose is to describe the framework within which data management occurs. (Earlier chapters have used data flow diagrams to illustrate specific applications. For instance, see pages 219 and 283 in Chapters 7 and 8.)

Figure 17.4 Partial System Diagram for an Accounts Payable Application
The system diagram is limited to showing major system components and relationships between them. The details of the system will be included in other diagrams and documents.

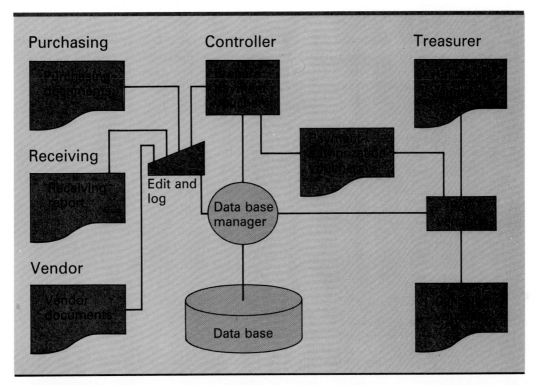

A typical application will almost certainly include several processes that update or draw upon the contents of various files, pass or receive data through interfaces with other applications, and create reports. Such an application will require a series of data flow diagrams to depict all of the intended relationships. Figure 17.5 is a partial data flow diagram illustrating an accounts payable process. The data flow diagram contains more information than a system diagram; it names the files, the processes, and perhaps also the reports. As an optional feature, it may show functional responsibility for various system elements.

A **process diagram** shows inputs, outputs, and activities within a single process. It lists the tasks a process must perform, so that the logic of the process can be designed. Thus the process diagram contains more information than the data flow diagram. The conceptual design should include one process diagram for each process shown in a data flow diagram. Figure 17.6 shows a process diagram.

The **narrative description** is a comprehensive but simple explanation of what the proposed system design will do and how, linking together all elements in the design. Because it is prepared last, the narrative can serve

Figure 17.5   Partial Data Flow Diagram for Accounts Payable Application
A data flow diagram shows the data-element groupings as files and shows which processes produce or use them.

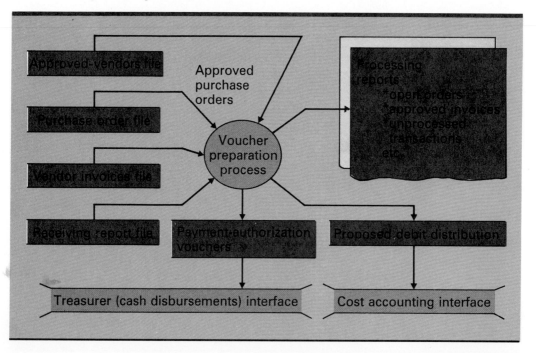

Figure 17.6   Partial Process Diagram for Voucher Preparation
The process diagram shows the activities within a process along with the data inputs and outputs. Each process shown in a data flow diagram will require a process diagram.

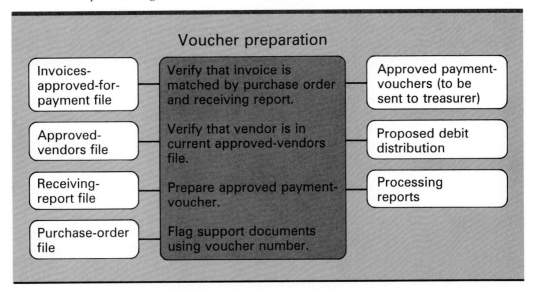

to catch omissions or inconsistencies in the various other descriptions in the conceptual design. Here is an excerpt from a typical narrative description:

> The Controller has identified a need for a voucher preparation process that will read a file of invoices and, if they represent items ordered and received from sellers according to approved purchasing and receiving procedures, calculate and prepare an approved voucher authorizing the treasurer to issue a check to the vendor, update the cash subledger and prepare a file of records for adjustment of seller's accounts. The Controller requires this process to include for payment only items on which a discount would be lost, or a penalty imposed, if payment does not reach the seller in five business days. The process must also forecast cash requirements up to five days in advance and produce daily reports of vouchers prepared, vouchers outstanding and cash requirements forecasted. The process must operate at each of the four regional controller headquarters and produce a daily summary report from these locations to national headquarters. It must be possible, from any of these locations, to make on-line inquiry as to the status of an account.

The final component of the conceptual design is the **system specifications**, an enumeration of all the parts and capacities of a system. The purpose of this component is to create an inventory of major system components that will be used to meet the performance requirements. Many people interpret *system specifications* to mean *hardware* specifications, but the specifications should also list applications, documentation, and even training specifications. For smaller systems, the specifications may include hardware details that ensure access to specific software choices during detail design; for example, specifying Apple, IBM, or other hardware compatibility. In general, specifications for large systems will list proportionately more software and documentation components. Here is an example of specifications for the hardware, software, and documentation components of a small system:

> An 80286-based microcomputer capable of running applications under MS-DOS version 3.1 or later operating system, with 640K bytes of RAM memory, 360K-byte internal 5.25-inch floppy disk drive, internal 20M-byte hard-disk drive, 2,400 baud modem, and 80-character-per-second or faster letter-quality printer with 12-inch carriage and automatic sheet feeder. The software will consist of the operating system and compatible versions of the MA-SQUARE spreadsheet, WORDY word processor, ELECTROTALK communications program, and SAVE'EM relational data base environment. Substitutions for any components must be approved in advance. No approval will be given for programs with fewer features than those listed. The accounting applications must be fully integrated with the general ledger and take full advantage of the features listed and be able to accept ASCII files prepared using the spreadsheet, word processor, and data base programs. The accounting software must include the following applications:

> General ledger
> Credit sales and accounts receivable
> Purchasing and accounts payable
> Inventory
> Cash receipts
> Cash disbursements

> The documentation for all equipment and software must be adequate for both technical analysis and training of staff. It should include tutorials for the data base and word-processor applications and a chart of accounts for the accounting application. Since additional branch-office locations may be opened in the future, the accounting documentation should explain how to include all of the accounts and reports required by branch offices in the chart of accounts.

In general, unless the conceptual design team strongly favors one conceptual design approach from the start, it will develop several (two to five) alternative conceptual designs—at least to the point at which the differences between them emerge strongly enough to be described and evaluated. During this exploratory process, many designs may be partially developed and discarded. Diagrams will be drawn, checked, corrected, rechecked, and corrected again; facts reviewed; and much effort put into developing workable, practical, effective conceptual designs. Figure 17.7 shows all the elements of the conceptual design phase of the systems design process in their proper relationship.

Figure 17.7 Conceptual Design
The conceptual design is a broad attempt to describe a system that meets the defined requirements. The conceptual design should answer all major questions about how a system will operate.

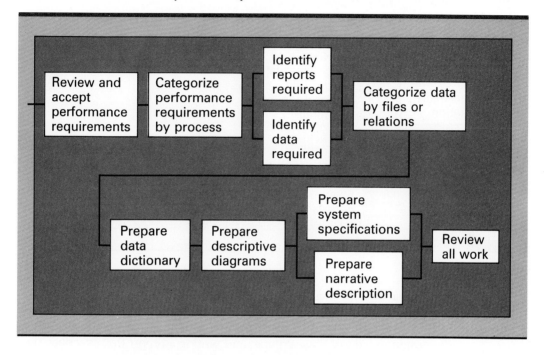

³, Feasibility Analysis of Alternatives

Before proceeding further, the designers compare alternative conceptual designs for feasibility. The purpose of feasibility analysis is to determine whether a proposed design will be implementable and if so, whether it will yield economic benefits. You may have many feasibility criteria; the ones you will rely on most consistently will be financial, time frame, technological, and organizational.

Feasibility analysis is not an exact science. Even a careful evaluation may fail to reveal pitfalls or fail to rank alternatives correctly. Management finds feasibility analysis difficult because it can implement only *one* system and cannot be certain how the discarded system designs would have performed. Even so, if experienced managers and consultants participate in a careful evaluation of the alternative conceptual designs, the chances of an unacceptable system being approved will lessen considerably. The consultant should regard feasibility analysis as a distinct and very important process. Since its results (whether positive or negative) are sure to be challenged, careful records should be kept to support all conclusions.

Figure 17.8 Feasibility Analysis
Feasibility analysis selects the best of competing designs. Several criteria may be used to test feasibility, including financial (cost), time-frame, technology, and organization compatibility.

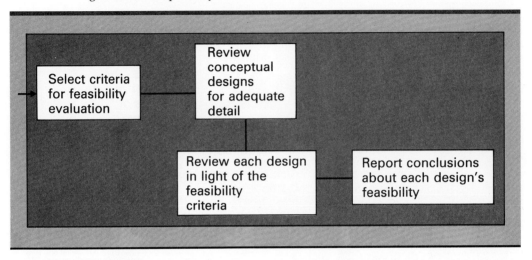

Feasibility analysis consists of selecting the criteria for feasibility and applying them to each conceptual design to establish that it is complete in respect to the details to be used in the evaluation, carefully considering the design in light of these criteria, and writing a report that describes the conceptual design's feasibility. The report should make comparisons among designs. Often only one completely new conceptual design is developed; in this case, it should be compared with the existing system as it would be enhanced to meet the defined requirements, if this is possible. Figure 17.8 shows these steps. A consultant involved in this phase should make recommendations but allow management to select the conceptual design.

Financial Feasibility.   **Financial feasibility** is a criterion for evaluating a conceptual design to determine its quality as an investment; the three factors in financial feasibility are that the proposed new system be affordable, economical, and an acceptable risk. You need to consider three types of cost:

- Investment to get the new system operational
- Additional operating costs attributable to the new system
- Operating-cost *savings* attributable to the new system

Beware of claims that a new accounting system will "save" money compared with the present system! But, it is reasonable to hope that future processing costs will be less than they would be if the old system were retained to do the same processing.

The analytical approach to computer system investments is the same incremental, net-present-value approach used in analysis of many other capital investments. In this approach, an internal rate of return is calculated by comparing the additional initial investment outlay with the sum of the discounted future net annual inflows and outflows of cash owing to the new system's operating economies (as compared with the system it is replacing). If the calculated internal rate of return is above the minimum acceptable cutoff return the managers use to evaluate investments, then the proposed system passes the financial feasibility test. Table 17.5 illustrates this approach used on a proposed investment in a system with a four-year useful life (in the table, the effects of income taxes are ignored and the inflow and outflow estimates are considered to be completely reliable). If the 24.8-percent internal rate of return calculated in Table 17.5 is above the cutoff point, and the total initial outlay is within the organization's ability to bear, then this alternative is financially feasible. The analysis of risk is straightforward if the information to support it is available. In general, a subjective analysis of risk may be preferable to an

Table 17.5   Financial Feasibility Analysis (figures in thousands)

Item	1987	1988	1989	1990	1991
Initial cash investment:					
Hardware	$12				
Software	6				
Site preparation	2				
Training and startup (including capitalized wages)	10				
Cash outlays to continue old system:					
Wages, salaries, benefits		36	48	65	88
Supplies, services, utilities		21	29	37	45
Total old-system operating outlays required		57	77	102	133
Cash outlays to operate proposed system:					
Wages, salaries, benefits		44	48	52	60
Supplies, services, utilities		15	20	27	36
Total new-system operating outlays required		59	68	79	99
Incremental cash inflow or (outflow)	**$(30)**	**(2)**	**9**	**23**	**34**

Internal rate of return: 24.8%
   (Found using a computer spreadsheet function applied to the boldface figures above)

objective analysis that is based on unreliable data. For an example of a subjective financial risk analysis, consider this process.

The following factors tend to increase the risk that actual costs will significantly exceed estimates. Score one point for each of these factors that is present:

1. Inexperienced system team
2. New organization
3. Lack of assistance from qualified consultants
4. Use of new or unproven products
5. Lack of experienced management in the areas to be served by the system
6. Weak management and financial controls
7. Lack of a strong financial position
8. Urgent time pressure to complete the system
9. High level of management turnover
10. Use of new, small, and financially weak suppliers

If your score is zero, there is little financial risk associated with your proposed conceptual design. A score of 1 or 2 indicates medium financial risk, and a score of 3 or more indicates high financial risk. If possible, the system designers should attempt to make changes that would place the conceptual design in the low-risk category.

Failing a financial feasibility test need not doom a system design. Sometimes, for example, a system offers unique abilities that the organization needs and cannot find elsewhere at any price. In such a case, if the management is able to assume the financial risk, it might decide to go ahead.

Time-Frame Feasibility.   **Time-frame feasibility** is a criterion for evaluating a conceptual design to determine whether it can be operational when it is needed. Occasionally the available time is dictated by the impending failure of the existing accounting system. For example, if a rapidly growing organization anticipates that normal operations will fully consume its system's **headroom** (available, unused disk space) in eight months, it will have a powerful incentive to convert to a new system before that time, and it must reject designs that may require longer than eight months to implement.

Systems projects are usually most successful when they are supported by sustained, intense effort of reasonably brief duration. This is because systems work is nonroutine, and it can therefore be somewhat disruptive to routine operating efficiency. Most organizations cannot sustain such disruption indefinitely. Therefore, the systems effort should last no longer than its complexity demands—as short a period as two or three months for a very simple system, or as long as two years or more for complex multimillion-dollar accounting systems.

Whatever limits time may place on the project, organizations should be careful to avoid one common mistake: an on-again, off-again effort that will leave everyone confused and doubtful of management's intent to complete the systems process.

Technological Feasibility.   When managers and consultants decide that a system has **technological feasibility**, they have decided that the technology required by the system is indeed available and appropriate. Technical evaluation is favorable when it shows that the capacities and capabilities of the proposed design and the requirements it is to meet complement each other. In other words, all its capabilities have contemplated uses, and all its requirements can be fulfilled using the system's designed-in capabilities. When managers and consultants decide that a system has technological feasibility, they agree that (a) the technology to make the system operate is available and (b) when applied in the system, the capacities and capabilities of the proposed design will enable it to meet the defined requirements. In other words, the requirements can be met using the system's designed-in capabilities and these capabilities can be provided by existing technology.

Rapid advances in systems design continue to make a wide range of products and technologies available to most users. As recently as 1979, microcomputers lacked hard disk drives or powerful data base programs. Today, both are available inexpensively for small computers. The range of technology has affected systems designers too. Some systems analysts now prefer microcomputer hardware and software over mainframes and minicomputers for many systems.

Nevertheless, some microcomputer technologies are still unsuitable for some applications. For example, local-area networks making use of current technology based on microcomputers, a bus linkage, and twisted-pair wire (see Chapter 16) will surely prove too slow for most managers if more than five to ten users are active simultaneously. Similarly, some very good accounting software relies on a 24-digit account number field; it would probably be technically infeasible to use this software when the design calls for a 32-digit or 8-digit number. Likewise, a 40M-byte disk will be insufficient for a projected system lifetime of 60 months if data is to be added to the disk at a net rate of 1M-byte per month. These examples do not rule out microcomputers. They simply serve to emphasize that one must be familiar with many technologies to choose the best for a particular application.

The best way to guarantee technical feasibility is to work closely with hardware and software vendors. They can usually be relied on to know what their products will do, the way their products interact with other products, and the circumstances under which their products should *not* be used. "Working closely" means you must disclose the proposed design to the vendor, including the parts the vendor won't supply, as well as a statement of the performance you expect from the total system. Responsible vendors—even small ones—typically discourage use of their products if the circumstances indicate the products would perform poorly. Responsible vendors will provide references and give demonstrations using data supplied by the customer.

Organizational Feasibility.   If a firm is managed well, evaluating **organizational feasibility** means determining whether the organization can implement and operate the proposed system. "Yes" answers to questions like those in Table 17.6 indicate compatibility between the organization and the system. As part of an organizational feasibility evaluation, management will also verify that there are sound responsibility relationships between system elements and organizational responsibility centers.

You have determined that the system is worth its price, can be up and running in a reasonable time, and is technologically possible. Will it also work well in the organization for which it is meant? It's easy for an organization to blame its poor performance on the accounting and other information systems. ("If only the computer had gotten me that report sooner . . .") But a poor driver couldn't drive competitively even in a sports car, and a poorly managed organization probably can't benefit from a fine accounting system. The better strategy is to upgrade and strengthen the organization before the start of accounting system design.

Table 17.6   Questions to Establish Organizational Feasibility
These questions should be addressed and answered formally by the system-development leadership.

- Has the organization recently evaluated and revised its internal controls?
- Have all affected managers participated in designing the new accounting system?
- Does the organization have the talent (internally or through vendors and consultants) to implement the system?
- Does the system provide support for the way the organization operates?
- Will the staff be able to master the system's operating procedures? If not, will the organization be able to hire additional staff who can operate the system?
- Have provisions been made to assure good employee relations during the difficult transition to the new system?
- Will the organization be able to cope with the effects of setbacks or failure during the systems process?

Even managers who assert their cooperativeness may exhibit (often to their own surprise) a hostility toward parts of the systems project. Some managers doubt their ability to supervise employees during a large-scale project, and may yearn for the security and lighter demands that a smaller-scale project would entail. In such instances, someone—perhaps one of the design consultants—must take on the task of individual one-on-one confidence building and persuasion for the sake of ensuring the project's success.

Summary

Information systems have a characteristic life cycle, which proceeds from design to startup, maturity and decline. Planning for design and implementation of a new system should begin before the existing system begins to decline. New systems offer greater power, more flexibility, and operating efficiencies. The systems design and implementation processes seek to develop a new information system that will serve the organization over a long term and also meet its immediate short-run operational requirements. Because systems design and implementation require advanced technical knowledge, management often utilizes consultants.

Systems design begins with fact finding and proceeds to a description of the specific performance the system must deliver. Then comes the creation of a conceptual design that will allow this performance and the evaluation of one or more conceptual designs. Fact finding relies on multiple sources of information, which should correlate and reinforce each other. Interviews with employees are a fact-finding methodology that systems designers consider especially important.

If the resources available for systems design and implementation are constrained, management must decide on the most important performance objectives and design the system to achieve these first. The cost range of a complete new system can be estimated by rules of thumb. These costs will include consultants' fees, management's time, hardware, software, forms and documentation, staff training, data conversion and system startup.

Before implementing a conceptual design, management will carefully evaluate its feasibility, comparing it (if possible) with other competing designs. Feasibility evaluation tests the financial, time-frame, technological, and organizational practicality of the design. To the extent that the investment and operating costs of a design can be estimated, its financial feasibility can be evaluated using net-present-value analysis, as for other capital investments. Evaluation of many other aspects of feasibility, such as financial risk, is more subjective and requires mature managerial judgment.

Key Terms

conceptual design
consultant
conversion
creation
data dictionary
data flow diagram
decline
detail design
engagement
feasibility analysis
financial feasibility
headroom
learning constant
learning effect
maturity

narrative description
organizational feasibility
process diagram
request for proposals (RFP)
requirements definition
scope
startup
system diagram
system performance requirements
systems development
system scope requirements
system specifications
technological feasibility
time-frame feasibility
vendor selection

Review Questions

1. Give at least three long-range reasons why it would be desirable for an organization to replace an existing accounting system with a new one.

2. What do you consider the two most important short-range objectives of designing a new accounting system?

3. What are the four periods in the system life cycle?

4. What is the learning effect? In which period of the system life cycle is the learning effect most prominent?

5. What are the six steps of the systems development process? In which period of the system life cycle do these steps occur?

6. Explain the following about a consulting engagement: the meaning of the phrase "objectives and scope," why management would hire a consultant to help with the systems process, the nature and function of a steering committee, and five examples of work an engagement might include.

7. Name five types of descriptive materials that would jointly comprise a conceptual design, and give a short definition or example of each one.

8. Why must a systems designer compile and use a data dictionary? List at least six characteristics of a data element that should appear in its data dictionary entry.

Discussion Questions

9. Do you think the system life cycle is inevitable? (That is, can you think of plausible circumstances in which an accounting system might last indefinitely?) What do you believe to be the major enemies of a long system life span?

10. Why is it difficult to estimate the cost of a new system? Why is it necessary, even so, to have estimates of system cost and other resource requirements?

11. Bedias Storage Systems, Inc., has revenues of $500,000 annually. Its financial vice president is convinced that a new accounting information system should be developed to replace the existing manual system. He thinks that $24,000 should cover the cost of the system. Is this a reasonable figure, based on the rule of thumb for cost estimation? Assuming this to be a reasonable figure, how much would be spent for hardware? How much for other system components? If system design hours equal total system cost/120, how many hours will Bedias require from consultants in this project? If the consultants charge $50 an hour, and after feasibility analysis Bedias decides not to proceed, how much will Bedias pay its consultants?

12. Why do personnel in the data processing, functional, and accounting departments often react negatively to a systems project? What specific forms do these negative reactions take? How can you cope with these effects if they do occur?

13. The president of Nameless Bank decided to review all accounting systems and revise or redesign them as required. The president called the controller and the director of data processing to inform them of this decision. Then he asked the sales department of a local computer vendor to conduct the review. The chief teller was assigned in-house responsibility for the systems review. "Call me when it's done," the president said. "Don't get too many of our people involved in it. These things can be very distracting, you know." How many errors did the bank president make? (List at least four).

14. Carol Jones is assistant operations supervisor at Midland Livery Company (MLC), a firm that dispatches minibuses and limousines in a medium-sized metropolitan area. She needs an up-to-date list of vehicles currently operating, the location of each, whether it is hired, where it is going, and when it will be available again (if unavailable now). Ms. Jones must compute the fares due and compare them with the amounts drivers report. Passengers pay in advance to MLC (or, with approved credit, are billed later); thus, drivers do not handle cash. The drivers are paid a percentage of the fares they earn. They receive a printed statement of their fares from Jones, and turn it in to the cashier to receive payment. Apply the four-step fact-finding

process described in the chapter to this fact situation to identify at least two information system performance requirements.

15. Write a narrative description of the process shown in the following diagram.

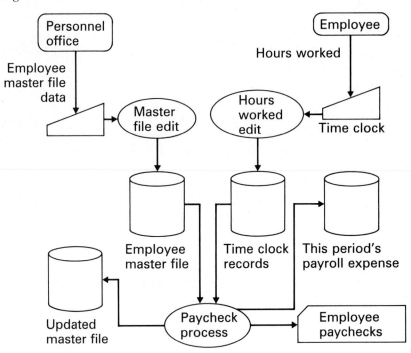

16. Classify each of the following performance requirements as a data processing requirement, a user operating requirement, or a top-management control requirement:
    (a) Accept 24-digit account numbers.
    (b) Compare actual and budgeted performance for each responsibility center.
    (c) Compute return on investment for each investment center.
    (d) Include an integrated test facility.
    (e) Classify customers according to any combination of twelve different attributes.
    (f) Alter reservation status of any passenger up to 5 minutes before gate departure.
    (g) Maintain an on-line historical record of three years of operation.
    (h) Show actual number of rejects and remanufactured items for each batch produced.

17. The figure on the top of page 645 shows the notations on a large sheet of brown paper taped to the wall of the system development team's headquarters.

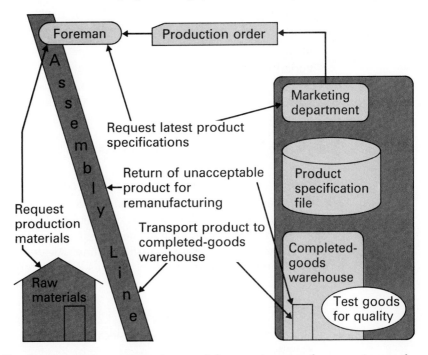

Do these notations suggest a need for any improved processing and control requirements? What are they?

18. The newly formed Dekalb Health Maintenance Organization (HMO) has just hired an experienced manager. This manager's predecessor was discharged after thirty days. The new manager must develop an accounting system to record cash receipts (mostly from members' payroll deductions) and pay bills (including physician salaries and fees). The system should be ready in ninety days, when the HMO will be formally organized. The manager has hired expert consultants to help select a proven existing product, supported by a major systems supplier, to adapt to this HMO; and to develop strong management and financial controls to go with it. Two other HMOs already exist in the same area, promising stiff competition.

    Evaluate the risk associated with this systems development project. For each high-risk factor you identify, suggest a possible remedy.

Problems

19. In periods 2 and 3 of the system life cycle, the learning effect is influential—but diminishing. Ferro Phone Company is training selected employees to enter transactions. The company notes that a certain employee enters the first 15 transactions in 60 minutes.

Required:

    Assuming a learning constant of 20 percent, how long will it take this employee to enter 120 transactions?

20. George West Company syndicates real estate projects. The company must keep accurate and detailed records of all expenses and render periodic statements to limited partners, the IRS, and certain creditors. At first the firm used a manual accounting system. Then, it engaged a service bureau (a company whose computer is programmed to keep separate books for a large number of clients). Recently it has decided to develop its own system.

    During the period when the accounting system will be used, average revenue will be about $18 million.

Required:

   (a) Estimate a range for the systems development costs.
   (b) Estimate a range for the total number of hours, and management's hours, devoted to systems development.
   (c) Estimate a range for consultant time. Assuming that actual consulting time is the midpoint of this distribution and that the consultants earn an average of $40 per hour, what will be the cash payment to consultants?

21. The Twilight Rhythm Night Club (TRNC) is an extremely popular entertainment complex with twelve locations in three neighboring cities. Your accounting firm has been engaged to develop a conceptual design for this business.

    TRNC does not have a computer system now. A central commissary purchases all food and supplies. Individual managers order from this commissary and receive daily deliveries. The central office has a talent department that hires entertainers. The managers choose among these entertainers and decide how long to book those they choose. Each manager has complete control over hiring all other personnel. All the locations operate on a reservation basis: patrons phone their reservation requests to a single number at the central office, which informs each location of its reservations at 7 P.M. daily.

Required:

Begin developing the conceptual design for TRNC's computerized information system:

   (a) State whether data base or file concepts are most appropriate.
   (b) State how often data updates should occur and whether they should be batch or on line.
   (c) Recommend whether record access should be sequential or direct.
   (d) Recommend whether files should be disk based or tape based and whether processing should be disk based or RAM based.
   (e) State whether processing should be centralized or distributed.
   (f) List all the data elements you can think of.
   (g) Identify the files or relations that will hold the data elements, and assign each data element to one or more of them.
   (h) Name each process required and briefly describe its purpose, the

files or relations it will use, and the reports it will produce. Limit yourself to the processes described. You need not draw any diagrams.

22. Quick-Publishers specializes in limited field-quality hardback and paperback editions of technical documents such as user's manuals for computers or machines. Each manuscript is treated as a new job. The writer or the writer's employer contacts the Q-P editor's office, which records the details of the job—author's name and address, billing address, and about twenty characteristics of the manuscript—such as length, type size, illustrations, and paper quality.

    Each manuscript goes through three processes: (1) editing, (2) composition, and (3) printing. For internal purposes, Q-P keeps track of the direct labor and material costs of each process for each manuscript. It does not apply indirect costs to individual processes but does apply them from a single indirect-cost pool to the manuscript as a whole. Each process has a manager, who receives a weekly report showing total direct costs incurred in that process, and the total applied to jobs. Each job has an editor, who receives a weekly report showing total costs applied to that job in all the processes.

    Q-P records its sale when the job is complete and has been accepted by the customer. At that point it removes the job costs from work in process to cost of goods sold, adds in the indirect costs, and computes a net contribution toward profit by that particular job.

Required:

(a) Draw a system diagram (using Figure 17.4 as a guide) showing all the operations described.

(b) Draw a partial data flow diagram (using Figure 17.5 as a guide) showing all the data-oriented processes and files you believe support the operations described.

23. Weatherford Optical Company has developed two conceptual designs for its computerized accounting and management information system. It is now evaluating their relative financial feasibility. The existing system cannot be made to meet the required performance specifications and will be discarded. The designs will provide comparable performance. Here are some data to assist in making this evaluation:

	System A	System B
Investment at start of year 1 to make system operational	$11,000	$17,000
Annual operating costs	26,000	19,000
(assume all are incurred at the end of the year in which they occur)		
Additional equipment required at end of year 3	9,000	4,000
System shutdown (years after startup)	5	5

Required:

Develop a financial feasibility analysis similar to the one shown in Table 17.5. Instead of calculating a rate of return, assume a required minimum internal rate of return of 20 percent. Then calculate the present value, at system startup, of all the costs associated with each alternative.

24. Starlight Management Company manages rental properties. It has a computer system that uses sequential file processing. The heart of this system is a tenant master file, containing a single large record for each tenant. The date and amount of each rent payment are entered in fields of this record, which holds three years of tenant payment history. The record also holds a substantial (but not unlimited) amount of expense information (taxes, utilities, repairs, management fee), the name and address of the landlord, and three years' history of remittances to the landlord. As billings, receipts and payments occur, the system creates a large update file. It sorts the tenant and tenant-update files into the same order, then transfers the update information into the master file. The tenant master file must be sorted into various sequences to (a) calculate, print, and remit statements and checks to landlords and (b) identify late or nonpaying tenants.

    Starlight has developed two conceptual designs. The first—an enhancement of the system described above—would replace the sequential file with an indexed, direct-access file. This file would have an index for each of the fields currently used for sorts, but update would still be on a batch basis. The second design is a multirelation data base, with separate relations for tenant information, landlord information, rental receipts, expenses, and payments.

    Some information about financial feasibility follows:

	Enhanced File System	Data Base System
Initial investment	$12,000	$20,000
Annual software lease	500	1,000
Annual additional wages & salaries	8,000	27,000
Annual additional supplies & services	4,000	5,000
Additional investment at start of year 2 (disk drive)	5,000	0
Additional investment at start of year 4 (CPU upgrade)	10,000	0
Additional investment at start of year 6 (disk drives)	15,000	0
Annual cash savings owing to shutdown of present system	0	(25,000)
System shutdown (years after startup)	7	7
Target rate of return (for discounting)	20%	20%

Required:

    (a) Prepare a financial feasibility analysis similar to that shown in Table 17.5. Calculate the net present equivalent of the costs and savings of each alternative as of the date of startup.

    (b) Discuss in a written statement of about 150 words the organizational feasibility of these two alternatives. Assume that the firm will grow about 20 percent annually for the next seven years.

25. North Central Auto Club of Pittsburgh has 12,000 members, who pay dues from $35 to $55 annually for a monthly newsletter and free towing, bail bonding, trip planning, and property insurance services. The club expects 5,000 new members each year for the next five years. The club now uses a service bureau, which charges $6 per member per year to keep accounting records and send out statements; this charge covers 700 bytes of disk storage per member to accommodate member data. North Central is responsible for its own cash receipts and check writing. Its annual in-house costs are $20,000 for a chief accountant, $16,000 for a clerk, $7,000 for supplies expense, and $3,000 for postage.

    The executive director proposes to process accounting records at the club's main office, where an unused 12-by-12-foot space is available, using a Solid State PC. This computer will have a color monitor, 16-bit CPU, 256K bytes of nonexpandable main memory, a 160-character-per-second dot matrix printer, one 360K-byte floppy disk drive, and one 10M-byte hard disk drive. With surge suppressor, appropriate furniture, and fire-resistant back-up data storage, the hardware will cost $17,000 on a one-time basis. The executive director will buy an already developed file-based accounting and membership software package from the Western Auto Club, which has a similar computer and serves 3,000 members at a cost of $12,000. This package will perform 90 percent of the functions now being performed by the service bureau and can be modified, for $17,000, to perform all the remaining functions. The executive director plans to hire a data processing director for $30,000 a year and an assistant for $17,000. Annual supplies and postage should cost about $2.50 per member.

Required:

    (a) Prepare a cost comparison of continued service-bureau use and adoption of the executive director's proposal.

    (b) Does anything about the executive director's proposal disturb you? If so, describe the disturbing factor(s).

    (c) Without prejudice for your response to *b*, suppose that the auto club's board of directors concludes that the executive director's proposal has the following defects: computer RAM is too small; hard disk capacity will be exceeded in a few months; printer is too slow to get statements out; cost of proposed software is relatively high. Explain how you would correct each of these deficiencies.

26. Panhandle Farmers Coop, in a remote wheat-raising area, has 300 farmer members who use the coop's grain storage and other services. The coop was formed in 1960. It has three full-time employees: a grain-elevator operator, a front-office manager, and a back-office clerk. The front-office manager, a retired farmer, has designed all existing systems since becoming manager in 1975. The grain-elevator operator has four year's experience.

    The coop has never had an audit but has operated satisfactorily since it was formed. It is governed by a 50-farmer board that meets twice annually. Its records are kept manually by a public bookkeeper in a nearby small town; her charges average $400 per month. The coop paid back as a dividend to members 10 percent of milling, storage, and marketing revenues, which amounted to $60,000 in its most recent year.

    The front-office manager has announced his intention to retire in six months. On behalf of the other employees, he has recommended to the board that the coop acquire a brand-name local-area network of three desktop computers linked to a fourth computer serving a 20M-byte hard disk and a laser printer. The network software would include a complementary basic network program plus a communications and terminal-emulator program; an accounting general ledger; a data base; and office-productivity programs. Each employee would have a computer and would use it for all transaction data entry and member inquiries. The system would also include a 1,200-baud modem for on-line connection to a commodities-price data service, so members could have the latest market information. The manager hopes no additional staff would be necessary.

    Required:

    (a) Using the price estimates on page 594, estimate the hardware and software cost of the proposed system.
    (b) Using the list of questions in Table 17.6, evaluate the organizational feasibility of the proposed system.

27. Hooks Farm Implement Co. (HFI) has developed a new system for financing its dealers' farm implements. The dealers forward merchandise orders through HFI sales representatives for their seasonal inventory requirements—diskers, shredders, cultivators, and so on—and execute 90-day trust certificates in return. These trust certificates make the dealers "trustees" for the equipment, to which HFI continues to hold legal title. As a dealer sells implements, HFI issues a revocation of the corresponding trust certificates. The dealer makes payment, assumes title, and passes it on to the purchaser (after full payment). When the trust certificates reach their 90-day maturity, HFI renews only 60 percent of the original certificate amount (less any sold). The dealer must purchase the implements not covered by trust certificates,

paying cash or signing equipment-secured six-month notes at 4 percent above prime rate annual interest. Each time the trust certificates mature, fewer of them will be renewed until (a) the merchandise is all sold, (b) the dealer has paid for the unsold merchandise, or (c) HFI holds the dealer's marketable notes for the remaining merchandise. In the case of a financially weak and sinking dealer, HFI may refuse to renew the six-month notes and instead recover the merchandise. This system works well in providing flexibility to dealers in financing and selling implements.

Required:

    (a) Draw a partial process diagram similar to Figure 17.6, showing the activities described.

    (b) Compile a data dictionary of at least ten data elements for the events described above. You will have to infer many of the required data elements, since they aren't explicitly mentioned above. For each element give the following information: (1) name, (2) how collected, and (3) used in what report or document.

28. Brewster Television Broadcasting operates a local-programming independent TV station serving an affluent suburban region. By policy, the station airs only 9 minutes of commercials per broadcast hour. The commercials may be as short as 15 seconds or as long as 60 seconds. The sales department solicits commercials and assists in their production. The station maintains a header file of sponsors and a related file in which a new record is created every time a commercial is shown for that sponsor. These two files are used to prepare statements to sponsors and also reports to management showing penetration of various local industries and identifying sponsors who don't pay quickly. When a sponsor pays for a commercial, the station cashier marks a field in the record of that commercial.

    The time between commercials is devoted to programs supplied by local producers. Each producer receives a flat reimbursement for the program, plus a 5-percent royalty on the collected billings for commercials shown during the program. The station maintains a header file of producers and another file of programs. The producer records are linked to the program records, which in turn are linked to the records of commercials run during that program. To figure the royalty, the station starts with a record in the producer file and identifies all collected commercial billings for that producer's programs since the last run date, then makes the royalty calculation. When the royalty has been paid, a field in the program record is marked "paid."

Required:

    (a) Prepare a data flow diagram similar to Figure 17.5 and a process diagram similar to Figure 17.6, for the billing and collection process.

    (b) Do the same for the producer-payment process.

Case: Straightway Van Lines (SVL)

SVL has seven trucks that move customer merchandise throughout North America. The vans follow approximate routes among public warehouses and customers, picking up and delivering shipments. The dispatcher must have an up-to-the-minute record of each truck's location, where it is traveling, what it is carrying, how much "open" space it has for additional shipments, and any delivery time commitments affecting route flexibility. Drivers work out their own routes. Each driver calls the dispatcher twice daily to report truck status and route plans and to learn of new pickups.

The driver collects shipping documents for each shipment and forwards his copy of the bill of lading to the SVL controller; it should match the copy the controller receives directly from the shipper. When the controller makes the match, the shipping charge is set up and billed as an account receivable.

The firm does not use computers now but wishes to do so. The firm wants to keep computerized records of committed and open space on the vans, route plans, pickups, and deliveries. SVL would like this system to integrate with the general ledger.

Required:

Using the information above, write at least twenty performance requirements for the new system. Distinguish between (1) requirements applying to the objectives and scope of the system and (2) tasks for the completed system to perform. In the latter category, provide for (a) keeping up with vans, (b) accounts receivable, and (c) order filling. Identify each requirement as a user-information requirement, an accountability-information requirement, or a control-information requirement.

Case: Itoh Trading Company[1]

Itoh operates men's clothing distributorships in Tokyo and Osaka. Its accounting system is computerized but relies on sequential files. Each season, the company displays fashions from factories in Taiwan, Singapore, China, and Korea and displays them at the industry exposition. Retailers visit the exhibits and place their orders. Orders come in at the rate of about 200 a day during the ten-day exposition. Each retailer writes up an order for each item of clothing ordered, specifying quantity, sizes, color, fabric, style, and quality class.

After the exhibition closes each day, Itoh's three data entry clerks create computer records of the orders. Because the transcription process is very slow, the orders aren't all transcribed until three weeks after the exposition closes. Then, the records are sorted by retailer and sent to the

---

[1]Adapted from a case by Junichi Akiyama, CPA; Chicago.

retailers for confirmation. When confirmed, orders are sorted by factory and forwarded to factories. The factory should confirm the order, but often declines part or all of an order owing to material or time shortages. When an order is confirmed, Itoh records it in the order file. Itoh then sorts the file and sends reports of the confirmed orders to retailers. If time is short, Itoh personnel telephone each retailer to inform them of the confirmed or refused status of their orders.

Each factory ships finished goods to a designated public warehouse at the port of entry. When an order is shipped, the factory sends Itoh a numbered invoice and shipping document. Itoh makes certain the shipment comes in through customs, gets into the warehouse, and is tagged properly. Then Itoh copies the shipping document, customs clearance, and warehouse-identification papers for both the warehouse and the retailer; prepares an invoice for the retailer; and indicates in the confirmed-order file that an invoice has been sent. Itoh's invoice accompanies the papers sent to the retailer.

The retailer must pick up the shipment at the warehouse. The warehouse assumes that anyone with papers matching those it received directly from the factory is authorized to receive the shipment. Often it is picked up by a common carrier. About 15 percent of shipments are not claimed from the warehouses. About 5 percent of merchandise picked up is returned to Itoh for a 20-percent credit. Depending on their credit arrangements with Itoh, retailers remit either checks or 60-to-90-day promissory notes.

Required:

For each of the exercises below, end the flowchart after Itoh forwards papers to the retailer.

(a) Draw a partial system flowchart, like Figure 17.4, for the processes described.
(b) Draw a partial data flow diagram, like Figure 17.5, for the processes described.
(c) Draw a partial process diagram, like Figure 17.6, for the processes described.
(d) The existing system has several shortcomings. Identify as many of them as you can, and propose corrections for them. Identify at least three difficulties. They may have separate causes, or a common cause.

CHAPTER 18

Implementing an Accounting System Design

Learning Objectives

After studying this chapter, you should be able to

- Prepare a plan for implementation: vendor selection, detail design, and conversion.

- Select system-development approaches, such as top-down or bottom-up, data oriented or application oriented; and conversion methods, such as block or parallel conversion.

- Carry out the plan, including detail design and its component steps such as training, preparing physical facilities, data conversion, and forms design.

- Evaluate the results in light of the original feasibility conditions established during the conceptual-design process.

- Provide for efficient, trouble-free system operation, including technical support for users.

Once a feasible system design has been selected, the people involved in the process usually breathe a sigh of relief. They should savor the moment, for there is much more work to come before a system is operational. The remaining work consists of identifying and handling the mass of detail—scheduling, detailed flowcharting, programming, equipment acquisition, staff training, documentation, testing, and coordination—required to complete the remaining three stages: vendor evaluation, detail design, and conversion. These three stages are referred to jointly as **implementation**—the process of making the system envisioned in the conceptual design operational.

Often the system-design managers, having agreed on performance objectives, will at this point disagree on the particular system configuration, hardware, and software that would best achieve the objectives. Such disagreement must be resolved constructively so that it does not lead to delays in detail design and conversion, incomplete evaluation of alternatives, abandonment of partially implemented systems, or full implementation of an ill-conceived and inadequate system. By concentrating on the process objectives and attempting to resolve conflicts as they arise, management can overcome disagreements and bring the system's detail design and conversion to a successful conclusion.

Overview of System Implementation

The conceptual design—the product of all the work discussed in Chapter 17—is nevertheless only a design. Shortly after completing the feasibility analysis, the system analyst must create a workable *implementation plan*. Regardless of the nature of the equipment and services, it will include planning for implementation, vendor selection, detail design, and conversion, as shown in Figure 18.1.

Depending on its complexity, implementation may call for securing proposals from vendors for specific equipment and services; evaluating vendor proposals and selecting vendors; drawing up a detailed system design; programming; testing the system; starting the system up and shaking out its initial defects; and conducting a postconversion review. After selecting the vendor(s) and determining the delivery schedules for equipment and services, you can update the implementation plan by scheduling every significant vendor-dependent event or process required for the detail design and conversion. The plan should incorporate time schedules, assign responsibilities, and provide for steering committee meetings to review progress.

Planning for Implementation

Planning for implementation consists of reviewing the feasibility evaluation and preparing a schedule for implementation, as shown in Figure 18.2. Small systems projects can be scheduled by listing the major steps, arranging them in the appropriate order, and checking them off as they are performed. Large projects may benefit from **critical-path scheduling** a planning procedure that reveals which implementation steps must be

Figure 18.1   Implementation
Implementation, the second half of the system creation process, requires planning based on prior work as well as selection of the right vendors to assist in detail design and conversion.

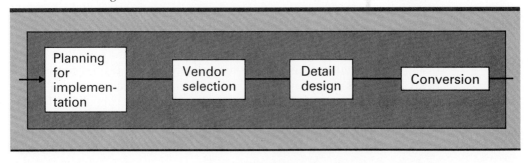

Figure 18.2 Planning for Implementation
Planning for implementation requires a review of the feasibility analysis results
and preparation of a schedule of required implementation activities.

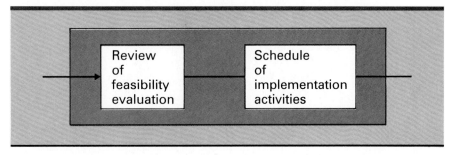

completed before others are begun and where potential bottlenecks are
likely to develop. Critical-path scheduling also serves as an orderly framework for planning and controlling implementation.

Critical-path scheduling is more easily understood if we consider an
example. The Albany Company has completed its conceptual design of an
accounting system enhancement that is to consist of new general journal,
cash, and accounts receivable applications. This enhancement will involve
the steps and amounts of time shown in Table 18.1.

Figure 18.3 shows the sequence of these steps, specifying those that
must be completed before others are begun. The circled numbers designate
the steps; the smaller superscript numbers indicate the number of weeks

Table 18.1 Steps and Times Required for Implementation
To be able to prepare a list of steps and completion times requires the systems
planners to become familiar with the implementation process.

Step	Time (in weeks)
1. Secure proposals from vendors	4
2. Evaluate proposals and select vendors	3
3. Detail design of general journal	7
4. Detail design of accounts receivable	5
5. Detail design of cash receipts	8
6. Programming and testing general journal	9
7. Programming and testing accounts receivable	4
8. Programming and testing cash receipts	6
9. Integrated testing of general journal, accounts receivable, and cash receipts	4

Figure 18.3   Critical-Path Diagram of Partial System Implementation
Critical-path diagrams can be done using microcomputer software. They help identify bottlenecks as well as areas where noncritical work can be deferred. In this
diagram, the critical path (bottleneck) runs through the steps 1, 2, 3, 6, and 9.

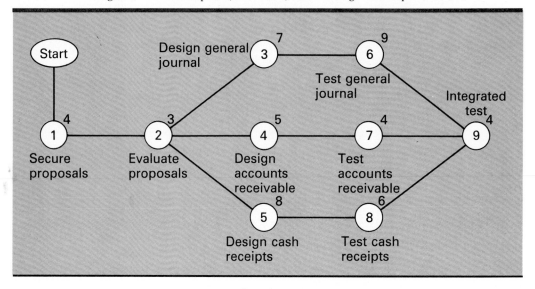

it will take to complete the step. As you can see, the system developers
must evaluate proposals and select vendors (step 2) before any detail design work can begin. Similarly, they must complete all testing of individual
applications (steps 6, 7, and 8) before integrated testing (step 9) can begin.
The three sequences of steps shown in Figure 18.3 are called *paths*. The
path components and completion times are as follows:

Path A:	1–2–3–6–9–	27 weeks
Path B:	1–2–4–7–9–	20 weeks
Path C:	1–2–5–8–9–	25 weeks

Path A is called the *critical path* because it requires the longest time to
complete. One could delay the design, programming, and testing of accounts receivable (Path B) up to seven weeks, and of cash (Path C) up to
two weeks, without prolonging the project. But delaying any step on Path
A would hold up completion of this entire phase of system implementation. Or, to put it another way, if the system developers could speed up
Path A by two weeks, they would finish this entire phase two weeks earlier
without needing to expedite other parts of the project. If the system developers found it necessary to curtail all detail design, programming and
testing (all the steps between 2 and 9) by *three* weeks, they would have to
compress general journal activities steps 3 and 6 by three weeks, cash steps

5 and 8 by one week, and accounts receivable steps 4 and 7 not at all. These are the kinds of scheduling insights that critical path scheduling fosters. Computerized critical-path programs exist for all sizes of computers. These programs enable one to track thousands of steps, to identify bottlenecks, and, if the relationships between step durations and costs are known, to search for the lowest cost schedule of implementation.

Management Structure of System Implementation

The management structure for detail design and conversion should resemble the management structure that developed the conceptual design. One person—a member of top management—should have overall responsibility. He or she could be a line manager representing functions directly affected by the new system, or a data processing manager representing the division that will support the system. In either case, the implementation director should have assistance from competent technical experts, usually headed by an independent consultant. The steering committee (composed of top management and technically qualified senior staff) that developed the conceptual design should continue to oversee its implementation. The steering committee should review all major milestones and serve as an intermediary between the technical experts and the system's eventual users.

Example.   To implement the step of securing proposals from vendors, the Albany Company's steering committee develops the following process:

1. The implementation director asks each steering committee member to submit the names of vendors to whom to send requests for proposals (RFPs). The director also consults with system experts and internal users not on the steering committee to get vendor names. All the names should be submitted by noon on March 15; the names and addresses of the vendors should be verified before sending out the RFP.

2. By March 22, the implementation director telephones each vendor on the list to describe the conceptual design and ascertain how likely they are to respond to the proposal. These calls may last an hour apiece and will probably shorten the list of vendors.

3. By March 22, the implementation director mails three copies of the RFP to each vendor on the shortened list. A cover letter explains that written responses are due by April 22 and that the vendor should send five copies of its proposal. The cover letter also specifies what information the proposal must contain and gives the name and phone number of the implementation director or another person who will respond to vendors' questions.

4. About March 30, the implementation director telephones the vendors to make certain they have received the proposal, to ask whether they will submit proposals, and to answer any questions they might have.

5. As written proposals arrive, the implementation director checks them off on the list of vendors. On April 20, the implementation director telephones any vendors that were expected to respond but have not done so, to make certain no serious proposals have been accidentally lost.

6. As proposals arrive, the implementation director attaches the evaluation instructions to each copy. By April 26, copies of the proposals are delivered to each member of the proposal evaluation team.

Each step in this example consists of a specific action that can be completed and a date by which completion is expected. When the action has been completed, a *milestone* has been passed. Thus the steering committee can determine whether the activity is complete and/or was completed on time. Top management support for precise definition of this type for all implementation activities helps ensure successful, on-time implementation.

Approaches to System Design

Management may select any of several strategies to guide it through the detail-design process. The *application-oriented* strategy was developed in the days of sequential-access file-processing systems, when only limited data analysis was possible without slowing down processing. In **application-oriented design**, data structures had to be carefully tailored to the requirements of each application; neither the applications nor the data structures could be altered without difficulty. **Top-down design** is a structured approach to detail design whereby the systems analyst, not the system users, decides most details of the new system. The analyst does so by subdividing the system into a number of hierarchical segments, resembling a preliminary outline of an article. Because the top-down approach is likely to result in a highly integrated system, it is the preferred approach. However, it carries greater risk in detail design, since its faults, if any, will pervade the completed system. **Bottom-up design** is an approach to detail design in which the system users, not the analyst, decide most details of the new system. Bottom-up design was not feasible in an application-oriented environment because of the conflicts it generated among users over the data to be collected, file and record design, and report preparation. Since the advent of data base processing, however, bottom-up design has become popular for detail design and implementation of user applications. Now system analysts can establish a pool of data for which each user may specify distinct applications. So long as the data base structure

Figure 18.4   System Design Philosophies
The philosophies that experience has shown work best are application-oriented, top-down; and data-oriented, bottom-up. Application-oriented philosophies are losing popularity except where they fit some unusual user criterion.

	Application oriented	Data oriented
	Input, output, and files are organized around processes.	Input, output, and processing are organized around a general and flexible data structure.
Top-down Experts specify most system details	Implementation tends to be smooth and efficient; the completed system is likely to work well but will require users to adapt to it.	Implementation tends to proceed efficiently; if the system requires changing, the changes may be made readily until performance is OK.
Bottom-up Users specify most system details	Implementation tends to be disorganized and inefficient; the results may be unsatisfactory and are not easily changed.	Implementation tends to be disorganized, but user criticisms are easy to respond to and the finished system is popular with users.

is appropriate for the data pool, users may create, change, or even discard and replace applications relatively easily. However, an application-oriented bottom-up approach may produce a minimally integrated, "sloppy" system. A **data-oriented design** philosophy aims to create a data structure that supports multiple and changing applications. A data-oriented, bottom-up approach characterizes an increasing share of new systems development projects today. Figure 18.4 illustrates these four approaches.

Vendor Selection

Every organization requires equipment and services from vendors to complete its systems process. The vendors in turn need to know the conceptual design, the time and cost restraints, and considerable other information about the proposed system. This section will explain how to communicate essential design requirements and other information to vendors, and how to evaluate their responses. Figure 18.5 shows the major steps in vendor selection. The organization ordinarily must include computer equipment, network and communications equipment, software, programming services, system testing, system documentation and training, and post-evaluation review in its planned system; each vendor's ability to supply these resources must be evaluated.

Figure 18.5 Vendor Selection
Vendor selection is the first priority after implementation planning. It is characterized by preparation of a Request for Proposal, and a structured review of any proposals received as vendor responses.

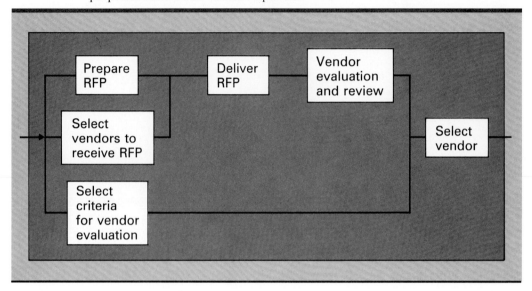

Securing Proposals from Vendors

Whether to use available software or develop custom programs depends on several factors. Small organizations generally cannot afford custom program development; indeed, this expensive step should not be necessary in most firms. The conceptual design should have been developed in such a way as to increase the likelihood that available system components can be adapted to meet its requirements. Small firms should consider programs available commercially or from similar organizations willing to license their custom-developed software.

A company with unique requirements may find that limited choice and the difficulty of adapting an available application make the use of commercial programs impractical. An organization with an unusual legally mandated data collection or reporting requirement may be forced to develop programs to assure compliance. But in general, the existence of so many reputable software firms trying hard to meet existing needs should motivate any organization to examine as many available products as possible.

At one extreme, a dentist's office should find an acceptable application among the dozen or so programs marketed for professional office scheduling and management, at well under $1,000 for the software only. In contrast, $1,000 would buy only about 30 hours of custom programmer time, which would cover only a small fraction of the cost of custom-developed software. At the other extreme, a huge firm such as General Motors or IBM wouldn't even consider commercial software to meet its global application requirements; even at a cost of millions of dollars, such firms develop their own custom systems.

When a decision has been made to acquire equipment, software, or specific services from vendors, management compiles a list of vendors it considers qualified, gives them complete information about the requirements, and encourages them to propose ways of meeting the requirements. Management expects to review the proposals and to select the one with the best combination of performance, risk, and cost.

The vendors on the initial list all receive the RFP describing the specific system requirements. Chapter 16 discussed only one aspect of the request for proposals, the definition of performance requirements. This chapter will focus on two other components, information about the acquisition process and about the vendor's promised performance. You could write a good request for proposals by following the lengthy outline in Table 18.2.

Table 18.2   Outline of a Request for Proposal
Given all the detail included in this RFP outline, a vendor can prepare a responsive proposal for the systems development team.

A.   About the acquiring organization and proposal process
1. Its name and address
2. Key facts about its operations (such as number of transactions per day, number of accounts, pages of reports per month)
3. Name of person responsible for systems process
4. Date proposal issued
5. Type of equipment and services desired (scope of the RFP)
6. Date of vendors' conference (a meeting with potential vendors to allow them to ask questions and clarify ambiguous or conflicting parts of the RFP)
7. Format of proposals (required content, forms to be filled out, guarantees and warranties, what the quoted cost should include)
8. Number of copies of proposal required (more than ten would be unusual)
9. Date and location for delivery of proposals
10. Date by which proposal selection will be announced

(continued)

Table 18.2 *(continued)*

B. Vendor's performance

1. Type of equipment and services the vendor must deliver, described in sufficient detail to allow the vendor to respond with assurance. If the vendor may make a choice, the RFP should so state. (For example, "Any 100Mb disk drive compatible with the Wang VS 130 computer and its peripherals.")

2. Qualifications expected of individuals working on this assignment and information about them the vendor should provide: name, years of experience, specialization, references

3. Dates vendor would begin and complete the work

4. Charges the vendor would make, including charges for extras and for work beyond the scope of the RFP requirements

5. Nature of expected responses to the performance requirements. A good format for responses is

    Y = requirement will be met
    N = requirement cannot be met
    X = requirement can be met with additional work or equipment

    (in which case the vendor should describe the additions and their cost over and above the costs quoted)

6. Invitation to the vendor to make explicit and specific representations, restrictions, reservations, warranties, and suggestions

C. System performance requirements

1. Mandatory requirements

2. Desirable requirements
   The RFP should group the mandatory and desirable requirements in some logical fashion, such as by process. Often the RFP provides a format for a response beside each requirement and asks the vendor to fill it in and return it or a copy in the proposal.

Evaluating Proposals, Selecting Vendors

Some time after the information listed in Table 18.2 has been transformed into an RFP and sent to qualified vendors, the organization can expect to receive usable proposals. Now the task is to identify the vendor most likely, judging from its proposal and other available information, to be able to satisfy the requirements at an acceptable cost.

Vendor Evaluation and Review Technique

Systems analysts typically have to explain and defend their choices of vendors to nontechnical executives. Therefore they want to select vendors objectively and to create an "audit trail" to support their choices. This is difficult to do, however, since many evaluation criteria, such as the apparent reliability of a vendor's maintenance services, are difficult to quantify. To achieve quantifiability and facilitate comparisons, analysts are willing to use evaluation techniques, such as rankings or points-scoring that introduce some arbitrariness and bias into the selection process. These evaluation techniques generate quantitative measures of subjective attributes of competing proposals so they may be ranked and a winning vendor identified. Collectively, these procedures are called the **Vendor Evaluation and Review Technique (VERT)**

As an outcome of the conceptual-design process, the organization will know what selection criteria are important to it and will use them to evaluate the proposals it receives. VERT will classify these criteria into broad categories. A typical classification would create separate categories for confidence in the vendor's long-run abilities and products, the vendor's ability to meet commitments required by the RFP, the estimated cost to complete and start up the system, and the number and importance of performance requirements the vendor can meet. These are summarized in Tables 18.3–18.7.

We will use as an illustration proposals from Vendors A, B, and C to the Ganado Consolidated School District. The school district hired a consultant to evaluate these proposals, which are not included because of their length; other details are omitted or simplified. VERT is only one of several ways to evaluate proposals, but it illustrates the key factors in any such process: objectivity, quantitative measures, and forced rankings.

To calculate a point score for each vendor proposal, the system analyst establishes a maximum number of points that can be assigned to each requirement or attribute. A proposal may receive any score from zero to the maximum on that requirement or attribute. The analyst assigns scores for all attributes in one classification, then for all attributes in the next classification, and so on, until all attributes have been evaluated. The sum of the points assigned to a particular proposal represents its score, and the proposal with the most points ranks highest. The point-assignment process may differ from one attribute to another; two methods are described in the illustration.

Confidence in the Vendor. The Ganado Consolidated School District expects the vendor to be in business long after the new information system is complete, to provide service, and to help the district use and expand

Table 18.3 Evaluation of Confidence in the Vendor, Using a Point System
All vendor evaluation processes, including this one, are intended to summarize proposal detail into a ranking in which the best proposal is ranked first. This table summarizes a ranking of vendors on the basis of several attributes that reflect the confidence one may have in the vendor as a supplier.

Attribute	Maximum Points	Vendor		
		A	B	C
Financial strength and credit rating	15	10	12	14
Years in business	4	4	4	4
Number of systems	3	3	2	2
Active users' association	3	0	0	3
Problem-resolution experiences	5	3	4	2
Age of products	2	1	1	2
Totals	32	21	23	27

the system. To evaluate the level of confidence a vendor merits, an analyst would consider the vendor's financial statements, credit standing, and references. These yardsticks are especially important if the vendor is small. Other factors are the number of years in business; the number of similar systems, hardware, and software the vendor has already installed; the existence of an active users' association or advisory group; references' descriptions of their problem resolution experiences, promptness of maintenance, and congruence between promised and actual performance. The age of the products, whether replacements are under development, and whether they will be compatible with older models are also important.

The VERT evaluation results shown in Table 18.3 compare Vendors A, B, and C on the attributes listed in the preceding paragraph. The analyst assigned scores by examining each vendor's proposal and exercising professional judgment. The analyst did not consider any of the vendors worthy of the maximum number of points for "financial strength and credit rating," but judged Vendor B's position strong enough to merit 12 of the 15 possible points. Vendor A appeared the weakest of the three. For "years in business," the analyst assigned one point for each year, up to a maximum of 4. All three firms have been in business for four or more years. For the number of systems the vendor has installed, the analyst assigns 3 points for 30 or more systems, 2 points for 20 or more, and 1 point for 10 or more. For the next attribute, the analyst assigns 3 points for a user association whose membership includes 50 percent or more of all the systems installed, 1 point for a user association with less than 50 percent membership, and 0 points if no association exists; only Vendor C has a user association. Having contacted the references furnished by each vendor, the analyst concluded that none had a perfect record of resolving problems; the points assigned are as shown. The analyst notes that Vendors A and B are both proposing components that have not been updated in three years, while Vendor C's components were updated last year. In sum, Vendor C is the apparent winner.

The Vendor's Ability to Meet Commitments.   The ability of the vendor to meet the time frame and other requirements of the project can be looked into by examining the qualifications of the vendor's staff and its backlog of orders or deliveries that must be completed before work commences on the Ganado Consolidated School District. Ganado's analyst should also consider how long the vendor's staff has been familiar with the Ganado proposal; their expertise becomes more important as the proposal becomes more complex. When contacting references, the analyst should ask them about their system installation experiences—specifically, whether the time schedule was met, and whether less experienced individuals were substituted for those described in the proposal. There is some risk in a brand-new system, and the analyst knows that the school district strongly prefers proven system components with which the vendor has some experience. Note, however, that both "brand-new" and "very old" entail risks.

The evaluation in Table 18.4 quantifies these factors. Vendor A ranks first, appearing to be the vendor most able to meet the RFP requirements. First, the analyst examined the qualifications of the staff the three vendors say they will assign to the Ganado system project. Vendor A would assign three people, of whom two are capable programmers; they have installed

Table 18.4   Evaluation of Vendor Ability to Meet Commitments
The highest total number of points signifies the vendor with the most ability to meet commitments.

Attribute	Maximum Points	Vendor		
		A	B	C
Staff qualifications	6	5	4	1
Time frame	10	10	5	10
Backlog	5	2	3	5
Staff experience	4	4	4	3
Customer experience	10	8	9	5
New products	3	3	3	2
Totals	**38**	**32**	**28**	**26**

eight other systems similar to this one and have twelve years of combined experience. Vendor B would also assign three people, who have installed twelve other systems similar to this one; only one is a programmer, but they have fifteen years of combined experience. Vendor C would assign only two people, one of whom has prior experience consisting of two similar installations and five years of other work. Next, Ganado's consultant looked at the time frame. Ganado felt it necessary to complete all work in eight months, a tight schedule. Both Vendors A and C could start immediately and proposed reasonable schedules with timely completion; Vendor B could not start for three months, and its schedule appeared unrealistic. Vendor C had no backlog of work to threaten the Ganado system's progress; the other two vendors did have backlogs. The consultant's staff experience ratings drew upon the information above. All three vendor's references had some reservations about their vendor's performance during the conversion process. Vendor C's references seemed to have had the worst experiences, and the analyst's follow-up suggested that these problems resulted from understaffing and overpromising, a situation likely to recur. The vendors were all familiar with the products they were installing, but A and B seemed most conversant.

Number of Requirements Met.   In general, unless the performance requirements are very simple, no vendor will offer to meet all of them. The Ganado system requirements are moderately complex, and none of the vendors has proposed to meet all of them. Thus, the consultant must compare the number and significance of the requirements different vendors offer to meet. Often the only evidence to evaluate is the vendor's own representations. Typically, organizations evaluate each requirement separately. VERT uses these individual evaluations in a two-step process of quantifying requirements compliance. The first step is to decide whether or not a given requirement has been met; then the numbers of mandatory and desirable requirements met in each proposal are counted and recorded. The second step is to assign the maximum number of possible points to the highest total, and zero points to the lowest total; each proposal in between is assigned a point total that represents its standing. Table 18.5 summarizes the results of evaluating performance requirement compliance.

The points awarded to Vendor A for meeting mandatory requirements were calculated according to the following formula, where X_A is the number of requirements met by Vendor A:

$$\text{Points assigned to Vendor A} = \frac{\left(\begin{array}{c}\text{Maximum} \\ \text{points possible}\end{array}\right) \times \left(\begin{array}{c}X_A - \text{lowest number} \\ \text{of requirements}\end{array}\right)}{\left(\begin{array}{c}\text{Highest number of} \\ \text{requirements met}\end{array}\right) - \left(\begin{array}{c}\text{lowest number of} \\ \text{requirements met}\end{array}\right)}$$

Table 18.5   Points Allocated for Requirements Met
The method for points allocation used here is different from that used in Tables 18.3 and 18.4. Here, the vendor meeting the most requirements receives the highest possible number of points; the vendor meeting the fewest requirements receives zero points. Other vendors receive points prorated to the number of requirements met. This assignment method tends to magnify the differences among vendors.

		Vendor		
Attribute		A	B	C
Mandatory requirements	75	70	45	75
Point total	20 (maximum possible)	17 in between	0 fewest requirements met	20 most requirements met
Desirable requirements	10	0	7	0
Point total	10 (maximum possible)	0 fewest requirements met	10 most requirements met	0 fewest requirements met

So, for example,

$$\text{Vendor A points} = \frac{20 \times (70 - 45)}{(75 - 45)} = 16.67, \text{ rounded up to } 17$$

The formula assures that the closer the vendor comes to meeting the maximum number of requirements, the more points the vendor will receive. If there were more than three vendors, all but the highest and lowest ranking would be calculated as shown above. With regard to desirable requirements, the maximum possible points was 10. Vendor B, which offered to meet the most requirements (7), received all 10 points; Vendors A and C, with the fewest (0), received 0 points.

Cost.   Cost must be considered in two ways: as quoted and as adjusted for modifications and options. The Ganado consultant found it very difficult to establish comparability, since the vendors proposed quite different ways to meet the school district's system requirements. In fact, true cost comparability is possible only if an organization specifies brand-name equipment or software, so that every vendor is compelled to propose identical products and services.

The consultant decided that the only way to achieve a useful comparison of costs was to compare vendors as if they were supplying the same items and meeting the same requirements. This meant modifying the less complete vendor proposals by calculating and incorporating the costs of additional services. To see how the consultant converted the final cost differences into evaluation point spreads, look at Table 18.6. The consultant began with the cost of each vendor's basic proposal, then identified the modifications that would make all the proposals produce the same final system. Next, the consultant asked each vendor the costs of these additional modifications and added them to the cost of the basic package. The consultant awarded the lowest-cost vendor (A) all 18 points, and highest-cost vendor (B) zero points. Vendor C, the in-between vendor, was awarded points using the following formula: X_n = the cost quoted by the vendor for whom points are being calculated. Then,

$$\text{Points assigned to Vendor N} = \frac{\text{maximum points} \times (\text{maximum cost} - X_n)}{(\text{maximum cost} - \text{minimum cost})}$$

So, for example,

$$\text{Vendor C points} = \frac{18 \times (21{,}000 - 18{,}000)}{(21{,}000 - 14{,}000)} = 7.7, \text{ rounded up to 8}$$

This formula assures that the closer the vendor is to the low bid, the more points the vendor will receive. Vendor A wins in this category.

Table 18.6 Evaluation of Cost Differences
Here, points are allocated as in Table 18.5. Before assigning points, the systems team must make certain all proposals are performance-equivalent, so their costs are comparable.

Attribute	Maximum Points	Vendor A	Vendor B	Vendor C
Basic package		$12,000	$ 8,000	$18,000
Modifications to meet mandatory requirements		$ 2,000	$ 9,000	0
Modifications to meet seven desirable requirements		0	$ 4,000	0
Dollar totals		$14,000	$21,000	$18,000
Point total	**18**	**18**	**0**	**8**

Table 18.7 VERT Point-Total Summary
The summary table indicates that, according to VERT, Vendor A ranks highest.

Attribute	Maximum Points	Vendor A	Vendor B	Vendor C
Confidence in vendor	32	21	23	27
Ability to meet commitments	38	32	28	26
Number of requirements met				
Mandatory	20	17	0	20
Desirable	10	0	10	0
Cost	18	18	0	8
Total	**118**	**88**	**61**	**81**

Interpreting VERT Results. When all of the requirements have been taken into account, VERT summarizes the point totals. Table 18.7 shows this summary.

The consultant's evaluation has awarded Vendor A the most points. Vendor A's strengths appear to be its ability to meet commitments and its reasonable cost. The consultant reexamines the analysis of the proposals to make certain that the point assignment, which has arbitrary aspects and reflects relatively few factors, appears consistent with common sense evaluation. The consultant has learned from experience not to trust a point-system evaluation that seems at odds with common sense! Point-system evaluation schemes are designed to encourage logic and objectivity, but they do so by forcing you to examine your premises and your reasoning. Point systems can only be helpful, not conclusive. Finally, the consultant presents the VERT analysis to the school board and explains each vendor's score. Additional evidence, including demonstration of existing systems and checks on vendor references, should also be presented as appropriate. Last, the consultant helps the school board select a vendor with whom to negotiate.

Management of Detail Design

The detail design must include literally every system detail—every line of every form, every procedure, every report, every control, every format, every responsibility, every position—of the completed system and how it will be developed and put in place. Detail-design management seeks to identify and decide on all that detail. But as you might expect, the system designers cannot realistically produce a complete detail design before con-

Figure 18.6   Detail Design
Detail design is the most complex part of implementation. Often, the system creation process seems to have bogged down here, in the mass of detail. It helps to remember that the system is being specified in progressively more detail until its operators are trained, its programs are written, its forms are designed, and its documentation is complete.

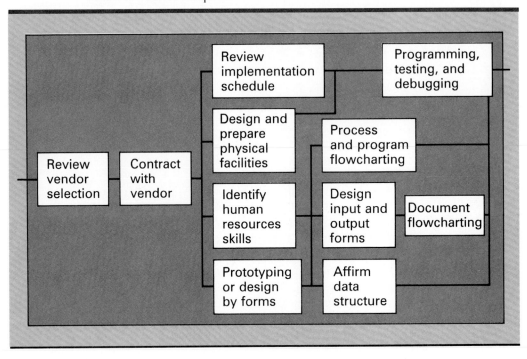

version begins. Although most of the detail design is finished shortly after vendor selection, a substantial portion, from 5 to 25 percent, continues into the conversion phase. Detail design and its supportive processes are shown in Figure 18.6.

Supportive Processes

The detail-design process relies on support from legal counsel for contracts, personnel for human resources, and engineering for site preparation. Certain support processes for detail design should be underway when the system details emerge. These stage-setting processes, which prepare the way for further detail design, include contract negotiation and signing with vendor(s), selection and training of human resources, and preparation of physical facilities.

Contract Negotiation and Signing with Vendor(s). After Ganado's school board has identified the leading candidate to provide the equipment, services, or systems it seeks, the school district will negotiate with that vendor to conclude a contract. The vendor's proposal is not itself a contract; it may even contain representations, claims, or statements the vendor is unwilling to include in a binding contract. The fee, the congruence between the vendor's proposal and Ganado's expectations, and the urgency of the system for Ganado will determine how quickly and seriously these negotiations proceed, and whether lawyers participate in negotiating and drafting the contract. If this were a more complex contract, lawyers should be involved on both sides to review and explain to their clients what it is they are agreeing to. In general, the school district and its consultant will try to incorporate the contents of the vendor's proposal into the contract. If negotiations proceed slowly or poorly, the consultant will update the point-system evaluation to reflect the contract commitments the vendor is actually proposing. If the vendor's score declines significantly below that of the runner-up, the school district might consider whether it would be better off changing vendors.

The consultant will make certain that Ganado's contract covers the following important points:

Dates when vendor performance must begin and be completed

Which members of the vendor's staff will be responsible for planning, designing, and converting the system

Amount of service or assistance the vendor will provide after conversion is complete

Whether the vendor may subcontract any portion of the contract

Complete descriptions of each aspect of vendor performance and its cost (often done by including performance requirements from the RFP and the vendor's responses from the proposal in the contract)

Specific penalties for every possible aspect of noncompliance with performance expectations and deadlines

Total cost of vendor performance

Selection and Training of Human Resources. In planning a system, it is easy to overlook definition of responsibilities, position descriptions, hiring qualified personnel, and training. In general, system users are unlikely to ask for as much help as they need. Without training, important features of the system will go unused, or be misused. The way to head off these potential problems is to approach use of the system as a human-resources–management challenge.

The Ganado consultant will encourage the school district to establish procedures that describe every intended use of the system. He will also see to it that the school district staff learns these procedures through training programs. The training programs will consist of modules covering distinctive tasks such as entering data, processing (sequence and frequency of running programs), generating and distributing output, authorizing system access, and dealing with system faults, malfunctions, and failures. The consultant will also be alert for peripheral topics, such as ordering computer supplies, that the staff should know about.

Training should begin early enough for it to end about the same time the system becomes operational. This training gives the staff self-confidence in use of the system during startup, and thus streamlines the early stages of system operation. Individual user training typically takes one to five days; operator training requires one to five weeks. If large portions of the system are custom-developed by the organization, the corresponding training will take approximately four times as long to develop as to conduct. If most of the system is acquired as packages from vendors, training programs too may be available through the vendor. At Ganado, the vendor will conduct all the training, modifying previously developed programs to incorporate details unique to the school district's system. This entire process—hiring new personnel and making them effective—may take one to six months.

Design and Preparation of Physical Facilities.   At Ganado School District, management has selected a basement room for the new system. Since preparation of a system-operations site often takes weeks, and since the site will be needed for data-conversion and training prior to startup, the consultant urged Ganado's management to begin site preparation early in the systems process. Management, aware that existing space might require renovation or additional construction, asked the consultant to help convert it into a suitable facility. This part of the detail-design and conversion process is commonly called **site preparation**, that is, the creation of a physical location suitable for a computer-based processing system.

Site preparation involves considerations of security, safety, space, and convenience. The site should be relatively inaccessible to the public and to unauthorized employees, through several doors, at least. If the offices of the organization cover several floors of a building, the system site should be above the ground floor, toward the center of the building. In this respect, the proposed site was less than ideal as a computer location. However, the basement was not subject to natural flooding and the water pipes were located at a safe distance from the room.

The consultant suggested that partitions be used to separate records storage from data processing. Other partitions would bar users, visitors, and messengers from every part of the office facility except a small reception area. Earthquakes, floods, fires, vandals, and terrorists were not considered likely; nevertheless, structural protections were added. Back-up data would be kept off-site in the vault of a nearby bank. The site would have adequate air conditioning, an independent temporary supply of electrical power, and a means of fire control that would be least harmful to the equipment and data storage media (carbon dioxide, certain foams, and powders are best). Finally, the center would be more than large enough for startup. Expansion would use up the excess area.

Creating the Major Detail-Design Components

For most systems analysts and consultants, a project "comes alive" when the hardware arrives and the software components begin to emerge in a recognizable form. After reviewing the conceptual design, the analyst begins working with the users to design user interfaces and with the programmers to design the logical processing and underlying data structures that support the user interfaces. In bottom-up design, the user interfaces will receive primary attention, and the analyst will utilize approaches called prototyping and design by forms. In top-down design, the analyst may concentrate first on decision tables and logical flowcharting, and secondarily on the user interfaces. Whatever the approach, actual programming, if required, will occur only after virtually all of the details of the new system have been finalized.

Prototyping

Prototyping is a relatively new systems development tool in which the analyst works with users to determine how the user interfaces should meet their requirements. The analyst then creates documents, screen forms, and processes that link data and information to the user interfaces. This is the approach the Ganado school district's consultant used. The consultant drew input and output screens on paper and showed them to the clerks and managers who would use the system. These people made repeated suggestions until they were satisfied that the screen forms would handle all the transactions and data search requirements. The consultant used the same approach with paper documents such as purchase orders, modifying facsimiles until they accommodated all necessary information and met with user approval.

The consultant relied on data flow diagrams and system diagrams from the conceptual-design phase to link each element of data to particular processes and files. In this way, the consultant learned what should happen to each data element from the time it was first recorded through its editing, storage, processing, and reporting. When every element could be traced in the data dictionary from user-approved entry or reporting forms through defined processes, files, and relations to user-approved files, the consultant judged the system to be successfully prototyped. To this pro-

Table 18.8   System Attributes Determined Through Prototyping
Although prototyping does not produce a complete system, it does allow users to specify many of the unique system details that the designers can add to the more-or-less standard design of a data base environment or other system framework.

- Content and appearance of screen input and output
- Content and appearance of documents
- Processing and conversion of data to information
- Records, files, and data bases used and their data elements
- Frequency of use
- Security requirements
- Back-up and recovery requirements

totype, the consultant added security, back-up, report frequency, and other elements to complete the system. Table 18.8 summarizes the system attributes determined through prototyping.

These attributes were also thought about during conceptual design, but in this later development step the system developers create actual prototype forms and reports like those the user will work with after the system is operational. When the user says, for example, "This is the way I want this report to appear, and I want to receive it every Monday," the developers describe and specify the procedures that will produce the report in that format and frequency. The result of prototyping is a series of forms linked to related processes, which in turn add, process, and update information in a defined data structure. The prototype "looks" like the final system, but it is not documented, tested, or refined to completion. These steps will be completed quickly once the organization accepts the prototype. Prototyping has been found to be a fast and cost-effective way to detail-design accounting systems in organizations where individual users can describe their needs.

Design by Forms

Design by forms is an approach to systems development in which, by working with data input, edit, search, and report formats, the user specifies all data elements and the data structures that contain them. Thus, in the sense that it does not involve very much programming, it is very closely related to prototyping. It usually takes place, however, in the context of a previously defined data base environment. Thus, it is useful in modifying an existing system as well as creating a new one. The analyst starts with a set of requirements, a data base, and previously defined relations, and works with users to develop the entry or report forms, and then to link them to the existing data base. If necessary, the data base could be altered by adding new data elements or relations. All processes would be linked to a form, and a given form could have more than one process linked to it. For example, suppose you are designing a new credit sales recording procedure. You have already defined a customer master file, an inventory-status file, an item-price file, and a transaction file. Now you are designing a credit sales order entry form and a means of using it.

When a credit sale commences, the sales clerk opens the sales form and enters the customer's credit number. When the clerk presses "enter," a short verification process opens the customer master file and searches it for the customer's credit number. If the number does not exist, the process displays the message "No such credit customer number" and waits for the clerk to enter another number. If the number does exist, the process reads the customer's credit status from the customer's master record. If the credit is not good, it displays the message "Valid customer number; credit limit exceeded" and returns to the start of the process. If the credit is good, the process fills in the customer's name on the screen (read from the customer's record in the master file) and allows the clerk to enter the identifying number and quantity of each item the customer wants to buy. For each item, another process opens the inventory-status file and checks that a record with this number exists and that enough items are in stock to fill this order. If either or both conditions are not met, the process displays an appropriate message. If the order can be filled, the process opens the item-price file and displays on the screen the name of the item, its unit price, and the total cost of all units ordered. When all items have been entered, the process totals the order (calculating tax and shipping if applicable). It then goes back to the customer master record and determines whether this order would cause the customer's credit limit to be exceeded. If so, it displays a message to that effect. Otherwise, the process will update the item-inventory-file records and the customer-master-file record, and be ready for another transaction. The original screen form remains visible at all times, and all processing and interchange of data take place through short processes, consisting of statements in a programming language, that are connected to the form. Once the sales clerk selects the screen form, all the processes associated with data on the form are automatically called up and invoked as needed.

The processes are usually programmed in a data base control language (DCL) unique to the data base environment being used. DCLs vary considerably, but may to some degree resemble an existing language such as COBOL, PASCAL, or C. Some DCLs are easier to learn and use than a full-blown programming language, because the work of designing forms and defining relations is handled by special parts of the data base environment. In addition, the often confusing use of "GO-TO" statements is avoided and data management is almost completely automatic.

Affirming the Content Specifications of Documents, Records, Files, and Data Bases

If prototyping is used, the system developer makes certain during that process that the content specifications of source documents, data capture documents, control documents, reports, records, files, and data bases are correct. Otherwise, the developer performs this step by a less user-intensive means, such as presenting data specifications to the key accounting managers and functional department supervisors, and with data-item checklists and, sometimes, simulation. Whatever the method, it is important to finalize these specifications before proceeding to program and software development.

Decision Tables

A **decision table** is a collection of rules in tabular format that relate the intended system actions to specific sets of conditions. The one illustrated in Table 18.9 was used by Ganado's consultant to partially describe its purchasing policies. Decision tables are not an alternative to logical flow-charting, but many systems experts use them to describe choice rules and criteria in a form programmers and documentation writers can under-

Table 18.9   Decision Table
Decision tables summarize how a system component will perform logically; the rules link conditions that are determined by processing conditions with actions that system software or managers take.

Decision Table									
Purchase-order approval policy Based on interview with purchasing manager 1-20-86		Rules							
		1	2	3	4	5	6	7	8
C o n d i t i o n s	1. Purchase request marked urgent?	Y	Y	Y	Y	N	N	N	N
	2. Request addressed to approved vendor?	Y	Y	N	N	Y	N	Y	N
	3. Request approved by department head?	Y	N	Y	N	Y	N	N	Y
A c t i o n s	1. Write purchase order to vendor	X				X			
	2. Write vendor approval form			X	X				
	3. Write department-head approval form		X		X				
	4. File this purchase request	X	X	X	X	X			
	5. Return request to sender						X	X	X

stand. Decision tables supplement flowcharts and help programmers understand the logic the programs must embody. Table 18.9 has three parts—conditions, actions, and rules—and was constructed from the transcript of an interview with Ganado's purchasing manager. The transcript read as follows:

> Purchasing management is my job. All departments have purchase-request forms, and anyone in any department can request a purchase by filling out the form and sending it to my department. A request can be urgent or not urgent, and we check for that first. Every request needs to be addressed to an approved vendor and approved by the department head. If a request is not urgent and is not addressed to an approved vendor or approved by the department head, we simply return it to the sender.
>
> If the department head approval is missing on an urgent request, we send the department head an approval form to sign. If an urgent request is not addressed to an approved vendor, we write a form for analyzing the vendor to see if it should be on the approved list. Whether or not the request is urgent, if everything is in order, we send it to the vendor. Oh, we also keep a file of the urgent purchase requests so we can follow up on them later.

In the *conditions* are the variables (facts not controllable by purchasing). The *actions* are the choices open to the purchasing department. The *rules* relate specific configurations of variables to specific actions. Table 18.9 shows three conditions, five actions, and eight rules. Theoretically, there can be as many as 2^N rules where N is the number of conditions. Usually, though, some of the possible configurations of conditions make no sense, so the number of rules is less than 2^N.

Process and Program Flowcharts

A **process flowchart** is a drawing that shows the data and operations of a single process. All process flowcharts follow a simple format such as in Figure 18.7. If a process is complex, several flowcharts may be needed to cover it completely. The process flowchart uses symbols such as those in Figure 18.9 on page 681, except that it does not show logic.

The **program flowchart**, a drawing that shows the data, steps, and logic of a process operation, does show logic and additional processing detail. The hierarchical relationships of these three types of descriptive figures is shown in Figure 18.8. Process and program flowcharting, along with decision tables, allow you to compare the system's activities with the checks of accounting, security, backup, and editing described in the performance requirements, which will constitute the data entry, processing, and reporting controls. The program flowchart also allows you to make certain that formulas and calculations are included in the instructions to the programmer.

Many people fear process and program flowcharts, possibly because they have been confronted with huge flowcharts of entire applications, no more digestible in a single sitting than a long novel. Flowcharts develop

Figure 18.7   Process Flowchart Format
The process flowchart shows the extent and sequence of activities needed to implement a process diagram (such as Figure 18.8).

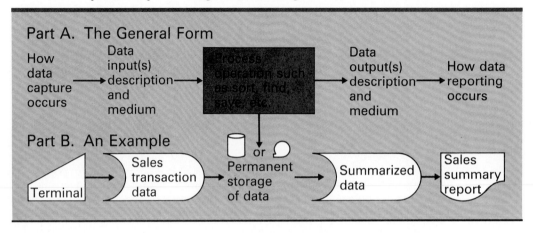

Figure 18.8   Relationship of Process Diagram, Process Flowcharts, and Program Flowchart
The process diagram, developed during conceptual design, contains the least detail. The additional detail required for process and program flowcharts must be developed through detail-design studies, interviews, and review.

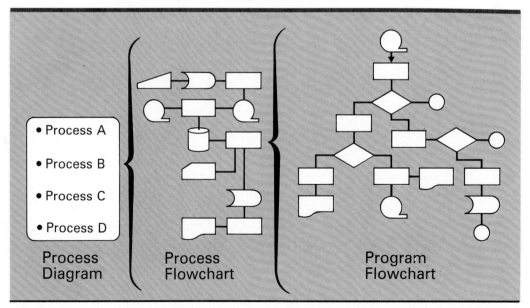

Figure 18.9 Symbols Used to Construct Process and Program Flowcharts
The symbols shown are used universally by systems analysts, and thus are a
concise way for analysts to express and receive understanding of a system design.

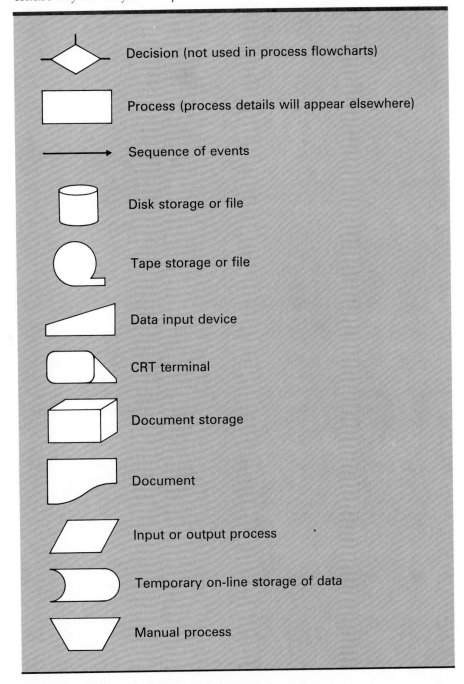

Decision (not used in process flowcharts)

Process (process details will appear elsewhere)

Sequence of events

Disk storage or file

Tape storage or file

Data input device

CRT terminal

Document storage

Document

Input or output process

Temporary on-line storage of data

Manual process

a page at a time, and this is the best way to understand and use them. A small flowchart is easy to grasp; it can serve as an effective medium of communication between system users, developers, and programmers. Figure 18.9 shows some of the symbols flowcharts employ. By proceeding manually through the processes and options shown on a flowchart (called a **walkthrough**), one can spot and correct errors and inconsistencies that would have been confusing and costly to correct later.

The program flowchart in Figure 18.10 shows the purchasing process just described by Mr. Thorne. Note that while it adheres closely to the decision table, it also shows the sequence of events. To make it easier to compare the flowchart to the decision table, the flowchart symbols have been labeled to refer to conditions (C) and actions (A) listed in the decision table. The statements in the flowchart can be extracted from it and listed in order; when this is done, they form the basis for **pseudocode**, a set of succinct instructions to the programmer using some of the syntax of the language in which the application will be programmed. Pseudocode brings the description of the system one step closer to the final programmed instructions.

Input and Output Forms

The design for an input or output form is often called a **template**. Whether adapting an existing form or designing a new template, the system developers should follow established principles of form design.

In explaining form design to the Ganado School Board, the consultant said, "It is good to preprint or display as much information as possible on the form, or on the screen display of the form, to preclude someone forgetting it or making a copying error each time the information is needed. No data element, such as the date, should have to be entered on the form more than once. I will solicit users' advice on each form's design and include on-line editing and error-trapping routines if it is a computer screen form. Each form will contain only the data items required by its function; additional items might confuse the form's users. On manually prepared forms, I recommend using a computer-readable data-entry method wherever possible."

Document Flowcharting

A document flowchart is a diagram illustrating where documents originate and where copies of them are sent. The most useful kind of document flowchart shows what happens to the copies of a single document from the time they are created until each of them is in a file or in the hands of an outside party. A consolidated flowchart for a single process shows the origins and fates of all documents in the process. Document flowcharts do not show logic or processing, nor do they show the components of a system. Figure 18.11 shows a document flowchart for purchasing.

Figure 18.10   Program Flowchart
The program flowchart includes logic and is, in a logic sense, equivalent to the decision table for the same system.

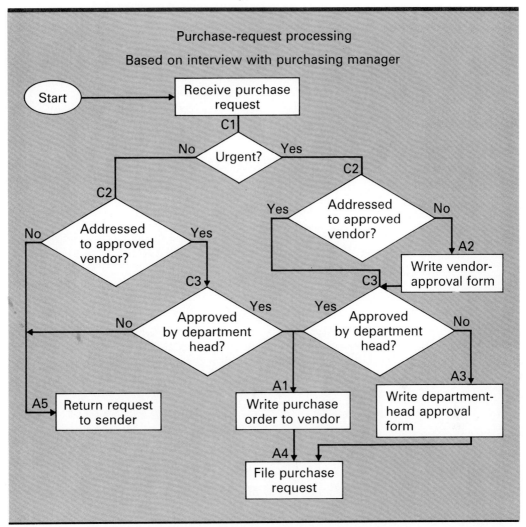

The Ganado consultant offered the school board the following advice about document flowcharts: "On a document flowchart, the columns refer to the responsibility centers that are the sources or destinations of documents. Try to arrange these so that the documents originate in the upper left-hand part of the flowchart and move, as much as possible, to the lower right-hand corner of the flowchart. Remember that every copy of every document must be traced from its originators into a computer file or storage cabinets. Do not include logic in your document flowcharts, and do not try to crowd many documents onto a one-page diagram."

Figure 18.11 Document Flowchart Showing Purchase Requisitions and Purchase Orders
This flowchart shows the purchase requisition that originates in the requesting department and the purchase order that the purchasing department prepares.

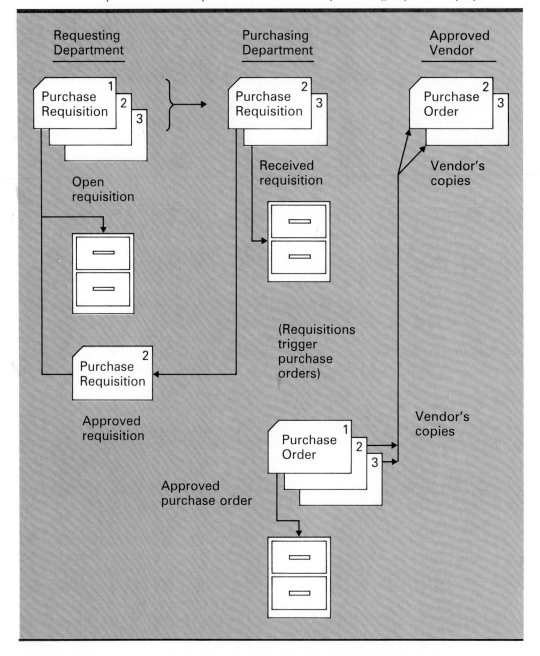

Programming, Modifying, Testing, and Debugging

Programming, whether it means modifying existing software or creating new software products, is one of the last stages of detail design. It occurs only after all other parts of the design have been assembled and approved. You might want to review some of the background on computer software in Chapter 4.

Computer programmers take the highly structured, user-approved system description evolved to this point, and from it they develop a set of interrelated instructions to a computer—a program. When a program has been completed and tested, it is ready for **conversion**, the final steps in system development that get the new system running. Conversion is akin to taking possession of an automobile and driving it until you are confident you can use it every day. It is the process of operating computer programs with real business transactions until they have proved themselves reliable enough to operate routinely without special attention. After conversion, the programs are part of the **installed system**, which processes data on a regular basis.

Programming languages are specifically designed to facilitate writing certain types of programs. For business systems, programmers usually favor assembler language, COBOL, C, and RPG. In fact, so many programs are written in COBOL that a serious business-applications programmer must know COBOL simply to understand these programs and make minor changes and enhancements to them.

Newer languages becoming available for accounting software differ from BASIC, FORTRAN, and COBOL in that they have a "structured" character. A **structured language** requires programmers to follow a set of rules in creating a program. This complicates the writing of short programs, which are so easy in BASIC, but simplifies writing longer programs. Many programmers feel that structured languages significantly reduce the effort of writing larger programs. New "object-oriented" languages such as SMALLTALK also appear to be gaining popularity.

A computer program for an accounting system may seem very complex and difficult when viewed in its entirety. In reality, though, the program was written one short segment at a time. Each segment corresponds to a specific process described in the system design and specifications. The programmers test each segment individually to be certain its internal logic contains no errors; that its variables are all in the data dictionary; that it uses data structures that contain values of these variables; and that it meets the performance requirements assigned to it. If the programmers find errors (whimsically called **bugs**; legend has it that a malfunction in an early computer was caused by a moth, which flew in, got off course, landed inside the computer, and formed a low-resistance electrical connection between two internal circuits), they track down their causes one by one and rewrite the program to eliminate them.

When the programmers have successfully tested all the segments in a process or part of a process, they test them in combination with each other. This is called **block testing.** Eventually, logically related blocks may be combined for a higher level of block testing. Although programming errors are usually eliminated at or below this stage, block testing may reveal that the performance of the combined blocks does not match the detail design. For example, a variable called BALANCE DUE in one block might be named AMOUNT BILLED in another block. To standardize the names, some reprogramming occurs.

As tests, the programmers use short files and records identical in their specifications to those the new accounting system will process. They may use test data designed to reveal whether controls are operating as expected, or they may even use random-number generators to create "unlikely" data that the system should be able to handle. They may use the system with large volumes of realistic data to see if the system meets the performance requirements and gives expected results when running at full capacity. Eventually, substantially complete processes will be tested. At that point, the work plan usually calls for the organization to accept the programmers' work. Testing of entire applications and systems is known as **acceptance testing**

In programming, as in auditing, one must keep detailed and complete working papers (records) describing all the variables, segments, blocks, tests, acceptances, errors noted, bugs found, and bugs corrected. There are various kinds of programs to facilitate the process, including programs that generate error-free lines of program to perform simple requirements, and programs that allow a newly coded routine to run one step at a time, making it easier to spot exactly when an error occurs. Programmers also make liberal use of **utilities**, which are routines to sort records, open and close files, and perform other tasks that may recur many times in a software program.

Relatively few organizations have sufficient ongoing need for programming to justify even one full-time programmer (annual salary: $30,000 and up). Most organizations turn to firms that specialize in programming or to individual contract programmers. Both cost $35 to $55 an hour, depending on the difficulty and duration of the job. Clearly, it is cost-effective to give the programmer a clear, complete system detail description.

Conversion

When at last the documents, equipment, forms, software, human resources, and facilities have been brought to a state of readiness, management must take the final steps of documentation, data conversion, system testing, startup and shakeout, and postconversion review. These steps are shown in Figure 18.12.

Documentation

The temptation to cut corners can become almost irresistible at this late stage. After all, doesn't everyone know how the system works? This may be true on the day the system is accepted, but organizations change, personnel changes, and people forget. Documentation will collectively serve as a crucial sustaining resource. **Documentation** is the written description of all system components, elements, structures, procedures, controls, and back-ups, including reference manuals, reference cards, operations descriptions, instructions for system components, labels on tapes and disk packs, "help" segments embedded in applications programs, and comments in the programs. Documentation anticipates the ignorance of new employees and managers by describing the systems processes, how to operate them (including such details as how to change the printer ribbon!), the locations of major system components, and how the major segments interface. It should anticipate power and component failures by describing detailed procedures for system startup and restart after a shutdown. It should prominently identify whom to call in case of a major breakdown or emergency. The documentation of processes operation should support both staff training and user access to all system features by showing every

Figure 18.12 Conversion
Because most of the implementation work has been done, little or no new work is necessary during conversion. Rather, the efforts of the systems staff help fit together system components, find and eliminate error, and evaluate the new system's performance.

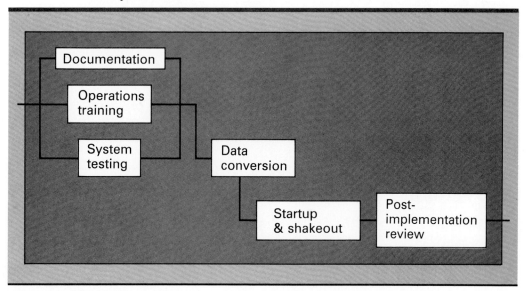

menu, describing what every option means, and explaining how to use the data entry screens. It must describe how backup, controls, and security controls operate. Other, more frequently revised documentation should outline the standard run schedule, including outputs and distribution.

Technical writers, supervised by systems experts, prepare the best documentation because they use simple, direct, explicit language. The systems analysts make certain the writers cover all necessary points from a user-oriented perspective. The key to good documentation is that systems expertise and writing expertise are both indispensable.

Conversion of Data to New Formats

If major differences exist between the old and new systems (altered data-item formats, new data items, new relations, or elimination of some data items), the data in the old system must be put in the structures defined for the new system. Data conversion is easiest if the new system uses the same computer as the old one. As a rule, however, system specialists can transform data electronically to a format usable on another computer. Data format conversion can take from less than an hour to many days, depending on the volume of data and the differences in format between the old data structure and the converted data structure. Users should verify data format conversion by comparing the specified conversion formats with test data from all converted files, then operating the processes with test data in the new formats. Actual conversion takes place in two stages, based on the frequency with which files are used. Less used files may be converted as convenient before the system becomes operational. Conversion of active on-line or operating files is virtually the last step before the new system becomes operational, after the old system has been decommissioned. On rare occasions, manual data entry proves to be the only way to incorporate data into the new system's files.

System Testing, Startup, and Shakeout

Although every step of the system development process points toward this transfer, its complexity requires that there be a comprehensive plan for achieving it. There are three broad strategies for system startup.

Block Conversion.   In **block conversion,** each stand-alone application or part of an application (and its operators and users) becomes operational when it passes acceptance testing. This continues until the entire system becomes operational. The blocks that depend on operationality of other blocks are converted last. For example, conversion of credit sales order entry would follow conversion of credit customer approval and reference. Block conversion does not risk the whole system at once if something doesn't work properly, and it doesn't require a lot of resources. Its disadvantages are that it prolongs the conversion process and, while it proceeds, the organization depends on two accounting systems, neither of which is complete.

Parallel Conversion. **Parallel conversion** makes one or more blocks of the new system operational without decommissioning the corresponding parts of the old system. The two systems, or fragments of them, operate on the same data for a period of time, during which their outputs are compared. Only when the new system has conclusively demonstrated a good record will the organization decommission the old system. Parallel conversion is inconvenient but virtually risk-free. This advantage may be offset by the extra cost (and confusion) of running two systems simultaneously.

"Cold-Turkey" Conversion. After successful acceptance testing, the controller may choose to dispense with the old system immediately. This **cold-turkey conversion** means startup of a system, or part of a system, without any back-up in the event the new system experiences failure. *If it proceeds successfully*, cold-turkey conversion offers the quickest and least disruptive route to bring up the new system. And the old system probably could be revived in whole or in part in an emergency if the new system should prove unreliable.

On the other hand, cold turkey is the highest risk route to new system startup. Nor does cold turkey work well with prototyping, design by forms, bottom-up system processes, or process-oriented system designs, all of which implement gradually and undergo modification to bring them closer to user requirements. In addition, cold-turkey conversion may mean delaying the benefits of fully operational status for accepted system components until all components have passed acceptance tests, which can take a long time. Cold-turkey conversion is popular with small accounting system projects; it is not popular with large systems because of the risk involved and the delays it entails if it fails.

Systems specialists usually rely on a combination of these strategies. For example, some modules may be run in parallel for a few days while others come up on a block basis. For new modules with no old system equivalent, cold-turkey conversion is the only choice.

Post–Detail Design and Conversion Review

Few periods in an accounting system manager's life are as exciting as the days after a new system becomes operational. Sound, competent work certainly contributes to a good conversion; however, one has to expect glitches. As they come to management's attention, they're listed, prioritized, and fixed. This period may last anywhere from a day to a month.

When the new accounting system appears to be running pretty smoothly, and operators and users are well on their way to mastering the system and using it productively, the time is ripe for management to schedule the **post implementation review (PIR)**, that is, review of the new system after it is operating normally to determine whether it needs any changes to achieve its original performance objectives. Omission of the PIR would leave management without a clear picture of whether it had gained what it expected from the systems process.

The best time for the PIR is likely to come two to six months after initial conversion. How long to wait, and whether the PIR lasts a few hours or several months, will depend on the system's complexity and how the organization has adapted to it. Its purpose is to determine whether the system has achieved the performance requirements defined during conceptual design. The reviewers will consider each requirement separately. If their verdict is negative, they must decide how important it is to improve performance of this objective and what additional steps will produce the improvement. In a sense, the PIR is a feedback control element on the entire system development and implementation process. Users, analysts, and consultants all learn from PIR how future projects may be designed and implemented with better results and less waste. The reviewers might use a format like the one in Table 18.10.

Management, not the consultants or the vendors, is responsible for conducting the PIR and following it up with appropriate action. However, the consultant can (and should) help out with the PIR.

For example, according to Table 18.10, the conceptual design included a performance requirement that a daily report of new authorized vendors be delivered to the purchasing director. The system as implemented issues this report weekly. This requirement thus receives an "N."

Table 18.10   Post Implementation Review Worksheet
Post implementation review not only uncovers major design failures; it is the fine tuning that tweaks a new system into a highly efficient, smooth running operation.

Performance Requirement	Met Satisfactorily? (Y/N)	Diagnosis If No	Priority (A = highest, C = lowest)	Recommended Action (given in exact steps)
Purchasing director receives daily report of new authorized vendors	N	Report generated only weekly	B	Revise run schedule for daily generation

The solution is to reschedule this report generator for daily runs. Even though this is a simple procedure, it receives a "B" priority because there are more important corrective tasks. The data processing director, upon receipt of the controller's Change Request Form, makes the change about four days after it's noted.

Summary

Turning a feasible conceptual design into an operational system requires careful planning and broad participation. Because implementation of a new system typically recurs only once every five to ten years, most organizations will not have the necessary experience and skills to conduct it satisfactorily. So management often relies on outside sources of expertise, particularly independent vendors and consultants. The consultants keep the process moving forward cost-effectively. They maintain contact between the users, the data processing department, the accountants, and the other technical experts such as systems analysts and programmers.

System implementation involves ongoing activities, such as site selection and staff training, and specific highly structured activities, including acquiring equipment and services from vendors, developing a detailed design, creating or modifying software, and documenting and testing the completed system. Implementation should take place in a way that minimizes the disruption and risk of disaster in data processing.

Management should follow up implementation with a hard-nosed review to determine which of the anticipated system benefits aren't present, and how best to bring them into existence.

Key Terms

acceptance testing
application-oriented design
block conversion
block testing
bottom-up design
bugs
cold-turkey conversion
conversion
critical-path scheduling
data-oriented design
decision table
design by forms
documentation
implementation
installed system

parallel conversion
post-implementation review (PIR)
process flowchart
program flowchart
prototyping
pseudocode
site preparation
structured language
template
top-down design
utilities
Vendor Evaluation and Review Technique (VERT)
walkthrough

Review Questions

1. What phase follows conceptual design? What are its five major objectives?

2. Name the four major stages in system implementation.

3. What processes must be covered in an implementation plan?

4. Explain the purpose of critical-path scheduling. What is the critical path?

5. What are the three main components of a request for proposal? What is the purpose of each component?

6. What are the major steps in selecting vendors to supply system equipment and services?

7. What is the VERT method for evaluating vendor proposals? Do you see any flaws in the point-evaluation method? Why is this method used? Can you think of a better method?

8. How does a steering committee help carry out the implementation plan? How does an implementation steering committee differ, if at all, from the conceptual-design steering committee?

9. What are the major steps in detail design? What is the end result of detail design?

10. What is prototyping? With what approach to detail design is prototyping associated? What design information is produced by prototyping? What work remains to be done after prototyping and before system startup?

11. What is a decision table? What is its purpose? What are its three major components?

12. What are the main steps in system conversion? What is the difference between cold-turkey and parallel conversion?

Discussion Questions

13. Look at Figure 18.3 on page 658, which illustrates a critical-path diagram. If evaluation of proposals requires 5 weeks instead of 3, how much longer will each path be? Will the critical path change? Why? If designing the accounts receivable application requires 10 weeks instead of 5, how much longer will the project take to complete? Will the critical path change? Why?

14. What factors help you evaluate a vendor's ability to meet commitments on your particular project? List and explain at least four of the factors mentioned in the text; *then add two more factors of your own and explain them.* If you were to allocate 40 total points to the vendor's ability to

meet commitments on your project, how would you weigh the factors you have listed for:

(a) a TV station planning to use the system for rapid billing of advertisers,

(b) a symphony association to use the system to keep track of pledges and payments against them, and

(c) a car manufacturer using just-in-time inventory management?

15. Which combinations of detail-design philosophies do the following situations represent?

(a) Bleakwood Company's programmers, acting on instructions from the chief financial officer and manufacturing vice president, have completed on schedule the design of a complex data structure to support an already approved manufacturing application.

(b) A committee of users at Jasper Company has discovered that several applications developed simultaneously cannot share data and must be extensively redesigned.

(c) China Grove Management is taking Friday off to celebrate the end of a three-month period of intense system development, during which they resolved many conflicting system requirements and successfully integrated diverse accounting applications.

(d) Circleville Implements Company has just accepted the resignations of two managers who could not adapt to the firm's new information system. They had no part in designing it, and the moderate changes they proposed could not be approved because extensive redesigning would have been required.

16. The Dessau Company decided to postpone site preparation and hardware delivery until the programs had all passed acceptance testing. Meanwhile, the firm would rely on the programmers to complete their testing on a similar computer in the programmers' office 550 miles away. What are some of the advantages and disadvantages of this decision?

17. One member of the Ganado School Board argued strongly that the district should not rely on computer screen forms for data capture or information reporting. He said, "If we can only record or report data through a computer screen, then if anything happens to the computer, we can't get our data! I hope you will design this system so that all data are first captured on paper, then transcribed into the system; and so that all reports are printed out before they are displayed on the computer screen."

As the school district's consultant, respond to these remarks.

18. Travis Merchants Bank prepared an RFP and sent it out to five vendors, three of whom responded with proposals. The proposal review produced the information shown in the table on the next page.

	Proposal A	Proposal B	Proposal C
Long-run confidence (30 points maximum)	22	25	15
Ability to meet commitments (40 points maximum)	38	25	30
Cost (10 points maximum)	$49,000	$55,000	$35,000
Number of requirements met (90 requirements maximum; 21 points maximum)	65	75	60

Required:

Calculate the points to allot for number of requirements met, add up the totals, and rank the proposals.

19. Travis Merchants Bank has selected Smith & Obote as a vendor and is preparing a contract for the vendor to sign. You want the vendor to begin work by June 1. The vendor has assigned Tom Smith to be in charge of the systems project. The vendor offered to perform requirements 1 through 10, 13 through 20, and 24 through 30 from the RFP. The bank wants Smith & Obote to agree to a $100-per-day penalty if it does not finish by December 1 and to do all the work itself. Smith and Obote quoted a fixed price of $24,000.

Required:

Rephrase this information into language suitable for a contract.

20. Sometimes the point-allocation method described in the chapter will not completely represent an organization's real preferences. For example, suppose the points fall as shown below:

	Vendor A	Vendor B
Confidence in vendor (maximum 20)	20	0
Ability of vendor to meet commitments (maximum 10)	10	0
Cost (maximum 40)	0	40
Number of requirements met (maximum 30)	20	15
Total (maximum 100)	50	55

Vendor B scored zero on two important categories, yet is ranked higher on points. These two vendors are the only choices; you must buy from one of them.

Required:

(a) Suggest how you could reweight the four categories to achieve a point score favoring Vendor A. In your opinion, is this "fair"?
(b) Suppose you used a nonlinear method of computing points. For example, suppose you square the number of points *not* earned by

each vendor and sum these squares. (For example, for number of requirements met Vendor A would have $(30 - 20)^2 = 100$ points.) The vendor with the fewest points computed this way would be preferred. Do this calculation. Does this "solve" the problem? In your opinion, is this fair?

21. Refer to the descriptions of the credit sales and accounts receivable records and files in Chapter 7, pages 220–225. This description is not a data dictionary, but it includes information from which a data dictionary could be prepared.

Required:

Prepare a data dictionary for the credit sales and accounts receivable application. Include in it only the following information: the data-item name, source document or application that originates it, file(s) in which it appears, report(s) in which it appears, and application(s) that use it. Do not include pointers.

22. Do the same for purchasing and accounts payable, using the descriptions of records and files in Chapter 8, pages 272–280.

23. Do the same for inventory and cost accounting, using the descriptions of records and files in Chapter 9, pages 319–322.

24. Calvert Paint Company mixes paints that other companies sell under their own brand names. To keep track of paint mixes for all its customers (each of whom may sell 50 to 100 unique colors), Calvert maintains a computer file of mix formulas. Recently, Calvert has been troubled by a trend among its customers to order much smaller batches more frequently. This slows down production, since batch preparation time doesn't depend on batch size.

Two systems vendors offer data base programs that allow faster access to formulas. The programs can also compare formulas to select those of different companies that are sufficiently similar to be mixed together, increasing batch size. Calvert is not sure how much confidence to put in these firms and has collected some information about them. It intends to give this information a 20-percent weight in a point-system evaluation of the vendors' systems.

Vendor A's system has been in use five years; Vendor B's program, two years. Vendor A does not upgrade its program, but it has a users' association of other paint-mixing companies that does share its own upgrades. Vendor B intends to issue an upgrade but has not done so, and no users' association exists for its system. Vendor A went into business years ago with its current system. Within the last year it has introduced an integrated accounting system, but Calvert will not be in the market for such a system for at least two years. Vendor B has been in business since 1960, specializing in accounting systems and technical support for its mainstay line of accounting systems. In 1965,

Vendor B was briefly in bankruptcy. The firm was acquired by a family that has operated it ever since. It does not issue financial statements. Both firms have acceptable credit ratings. Vendor A's users' association has 42 members out of the 80 systems it has installed. Vendor B has installed 51 systems. Calvert was told by Vendor A customers that its system was highly satisfactory only with extensive support from Vendor A consultants, which Vendor A provides. Vendor B customers had no difficulty with its system, did not receive any consulting support, but felt in need of additional speed and reporting features, which Vendor B kept promising would be in the coming upgrade.

Required:

Develop a point-evaluation scheme to quantify the relative confidence Calvert should have in these two vendors.

25. At State University, students register a month before classes start. Each student completes a multicopy course-request form. This form has space for the student's name, social security number, billing address, class, major, and preferential status, if any. It provides space for the student to select up to eight courses. The student lists the course name and section identification number (the university computer maintains a record of the meeting time, prerequisites, and room size in which this number is the record key). The student keeps one copy, and the student's college keeps one copy. The registrar keeps the original and uses it to create a series of direct-access course-request records that the course-scheduling program uses to compute each student's schedule. Meanwhile, the last two copies of the course-request form go to the college bursar.

The bursar computes the student's bill and sends it (along with one copy of the course-request form) to the student, who must pay within 30 days, using the course-request form copy as a remittance advice. When the student pays, the bursar sends the remittance advice (copy of the course-request form) to the registrar, who matches it with his copy of the same form. The registrar mails the actual schedule to all paid students the week before classes start. If there were any discrepancies between courses billed and courses actually scheduled, the bursar will send such students a refund covering the discrepancy.

Required:

Prepare a document flowchart showing what happens to each copy of the course-request form.

26. Red Rock Record Store keeps some 70,000 record and tape titles in stock. To help find titles requested by customers, the firm has implemented a stand-alone computerized inventory-location system. This system allows fast, accurate service, so the firm has paid a lot of attention to its reliability and security. You have been called in to provide

an independent post implementation review to evaluate these aspects of the system.

You find that the three computer terminals in the sales area (used by clerks to locate records and record sales) are separated from customers by shatter-resistant glass. The three inventory-record maintenance terminals are located in the back of the store. Armored cables from all terminals lead directly to the computer room, located below ground level. This room is actually two rooms, constructed of 6-inch-thick steel-reinforced concrete, both temperature and humidity are controlled by a dual-compressor system with back-up electrical generator. In one room resides the computer itself, a microcomputer with one megabyte of RAM and two 30-Mb hard disks to provide on-line storage. This room has its own uninterruptible power supply with surge protectors. It has a carbon dioxide gas fire extinguishing system (carbon dioxide will not harm the equipment or data) and emergency oxygen supplies for the operators. There is a kitchenette so they need not leave the computer unattended in order to eat. In the other room is a 25-cubic-foot, 6-ton fireproof safe, where all operating programs are kept. (Back-up program copies are made daily and kept at a secure off-site location.) Both rooms may be locked from inside by the two computer operators, to seal them off from fire or disturbance. The rooms may be opened from outside only by a special combination lock, and only the company president knows its combination. All salespeople, terminal operators, and computer operators are bonded and undergo one week of competency training annually. Although there have been no losses of data since implementation, development of the new system was very expensive. Management is beginning to wonder if all the features included in the new system were really necessary; that is, management would like to know if the new features remedy actual weaknesses.

Required:

Identify the security measures in the description above. Classify each as necessary or not necessary. Give a short explanation of each "not necessary" classification (there are five "not necessary" measures). Explain how systems development could have been controlled and conducted so as not to produce a design that included so many unnecessary features.

27. During work on the accounting system of Mathis Dentist's Supply, the cashier's function was reviewed. Management wanted to computerize and automate the credit-verification part of the cashier's job. They wrote out the following description of the cashier's function:

    "The cashier first makes certain the customer has completed a three-part form. If not, the customer must return to the order taker. Next the cashier determines how the customer wishes to pay. If he or she wants to use credit, the cashier checks to be certain the customer has credit. If not, the cashier offers the option of cash or charge. If charge, the cashier asks for a credit card and verifies that the card is valid. If the card is not valid or the customer indicates a cash sale, the cashier may accept currency or a check. For a check over $50, the cashier verifies that the customer is in good standing with the bank and the merchants' association. If the customer does not have credit with Mathis, the cashier offers a credit application. If the customer has completed a credit application, the cashier refers him or her to the credit officer. If the customer has credit and wishes to use it, the cashier accesses the customer's computer record and enters "X" in the "Use Credit?" field. The cashier then stamps the three-part form. If the customer wishes to charge and has a valid charge card, the cashier completes the charge form, has the customer sign it, gives the customer the top copy and carbons, and places the other copies in the cash register.

Required:

Prepare a decision table incorporating all the above procedures and rules.

28. At the Segovia Restaurant Supply Company an apparent major weakness was discovered when the consultants conducted a walkthrough of the credit sales application. The weakness appears in the following anecdote:

Lowe, a restaurant owner, opened a charge account. A week later, he appeared at the order taker's desk and ordered 300 sets of premium-quality stainless-steel tableware at a cost of $11.00 each. The order taker took all the appropriate information and gave Lowe the three-part form. Lowe took the form to the cashier and indicated that it would be a credit sale. The cashier recorded this information in the computer record and stamped the three-part form. Lowe received his order and left. A week later, Lowe appeared with the invoice, saying "There must be a mistake. I charged this order to my Moneybucks credit card. You are trying to bill me twice! I insist you cancel this charge." When a search for the Moneybucks charge form was unsuccessful, Lowe said, "You must have lost it." The company knew it had been "had," but without some evidence of Lowe's verbal acceptance of the charge, could not collect from him.

Required:

(a) Identify the weakness.
(b) Describe a new procedure or change that would correct the weakness without forcing the company to abandon its accounting system.

Case: San Angelo Lumber Company, Part 1

San Angelo Lumber Company has implemented an integrated accounting and control system designed to reduce loss by pilferage and incorrect order filling. A customer must first see an order taker. The order taker, using an on-line terminal to check inventories and prices, enters the contractor's order. The computer creates an order record and then prints out the order on a three-part form, which the customer carries to a cashier located elsewhere in the store. The customer can pay in any of three ways: with approval, on 30-day revolving credit; with a recognized credit card; or with cash. The means of payment is entered into the sale record, which is created at the same time as on-line adjustments to the computer-kept inventory records.

The cashier stamps *paid* on all three parts of the form. The customer carries the form to the yard manager, who fills the order, stamps all three parts, keeps one, and sends the customer to the gate (a high fence encloses the yard). The gate guard takes one copy of the form, compares the order to the items and quantities on the form and, if all is in order, allows the contractor to proceed. The lumberyard accountant later compares the guard's copy of the form, the yard manager's copy, and the computer record.

The consultants' post implementation review of the system produced the following list of points:

- The cashier and the gate guard are in the same room.
- The approved-credit file is not on-line.
- The accountant spends a great deal of time matching all the forms and computer records.
- The three-part form doesn't have a sequential number printed on it.
- The three-part form doesn't have a date on it.
- The data processing operator is two weeks behind posting new inventory deliveries.
- Five partial refunds were given to customers who returned their copies of the form with the gate guard's notation that the quantities in their trucks at the gate inspection were less than the quantities they had paid for.

Required:
(a) Draw a process diagram illustrating how the lumberyard takes, fills, and verifies a customer's order and credit.
(b) Point out three weaknesses identified by the consultants.

(c) Evaluate each point raised by the consultants: Does it actually represent a system weakness? How important do you think it is? How would you correct it?

Case: San Angelo Lumber Company, Part 2

The San Angelo Lumber Company also asked the consultants to develop a budgeting system for purposes of preparing and reviewing performance reports. The consultants decided to start with sales to contractors. The key to the plan was a file containing estimates of sales to contractors classified according to:

- Contractor size
- Credit, charge, or cash sale
- Local (San Angelo only) or regional contractor
- Month of the year
- Type of merchandise (lumber, hardware, roofing, tools, supplies, etc.)

Required:

(a) Discuss, as specifically as you can, how sales and accounts receivable must operate in conjunction with the budgeting system to produce sales-performance reports. Prepare a system diagram, and use whatever narrative and descriptive formats you prefer.
(b) Prepare a format for one sales-performance report. To whom should this report be sent? Explain how your report enhances financial control.

Case: San Angelo Lumber Company, Part 3

The San Angelo Lumber Company contractor-sales accounting, budgeting, and financial-performance systems have been completed and are operating satisfactorily. Now the company wants to know the *profitability* of each of its types of sales; this will involve matching the cost of lumber, and so on, with sales. The consultants have proposed two conceptual designs for doing this:

Design A: Maintain perpetual inventory files, showing the actual cost of each item in stock (for very low-cost items such as nails, the individual item would be the box, carton, or barrel) as derived from vendors' invoices. Upon sale, transfer these actual costs to the proper category of sale. Program the computer to add up the costs in each category and subtract the total from corresponding sales revenues to obtain that category's contribution to profit. For example, if sales in the category "credit roofing-materials sales to large out-of-town contractors in December" are $3,400, and related costs are $2,100, its contribution is $1,300. Contractor returns would be deducted from both sales and cost of sales.

Design B: As purchases occur, classify them according to the type of item they represent. As sales occur, allocate the average cost of all items of a given type to that category of sale. Calculate the contribution as in Design A.

Discuss the apparent advantages and disadvantages of each design, including relative cost, complexity, precision, and reliability. If any useful information would be omitted from performance reports by either plan, identify it.

Comprehensive Case

Sports Products, Inc.

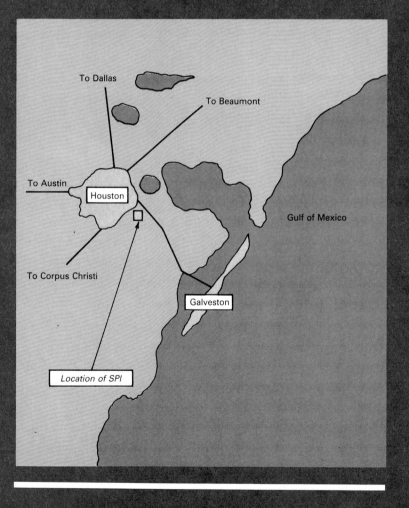

Introduction

Tom Smith founded Sports Products, Incorporated (SPI), in 1975 in Houston, Texas, as a producer of fiberglass motorboats. The company has been successful since its start. In 1977 SPI began to make small sailboats, and in 1978 it discontinued the motorboat line. So that it could outfit sailboaters completely, SPI in 1980 expanded its product line to include marine equipment and nautical clothing. The company grew and moved to larger locations in 1978 and 1982. The inset on page 702 shows SPI's present location near Houston.

Of all its products, only sailboats are produced by the company, in a factory behind the sales showroom. The marine equipment and nautical clothing are purchased from distributors. Inventories are kept in a warehouse near the showroom and boat factory. All managerial and administrative facilities are located in an office building at the same site. Figure 1 shows the physical layout.

Figure 1

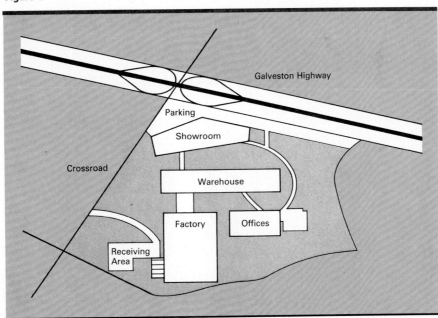

Table 1   SPI Sales, 1983–1987 (in thousands)

	1983	1984	1985	1986	1987
Sailboats	$1,300	$1,400	$1,400	$1,450	$1,550
Marine Eqpt	350	460	600	640	710
Nautical clthng	400	430	470	550	530
Total sales	$2,050	$2,290	$2,470	$2,640	$2,790

SPI prepares an annual budget in December for the calendar year. Sales are seasonal, with most activity from March to September. The boat factory operates at a steady rate, although SPI watches the sales rate in March and April and changes the rate of production if actual sales differ significantly from budgeted sales. Thus, sailboat inventories are at their highest in early March and at their lowest in early October. All other items are ordered from distributors so as to have about a seven-day supply at the present selling rate. Sales for the past five years for the three major product lines are shown in Table 1 and, graphically, in Figure 2.

Figure 2   SPI Sales, 1983–1987 (in thousands)

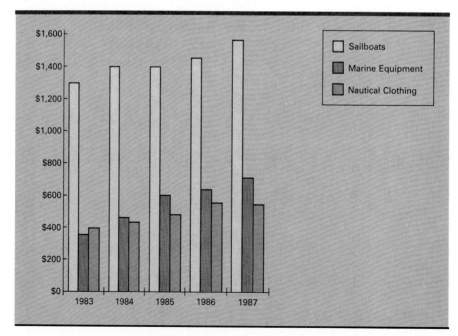

Figure 3   Organization Chart for Sports Products, Inc.

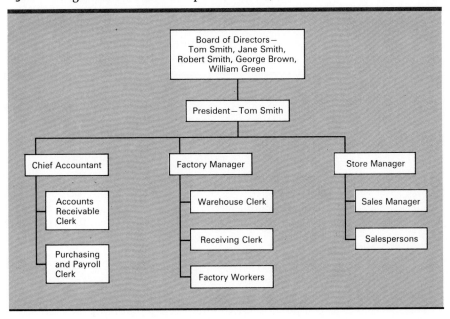

SPI management's objective is to enjoy profitability and moderate growth in the marine-recreational markets as a family-owned and family-operated business. Simplified 1987 financial statements for SPI appear in Exhibit 1 on pages 706–707. The company's organization is simple, reflects family involvement, and has been stable in the form shown in Figure 3 for several years.

The company president, Tom Smith, owns 55 percent of the stock. Other family members in management own the remainder. All family members in management have earned university degrees in business and have several years of experience in their present positions. All of them are active recreational sailors.

The company has experienced competition from several other marine sporting-goods companies. However, owing to the quality and reasonable prices of its products, it continues to expand. The company's debt is limited to the amount necessary to finance inventory growth during the winter and fall months. This debt is retired by June each year. The management is financially conservative.

SPI's accounting system is manual and consists of general ledger, general journal, accounts receivable subsidiary ledger, purchases journal, and cost accounting subsidiary ledger. During the next year, the firm plans to convert to an accounting system based on an as yet unselected com-

Exhibit 1   SPI's Financial Statements for 1987

Sports Products, Incorporated
Income Statement
Year Ended December 31, 1987

	Sailboats	Marine Equipment	Nautical Clothing	Totals
Revenue	$1,550	$710	$530	$2,790
Less direct variable costs				
Materials	210	350	240	800
Manufacturing wages	450			450
Selling costs	220	175	110	505
Contribution before				
fixed direct costs	670	185	180	1,035
Less fixed direct costs				
Salaries	225	85	55	365
Other overhead	270	75	65	410
Contribution after all				
product-line costs	175	25	60	260
Less non-product-line costs				
Administrative costs				135
Interest				55
Income taxes				45
Addition to retained earnings				$ 25

mercial software package and running on one or more networked micro-computers. SPI has never had a financial audit or survey of internal controls. Although management has not had any bad experiences caused by the present information system, it is looking forward to seeing how much support it can design into the new system.

Credit Sales and Accounts Receivable

All sales occur in the showroom; only merchandise currently in stock is sold (no backorders). After the customer has selected merchandise, the salesperson carries out the following steps:

Exhibit 1 *continued*

Sports Products, Incorporated
Balance Sheet
December 31, 1987

Assets

Cash		$ 155
Short-term securities		558
Accounts receivable (net)		75
Manufacturing materials inventories		5
Completed sailboat inventory		200
Marine equipment inventory		5
Nautical clothing inventory		4
Real property		125
Buildings		495
Equipment		235
Provision for depreciation on buildings and equipment	(377)	
Intangible assets		15
Total assets		$1,495

Equities

Trade accounts and wages payable	$ 155
Notes payable	550
Original investment	250
Accumulated retained earnings to 12-31-86	515
1987 addition to retained earnings	25
Total equities	$1,495

---

1. Identifies the customer and completes the top part of a sales invoice form (shown in Figure 4).

2. Identifies the merchandise the customer has selected and fills in the item code, item description, quantity, and price on the sales invoice.

3. Calculates the total amount of the sale, including tax, and enters this on the sales invoice.

4. Informs the customer of the total and asks how the customer will pay—cash, check, SPI credit, or major credit card—and enters this information on the sales invoice as follows:

   a. Check or major credit card: The salesperson accepts the check, records the customer's identification, verifies with the credit bureau that the customer's credit record is satisfactory, and secures approval of the sales manager to complete the sale.

   b. SPI credit: The salesperson calls the accounts receivable clerk to verify the credit.

5. The salesperson completes the sale by accepting the customer's cash or check or by completing an appropriate imprinted charge form and getting the customer's signature on it, and delivering the merchandise to the customer along with copy A of the sales invoice. Copy B is kept in the showroom sales file, and copy C is sent to the accounts receivable clerk. The charge form used for both major and SPI credit is shown in Figure 5.

    The collected B copies of sales invoices form the sales journal. At the close of each day, the sales manager uses the B copies to prepare a sales summary, using the first two digits of the item identification code to show sales by major categories. About 500 sales occur each week, of which about 20 percent are paid by cash, 20 percent by check, 40 percent by major credit, and 20 percent by SPI credit. The form used by the sales manager

Figure 4   SPI Sales Invoice

Sales Invoice

Date: _____ Clerk ID: _____   No. 99165   Copy A

Sold by   SPORTS PRODUCTS, INC.
        14000 Gulf Freeway
        Houston, Texas 77056
        713-555-1212

To: _____
Street _____
City/State/ZIP _____
Phone: _____

Item code	Item description	Quantity	Price each	Total price
	Sales tax			

Payment ☐ Cash ☐ CC(_____)
Check one ☐ Check ☐ SPI Charge

Total sale

SPI credit/check OK by _____

Figure 5 **SPI and Major Credit Card Charge Form**

Customer Copy

Account
or card
number

Date	Clerk
Description	Auth. no.

SPORTS PRODUCTS, INC.
Houston, Texas 77056

The issuer of the card identified on this item is authorized to pay the amount shown as TOTAL upon proper presentation. I promise to pay such TOTAL subject to and in accordance with the agreement governing use of my credit.

Purchases & services		
Tax		
TOTAL		

Signature X________________________

Please Retain This Copy for Your Records ☐ SPI CHARGE ☐ OTHER

to prepare the daily sales summary from the sales journal is shown in Figure 6.

The clerks clear the cash register at the end of each day and complete (a) a short form shown in Figure 7 reconciling cash register contents to the sales invoices, (b) a deposit slip for the cash and checks, and (c) a transmittal form for major credit card invoice slips (this form and the deposit slips are provided by SPI's bank). A clerk carries the deposit and credit card invoices to the bank. (The bank, as agent for the credit-card companies, credits SPI's account for the sales proceeds, less a fee.)

SPI has about 500 approved credit customers. The collected C copies of sales invoices are examined, and those indicating SPI charge are used to post the accounts receivable subsidiary ledger. The subsidiary ledger is actually a series of folders, one for each customer. Each folder contains a summarizing form that shows the customer name and billing address, and a number of lines for recording transactions and resulting balances. This summarizing form is shown in Figure 8.

The accounts receivable clerk posts credit sales and finance charges to these forms daily. When a credit sales invoice has been posted, it is stamped *posted* and placed in the folder in invoice-number sequence.

SPI uses cycle billing; that is, the accounts receivable clerk prepares and mails statements for a different group of thirty customers each day.

Figure 6 Daily Sales Summary

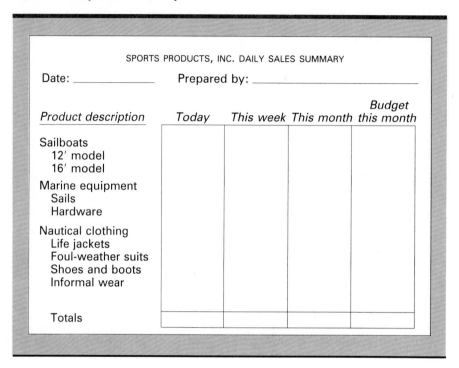

SPORTS PRODUCTS, INC. DAILY SALES SUMMARY

Date: _____ Prepared by: _____

Product description	Today	This week	This month	Budget this month
Sailboats				
12′ model				
16′ model				
Marine equipment				
Sails				
Hardware				
Nautical clothing				
Life jackets				
Foul-weather suits				
Shoes and boots				
Informal wear				
Totals				

Figure 7 Cash Register Clearing Form

CASH REGISTER CLEARING FORM

Clerk: _____ Date: _____

Balance in register per clearing form of date _____	$
Sales per cash register tape	$
Refunds, payouts, etc.	$
Less cash withdrawn for deposit	$ (_____)
Balance remaining in cash register per this date	$ _____

Figure 8 **Permanent Credit Record**

PERMANENT CREDIT RECORD

Name				Home Phone	

Address				Office Phone	

City	State	ZIP	Employer		

Credit Limit	Approved by	Date	

Date	Charge/ Remittance No.	Previous Balance	Debit	Credit	Balance	By

The clerk does this by using a customer's summary form to complete the customer statement shown in Figure 9.

If, when preparing statements, the accounts receivable clerk sees that a customer has not paid within 25 days, the chief accountant adds to the customer's account a service charge for that month of 1.5 percent of the unpaid balance. If a customer does not make a payment on an outstanding balance for two months, the accounts receivable clerk adds that customer's name to a list of persons to receive a phone call and letter from Tom Smith.

Purchasing and Inventory

Each day, the sales manager and clerks continually replenish showroom inventory from the warehouse. The sales manager also surveys the warehouse retail stock quantities for about one-fifth of all items that must be ordered. In this way, all items are surveyed once a week. The survey requires about 60 minutes to complete. In deciding whether to reorder each item, the sales manager relies on his "feel" for sales volume and how far in advance the item must be reordered. The factory manager is re-

Figure 9 **SPI Customer Statement**

SPORTS PRODUCTS, INC.
14000 Gulf Freeway
Houston, Texas 77056

Date:

Customer name & address
go in this space

Amount due: $ _____

Amount remitted: $

Please return this portion with your payment.

Summary of activity:

Balance due on previous statement	$
Credit sales	$
Finance charges	$
Returns and allowances	$
Cash payments	$
Balance due with this statement	$ _____

Terms: Balance due 25 days after date above. Save this part for your
records.

sponsible for reviewing materials and supplies inventories and maintaining sufficient levels to support planned production without interruption for one month. At the end of the week, the sales and factory managers provide their reorder recommendations to the purchasing clerk, who completes purchase orders to approved suppliers.

The sales manager places the recommendations on the form shown in Figure 10, completing the first three columns only. The purchasing clerk completes the final column, using the name of an approved vendor associated with the item being ordered. This name is taken from a file maintained by the purchasing clerk in two parts. The first part is a file of items normally stocked and sold, or used in producing sailboats; each record in this file corresponds to one such item and contains the item number, description, and vendor name. The second part is a file in which each record corresponds to an approved vendor and contains the vendor name and address and the numbers of items that vendor normally supplies. At the present time, some 1,700 different items are supplied by 11 vendors. Each vendor is assigned a 2-digit code. The item-identifying codes have the structure AB = CDE = FG, broken down as shown on the next page.

AB = the broad category
00 = the control account for inventory; not used to identify
     individual items
01–19 = unassigned
20–39 = marine equipment
40–59 = nautical clothing
60–69 = direct materials for use in manufacturing sailboats
70–79 = indirect materials for use in manufacturing sailboats
80–99 = office supplies and other items not purchased for resale
CDE = a subcategory to designate a particular type of item
FG = a code used to identify the vendor of the item

After identifying the vendor for each item recommended for purchase, the purchasing clerk places all the items to be purchased from one vendor on a purchase order to that vendor and mails the vendor one copy of the purchase order. A copy of each purchase order also goes to the purchasing clerk's files, the receiving clerk, and the accounts payable clerk.

The vendor will, after receiving the purchase order, prepare and ship the order. With the order will be the vendor's packing slip, listing the items in the shipment. In addition, the vendor sends an invoice, which also serves as a shipping notice, to SPI's accounts payable clerk. When the

Figure 10 Purchase Order Recommendation Form

SPORTS PRODUCTS, INC.   PURCHASE RECOMMENDATION

Date: _____   Recommended by: _____

Item No.	Description	Quantity	Vendor

order arrives, it is met and, if it references a purchase order on file, accepted by the receiving clerk. The receiving clerk opens the order, verifies that the packing slip accurately describes its contents, and sends the packing slip and shipping documents furnished by the shipper as a receiving report to the accounts payable clerk. After the receiving clerk accepts incoming shipments of materials and supplies, they are placed in the warehouse. Another employee supervises the warehouse, placing incoming shipments on the shelves, issuing retail goods to salesclerks, and issuing supplies and materials for sailboat production.

If the accounts payable clerk has available the original purchase order, the vendor's invoice, and the receiving report, the clerk can verify that (a) an order was placed, (b) a shipment fitting the description of merchandise ordered has been received, and (c) an invoice accurately charging for the merchandise has also been received.

If these conditions are met, the clerk attaches these documents to a voucher, fills in the voucher information, and sends the voucher and attachments to the chief accountant, asking that the vendor be paid. A standard journal entry sets up the voucher as an account payable:

Factory Direct Materials Suspense	$
Factory Indirect Materials Suspense	$
Marine Equipment	$
Nautical Clothing	$
Office Supplies and Other Items Not Purchased for Resale	$
Accounts Payable (vendor code)	$

Every month, the accounts payable clerk prepares reports giving the following information: total purchases of marine equipment, nautical clothing, factory materials and supplies, and administrative supplies.

Cash Receipts and Payments

The remittance advice and payment are received by the chief accountant, who opens the mail and prepares a daily deposit of the remittances it contains. This deposit goes to the bank before noon and so is separate from the deposit of daily sales receipts. The chief accountant sorts the remittance advices and posts them to the appropriate customer accounts receivable. The total of these credits to accounts receivable should equal the total of that day's bank deposit of cash received by mail.

The chief accountant is responsible for paying expenses and for operating SPI's accounting systems. The chief accountant prepares and signs checks to creditors based on properly prepared vouchers from the purchasing clerk. The chief accountant writes the check number on the voucher, writes the voucher number on the check, stamps *cancel* on the voucher, sends the check to the creditor, and files the voucher.

Payroll

Seven employees work in the factory. Along with the four salespersons, three clerks, and the managers, they are paid weekly. The purchasing clerk maintains a file containing, for each employee, a record with the person's name, address, salary, deductions, and other payroll information. An example of such a record is shown in Figure 11.

The purchasing clerk prepares payroll data, to be processed by Cox & Box, an accounting and service bureau company. SPI's procedure is typical of many small and medium-size businesses that do not prepare

Figure 11 SPI Employee Record

SPI EMPLOYEE RECORD

Name

Year: 19____

SSN _ _ _ - _ _ - _ _ _ _

Address

Position	Date	Salary/hr	Appr. by

City   State   ZIP

In case of emergency contact:

Number of dependents [   ]   Date hired: _ - _ - _

Medical plan   A ☐   B ☐   C ☐

Life insurance: $ _____ ,000   Beneficiary: _____

Other Deductions (Explain):

Record of Salary Paid

Pay period	Gross pay	Income tax	OASI	Medical	Life	Other	Net pay

payroll internally. The outside firm accepts payroll data from SPI; calculates payroll information; writes and delivers payroll checks; prepares vouchers for checks remitting payroll withholdings to OASI, IRS, and insurance companies; and prepares journal entries that the chief accountant will post, reflecting payroll liabilities and expenses.

Because all employees are salaried and work a regular forty-hour week, there is no need to keep track of hours worked. However, pay rates change, bonuses are paid, new employees are hired, and old ones quit or retire. Therefore, the purchasing clerk updates the employee master file weekly to be certain the payroll is prepared using current information. At the end of each pay period Cox & Box receives the current version of this file in addition to the current list of employees on the form in Figure 12, which shows the current period's payroll information.

The service bureau returns the paychecks, the updated payroll file, and a journal entry for recording payroll in the general journal. The journal entry format is specified by SPI as follows:

(1)	Gross Factory Direct Labor Payroll Suspense	$	
	Gross Factory Indirect Labor Payroll Suspense	$	
	Gross Sales Payroll Expense	$	
	Gross Administrative Payroll Expense	$	
	Income Tax Withheld Liability		$
	OASI Withheld Liability		$
	OASI—Employers Liability		$
	Medical Insurance Withheld Liability		$
	Medical Insurance—Employers Liability		$
	Life Insurance Withheld Liability		$
	Life Insurance—Employers Liability		$
	Other Withholdings Liability		$
	Salaries Payable to Employees		$
	To record payroll for week of __, 19__.		
(2)	Salaries Payable to Employees	$	
	Cash		$
	To record pay checks to employees.		

Manufacturing the Sailboats

Two sailboat models—12 foot and 16 foot—are produced. The manufacturing process takes place in the factory and is very simple. The fiberglass molds for hulls and decks are filled with woven fiberglass cloth and loose fibers and then sprayed with resin. The mixture is allowed to harden, then the molds are removed, cleaned, and set aside for reuse. The hull and deck of each boat are glued, then riveted, together. The metal hardware—such as the motor mount, cleats, seats, tiller, rudder, mast step, blocks, and trim—are attached. Each sailboat is mounted on a boat trailer, which

Figure 12 Payroll Form

Cox & Box Service Bureau Payroll Form

Name	Status Changes?	Hours Worked	Adjustments
Allen, William			
Bizzell, Susan			
Catt, Morris T.			
Davidson, Helen			
Fonken, Johann			
Glenn, Joshua			
Green, William			
Kelley, Donn			
Kielberg, Barbara			
Lowell, John			
Mahoney, Mary			
Morris, David			
Smith, Esther			
Smith, Robert			
Smith, Tom			

is purchased complete from a trailer producer. Quality control checks are made throughout this process and, after a final inspection, the boat-trailer combination is moved to the warehouse, where it remains until it is sold.

SPI has made a bill of materials for each boat model. The factory produces only one model at a time, at a rate of eight per week. Before a production run, SPI decides how many units to produce and the starting date for the run. The factory and sales managers consult the budget and recent sales figures, and plan boat production for three months in advance. The factory manager prepares work orders, which identify the model to be produced, the number of units to produce, and the date when the units all should be completed. Next, the factory manager, using the bill of materials for the boat model specified in the work order, prepares a materials requisition for the warehouse. One requisition is prepared at the start of the week, and occasionally other, smaller ones will be required during the week, usually to compensate for waste or spoilage.

In the factory, there are several cost pools, which include individual costs as follows:

DLC   Direct labor—hull layup, assembly, finishing

ILC   Indirect labor—quality control, employee benefits, factory administration

DMC   Direct materials—fiberglass, resin, fittings, trim

IMC   Indirect materials—fasteners, rags, cleaners

OHC   Overhead costs—depreciation, maintenance, warranties, taxes

These costs pools are debited with the costs of all related items as soon as the voucher is canceled. That is, as soon as possible after a voucher or payroll is paid, an allocating entry is made that places the expenses in the appropriate cost pools. For example, if $13,000 in materials and supplies have been ordered from Marine Suppliers, Inc., received, invoiced, and paid for, the allocating entry might be:

DMC	$4,500	
IMC	7,000	
Administrative Supplies	1,500	
Purchases (from Marine Suppliers, Inc.)		$13,000

A factory payroll is divided among direct and indirect labor cost pools as shown in the payroll liability entry. For example, in the week of January 22, the amounts debited to suspense in these pools were:

DLC	$8,000
ILC	4,000

The five factory cost pools are allocated among boats produced thus:

Boat Model	DLC	ILC	DMC	IMC	OHC
1	$200	$200	$300	$300	$ 400
2	300	200	600	800	1,000

At the end of each month, the chief accountant notes the number of units of each model that have been completed and transferred to the warehouse. Thus, in this case he would withdraw from each cost pool (and place in Finished Boats Inventory) the unit costs shown, multiplied by the number of units completed.

Relative to the number of boat units completed, very few boat units were left incomplete at the end of the month under discussion. For each such unit, 100 percent of the DMC costs shown were removed from the DMC cost pool. Then the unit's percentage of completion was estimated. That percentage was multiplied by the costs shown in each of the other four cost pools, removed from them, and in combination with the DMC costs, added to Inventory—Incomplete Work Orders.

At the end of the month, if any costs remain in a cost pool, the chief accountant reports them to the factory manager and the president as a performance variance. In summary, the costs are handled as follows:

Add:	debits from	Payroll
		Taxes Paid
		Vouchers Paid
		General journal entries
Subtract:	credits from	Finished Boats Inventory
		Incomplete Work Orders
Difference:	Favorable performance variance (if credit balance)	
	Unfavorable performance variance (if debit balance)	

Assignments for Sports Products, Inc.

These case assignments work most effectively if they are completed as part of the work for the chapter to which they pertain.

Chapter 1

First read the case from beginning to end. Then prepare to discuss the following questions, either in class or as a member of a group:

1. Who are the primary users of the SPI accounting system?
2. What are the objectives of the SPI accounting system?
3. What are the boundaries of the SPI accounting system?
4. What are the information requirements of SPI management?
5. Can the information requirements be fulfilled?

Take notes on the discussion, and after it is over, write up your notes as a memorandum to SPI's management.

Chapter 2

1. Examine the SPI organization chart. Does this company have a functional or a market-oriented organizational structure? Draw an organization chart for SPI that reorganizes the company according to the other structure.

At SPI, the sales manager is responsible for replenishing showroom inventory from the warehouse.

2. Draw a data flow diagram of the purchasing and receiving process, including voucher preparation, as described in the case.
3. List all documents that are generated or used in the purchasing and receiving process. Beside each document, list the titles of persons who create, use, or receive that document, or a copy of it.
4. Does the decision to replenish showroom stock involve risk? If so, what is the nature of the risk? If not, select another decision made at SPI that does involve risk and describe its nature.
5. One product sold in the showroom is nautical clothing. The sales manager is deciding how much clothing to order. The rule for ordering is "order enough each month so that the order plus the amount on hand equal the next month's expected sales volume." The manager has prepared three estimates of next month's sales volume: conservative, $70,000; most likely, $90,000; optimistic, $120,000. The amount of clothing on hand now is $60,000. Costs of keeping the nautical clothing inventory amount to 1 percent per week of the average amount on hand. Any inventory in excess of next month's sales volume must be

placed on sale at 5 percent off. Prepare a matrix, similar to Figure 2.5, describing the costs of this decision, given the three possible sales-volume levels and three possible order-size levels.

Chapter 3

SPI must prepare a financial budget for the coming year. Its market analysis suggests that selected sales and cost figures will change from last year as shown in Table 2.

Table 2

	Sailboats	Marine Equipment	Nautical Clothing
Revenue change	+10%	+5%	−8%
Direct variable costs			
Materials	+10%	+7%	+1%
Manufacturing wages	+2%		
Selling costs	−6%	+5%	−4%
Fixed direct costs			
Salaries	−15%	+5%	no change
Other overhead	no change	+2%	+10%
Ending inventories			
Manufacturing materials	−15%		
Completed sailboats	−10%		
Marine equipment		−25%	
Nautical clothing			+25%
Non-product-line costs			
Administrative		+15%	
Interest		−10%	
Income taxes		35% of income before taxes	

Using this information, prepare a pro forma 1988 income statement, including 1988's estimated addition to retained earnings. In addition, use the budgeted cost of sales and ending inventory figures to budget purchases of manufacturing materials, marine equipment, and nautical clothing.

Chapter 4

This assignment will require you to obtain information about computers from a library, computer store, or computer consultant. Assume that SPI will require a microcomputer with a power-supply protector, color RGB monitor, 32-bit CPU, 2Mb RAM memory, 80Mb disk drive with tape back-up, and high-capacity desktop laser printer.

Identify at least one complete hardware system with these components. Give the individual and combined costs of all the components and as many additional specifications as possible. If manufacturers' literature is available, obtain and include it in your report.

Chapter 5

1. Give examples taken from the payroll application of the following processing operations: capture, process, store, update, delete, report generation, search.
2. In the payroll application, draw a data flow diagram that shows the major files and processes.
3. For each major file shown in your data flow diagram, name the component fields in each record, and identify one of them as the record key.
4. If records in any of the files above should be linked together, identify the links.

Chapter 6

SPI has decided to develop a group account number code. This code will link all general ledger control accounts, subsidiary ledger accounts, and accounts used in manufacturing. The code can include both numbers and letters. Groups will be separated by dashes. The group in the code that will identify the general ledger account will have 2 characters. In addition to the general ledger accounts shown in the financial statements and mentioned in the case description, the general ledger includes control accounts for Purchases, Work in Progress, and perhaps others.

1. Prepare a chart of accounts for SPI. First, identify all the general ledger control accounts that you can think of. For each control account, include all the subsidiary ledger or journal accounts that you feel are indicated.

2. Design an account code with sufficient groups and characters to cover all the accounts. A 7-character group in the code will identify items purchased (this use is mentioned in the case); this same group can be used for other purposes (such as customer credit account numbers) when the control account group does not have the value assigned to the purchases journal. You may place any number of groups—three, six, or even more—in the code.

3. Explain your code. As a check on its completeness, make certain it provides for a unique identifier for every credit sale, cash receipt, payroll check, and vouchered cash disbursement.

Chapter 7

1. Develop process descriptions for each process in SPI's credit sales and accounts receivable application. Note that the description does not specifically identify these processes; you will have to look in Chapter 7 in the text and decide for yourself what processes are present at SPI and what materials about them belong in the descriptions.

2. Robert Smith, the founder's son and chief accountant at SPI, has questioned whether it is cost-effective for the company to operate its own customer credit service and seeks your advice. He gives you the following information in addition to that contained in the case. He has proposed replacing SPI's service by using the Saltwater Acceptance Company, which specializes in consumer finance. Under the proposal, SPI credit customers would continue to charge their purchases, but their payments would be made to a lockbox operated by Saltwater, which would forward the remittances to SPI minus an 18-percent service charge. Saltwater would also take over credit approval and collection of bad debts. SPI's uncollectible accounts currently average 3.5 percent of sales. If the change is made, the accounts receivable clerk, whose annual salary is $20,000, would no longer be required; nor would forms, postage, and supplies costing $8,000 per year. If, instead of using Saltwater, credit approval and credit sales processing are included in the new computerized system, the estimated incremental costs will be $5,000 to purchase the software, $500 per year to maintain it, and $4,000 per year in clerical and materials costs. Robert Smith would train the accounts receivable clerk to be the data processing supervisor for the computerized system. What is your advice to Robert?

Chapter 8

1. Refer to the data flow diagram of the purchasing and inventory application you drew earlier as part of the Chapter 2 assignment. Or, if your instructor did not assign this task to you, refer to the data flow diagram in Chapter 8 of the text. On whichever diagram you use there are a number of processes. Draw a process diagram for each process, showing the requirements each process performs and the files and documents that are its inputs and outputs.

2. List the attributes in each file shown in your data flow diagram. Indicate in each file which attribute will be the primary key. Indicate from what form, on-line operation, or calculation each attribute originates. For an attribute that will appear in reports, indicate which reports.

3. Examine the source documents shown in the case. Do they provide for all necessary transaction data to be captured? If not, what attributes are missing?

Chapter 9

In a recent month, in which 26 Model 1 and 22 Model 2 sailboats were completely produced and transferred to completed sailboat inventories, the following compound journal entry was made:

DLC	$12,800	
ILC	9,500	
DMC	22,500	
IMC	25,200	
OHC	11,450	
Gross Factory Payroll Expense		$27,500
Purchases		49,100
Depreciation Expense		3,800
Other credits		1,050

Beginning-of-month account balances were as follows:

	Debit	Credit
DLC	$ 0	
ILC 0	0	
DMC	400	
IMC (credit balance)		300
OHC 250	250	

No partially completed boats existed at the end of the month.

1. Using the allocation standards from page 718, calculate the distributions from the cost pools, the ending balance of each cost pool, and the performance variances in manufacturing.

2. Design forms for (a) the work order, (b) the bill of materials, and (c) the materials requisition.

3. At SPI, the supervisor completes a labor distribution form at the end of each day. This form assigns all *hours* worked that day (based on the supervisor's observations) to specific cost pools. Design this form and suggest how it could be used to calculate the actual costs placed in each pool's suspense account (the debits in the accounting entry shown above).

Chapter 10

No assignment; SPI does not operate any funds.

Chapter 11

1. Chief accountant Robert Smith has decided to consider a plan for the proposed data processing department. He has asked for your input to this plan in the form of answers to the following questions:

   a. Where on the physical site should the data processing department be located?

   b. How should this department be organized (what responsibilities will it have)?

   c. To whom should the data processing department report?

   d. Who will be the users of data processing services?

2. A tentative data processing department operating budget must be estimated. The budget can be estimated using the following industry wide average annual or per-transaction costs:

Cost per SPI approved credit customer	$32.00
Processing cost per credit sale	0.50
Processing cost per sales transaction (in addition to credit processing cost)	0.25
Annual cost per approved vendor	85.00
Processing cost per credit purchase order	18.00
Processing cost per boat manufactured	22.00
Processing costs per employee (for payroll)	60.00

   Using these figures and information in the case, estimate the annual data processing budget. Identify and describe any uncertainties that may limit the accuracy of your estimate.

3. What do you think will be the best way for SPI to control data processing costs? Answer this question in detail, including such illustrative performance reports and calculations as you think necessary.

Chapter 12

1. Study the description of SPI's payroll application. Produce a list of at least eight control objectives that should apply to this (or any) payroll application. Each of the following control types should be represented by at least one objective (an objective may represent more than one type):

input	process-specific
processing	accounting
output	asset access
applicationwide	transaction-authorization

   State the control types each objective represents.

2. Identify the preventive, feedback, and comparative elements that correspond to each objective above.

3. Indicate whether the objectives and other elements identified in 1 and 2 exist or do not exist at SPI.

Chapter 13

1. Although SPI doesn't yet have its computer, its control weaknesses and risks make it vulnerable to employee crime. Identify five situations where such crime is possible at SPI. For each situation, explain briefly what the crime would be, why the crime is possible, and what controls would tend to prevent or detect it.

2. In the store, clothing sells at a 150-percent markup over invoice cost, less any sale discounts. Thus, retail sales of $2,500 should have had an invoice cost of $1,000. The table below shows data that have been developed concerning retail sales for four recent months.

	Month 1	Month 2	Month 3	Month 4
Adjusted markup in effect	150%	140%	130%	140%
Observed beginning inventory at retail	$ 9,000			
Observed ending inventory at retail				$ 7,000
Clothing purchases at invoice cost	18,000	17,000	19,000	20,000
Cash and check sales at retail, per cash register clearing forms	18,000	16,000	16,000	14,000
Major credit card and SPI charge sales at retail, per charge forms	27,000	28,000	30,000	31,000
Disputed credit charges and delinquent accounts	500	1,200	2,100	3,500

Give your best and most detailed explanation of what has happened and of the control(s) whose absence allowed it to happen.

Chapter 14

At SPI, the present accounting system is, of course, manual, and there is no internal auditor. Recently, the chief accountant visited a business very similar to SPI. This business is now using one of the accounting software packages that SPI might consider. This program does *not* integrate with the cash register; the cash-register clearing form is, however, used to capture credit sales data and a copy of the bank-deposit slip can be used to capture cash receipts data. At SPI, the data entry from both documents would have to be done by the accounts receivable clerk.

The software package includes one floppy disk and two copies of an instruction manual. The floppy disk is not copy-protected. Although no backup disk is provided, the user can make copies as needed. The programs are written in assembly language; the source code is on the disk as a text file (in ASCII code). The lines of code are interspersed with lines of explanatory comment. SPI's chief accountant, though not an EDP expert, was able to follow the logic of the program when shown a listing of it which the company had prepared from the floppy disk. Nevertheless, the chief accountant was glad that the purchasing and payroll clerk, who is a computer hobbyist, would be able to modify the code to meet any special or unusual SPI requirements. The chief accountant also noted that the software company provided up to five hours of free consultation to new users of its software.

1. Assume that SPI acquires this system. Discuss the control situation relative to this software, identifying any control weaknesses you feel should be anticipated.
2. State control objectives for the custody and use of this software.
3. Develop procedures to implement the control objectives listed for part 2.
4. Write a set of audit steps that will determine whether the software-control procedures are reliable.

Chapter 15

George Brown, a director of SPI, feels that the SPI purchasing activity could be supplemented using an expert system. Actual purchasing levels are determined by the sales manager on the basis of "feel" for sales volume. Brown wants (at the very least) to document the expertise used by the sales manager. After consulting with a friend whose company had developed an expert system in another area, he wrote the following memo to the sales manager:

> I am interested in developing an expert system for use in controlling inventory, or at least purchasing, and I need your help. Can we meet to develop a complete description of your inventory ordering policies? I will phone in a day or so, so we can set a time.

When the two met, the sales manager said, in part,

> I try to keep a one-month supply of inventory on hand. I can visually inspect all the items, and I inspect every item once a week. Of course, the 'trick' is

to estimate sales in the next month, and estimate them correctly. Here are some of the rules I use:

If the stock quantity on hand is less than sales the last four weeks, I look to see if there are any open orders for that item. If not, I order a two-week supply based on the average weekly selling rate of the last two weeks. If the sum of quantity on order plus quantity on hand is equal to or greater than the last four weeks' sales, but less than 120% of that amount, I order a three-week supply based on the last two weeks' average weekly selling rate. If the sum of quantity on order plus quantity on hand is more than 120% of the last four weeks' sales, I do not place an order. And of course, if the amount on hand, without considering open orders, is more than the last four weeks' sales, I do not place an order.

Now, the above applies only to nonseasonal items. There are two other types of items: slightly seasonal, and highly seasonal. Here's how their treatment differs:

For slightly seasonal items, I go through the same process except I don't use sales of the last four weeks as the basis for comparison. Instead, I use sales during the corresponding year-ago four-week period. The order quantity (when an order is necessary) will be either 100% or 150% of sales in the corresponding year-ago two-week period.

For highly seasonal items, I use the sales of the corresponding year-ago four-week period, just as for slightly seasonal items. However, I determine the order quantity (when an order is necessary) as either 100% or 150% of sales in the corresponding year-ago two-week period *starting with this week*. This is necessary because of the rapid fluctuations in sales of highly seasonal items.

Oh—and there are always a few items that don't fit any of these rules. ɪ identify them as the ones whose inventory level is less than last week's sales and for which sales last week were 300% or more of sales the week before that. For these items, I order four times as much as last week's sales.

I hope this explanation helps you!

1. What will be the questions (and range of responses) in a consultation if an expert system is developed for this application?

2. What actions will this expert system be able to recommend?

3. Organize the questions, responses, and actions as they are arranged in Figure 15.3.

4. *Optional:* If you have access to a simple expert system, such as VP-EXPERT, develop the system called for here.

Chapter 16

SPI has decided that its new system will be based on a local area network concept.

Review the case, then propose and justify
   a. A LAN design concept
   b. The nodes and their locations

   c. The type of cabling, connections, and network software

   d. An estimate of the cost of the components in (b) and (c)

2. Be as specific as possible (brand names, model numbers) in your responses. Get the detail from cooperative vendors and from widely available technical publications. For example, you could select a star concept with six workstation nodes and one printer node in each building. Then, you could connect these with twisted-pair cable. Additional detail would identify other nodes and give their specifications. The more detail you can gather and apply, the better.

Chapter 17

SPI president Tom Smith has asked you to be a consultant assisting the company in preparing a conceptual design for the contemplated new accounting system.

1. Draft a letter of engagement that describes the scope of your work, the steps you will take, and the outputs you will deliver.

2. Write at least fifty performance requirements, including at least eight for each major application. Organize these requirements by application.

3. Prepare a data dictionary for the proposed SPI system. Preparing the data dictionary may also require you to prepare system and data flow diagrams.

4. Estimate the outlay cost range of the new system for SPI, and classify the costs according to hardware, your fees, and other appropriate categories.

Chapter 18

SPI was pleased with your work on the conceptual design and wishes for you to continue advising them during vendor selection and detail design.

1. Prepare a rough draft, in outline form, of the Request for Proposal that will be sent to vendors. Include as much SPI-specific material as possible in this outline.

2. Assume that a vendor has been selected and a contract signed. Prepare a plan for the conduct and completion of a detail design, implementation, and startup. The plan should list every report you think SPI should have. You may assume that the vendor selected is proposing a commercial software accounting system that will not require programming but will require customizing. This customizing will require 10 hours per report and will all be done by the same person. This plan should begin on June 1, 1988 and provide for all work except postimplementation review to be done by December 1, 1988.

3. Looking ahead, imagine that the post-implementation review has been completed. The following items were noted:

  - There was a requirement that "All direct and indirect materials purchases will be placed in suspense accounts at standard cost and the difference, if any, placed in a Purchase Price Variance account for later analysis. All other purchases shall be accounted for at actual purchase price." This requirement has not been implemented.

  - There was a requirement that "Manufacturing personnel be able to modify the bill of materials in any work order to reflect substitution of materials or special manufacturing or design requirements." This requirement has been implemented; however, the need for prior manufacturing management approval of such changes was not anticipated and numerous unauthorized changes have been made, not only in work orders, but in the master bill of materials file records themselves.

  - There was no requirement that vouchers be canceled as checks are printed to pay approved vouchers. This step is being done by manually entering the detail of debits to the accounts payable subsidiary ledger.

Evaluate each of these items and suggest appropriate follow-up action, if any.

Glossary

Acceptance testing The use with realistic data to see if a new system can meet the performance requirements and respond acceptably when running at full capacity

Access The use of assets, including production, processing, and transfer to an outside party

Access security Measures that limit physical or logical opportunities to see, use, or abuse computers, programs, and records

Account A classification, used in an accounting system, to summarize the amount of a particular type of revenue, expense, asset, or liability

Account payable Payment due a seller for goods or services received by the purchaser

Accounting A standardized process, governed by principles and rules, for recording, classifying, summarizing, and reporting financial data and information used in management processes

Accounting control An internal control that describes a standard for collecting, classifying, processing, and reporting transactions and other data so that when financial statements are prepared, they will be consistent with generally accepted accounting principles

Accounting entry Transaction details organized so they can be recorded in a journal

Accounting model The rules that determine how an accounting system collects, processes, and reports for a specific organization

Accounting system A set of elements—goals, policies, accounting principles, equipment, documents, and controls—that can jointly perform accounting functions

Accounts receivable control account A general ledger account containing the sum of all shipping advices for which reimbursement has not yet been received

Acoustic modem An electrical connection between a phone handset and a computer that converts sound to electrical impulses and vice versa

Adjusting entries Accounting entries that are required as a result of time's passage or of internal operations

Aging of accounts receivable The process for determining and reporting how long ago each credit purchase was made

Allocated costs Costs classified together and assigned to work centers on a meaningful but often arbitrary basis

Allowance for doubtful accounts Estimate of the amount of accounts receivable that will prove to be uncollectible

Alphabetic-or-numeric test Examination of entered data to determine if it is all alphabetic or all numeric and compare the result to the specification of the field in which the data are to be placed

Alternative A value assigned by a decision maker to a controllable variable

Analog Represented by continuously varying (not digital) quantities or values

Analytic evidence Evidence that reveals whether system controls are of adequate design

Analytic follow-up Regular, periodic studies of performance over several periods to detect patterns that should be encouraged or eliminated

Analytic review In an audit, evaluation of the adequacy of controls design

Application A specialized part of the accounting system; also, a computer program that produces information

Application controls Controls specific to a particular application

Application-oriented design An older system-design strategy in which input, output, files, and data structures had to be tailored to the requirements of each application

Appropriation Legal authorization to spend money

Appropriation free balance The balance of appropriated but unencumbered funds

Approved credit Permission to purchase without immediately paying cash

Approved-credit-customer master file Records describing individuals or organizations authorized to purchase on credit

Approved seller Another organization, from which purchases of specific items are authorized

Arithmetic-logic unit (ALU) The part of the CPU that can carry out arithmetic operations and make logical comparisons

Artificial intelligence Ability of a computer system to perform tasks normally associated with human intelligence

ASCII American Standard Code for Information Interchange, the code used to assign binary values to letters, numbers, and symbols

Assembly language Command symbols used by programmers to control the processor

Asset Property of an organization that can be used to produce revenue

Asset accountability Maintaining a set of accounting records that describe the organization's assets accurately

Asynchronous Signal transmission controlled by start and stop bits; the rate of transmission is not a function of time

Attribute A column of data items in a relation

Audit A methodology to collect and analyze evidence on consistency and other attributes of business information, in part by examining the system that prepared the information, through an intensive study of the system records and other evidence

Audit cost effectiveness The ability of an audit to produce benefits in excess of its cost

Audit field work specification In an audit, the auditor's selection of the necessary tests of controls

Audit objectives The purposes of the audit, which define its scope and the controls whose performance it will examine

Audit opinion The professional judgment of the auditor, based on evidence collected during an audit

Audit plan A list of procedures for collecting evidence to show whether a system (or part of a system) works as it should

Audit trail The documentation that describes a transaction's history, which auditors use to trace system outputs back from account balances to their component transactions and verify their authorization and processing

Auditing Carrying out an audit

Auditing around the computer Testing to verify that the results of specific routine processing, already done on a computer, can be duplicated by manual processing

Auditing through the computer Using test data to probe how the computer would process actual data. The test data is selected so that outputs will be correct if proper controls are in place, but distorted if they are not

Auditing with the computer Using a computer to conduct an audit

Authorization Approval for a transaction to take place

Back-up files File duplicates made to control data security and protect against data loss

Balance-forward design A process design in which only the current amount due appears in the computer file for each credit customer

Balance sheet An accounting statement showing assets, liabilities, and equities

BASIC Beginner's All-purpose Symbolic Instruction Code, a popular language for writing short computer programs

Basic input-output system (BIOS) ROM-based code that relates the operating system to the arithmetic-logical unit of the CPU

Batch process In manufacturing, a production method that carries one set of units to completion, then starts another

Batch processing In data processing, a design in which records of similar transactions are saved for processing in one run

Baud One change per second in an electronic signal, equivalent to one bit

Baud rate Number of changes in an electronic signal transmitted each second

Behavioral decision model A model that emphasizes the relationship between variables influencing human information processing

Bill of lading A document accompanying a shipment, instructing the shipper where and how to deliver it

Binary number system A number system with only two numerals, 1 or 0

Bit An electronic component in a computer that can be on or off, corresponding to values of 1 or 0

Block code Blocks of numbers set aside to identify similar accounts

Block conversion Making a system operational one segment or block at a time

Block testing Testing the performance of several program segments together as a block

Blocking factor Number of records per sector or block of external storage

Bottom-up design An approach to detail design in which the system users—not the analyst—decide most of the details of the new system

Budget A detailed quantitative organization operating plan

Budget organization The structure and contents of the budget

Budget process The sequence of events that occurs in the preparation of a budget

Budgeting unit A responsibility center that prepares a budget

Buffer Temporary storage for data, input, or output

Bugs Errors in a computer program

Bus network A cable with interfaces to which nodes may be connected; the cable transports signals between nodes in the form of packets, or sets of characters

Byte A combination of bits used to represent letters, symbols, and numbers; a byte usually consists of 8 bits

Byte-count test Comparison of the length of the in-use and back-up copies of a program

Bytes per character The number of bytes required to represent a unique character

Cache A segment of memory reserved for frequently used program segments or data expected to be processed

Capture The collection of all data required for a complete accounting entry

Carrier sense multiple access/collision detection (CSMA/CD) A means of organizing messages in a network that allows nodes to send only when the links between them are not carrying any messages

Cash remittance A cash payment on account by credit customer

Cash statement An accounting statement showing sources and uses of cash

Centralized data processing A system design in which one location possesses all or nearly all of the data processing capacity

Certified Public Accountant (CPA) A designation of accounting professionals who meet legal standards in one of 54 U.S. state and territorial jurisdictions

Channels The means of moving data between network nodes

Chart of accounts The systematic rules used to assign codes to accounts; also, a diagram of all the accounts and their relationships

Check-digit test A value computed by a formula when a number is created, then recomputed and compared to the original value whenever the number is used; the purpose is to verify correct entry of the number

Clear-to-send/none A common asynchronous-network handshake convention

Clock Computer segment that gives a signal used to time its operations

Closed architecture A system wherein the designers do not intend any additional components to be connected to the CPU

Closed system One that does not interact with its environment

Closing entry A journal entry made after financial statements have been prepared, to "reset" revenue and expense accounts to zero

COBOL Common Business Oriented Language, a language developed by the Conference on Data System Languages for use in business data processing applications

Cold-turkey conversion Startup of a system, or part of a system, without any back-up in the event the new system experiences failure

Collections report Report showing the schedule of expected cash flow from accounts receivable during a particular period

Committed cost A cost that cannot be changed within the time period specified by the commitment

Communications Transfer of messages between stations or nodes

Communications program Software that enables a computer to send and receive messages as part of a network

Compilation A restructing into financial-statement format of what the client claims are its records, resulting in a disclaimer by the CPA that any investigative work has been done

Compliance Conformance of organizational activities to budget or plans

Computer-assisted auditing Use of computer-based sampling plans and other audit-productivity aids

Computer crime Any deliberate act, requiring knowledge of how a specific computer works, that deprives the rightful owner of a benefit such as use of the computer, or use of computer-produced information, or the exclusive use of information or other property

Conceptual design The second step of the design phase in a system's creation, laying out the broad design principles

Conclusions In an expert system, the set of possible expert-system outputs

Consultant An independent professional with specific expertise who applies that expertise by advising clients

Continuous process A production method that turns out a steady stream of output in which one unit is indistinguishable from another

Control The ability to regulate, consisting of the means to assure a desired outcome and/ or to identify and correct the failure to achieve a desired outcome

Control account A general-ledger account whose balance summarizes the balances of all accounts in a particular subsidiary ledger

Control element Any of the four parts of a control: objective, preventive, feedback, follow-up

Control objective A statement of the performance desired from some process in a system

Control process Procedure that implements a control

Control time horizon Length of time into the future for which planning occurs

Control-total test Test to assure that all items in a given set or batch are processed

Control unit The part of the CPU that issues commands

Controllable cost A cost for which a work center is responsible

Conversion The third step in the implementation phase in which the new system is placed in operation, becomes a working system, and its performance is evaluated

Correct-file test A procedure to make certain the correct copy of a file is used in processing

Cost accounting Techniques used to estimate and control manufacturing costs

Cost-allocation base *See* Cost-allocation basis

Cost-allocation basis An objective and reasonable measure of the extent to which costs centers are individually responsible for the incurrence of indirect costs

Cost-allocation rate Dollars taken from the cost pool and distributed to the work center for every unit of the cost-allocation basis

Cost center A unit of an organization with responsibility for control over certain costs

Cost pool Costs of similar resources that are treated alike by the cost-accounting process. Also called Suspense account

Cost variance A variance between actual cost and standard cost

CPU   In a computer, the combination of control unit, arithmetic and logic processor, input-output interfaces, RAM, ROM, motherboard, clock, and perhaps other components

Creation   Period in the system life cycle, the process of designing and implementing a new system

Credit   An increase in equities, or decrease in assets

Credit sale   A transaction in which merchandise is exchanged for a promise to pay cash later

Critical-path scheduling   A planning procedure that reveals which implementation steps must be completed before others are begun and where potential bottlenecks are likely to develop

Customer account   A record of the balance owed by a credit customer

Cycle billing   Processing strategy in which statements are prepared and mailed to a few customers each day, rather than all customers on the same day

Data   Qualitative and quantitative measurements recorded in durable and usable form, but unprocessed and of uncertain significance

Data base   A collection of data organized to allow processing in different ways and to minimize data redundancy

Data base environment   The procedures and programs for entering, storing, and retrieving data and information in the specific ways required by applications

Data base manager   A computer program that interfaces between data and processes that use the data; also, a person responsible for administering data processing

Data dictionary   A component of system conceptual design, a collection of the names and descriptions of the data elements found in the system

Data element   A unit of data containing one or more data items

Data entry   Organizing data in system-usable format, usually on source documents or magnetic media

Data flow diagram   A component of the system's conceptual design that graphically shows the data groupings and processes that create, modify, and use data in an application

Data item   One value of a variable

Data-oriented design   A system design philosophy that aims to create a data structure that supports multiple and changing applications

Data processing   The activities that convert data into information: recording, classifying, processing, and reporting

Data processing control   An internal control that describes a standard for data processing activity, which must take place in accordance with management policies and objectives

Data processing efficiency   The difference between the cost of data processing and costs distributed to users of data processing services

Data processing function   System that processes data into information

Data-processing operations department   Conducts the day-to-day activities of EDP, including archival storage, the library of operating programs and files, data-capture activities, and data-processing management

Data-processing systems development process   The process of planning and preparing a new or improved system and making it operational

Data processing technical support department   Assists users in taking advantage of existing data-processing capabilities

Data security   Measures to assure that data may be created, deleted, or altered only in authorized fashion

Data structure   The way data items are related to one another

Debit   An increase in assets, or decrease in equities

Debit memorandum   A document informing the seller that the buyer is rejecting a shipment in whole or in part and is decreasing all or part of the seller's invoice

Debugging   Troubleshooting a computer-based process; locating bugs

Decision   A choice among alternatives

Decision maker   One who chooses an alternative and is responsible for its consequences

Decision objective   The goal or target a decision maker hopes to achieve

Decision relevance   A property of information that may affect a particular decision

Decision rule   A guideline for decision making relating the expected payoff, or independent-variable values, of the alternative selected

Decision-support system   A collection of data, information, and processes specifically intended to provide relevant information for managers with known responsibilities

Decision table   A collection of rules in tabular format that relate the intended system actions to specific sets of conditions

Declarative language   A language that enables the programmer to describe the structure of a problem; i.e., a spreadsheet implementation of a budget

Decline   Period 4 in the system life cycle, during which the system's performance declines and management becomes unwilling to devote additional resources to it

Design by forms   An approach to systems development in which, by working with data input, edit, search, or report formats, all data elements and (to some extent) data structures, are specified by the user

Detail design   The second step in systems creation, devoted primarily to programming (if required), documentation, and training to ensure that a system meets performance objectives within conceptual-design constraints

Deterrent   Any control, barrier, or condition that tends to make commission of a crime more difficult or less attractive

Digital   A variable whose discrete changes can be assigned the value of either 1 or 0; *compare with* Analog

Direct access   Ability of a computer to locate a record without first examining other records before or after it in memory

Direct-connect modem   A device that transmits phone-line signals to and from a computer in electrical form, without ever converting them into sounds

Direct cost   Costs that are proportional to the rate or level of output; that increase by the same amount per unit of output

Direct data-processing costs   Costs that are proportional to the volume of data processing output

Direct testimony   Firsthand verbal evidence of an incident, e.g., A confesses an act to B

Discretionary cost   Costs that can be increased, decreased, or cancelled during a given time interval

Disk cache   Either part of RAM or a separate small memory used to hold programs or data normally kept in external storage but likely to be required next by the operations under way

Disk drive   An external storage device

Distributed data processing   A system design in which data processing capacity is divided up among several locations

Distribution   Allocation of costs to specific work centers or work orders

Distribution account   A credit-balance account showing the sum of costs which have been distributed (debited) to other accounts

Distribution test   A test to assure that reports go to those for whom they are intended and no one else

Documentation   Written descriptions of all system components, elements, structures, procedures, controls, and back-ups

DOS   Disk operating system, same as Operating system

Double entry   Dual classification of transactions in accounting entries

Double-entry rule   The concept that changes must offset each other within an accounting entry

Dynamic data base   The facts associated with an individual application of an expert system and the conclusions the expert system reaches based on these facts and on the static data base

Echo   An error-detection procedure whereby the receiver returns the received data to the sending computer for comparison with the transmitted data

Economic order quantity (EOQ) The order size that, under certain conditions, will yield the lowest combined cost of ordering and carrying inventory in stock

EDP Electronic data processing

EDP audit An audit of EDP controls

EDP controls Procedures to assure that the use of computers in data processing takes place in accordance with management objectives and policies

Efficiency variance A cost variance that is positive (a credit) when efficiency is at or above the acceptable level and negative (a debit) when it is not

Electronic mail A system in which each user has a private file in which other users can place messages and only the user with the proper password (or address) can read the messages

Element The smallest part of a system that can be used in a system description or design

Encumber To create an encumbrance

Encumbrance A commitment of appropriate funds to use for specific programs and activities

Engagement The relationship between a consultant and management

Entity diagram A pictorial representation of the entities comprising a system

Entry An accounting representation of a transaction

Equal-length records A file consisting of records, each of which is allocated the same number of bytes of storage space

Equity Any claim upon assets by creditors or owners

Error Accidental handling of a transaction in an inaccurate or unapproved fashion

Exchange entry An accounting entry arising from exchanges with independent outside parties

Expected value Present equivalent of future cash flows, which is less than the undiscounted sum of such cash flows

Expenditure Use of funds as designated by an encumbrance

Expert knowledge Rules relating observations to conclusions

Expert system A computer program capable of selecting conclusions based on situation-specific input data, processed according to previously learned rules

External storage Memory outside the CPU

Feasibility analysis The third step in the design phase of systems creation, determining whether and to what degree the proposed conceptual designs are acceptable

Feedback The ability of a system to analyze information and modify its outputs accordingly, in order to achieve a specific immediate result such as a change in the system's responses to the environment

Feedback element The actual, observed value a selected variable will have (for comparison with the preventive element)

Feedforward The ability of a system to modify its outputs in response to information to achieve a specific future result

Field Smallest meaningful unit of data recognized by humans; building blocks for records

Fifth-generation computer Computers under development especially intended for use in artificial intelligence applications

File A collection of related records

File index A file of short records, each containing the record key and the disk location of a longer record in the main file

File maintenance Changing records in a file to reflect recent transactions or changes in company policies

Financial audit An audit by CPAs to determine if the financial statements are consistent and objective

Financial control Control that helps assure the availability of financial resources to carry out management's operational plans

Financial feasibility A criterion for evaluating a conceptual design to determine its quality as an investment; the three factors in financial feasibility are that the proposed new system be affordable, economical, and an acceptable risk

Financial planning model A set of equations describing relationships between an organization and its environments

Flag A type of variable that is set to a value that corresponds to an operation's outcome

Flexible budget A budget for calculating the inputs that should have been used to produce the actual output

Floppy disk drive Disk drive using a flexible plastic iron-oxide-coated disk

Follow-up element Deciding, based on a comparison of expected and observed variable values, whether a control objective was achieved

Full duplex Simultaneous two-way transmission

Functional divisions Usually refers to marketing, manufacturing, and finance; also, less properly, to any top-level divisions of an organization

Fund The basic unit of fund accounting; a set of resources committed to specific purposes

Fund accounting A system of accounting in which each fund's receipts, expenditures, assets, and liabilities are kept separately

Fund balance The total amount of a fund

Fund identifier A portion of the account number whose value is unique to each fund

Funding authority An entity that collects or earns revenues and designates how much and for what purposes an organization may use them

Garbage Irrelevant, unwanted, and meaningless data, often deliberately or carelessly placed into a system

Gateway A connection that forms a bridge or interface from one network to another

General data-processing controls Controls that apply to all data processing activities, such as system development, back-up and security, and technical support

General ledger The ledger containing all accounts in the trial balance

Generally accepted accounting principles (GAAP) The shell of assumptions, principles, and rules that govern preparation of all organizations' financial statements

Goal congruence A lack of conflict among goals of different persons, so that advancing one's own goals also advances goals of others

Goal setting The process of selecting goals and objectives that will sustain the organization's existence without taking unnecessary chances

Group code One or more characters within an account number, used to designate similar accounts

Hacker Someone who seeks unauthorized logical access to computer systems via phone-line connections

Half duplex Two-way transmission, but only in one direction at a time

Handshake In asynchronous transmission, a protocol for controlling flow of data in which the receiving computer instructs the sending computer to pause, then resume sending data

Hash-total test A processing total, used to determine whether the identity of items in a set remains unchanged throughout processing

Hashing Assigning each record a disk address based on its primary key

Header record A record containing information common to other records that are linked to it

Headroom Available unused disk space

Hearsay evidence Indirect verbal evidence of an incident where, for example, B testifies that A confessed the incident to B

Hierarchical data base A data structure in which records in one relation own records in other relations, as established by links

Host A computer running software that is under the control of another computer

Host environment The operating capabilities of a phone-line-based network

Host program Software that allows one node to control software being run by another node (the host computer)

IF . . . THEN One structure for rules in an expert system

Imperative language A computer-programming language that allows one to instruct the computer on how to solve a problem

Implementation   The process of making operational the system envisioned in the conceptual design

Income statement   An accounting statement showing changes in assets and equities in the form of revenues, expenses, and profits

Independent auditor   An auditor not controlled or supervised by the entity being audited

Independent variables   The variables whose values aren't known until after a decision alternative is selected; the key factors not controllable by the decision maker

Index   A series of short records showing the locations in storage and sequence of access of longer records

Index-sequential-access method (ISAM)   A means of organizing files so as to find records rapidly in a specific order; the records are both indexed and in sequence of the primary key values

Indexed file   A file with an associated index that speeds access to records or allows access to records in a desired sequence

Indirect addressing   Storing the location (address) of one record in a location referenced in an index

Indirect costs   Costs that are more strongly a function of the passage of time than of output rate; they tend to be the same per unit of time and to be unaffected by output rate

Indirect data-processing costs   Costs that are not proportional to data-processing output; they are about the same each period and are unaffected by the output rule

Information   An input to a system capable of causing the system to change its response or output to the environment; for example, a stimulus capable of changing a person's or system's behavior

Information processing   Conversion of information into decisions by managers or computers

Information retrieval   Recovery of record or file contents

Input   A phenomenon that has a measurable effect on a system

Installed system   A system that processes data on a regular basis

Integrated test facility (ITF)   Real-time testing under actual processing conditions by inserting simulated transactions into the stream of real transactions to see if the features they contain will trigger controls properly

Internal audit   An examination of operational compliance with internal controls; acts as both preventive and feedback elements of many management and financial controls

Internal auditor   An auditor employed by the entity being audited

Internal control   Any control that describes a standard for a day-to-day operation or activity of a specific organization segment

Internal entry   An accounting entry resulting from purely internal activities; i.e., not involving third parties

Internal-audit function   An audit facility within an organization; not the independent-audit function

Internal storage   Memory inside the CPU

Inverted file   A file with a secondary key index, or one whose records have been sorted into secondary key order. Also called *sorted file*

Investment center   Any department with authority to control and use assets

Invoice   A source document showing that a sales or purchase transaction has occurred and containing the information necessary to record that transaction

Job-queue manager   A design feature that analyzes the jobs and arranges them according to rules designed into it

Journal   Storage for accounting record in which transactions of a particular type are entered and described in the order in which they occurred

Journalizing   Process of placing an accounting entry into a journal

Just-in-time   A strategy of purchasing, production, and inventory management that emphasizes efficiency, quality, and low inventories

Key field   Any record key used to order or sort records

Kilobyte   1,024 bytes

Kiting   Taking advantage of normal delays in processing financial documents to create the appearance of assets that do not exist

Knowledge processing   The use in the management process of expert knowledge, judgment, experience, computer-processed information, decision structure, and management objectives

Language   A set of acceptable statements and syntax for writing computer programs

Lapping   Use of current cash receipts to replace earlier receipts that were used for unauthorized (usually personal) purposes

Late payment   A cash remittance on account that arrives after the due date

Laundering   A set of practices intended to obscure the true source of money

Lead time   The interval between placing an order and receiving the shipment

Learning constant   In the learning-effect model, the fixed proportion of decline in time required to produce a unit of output

Learning effect   The phenomenon of rapid initial progress toward increased internal productivity and efficiency in a new system

Ledger   A collection of accounts

Legislative budget board   A staff agency that studies and coordinates all the budget requests of individual units before they are presented to the legislature or other funding authority

Length test   An edit test to verify that data entered contains a specific number of characters

Line end   A signal indicating completion of a transmitted line of data

Link   Any means of connecting one record to another; a pointer

LISP   List-processing artificial language used in programming artificial intelligence applications

Local-area networks (LAN)   Networks whose nodes are relatively close to each other and that typically use direct-communications devices

Lockbox   An arrangement whereby a bank or other agent collects and deposits a firm's customer cash remittances

Logical access security   Assurance that electronic access to data and software will be for authorized purposes only

Management controls   Controls on organizational structures, long-range planning, and staffing top-level positions; these controls operate at higher management levels and over longer time spans than most other controls

Management information   A system designed to provide managers with information likely to change their behavior; i.e., help them carry out their responsibilities

Management program   A sequence of activities usually extending over several periods, coordinated to achieve selected management objectives

Management utility   A center that provides services on demand to other centers

Master file   A file containing relatively permanent, frequently used information about a set of entities

Master record   A master file record containing permanent, frequently used information about one entity, such as an employee, customer, product, or vendor

Material requisition   A document used by operating departments to inform purchasing about materials, supplies, or services they need to operate

Matrix management   A type of project management in which all projects worked on by several responsibility centers are managed and accounted for in a similar way, enabling comparison of their revenues and costs on a two-dimensional matrix

Maturity   Period 3 in the system lifecycle, which operates reliably with only minor deterioration or enhancement

Maximax strategy   A decision-making strategy with the objective of maximizing the maximum possible benefit

Maximin strategy   A decision-making strategy with the objective of assuring that the minimum gain is as large as possible

Megabyte   1,024 kilobytes

Memory chip   The integrated circuit that stores data

Menu   A list of options presented to the user

Mission   An NFP organization's guiding purpose

Model   A representation, as in "an accounting system is a model of an organization"

Modem   An interface device between a computer and a phone line that converts signals between digital and analog

Motive   An objective or incentive to commit a crime

Multiplexer   An interface device that combines input from two or more communications channels into one channel, or splits messages on one channel into messages for two or more channels

Multiprocessing   An approach to accommodating several different users by linking several CPUs under common control to execute programs simultaneously

Multiprogramming   An approach to accommodating different users by installing several processors in the CPU for program execution

MYCIN   An expert system developed to diagnose bacterial infections

Narrative description   A component of system conceptual design, a comprehensive but simple explanation of what the proposed system design will do; also links together all elements in the design

National Accounting and Auditing Retrieval System (NAARS)   A nationwide DSS; database of comparative information for use in the latter stages of an audit

Natural languages   The languages that people use to communicate with each other, in contrast with the artificial languages employed in computer programming

Network   Nodes that collect, store, process, or use data or information, linked by data-carrying channels

Networking   The combination of one or more computers with stations for input and output

Nodes   The logical devices in a network

Noise   Useless or unwanted data, often resulting from poor system design that cannot reject certain inputs

Noncontrollable costs   Costs that a work center cannot influence

Nonrelevant costs   Costs whose magnitude will not be affected by the alternatives selected in a decision. Costs that are nonrelevant in one decision may be relevant in other decisions

Not-for-profit (NFP)   An organization not intended to pursue profit

Not sufficient funds   A reason given by a financial institution for not honoring a check (the customer's account balance is too low)

NSF   Abbreviation for *not sufficient funds*

Objective   A unifying reason for a system to exist; a future and desirable state for the system

Object-oriented language   A computer programming language that treats data as objects to which various routines may be applied

Office network   A network customized to provide information support for people performing diverse tasks in close proximity, e.g., on the same floor or in the same building

On-demand report   Information issued only when requested

On-line system   A system in which files and records may be used as they are needed for management purposes

Open architecture   A design feature that allows the end user of the computer system to connect additional components to the CPU

Open-invoice design   A process design whose computer records contain data required to reconstruct current balance in a customer account

Open purchase order   A purchase order against which shipments are still incomplete

Open system   One that exchanges elements with its environment

Operating system   A software program that enables the CPU to run application programs; same as DOS

Operational audit   Audit performed by internal auditors, with the aim of enhancing operating management's success in achieving top management's objectives

Opportunity   A chance to commit a crime

Optical disk   A storage device that retains data in optically readable form

Optimizing   Seeking the very best level of payoff in one or a series of decisions

Order point   The inventory level at which an item should be reordered

Organization   An association of people, some of whom are managers

Organizational feasibility   A criterion for evaluating a conceptual design to determine whether an organization can implement and operate the proposed system

Output   A phenomenon produced by the system which has an observable effect on the environment

Overhead   Indirect costs, allocated to production as if they were direct costs

Overhead distribution   Allocation of overhead costs

Packing slip   A document accompanying a shipment, listing its contents and referencing the purchase order that serves as the seller's authority to ship them

Parallel conversion   Making one or more blocks of a new system operational without decommissioning the corresponding parts of the old system

Parity bit   A bit added to a character to help ensure accurate transmission

Parity check   An error-detection procedure that adds an extra (parity) "on" bit to characters as needed to give them all an odd, or all an even, number of "on" bits

PASCAL   A general-purpose structured programming language, named after the French scientist Blaise Pascal

Payoff   A consequence experienced by a decision maker

Payoff threshold   The minimum payoff expected value that would make an individual consider committing a computer crime

Performance report   Statements for internal use within a business; they compare expected and actual results of operation

Performance reporting   The use of performance reports to compare actual operations with a budget, as part of the control process

Peripherals   Computer hardware controlled by the CPU including external storage, input-output devices, and the connections among them

Periodic report   Information issued at regular intervals

Physical access security   Measures to make a data-processing site less subject to disruption due to natural disasters or mechanical failure (such as air conditioning or power failure), or to unauthorized intrusion

Pixel   The smallest addressable point on a monitor screen

Planning   Systematic setting of goals and anticipation of activities that will lead to their achievement

Plotter   An output device that can produce graphs, line drawings, abstract forms, or lettering

Pointer   A field in a record which indicates a related record

Points-system evaluation   Any of the proposal-evaluation methodologies that assign points to indicate the extent to which a proposal possesses particular attributes

Post-implementation review (PIR)   Review of a new system after it is operating normally to determine whether it needs any changes to achieve its original performance objectives

Posting   Transferring data from journals to the appropriate subsidiary ledgers

Premises   The values of variables that describe specific fact situations which a knowledge-processing program must perform

Preventive element   The value a selected variable is expected to have if the control objective is achieved (to compare with the follow-up element)

Primary key   The record key which must be a unique value for each record

Printer buffer   A form of RAM memory which contains a print file from which a printer draws the data to be printed

Printer   An output device that produces reports on paper

Process   A sequence of operations such as commands and procedures intended to produce certain results routinely, such as order entry or credit verification, as part of an accounting application

Process diagram   A component of system conceptual design that shows the data inputs, outputs, and activities within a single process

Process flowchart   A drawing that shows the data and operations of a single process

Process relevance   A characteristic of information that enables a manager to administer and control a specific process or to carry out sets of related decisions

Processing   The conversion of raw transaction data into forms useful to management activities

Processing controls   Internal controls applicable to data-processing operations

Processing report   A report of programs run and files updated

Processor chip   Logic circuits contained in the computer

Product specifications   A description of a product's components and expected performance, and of the manufacturing operations required to produce it

Production line   A means of production whereby a product being assembled passes from one work center to another until completed

Pro forma statements   Prospective financial statements projecting circumstances at a future date

Program   A sequence of interrelated instructions to a computer, which have the objective of producing specific outputs, such as a report

Program flowchart   A drawing that shows the data, steps, and logic of a process operation

Program-logic test   A comparison to see if the operating version of a program is identical to the archival version

Programmer   One who converts processing objectives into a program to achieve the outputs

Programming   The process of creating programs

Programming language   A set of human-understandable statements and logical instructions that can be combined to accomplish specific processing objectives

PROLOG   Artificial declarative language useful in writing expert systems applications in both the United States and Japan

Prompt-payment discount   Reduction of an invoice amount if payment occurs before a certain date; may be offered by the seller

Proposal-evaluation process   Evaluation of vendor proposals for the purpose of identifying the vendor with whom system development will proceed on the most timely, cost-effective, and successful basis

Proprietary network   A network completely under the control of, and for the use of, private parties

Protocol   The rules that govern transmission of messages

Prototyping   A relatively new system-development tool in which the analyst works with users to determine how the user interfaces should meet their requirements

Pseudocode   Succinct instructions to the programmer using some of the syntax of the language in which the application will be programmed

Purchase order   A document used by the purchasing department that provides a seller a written description of supplies or services, specifying items and quantities, that the buyer is offering to purchase

Purchasing and accounts payable   The activity which acquires material resources; the accounting application that records this activity

Purchasing function   A center in an organization responsible for identifying and acquiring specific materials, suppliers, and services, which an organization needs to function

RAM   Random access memory; internal temporary memory

RAM disk   Special memory in the CPU used to store data from external storage

Random sampling An audit test of a portion of total transactions, from which inferences are made about all transactions

Range test A data-entry or edit test that checks to see if a recorded value falls within preset limits and rejects (does not record) it if it does not

Real-time processing A design in which files are updated at the moment of a transaction

Receiving function A center in an organization responsible for examining and accepting incoming shipments

Receiving report A record itemizing and linking services received or the contents of an incoming shipment to a purchase commitment, prepared by the receiving department

Record A set of field values

Record key Any data in a record used to determine its order in sequence or to identify it

Recording Creating a documentary or computer record of the data in a transaction

Relation Any common property, such as equality, greater than, less than or occurrence in the same transaction, that links two or more objects, including data items and elements

Relational data base A data structure in which the relations between objects are based on properties that objects have in common, which may be utilized or redefined during data processing

Relevance Information's property of being pertinent to specific circumstances

Relevant costs Costs whose magnitude will depend on the decision alternative that is selected. Costs that are relevant in one decision may not be relevant in other decisions

Remedial follow-up Efforts to correct faults uncovered by other kinds of review

Remittance A cash payment received from a debtor or customer

Remittance advice Documentary evidence accompanying cash payment, and identifying the payor, amount of payment, and reason for paying

Report generation Formatting and creation of screen or printed output

Report period The interval between performance reports

Request for proposals (RFP) A document describing the conceptual design, including performance requirements, for the use of suppliers, consultants, and programmers invited to propose their products or services to meet the system's performance requirements

Requirements definition The first step in the design phase of systems creation, devoted to determining system scope and performance requirements

Resource locking System feature that limits use of data or devices to only one user at a time and thus prevents one user from altering data someone else is using

Resources Means available to management to pursue objectives or implement controls— such as time and system design

Responsibility center A position or department in an organization with decision-making authority and other specified duties, and accountability for how these are done

Return authorization Permission to return merchandise to the seller

Return of merchandise Sending unwanted or unacceptable items back to the seller

Reversing entry An accounting entry that nullifies a previous entry, which was perhaps made in error

Review A limited examination of financial statements and supporting records; the CPA who does the review must disclose that no audit has been conducted on the financial statements. In a review the CPA does not search for evidence of material misrepresentations

Ring network A design that connects all nodes to a circular cable or bus

Risk Inability of the decision maker to anticipate the impact of independent variables on the success of a decision's outcome; also, in control evaluation, any situation in which additional control would result in a potential savings

Risk management Use of information to pinpoint and reduce risk in decisions to acceptable levels

Robotics   The technology of designing, building, and using robots

ROM   Read-only memory; internal permanent memory

Rounding   A fraudulent practice in which the perpetrator calculates amounts to the nearest cent or dollar, accumulating the fractional overages and crediting them to the perpetrator's account

Routine follow-up   The review of periodic performance on a regular basis by the manager and the manager's immediate superior

Rules   In an expert system, the relationships between premises and conclusions

Sales returns and allowances   Reductions in a customer's outstanding balance due to merchandise returns, discounts, and rebates

Satisficing   Seeking an acceptable, rather than optimal, level of payoff in one or a series of decisions

Scope   In a consulting engagement, the matters on which management wishes advice from consultants

Screen form   A computer-monitor display that prompts the user to enter specific data

Search   An organized process of seeking a specific field value or identified record

Search criterion   The value of the record key in the record to be located

Secondary key   A second key field, for which a separate index is kept linking its value to the primary key field value in the same record; assists in searching for a record when the primary attribute isn't known. Similar to Inverted file

Sequential access   Ability to locate records in a sequence determined by their order on the storage media, or in order of the values of a common field

Seller   A vendor or supplier from whom the buyer purchases goods and services

Seller invoice   A document sent by the seller to the buyer, indicating that the seller considers payment due for specific goods or services

Server   A network node that provides, allocates, or manages shared resources to other network nodes

Shared resource   The specific service or capacity provided by a server. Examples of resources that may be shared are printer capacity and external storage

Shipping advice   A document sent by the seller to inform the buyer that a shipment has been sent, what it consists of, and what amount due will appear on the invoice for this shipment

Simplex   Pure one-way transmission, such as by a radio; transmission in the other direction is not possible

Site preparation   Creation of a physical location suitable for a computer-based processing system

Sorted file   *See* Inverted file

Source document   Any form, approval, or paper that supports a transaction and its processing, and especially those used to record detail for the first time, as the transaction occurs

Standard costs   The cost of inputs per unit of output, if manufacturing proceeds as efficiently and competently as management expects

Standard Industrial Classification   Categories that describe different types of economic activity in the United States

Star network   A network design in which every node is directly connected to the central point, which must be a server

Start and stop bits   One or two bits added at the beginning and end of each character transmission by asynchronous devices

Startup   Period 2 of the system life cycle, during which it experiences rapid gains in productivity and efficiency

Statement of cash flows   A financial statement showing how operating, investing, and financing activities during a period have affected cash

Statement of retained earnings   An accounting statement showing changes in the owner's equity built up through earnings

Static data base   In an expert system, the permanent rules and expert knowledge used to analyze each situation

Statistical decision model   A model that lends itself to quantitative analysis of the costs, benefits, and risks associated with available choices

Steering committee   The joint management-vendor-consultant group that provides leadership and coordinates system development

Structure   Assignment of responsibilities within organization for specific jobs, tasks, projects, and processes

Structured language   A language that requires programmers to follow a set of rules in writing a program

Subsidiary ledger, or subledger   A ledger containing only those accounts used in a particular management activity

Sunset review   A control process that specifies a finite lifespan for a government agency, after which the agency is allowed either to expire or is re-established

Support   Relationship of accounting function to a specific process that results in recording the details of the process and in reports that help managers control the process

Surprise tests   Tests undertaken without prior warning to the audited unit, and in which the element of surprise is important to the effectiveness of the test

Suspense account   Another name for a cost pool

Synchronous   Transmission of a fixed number of characters per time interval; compare to asynchronous

System   A group of related elements that can be distinguished from its environment

System boundary   What separates a system from its environment

System diagram   A diagram showing the general relationships among the major components of the system

System life cycle   The creation, start-up, maturity, and decline stages through which a system passes

System performance requirements   Tasks within the system scope that a completed system will be expected to perform

System scope requirements   Requirements that apply to the objectives and scope of a new system

System specifications   A component of con-

ceptual design, an enumeration of all the parts and capacities of the system

System-user interface   The means of passing data into a system and getting it back

Systems development   The process of planning and preparing a new or improved system and making it operational

Tape drive   In a computer, the unit that passes a tape past the read-write head

Technological feasibility   A criterion for evaluating a conceptual design to ensure that the technology exists to make the design operate, and to be sure the design's capacities and capabilities match the requirements defined for it

Template   The design for an input or output form

Terminal emulator   Software that enables one computer to transmit signals identical to those of a certain kind of terminal that can be received by another computer

Test data   Simulated transactions expressly designed by auditors to probe for possible weaknesses in controls

Test evidence   Evidence that tells the auditor whether system controls work reliably

Test of authorization   Audit test to see if the operating version of software is the authorized version

Test of controls   Audit procedures that gather test evidence

Test of transactions   Examination of actual transactions to find evidence about how data-entry and processing controls operate

Time-frame feasibility   A criterion for evaluating a conceptual design to determine whether it can be operational when it is needed

Time-interval entries   Accounting entries that arise from the passage of time

Token-passing   A network design in which a special signal, the token, indicates the end of a group of messages. The token signals a receiving node to insert a message if it has one, then retransmit the messages it did not originate or which are addressed to other nodes

Top-down design A structured approach to detail design whereby the system analyst—not the system users—decides most details of the new system

Top management controls Controls that regulate the basic distinguishing features of the enterprise: its mission, long-range goals and objectives, organizational structure, position descriptions, and staffing

Topology The network design: star, ring, or bus

Track A circular sequence of sectors on a hard or floppy disk

Transaction An event involving a change in resources, usually an exchange or transfer of either an asset or a claim on an asset, or offsetting changes in the status of assets (or claims on assets)

Transaction processing Recording the details of a transaction, then restating them as an accounting entry, then classifying and summarizing them to become part of an accounting system's contents

Transmission mode How data communication occurs—such as through full duplex, half duplex, or simplex

Trees The combined branchlike connections in a hierarchical database

Trial balance The accounts and their balances used to prepare all major internal and external accounting statements

Trojan Horse technique A programmer's placement of unauthorized instructions in a computer operating system, for future use in gaining access to restricted information

Turnaround document A document for control purposes designed by one party (in this case, the creditor) to be returned by another party (the customer)

Twisted-pair An inexpensive form of cabling used in low-capacity network applications

Unposted-transactions file In a batch-processing system, data on similar transactions which have been saved to process (post) all at once

Unposted-transaction procedure A process-ing control to make certain that only complete transactions are recorded, that all complete transactions are recorded, and that no transactions are lost

Unprocessed transactions Transaction data that could not be used to update files, usually due to errors or omissions

Update A change in data to keep it current and useful

Update file A file of records containing current information that supplements the information in at least one master-file record

Updating A process in sequential file processing that requires that the records in each file be arranged in the order they are to be processed

User advisory group A group of users who provide formal feedback and assistance to the data-processing function

User interface The boundary between human user and computer, through which the two communicate

Utilities Routines consisting of computer instructions, used to perform sorts, open and close files, and accomplish other tasks which occur repetitively in a computer program

Valid-combinations test A data-entry or edit control to detect improper data combinations by comparing the data entered to a list of data combinations that should not occur

Valuation account An account whose balance is used to estimate the book value of an asset; usually has the words ''Provision for'' or ''Allowance for'' in its title

Value-added A way of pricing a consulting engagement, in which the consultants charge a percentage of what they believe to be the benefits they have provided

Value test A data-entry or edit test that compares data to a table of values and accepts it only if it agrees with one of the values in the table

Vendor contract The legal document between the vendor and organization developing a new system, spelling out the agreement between them

Vendor Evaluation and Review Technique (VERT) Procedures for evaluating vendors and their proposals

Vendor selection The first step in the implementation phase of systems creation; selecting the consultants, suppliers, and programmers who will assist in the remaining steps

Verification test An output control to verify whether accounting controls are being applied during processing; for example, checking to see if prenumbered forms are dated in numerical sequence

Virus Machine-language code that replaces software or data with a copy of itself, without authorization

Voucher A document used to organize information supporting a cash payment to a creditor

Walkthrough A manual comparison of the processes and options of a process or program flowchart with the system requirements, conducted to spot errors and inconsistencies before system detail design proceeds further

Weakness Any control risk in which the potential savings from implementation exceed the probable cost of installing and operating the control; see *Risk*

Weighted-outcomes strategy A way of increasing the average benefit from a repeated decision when the decision maker concludes that the outcomes are not all equally likely and can be assigned weights describing their relative likelihood

Wide-area networks Computer networks scattered over a wide geographical area

Work center Responsibility center charged with specified production tasks; also is usually a cost center and is held responsible for costs incurred while performing these tasks

Work in process Partially manufactured and incomplete units or materials

Work order Authorization to produce a certain quantity of a specific product

Working-capital statement An accounting statement showing increases and decreases in working capital

Working papers Records of audit procedures, the evidence that resulted from them, and the conclusions drawn therefrom

Worm code Machine-language code that erases software or data in core memory or stored externally, without authorization

Writeoff Reduction of an account balance

Xon-Xoff A common handshake convention

Zero-based budgeting The process of building up a budget based on each unit's objectives, rather than on the last period's budget

Bibliography

CHAPTER 1

Ackoff, R. L. "Management Misinformation Systems." *Management Science,* December 1, 1967, 147–156.

Ackoff, R. L. "Towards a System of System Concepts." *Management Science,* July 1971, 661–671.

Asimov, Isaac. "What Humans Will Never Need Computers to Do." *Computerworld Celebrating the Computer Age: Man, Computers and Society,* November 3, 1986, 20–22.

Bequai, August. " 'Information Man' Struggles to Control Information Society." *Computerworld Celebrating the Computer Age: Man, Computers and Society,* November 3, 1986, 84–88.

Bertalanffy, Ludwig von. *General System Theory.* New York: George Braziller, 1968. 289pp.

Bodnar, George H. and Hopwood, William S. *Accounting Information Systems,* 3d ed. Boston: Allyn and Bacon, 1987. 892pp.

Boulding, K. E. "General Systems Theory—The Skeleton of Science." *Management Science,* April 1, 1956, 197–208.

Churchman, C. West. *The Systems Approach.* New York: Dell, 1968.

Cushing, B. E. and Romney, Marshal B. *Accounting Information Systems and Business Organizations,* 4th ed. Reading, MA: Addison-Wesley Publishing Company, 1987. 906pp. Chapter 1.

Hicks, Jr., James O. and Leininger, Wayne E. *Accounting Information Systems,* 2d ed. St. Paul, MN: West Publishing Company, 1987. 748pp. Chapters 2, 11, 15.

Hopwood, Anthony G. "Toward an Organizational Perspective for the Study of Accounting and Information Systems." *Accounting, Organizations, and Society,* no. 1, 1978, 3–13.

Horngren, Charles T. and Foster, George. *Cost Accounting: A Managerial Emphasis,* 6th ed. Englewood Cliffs, NJ: Prentice-Hall, 1987. 980pp. Chapter 1.

Lee, John Y. *Managerial Accounting Changes for the 1990s.* McKay Business Systems, 1987. 87pp.

Moscove, Stephen A. and Simkin, Mark G. *Accounting Information Systems,* 3d ed. New York: John Wiley & Sons, 1987. Chapter 1.

Parker, Donn B. "20 Principles for Selecting Information Safeguards." *Journal of Accounting and EDP,* Fall 1986, 25–33.

Price, Wilson T. *Data Processing: The Fundamentals.* New York: Holt, Rinehart and Winston, 1982. 185pp.

Satchell, Steve. "IBM's New 80286 PC Ushers in Next Generation." *Infoworld,* April 20, 1987, 65.

Shouldice, Mike and Harvat, Mike. "Software Installations as an Accounting Firm Service." *Journal of Accounting and EDP,* Spring 1987, 44–46.

Wilkinson, Joseph W. *Accounting and Information Systems,* 2d ed. New York: John Wiley & Sons, 1986. 980pp. Chapters 1, 2.

Zivic, Louis J. (ed.) *Computers in Business.* Guilford, CT: Dushkin Publishing Group, Inc., 1986. 241pp.

CHAPTER 2

Ackoff, R. L. "Management Misinformation Systems." *Management Science,* December 1967, B147–B156.

Angus, Jeff. "Congress in Accord over PC Database Solution." *Infoworld,* July 13, 1987, 35.

Anthony, Robert M., Dearden, John, and Bedford, Norton. *Management Control Systems,* 5th ed. Homewood, IL: Richard D. Irwin, 1984. 851pp.

Bodnar, George H. and Hopwood, William S. *Accounting Information Systems,* 3d ed. Boston: Allyn and Bacon, 1987. 892pp. Chapter 2.

Buckley, J. W. "Goal-Process-System Interaction in Management." *Business Horizons,* December 1, 1971.

Cushing, B. E. and Romney, Marshal B. *Accounting Information Systems and Business Organizations,* 4th ed. Reading, MA: Addison-Wesley Publishing Company, 1987. 906pp. Chapter 2.

Cyert, R. M. and March, J. G. *A Behavioral Theory of the Firm.* Englewood Cliffs, NJ: Prentice-Hall, 1973.

Fasci, M. A. and Willis, D. "Evaluating EDP Reports for Strategic Decision Making." *Financial Executive,* May 1981.

Feltham, G. A. "The Value of Information." *The Accounting Review,* 1968, 684–696.

Gorry, G. A. and Morton, M. S. S. "A Framework for Management Information Systems." *Sloan Management Review,* Fall 1971.

Hicks, Jr., James O. and Leininger, Wayne E. *Accounting Information Systems,* 2d ed. St. Paul, MN: West Publishing Company, 1987. 748pp. Chapter 1.

Johnson, R. A., Kast, F. E., and Rosenzweig, J. E. "Systems Theory and Management." *Management Science,* January 1, 1964, 367–384.

LaPlante, Alice. "Deloitte Haskins & Sells Decentralizes PC Support." *Infoworld,* March 2, 1987, 33.

LaPlante, Alice. "Firms Miss Full Return on Investment, Study Says." *Infoworld,* May 11, 1987, 37.

Markus, M. Lynne. *Systems in Organizations: Bugs + Features.* Boston: Pitman Publishers, 1984. 243pp.

Moscove, Stephen A. and Simkin, Mark G. *Accounting Information Systems,* 3d ed. New York: John Wiley & Sons, 1987. Chapter 2.

Ouchi, William G. "A Conceptual Framework for the Design of Organizational Control Mechanisms." *Management Science,* September 1979, 833–848.

Picher, Oliver, Lubrano, Cynthia, and Theophano, Rochelle. "The Promise of Application Software." *Applications Software Today,* Summer 1987, 37.

Skinner, B. F. "Technology: How Is It Changing the CFO's Job?" *Financial Executive,* May 1986, 21–24.

Warner, Edward. "Executive Information Systems Gaining Favor." *Infoworld*, December 15, 1986, 39.

CHAPTER 3

Anthony, Robert M., Dearden, John, and Bedford, Norton. *Management Control Systems*, 5th ed. Homewood,IL: Richard D. Irwin, 1984. 851pp.

Beniger, James. "Information Society and the Control Revolution." *Computerworld Celebrating the Computer Age: Man, Computers and Society*, November 3, 1986, 147–150.

Beyer, Robert and Trawicki, Donald J. *Profitability Accounting for Planning and Control*, 2d ed. New York: The Ronald Press, 1972. 403pp.

Bodnar, George H. and Hopwood, William S. *Accounting Information Systems*, 3d ed. Boston: Allyn and Bacon, 1987. 892pp. Chapter 7.

Clancy, Donald K. "The Management Control Problems of Responsibility Reporting." *Management Accounting*, March 1978, 35–40.

Clukey, Lee Paul. *UNIX & XENIX Demystified*. Blue Ridge Summit, PA: TAB Books Inc., 1985. 243pp.

Cushing, B. E. and Romney, Marshal B. *Accounting Information Systems and Business Organizations*, 4th ed. Reading, MA: Addison-Wesley Publishing Company, 1987. 906pp. Chapter 20.

Held, Gilbert. *IBM PC: User's Reference Manual*. Rochelle Park, NJ: Hayden Book Co., 1985. 453pp.

Hildebrand, George. *Using Microcomputers in Managerial Accounting*. Santa Cruz, CA: Mitchell Publishing, 1985.

Horngren, Charles T. and Foster, George. *Cost Accounting: A Managerial Emphasis*, 6th ed. Englewood Cliffs, NJ: Prentice-Hall, 1987. 980pp. Chapters 5, 6, 7.

Jones, Reginald L. and Trentin, H. George. *Budgeting—Key to Planning and Control*. American Management Assoc. Inc., 1971. 308pp.

Kaplan, R. S. "The Evolution of Management Accounting," *The Accounting Review*, June 1984, 390–418.

Loebbecke, James K. and Vasarhelyi, Miklos A. *Microcomputers: Applications to Business Problems*. Homewood, IL: Richard D. Irwin, 1986. 287pp.

Maciariello, Joseph A. *Management Control Systems*. Englewood Cliffs, NJ: Prentice-Hall, 1984. 591pp.

Maller, Steven. *Mastering Omnis 3*. Blue Ridge Summit, PA: TAB Books Inc., 1986. 208pp.

Moscove, Stephen A. and Simkin, Mark G. *Accounting Information Systems*, 3d ed. New York: John Wiley & Sons, 1987. Chapter 3.

Potter, E. E. "How to Integrate and Consolidate General Ledger Systems for Financial Control." *Journal of Accounting and EDP*, Spring 1987, 4–10.

Sorensen, Karen. "Special Report: Dot-Matrix Printers." *Infoworld*, July 28, 1986, 29.

Welsch, Glenn A. *Budgeting: Profit Planning and Control*, 4th ed. Englewood Cliffs, NJ: Prentice-Hall, 1976. 602pp.

Wilkinson, Joseph W. *Accounting and Information Systems*, 2d ed. New York: John Wiley & Sons, 1986. 980pp. Chapters 5, 6, 15.

Zircher, J. R. "The EDP Technician, the Accountant, and Internal Control." *Management Accounting*, September 1975, 38–40.

CHAPTER 4

Anderson, Kevin and Bernard, Alan. "Developing Standards for Microcomputer Acquisition and Use." *Accounting and EDP*, Summer 1985, 57–59.

Babbage, Henry P. *Babbage's Calculating Engines.* Los Angeles, CA: Tomash, 1982. 369pp.

Bodnar, George H. and Hopwood, William S. *Accounting Information Systems*, 3d ed. Boston: Allyn and Bacon, 1987. 892pp. Chapters 8, 9.

Cushing, B. E. and Romney, Marshal B. *Accounting Information Systems and Business Organizations*, 4th ed. Reading, MA: Addison-Wesley Publishing Company, 1987. 906 pp. Chapter 5.

Date, C. J. *Database, a Primer.* Reading, MA: Addison-Wesley Publishing Company, 1983. 265pp.

Fife, D. W., Hardgrave, W. T., and Deutsch, D. R. *Database Concepts.* South-Western Publishing Co., Cincinnati: 1986, 294pp.

Harrar, George. "In the Beginning . . . An Interview with J. Presper Eckert, Co-Inventor of ENIAC." *Computerworld Celebrating the Computer Age: Man, Computers and Society*, November 3, 1986, 3–10.

Heckel, Paul. *The Elements of Friendly Software Design.* New York: Warner Books, 1984.

Hicks, Jr., James O. and Leininger, Wayne E. *Accounting Information Systems*, 2d ed. St. Paul, MN: West Publishing Company, 1987. 748pp. Chapters 4, 6, 7.

Howe, D. R. *Data Analysis for Data Base Design.* London: Edward Arnold, 1983. 307pp.

Illingworth, Valerie, Glaser, Edward L., and Pyle, I. C. *Dictionary of Computing*, 2d ed. Oxford, United Kingdom: Oxford Science Publications, 1986. 416pp.

King, Steve. "Ooops! Programs That Retrieve Deleted Data." *Infoworld*, July 20, 1987, 39.

Lach, Eric. "Word Processing Accessories." *Infoworld*, December 15, 1986, 47.

Levinson, Sherwin and Wood, Lamont. "Laptop." *Infoworld*, September 7, 1987, 47.

Loebbecke, James K. and Vasarhelyi, Miklos A. *Microcomputers: Applications to Business Problems.* Homewood, IL: Richard D. Irwin, 1986. 287pp.

Milburn, Ken. "Multiscanning Monitors." *Infoworld*, August 17, 1987, 39.

Moscove, Stephen A. and Simkin, Mark G. *Accounting Information Systems*, 3d ed. New York: John Wiley & Sons, 1987. Chapters 17, 19, 20.

Plemmons, Patrick et al. *Essential Applications for the IBM PC and XT.* New York: Simon & Schuster, 1984. 235pp.

Rinder, Robert M. *A Practical Guide to Small Computers*, rev. ed. New York: Monarch Press, 1983. 285pp.

Satchell, Stephen. "Fast Hard Disk Drives for the AT." *Infoworld*, May 4, 1987, 43.

Satchell, Stephen. "Tape Backup Systems for the IBM PC and Compatibles." *Infoworld*, August 3, 1987, 33.

Satchell, Stephen. "386 System Offers High Quality, Speed, Price." *Infoworld*, August 10, 1987, 61.

Warner, Edward. "Spreadsheets." *Infoworld*, February 9, 1987, 43.

Wilkinson, Joseph W. *Accounting and Information Systems*, 2d ed. New York: John Wiley & Sons, 1986. 980pp. Chapters 7, 8, 9, 10.

CHAPTER 5

Bodnar, George H. and Hopwood, William S. *Accounting Information Systems,* 3d ed. Boston: Allyn and Bacon, 1987. 892pp. Chapters 10, 14.

Borland International. *REFLEX for the MAC.* Scotts Valley, CA: Borland International, 1986. 327pp.

Brink, Victor Z. and Witt, Herbert. *Modern Internal Auditing: Appraising Operations and Controls.* New York: John Wiley & Sons, 1982. 882pp.

Burns, R. N. and Dennis, A. R. "Selecting the Appropriate Applications Development Technology." *Data Base,* Fall 1985, 19–23.

Cornick, Delroy L. *Auditing in the Electronic Environment.* Mount Airy, MD: Lomond Publications Inc., 1981. 316pp.

Crabb, Don. "Four LAN Databases for the Power User." *Infoworld,* May 25, 1987, 41.

Cushing, B. E. and Romney, Marshal B. *Accounting Information Systems and Business Organizations,* 4th ed. Reading, MA: Addison-Wesley Publishing Company, 1987. 906pp. Chapters 6, 9.

Davis, Keagle W. and Perry, William E. *Auditing Computer Applications—A Basic Systematic Approach.* New York: John Wiley & Sons, 1982. 661pp.

Everest, Gordon C. *Database Management.* New York: McGraw-Hill, 1986. 816pp.

Gilmour, Robert W. *Business Systems Handbook.* Englewood Cliffs, NJ: Prentice-Hall, 1979, 229pp.

Grosch, Herbert. "Machines May Think Better Than, But Never The Same As, Humans." *Computerworld Celebrating the Computer Age: Man, Computers and Society,* November 3, 1986, 52–53.

Halper, S., Davis, G., O'Neil-Duane, P., and Pfau, P. *Handbook of EDP Auditing.* Boston: Warren, Gorham & Lamont, 1985.

Hicks, Jr., James O. and Leininger, Wayne E. *Accounting Information Systems,* 2d ed. St. Paul, MN: West Publishing Company, 1987. 748pp. Chapters 8, 9.

Hoffer, J. A. "Database Design Practices for Inverted Files." *Information & Management,* vol. 3, 1980, 149.

Kroenke, David. *Database Processing,* 2d ed. Chicago: Science Research Associates, 1983. 607pp. Chapter 1.

Martin, James. *The Principles of Data-Base Management.* Englewood Cliffs, NJ: Prentice-Hall, 1976. 352pp. Chapters 1, 6, 9, 10, 11.

Moscove, Stephen A. and Simkin, Mark G. *Accounting Information Systems,* 3d ed. New York: John Wiley & Sons, 1987. Chapter 5.

Petreley, Nicholas. "Relational Databases." *Infoworld,* August 24, 1987, 47.

Smith, James F. and Mufti, Amer. "Using the Relational Database." *Management Accounting,* October 1985.

Stern, Myles. "A Data Base Primer for Accounting." *Accounting and EDP,* Summer 1985, 14–21.

Ullman, Jeffrey D. *Principles of Database Systems,* 2d ed. Rockville, MD: Computer Science Press, 1982. 484pp.

Wilkinson, Joseph W. *Accounting and Information Systems,* 2d ed. New York: John Wiley & Sons, 1986. 980pp. Chapters 3, 4, 11, 12.

CHAPTER 6

Bodnar, George H. and Hopwood, William S. *Accounting Information Systems*, 3d ed. Boston: Allyn and Bacon, 1987. 892pp. Chapter 3.

Chalmers, Leslie. "End-User Computing and Data Security—Can You Have Both?" *Journal of Accounting and EDP*, Summer 1986, 62–65.

Cushing, B. E. and Romney, Marshal B. *Accounting Information Systems and Business Organizations*, 4th ed. Reading, MA: Addison-Wesley Publishing Company, 1987. 906pp. Chapters 3, 7.

Eliason, Alan L. *Online Business Computer Applications*, 2d ed. Chicago: Science Research Associates, 1987. 503pp. Chapters 1, 2.

Grabski, Severin V. "Auditor Participation in Accounting Systems Design: Past Involvement and Future Challenges." *Journal of Information Systems*, Fall 1986, 3–23.

Hedge, Gary W. "Designing Modern Accounting Software." *Applications Software Today*, Summer 1987, 47.

Hicks, Jr., James O. and Leininger, Wayne E. *Accounting Information Systems*, 2d ed. St. Paul, MN: West Publishing Company, 1987. 748pp. Chapter 18.

Horngren, Charles T. *Cost Accounting—A Managerial Emphasis*. Englewood Cliffs, NJ: Prentice-Hall, 1982. 997pp.

Kroenke, David. *Database Processing*, 2d ed. Chicago: Science Research Associates, 1983. 607pp. Chapter 3.

Needle, Sheldon P. "A Guide to Accounting Software for Microcomputers." *CTS*, 1984.

Matz, Adolph and Usry, Milton F. *Cost Accounting—Planning and Control*. Cincinnati: South-Western Publishing Co., 1984. 786pp.

McMickle, Peter L. "Paradox Simplifies Development of Microcomputer Accounting Packages." *Journal of Accounting and EDP*, Winter 1987, 63–66.

Moscove, Stephen A. and Simkin, Mark G. *Accounting Information Systems*, 3d ed. New York: John Wiley & Sons, 1987. Chapter 4.

Wilkinson, Joseph W. *Accounting and Information Systems*, 2d ed. New York: John Wiley & Sons, 1986. 980pp. Chapter 13.

CHAPTER 7

Bodnar, George H. and Hopwood, William S. *Accounting Information Systems*, 3d ed. Boston: Allyn and Bacon, 1987. 892pp. Chapters 5, 12.

Cushing, B. E. and Romney, Marshal B. *Accounting Information Systems and Business Organizations*, 4th ed. Reading, MA: Addison-Wesley Publishing Company, 1987. 906pp. Chapter 16.

Davis, James R. and Cushing, Barry E. *Accounting Information Systems: A Book of Readings with Cases*, 2d ed. Reading, MA: Addison-Wesley Publishing Company, 1987. 359pp.

Eliason, Alan L. *Online Business Computer Applications*, 2d ed. Chicago: Science Research Associates, 1987. 503pp. Chapters 4, 5, 6.

Forsythe, Richard (ed.) *Expert Systems: Principles and Case Studies*. New York: Chapman & Hall, 1984. 228pp.

Hicks, Jr., James O. and Leininger, Wayne E. *Accounting Information Systems*, 2d ed. St. Paul, MN: West Publishing Company, 1987. 748pp. Chapters 19, 20.

Management Science America. *Accounts Receivable II: Commercial System.* Atlanta: Management Science America, 1986.

Management Science America. *Realtime, Online Accounts Receivable.* Atlanta: Management Science America, 1986.

Moscove, Stephen A. and Simkin, Mark G. *Accounting Information Systems,* 3d ed. New York: John Wiley & Sons, 1987. Chapter 6.

NCR Corporation. *NCR Interactive Accounts Receivable System.* Dayton, OH: NCR Corporation, 1977.

O'Shea, Tim and Eisenstadt, Marc (eds.) *Artificial Intelligence: Tools, Techniques, and Applications.* New York: Harper & Row, 1984. 497pp.

Rushinek, A. and Rushinek, S. F. "Accounting and Billing Software and User Reactions: An Interactive Diagnostic Audit Trail." *Information & Management,* vol. 9, 1985, 9.

Spencer, Donald D. *The Illustrated Computer Dictionary.* Columbus, OH: Charles E. Merrill, 1980. 187pp.

Vickman, Thomas M. *Handbook of Model Accounting Reports and Formats.* Englewood Cliffs, NJ: Prentice-Hall, 1987. Chapters 3, 4, 5, 15.

Wilkinson, Joseph W. *Accounting Information Systems,* 2d ed. New York: John Wiley & Sons, 1986. 980pp. Chapters 14, 16.

CHAPTER 8

Bodnar, George H. and Hopwood, William S. *Accounting Information Systems,* 3d ed. Boston: Allyn and Bacon, 1987. 892pp. Chapters 5, 6.

Cushing, B. E. and Romney, Marshal B. *Accounting Information Systems and Business Organizations,* 4th ed. Reading, MA: Addison-Wesley Publishing Company, 1987. 906pp. Chapter 17.

Eliason, Alan L. *Online Business Computer Applications,* 2d ed. Chicago: Science Research Associates, 1987. 503pp. Chapters 9, 10.

Hicks, Jr., James O. and Leininger, Wayne E. *Accounting Information Systems,* 2d ed. St. Paul, MN: West Publishing Company, 1987. 748pp. Chapter 19.

Honeywell Information Systems. *Accounts Payable Systems Handbook.* Waltham, MA: Honeywell Information Systems, 1976.

Management Science America. *Accounts Payable II.* Atlanta: Management Science America, 1986.

Needle, Sheldon. "IBM's New Accounting Package: An Evaluation." *The Journal of Accountancy,* July 1985, 86–94.

Wilkinson, Joseph W. *Accounting and Information Systems,* 2d ed. New York: John Wiley & Sons, 1986. 980pp. Chapters 17, 18.

Vickman, Thomas M. *Handbook of Model Accounting Reports and Formats.* Englewood Cliffs, NJ: Prentice-Hall, 1987. Chapter 10.

CHAPTER 9

Bodnar, George H. and Hopwood, William S. *Accounting Information Systems,* 3d ed. Boston: Allyn and Bacon, 1987. 892pp. Chapters 6, 13.

Burke, Thomas J. M. and Lehman, Maxwell (eds.) *Communications Technologies and Information Flow.* New York: Pergamon Press, 1981. 151pp.

Carter, Roger. *Business Administration: A Textbook for the Computer Age.* Rockville, MD: Computer Science Press, 1984. 200pp.

Closs, David J. "Designing Computerized Inventory Management Systems." *Accounting and EDP*, Summer 1985, 22–29.

Cushing, B. E. and Romney, Marshal B. *Accounting Information Systems and Business Organizations*, 4th ed. Reading, MA: Addison-Wesley Publishing Company, 1987. 906pp. Chapter 18.

Dena, James A. and Smith, Lawrence Murphy. "Designing and Implementing an Integrated Job Cost Accounting System." *The Journal of Information Systems*, Fall 1986, 102–112.

Deran, David R. "Cost Control Through Control Reporting." *Management Accounting*, April 1982, 29–33.

Eliason, Alan L. *Online Business Computer Applications*, 2d ed. Chicago: Science Research Associates, 1987. 503pp. Chapters 8, 12.

Gessner, Robert A. *Manufacturing Information Systems*. New York: John Wiley & Sons, 1984. 221pp.

Goletz, W. K. and Muir, William T. "Implementing a Manufacturing Management System." *Price Waterhouse Review*, no. 1, 1983, 16–25.

Hicks, Jr., James O. and Leininger, Wayne E. *Accounting Information Systems*, 2d ed. St. Paul: MN: West Publishing Company, 1987. 748pp. Chapter 21.

Horngren, Charles T. and Foster, George. *Cost Accounting: A Managerial Emphasis*, 6th ed. Englewood Cliffs, NJ: Prentice-Hall, 1987. 980pp. Chapters 4, 12, 13, 17.

Howe, D. R. *Data Analysis for Data Base Design*. London: Edward Arnold, 1983. 307pp.

Leavitt, Gary S. and Sapp, Richard W. "Who's Minding the Store? Inventory Control for Bars and Clubs." *Management Accounting*, November 1980, 13–24.

Martin, James R. "Integrating the Major Concepts and Techniques of Cost and Managerial Accounting: A Recommendation." *Issues in Accounting Education*, Spring 1987, 72–84.

Moscove, Stephen, Crowningshield, Gerald, and Gorman, Kenneth. *Cost Accounting with Managerial Applications*. Boston: Houghton Mifflin, 1985. Chapter 17.

Rhodes, David et al. *Computers, Information and Manufacturing Systems*. New York: Praeger, 1984. 152pp.

Sullivan, Kenneth M. *Practical Computer Cost Accounting*. New York: Van Nostrand, 1983. 298pp.

Vickman, Thomas M. *Handbook of Model Accounting Reports and Formats*. Englewood Cliffs, NJ: Prentice-Hall, 1987. Chapters 6, 7, 8, 9, 16.

Vollum, Robert B. "Cost Accounting: The Key to Capturing Cost Information on the Factory Floor." *Accounting and EDP*, Summer 1985, 44–51.

Wilkinson, Joseph W. *Accounting and Information Systems*, 2d ed. New York: John Wiley & Sons, 1986. 980 pp. Chapters 19, 20.

CHAPTER 10

Biggs, Charles L., Birks, Evan, and Atkins, William. *Managing the Systems Development Process*. Englewood Cliffs, NJ: Prentice-Hall, 1980. 408pp.

Collins, Stephen H. "Governmental Accounting and Auditing." *The Journal of Accountancy*, no. 117, 1986, 92–97.

Davidson, Sidney and Weil, Roman L. (eds.) *Handbook of Modern Accounting*, 3d ed. New York: McGraw-Hill, 1983. Chapters 41, 42.

Fanning, David (ed.) *Handbook of Management Accounting*. Aldershot, United Kingdom: Gower Publishing Company, 1983. Chapter 21.

General Accounting Office. "Social Security Administration's Progress in Modernizing Its Computer Operations." *Information & Management,* vol. 9, 1985, 283.

Hancock, Sidney. "An Approach to Hospital Data Processing Development." *Management Accounting,* March 1978.

Hay, Leon. *Accounting for Governmental and Non-Profit Entities,* 6th ed., Homewood, IL: Richard D. Irwin, 1980.

Ives, Martin. "Accountability and Governmental Financial Reporting." *The Journal of Accountancy,* October 1987, 130–135.

Mann, Steve. "The Accounting Software Match Game." *Macworld,* October 1987, 136–149.

Moscove, Stephen A. and Simkin, Mark G. *Accounting Information Systems,* 3d ed. New York: John Wiley & Sons, 1987. Chapter 16.

National Commission on Governmental Accounting. *Governmental Accounting and Financial Reporting Principles, Statement 1.* Chicago: Municipal Finance Officers Association, 1979.

Novak, Stephen R. *Field Auditor's Manual and Guide.* Englewood Cliffs, NJ: Institute for Business Planning, 1980. Chapters 18, 19.

CHAPTER 11

Ahituv, N. and Hadass, M. "Organizational Structure of a Complex Data Processing Department." *Information & Management,* vol. 1, 1978, 53.

Allen, Brandt. "An Unmanaged Computer System Can Stop You Dead." *Harvard Business Review,* November 12, 1982.

Bodnar, George H. and Hopwood, William S. *Accounting Information Systems,* 3d ed. Boston: Allyn and Bacon, 1987. 892pp. Chapters 9, 11.

Brill, Alan E. *Building Controls into Structured Systems.* New York: Yourdon Press, 1983. 149pp. Chapters 1, 4, 5.

Calvo, Melissa. "Modems and Communications Software." *Infoworld,* September 15, 1986, 25.

Cortada, James W. *EDP Costs and Changes: Finance, Budgets & Cost Control in DP.* Englewood Cliffs, NJ: Prentice-Hall, 1980. 287pp.

Cushing, B. E. and Romney, Marshal B. *Accounting Information Systems and Business Organizations,* 4th ed. Reading, MA: Addison-Wesley Publishing Company, 1987. 906pp. Chapter 10.

Drury, D. H. "Conditions Affecting Chargeback Effectiveness." *Information & Management,* vol. 6, 1982, 317.

Flynn, Laurie. "Firms Often Misjudge the Complexity of LANs." *Infoworld,* October 20, 1986. 21.

Franci, Thomas J. et al. *Planning, Budgeting, and Control for Data Processing.* New York: Van Nostrand, 1984. 180pp.

Garner, Rochelle. "Spreadsheet Products." *Infoworld,* November 10, 1986, 51.

Gilmour, Robert W. *Business Systems Handbook.* Englewood Cliffs, NJ: Prentice-Hall, 1979. 229pp.

Hicks, Jr., James O. and Leininger, Wayne E. *Accounting Information Systems,* 2d ed. St. Paul, MN: West Publishing Company, 1987. 748pp. Chapter 12.

Holmes, F. W. "Auditing from the DP Manager's Viewpoint." *The Internal Auditor,* November/December 1975, 29–34.

Kroenke, David, *Database Processing,* 2d ed. Chicago: Science Research Associates, 1983. 607pp. Chapter 14.

Loew, Gary W. "Budgeting a 'Top-Down, Bottom-Up, Top-Down' Process." *The CPA Journal,* September 1987, 98–99.

Moscove, Stephen A. and Simkin, Mark G. *Accounting Information Systems,* 3d ed. New York: John Wiley & Sons, 1987. Chapter 15.

Needle, David. "Presentation Graphics Software." *Infoworld,* September 22, 1986, 35.

Perry, William E. *Data Processor's Survival Guide to Accounting.* New York: John Wiley & Sons, 1985. 325 pp.

Perry, William E. *EDP Administration and Control.* Englewood Cliffs, NJ: Prentice-Hall, 1985. 354pp.

Perry, William E. "Software Maintenance—An Unexplored Audit Area." *Journal of Accounting and EDP,* Summer 1986, 59–61.

Price Waterhouse & Co. *Management Controls for Data Processing,* 2d ed. White Plains, NY: IBM Corporation, 1976. 95pp.

Rittenberg, L. E. and Litecky, C. E. "Analysis of Current Data Processing Weaknesses." *EDP Auditor,* Spring 1980, 33–42.

Selig, Gad J. "Strategic Planning for Information Resource Management." University Microfilm, 1983, 257pp.

Sorensen, Karen. "Dot-Matrix Printers." *Infoworld,* July 28, 1986, 29.

Sorensen, Karen. "Laser Printers," *Infoworld,* November 17, 1986, 55.

CHAPTER 12

Bodnar, George H. and Hopwood, William S. *Accounting Information Systems,* 3d ed. Boston: Allyn and Bacon, 1987. 892pp. Chapters 4, 11.

Brill, Alan E. *Building Controls into Structured Systems.* New York: Yourdon Press, 1983. 149pp. Chapters 6, 7, 8.

Chalmers, Leslie E. "The Data Encryption Standard." *Journal of Accounting and EDP,* Fall 1986, 65–67.

Cushing, B. E. and Romney, Marshal B. *Accounting Information Systems and Business Organizations,* 4th ed. Reading, MA: Addison-Wesley Publishing Company, 1987 906pp. Chapters 4, 14.

Davidson, Sidney and Weil, Roman L. (eds.) *Handbook of Modern Accounting,* 3d ed. New York: McGraw-Hill, 1983. Chapter 39.

Fanning, David (ed.) *Handbook of Management Accounting.* Aldershot, United Kingdom: Gower Publishing Company, 1983. Chapter 22.

Gal, G. and McCarthy, W. E. "Specification of Internal Accounting Controls in a Database Environment." *Computers & Security,* 1985, 23–32.

Harper, Jr., Robert M. "Internal Control of Microcomputers in Local Area Networks." *The Journal of Information Systems,* Fall 1986, 67–80.

Hicks, Jr., James O. and Leininger, Wayne E. *Accounting Information Systems,* 2d ed. St. Paul, MN: West Publishing Company, 1987. 748pp. Chapters 15, 16.

Horngren, Charles T. and Foster, George. *Cost Accounting: A Managerial Emphasis,* 6th ed. Englewood Cliffs, NJ: Prentice-Hall, 1987. 980pp. Chapter 27.

Joseph, W. Gilbert. "Appraising the Control Environment for Accounting Programs." *Journal of Accounting and EDP,* Summer 1986, 7–14.

LaPlante, Alice. "Security Firm Develops Retina-Scanning Device." *Infoworld,* January 26, 1987, 35.

Loebbecke, James K. and Zuber, George R. "Evaluating Internal Control." *The Journal of Accountancy,* February 1980, 49–57.

Moscove, Stephen A. and Simkin, Mark G. *Accounting Information Systems,* 3d ed. New York: John Wiley & Sons, 1987. Chapters 7, 8.

Sperry, John and Hicks, Donald W. "Do Your Data Files Contain Errors?" *Journal of Accounting and EDP,* Spring 1987, 36–38.

Stanford, Eric. "Management Control Risks in Microcomputing Systems." *Accounting and EDP,* Summer 1985, 38–43.

Warner, S. "Accounting Control Problems in Systems Using Minicomputers." *The Internal Auditor,* June 1981, 46–50.

Weiss, Jirl. "Firms Find Hidden Costs in Employee Use of PCs." *Infoworld,* April 13, 1987, 31.

CHAPTER 13

Bacon, Chris N. "Six Opportunities for DP Fraud." *Journal of Accounting and EDP,* Summer 1986, 42–46.

Bequai, August. *Computer Crime.* Lexington, MA: Lexington Books, 1978. 207pp.

Bequai, August. *How to Prevent Computer Crime: A Guide for Managers.* New York: John Wiley & Sons, 1983. 308pp.

Bodnar, George H. and Hopwood, William S. *Accounting Information Systems,* 3d ed. Boston: Allyn and Bacon, 1987. 892pp. Chapter 16.

Cony, Ed and Penn, Stanley. "Tale of a Kite: How 2 Depositors Ran a Giant Check Scheme at 2 New York Banks." *The Wall Street Journal,* August 11, 1986, 1, 8.

Coughlan, John W. "The Fairfax Embezzlement." *Management Accounting,* May 1983.

Crabb, Don and the Review Board. "Schwab's Financial Software Is Good Value." *Infoworld,* June 2, 1986, 46.

Duyn, J. A. van. *The Human Factor in Computer Crime.* Princeton, NJ: Petrocelli, 1985. 162pp.

Ernst & Whinney. *Computer Fraud.* Cleveland: Ernst & Whinney, 1987. 54pp.

Gurry, E. J. "Locating Potential Irregularities." *The Journal of Accountancy,* September 1975, 111–114.

Jacobs, Sanford L. "How to Prevent an Employee from Ripping Off the Firm." *The Wall Street Journal,* May 10, 1982, 21.

LaPlante, Alice. "Computer Fraud Threat Increasing, Study Says." *Infoworld,* May 18, 1987, 47.

LaPlante, Alice. "PC LAN Security a Hot Issue at Seminar." *Infoworld,* December 21, 1987, 33.

Levy, Marvin M. "Financial Fraud: Schemes and Indicia." *Journal of Accountancy,* 1985.

Manzi, Jim and Osborne, Adam. "The Look and Feel Debate." *Infoworld,* March 30, 1987. 8.

Moscove, Stephen A. and Simkin, Mark G. *Accounting Information Systems,* 3d ed. New York: John Wiley & Sons, 1987. Chapter 9.

Nasuti, Frank W. "Investigating Computer Crime." *Journal of Accounting and EDP,* Fall 1986, 13–19.

National Commission on Fraudulent Financial Reporting. *Report of the National Commission on Fraudulent Reporting (Exposure Draft).* Washington, D.C.: National Commission on Fraudulent Reporting, May 1, 1987. 191 pp.

Petreley, Nicholas and the Review Board. "Rbase V: Functional, Easy to Use." *Infoworld,* September 22, 1986, 49.

Srinivasan, C. A. and Dascher, P. E. "Management of Computer Security: An Auditing Viewpoint." *Magazine of Bank Administration,* March 1980, 50–53.

Welsch, Mark J. "PC and AT Compatibles." *Infoworld,* July 14, 1986, 29.

CHAPTER 14

AICPA Auditing Standards Executive Committee. *Statement on Auditing Standards 1: Codification of Auditing Standards and Procedures.* New York: AICPA, 1973. 235pp.

Auditing Standards Board. "Statement on Auditing Standards 48: The Effect of Computer Processing on the Examination of Financial Statements." New York: AICPA, 1984. 9pp.

Blanding, Steven E. "Audit, Control, and Security of Micro-Mainframe Systems." *Journal of Accounting and EDP,* Fall 1986, 54–59.

Bodnar, George H. and Hopwood, William S. *Accounting Information Systems,* 3d ed. Boston: Allyn and Bacon, 1987. 892pp. Chapter 21.

Brill, A. E. "EDP Auditors' Tales of Horror." *Journal of Systems Management,* January 1982, 20–22.

Brill, A. E. *Building Controls into Structured Systems.* New York: Yourdon Press, 1983. 149pp. Chapters 2, 3, 9.

Brown, Jr., N. "Making the EDP Audit Specialist Part of the Audit Team." *The Internal Auditor,* February 1987, 11–15.

Colbert, John L. "Audit Risk—Tracing the Evolution." *Accounting Horizons,* September 1987, 49–57.

Computer Services Guidelines: Management Control and Audit of Advanced EDP Systems. New York: American Institute of CPAs, 1977.

Cushing, B. E. and Romney, Marshal B. *Accounting Information Systems and Business Organizations,* 4th ed. Reading, MA: Addison-Wesley Publishing Company, 1987. 906pp. Chapter 15.

Dowell, C. D. and Hall, J. A. "EDP Controls with Audit Cost Implications." *Journal of Accounting, Auditing, and Finance,* Fall 1981, 30–40.

Elliot, Robert K. and Jacobson, Peter D. "Audit Technology: A Heritage and a Promise." *Journal of Accountancy,* May 1987, 198–217.

Gafford, W. Wade and Carmichael, D. R. "Materiality, Audit Risk, and Sampling: A Nuts-and-Bolts Approach (Part One)." *The Journal of Accountancy,* October 1984, 109.

Goossens, B. and Schouten, N. "Using the Computer for Audit." *Information & Management,* vol. 4, 1981, 3.

Halper, S., Davis, G., O'Neil-Duane, P., and Pfau, P. *Handbook of EDP Auditing.* Boston: Warren, Gorham & Lamont, 1985.

Hicks, Jr., James O. and Leininger, Wayne E. *Accounting Information Systems,* 2d ed. St. Paul, MN: West Publishing Company, 1987. 748pp. Chapter 17.

Hubbert, J. F. "Establishing an EDP Audit Function." *EDPACS: The Audit, Control, and Security Newsletter,* June 1982, 9–14.

Johnson, B. "New World of Corporate DP Auditors Sighted." *Computerworld,* May 18, 1981, 23.

LaPlante, Alice. "Micros Earn Their MBAs." *Infoworld,* February 3, 1986, 24.

Leichti, Janet L. "How to Evelute Inherent Risk—and Improve Your Audits." *The Practical Accountant,* March 1986, 59–64.

Methodios, I. "Internal Controls and Audit." *Journal of Systems Management*, June 1976, 6–14.

Moscove, Stephen A. and Simkin, Mark G. *Accounting Information Systems*, 3d ed. New York: John Wiley & Sons, 1987. Chapter 10.

Perry, W. E. "The Four Phases of EDP Auditing." *EDPACS: The Audit, Control, and Security Newsletter*, May 1975, 1–8.

Porter, W. Thomas and Perry, William E. *EDP Controls and Auditing*, 5th ed. Boston: Kent Publishing Company, 1987. 607pp.

Price Waterhouse & Co. *Management Controls for Data Processing*, 2d ed. White Plains, NY: IBM Corporation, 1976. 95pp.

Sorensen, Karen. "Expert Systems Introduced for IBM RT PC, Mac +." *Infoworld*, February 3, 1986, 10.

Sorensen, Karen. "Fifth Generation: Slow to Rise." *Infoworld*, June 9, 1986, 35.

Welch, Mark J. "Data Storage: Hard Disk, Tape Backup Choices Grow." *Infoworld*, June 16, 1986, 37.

CHAPTER 15

Bailey, A. D. et al. "Auditing, Artificial Intelligence and Expert Systems." *Decision Support Systems: Theory and Practice*, June 1, 1985.

Blanning, R. W. "Management Applications of Expert Systems." *Information & Management*, vol. 7, 1984, 311.

CODASYL (Conference of Data System Language). *Framework for Distributed DB Systems*. Association for Computing Machinery, 1985. 134pp.

Cohen, Paul and Feigenbaum, Edward. *The Handbook of Artificial Intelligence: II.* Palo Alto, CA: William Kaufman, Inc., 1982. 428pp.

"Computers: When Will the Slump End?" *Business Week*, April 21, 1986, 58.

Conlon, Tom. *Learning Micro PROLOG*. Reading, MA: Addison-Wesley Publishing Company, 1985. 183pp.

Elliot, R. K. and Kielich, J. A. "Expert Systems for Accountants." *Journal of Accountancy*, September 1, 1985, 126–134.

Fiderio, Janet, "Tying Minds Together . . . An Interview with Joshua Lederberg." *Computerworld Celebrating the Computer Age: Man, Computers and Society*, November 3, 1986, 25–26.

Forbes, Jim. "Police Set Up Bulletin Board Stings." *Infoworld*, April 7, 1986, 5.

Forbes, Jim. "A Day in the Life of a Venture Capitalist." *Infoworld*, April 28, 1986, 38.

Ford, F. N. "Decision Support Systems and Expert Systems: A Comparison." *Information & Management*, vol. 8, 1985, 21.

Garsombke, Perrin and Parker, Larry M. "Decision Support and Expert Systems: Auditing in the Information Age." *Journal of Accounting and EDP*, Winter 1987, 20–25.

LaPlante, Alice. "Third-Party Maintenance Services." *Infoworld*, May 12, 1986, 43.

Lima, Tony. "Dbase III Plus Takes Heavyweight Title." *Infoworld*, April 7, 1986. 41.

Mace, Scott and Crabb, Don. "Getting Your Finances in Order." *Infoworld*, April 4, 1986, 26.

Mace, Scott and LaPlante, Alice. "CEOs Say Products Poorly Tested." *Infoworld*, May 12, 1986, 1.

Mace, Scott and Miller, Michael J. "Database Management Software." *Infoworld*, May 5, 1986, 39.

O'Shea, Tim and Eisenstadt, Marc (eds.) *Artificial Intelligence: Tools, Techniques, and Applications.* New York: Harper & Row, 1984. 497pp.

Petrosky, Mary and Crabb, Don. "Linking Up the Office: Buyers Face Tough Choices." *Infoworld*, March 24, 1986, 25.

Simon, Ruth. "The Morning After." *Forbes*, October 19, 1987, 164–168.

Sullivan-Trainor, Michael. "Marvin Minsky: Pioneer of AI—Making Machines Do What They Can't Do Yet." *Computerworld Celebrating the Computer Age: Man, Computers and Society*, November 3, 1986, 55–56.

Ten Dyke, R. P. "Outlook on Artificial Intelligence." *Journal of Accounting and EDP*, Summer 1985, 30–37.

Wolfe, C. and Viator, R. "Expert Systems in Accounting Perspective." *Journal of Accounting and EDP*, Summer 1986, 47–51.

CHAPTER 16

Bartik, Jean. "IBM's Token Ring: Have the Pieces Finally Come Together?" *Data Communications*, August 1984, 125–139.

Bodnar, George H. and Hopwood, William S. *Accounting Information Systems*, 3d ed. Boston: Allyn and Bacon, 1987. 892pp. Chapter 15.

Callas, Melinda and Skolnik, Sheryl. "Establishing and Controlling the Micro-Mainframe Link." *Journal of Accounting and EDP*, Summer 1985, 4–13.

Calvo, Melissa. "On-Line Services." *Infoworld*, November 3, 1987, 36.

Cerullo, Michael J. "Data Communications: Opportunities for Accountants." *The CPA Journal*, April 1984.

Crabb, Don. "Accounting Cheap, Easy for Dac's Easy." *Infoworld*, September 23, 1985, 35.

Crabb, Don. "Integrated Applications: LAN Programs with Something for Everyone." *Infoworld*, June 29, 1987, 33.

Cushing, B. E. and Romney, Marshal B. *Accounting Information Systems and Business Organizations*, 4th ed. Reading, MA: Addison-Wesley Publishing Company, 1987. 906pp. Chapter 8.

Forbes, Jim. "Decision Support Software: Still Hanging in Balance." *Infoworld*, December 23, 1985, 27.

Forsyth, Richard. *Expert Systems: Principles and Case Studies.* New York: Chapman and Hall, 1984. 231pp.

Gale, Andrew P. "Data Bases: An Accountant's Choice." *The Journal of Accountancy*, October 1985, 119–124.

Goodman, Hortense. "NAARS: the CPA's Electronic Shoebox." *The Journal of Accountancy*, October 1985, 125–133.

Hicks, Jr., James O. and Leininger, Wayne E. *Accounting Information Systems*, 2d ed. St. Paul, MN: West Publishing Company, 1987. 748pp. Chapter 10.

Howe, D. R. *Data Analysis for Data Base Design.* London: Edward Arnold, 1983. 307pp.

Kellner, Mark A. "Communications Software." *Infoworld*, March 2, 1987, 39.

Leigh, William E. and Doherty, Michael E. *Decision Support and Expert Systems.* Cincinnati: South-Western Publishing Co., 1986. 454pp.

Massey, L. Daniel. *Managing the Human Element in EDP.* Braintree, MA: D. H. Mark Publishing Co., 1969. 122pp.

Moore, Carl, Jaedicke, Robert, and Anderson, Lane. *Managerial Accounting,* 6th ed. Cincinnati: South-Western Publishing Co., 1984. 665pp.

Moscove, Stephen A. and Simkin, Mark G. *Accounting Information Systems,* 3d ed. New York: John Wiley & Sons, 1987. Chapter 18.

Petrosky, Mary. "The Thankless Job of LAN Administrator." *Infoworld,* January 6, 1986, 23.

Ranney, Elizabeth. "Data Security Violated Mostly on the Inside." *Infoworld,* September 23, 1985, 1.

Ranney, Elizabeth. "Networks Pose New Threats to Data Security." *Infoworld,* February 10, 1986. 23.

Spencer, Donald D. *The Illustrated Computer Dictionary.* Columbus, OH: Charles E. Merrill, 1980. 187pp.

Spiegelman, Lisa. "Sun Announces Products to Link PCs, MACs in LAN." *Infoworld,* June 15, 1987, 25.

Vanacek, Michael T., Zant, Robert M., and Guynes, Carl Stephen. "Distributed Data Processing: A New Tool for Accountants." *The Journal of Accountancy,* October 1980, 75.

CHAPTER 17

Angus, Jeff. "Firms Choose Decentralized PC Accounting." *Infoworld,* May 11, 1987, 37.

Bodnar, George H. and Hopwood, William S. *Accounting Information Systems,* 3d ed. Boston: Allyn and Bacon, 1987. 892pp. Chapters 17, 18.

Burke, Thomas and Lehman, Maxwell (eds.) *Communication Technologies and Information Flow.* New York: Pergamon Press, 1981. 151pp.

Clarke, Raymond T. and Associates. *Systems Life Cycle Guide.* Englewood Cliffs, NJ: Prentice-Hall, 1987.

Couger, Dan, Colter, Mel, and Knapp, Robert. *Advanced System Development/Feasibility Analysis.* New York: John Wiley & Sons, 1982. 506pp.

Cushing, B. E. and Romney, Marshal B. *Accounting Information Systems and Business Organizations,* 4th ed. Reading, MA: Addison-Wesley Publishing Company, 1987. 906pp. Chapter 11.

Davis, Carl G. et al. (eds.) *Entity-Relationship Approach to Software Engineering.* Amsterdam: Elsevier, 1983, 867pp.

Dolan, Kathleen. *Business Computer System Design.* Santa Cruz, CA: Mitchell Publishing, 1984. 323pp.

Eliason, Alan L. *Online Business Computer Applications,* 2d ed. Chicago: Science Research Associates, 1987. 503pp. Chapter 3.

Gilmour, Robert W. *Business Systems Handbook: Analysis, Design, and Documentation Standards.* Englewood Cliffs, NJ: Prentice-Hall, 1979. 229pp.

Hicks, Jr., James O. and Leininger, Wayne E. *Accounting Information Systems,* 2d ed. St. Paul, MN: West Publishing Company, 1987. 748pp. Chapters 11, 13.

Kole, M. A. "Going Outside for MIS Implementation." *Information & Management,* vol. 6, 1983, 261.

Kroenke, David. *Database Processing,* 2d ed. Chicago: Science Research Associates, 1983. 607pp. Chapter 2.

Kull, David. "Anatomy of a 4GL Disaster." *Computer Decisions,* February 11, 1986, 58–65.

LaPlante, Alice. "Productivity Tools Speed Systems Development." *Infoworld*, December 22, 1987, 25.

Martin, James. *Application Development Without Programmers*. Englewood Cliffs, NJ: Prentice-Hall, 1982.

Moscove, Stephen A. and Simkin, Mark G. *Accounting Information Systems*, 3d ed. New York: John Wiley & Sons, 1987. Chapters 11, 12.

1981–82 MAS Technical and Industry Consulting Practices Subcommittee. "MAS Practice Aid 1: EDP Engagement: Systems Planning and General Design." New York: AICPA, 1982. 23pp.

O'Shea, Tim and Eisenstadt, Marc. *Artificial Intelligence: Tools, Techniques, and Applications*. New York: Harper & Row, 1984, 497pp.

Revell, N. "Managing the Development of Database Systems." *Information & Management*, vol. 4, 1981, 197.

Rittenberg, L. E. *Auditor Independence and Systems Design*. Altamonte Springs, FL: Institute of Internal Auditors, Inc., 1977.

Strosberg, Linda. *Big Decisions for Small Business: What You Should Know Before You Buy a Computer*. New York: Harper & Row, 1984. 144pp.

CHAPTER 18

Angus, Jeff. "Info Center Managers Increase PC COBOL Use." *Infoworld*, February 16, 1987, 33.

Bally, L., Brittan, J., and Wagner, K. H. "A Prototype Approach to Information Systems Design and Development." *Information & Management*, vol. 1, 1977, 21.

Biggs, C. L., Birks, Evan G., and Atkins, William. *Managing the Systems Development Process*. Englewood Cliffs, NJ: Prentice-Hall, 1980. 408pp.

Bodnar, George H. and Hopwood, William S. *Accounting Information Systems*, 3d ed. Boston: Allyn and Bacon, 1987. 892pp. Chapters 19, 20.

Clark, David M. "Guidelines for Software Package Selection." *Journal of Accounting and EDP*, Spring 1987, 18–26.

Cushing, B. E. and Romney, Marshal B. *Accounting Information Systems and Business Organizations*, 4th ed. Reading, MA: Addison-Wesley Publishing Company, 1987. 906pp. Chapters 12, 13.

Earl, M. J. "Prototype Systems for Accounting, Information, and Control." *Accounting, Organizations, and Society*, March 1978, 161–170.

Florida Software Service. "PAYCER, General Purpose Payroll System: Detailed System Description." Orlando, FL: Florida Software Service, n.d.

Gilmour, Robert W. *Business Systems Handbook: Analysis, Design, and Documentation Standards*. Englewood Cliffs, NJ: Prentice-Hall, 1979. 229pp.

Hicks, Jr., James O. and Leininger, Wayne E. *Accounting Information Systems*, 2d ed. St. Paul, MN: West Publishing Company, 1987. 748pp. Chapter 14.

Jansom, M. "Applying a Pilot System and Prototyping Approach to Systems Development and Implementation." *Information & Management*, vol. 10, 1986, 209.

Mathieson, R. "Systems and Installation Review." *The Accountants Magazine*, March 1979, 112–114.

McCarthy, William E. "An Entity-Relationship View of Accounting Models." *Accounting Review*, October 1979.

Moscove, Stephen A. and Simkin, Mark G. *Accounting Information Systems*, 3d ed. New York: John Wiley & Sons, 1987. Chapters 13, 14, 15.

Naumann, J. D. and Jenkins, A. M. "Prototyping: The New Paradigm for Systems Development." *MIS Quarterly*, September 1982, 29–44.

1982–83 AICPA Computer Applications Committee. "MAS Practice Aid 5: EDP Engagement: Assisting Clients in Software Contract Negotiations." New York: AICPA, 1984. 21pp.

Porter, W. Thomas and Perry, William E. *EDP: Controls and Auditing*. Boston: Kent Publishing Company, 1984. 571pp.

Stone, Paula S. "Lack of Training Can Result in Financial Losses." *Infoworld*, July 20, 1987, 35.

Touche Ross & Co. *Flowcharting*. New York: Touche Ross & Co., 1977. 105pp.

Index